The High Tide of British Trade Unionism

The High Tide of British Trade Unionism:
Trade Unions and Industrial Politics, 1964–79

Edited by

JOHN McILROY
NINA FISHMAN
ALAN CAMPBELL

MERLIN PRESS

© Editors and contributors, 2007
First published 1999 by Ashgate
First paperback edition published in 2007
by The Merlin Press
96 Monnow Street
Monmouth
NP25 3EQ
Wales

www.merlinpress.co.uk

ISBN. 9780850366020

British Library Cataloguing in Publication Data
is available from the British Library

Cover photo © Associated Newspapers Ltd.
with thanks to TUC Library Collections

Printed in Great Britain by Lightning Source UK, Milton Keynes

Contents

PART THREE Case Studies, 1964–79

Tables

Abbreviations

ACAS	Advisory, Conciliation and Arbitration Service
ACP	Advisory Committee on Policy
ACTT	Association of Cinematograph and Allied Technicians
ACTU	Association of Catholic Trade Unionists
AEF	Amalgamated Engineering and Foundry Workers' Union
AES	Alternative Economic Strategy
AESD	Association of Engineering and Shipbuilding Draughtsmen
AEU	Amalgamated Engineering Union
AFL	American Federation of Labor
AFL-CIO	American Federation of Labor – Congress of Industrial Organizations
APEX	Association of Professional Executive, Clerical and Computer Staff
ASLEF	Associated Society of Locomotive Engineers and Firemen
ASSET	Association of Supervisory Staffs, Executives and Technicians
ASTMS	Association of Supervisory, Technical and Managerial Staffs
ASW	Amalgamated Society of Woodworkers
AScW	Association of Scientific Workers
ATTI	Association of Teachers in Technical Institutions
ATUA	All Trade Union Alliance
AUCCTU	Soviet All Union Central Council of Trade Unions
AUEW	Amalgamated Union of Engineering Workers
AUEW(E)	Amalgamated Union of Engineering Workers, Engineering Section
AUFW	Amalgamated Union of Foundry Workers
BBC	British Broadcasting Corporation
BDC	Biennial Delegate Conference
BEC	British Employers' Confederation
BISAKTA	British Iron, Steel and Kindred Trades' Association
BL	British Leyland; Broad Left
BMC	British Motor Corporation
BTC	British Transport Commission
CATU	Ceramic and Allied Trades Union
CAWU	Clerical and Administrative Workers' Union
CBC	Central Bus Committee of the Transport and General Workers' Union
CBI	Confederation of British Industry

CCU	Civil Contingencies Unit
CEGB	Central Electricity Generating Board
CEU	Constructional Engineering Union
CGT	Confédération Générale du Travail
CIR	Commission on Industrial Relations
CLP	Constituency Labour Party
CND	Campaign for Nuclear Disarmament
Confed	Confederation of Shipbuilding and Engineering Trade Unions
CP	Communist Party of Great Britain
CPC	Conservative Political Centre
CPS	Centre for Policy Studies
CPSA	Civil and Public Services Association
COHSE	Confederation of Health Service Employees
CRD	Conservative Research Department
CSEU	Confederation of Shipbuilding and Engineering Unions
CWU	Chemical Workers' Union
DATA	Draughtsmen's and Allied Technicians' Association
DC	District Committee
DE	Department of Employment
DEA	Department of Economic Affairs
DGB	Deutscher Gewerkschaftsbund
DMA	Durham Miners' Association
DO	Divisional Organizer
DPC	District Party Committee of the CP
EATSSNC	Engineering and Allied Trades Shop Stewards' National Council
EEC	European Economic Community
EEF	Engineering Employers' Federation
EETPU	Electrical, Electronic, Telecommunication and Plumbing Union
EIS	Educational Institute of Scotland
EPEA	Electrical Power Engineers' Association
ETU	Electrical Trades Union
ETUC	European Trade Union Confederation
EVWs	European Volunteer Workers
FBI	Federation of British Industry
FBU	Fire Brigades' Union
Fed	South Wales Miners' Federation
F&GP	Finance and General Purposes Committee
FTAT	Furnishing Timber and Allied Trades Union

GC	General Council
GCA	Glasgow City Archives
GEC	General Executive Council
GMWU	General and Municipal Workers' Union (see also NUGMW)
HRM	Human Resource Management
ICFTU	International Confederation of Free Trade Unions
IEA	Institute of Economic Affairs
IGF	International Graphical Federation
ILO	International Labour Organisation
ILP	Independent Labour Party
IMG	International Marxist Group
IRD	Information Research Department
IRIS	Industrial Research and Information Services
IRSF	Inland Revenue Staff Federation
IS	International Socialists
ISF	International Solidarity Fund
ITF	International Transport Workers' Federation
ITS	International Trade Secretariats
IWC	Institute for Workers' Control
JPC	Joint Production Committee
JSS	Joint Shop Stewards
KFL	Kenya Federation of Labour
KPD	Kommunistische Partei Deutschlands (German Communist Party)
LCC	London County Council
LCDTU	Liaison Committee for the Defence of Trade Unions
LGOC	London General Omnibus Company
LISSDC	London Industrial Shop Stewards' Defence Committee
LO	Landsorganisationen i Sverige
LPC	Local Party Committee of the CPGB
LPCR	Labour Party Conference Report
LRC	Labour Representation Committee
LRD	Labour Research Department
LTE	London Transport Executive
MDW	measured day work
MFGB	Miners' Federation of Great Britain
MLSA	Ministry of Labour Staff Association
MRC	Modern Records Centre
NAFF	National Association for Freedom

NALGO	National Association of Local Government Officers' Association
NAPE	National Association of Port Employers
NASD	National Amalgamated Stevedores and Dockers
NCB	National Coal Board
NCLC	National Council of Labour Colleges
NDLB	National Dock Labour Board
NEC	National Executive Committee
NEDC	National Economic Development Council
NEDDY	National Economic Development Council
NEDDYS	sector- or industry-based economic development committees serviced by NEDC secretariat
NF	National Front
NGA	National Graphical Association
NIC	National Industrial Commission
NIRC	National Industrial Relations Court
NJC	National Joint Council
NMLH	National Museum of Labour History
NPWU	National Passenger Workers' Union
NSMM	National Society of Metal Mechanics
NSP	National Society of Painters
NUB	National Union of Blastfurnacemen
NUBE	National Union of Bank Employees
NUBSO	National Union of Boot and Shoe Operatives
NUDAW	National Union of Distributive and Allied Workers
NUDBTW	National Union of Dyers, Bleachers and Textile Workers
NUFTO	National Union of Furniture Trade Operatives
NUGMW	National Union of General and Municipal Workers (see also GMWU)
NUHKW	National Union of Hosiery and Knitwear Workers
NUJ	National Union of Journalists
NUM	National Union of Mineworkers
NUPE	National Union of Public Employees
NUR	National Union of Railwaymen
NUS	National Union of Seamen (later Seafarers)
NUSMW	National Union of Sheet Metal Workers and Braziers
NUT	National Union of Teachers
NUTGW	National Union of Tailors and Garment Workers
NUVB	National Union of Vehicle Builders
OECD	Organisation for Economic Co-operation and Development

PEP	Political and Economic Planning
PLP	Parliamentary Labour Party
POEU	Post Office Engineering Union
PPS	Parliamentary Private Secretary
PTU	Plumbing Trades Union
RCP	Revolutionary Communist Party
RSL	Revolutionary Socialist League
RTUO	Revolutionary Trade Union Opposition
SDP	(British) Social Democratic Party
SEEA	Scottish Engineering Employers' Association
SLL	Socialist Labour League
SOGAT	Society of Graphical and Allied Trades
SPGB	Socialist Party of Great Britain
SS	steamship
STA	Socialist Teachers' Alliance
STUC	Scottish Trades Union Congress
SWP	Socialist Workers' Party
TASS	Technical and Supervisory Section of AUEW
TGWU	Transport and General Workers' Union (also T&G)
TSSA	Transport Salaried Staffs Association
TUC	Trades Union Congress
TWU	Tobacco Workers' Union
UCATT	Union of Construction, Allied Trades and Technicians
UCS	Upper Clyde Shipbuilders
UPW	Union of Post Office Workers
USB	United Society of Boilermakers
USDAW	Union of Shop, Distributive and Allied Workers
UTFWA	United Textile Factory Workers' Association
WEA	Workers' Educational Association
WETUC	Workers' Educational Trade Union Committee
WFTU	World Federation of Trade Unions
WLBTU	Watermen, Lightermen, Tugmen and Bargemen's Union
WRP	Workers' Revolutionary Party
WSL	Workers' Socialist League

Contributors

Alan Campbell is Reader in Labour and Social History, University of Liverpool. He is the author of the two-volume *The Scottish Miners, 1874–1939* (2000).

Nina Fishman is Honorary Research Professor in History, University of Swansea, and author of *The British Communist Party and the Trade Unions, 1933-45* (1995).

John Foster was until recently a Professor in the Department of Applied Social Studies, University of Paisley. He is the co-author of *The Politics of the UCS Work-In* (1986) and *Track Record: the story of the Caterpillar occupation* (1988).

Richard Hyman is Professor of Industrial Relations at the London School of Economics. His books include *The Political Economy of Industrial Relations* (1989) and *Understanding European Trade Unionism: between market, class and society* (2001).

Ken Lunn recently retired as a Reader in the Department of Social and Historical Studies, University of Portsmouth. He is a former editor of *Immigrants and Minorities*.

Dave Lyddon is a Senior Lecturer in Industrial Relations at Keele University and editor of *Historical Studies in Industrial Relations*.

John McIlroy is Professor of Industrial Relations at Keele University. His books include *Industrial Politics and the 1926 Mining Lockout: the struggle for dignity* (2004).

Mike Savage is Professor of Sociology at the University of Manchester. He is the author of *Class Analysis and Social Transformation* (2000) and *Globalisation and Belonging* (2005).

Andrew Taylor is Professor of Politics at the University of Sheffield and author of the two-volume *The NUM and British Politics* (2003 and 2005).

Robert Taylor was formerly Employment Editor of the *Financial Times*. His books include *The TUC: from the general strike to new unionism* (2000).

Andrew Thorpe is Professor of History, University of Exeter. He is the author of *A History of the British Labour Party* (2nd edn, 2001) and *The British Communist Party and Moscow, 1920–43* (2000).

Charles Woolfson is Professor of Labour Studies, University of Glasgow. He is co-author of *Paying the Piper: capital and labour in Britain's offshore oil industry* (1996).

Chris Wrigley is Professor of Modern British History at the University of Nottingham. He is editor of the three-volume *History of British Industrial Relations* (1982, 1987, 1996) and author of *British Trade Unions since 1933* (2002).

Introduction to the Paperback Edition:
Reflections on British Trade Unions and Industrial Politics

John McIlroy

The two companion volumes addressing industrial politics in the post-war era, *The Post-War Compromise* and *The High Tide of British Trade Unionism*, were first published in 1999.[1] They attracted both commendation and criticism. Most of the reviewers were kind. Neville Kirk, a professor of labour history, felt that the texts constituted 'a major contribution towards filling the many gaps in our understanding of post-war trade unionism and politics. They also provoke many new questions and open up important areas of research.'[2] The economic historian Alan Fowler described *The Post-War Compromise* as 'a most welcome addition to the literature ... this volume will provide future scholars with a far greater understanding of the post-war period than has yet been available.'[3]

The insightful student of the politics and sociology of industry Colin Crouch found the books 'deeply empirical and detailed, scrupulously scholarly ... They tell it how it was.'[4] Mike Terry, a professor of industrial relations, characterized *The High Tide of British Trade Unionism* as 'scholarly and precise ... [the essays] add greatly to our knowledge of the period under review, extending our understanding of the familiar and exposing much that lay hidden ... It is a fascinating volume that will engage all readers with its mix of meticulous research and lucid exposition. Together with its companion volume it will no doubt come to serve as one of the definitive assessments of post-war trade unionism.'[5]

In the introduction to the two books we were at pains to stress that they made no claim to provide a comprehensive account of the trade unionism of this period, still less its social and political context and its impact on the economy. Eric Hobsbawm believed that we were excessively modest in characterising much of the work as 'first accounts of neglected byways'.[6] Needless to say, at least one reviewer succumbed to the perennial malady of that trade by suggesting that we should have edited two very different books covering, *inter alia*, globalization; class mobility; popular attitudes; 'sheer [*sic*] generational change'; the role of trade unionists as consumers; and 'the changing developmental role of government'.[7] More reasonable was the observation that the activities of black and Asian trade unionists, women employees and 'white-collar workers in general' during these years merited greater attention.[8]

Within the confines of our texts there should certainly have been more on the link between the unions and the Labour Party which by 1979 contributed so much to the discourse of 'ungovernability'; on labour legislation and the role of the judiciary, a topic of undoubted political importance throughout the period; on industrial democracy, not only on the Bullock Report of 1977 but also on initiatives from below; as well as greater attention to the alternative economic strategies, predicated as a means of mobilizing trade unionists for radical change, which transcended existing approaches to reform. A rounder treatment of the period would need to pay fuller attention to the context and content of social change, the changing culture of working-class communities and the lives and experiences of political and industrial activists, as well as those they represented.[9]

* * * * *

Lord Morgan generously praised many of the contributions. He claimed that others were too concerned with 'justifying rank-and-file militancy as a reasonable response to anti-inflation policies'.[10] Morgan was particularly perturbed at McIlroy and Campbell's discussion of the 'Winter of Discontent', 1978–9, in their survey, 'The High Tide of Trade Unionism', omitting to inform readers that, among other things, that chapter critically engages with his own examination of those events.[11] In his account, the Labour Prime Minister James Callaghan, the subject of a major biography by Morgan, is a tragic hero brought down by the trade unions, personified by the irresponsibility of Moss Evans, general secretary of the Transport and General Workers' Union (TGWU), and Alan Fisher, general secretary of the National Union of Public Employees.[12]

In his biography, Morgan notes the risk that Callaghan ran in unilaterally imposing a 5 per cent pay limit against the opposition of both the TUC and the Labour Party when inflation was running at almost twice that amount. He records Callaghan's miscalculation in refusing to call a general election in autumn 1978. He even recognizes that beneath the high politics that he chronicles 'lay the pent-up anger of public sector service workers after three years of pay restraint'.[13] He is very clear who the villains of the piece are. In Morgan's narrative, exercise of 'the irresponsible power of the over mighty unions' paves the way for Thatcherism. Trade unionists succumb to a 'feverish madness' and 'commit hara kiri', in the process derailing a government 'helpless in the face of the undisciplined brute force of union power'.[14] Evans and Fisher are found wanting, judged by the ahistorical standards of Callaghan's and Morgan's model union leaders, Ernest Bevin, Arthur Deakin, Sir William Lawther and the later Jack Jones.[15]

In their essay McIlroy and Campbell looked at matters differently and, we would submit, rather more convincingly. They commenced not with explanations in terms of pathology or the death wish of irresponsible union leaders but with analysis rooted in the structural situation constraining the actors of 1978–9 and the interplay of agency with context. The power of the unions, even at their high tide, and their leaders' ability to mobilize it for agreed objectives, remained limited, secondary and, it should be stressed, diffuse.[16] Until the end of our period the decentralization of union structure and collective bargaining, and the confines of sectoral and workplace consciousness as well as the weaknesses of state policy, and persisting economic pressure, militated against concertation and social contracts. Whatever else they are in business for, union leaders are essentially preoccupied with securing real wage increases. Real wages had fallen in 1976 and fallen sharply in 1977. Attributed to government policy, this aroused understandable resentment among trade unionists. Yet a new wage limit of 5 per cent for 1978–9 was introduced when prices were rising at around 9 per cent.[17] As Andrew Thorpe comments in his chapter in *The High Tide*: 'To most informed observers, the new limit seemed utterly unrealistic.'[18] Faced with further initiatives to control wages, trade unionists, often far from militant, responded with industrial action to an inflationary situation which was not of their making and over which they possessed little control.[19]

In explaining rank-and-file action, McIlroy and Campbell stated (although not in direct reference to 1978–9), that 'economic rationality provides a plausible explanatory starting point'.[20] But not, we hasten to add, a concluding point. Politics is part of the business of union leaders and union leadership requires relating wage policy to other issues including the social wage, public expenditure and the welfare state. By 1978, although there was as always differentiation within the unions, the trade-off between the pay packet and the social wage was deteriorating; the turn to monetarism supervised by the Chancellor, Dennis Healy, was emerging. Fundamentally, in terms of what happened the union leaders of 1978–9 were neither autocrats nor simply conduit pipes for their members' aspirations. There are always limits to the most vigorous leadership over wages in economic organizations which, to one degree or another, acknowledge the demands of democracy and which were at the time relatively fragmented and often decentralized as far as decision-making and action went.[21]

The firm smack of government of Bevin, Deakin and Lawther resounds nostalgically from the 1930s through the 1950s. But those were different times and different unions. The writ of the grandees of the past was perhaps more contested than Morgan allows. Moreover, as Thorpe observes of Morgan's contemporary exemplar, Jack Jones, by 1977 he 'had no choice but to back away from the kind of "one-way" incomes policy which came to dominate the scene after 1976'.[22] Ultimately he had to accept the mandate of the TGWU conference. In the end, despite some politicking, he had to respect his members' rejection of wage controls. Evans was more sceptical about government policy; the constraints of union democracy were again paramount.

Trade unionists are not, as far as we are concerned, above criticism. The Labour government had its achievements and it was operating within the rigours of the changing world economy and intensifying international competition. But explanation – and judgement – of the 'Winter of Discontent' has to start with the policy of that government and its leaders and the choices made by Callaghan and his Cabinet in the troubled context of 1978, as well as the difficult inheritance of the earlier 1970s. Our understanding is not greatly furthered by interdictions against 'over mighty unions' and the 'irresponsibility' of union leaders who failed to impose their will against their members' wishes.[23]

Morgan asserts that McIlroy and Campbell 'attempt to deny that the Winter of Discontent … had much impact on the unions' reputation. They also believe that the poll evidence that Labour could handle the unions better half justifies the strikes …'.[24] We refer readers to what we wrote. The episode, we emphatically concluded, 'undoubtedly played a role in the Conservative victory at the polls'.[25] But rigorous explanation needs to register the nuances. If the 'Winter of Discontent' was in itself the unique, transformative agent of much mythology and not a little history, it is difficult to understand why, in April 1979, Labour once more headed the Conservatives in the polls. It is hard to comprehend why, during the election campaign itself, Labour was still judged more capable than the Conservatives of handling the unions.[26] And if Morgan consults the contributions which he claims refute our views, he will discover that he is mistaken: they do not dissent from our comments and conclusions.[27]

* * * * *

Specific strictures apart, the only largely hostile review of the two volumes came from the journalist John Lloyd.[28] It was embedded in reflection on the decline of the trade unionism he had reported on as an industrial correspondent during the 1980s. It is, he contends, a reverse for which the unions bear a significant share of the blame.[29] Within this problematic, Lloyd is exercised by our critical probing of New Labour's mythmaking about the trade unionism of the 1960s and 1970s. He overlooks our rider: '… we should remain alert to the recrudescence of currently less influential left-wing fables such as the inevitability, despite everything that has happened, of the revival of labour's progress or the essential, if presently invisible, revolutionary instincts of the rank and file trade unionist.'[30]

All history, Lloyd pronounces, is partisan and 'the majority' of the essays in these two volumes are not only 'militantly partisan' but further a particular political agenda.[31] This verdict is at odds with the judgements of other reviewers. One of them recognised 'a disparate group of labour historians, political scientists, management studies and industrial relations specialists'.[32] Another registered 'the diversity of approach and coverage in the contributions'.[33] The latter approved the editors' restraint in declining to produce a directed text 'smoothed for consistency'.[34] A glance at the contributors and what they have written here and elsewhere sustains this assessment. They hold different views in relation to history and politics: if they are united, it is only, in differing degrees, by their critical, sometimes very critical, advocacy of trade unionism.

In a broader sense Lloyd is repeating a commonplace of historiography: the values, preconceptions and politics of the historian are there in the writing of history, in selection, analysis and evaluation. Reconstruction inevitably includes an element of construction. Perhaps, as Lloyd claims, a critical stance towards New Labour (or, in Lloyd's case, a supportive stance) may influence matters. We measure this by the extent to which the historian's product, whatever the historian's commitments, passes the scholarly tests of evidence, interpretation and analysis. Here Lloyd is less than convincing. His assertions are rarely encumbered by evidence and sometimes elide history. Take this example: '... the unions again and again spurned the opportunity, in whatever guise it was offered, to take any responsibility for production, or to be party to any agreement in which a Labour government would plan output and growth.'[35]

Quite apart from the evasive grandiloquence, 'responsibility for production', something that was never on offer, this is caricature. A terse correction might go: the evidence discloses that between 1964 and 1966 trade unionists agreed to support Harold Wilson's National Plan, the National Economic Development Council (NEDC), the work of the National Prices and Incomes Board and the government's proffered 'planned growth of incomes'. Whatever their divisions, deficiencies – in terms of the structures of collective bargaining and trade unionism– and doubts, they supported government projects for planning prices, profits, wages, income and wealth. Blown off course in 1966, the government placed deflation and statutory control over pay, at the expense of control over prices, profits and redistribution, at the centre of economic management. Planned growth of incomes dwindled into rhetoric; consensual restraint transmuted into coercion. Recent research perhaps goes too far in contending that confusion in the government over the purpose of incomes policy was more important than the response of trade unions and employers and that by 1970 'there were very few proponents of wage and price control left within government'.[36]

In opposition the unions worked closely with Labour's leadership to produce the Social Contract strategy. Between 1974 and 1976 it had its successes, particularly with pay restraint. Again a sterling crisis struck and again radical designs were deserted. The 1975 Industry Act, the National Enterprise Board, planning agreements, redistribution of income and wealth – in sum the radical edge of Labour's strategy – were overshadowed by emphasis on wage controls, fiscal rectitude, tightening of public expenditure and a turn to monetarism. Union leaders continued to cooperate. But by 1978 pressure from below rendered this precarious. Some opportunities were in retrospect disregarded, notably Lord Bullock's proposals on industrial democracy. But that was 1977–1978 not 1974 or 1964. Despite helpful reforms, the overarching reality that trade unionists ultimately faced in 1964–70 and again in 1974–9 was downward pressure on wages from governments retreating from radicalism.[37]

A not uncritical reviewer acknowledged: '… as Dave Lyddon points out in an essay that sets out to rescue the 1972 high point of militancy from inaccurate accounts by lazy historians, what deserves our attention is at least as much that "glorious summer" as the all too often remembered "winter of discontent" seven years later.'[38] Lloyd, in contrast, takes exception to Lyddon's admiration for the militancy of 1972. This does not take us very far. Those of a different persuasion may object to Lloyd's aversion to it. Unlike Hinton, Lloyd takes issue with Lyddon's criticism of the depiction of key events of the 1970s by politicians, union leaders and 'lazy historians'. The difference is that Lyddon provides quotation and citation of 'inaccuracies': Lloyd does not.[39]

One reviewer felt that: 'The excellent survey chapters make the editors' case for the need for far more detailed narrative work on the post-war period. The accounts here are balanced and reflective.'[40] Another declared that both surveys 'nicely provide an integrative core and balance to the broad and diverse concerns of other contributors'.[41] Lloyd again disagrees. The only evidence he deploys to explain his dissent is a single sentence from McIlroy and Campbell's survey, 'The High Tide', to the effect that incomes policies were generally temporary expedients centred on wage restraint while their articulation with prices, profits, the social wage and the redistribution of income and wealth was slight and rhetorical.[42] Lloyd claims this as evidence for the view, which he again attributes to the majority of contributors, that Labour governments 'were never serious about running a corporatist policy'.[43] The sentiments in our sentence are, he asserts, not substantiated elsewhere in the text; indeed, they are, he believes, contradicted in the essays by Thorpe and Andrew Taylor and Robert Taylor in the same volume.[44]

The test of the seriousness of Labour governments is what they did, or what they assiduously endeavoured to do, in terms of developing corporatism. The pages from which Lloyd extracts McIlroy and Campbell's sentence detail, with extensive reference, how incomplete and fragile corporatist initiatives in Britain were. These pages remark on successive governments' attention to controlling labour at the expense of controlling capital, the absence of any *dirigiste* National Economic Forum or National Economic Assessment with teeth, and the inadequacies of the NEDC as an instrument of decision-making and intervention. They go on to note that both employers and unions were ill-equipped to play a viable part in long-term, strategic concertation; and they record that by the end of the period capital was moving away from corporatist solutions to its problems.[45]

Thorpe certainly, as Lloyd suggests, opens his account with the pronouncement that in 1974, '... there was an explicit commitment that pay restraint would not be a one-way street'.[46] But Thorpe then rehearses Labour's policies on the social wage before concluding that the cuts and fiscal stance adopted in autumn 1976 'effectively marked the end of the government side of the Social Contract ... the restraint of income growth would provide more of a priority than ever. In this sense *incomes policy once again became a one-way street* ...'[47] (emphasis added). Andrew Taylor does indeed observe that in 1972 the Conservative Prime Minister Edward Heath attempted to draw the unions into corporatism. But he adds: '... the Industrial Relations Act and the TUC's insistence on statutory price control and voluntary pay restraint remained insuperable obstacles to an agreement.'[48] This was not the spurning of an opportunity. In the prevailing circumstances union leaders could do little else: the Act was an insuperable obstacle of Heath's making. Robert Taylor, Lloyd's third supposed witness, has nothing of substance to say on the matter. While Taylor does not exonerate union leaders he presents a rather more nuanced account of their difficulties quite distinct from simplistic 'the unions were to blame' paradigms.[49]

Trade unionists wielded restricted, reactive, fragmented, largely negative, power over the market, which they were unable to co-ordinate and develop into positive political power over the state. They cannot be artificially extrapolated from the matrix of inter-relating actors and interactive pressures configuring the crisis of the labour movement in the late 1970s and 1980s, still less conjured into a major contributory factor for the decline of collectivism at the expense of more qualitatively powerful protagonists. To take a further step and blend explanation with blame compounds the error. James Hinton's review endorses one message of our books in providing an antidote to the 'it's largely the unions' fault' approach: 'The most important explanations of the inability of the unions to translate their growing power into structural reform lie with the state and capital – forces beyond their control and largely beyond the brief of these volumes. Labor governments proceeded on the basis of incomes policy devised as short-term crisis management rather than any fundamental thinking about the refashioning of the state.'[50] As Brian Towers, another reviewer, put it: 'it is laying "very rough hands on history", as the late and much missed Henry Phelps Brown would have said, to find villainy in only one place.'[51]

* * * * *

Our purpose in these volumes was to record the marginal as well as the mainstream. In that context we readily concede the point made by Hinton that we could have made more room for discussion of the 'new social movements', which emerged from the late 1960s.[52] Vietnam, the peace movement, what became the green movement, the women's liberation movement, the Working Women's Charter Campaign, the National Abortion Campaign, a range of movements centred on sexual orientation, black consciousness, international solidarity, tenants' associations, theatre groups and alternative newspapers, all had an impact on contemporary trade unionism. They sometimes criss-crossed with union campaigns and initiatives, such as the workers' alternative plans discussed by Richard Hyman in his 'Afterword' to *The High Tide of British Trade Unionism*.[53] They enriched, sometimes belatedly, aspects of trade unionism. The women's movement, particularly its more radical varieties, laid the basis for growing consciousness of the diversity of oppression in the unions and their extensive institutional restructuring to counter inequality in the last years of the century. As Chris Wrigley concludes in his chapter on women in the same volume, external forces stimulated internal change.[54]

In this sense the women's movement was 'a social force'. As a movement – diffuse, disparate, minimally organized – it existed on a different plane to organized labour which arguably offered the best arena for pressing and realising its demands. Like trade unionism, social movements have their limits. Nor can oppression based on gender or ethnicity –significant as this is, it remains patterned by class – in itself stand convincing comparison with class as a potential motor for transformative social change. Capitalism can never terminate, although it may ameliorate, class exploitation. It can and it has assimilated movements based on gender and ethnicity.[55]

In the writing of labour and social history there is, as we noted in our 1999 introduction to these volumes, a deficit in work on gender and ethnicity. Hinton's view that in repairing it class analysis and gender analysis should be seen as 'complementary' is imprecise and may be perceived as denying the ultimate paramountcy of class as an analytical tool and conciliating identity history. In his recent writing, Hinton is similarly reticent: 'Much recent scholarship has been concerned to downgrade the explanatory power of the concept of class ...

the category of gender cannot usefully be given precedence over the category of class ... if class was gendered then gender was also "classed".'[56] Certainly they interact. But which category is analytically prior? The task, surely, is to structure the intersections and integrate gender into the concept of class.[57]

Several reviewers recognised and endorsed our desire to examine the post-war years on their own terms. We wanted to convey how things were then for actors whose formative experiences stretched even further back into the past, men and women who did things differently in the topography of 'a foreign country'. This was a reaction to narratives in which 'the period has typically been viewed as a necessary preface to the demise of the British labour movement'.[58] We wanted to avoid teleologies and meta-narratives, whether of the 'irresistible rise and rise of neo-liberalism' or 'the forward march of labour halted' genre, in which the downfall of the unions in the 1980s was largely determined by the events of the post-war period. Partly because of this we essayed terse counterfactuals. Rejecting pristine and conservative conceptions of balance and relevance, utility and public policy, we included essays on the Communist Party and the Trotskyists. History is about the losers as well as the winners.

Nonetheless, we glanced towards the future in assessing the strengths and weaknesses of trade unionism in 1979. So did several of our contributors, on whom no particular approach was incumbent. Despite this, Colin Crouch, who acknowledged 'it is not the primary task of the authors ... to provide answers to how what was in 1945 arguably the world's most important trade union movement, came to such a pass',[59] and Mike Terry, both suggested the need for further consideration of the direction which trade unionism was taking in 1979, and whether and how the impasse of the late 1970s 'paved the way for the 1980s'.[60]

It is important to re-emphasise that what happened in the 1980s depended crucially on the circumstances and struggles of that decade and can only be understood through a proper historical account of that decade. It is a truism that Thatcherism was neither *ab initio* a fully fledged ideology nor a *blitzkrieg*: it represented, despite preparations, increasingly confident groping towards a new politics; it developed and unfolded incrementally in sustained engagement with the labour movement; it was different in 1989 than in 1979; and it was never fully coherent. The reverses unions suffered occurred on the terrain of that decade, on territory newly treacherous to trade unionism, reconfigured by economic policy, large-scale unemployment, industrial restructuring, the increasing marginalization of the Labour Party and the Falklands War. They had more to do with the printworkers' dispute of 1982 than the strikes of 1972, more to do, even more crucially, with the miners' strike of 1984–5 than the miners' strike of 1974.[61] The recent past remained relevant. So, too, did the more distant past and *la longue durée* of British industrial relations, a largely evolutionary trajectory which the state was increasingly determined to rupture.[62]

It is important to recognise the elements of truth in the arguments, most powerfully proposed by Colin Crouch, that as the 1970s moved to their turbulent close, the potential of existing trade union ideologies of mission and mobilisation was becoming exhausted.[63] Like others, we have been educated by subsequent experience. We understand to a far greater degree than we did the complexities and limitations of industrial struggle within never to be underestimated capitalisms as well as the inadequacy of much that once passed for radicalism and militancy as a road to socialist change. We appreciate the need for deeper, more extensive, transformative ideological shifts as a condition for progress and the necessity for greater control and co-ordination within the labour movement, as well as critical but ambitious engagement with the state. We can learn but we cannot go back. And some of these arguments appear pessimistic in relation to the 1970s, overly informed and sometimes flawed by hindsight and backward projection of what we know now. If we compare British trade unionism at that time with its position both earlier and later in the twentieth century, it is difficult to agree (without over-estimating their influence) that unions were already Emperors with no clothes.[64]

There was unity and class consciousness as well as fragmentation, solidarity as well as sectionalism. In 1979 British trade unionism was, in one sense, moving in the direction of a stronger, more inclusive collectivism, better able to provide, albeit still inadequate, protection to workers against the vicissitudes of an inequitable, exploitative class society. If restricted, variable and contingent, its reach, its legitimacy, its social presence, measured by membership, density, legislation and access to government, its potential to mobilize its members and its ability to bargain successfully with the state, were greater than at any other time in its history. What was in question was its structure, its purpose, its politics, and the nature of its power, as well as its impact on capital and profit levels.

Post-war labourism and post-war trade unionism tried but failed to secure a satisfactory trade-off between planning capitalism efficiently, voluntarism and 'free collective bargaining'. The results, an uneasy mix of flaking collective *laisser-faire* and incomplete corporatism, were increasingly viewed as stifling economic regeneration. Strong, uncoordinated collective bargaining was seen as economically dysfunctional. Trade unionism was increasingly perceived as generating inflation, constricting the freedom of business and the market, and obstructing government. Its specific strengths and weaknesses are outlined in the survey chapter in *The High Tide of British Trade Unionism*.[65] The latter were differently elaborated by other contributors, particularly by Richard Hyman in his 'Afterword'.[66]

They ranged from problems of sectional bargaining, organization and consciousness, failure to develop structures and strategies of co-ordination adequate to articulate either successful antagonism or political exchange with the state, the unevenness of militancy, its tensions with concertation and its singular failure to produce substantial political radicalisation, to the enrolment of members, often by management in closed shops, rather than the ideological making of trade unionists, and the brittleness of solidarity between them. They included incapacity to effectively link the trade union and Labour Party left, take industrial democracy and new forms of workers' control over production sufficiently seriously, and appreciate the significance of internationalism and Europe.

Both strengths and weaknesses must be weighed within an understanding of the nature and historic limits of British trade unionism: it has been an agency of real but circumscribed class cohesion, an agency of real but restricted social change.[67] And they must be assessed in the context of the power of the state and capital and their historic inhibitions about strategic co-ordination, inhibitions which could not be reassured by the confused choreography of concertation during the 1960s and 1970s. There developed increasing awareness among elite opinion makers, employers and politicians beyond the ranks of Conservatism that it was time to turn from the post-war compromise, time to turn instead towards the liberation of the corporation and the remaking of the market, time to turn towards privatization, deregulation and globalization.[68]

If the debilities of the trade unions pre-Thatcher played a role in the events of the 1980s, they did not play a primary role. The leading actors in the drama were not trade unionists but politicians and capitalists. We also recorded that by 1979 management was harvesting the fruits of more strategic approaches to regaining control of the workplace, formalizing single-employer bargaining at company and enterprise level, weakening union workplace organization and eroding the sinews of mobilization.[69] It was moving away from its never powerful belief in co-ordination, and even employer coalitions, towards freedom and company autonomy. The prolonged crisis of planning, the faltering corporatist experiment, the periodic challenges to the state, the pressure on profits, the resilience, unpredictability and economic consequences of fragmented collective bargaining, recurring stagflation: all of this, in the context of Britain's decline in a changing world economy, made strong trade unionism appear a liability. Politically packaged, this perspective influenced the turn to Thatcherism and the construction of consent.

It was, in retrospect, the moment of neo-liberalism, just as 1945 had been the moment of social democracy. We must not lose sight of national particularities and national tempos as one kind of international capitalism turns into another. But 'future historians may well look upon the years 1978–80 as a revolutionary turning point in the world's social and economic history'.[70] Few saw it then.[71]

Suitably amplified, the problems of post-war trade unionism stimulated change. They did not help in combating it, although the resistance of the 1980s should not be passed over lightly. Without disregarding the necessity for a detailed history of the period, what was ultimately involved was perhaps something more fundamental: the fragility of trade unionism nurtured by a collectivist, consensual state when confronted by capitalist restructuring and a hostile, confrontationist, market-oriented state. In the 1960s and 1970s, myth maintained that significant curtailment of trade unionism was too costly: it had to be moulded, integrated or for some placated. As the 1980s demonstrated, that only went for the social democratic state, for the post-war compromise, for a certain balance of class forces, for a relatively benign attitude towards collectivism and coercion.

Conservative neo-liberalism 'affirmed that in the twentieth century as in the nineteenth, it has proved immensely difficult – perhaps impossible – for organized labour to defeat a strategic attack led by the state which fused politics and economics in an extended, sophisticated assault.'[72] The degree to which British trade unionism had been fostered by the state became apparent as the state withdrew support and legitimacy. This is not to deprecate the creative power of workers' self-activity. It is rather to acknowledge that agency operates in contexts facilitative or constrictive, to judge that in the face of neo-liberalism British trade unionism was 'confirmed as the bearer of a secondary, derivative, negative, limited power, severely circumscribed by economic change and state initiatives'.[73]

* * * * *

Since 1999 a variety of texts relevant to the history of post-war trade unionism have appeared.[74] Popular histories still arguably pay inadequate attention to the subject despite its contemporary significance. Dominic Sandbrook's *Never Had It So Good* is very much in tune with current pre-occupations, with cultural history of the popular kind and representations mixed with a dash of high politics.[75] Most of the relatively little it has to say about trade unionism is drawn from popular contemporary sources while it has rather a lot to say about *I'm All Right, Jack,* admittedly a marvellous film. The same goes, on the whole, for Sandbrook's engaging companion volume dealing with 'the swinging sixties', while Peter Hennessy's fascinating history of the 1950s is also relatively restrained on trade unions.[76]

Three general surveys of trade union history have been published. Chris

Wrigley's brief synopsis of the years since 1933 is effectively organized around issues such as strikes, incomes policies and legislation and is strong on the economic impact of trade unionism.[77] In contrast, Hamish Fraser traverses the three centuries from 1700. This is well-researched, accessible, empirical history, enlivened by examples from Scotland, which centres on collective bargaining and industry sometimes at the expense of the unions' political role. Some forty-three pages are devoted to 1945–79 and this makes for broad sweep treatment, more descriptive than analytical, with occasional over-emphasis on 'restrictive practices' and unofficial strikes.[78]

Alistair Reid's *United We Stand* is the successor volume to Henry Pelling's durable *History of British Trade Unionism*: it covers developments from the late 1600s to the present in less than 450 pages.[79] Like Fraser, Reid is constrained by the difficulty of doing justice to three packed centuries in a single text. Moreover, his eschewal of Pelling's chronological approach and his attempt to separate out the stories of different types of trade unionists – contentiously defined – and narrate them sequentially, produces fragmentation, overlap and sometimes neglect of the commonality and centrality of key episodes. Reid's examination of post-war events can be cursory. *In Place of Strife* and the struggles around the Industrial Relations Act 1971 each receive a couple of paragraphs and the miners' strikes of 1972 and 1974 take up a couple of pages in total.[80] His attempt to rehabilitate moderation and bread-and-butter trade unionism amongst the alarums and excitements of mobilization is laudable if occasionally intrusive. It is a truism that trade unionism reflects a variety of goals and is, in essence, neither militant nor moderate. At times authorial antipathy towards the struggles and socialist alignments which co-existed with, and in certain periods transcended, acquiescence, ensures that co-operation is emphasised against conflict.[81]

The field of industrial relations continues to benefit from the work of scholars in adjacent disciplines. The political scientist Chris Howell has written an important overview of the role of the state in British industrial relations.[82] Revising conventional accounts of state abstention, voluntarism and collective *laisser-faire*, Howell rehabilitates the interventionist role of the state from the cautious initiatives of the 1890s through Whitley and Donovan to neo-liberalism. He highlights the importance of the institutions the state created in constituting industrial relations systems, if not their outcomes. The corporatist experiment – is it more useful, as Howell does, to see it as a distinctive system or regime, rather than a tendency within, although pushing against, the limits of the regime of collective *laisser-faire*? – broke down because of its contradictions. The state's strategic sponsoring of trade unionism was increasingly perceived as dysfunctional in terms of economic efficiency and productivity and, as international competition intensified, employers turned to undermine both corporatism and collective bargaining. By depriving trade unionism of its props, they demonstrated that its autonomous strength had been exaggerated. We made similar points earlier.

Explorations of trade unionism need to transcend the conventional treatment of the state by industrial relations scholars: they should consider its role in legitimation and coercion and, pertinently here, taxation, social security and welfare regimes. This is one of the numerous lessons reinforced by reading Simon Deakin and Frank Wilkinson's imposing *Law of the Labour Market*.[83] A labour lawyer and labour economist respectively, their book represents a wide-ranging synthesis which, like Howell's work, foregrounds the creative role that the state and social regulation have played, in interaction with private regulation, in developing the role of the market and influencing industrial relations. Focusing on the historical development of the contract of employment, they examine the interplay of labour law, the welfare state and collective bargaining in the formation of employment relations. They stress the limitations of collective bargaining in terms of trade union objectives, wider economic planning and counter-inflation policy, and eschew both neo-liberal policies and the lost world of corporatism in favour of a middle way, a system of social rights which far from impairing market regulation can complement it.

In a different vein, the industrial relations academics Ralph Darlington and Dave Lyddon have extended the latter's study of that *annus mirabilis* of militancy, 1972, in *The High Tide of British Trade Unionism*, into a meticulously detailed, book-length account of events. If some will question its emphasis on rank-and-file activism and belief in militancy as a precursor or necessary component of class-based political action, it provides a valuable addition to the literature on strikes and strike strategy.[84] Paul Smith's research into road haulage has resulted in an impressive study of the evolution of industrial relations at national and local level illuminated by analysis of theories of trade unionism. For our purposes it is particularly useful on the 'Winter of Discontent'. Like much work in industrial relations it is underpeopled.[85] The political scientist Andrew Taylor writes top-down, institutional history. His two volumes on the National Union of Mineworkers (NUM) shed new light on the experience of nationalization and the impact of state policy, NUM policy, the development of factionalism and the important internal as well as the significant external conflicts of the 1960s and 1970s.[86] Keith Gildart's volume on the tiny North Wales coalfield usefully rounds out our knowledge of miners' activities in the regions during the post-war years.[87]

Understanding the development of the TUC is indispensable to comprehending the reconstruction of collective *laisser-faire* after 1945, the detail of the post-war compromise and the burgeoning of corporatism from the early 1960s. Building on his analysis of George Woodcock in *The High Tide of British Trade Unionism*, Robert Taylor has provided us with an extended, accessible analysis of TUC initiatives throughout the period. Replete with shrewd and vivid portraits of protagonists, it is perhaps stronger on the conflicts of the later years.[88]

The advent of New Labour provoked a spate of publications, some of which interrogated its antecedents, and this was reinforced by a number of books published to mark the party's centenary. Recent scholarship on the Labour Party sometimes suffers from a constriction of focus. It is difficult to deny that the trade unions were part of the marrow of labourism or that trade unionists were key actors in the party. It is, consequently, hard to understand why some of these volumes treat trade unionism in perfunctory fashion. There is nothing of substance about it in the history of the Labour Party in Wales while in *Labour's First Century* a few pages in a single chapter cover the period 1945–79, a time when trade unionism constituted an unavoidable landmark in the landscapes of labourism, not to speak of the wider polity.[89] Despite the centrality of 'the trade union question' to the concerns of the Wilson administrations, a recent three-volume history of the 1964–70 Labour governments contains sparse address of trade unions and their links with the party.[90] Its revisionist claims to rehabilitate the limited achievements of the Wilson administrations in economic policy may have some merit. They are questionable with regard to industrial relations.[91]

The more comprehensive centenary volume edited by Brian Brivati and Richard Heffernan has a valuable chapter on 1945–64 and a slighter survey of the rest of the century.[92] The position may be different today but in the 1950s and 1960s trade unionism was an integral part of the culture of the left. Nonetheless, a recent monograph on the subject has scarcely anything to say about it.[93] In contrast, James Cronin makes a valiant attempt to integrate analysis of the unions' role into his assessments of the Wilson and Callaghan governments. He emphasises the extent to which moving away from the intractabilities of 'the contentious alliance' with the unions, perceived as antagonistic to winning elections, good policy and good government, distancing the party from the unions and repudiating class, was central to defining the New Labour project. Cronin provides insightful reading on the economic dilemmas, the incomes policies and the confrontations over legislation of the post-war years.[94]

The final two volumes of the 'official' history of the Communist Party add to the detail of the industrial politics of the period,[95] although there has been little new on Trotskyism.[96] Attention to factional organization and the political process in trade unions[97] and the role of political activists in the unions and the workplace,[98] has been sustained, but slight. In terms of serious investigation of the circumstances that mould militants and militancy, make moderates and moderation, the literature remains vestigial and undeveloped. The influences that created activism in different periods, the forces that maintain or transform the trajectories of individual activists, the interactions and tensions between their union activities and their political allegiances, require further exploration.[99] We need more biographies, more prosopographies and greater address of the varieties of militancy and moderation as well as the attitudes towards them of union members. Conventional biographies continue to appear in abundance. In contrast with the multiplying lives of politicians – Clement Attlee, Harold Macmillan, Barbara Castle, Wilson, Heath, Callaghan, Michael Foot – extended studies of union leaders, let alone activists, have remained at a premium.[100] However the *Dictionary of Labour Biography* maintains its useful role.[101]

* * * * *

This brief survey suggests that, whatever its difficulties, the history of labour and industrial politics remains very much alive. We conclude with a plea for breadth, range and historical imagination in research and writing, and recognition of values as well as acknowledgement of variety and commonality in trade unionism. An emphasis on industrial politics, as we suggested in our 1999 introduction, requires an inter-disciplinary approach. Historians are often at their best when they work across boundaries and synthesize the insights of different fields and disciplines. If the labour movement has often seemed a pallid simulacrum of what the words conjure up, the term is suggestive of the integration necessary in historical writing about industrial politics. To take one example, in telling the story of the Labour Party, historians cannot, at least not with any conviction, treat trade unionism as playing a minor part nor can they treat it as a monolith: they need to address trade unionism and its complexities and divisions as an integral aspect of the party narrative. What is connected should not be sundered.

Eric Hobsbawm remarked, '… *even the recorded past* changes in the light of subsequent history.'[102] (original emphasis) Some of the studies discussed above were written in the context of the emergence of New Labour, a development which has led historians to reconsider Labour's past. If for some the triumphant advent of New Labour represented, like Hobsbawm's illustration, the collapse of the Soviet Union, the closure of an historic period or 'the strange death of social democracy', others stressed its continuity with earlier phases of labourism and Labour's links with liberalism.[103]

Caution may be in order. If there are continuities between today and yesterday – and the Labour Party and the trade unions have unquestionably reinvented aspects of their ideology, politics and political practice throughout their history

– New Labour may be persuasively represented as a novel reaction to a novel context, the brave new world of neo-liberalism. To assimilate recent innovation to the liberalism or even the revisionism of Labour's past risks entering the realm of the ahistorical.[104] It may also be premature: how rooted is 'Blairism'? Is Old Labour dead and gone, with Nye Bevan in the grave? An evanescent present can be an unreliable guide to such questions. Those who prophesied a renewal of the radical Liberalism of the early twentieth century, the dissolution of the party's alliance with the unions and the success of Tony Blair, already have much to think about.[105]

But looking at the past with an eye on the present is not, as Herbert Butterfield had it, the greatest of all historical sins.[106] Current pre-occupations can be a stimulus to reconstructing the past and informing us about the present. So long as we accept that the past possesses its own integrity. If we impose our vision of the present onto the past we run the risk of violating that integrity. Historians should travel across time as well as across boundaries. They should treat the past on its own terms. If we employ historical imagination to reconstruct it, rather than too easily understanding it in terms of today and ransacking it for contemporary parallels, lessons may still emerge. They are likely to be complex, conditional, contingent and contradictory.

Relevance is contested and changing. What some perceive as relevant today may not have been perceived as relevant yesterday nor appear relevant tomorrow.[107] Acknowledgement of forgotten movements and lost causes, recognition of the Digger, the Leveller, the stockinger, the handloom weaver, is more than antiquarian whimsy: it is a central aspect of the heritage of labour and social history. In the same spirit, the casual docker, the aristocratic tool-room worker, the black-coated clerk, the female sewing machinist, the black bus conductor and the Trotskyist militant of the post-war period, demand rescue from the condescension of posterity and, in some cases, the twenty-first century historian.[108]

For the wheel turns bringing new fashions, new professional cultures, new academic networks, new gatekeepers.[109] This may militate against certain subjects and certain approaches. One wonders how the work of Edward Thompson, Eric Hobsbawm, Christopher Hill and John Saville would be received if it was published for the first time today.[110] A fair assessment would honour its breadth, its analytical insight and its vindication of the use of an open and creative Marxism. Contemporary critics are worried by its teleological aspects, the socialist values which impregnate it and their impact on subsequent historians of labour.[111] Reappraisal is healthy and history should not ultimately be measured against what ought to have happened, whatever we think that should have been. But all historians mediate between themselves, their readers and the 'facts'. Evaluation is not exclusive to socialist historians. It is inescapable.[112] The temptation to depict assessments, which employ criteria that we find disagreeable, as illegitimate intrusions into the province of the value-free historian may miss the point in making a partisan point. Commitments, conceptions of progress, yardsticks of one kind or another are pervasive. They can be creative if open to scrutiny, conscious and controlled. If we remember this then the history of labour may possess not only a path breaking past but a vibrant future.

Notes

This paperback edition has been produced using images of the original pages published in 1999.
Place of publication is London unless otherwise indicated.

1   A. Campbell, N. Fishman and J. McIlroy (eds), *The Post-War Compromise: British trade unions and industrial politics, 1945–64* (2007) first published by Ashgate as A. Campbell, N. Fishman and J. McIlroy (eds), *British Trade Unions and Industrial Politics, vol. 1: the post-war compromise, 1945–64* (Aldershot, 1999); J. McIlroy, N. Fishman and A. Campbell (eds). *The High Tide of British Trade Unionism: trade unions and industrial politics, 1964–79* (2007) first published by Ashgate as J. McIlroy, N. Fishman and A. Campbell (eds), *British Trade Unions and Industrial Politics, vol. 2: the high tide of trade unionism, 1964–79* (Aldershot, 1999).
2   N. Kirk, review, *International Labor and Working-Class History*, 63, 2003, p. 166.
3   A. Fowler, review, *Historical Studies in Industrial Relations*, 9, 2000, pp. 171, 175.
4   C. Crouch, 'Once upon a time, trade unions ...', *Political Quarterly*, 71, 2000, p. 362.
5   M. Terry, review, *Historical Studies in Industrial Relations*, 11, 2001, pp. 148, 155. See also the reviews by I. Aitken, 'New Labour may not like us ...', *Guardian*, 26 April 2000, J. Tomlinson, 'Rough and tumble on the shop floor', *The Times Higher Education Supplement*, 29 September 2000, R. Darlington in *Socialist Review*, January 2001 and H. Ratner in *Revolutionary History*, 8, 2, 2002. See also *Labour Research*, May 2000.
6   E. Hobsbawm, 'Afterword', in Campbell *et al.*, *Post-War Compromise*, p. 314, and J. McIlroy *et al.*, 'Introduction: approaching post-war trade unionism', p. 13.
7   K. O. Morgan, review, *Labour History Review*, 65, 3, 2000, p. 387.
8   Kirk, review, pp. 166–7 and T. Bergholm, review, *Scandinavian Economic History Review*, xlix, 2, 2001, p. 100
9   Cf Hobsbawm, 'Afterword'.
10   Morgan, review, p. 386. His distaste for the many index entries referring to the Communist Party and the Trotskyists is suggestive of the allegiance to top-down history and high politics evident in his published work.

11 J. McIlroy and A. Campbell, 'The high tide of trade unionism: mapping industrial politics, 1964–79' in McIlroy *et al.*, *High Tide*, pp. 116–18.

12 K. O. Morgan, *Callaghan: a life* (Oxford, 1997), pp. 626–76.

13 Ibid., p. 673.

14 Ibid., pp. 664, 657, 650, 672.

15 Ibid., pp. 343, 658.

16 Cf McIlroy and Campbell, 'High tide', p. 101.

17 Cf ibid., pp. 113 and 123, Table 4.4.

18 A. Thorpe, 'The Labour Party and the trade unions', in McIlroy *et al.*, *High Tide*, p. 145: '… it was to assert a fairly naked truth to argue that, for many workers, years of pay restraint had brought few real benefits and not a few costs … This time there was no question of union agreement' (ibid.).

19 Cf McIlroy and Campbell, 'High tide', pp. 110–11.

20 Ibid., p. 110.

21 Cf The 5 per cent norm 'certainly put any trade union leader who wished to support government policy in an extremely difficult position. Few would have the authority to control the demands of their members to this degree and their position would be impossible if other union leaders had not even the will to support the policy' (D. Barnes and E. Reid, *Governments and Trade Unions: the British experience, 1964–79* (1980), p. 214).

22 Thorpe, 'Labour Party', p. 146.

23 Cf 'While the 1979 "winter of discontent" was certainly less decisive than is claimed by subsequent mythologies, there is little doubt that Callaghan's political miscalculations (which more than any "irresponsibility" on the part of union leaders or members, was, as Andrew Thorpe shows, largely responsible for the crisis) contributed to the Tories' eventual success …' (J. Hinton, review, *Albion*, 33, 2, 2001, p. 357).

24 Morgan, review, p. 386.

25 McIlroy and Campbell, 'High tide', p. 117.

26 Ibid., pp. 117–8.

27 Cf Thorpe, 'Labour Party', pp. 145–7; A Taylor, 'The Conservative Party and the trade unions', in McIlroy *et al.*, *High Tide*, pp. 176–8 and p. 180, Table 6.2, which confirms that the indicators of the public esteem for trade unions recorded in opinion polls were the same in August 1977 as in August 1979. There is no reference to the 'Winter of Discontent', let alone refutation of McIlroy and Campbell's views, in R. Taylor, '"What are we here for?" George Woodcock and trade union reform', in McIlroy *et al.*, *High Tide*, although they take issue with some of the comments he has made elsewhere – see McIlroy and Campbell, 'High tide', pp. 116–17.

28 J. Lloyd, 'All together now', *London Review of Books*, 19 October 2000. Lloyd commends Nina Fishman's chapters in *Post-War Compromise* and appears to exclude from censure those by Geoffrey Goodman (ibid.), Alan McKinlay and Joseph Melling (ibid.) and Robert Taylor (*High Tide*) and to some extent that of Mike Savage (ibid.).

29 Lloyd states that the contention 'that it was the unions' own fault – contains something of the truth … organised labour bears part of the responsibility for its

own marginalisation' (Lloyd, 'All together now', pp. 32–3). But the thrust of his essay indicts the unions and nowhere does he refer to any other actor or any other factor as playing a part in union decline.

30   McIlroy *et al.*, 'Introduction', p. 2.
31   Lloyd, 'All together now', p. 33.
32   B. Towers, review, *Industrial Relations Journal*, 32, 4, 2001, p. 349.
33   E. Sullivan, 'Chronicling labour: recent writings', *Journal of Contemporary History*, 40, 2, 2005, p. 402.
34   Ibid., pp. 402–3. Cf 'Most tastes are well catered for': Kirk, review, p. 166.
35   Lloyd, 'All together now', p. 32.
36   G. O'Hara, '"Planned growth of incomes" or "emergency gimmick": the Labour Party, the social partners and incomes policy, 1964–70', *Labour History Review*, 69, 1, 2004, p. 59. O'Hara's insistence that 'agreement was fleeting mainly because the Labour Party in government was uncertain in its theoretical outlook as to what prices and incomes policy was actually for' and that in assessing policy failure this confusion was 'just as important as the structure of British capital, industrial relations and labour politics' (ibid., pp. 61, 62) remains unconvincing.
37   See Thorpe, 'Labour Party', pp. 133–50; see also L. Panitch, *Social Democracy and Industrial Militancy: the Labour Party, the trade unions and incomes policy, 1945–74* (Cambridge, 1976); Barnes and Reid, *Governments and Trade Unions*; D. Coates, *Labour in Power?: a study of the Labour Government, 1974–79* (1980); J. Cronin, *Labour and Society in Britain, 1918–79* (1984), pp. 193–205; D. Coates, *The Crisis of Labour: industrial relations and the state in contemporary Britain* (1989), pp. 37–159; J. McIlroy, *Trade Unions in Britain Today* (2nd edn, Manchester, 1995), pp. 186–207; P. Bell, *The Labour Party in Opposition, 1970–74* (2003); J. E. Cronin, *New Labour's Pasts: the Labour Party and its discontents* (Harlow, 2004), pp. 1–202.
38   Hinton, review, p. 360.
39   Lloyd, 'All together now', p. 33; D. Lyddon, '"Glorious summer": the high tide of rank and file militancy', in McIlroy *et al.*, *High Tide*.
40   Towers, review, p. 349.
41   Kirk, review, p. 166.
42   McIlroy and Campbell, 'High tide', p. 96.
43   Lloyd, 'All together now', p. 33.
44   Ibid.
45   McIlroy and Campbell, 'High tide', pp. 96–7.
46   Thorpe, 'Labour Party', p. 142.
47   Ibid., p. 144.
48   Taylor, 'Conservative Party', p. 161.
49   Taylor, 'What are we here for?' Some of Lloyd's extensive engagements are with straw men: '… it's wrong to argue that the unions hadn't benefited from Labour legislation or that there was nothing to gain from further cooperation …' ('All together now', p. 33). It remains unclear whom he is arguing against. He also notes that Harold Wilson's 'National Dividend' of 1967 is not mentioned in our book and implies that the unions 'killed it off'(ibid., p. 32). Wilson's vague suggestion was for the long term (unlike his contemporary proposals for the statutory restriction

of wages) and met with immediate opposition from the Confederation of British Industry as well as the TUC. The latter deemed it 'administratively impractical' but nevertheless remained committed to voluntary wage vetting (*The Times*, 4, 6 March, 3 April 1967; Panitch, *Social Democracy*, pp. 141, 296, n.9).

50   Hinton, review, pp. 357–8.

51   Towers, review, p. 348.

52   Hinton, review, p. 359. And I readily concede Hinton's point that my dismissal was unduly peremptory given the 'admirably balanced commentaries' on other marginal movements (ibid.).

53   R. Hyman, 'Afterword', in McIlroy *et al.*, *High Tide*, p. 359.

54   C. Wrigley, 'Women in the labour market and in the unions', in McIlroy *et al.*, *High Tide*, pp. 60–1. But the distance of feminism then from feminism now may be evoked by reading S. Rowbotham, L. Segal and H. Wainwright, *Beyond the Fragments: feminism and the making of socialism* (1979).

55   For the contemporary relevance of class analysis from a range of perspectives, see E. Meiksins Wood, *Democracy Against Capitalism: renewing historical materialism* (Cambridge, 1995); G. Marshall, *Repositioning Class: social inequality in industrial societies* (1997); R. Crompton, *Class and Stratification: an introduction to current debates* (2nd edn, Cambridge, 1998); F. Devine *et al.*, *Rethinking Class: culture, identities, lifestyle* (Basingstoke, 2005). For discussions of gender, see, for example, A. Baron (ed.), *Work Engendered: towards a new history of American labor* (Ithaca, NY, 1991); A. Kessler-Harris, 'Treating the male as "other": redefining the parameters of labor history', *Labor History*, 34, 2/3, 1993, pp. 190–204.

56   J. Hinton, *Women, Social Leadership and the Second World War: continuities of class* (Oxford, 2002), p. 9.

57   Our doubts as to his position are intensified by Hinton's apparent rejection of class as a structure: 'It is not however my intention to reassert a foundational concept of class as a precursive reality structuring social and political life ... class was, amongst other things, a matter of identity' (ibid., p. 10).

58   McIlroy and Campbell, 'High tide', p. 113.

59   Crouch, review, p. 362.

60   Terry, review, p. 150.

61   For a brief summary see McIlroy, *Trade Unions in Britain Today*, particularly pp. 194–222.

62   See, for example, A. Fox, *History and Heritage: the social origins of the British industrial relations system* (1985).

63   Crouch, review, p. 63. This was, of course, the contemporary position of Hobsbawm although, as discussed in McIlroy *et al*, *High Tide*, his evidence was contentious.

64   Crouch, review, p. 364. He invokes Richard Hyman in support, quoting Hyman's observation that 'by the 1970s unions seem to have lost their former status as influential components of civil society'. Hyman, 'Afterword' p. 362 was referring specifically to England, and excluding Scotland and 'perhaps' Wales. Again, if we compare the 1970s with the rest of the century this judgement seems questionable.

65   McIlroy and Campbell, 'High tide', pp. 106–19.

66   R. Hyman, 'Afterword'. pp. 355–9; see also Thorpe, 'Labour Party', pp. 142–7.
67   For a recent discussion, see P. Smith, *Union Organization and Union Leadership: The Road Haulage Industry* (2001), pp. 7–30.
68   G. Duménil and D. Lévy, *Capital Resurgent: roots of the neo-liberal revolution* (Cambridge, Mass., 2004); D. Harvey, *A Brief History of Neo-Liberalism* (Oxford, 2005); A. Glyn, *Capitalism Unleashed* (Oxford, 2006).
69   McIlroy and Campbell, 'High tide', pp. 97–8; Hyman, 'Afterword', pp. 357–8; J. McIlroy, Notes on the Communist Party', in McIlroy *et al.*, *High Tide*, pp. 245–8; J. McIlroy, '"Always outnumbered, always outgunned": the Trotskyists and the trade unions', in ibid., pp. 279–83.
70   Harvey, *A Brief History*, p. 1.
71   Hyman refers to Hugh Clegg and Royden Harrison, well known professors of industrial relations and social and labour history respectively. To take another example, Colin Crouch hazarded some 'combination of monetarism and attempts at straightforward corporatism' would characterize the 1980s (C. Crouch, *The Politics of Industrial Relations*, Manchester (1979), pp. 195–6).
72   J. McIlroy, 'Still under siege: British trade unions at the turn of the century', *Historical Studies in Industrial Relations*, 3, 1997, p. 103.
73   McIlroy, *Trade Unions in Britain Today*, p. 398. Unemployment was important in weakening the unions. But the state can influence or refuse to influence the level of unemployment. Adoption of neo-liberal economics restrained inflation, real wages rose for key groups of workers, employment levels and compositional changes in the labour force, in the context of union exclusion, restrictive legislation and economic policy, shifted the balance of forces. Cf H. Gospel, 'Markets, firms and unions', in S. Fernie and D. Metcalf, *Trade Unions: resurgence or demise?* (2005), pp. 35–9.
74   Lack of space does not permit address of recent periodical literature; for this see, particularly, the annual bibliographies published in *Labour History Review* and the indexes to *Historical Studies in Industrial Relations*.
75   D. Sandbrook, *Never Had It So Good: a history of Britain from Suez to the Beatles* (2005). Sandbrook draws largely on A. Sampson, *Anatomy of Britain* (1962) and also on M. Shanks, *The Stagnant Society* (Harmondsworth, 1961). There are isolated references to the work of academics Hugh Clegg and Henry Phelps Brown.
76   D. Sandbrook, *White Heat: a history of Britain in the swinging sixties* (2005); P. Hennessy, *Having It So Good: Britain in the fifties* (2006) presents a portrait of trade unions as political actors, drawing usefully on Cabinet papers but not on academic work, saving R. Taylor, *The Trade Union Question in British Politics* (Oxford, 1993).
77   C. Wrigley, *British Trade Unions since 1933* (Cambridge, 2002).
78   W. Hamish Fraser, *A History of British Trade Unionism, 1700–1998* (Basingstoke, 1999), pp. 191–235.
79   A. J. Reid, *United We Stand: a history of Britain's trade unions* (2004).
80   Ibid., pp. 301–2, 327–8.
81   Reid warns readers that the growth of shop floor bargaining after 1945, 'had very little to do with any mood of revolutionary revolt' (ibid., p. xv). Moreover, the

miners' strikes of the 1970s were 'less a result of popular insurgency than of the excessively confrontational attitudes of those managing the industry' (ibid.) Some historians may be surprised to learn that: 'Most previous discussions of the history of trade unions in Britain have portrayed a unitary figure of "the working class" in either a heroic or sinister light, implying that its members came from somewhere different from the rest of the population and may indeed have been not quite human' (ibid., p. ix).

82 C. Howell, *Trade Unions and the State: the construction of industrial relations institutions in Britain, 1890–2000* (Princeton, NJ, and Oxford, 2005). Similar points have been made in earlier literature; see K. D. Ewing, 'The state and industrial relations: "collective laissez-faire" revisited', *Historical Studies in Industrial Relations*, 5, 1998; N. Fishman, 'A vital element in British industrial relations: a reassessment of Order 1305, 1941–51', *Historical Studies in Industrial Relations*, 8, 1999. But Howell's work constitutes a powerful, synthetic elaboration.

83 S. Deakin and F. Wilkinson, *The Law of the Labour Market: institutions, employment and legal evolution* (Oxford, 2005).

84 R. Darlington and D. Lyddon, *Glorious Summer: class struggle in Britain, 1972* (2001).

85 Smith, *Unionization and Union Leadership*.

86 A. Taylor, *The NUM and British Politics, vol. 1: 1947–1968* (Aldershot, 2003); *vol. 2: 1968–1995* (Aldershot, 2005).

87 K. Gildart, *The North Wales Miners, 1945–1996: a fragile unity* (Cardiff, 2001).

88 R. Taylor, *The TUC: from the general strike to new unionism* (Basingstoke, 2000). On the neglected area of trade union education, see J. Fisher, *Bread on the Waters: a history of TGWU education, 1922–2000* (2005), pp. 92–209.

89 D. Tanner *et al* (eds), *The Labour Party in Wales, 1900–2000* (Cardiff, 2000); A. Reid, 'Labour and the trade unions', in D. Tanner *et al.* (eds), *Labour's First Century* (Cambridge, 2000), pp. 230–33.

90 S. Fielding, *The Labour Governments, 1964–70, vol. 1: Labour and cultural change* (Manchester, 2003); J. W. Young, *The Labour Governments, 1964–70, vol. 2: international policy* (Manchester, 2003; J. Tomlinson, *The Labour Governments, 1964–70, vol. 3: economic policy* (Manchester, 2003). For example, *In Place of Strife* attracts little over a page in volume 1 (pp. 105–6) and four pages in volume 3 (pp. 142–5). For a recent analysis, see R. Tyler, '"Victims of our history"? Barbara Castle and *In Place of Strife*', *Contemporary British History*, 20, 3, 2006.

91 A possible example is the long-term impact on industrial relations reform of the proposals of the Donovan Commission. But Wilson was not prepared to wait for the voluntary implementation of these recommendations. *In Place of Strife* was 'In Place of Donovan'. P. Jenkins, *The Battle of Downing Street* (1970), pp. 26–43.

92 R. Taylor, 'Trade union freedom and the Labour Party: Arthur Deakin, Frank Cousins and the Transport and General Workers' Union, 1945–64', in B. Brivati and R. Heffernan (eds), *The Labour Party: a centenary history* (Basingstoke, 2000); S. Ludlam, 'Norms and blocks: trade unions and the Labour Party since 1964', in ibid. See also A. Seldon and K. Hickson (eds), *New Labour, Old Labour: the Wilson and Callaghan governments, 1974–79* (2004), particularly the chapters by Robert Taylor and Jim Tomlinson.

93   L. Black, *The Political Culture of the Left in Affluent Britain, 1951–64: old Labour, new Britain* (Basingstoke, 2003).

94   Cronin, *New Labour's Past*. See also S. Ludlam, 'Too much pluralism, not enough socialism: interpreting the unions-party link', in J. Callaghan *et al.* (eds), *Interpreting the Labour Party: approaches to Labour Party history* (Manchester, 2003); E. Shaw, 'Lewis Minkin and the party-unions link', in ibid.

95   J. Callaghan, *Cold War, Crisis and Conflict: the history of the Communist Party of Great Britain 1951–68* (2003); G. Andrews, *End Game and New Times: the final years of British Communism 1964–91* (2004). The former makes no reference to R. Stephens, 'Cold War politics: Communism and anti-Communism in the trade unions', in Campbell *et al.*, *Post-War Compromise*. Other pertinent publications also go uncited, for example, J. McIlroy, 'Reds at work: Communist factory organisation in the Cold War 1947-56', *Labour History Review*, 65, 2, 2000; J. McIlroy, ' "Every factory our fortress": Communist Party workplace branches in a time of militancy, 1956-79, part 1: history, politics, topography', *Historical Studies in Industrial Relations*, 10, 2000; and J. McIlroy, 'Every factory our fortress": Communist Party workplace branches in a time of militancy, 1956-79, part 2: testimonies and judgements', *Historical Studies in Industrial Relations*, 12, 2001. In contrast, Geoff Andrews generously acknowledges McIlroy, 'Notes on the Communist Party', and other relevant work: 'The first in-depth study of the party's industrial strategy during the 1960s and 1970s, carried out by John McIlroy, has made a major contribution towards understanding the complexities of this period, by bringing much new evidence to light ...'. (ibid., p. 106).

96   There is some material in T. Cliff, *A World to Win: life of a revolutionary* (2000), and T. Grant, *History of British Trotskyism* (2002); and see, for example, J. McIlroy, 'The revolutionary odyssey of John Lawrence', *Revolutionary History*, 9, 2, 2006; J. McIlroy, 'A Communist historian in 1956: Brian Pearce and the crisis of British Stalinism', *Revolutionary History*, 9, 3, 2006

97   G. Gall, *The Meaning of Militancy? Postal workers and industrial relations* (Aldershot, 2003).

98   S. Cohen, *Ramparts of Resistance: why workers lost their power and how to get it back* (2006). R. Darlington, 'The agitator 'theory' of strikes re-evaluated', *Labor History*, 47, 2006.

99   Cf McIlroy, 'Notes on the Communist Party', p. 216. A number of largely uncritical autobiographies have been published: for example, F. Westacott, *Shaking the Chains: a personal and political history* (Chesterfield, 2002); N. Harding, *Staying Red: why I remain a socialist* (2005).

100 See, for example, A. Perkins, *Red Queen: the authorized biography of Barbara Castle* (2003); D. Howell, *Attlee* (2006); F. Beckett, *Macmillan* (2006); H. Conroy, *Callaghan* (2006); D. McShane, *Heath* (2006); P. Routledge, *Wilson* (2006); K. O. Morgan, *Michael Foot* (2007).

101 K. Gildart *et al.*, (eds), *Dictionary of Labour Biography, vol. 11* (Basingstoke, 2003); K. Gildart and D. Howell (eds) *Dictionary of Labour Biography, vol. 12* (Basingstoke, 2005). Volume 11 has entries relevant to this period on the engineering workers' leader, Jack Tanner, by Nina Fishman, the TGWU officials, Huw Edwards and Thomas Jones, and the mining trade unionist Tom Stephenson,

by Keith Gildart. Volume 12 has entries on the Scottish miners' leader, Abe Moffat, by myself and Alan Campbell as well as my piece on the Trotskyist and trade union educator, Jock Haston. See also my entry on the engineering union's Reg Birch and myself and Campbell on miners' leader Michael McGahey in volume 13 (forthcoming, Basingstoke, 2008). Also of interest is Joe Melling's work on the white-collar trade unionist, Clive Jenkins: see, for example, J. Melling, 'Leadership and factionalism in the growth of supervisory trade unionism: the case of ASSET, 1939–1956', *Historical Studies in Industrial Relations*, 13, 2002; J. Melling, 'Managing the white-collar union: salaried staff, trade union leadership and the politics of organised labour in post-war Britain, c1950-1968', *International Review of Social History*, 48, 2003.

102 E. Hobsbawm, 'The past as history', in E. Hobsbawm, *On History* (1997), p. 235.

103 S. Fielding, *The Labour Party: continuity and change in the making of 'New' Labour* (Basingstoke, 2003).

104 R. Toye, '"The smallest party in history"? New Labour in historical perspective', *Labour History Review*, 69, 1, 2004.

105 In a different way we may note the persistent attempts by industrial relations scholars to predicate the resurgence of contemporary trade unionism on the basis of short-term, sometimes ephemeral, indicators. See, for example, E. Heery, J. Kelly and J. Waddington, 'Union revitalization in Britain', *European Journal of Industrial Relations*, 9, 1, 2003; for a corrective, see A. Charlwood, 'The new generation of trade union leaders and prospects for union revitalization', *British Journal of Industrial Relations*, 42, 2, 2004.

106 H. Butterfield, *The Whig Interpretation of History* (1931), pp. 11–14, 62–3, 111.

107 Cf S. Fielding, 'Interesting but irrelevant', *Labour History Review*, 60, 3, 1995; J. Saville, 'The crisis in labour history: a further comment', *Labour History Review*, 61, 3, 1996.

108 Cf. The invocation of 'quirkiness' to characterise our attention to Stalinists and Trotskyists in Crouch, review, p. 364

109 Cf R. J. Evans, *In Defence of History* (1977), pp. 191–203.

110 Cf Fielding, 'Interesting but irrelevant'; Saville, 'The crisis in labour history'.

111 Cf D. Howell, 'Reading Alastair Reid: a future for labour history?', in N. Kirk (ed.), *Social Classes and Marxism* (Aldershot, 1996). For self-styled revisionism see A. Reid, 'Marxism and revisionism in British labour history', *Bulletin of the Society for the Study of Labour History*, 52, 3, 1987; A. Reid and E. F. Biagini, 'Currents of radicalism 1850-1914' in A. Reid and E. F. Biagini (eds), *Currents of Radicalism: popular radicalism, organised labour and party politics in Britain, 1850-1914* (Cambridge, 1991). A. Reid, 'A new paradigm for British labour history', *History Compass*, 3, 2005, pp. 2, 19–20.

112 Alistair Reid, who emphasises continuity and the resilience of liberalism in British labour history and contends that scholars in the Marxist tradition are handicapped in writing history by their politics, may provide a case in point. For example, he summarises the agitation against the 1971 Industrial Relations Act thus: 'Since this was a campaign of industrial and extra-parliamentary action, it could be portrayed as having extremist overtones, but in reality it showed marked continuities with

all the most respectable traditions of craft unionism and parliamentary liberalism, earlier enshrined in the statutory provisions of 1871, 1875 and 1906.' ('A new paradigm', p. 11). Reid makes a judgement, and it is partial. The drive to restore voluntarism and its continuity with the past and with liberal values is evaluated as significant and real. But this is at the expense of what was strikingly new and startling different. Militant political strikes, often organised from below, which challenged the state, were at the heart of the events that Reid characterises here. Allowing for the fact that craft unionists were sometimes not quite as respectable as they led liberals to believe, the strikes of the early 1970s hardly 'showed marked continuities with all the most respectable traditions of craft unionism and parliamentary liberalism'. Strikes, not to say strikes of this kind and on this scale, were absent from the campaigns of the 1870s and 1906. Reid's one-sided evaluation – underlining what was similar at the expense of what was distinctive – may be read as reflecting his predispositions and determination to discern 'the persistence of liberalism' (ibid., p. 20).

Preface to the 1999 Edition

The idea of this book and its companion volume, *British Trade Unionism and Industrial Politics: the high tide of trade unionism, 1964–79*, came from a conference we organized on the theme of 'British Trade Unionism, Workers' Struggles and Economic Performance, 1940–1979', held at the University of Warwick in September 1997. The event strengthened our belief that it was more than time for historians to begin taking stock of the trade unionism of these decades in more detailed and extensive fashion. The war years are of great significance but constitute a discrete period. The literature discussing the elusive relationships between trade unions and national economic performance is a burgeoning industry. Hence our emphasis in these texts upon the politics of trade unionism, conceived not only in terms of relations with the state but in terms of factionalism, the dynamics of industrial struggles and the allegiances of union activists.

Many of our chapters started life as conference papers, others were specially commissioned for these volumes. These two collections of essays make no claim to be comprehensive. We have revisited well-trodden ground and also provided first accounts of neglected byways, although we are under no illusions that key areas still require excavation and others more research. We have attempted to sketch in some of the background to the period in the survey chapters which preface the case studies. The books are most profitably read together but each stands independently in its own right.

We would like to express our gratitude to Dave Lyddon, Paul Smith, Richard Storey and Chris Wrigley who were involved with us in organizing the Warwick conference. Thanks are also due to the Modern Records Centre and the School of History, University of Warwick, the Society for the Study of Labour History, *Historical Studies in Industrial Relations*, the Barry Amiel and Norman Melburn Trust and the University of Stirling, who all supported the conference in a variety of ways. We are personally indebted to the Society for commissioning these texts as part of the Studies in Labour History series, and to Chris Wrigley, its President, who has supported us through a difficult gestation period. As a publisher, Alec McAulay has given unique and enduring support to labour history and we wish to thank him for his tolerance, good humour and hospitality.

The sustenance of labour history and its extension to new periods such as the

xli

second half of the twentieth century is dependent not only on the willingness of trade unionists and politicians to reflect on the past and the efforts of researchers to record it. They hinge also on the tireless endeavours of those 'active citizens' who have organized the Society for the Study of Labour History, its conferences and publications, over four decades – sometimes at the expense of their own research. And of course on the unstinting efforts of archivists, who in their own way facilitate the making of labour history, not only in well known establishments such as the Modern Records Centre and the National Museum of Labour History, but in hundreds of local archives. It is to these men and women that this book is dedicated.

John McIlroy, Alan Campbell, Nina Fishman, December 1998

Introduction:
Approaching Post-War Trade Unionism

John McIlroy, Alan Campbell, Nina Fishman

In the last decade of the twentieth century myths about the role of trade unions in the preceding post-war era were extended and lodged themselves deeper in public consciousness. The common sense of Thatcherism had long held the 1950s to be the locust years of lost opportunity in which Conservative administrations embraced social democracy and legitimized and stimulated collectivism and union power in ways inimical to the economic and political health of the nation. The 1960s and 1970s were depicted as a period of hedonism, indiscipline, appeasement. Edward Heath's 'U-turn' in 1971–2, his subsequent succumbing to the miners in 1974 and the 'Winter of Discontent' of 1978–9 were foundation legends of the new Conservatism. As the 1990s developed, Labour Party leaders began to subscribe to similar readings of history, signalling their own adaptation to neo-liberalism. Finally union leaders, traditionally renowned for celebratory accounts of labour's past, nailed their colours to the same mast. The 'magnificent journey', it seemed, had crashed into the buffers in 1979. A completely new beginning was necessary and timely.

From 1994, TUC leaders questioned the rationale and value of union policy in the 1960s and 1970s, branded the period 'the bad old days' and suggested that the central thrust of TUC strategy in the post-war era – the drive to secure working-class influence over the state – was 'a mistake, one which should never be repeated'.[1] For New Labour leader Tony Blair, Conservative governments since 1979 had improved industrial relations and moulded more responsible and efficient trade unionism. If the language employed was furtive in comparison with the saloon bar hyperbole of Thatcherism, its purposes in determining the parameters of policy and reducing the currency of debate were all too clear. In Blairspeak, the negative pre-1979 and positive post-Thatcher properties of trade unionism were asserted, unargued, unevidenced but coded: on the one hand, 'flying pickets ... closed shop ... relations with the state too close for comfort', and on the other, 'ballots ... fairness not favours'. The union struggles of recent history and their protagonists were, for Blair, his government and supporters, simply 'ghosts of time past ... it is time to leave them where they lie'.[2]

Just as much as Thatcherism, New Labour and New Unionism have defined their projects in opposition to a past selectively rendered. All these rhetorics underline once more the intense relevance of interpretations of the past for politicians and trade unionists, members as well as leaders, as a source of meaning and validation for action in the present. This development suggests again the value of close scrutiny of contemporary history, and the essential role of scholars in recreating and analysing the complexities of yesterday's issues, events and personalities, failures and successes. It foregrounds the necessity to recover the diminishing role of historians in assessing and challenging appropriations and partisan recovery of the recent past which may close off alternatives and provide a false basis for future strategy and policy by political and union activists. It is worth adding that we should remain alert to the recrudescence of currently less influential left-wing fables such as the inevitability, despite everything that has happened, of the revival of labour's progress or the essential, if presently invisible, revolutionary instincts of the rank and file trade unionist.

The hazards of engagement with the history of our own times have been recently and eloquently re-argued.[3] The problems – from our own proximity and personal experience, which can constrain detachment, to the difficulties of access to participants and documentation – are numerous. Yet the dangers of leaving the field to self-interested mythmakers justify the preliminary work of clearing the ground and beginning a more rigorous scrutiny of the fortunes of post-war trade unionism. If the labour movement is to have a future, it requires a more detailed, more balanced account of its past.

This aspiration is reinforced by the general neglect of trade unionism by social scientists and historians in recent years and specifically the relative paucity of work on the post-war era, 1945–79. The interest sociologists took in this area in the 1970s has diminished.[4] With the exception of Lewis Minkin's monumental work on relations between unions and the Labour Party and the extended survey edited by Pimlott and Cook, covering the period from the early eighteenth century but containing several chapters dealing with the period 1945–79, much the same could be said about political scientists. As with sociology, there is only a sparse periodical literature devoted almost wholly to developments in trade unionism in the 1980s.[5] In contrast, economists continue to take an interest in trade unionism, if largely through a specialized literature dealing with wage movements, bargaining models, the consequences of state policy and the impact of unions on the firm and the national economy. The totalized, problem-centred synthesis associated most recently with the labour economist, the late Henry Phelps Brown, is rarely emulated today.[6]

Industrial relations has continued to constitute the heartland for the study of trade unionism. It still produces a rich periodical and monographic literature dealing with diverse aspects of current trade union organization and practice. Yet it is adjudged by leading practitioners as a subject in some disarray. It has proved unable to come to terms with central questions: the role of the state; the political alignments of trade unions; power, conflict and change in the workplace; and the social processes of worker mobilization. Since the 1980s its core concerns, always broadly managerialist and pre-occupied with public policy but set within a pluralist framework which privileged collectivism, have shifted. Industrial relations, in the workplace and in the university, has been in decline. It has been beset, within and without, by the growth of Human Resource Management (HRM) which, with its crude unitarist paradigm, reduces trade unionism to the margins. The growth of HRM has unfortunately overshadowed a more beneficial, novel strand in the discipline which has involved more sophisticated interest in enterprise organization and managerial strategy.[7]

Industrial relations academics, an observer faithfully recorded forty years ago, 'think in constricted terms, nearly always in the present tense ... the sense of history, with its depth, reach and contemplative spirit, fails to stir.'[8] Texts addressing the past, even the post-war period, have been rare and have constituted a small fraction of the output of industrial relations, as a glance at its major journals will confirm. Alan Fox's magisterial *History and Heritage* deals with the years after 1945 in broad sweep; the late Hugh Clegg brought his three-volume *History of British Trade Unions* up to 1951; and Terry and Edwards have produced a valuable collection of essays on the hidden history of union workplace organization in the post-war decades. Valuable histories of individual unions which cover this period have continued to appear in healthy numbers, although they are sometimes overlooked.[9]

Nor has the study of trade unionism found a safe refuge in labour history. Here too there has been much talk of 'crisis'.[10] The shift in disciplinary concerns in the 1960s from an institutional emphasis on unions and political parties to a new concern with working-class experience and culture, stimulated by the publication of Edward Thompson's *The Making of the English Working-class* in 1963, was increasingly questioned by the 1980s. Concerned at the direction the discipline had taken, critics indicated the hazards inherent in the redefinition of labour history as the social history of the working-class, and worried about the extent to which labour history's political concerns had been dissolved in the 'general celebration of working-class life'. Selective appropriation from Thompson's own highly politicized writing had led to a de-politicization of the subject,

> and a radically de-institutionalised understanding of politics, in which the possible sources of working-class oppositional impulse are displaced from the recognized media of political parties and trade unions into a variety of non-institutional settings, embracing behaviour previously regarded as 'non-political' – eg crime, street violence, riots, industrial sabotage, mental illness, etc.[11]

In this context, Zeitlin urged a return to the institutional history of industrial

relations while Kimeldorf argued for bringing the analysis of trade unionism back to the centre of historical exploration.[12]

None the less, studies of working-class experience, housing, education,
gender, ethnicity, and of course language, continue to proliferate to the relative neglect of scholarship on trade unions. In the *Labour History Review's*
annual bibliographies for recent years, far fewer contributions are listed under 'trade unionism' – quite widely defined – than under 'popular culture,
leisure, sport and religion'.[13] For the post-war period, there have been some
attempts to address areas of trade union development but much remains to
be done. The late Henry Pelling updated his classic survey, *A History of
British Trade Unions*, to cover the 1960s and 1970s. There has been a new
general study by Laybourn, and Wrigley has published a valuable collection
of documents on mainstream trade unionism. Writing in the aftermath of the
decisive defeat of the 1984 miners' strike, John Saville delivered a concise,
insightful critique of the twentieth century labour movement. More special-
ised studies have been provided by Hyman on unions in the late 1940s and
by Tomlinson on the high politics of union-government relations under the
Attlee administration, while Tolliday, Zeitlin and Lyddon have begun to examine workplace organization. One of the most impressive contributions,
out of print and often overlooked, is Cronin's synthetic, rounded history of
Labour and Society which devotes most of five chapters to the post-war
period and tells us a great deal, albeit sometimes indirectly, about the predicament of trade unionism and its essential context.[14] But despite rhetorical
attention, neglected areas have continued to be uncultivated: recent decades
have seen few significant studies of the experiences of women and black
workers in trade unions between 1945 and 1979. Nor has the role of political activists in the post-war unions yet been fully addressed. Although general
surveys of the Communist Party (CP) have appeared by Thompson and
Branson (whose book ends in 1951), as well as a case study of engineering
in the 1940s by Hinton, we still lack an appreciation, based on detailed ar-
chival excavation, of the role of the CP in industry throughout the post-war
period comparable with studies of the party's earlier activities.[15]

Economic and social history more generally has neglected the study of
trade unionism over the last decade. Symptomatic of this tendency is a recent collection of essays on *Twentieth Century Britain: economic, social
and cultural change*, a 500-page volume with clear ambitions to be seen as
an authoritative text (the authors were assembled by the Economic History
Society). There is no reference to the shop stewards' movement of the First
World War; there is no index entry on the Communist Party, although it is
briefly mentioned in a chapter on inter-war unemployment which contains
two inconclusive paragraphs on the National Unemployed Workers' Movement. In the chapter 'Crisis and turmoil? 1973–93', two pages are devoted
to industrial relations: they mention neither shop stewards nor the 1984–5
miners' strike.[16] Such deficiencies have been partially repaired by inter-dis-

4

ciplinary work and by contributions from outside the universities. We are referring here to Chris Wrigley's edited *History of Industrial Relations*, the third volume of which covers the period 1940–79 and draws on contributions from historians and industrial relations scholars, and the well-known journalist Robert Taylor's volume in the series sponsored by the Institute of Contemporary British History.[17]

This uneven but overall far from impressive picture must be set within a general sense of malaise in labour studies in the 1990s, which has produced some heart-searching. The decline of class and the social weight of trade unionism; the political shift to the right; the collapse of the Soviet bloc; labour history's neglect of women and ethnic minorities; and the firm yoking of research funding to managerial agendas: all are commonly implicated.[18] It is far from obvious why the decline of trade unionism and socialist radicalism should of itself cause committed scholars to lose interest in serious research concerns. The alleged decline of class constitutes a good positive example: it has been vigorously combated in a growing inter-disciplinary literature.[19] The secular decline of labour in the United States since the 1950s has not stemmed a fertile stream of labour studies there. One wonders whether for some the essential historical sense of time, and the intuitive feeling for history's upturns and downturns has become coarsened and attenuated. Are Edward Thompson's and Christopher Hill's concern with lost causes and Eric Hobsbawm's belief that nothing sharpens the historical mind like defeat merely residues from a more principled era?[20] The events of 1956 stimulated the intellectual and political revitalization of many of labour history's formative spirits. It is difficult to understand in the context of labour history and industrial relations why the collapse of Stalinism should have dissipated interest in these fields unless there were many more closet Stalinists than we previously conceived. Labour history's neglect of women and minorities is indubitable: what is in contention is the means by which this should be redeemed. Once more the reinvigoration of class analysis suggests that, on any account, the revitalization of traditional approaches has more to offer the committed historian than emphases on patriarchy and identity. Heralded as an alternative to the durable duality of class and labour movement as the subject of politics and history, social movements based on gender and ethnicity have demonstrated sectionalism, subordination and compatibility with capitalism. Despite their incalculable educational impact, they are no substitute for the potential universality of movements and history rooted in class.

As for research funding, academics play some role in setting its parameters and are under no direct or overpowering compulsion to take the neo-liberal shilling. Their freedom in this sphere alerts us to a missing element – somewhat ironically, given the emphasis potential protagonists place upon it in their academic work – human agency. An increasingly overlooked but central factor since 1979 has been the refusal of resistance to trends in the

5

universities – trends inimical not only to radically committed scholarship but to the liberal academy itself – by social scientists and historians who once eagerly supported struggle in factories and offices. As David Howell has pointed out, the 'Third Way' – the attempt to subvert the assumptions, language and priorities of the funding agencies by critically emulating them – usually leads to the appropriation of the would-be appropriators.[21]

The debilities of labour studies in terms of both coverage and method have to be located within state policies and academic responses to them. Both have influenced diminished autonomy, reinforced cultures of deference to power, conformity and managerialism and stimulated a growing allegiance to 'relevance', increasingly defined as contributing to the state's political agendas and the resurgence of British capital. The competing post-modernist tendency to take refuge from reality and seek solace in 'virtual' control of events, play and 'discourse', has been only minimally apparent here. In its more moderate variants, post-modernism can help counteract simplistic ideas about human progress, the natural advance of labour, the inevitability of trade unionism. We can retrieve from post-modernism – as from older philosophies of history – reaffirmation of the tenuousness of our recovery of the past as it was, the space for competing narratives and interpretations, the importance of language. Critical engagement with the literary techniques of post-modernism, its passion for buried episodes, lost lives and storytelling, as practised by, say, Orlando Figes in *A People's Tragedy*, his enthralling, if for some of us politically dubious and over-inventive, study of the Russian revolution, may help to produce richer history and better writing.

There remains, nevertheless, the intellectual necessity to confront and reject post-modernism's epistemological core and its approach to history. Here we encounter the mistaken view – vigorously rebuffed by the post-modernists themselves – that labour historians should welcome and utilize the post-modernists' 'exciting' contribution to modern labour history. Some have urged that in resisting post-modernism's 'theoretical pretensions', we should accept that, in spite of its nihilism, epistemic relativism, rejection of class, 'its focus and practice ... should be embraced within the widening agenda of labour history'. The specific contention, based upon, in this case, an unwarranted division between post-modernists' theory and practice, is that recent work, notably by Patrick Joyce and James Vernon, helps us 'to appreciate the complex interaction of language and social structure, to examine more thoroughly the link between structure and action, the medium between material conditions and consciousness'.[22] If historians have always struggled with these relationships, they are precisely what post-modernists are *not* about. As one incisive review of their recent contributions to labour history put it,

What is disappointing, however, is that the prominence given to language in these new accounts does not actually help to meet the need to examine these complex connections. The stress on language all too easily slides into a form of linguistic

6

determinism, in which the historical impact of any non-linguistic realm is obscured, denied or declared unknowable. The turn against social class, in favour of a form of historical research in which only the concepts, idioms and grammars used in discourse are regarded as open to examination, is profoundly disabling.[23]

The more popular labour history is, the better, provided, of course, this is consonant with its rigour and integrity. But the health of a discipline must not be confused with its popularity or its ability to adapt to, as distinct from take the measure of, the latest intellectual fashion. Identity history which deserts universalism and privileges the particular, whether ethnicity, gender, sexuality, whatever, is subversive of good history.[24] The lure of post-modernist novelty should not lead us to trim, still less desert, basic touchstones, from class to the reality of the past and our ability to know it. There are incontestably real difficulties and fundamental problems in labour history – not least in the lack of recent attention to labour movements, with their aspiration and, sometimes, ability to transcend particularism – even if it is a little premature to speak of fatal crisis. New work of diversity and originality is still being produced, if on a smaller scale than we would like. The stream of studies of trade unionism has not yet dried up. Academics are still taking ambitious initiatives, witness the revamping of the *Labour History Review*, the recent establishment of the already thriving journal *Historical Studies in Industrial Relations*, the continuing vigour of the *International Review of Social History* and the welcome attention which *Twentieth Century British History* is paying to the labour movement.[25]

Our purpose in these two volumes is to extend this existing work and to fill gaps within it. But we also want to begin to build on strengths and compensate for weaknesses in its method and approach. Willman and Winch's *Innovation and Management Control: labour relations at BL Cars* (1985) may be taken as exemplifying the problems with even more sophisticated industrial relations research.[26] Unlike many of the surveys which dominate the industrial relations literature and which de-emphasize social action, it promises an in-depth historical analysis based on research conducted over three years. The study, focused on the development of the Metro model which was intended to restore profitability to the crisis-ridden British Leyland, covers the period from the early 1970s to the early 1980s. The account starts from, and remains heavily weighted towards, management's perspective. In terms of the relative absence of emphasis on management strategies from industrial relations research in the past, this rehabilitation is healthy.

However, it is achieved at the expense of adequate treatment of trade unionism. While fourteen stewards and three full-time officials were interviewed, this contrasts unfavourably with thirty-two BL managers, and footnote references to sources are biased towards the latter group. The texture is thin, the writing brusque and flesh and blood actors largely non-existent. Internal divisions amongst stewards in the plant and their relation, on the one hand, to members, and, on the other, to the AUEW and the TGWU, as well as the politics of these two unions, are briefly mentioned but far from fully developed. The BL Combine Committee is given a few lines, the victimization of Derek Robinson a page, in an account which contrasts unfavourably with those proffered by managers and trade unionists.[27] Robinson is typically referred to anonymously as 'the Longbridge convenor'. His membership of the Communist Party and the significant role CP members played in building and sustaining the stewards' organization in the plant is simply not mentioned.

The book's central section is referred to by Zeitlin as ' a detailed account of industrial relations at British Leyland in the late 1970s and early 1980s'.[28] It merits this evaluation only in an institutionalized and historically impoverished way. The narrative's connection with conflicts outside the plant to which the struggles depicted here were intimately related – the sharp conflict over the role of the state between corporatist and neo-liberal tendencies, internal union politics, the collapse of the Social Contract – is tenuous. Although the plant battles over participation, productivity and the activity of the National Enterprise Board were an integral part of wider agendas and struggles, these are only dimly echoed here. Strong on accounts of bargaining structures and procedures, management strategy and technological innovation, the text has difficulty in dealing with human agency, with alternatives and choices, with politics and with history. Whilst the authors are concerned to demonstrate 'how deep rooted historically were the trends that fostered labour relations problems', their histories of union organization and its protagonists are pallid and sometimes unsure: 'Another characteristic of the industry, the reliance on the shop steward system to express union demands may have originated in the wartime period'. Comparisons with Richard Croucher's well peopled, thick textured, wide canvassed *Engineers at War* (1982) are irresistible. More space is devoted by Willman and Winch to the engineering process of constructing the Metro than the political processes of the joint shop stewards' committee.[29] We make these criticisms at some length, not to dismiss what remains a valuable case study in industrial relations, but to illustrate that discipline's lack of a historical imagination even in its better work.

Some of these problems – from industrial relations' engagement with trade unions rather than labour movements, its neglect of the state, the influence of the past, the values and motivations of its actors, suggest the need for a multi-disciplinary approach. They have received attention in the past and it has recently been renewed. Lyddon and Smith have asserted the importance of history in industrial relations and, with their colleagues, have sought to remedy its absence through the important publication of *Historical Studies in Industrial Relations*.[30] However, the question remains: what kind of history, what kind of conceptual framework? It is, of course, possible, at least 'in principle', to insert class struggle into the mechanical categories of

Dunlop's system·of industrial relations as David Brody has suggested, though it is not necessarily desirable. Or, as Lyddon more fruitfully argues, by developing the insights of the Webbs, Allan Flanders and Hugh Clegg and in opposition to the neo-institutionalism of Jonathan Zeitlin, to centrally locate the history of trade unions within 'a very comprehensive classification of internal and external job regulation'. Although Lyddon is 'mindful' of Montgomery's caution regarding the dangers of 'an exclusive focus on industrial relations', this remains a potential hazard of such a strategy. A historical vision confined to the processes of regulation in the workplace and the industry, even one encompassing the role of the state, may remain in practice unnecessarily limited.[31] For, at least to date, the history of industrial relations has tended to address the historicized problematics of contemporary industrial relations. Thus we get Clegg's immensely valuable but nevertheless restricted history of industrial relations from above. Even Terry and Edwards' pioneering collection has, on close scrutiny, too little to say either about workplace politics or politics beyond the factory, and still feels the need to justify itself as 'a guide to good policy making'.[32] Even the class struggle component of industrial relations literature has possessed a restrictive bias towards the workplace and a partial, circumscribed and, for many, esoteric conception of politics.

We would endorse the sentiments of Alan Fox (and the scope of his essay in realizing them) which insists on an integrated approach in examining historically the social context of industrial relations but also,

> involves dwelling at some length upon matters not normally discussed in industrial relations literature. Political theory, upper class strategies of rule, the nature of the British state, the nature of English law, the Victorian middle class concept of service, social imperialism, the personality and political convictions of Stanley Baldwin, the reasons for the failure of British fascism: these are among the themes I have found relevant for understanding why the industrial relations system grew as it did and not in some other way.[33]

This is essentially and extensively a political agenda, if one which conceives of a politics deeper than many contemporary political scientists envisage. We would embrace but go beyond this formulation to argue for a multilayered concern with social and economic, as well as political, factors. We are looking for a totalized approach, a return to the broad vision of political economy. We would agree with Richard Price: advocacy of the primacy of politics in writing history, and certainly politics as discourse, politics autonomous and free-floating from structure, may be self-defeating. He remarks that it is unclear how strikes fit entirely into 'that lockbox' and observes pertinently that 'politics tends to be confined to institutions rather than action and behaviour'.[34] But whilst we need to embed our analysis in economics, politics plays an intrinsic role in the mobilization of industrial action, in the form that action takes, in its progress, its resolution and its consequences. There is no need at all for politics to be confined to institutions – although let us not downplay the importance of institutions. Whilst we must address the wide range of factors stimulating and constraining social action, politics is certainly there, very close to its heart, in the values of protagonists and in the structures they make and confront.

What appears to us most fruitful in writing the history of trade unions and trade unionists, a history soaked in politics, is thus a multi-factor approach which emphasizes politics. The traditional, essential subject of history is politics, for it is through politics that change takes place, it is through politics that change in other realms, economic, technological, social, is mediated. It seems artificial and constricting to conceive of the history of trade unions or industrial relations as a distinct field, set apart from labour history. To attempt to press this necessarily diverse subject matter solely into the boundaries of job regulation or an industrial relations history demarcated from the wider field of labour history appears to deny its breadth and its freedom. This is not to reject the utility of a dedicated journal but to address its scope. The kind of approach Fox offers is most fruitfully conceived of, we would argue, as the history of industrial politics, essentially imbricated with the broader field of labour history.[35]

To adopt this emphasis is consciously to redress the conventional focus of industrial relations by a consideration of industrial politics, from above and from below. This necessitates an examination of politics not only at the level of the state, but inside unions and parties. It requires address of politics not only inside these institutions but also inside the workplace, and in the values and actions of trade unionists. Our concern must be not only with the politics of the labour movement, its activists and the broader working-class but with the politics of capital and the management of labour, an area that has been relatively ignored.[36] David Marsh recently reproached industrial relations scholars for their limited interest in political issues and the literature of political science – ironically in a study of trade unionism with scarcely a word to say about politics inside unions. Political scientists, for their part, have neglected trade unions and their history. When unions have attracted their attention they have all too often been examined in a shallow fashion, their relations with the state being considered to the virtual exclusion of most other aspects of union activity.[37]

But Marsh has a point. Some years ago a monograph appeared analysing conflicts inside the AUEW, centred on a study of one district committee from the 1940s to the 1970s. The limited and disparate literature on factionalism in trade unions was outlined. There were brief references to 'the left-wing faction' and CP members. Indeed factional membership was stated to be one of the 'four structural dimensions of Committee membership'. Although the district and the committee researched – Manchester –

were perhaps the strongest base of 'the Broad Left' in Britain, the organization of the faction and the manner in which membership of it impinged upon the actions of the committee's members went unexamined. This was despite the existence at the time of a detailed study of the Broad Left in Manchester, a rich fugitive literature and the availability of key protagonists. Important political actors, right-wing as well as left, occasionally intrude into the text; but their voices are mute, their politics, and the impact of those politics on their trade unionism, are scarcely mentioned. In terms of their contribution to understanding conflict, it is instructive to place the institutional, impersonal account given of the Platts (Barton) Ltd closure in 1956 alongside the later view of politics from below embodied in the testimony of the Trotskyist senior steward, who of course is absent from the academic text. The politics of internal conflict in unions is, at least in recent literature, generally neglected.[38]

When industrial relations writers have addressed the political aspects of trade unions, they have largely operated one-dimensionally, employing a partial focus on politics which sometimes eschews consideration of the practice and organization of reformism – which is politics for most trade unionists – and which primarily discusses the potential contribution which tendencies in trade unionism may make to revolutionary change.[39] Conventional, 'actually existing' politics have been judged in practice as peripheral to industrial relations. Yet exchange with the state and political parties, the political process inside unions, factionalism, the political allegiances of activists, the role of political parties and their impact in the workplace should surely constitute an integral, indispensable component of the study of trade unionism.

At least some contributions to the long debate on writing labour history are tinged with a somewhat dogmatic prescription of particular paths and panaceas. We are instead pointing towards a framework which we feel will produce fruitful work without detracting from diversity and pluralism, a directive emphasis on the history of trade unionists rather than trade unionism. But this framework draws our attention to related silences. The need for studies of the organizational culture of unions, how the values of trade unionists and the structures and ethos which these values shape change over time and the factors which influence the forms they take, has been urged but not realized. Long-running debates on bureaucracy and rank and file have far outpaced empirical studies.[40] No writer in recent decades has sought to expand the boundaries of the history of the single union, to develop general theory with the ambition deployed by Turner in the 1960s. There has been no attempt to ponder the life and career of union leaders for similar purposes in the style once essayed by Vic Allen. Writing in 1964, Eric Hobsbawm highlighted the dearth of studies of union leadership.[41] The absence remains acute. Despite their importance, we have no published studies on Jack Jones or Hugh Scanlon – or any other leader of the period with the exception of Arthur Scargill.[42]

Despite the sterling efforts of John Saville, Joyce Bellamy and their contributors to the multi-volume *Dictionary of Labour Biography*, the lack of sufficiently extensive materials for rigorous, comparative prosopography has circumscribed the use in practice of important theoretical tools such as generational analysis. We still have inadequate information on the lay activists, despite acknowledgement of their importance, along with national leaders, in working-class mobilization. The stress on the active – not always militant – minority is sometimes criticized on the grounds that they were untypical and exceptional. Again the problem is one of integration. The active minority's importance lies precisely in their immense significance to the development and sustenance of consciousness and action. What made them, what motivated them, as well as the complex processes of interaction, in the workplace and beyond it, between members, representatives and officials are central to understanding trade unionism. And of course we cannot understand these relationships of power, authority and legitimacy unless we relate them to wider processes involving political parties, capital and the state.[43]

David Montgomery asserts that 'what needs to be kept in mind is that unions are but one instrument – one extremely important instrument – of working-class mobilization ...'.[44] We would rebalance his specification. Our claim for twentieth-century Britain is that trade unionism, grasped in its industrial and political dimensions, has been the primary, fundamental instrument for attracting workers' allegiance and realizing workers' goals. By far the largest voluntary movement and with a strong associational culture, it has been the key means of creating class unity and action. We would, however, endorse Montgomery's plea for a history which situates unions within the complex web of community associations, parties, employers, economy and state.[45] *Starting from* trade unionism as the bedrock, the animating core of the labour movement, still seems to us the most fruitful way to proceed.

In beginning to develop these approaches we have related our two volumes to the existing work covering the period 1945–79. Pelling's treatment justifiably emphasizes high politics to a greater degree than for the earlier period of his study. The same is true of Fox as he develops the compelling themes of his probing interrogation of two centuries. Robert Taylor likewise largely addresses 'the complex relationship between governments and organized labour and narrates the flow of events'.[46] Wrigley and his colleagues cover similar ground although their volume also provides valuable analyses of strikes and social welfare as well as case studies of the docks, car manufacture and road haulage. The breadth of Cronin's fertile treatment of these decades prohibits him from any detailed address of developments within individual unions. As he is addressing a packed century and four countries, Phelps Brown's discussion of the post-war era requires re-examination and expansion. Pimlott and Cook's collection contains several valuable chapters

12

of relevance: an essay by Robert Taylor on 'the trade union problem' and a brief overview by Ken Coates of 1945–60.

In the light of this literature, we have included in these volumes more detailed analyses by authoritative scholars of the industrial politics of the Conservative and Labour Parties. But we also have studies of the relatively obscure industrial activities of the Communist Party and the Trotskyists. There are contributions on ethnicity, gender and internationalism, as well as case studies of neglected but important strikes, individual unions and the role of the TUC. There is novel analysis of the use of language by militants to mobilize support; of class and work culture; the role of the labour correspondent; workers' education; the politics of academics and their influence on state policy.

Our contributors are drawn from a range of disciplines – industrial relations, sociology, labour history, political science, management studies. Our hope is that these texts will appeal to students of each of these subjects. The essays are thus diverse and far reaching, dealing anew with ground previously tilled as well as with neglected areas. We attempt to address the mainstream and the marginal. Our subject is the politics – in the fullest sense of the term – of trade unionism, treated as an autonomous and still exciting subject for study which may provide lessons for future architects of labour movements. Perhaps unfashionably, the diverse activities and complex experience of trade unionists have not been winnowed here to provide evidence of their impact upon productivity, the enterprise and the fortunes of national capital, an exercise currently popular with academics from a variety of disciplines, nor re-interpreted in such a way that they might be accommodated, however imperfectly, within contemporary economic theories.[47] Neither do we make any claim to provide a full account of the trade unionism of these years, although the survey chapters in each volume map out brief overviews. A comprehensive, panoramic history requires as a preliminary the deep quarrying of its component blocks; it is in this spirit that we offer these essays, as a further step towards constructing both a broad and detailed picture of industrial politics during these years. If the labour movement is to continue to be relevant to working people, its partisans must understand what happened to it and why. Labour history still has a vital role to play in this process.

Notes

1. See, for example, J. Monks, 'No shopping list', *New Statesman*, 8 September 1995; 'Interview with John Monks', *New Statesman*, 6 September 1996; J. Monks, 'Gains and losses after twenty years of legal intervention', in W. McCarthy (ed.), *Legal Intervention in Industrial Relations: gains and losses* (1992).
2. Quoted in J. McIlroy, 'The enduring alliance? Trade unions and the making

of New Labour, 1994–97', *British Journal of Industrial Relations*, 36, 4, 1998, p. 542.

3. E. Hobsbawm, 'The present as history', in E. Hobsbawm, *On History* (1997).
4. See, for example, the studies of trade unionism in the workplace, notably T. Lane and K. Roberts, *Strike at Pilkingtons* (1971); H. Beynon, *Working for Ford* (Harmondsworth, 1973); A. Pollert, *Girls, Wives, Factory Lives* (1981); T. Nichols and P. Armstrong, *Workers Divided* (1976); and wider attempts to analyse trade unionism such as A. Fox, *A Sociology of Work and Industry* (1971); R. Hyman, *Marxism and the Sociology of Trade Unionism* (1971) and *Industrial Relations: a Marxist introduction* (1975); V. L. Allen, *The Sociology of Industrial Relations* (1971); J. A. Banks, *Trade Unionism* (1974); S. Hill, *Competition and Control at Work* (1981); C. Crouch, *Class Conflict and the Industrial Relations Crisis* (1977) and *Trade Unions: the logic of collective action* (1982); not to speak of the influential work of Goldthorpe and his colleagues – see J. Goldthorpe et al., *The Affluent Worker: industrial attitudes and behaviour* (Cambridge, 1968), *The Affluent Worker: political attitudes and behaviour* (Cambridge, 1968), and *The Affluent Worker in the Class Structure* (Cambridge, 1969); but see now F. Devine, *Affluent Workers Revisited: privatism and the working-class* (Edinburgh, 1992) and D. Gallie, R. Penn and M. Rose (eds), *Trade Unionism in Recession* (Oxford, 1996).
5. L. Minkin, *The Labour Party Conference* (Manchester, 1980) and *The Contentious Alliance: trade unions and the Labour Party* (Edinburgh, 1991); B. Pimlott and C. Cook (eds), *Trade Unions in British Politics: the first 250 years* (2nd edition, 1991): whereas the balance of the first edition of this book, published in 1982, was tilted towards the period before 1945, additions to the second edition focused on the years after 1979. See also M. Moran, *The Union of Post Office Workers: a study in political sociology* (1974) and *The Politics of Industrial Relations* (1977); A. Taylor, *Trade Unions and the Labour Party* (1987); D. Marsh, *The New Politics of British Trade Unionism* (1992).
6. Recent surveys include J.H. Pencavel, *Labour Markets under Trade Unionism* (Oxford, 1991); A.L. Booth, *The Economics of the Trade Union* (Cambridge, 1995). An outstanding, wide-ranging analysis is H. Phelps Brown, *The Origins of Trade Union Power* (Oxford, 1983).
7. J. Kelly, 'Does the field of industrial relations have a future?', unpublished paper to the British Universities Industrial Relations Association Annual Conference, Oxford 1994, and see now J. Kelly, *Rethinking Industrial Relations* (1998). Industrial relations academics have produced books on aspects of trade unionism in the 1990s which contain some historical material; see, for example, P. Ackers et al., *The New Workplace and Trade Unionism* (1996); J. Kelly and E. Heery, *Working for the Union: British trade union officers* (Cambridge, 1994); R. Darlington, *The Dynamics of Workplace Unionism* (1994); R. Undy *et al.*, *Managing the Unions: the impact of legislation on trade unions' behaviour* (Oxford, 1996). General accounts of contemporary trade unionism have come from the margins of the industrial relations field; see, for example, R. Taylor, *The Future of the Trade Unions* (1994) and J.

14

McIlroy, *Trade Unions in Britain Today* (Manchester, 1995).

8. M. Neufeld, 'The sense of history and the annals of labor', *Proceedings of the American Industrial Relations Research Association*, 1961, quoted in D. Brody, 'Labor history, industrial relations and the crisis of American labor', *Industrial and Labor Relations Review*, 43, 1, 1989, p. 7.

9. A. Fox, *History and Heritage: the social origins of the British industrial relations system* (1985); H.A. Clegg, *A History of British Trade Unions since 1989, vol. 3, 1934–51* (Oxford, 1994); M. Terry and P. Edwards (eds), *Shop floor Politics and Job Controls* (Oxford, 1988). For individual union histories see, for example, J. Gennard, *A History of the National Graphical Association* (1990); J. Gennard and P. Bain, *A History of the Society of Graphical and Allied Trades* (1995); A. Marsh and V. Ryan, *The Seamen: a history of the National Union of Seamen, 1887–1987* (Oxford, 1988); J. E. Mortimer, *History of the Boilermakers' Society, volume 3: 1940–89* (1994); A. Marsh, *The Carpet Weavers* (Oxford, 1995). Perhaps the most successful recent work in this genre is K. Coates and T. Topham, *The Making of the Labour Movement: the formation of the Transport and General Workers' Union* (Nottingham, 1994).

10. See, for example, D. Howell, 'Editorial', *Labour History Review (LHR)*, 60, 1, 1995; 'Comments' by M. Chase, S. Fielding, K. Flett and J. Halstead & D. Martin, *LHR*, 60, 3, 1995; J. Saville, 'The "crisis" in labour history: a further comment', *LHR*, 61, 3, 1996.

11. G. Eley and K. Neild, 'Why does social history ignore politics?', *Social History*, 5, 2, 1980, pp. 264, 267. See also R. Price, 'The future of British labour history', *International Review of Social History*, 34, 1991, for a renewal of such concerns.

12. J. Zeitlin, 'From labour history to the history of industrial relations', *Economic History Review*, 40, 2, 1987; H. Kimeldorf, 'Bringing the unions back in (or why we need a new old labour history)', *Labor History*, 32, 1, 1991. As is apparent below, we do not endorse the narrowing of labour history's agenda implicit in Zeitlin's prescriptions.

13. In 1990, for example, there were 29 entries under 'trade unionism' compared with 81 on 'popular culture, leisure, sport and religion', (*LHR*, 55, 2, 1990); in 1993 the comparable figures were 11 and 45 (*LHR*, 58, 2, 1993); in 1997, 25 and 56 (*LHR*, 62, 2, 1997), although the former figure was inflated by 8 entries relating to articles in *Historical Studies in Industrial Relations*: see below, note 35.

14. H. Pelling, *A History of British Trade Unionism* (5th edition, Harmondsworth, 1992); K. Laybourn, *A History of British Trade Unions, 1770–1990* (Stroud, 1992); J. Saville, *The Labour Movement in Britain* (1988); R. Hyman, 'Praetorians and proletarians: unions and industrial relations', in J. Fyrth (ed.), *Labour's High Noon: the government and the economy, 1945–51* (1993); J. Tomlinson, 'The Labour government and the trade unions, 1945–51', in N. Tiratsoo (ed.), *The Attlee Years* (1991); S. Tolliday and J. Zeitlin (eds), *Shop Floor Bargaining and the State: historical and comparative perspectives* (Cambridge, 1985); D. Lyddon, 'The car industry, 1945–79: shop

stewards and workplace unionism', in C. Wrigley (ed.), *A History of British Industrial Relations, 1939–79: industrial relations in a declining economy* (Cheltenham, 1996); C. Wrigley (ed.), *British Trade Unions, 1945–95: documents in contemporary history* (Manchester, 1997); J. Cronin, *Labour and Society in Britain, 1918–79* (1984).

15.   On ethnicity there is very little by labour historians, although useful material is contained in general works such as R. Ramdin, *The Making of the Black Working-class in Britain* (Aldershot, 1987) and top-down surveys such as R. Miles and A. Phizacklea, 'The TUC and black workers', *British Journal of Industrial Relations*, 16, 2, 1978. There is a similar absence of substantial historical studies of women trade unionists, 1945–79. For surveys see S. Boston, *Women Workers and the Trade Unions* (1980); S. Lewenhak, *Women and Trade Unions* (1977); A. Wilson, 'Finding a voice: Asian women in Britain', in Feminist Review, *Waged Work: a reader* (1986). For the experience of one industry, see C. Cockburn, *Brothers: male dominance and technological change* (1983). W. Thompson, *The Good Old Cause: British Communism, 1921–91* (1992); N. Branson, *History of the Communist Party of Great Britain 1941–51* (1997); J. Hinton, *Shop floor Citizens: engineering democracy in 1940s Britain* (Aldershot, 1994). For studies of the CP before and during the Second World War, see N. Fishman, *The British Communist Party and the Trade Unions, 1933–45* (Aldershot, 1995) and R. Croucher, *Engineers at War* (1982).

16.   P. Johnston (ed.), *Twentieth Century Britain: economic, social and cultural change* (1994).

17.   Wrigley, *History*; R. Taylor, *The Trade Union Question in British Politics: government and unions since 1945* (Oxford, 1993).

18.   Howell, 'Editorial'; Kelly, 'Does the field of industrial relations have a future?'; A. Campbell, 'The pasts and the futures of British labour history', unpublished paper delivered to the Ninth British-Dutch Conference on Labour History, Bergen, September 1994.

19.   See, for example, the essays in N. Kirk (ed.), *Social Class and Marxism: defences and challenges* (Aldershot, 1996).

20.   Hobsbawm, *On History*, p. 239.

21.   Howell, 'Editorial'.

22.   J. Belchem, 'Reconstructing labour history', *LHR*, 62, 3, 1997, pp. 320–1.

23.   M. Savage and A. Miles, *The Remaking of the British Working-class, 1840–1940* (1994), p. 17. We don't address post-modernism in history further here, not because we feel it is not worthy of detailed attention but because of its minimal impact so far on our specific subject matter. Most of the historical writing influenced by post-modernism which is relevant to labour history is concerned with the nineteenth century. Labour history's encounter with post-modernism has been belated and limited. For example, the only contribution in *LHR* over the last decade which specifically engages with it has been Belchem, 'Reconstructing labour history'. Post-modernism has imposed only tangentially on industrial relations, and then largely in terms of related analyses of 'post-Fordism' and 'new times' which posit epochal change in

capitalism since the 1970s: see, for example, S. Crook et al., *Post-modernization: change in advanced societies* (1992). For a rare attempt to write the history of industrial relations in a post-modernist vein see, C. Hay, 'Narrating crisis: the discursive construction of the winter of discontent', *Sociology*, 30, 2, 1990. For an excellent general assessment of post-modernism's contribution to historical endeavour, see R.J. Evans, *In Defence of History* (1997).

24. E. Hobsbawm, 'Identity history is not enough', in *On History*; Evans, *Defence of History*, pp. 215–18.

25. Although the fickleness of fashion has ensured the loss of *History Workshop Journal* as a major support for labour studies. Recent work on trade unions from labour historians includes Hinton, *Shop floor Citizens*; Fishman, *The British Communist Party and the Trade Unions;* A. Campbell, N. Fishman and D. Howell (eds), *Miners, Unions and Politics, 1910–47* (Aldershot, 1996). For work in industrial relations which suggests an historical approach, see J. Kelly, 'Long waves in industrial relations: mobilization and counter-mobilization in historical perspective', *Historical Studies in Industrial Relations (HSIR)*, 4, 1997; D. Lyddon, 'Industrial relations theory and labor history', *International Labour and Working-class History*, 46, 1994. However one must be concerned at the fact that the 3 volumes and 9 issues of *LHR* published since its revamp have included 21 articles, only 1 of which was a study of trade unionism: R. Stevens, 'Containing radicalism: the Trades Union Congress Organization Department and trades councils, 1928–53', *LHR*, 62, 1, 1997.

26. P. Willman and G. Winch, *Innovation and Management Control: labour relations at BL Cars* (Cambridge, 1995).

27. See, for example, the detailed and gripping account in M. Edwardes, *Back from the Brink* (1983); for a superior account of developments from the union side, see A. Thornett, *Inside Cowley. Trade union struggle in the 1970s: who really opened the door for the Tory onslaught* (1998).

28. Zeitlin, 'From labour history', p. 171, n. 47.

29. Willman and Winch, *Innovation*, pp. 1, 67. Compare their detailed treatment of industrial engineering, pp. 194–9, with their superficial attention to aspects of steward organization, pp. 159–61, 180–2.

30. D. Lyddon and P. Smith, 'Editorial', *HSIR*, 1, 1996.

31. Brody, 'Labor history', pp. 12–13; Lyddon, 'Industrial relations theory', pp. 136–7.

32. Terry and Edwards, *Shop floor Politics*, p. 3; of the case studies in this volume, only S. Jefferys, 'The changing face of conflict: shop floor organization at Longbridge, 1939–80' touches, and then only briefly, on the role of the Communist Party in the plant.

33. Fox, *History and Heritage*, p. xii, quoted, slightly abbreviated, in Lyddon and Smith, 'Editorial', p. 8.

34. Price, 'Future of British labour history', p. 256.

35. The value of *HSIR* is attested by its coverage of trade unionism in comparison with other journals. Its first 5 issues contained 16 articles, 11 of which

17

dealt with aspects of trade unionism. This understates the position as other articles dealing with management have been of relevance and trade union issues have also been addressed in review essays.

36. But see, for example, C. Crouch, *The Politics of Industrial Relations* (1978), pp. 148–58; S. Tolliday and J. Zeitlin (eds), *The Power to Manage? Employers and industrial relations in comparative-historical perspective* (1991); W. Grant, *Business and Politics in Britain* (1993); J. Melling and A. McKinlay (eds), *Management, Labour and Industrial Politics in Modern Europe* (Cheltenham, 1996).

37. Marsh, *New Politics of British Trade Unionism*, pp. xvii–xix. For his examples of the writing of political scientists on trade unionism in the 1980s, Marsh has to rely on brief references to D. Kavanagh, *Thatcherism and British Politics* (1987); A. King, 'Mrs Thatcher as political leader' in R. Skidelsky (ed.), *Thatcherism* (1988); and A. Gamble, *The Free Economy and the Strong State* (1988). For the earlier period he relies on Minkin and writers outside the mainstream of British political science such as K. Middlemas, *Politics in Industrial Society* (1979) and G. Dorfman, *British Trade Unionism against the TUC* (1983).

38. L. James, *Power in a Trade Union: the role of the District Committee in the AUEW* (Cambridge, 1984), pp. 3–5, 46; M. Armstrong, 'The History and Organization of the Broad Left in the AUEW (Engineering Section) until 1972, with special reference to Manchester', unpublished MA thesis, University of Warwick, 1978; see also J. McIlroy, 'Notes on the Communist Party and industrial politics', in this volume. James thanks Eddie Frow for his help with this work. Frow was one of the architects of the faction and interviewed as such by Armstrong (*Power in a Trade Union*, p. vii). For the Platt's closure, see James, *Power in a Trade Union*, pp. 75–8, and H. Ratner, *Reluctant Revolutionary: memoirs of a Trotskyist, 1936–60* (1994), pp. 172–84.

39. See, for example, Hyman, *Industrial Relations*; J. Kelly, *Trade Unions and Socialist Politics* (1988).

40. E. Heery and J. Kelly, 'Professional, participative and managerial unionism: an interpretation of change in trade unions', *Work, Employment and Society*, 8, 1, 1994; P. Smith, 'Change in British trade unions since 1945', *Work, Employment and Society*, 9, 1, 1995; J. Zeitlin, '"Rank and filism" in British labour history, *International Review of Social History*', 34, 1989, and the responses by Richard Price and James Cronin in that same volume and by Richard Hyman in the subsequent issue; for one attempt at a sustained empirical examination of some of the issues raised in that debate, see M. Leier, *Red Flags and Red Tape: the making of a labour bureaucracy* (Toronto, 1995).

41. H. A. Turner, *Trade Union Growth, Structure and Policy: a comparative study of the cotton unions* (1962); V. Allen, *Trade Union Leadership: based on a study of Arthur Deakin* (1957); E. Hobsbawm, 'Trade union historiography', *Bulletin of the Study for the Society of Labour History*, 8, 1964, p. 33.

42. P. Routledge, *Scargill: the unauthorized biography* (1993). On Jones there is only J. Jones, *Union Man: an autobiography* (1986), and on Scanlon, K.

Ryan, 'The power of the presidency: an evaluation of Hugh Scanlon's early leadership', unpublished paper delivered to the conference on British Trade Unionism 1940–79, University of Warwick, 1997.

43.   On this point see D. Montgomery, *The Fall of the House of Labor: the workplace, the state and American labor activism, 1865–1925* (New York, 1987), p. 2; J. McIlroy, 'Still under siege: British trade unions at the turn of the century', *HSIR*, 3, 1997, pp. 118–21; Saville, 'The "crisis" in labour history', pp. 322–3.

44.   D. Montgomery, 'The limits of union-centred history: responses to Howard Kimeldorf', *Labor History*, 32, 1, p. 116.

45.   Ibid; J. McIlroy, review of Wrigley, *History*, in *HSIR*, 2, 1996, pp. 169–70.

46.   Taylor, *Trade Union Question*, p. 4.

47.   There is a voluminous literature on the general topic of economic decline which is usefully surveyed by M. Dintenfass, *The Decline of Industrial Britain, 1870–1980* (1992); see also D. Coates and J. Hillard (eds), *The Economic Decline of Modern Britain: the debate between left and right* (1986); D. Coates (ed.), *Industrial Policy in Great Britain* (Basingstoke, 1996); Melling and McKinlay, *Management, Labour and Industrial Politics*.

PART ONE

Overviews, 1945–79

CHAPTER ONE

Sociology, Class and Male Manual Work Cultures

Mike Savage

Understanding the fortunes of trade unionism between 1945 and 1979 offers serious difficulties of historical interpretation. Looking backward to the interwar years, these were the culminating years of the 'forward march of labour' when trade unions reached their peak levels of support and influence.[1] Union membership peaked in 1979, when over half the workforce was unionized and the Labour Party itself was, though not the dominant political party, a serious political force. Governments felt that there was no choice but to deal with unions as one of the main power brokers in the country and the 1970s saw corporatist policy making reach unprecedented levels.[2] Looking forward, however, to the Thatcher era, these were also the years when cracks in the labour movement became evident. Certainly, these cracks – which, to be sure, some writers denied the existence of – were to become fractures only in the 1980s and beyond. None the less, debates about the significance of 'affluence', the implications of the new mass media, the development of youth culture and of unorthodox political currents and forms such as the New Left, feminism and pacifism, all hinted that established forms of working-class collective action were under challenge.

If we seek out potential seeds of decline amidst the strengths displayed by the labour movement in this period, one idea above all others commands attention. This is the belief that the collective work and class cultures which had supposedly spawned the labour movement were fading and that individualistic orientations and actions were becoming steadily more prominent. From the vantage point of the 1990s, the idea that contemporary social life gives the individual unprecedented prominence is commonplace. Many of the recent sociological glosses on the main elements of contemporary social change explicitly or implicitly endorse the view that collective solidarities have faded. Ulrich Beck and Anthony Giddens are particularly well known for arguing that the rise of 'reflexivity', 'individualisation' and 'life politics' have stripped down traditional class allegiances and solidarities.[3] In the field of industrial relations, conceptions of the 'new individualism' have become one of the talking points in considering the reasons for the contemporary travails of trade unions.[4]

It can be argued that the 1950s and 1960s were a critical turning point in the elaboration of the idea that individualized identities were gaining prominence and that these spelled the erosion of class loyalties. This essay is a contribution to thinking about the key features of male manual work cultures, in ways which may further our understanding of the cultural roots of trade unionism. The aim is not to offer an original, source-based contribution to an examination of male manual work cultures, but to offer a series of critical reflections on how we can read the sociological accounts of these cultures which were produced in abundance in those decades. I will argue that for all their value and importance, these studies have left us a problematic intellectual legacy. A set of conceptual oppositions were set in place during this formative intellectual period which has ultimately provided us with an inadequate understanding of the relationship between work, class, and culture. The task I set myself here is to consider how we read the research contributions of the time *historically*, that is to say not as a contribution to the development of sociological research traditions but as documents whose meaning needs to be uncovered by placing them in their historical and intellectual context.[5]

The main argument I seek to develop is as follows. The contemporary emphasis on the alleged decline of collective solidarities and the rise of individualism has its intellectual roots in debates about work cultures that developed in the 1960s. I want to challenge the historicism that colours this work and the way such research has been enshrined in subsequent debates. Following Marshall and his associates, I will argue that in the 1960s a series of dualistic oppositions were put in place which conflated a number of quite distinct processes: the traditional, the collective, the solidaristic and the 'class member', were contrasted with the modern, the individual, the instrumental and the 'non-class member'.[6] These oppositions, I want to argue, have left a powerful legacy. It is not much of an exaggeration to say that the recent, rather unsatisfactory, debate on class in British sociology continues to be dependent on the conceptual frame they provided, in seeing class identities as somehow dependent on a collective, rather than an individual basis.[7] However, if we are to understand the contradictory nature of male manual work cultures both in the period between 1945 and 1979, and more recently, we need to rethink the relevant conceptual tools afresh and examine the complex inter-relationship between individual identities and social class.

The chapter is organized as follows. In the first part I describe some of the major research works of the period, in order to draw attention to the distinctive intellectual moment within which these writings were formed. In the second section I go on to consider the emerging opposition between *individual* and *collective* cultures which increasingly came to colour these studies. My third section argues that, rather than contrasting the collective and the individual, and class and non-class, we should explore their inter-relationship. I suggest that the idea of 'rugged individualism' offers one way of doing so. The final section draws out some possible ramifications of this understanding of work cultures and leads to some brief conclusions.

24

The sociological analysis of work cultures 1960–79

Anyone examining the character of work cultures in the period after 1945, and especially after the mid-1950s, has a resource that was not available to historians of earlier periods. The post-war years saw the emergence of a remarkable wave of sociologically informed studies of work and employment that claimed to represent a bright new future for social scientific research. It can indeed be argued without much exaggeration that the period from 1955 to 1975 was the golden age of British occupational and industrial sociology. There was, of course, an older tradition of social scientific research, associated for example with Booth and Rowntree's poverty studies, which as Yeo has recently shown was committed to a politics of 'class communion' and which invoked middle-class moralistic understandings of working-class life.[8] By contrast, after the Second World War, a new series of pioneering sociological studies *claimed* to be concerned to understand male manual workers *in their own terms* and proved pivotal to the elaboration of a sociological research agenda of unprecedented breadth and depth. Dennis et al.'s *Coal is Our life*, Lupton's ethnographic shop floor research, Goldthorpe and Lockwood's 'affluent worker' studies, Runciman's study of *Relative Deprivation and Social Justice*, and Beynon's study of assembly line cultures in *Working for Ford*, were all part of this trend. They were undoubtedly diverse in methodology, politics, and in theoretical inspiration. None the less, they all shared one central commitment: to pioneer a methodologically rigorous way of looking at male manual cultures 'from the inside'.[9]

These studies were informed by fascination as to how the 'modernization' of British social life would affect various social and cultural features of British society. One line of inquiry, which drew on Glass's social mobility research at the London School of Economics, was interested in the implications of the rise of a middle-class, white collar workforce.[10] Another line of approach was through the debate on working-class 'affluence', which first came to popular attention as a result of the difficulty experienced by the Labour Party in breaking Conservative hegemony in the period between 1951 and 1964.[11] Another focus of interest, manifest in the work of Hoggart, Williams and in Dennis and his associates, lay in considering how working-class values might offer an alternative to those offered by modern, commercial, mass, society.[12] Whichever line of inquiry was adopted, there was a common focus on understanding change through the prism of the self-understanding of the working class. Yeo links this moment to the rise of a new breed of academics from working-class backgrounds, educated largely in the grammar schools, who were determined to resist the conceptual labelling of middle-class outsiders.[13]

The emergence of this new stream of work was not simply the inevitable product of dramatic social change in Britain. Notwithstanding the concerns

25

of the sociologists with British 'modernity', it is worth emphasizing that the period between 1945 and 1970 did *not* see dramatic occupational or industrial restructuring, certainly nothing on the scale of what was to come in the 1980s and 1990s. Between 1951 and 1971 the percentage of workers in manufacturing fell hardly at all (from 37.2 per cent to 34.9 per cent). Admittedly, some sectors saw significant declines, notably textiles and mining, and there were significant trends towards the expansion of the white collar workforce, though from a relatively small base.[14] There was also a marked increase in the number of women employed in the labour market, and a general increase in real wages. But, notwithstanding the general fascination with the idea of working-class affluence, male manual wages did not increase markedly in relative terms between the mid-1950s and 1970s.[15]

We need to understand the sociological study of work cultures and values not primarily as a detached set of reflections about social change, but rather as intellectual interventions in political and academic disputes. The political issues at stake are fairly familiar and were indeed openly acknowledged at the time. They included arguments associated with the 'New Left' which claimed that the labour movement's relationship to its working-class constituency was more fraught and fragile than some assumed.[16] Another, more mainstream, set of concerns, lay in fears that the Labour Party's electoral base was weakening.[17] The academic issues are less well appreciated. Political questions were refracted within disciplinary debates about the status of 'sociology' in social science research. From the early 1960s to the mid-1970s, sociology changed from being a marginal academic subject taught in only a handful of university departments to being a mainstay of the social sciences with significant departments at nearly all universities outside Oxbridge. This was also the period in which the sociological agenda was championed primarily by its claims to give distinctive insights into the study of male manual work cultures.[18] The study of male manual work cultures allowed the intellectual collision of two rather different visions of sociology. A form of activist Marxism, which linked academic study to socialist political concerns, jostled with a more orthodox sociological perspective, which championed the use of survey methods, the deployment of sophisticated forms of Weberian, rather than Marxist, theory, and in a few cases the use of ethnographic theory or methods.[19] In this crucible, modern British sociology was forged.

These studies of male manual work cultures therefore came to possess critical, pioneering importance. They were concerned with establishing the place of 'upstart' sociology by showing how it could shed new and distinctive light on current social changes. Hence, the pre-occupation with emphasizing the significance of the *new* social developments. Hence also the concern with distinguishing the modern from the traditional, and with justifying the sociological perspective in terms of its ability to shed light on contemporary social change. These concerns, deeply embedded in the intellectual framework of the explorers of work culture, led them to develop conceptual oppositions in terms of a difference between the 'traditional' and the 'modern'. This was to have major repercussions for emphasizing the distinction between the collective and the individual in ways which have had a long-term impact.

The emergence of 'instrumentalism': sociological conceptions of class and identity in the analysis of male manual work cultures

As the sociological study of work cultures developed in the 1960s, it is possible to trace its engagement with the idea of the class conscious, collective, male, manual worker. This engagement proved foundational in our understanding of male manual work cultures, but the real legacy of this moment is not always fully recognized. The idea of male manual work as being essentially a collective and collaborative enterprise, which binds people into some kind of collective awareness has a number of intellectual sources. Empirically, one of the mainsprings comes from the various community studies. The most famous of these is perhaps *Coal is our Life*. This examined the way that the experience of mining created cultures of collectivism. Miners, engaged in hazardous work, learnt to trust each other and to form a solidaristic work culture which distrusted supervisors and managers and was conducive to radical trade unionism. Miners' work cultures were also integrally tied to the social world of mining villages, so allowing the bonds of the workplace to mesh with those of the local neighbourhood. The collectivism which resulted was highly gendered, and the authors of *Coal is our Life* were unusually prescient in emphasizing the patriarchal nature of mining cultures, but this allowed still further the culture of male work solidarity to hold sway in its sphere.

However, this study should not be singled out. It can be argued that this claim about the collectivist nature of working-class culture was a fundamental part of all the community-based studies: indeed, it can be argued that this notion must be foundational for work of this type.[20] Horobin's 1957 study of occupational communities amongst the Hull fishermen, and Cannon's 1967 examination of how compositors were bound into an occupational community based around the print workers' 'chapel', were premised on being able to detect some kind of unifying feature – whether it be based on neighbourhood or work cultures – which bound workers together.[21]

Alongside these empirically focused studies was a current of political/theoretical work which elaborated the idea of the collective nature of male manual cultures as part of a broader political project. Here the aim was to use working-class collectivism as a foil in order to provide a cultural critique of the competitive and individualistic character of capitalist, middle-class, Britain. The work of Richard Hoggart had a key role here, specifically in his attempt to see his own working-class upbringing in Leeds as a counter to the commercializing and Americanizing influences found elsewhere in British society. For Hoggart,

> In any discussions of working-class attitudes much is said of the group sense, the feeling of being not so much an individual with a 'way to make' as one of a group whose members are all roughly level and likely to remain so ... [this feeling] arises from a knowledge, born of close living together, that one is inescapably part of a group.[22]

This idea is perhaps found more clearly and directly in the writings of Raymond Williams. For Williams, working-class culture,

> is not proletarian art, or council houses, or a particular use of languages; it is rather, the basic collectivist idea, and the institutions, manners, habits of thought and intentions which proceed from this. Bourgeois culture, similarly is the basic individualist idea ... the culture which it (the working-class) has produced ... is the collective democratic institution, whether in trade unions, the co-operative movement or political party.[23]

This is a very important intellectual move. Like Hoggart, Williams articulates a vision of the essential collectivism of working-class culture in opposition to the individualism of orthodox middle-class cultures as providing a lever for cultural critique. But, what we see here is the use of the idea of the collective working-class as a receptacle for a political project, thereby allowing working-class culture to be used as critique.

Today, this view of the essential collectivism of working-class culture is largely discredited. Or, rather like Williams' own account of the English rural golden age, the actual empirical instances of working-class collectivism retreat into the dim and distant past, or to fewer and fewer cases, as research develops and shows that in reality things were always more complex than the stereotypes suggest. Lockwood, in 1966, was one of the first sociologists to delimit the kinds of situations that might produce traditional, collective working-class cultures. He suggested three examples of 'proletarian traditional' class imagery, amongst miners, dockers and shipbuilders. Thirty years later, we know that mining areas were heterogeneous and that many of them, for instance the Midlands, did not fit the collective ideal.[24] Research has emphasized that the history of dock workers was characterized by a marked difficulty in organizing collectively and continued battles to overcome apathy in the early decades of the twentieth century, and that shipbuilders were characterized by chronic sectionalist and demarcation conflicts.[25] Much the same point has been made with respect to working-class communities, which have shown to be divided by age, gender, religion and ethnicity.[26]

But this is not my main point here, since it is hardly an original endeavour to attack, once again, the stereotype of the collective working-class. What is pertinent to point out is that the development of these sociological studies helped play a key role in attacking the view of male, manual work cultures as collective by seeing such cultures as historical residues, being replaced by modern, non-collective work cultures. Goldthorpe and Lockwood's *Affluent Worker* volumes proved particularly influential. They were the epitome of the sociological moment described earlier. They used new, scientific research methods (the sample survey). Theoretically they endorsed the neo-Weberian view, emphasizing that workers' values and attitudes could not be read off from their social situation. They helped found a distinctive sociological interpretation of work cultures organized around the idea of looking at 'orientations to work'. However, their ideas were still constructed in critical dialogue with older collective notions of class cultures, *and they still bear these hallmarks.*[27] It is therefore important to return to this well-known study to examine how the subsequent debate on its findings has skewed discussion in problematic ways.[28]

The most obvious way in which the new 'sociological' approach can be seen to wrestle with the older legacy of the communal and collective analysis of class cultures can be perceived in Lockwood's influential theoretical account which delineated three different types of 'images of society' and which fed into the arguments about the affluent workers. Firstly, there were 'traditional proletarians' who held a vision of the social world defined in terms of power, of 'us' and 'them'. 'Deferential workers' saw society organized around distinctions of prestige, with higher and lower status orders. The new 'affluent workers' held a conception of the social world which divided groups according to their pecuniary position. Goldthorpe and Lockwood's study of workers in three Luton industries argued that these workers tended to have instrumental orientations to work, that they lived privatized lives and that they possessed weak attachments both to work itself and to their fellow workers. This latter orientation could at times lead to trade union militancy, and it could lead to continued loyalty to the Labour Party, when it could be shown that instrumental purposes could be served by such movements. However, this instrumentalist perspective was not conducive to strong forms of class consciousness or identity.[29]

Goldthorpe and Lockwood's formulations depended for their novelty on contrasting their Luton workers with the idea of the 'collective' working-class. Yet since this idea itself was a problematic one, so their idea of the instrumental worker was built on unstable foundations. I do not want to focus here on the empirical claims associated with instrumentalism itself. As Devine observes, the term was a loose one, which could be bent to anyone's particular perspective. Goldthorpe and Lockwood themselves made it clear that they came to the conception of instrumental orientations to work late in their research, and that therefore they were not able fully to test the concept which they had developed. Westergaard saw the account of instrumentalism as being quite compatible with an accurate, class conscious recognition by

29

workers of the reality of the cash nexus of capitalist society. The value of the term lay in the way it served as an intellectual foil, with the result that its attraction seemed to owe as much to problems in older ideas about male manual values than to its own merit.[30]

The important conceptual point, associated with the idea of instrumentalism, concerned its claims about the salience of class identity and awareness. The concept of instrumentalism endorsed the view that male manual workers were not, by and large, class aware, and that their self-interested actions eclipsed class awareness. The clearest indication of this is Goldthorpe's later reading of how sociologists have analysed the working-class. Goldthorpe emphasized that Marxist and 'organicist' writers had used the working-class as a vehicle for their own political aspirations for social change. In Goldthorpe's own view, the working class has its own distinct agenda. Within it, class conflict,

> reflect[ed] a heightened dissent over distributional, and in turn industrial rela-
> tions issues – which presupposed ultimate goals that were largely held in com-
> mon; for example those listed by Crosland of 'choice, leisure, comfort privacy
> and a more spacious family life', plus, I would want to say, greater control over
> one's destiny in working life. There are, moreover, goals that imply an individu-
> alistic, or privatised, rather than a communal frame of reference.[31]

For Goldthorpe, a male, manual working class with the same values as the middle-class could, none the less, engage in class actions because its different structural locations compelled it to do so. Instrumentalism does not necessarily revoke class awareness.

Although there was intense criticism of Goldthorpe and Lockwood's work, it is striking that much of this criticism, has, in a sense, followed the same line of reasoning. This logic has been to recognize that cohesive class identities do not generally exist, but to argue the centrality of class means that class sentiments retain the potential to become salient in particular social settings. This is true for Westergaard's well known observation that Luton's affluent Vauxhall carworkers found it quite possible to sing the 'Red Flag' when they came out on strike shortly after the fieldwork by Goldthorpe and Lockwood's team had been completed. It was also manifest in the debate on class imagery which followed publication of Lockwood's typology of work-ing-class images of society. Lockwood's arguments depended on a particular way of conceptualizing class imagery, what has subsequently been labelled the 'structure-consciousness-action' model.[32] In this model a particular set of circumstances gives rise to a particular image of the society, which in turn leads to certain forms of political agency. This model depended on the images of society having a certain consistency in order for them to play the key mediating role between people's social environment and their actions. Subsequent research has showed decisively, however, that no consistent attitudes could be found. It simply proved empirically impossible to clearly distinguish workers with 'power', 'prestige' or 'instrumental' images. Responses reflecting all three kinds could be found mixed together in complex and frequently contradictory images of society.[33]

Two responses to this finding are possible. One way, which I shall explore below, is to reconsider Lockwood's typology itself and to think about whether instrumentalism may actually be logically consistent with forms of class awareness and thereby to probe how 'individualistic' identities may be compatible with class identities. The route followed by most subsequent writers, however, has been to turn attention away from exploring attitudes and culture towards looking at what workers did in practice. A good example of this is Marshall's argument that it was useful for researchers to examine ethnographically the kinds of social actions workers engaged in, as these may display more cultural coherence than responses to surveys might suggest.[34]

I want to argue that by setting up influential oppositions between collective working-class values on the one hand and instrumental ones on the other, we have not developed an adequate understanding of working-class *individualism* – a term which I want to suggest has resonances *both* with the collective class cultures elaborated by Hoggart, for instance, *and* the instrumental ones elaborated by Goldthorpe and Lockwood. It is certainly true that protagonists of the collective perspective did not have a ready handle on how male manual cultures were tied up with the quest for individual integrity, self-esteem and identity. By seeing individualism as a characteristic of 'middle-class' cultures, it became difficult, conceptually, to register the salience of individualistic strains in working-class culture. On the other hand, the writers endorsing ideas of working class instrumentalism have no ready way of interpreting the more expressive and moral concerns about sustaining dignity and self-respect, which in many ways were not instrumental at all. Nor do they recognize how modes of class awareness and identity are compatible and indeed can be inherent in, modes of instrumental reasoning.

'Rugged individualism'

During research I carried out in the early 1990s on the restructuring of banking, I interviewed employees about their careers, their attitudes towards their careers, and their perception of changes in their working lives.[35] One man interested me particularly: he was a senior clerk, in his mid-forties, who, unlike most of his male contemporaries, expressed no desire to move into management. I asked him whether he identified with the bank's clerical staff or managers:

I would personally identify with the staff, I mean I have never wanted to go beyond where I am now.
Q: Why is that?
It has never appealed to me, because of the way I look at work it is only a means to an end to me. It has always seemed, for many years, it has always seemed to me that if you aspire to the management side of it you have to devote more of your own time and personality to the bank, which I am not prepared to do.[36]

This is an interesting statement. In some ways John is the archetypal instrumental worker (it is 'a means to an end'). *However*, this notion is also linked to a class-based perception about *individuality*. John believed that retaining his individuality depended on his not becoming part of management. Becoming a manager involved losing part of himself, losing a core sense of his own individuality and autonomy, becoming, in some sense, a 'company man'. Being a real, autonomous, individual depended on being one of the staff, being in a situation where you did not have to 'sell your soul'. What is interesting here is the way that an instrumental set of attitudes was associated with a concern to retain individual autonomy *and* invoked a sense of class. The kind of class sentiment invoked was not that of class solidarism but of class differentiation, with a keen perception that 'middle-class' jobs were defined in terms of their inability to allow individuals to be themselves.

This suggests that instrumentalism, individualism and class awareness may be linked *integrally* (not contingently) together in ways which are quite at odds with, say, Lockwood's depiction of working-class images of society, or Goldthorpe's emphasis on the similarity of working- and middle-class values towards work. Far from individualism eroding class awareness, it may actually consolidate it. In this paper I can present no substantive evidence to develop this point, but considerable incidental back-up is available. Take, for instance, Arthur Seaton, Alan Sillitoe's leading character in his famous novel, *Saturday Night and Sunday Morning*. Seaton seems to adopt an instrumental attitude to his work. He has no loyalty to anyone but himself. Although a Communist sympathizer he has no loyalty to his class, and indeed he scorns the narrow, conformist practices in working-class communities. His politics is essentially of the 'stuff you all' type. But there is also a strong sense of 'them' and 'us', and his sense of individualism is linked, it might be argued, to a perception of how to break out of his class situation.

More sociological studies also give evidence of this kind of outlook. Beynon's study of work cultures on the assembly line and the sociology of the shop stewards' movement in Ford's Halewood plant in the later 1960s also backs up this point very well. Car workers are of course an interesting case. As they worked in a car factory, one might expect them to be instrumentalists. But in reality a militant shop floor culture was generated, linked to the kind of 'them and us' power imagery which Lockwood saw as part of

32

the traditional proletarian culture. Of course it might be possible to explain this by noting that Halewood was located near an old, working-class, city (Liverpool) rather than a new, modern town (Luton). However, it is worth noting even here that many of Halewood's workers probably came from the new overspill estates in Speke and Kirkby, i.e. the kind of 'council, or private, low-cost housing estates' which Lockwood saw as typical of the new instrumental workers. But this is not my main point, which is rather that Beynon emphasized the powerfully individualistic – but not instrumentalist – ethos which lay at the centre of the shop floor culture. Beynon emphasizes that the shop stewards were not some 'hang over' from 'traditional working-class' cultures. They followed fashion, wore smart clothes and exemplified the new pop culture sweeping Britain in the 1960s. They were profoundly concerned to emphasize their individuality. One of the indications of this lay in the attitudes of the workers to promotion. For, although working conditions were grim, it was striking that most workers had no interest in 'escaping the line' through attempting to gain promotion to more senior jobs. The shop stewards he talked to were especially insistent on this point:

> The (shop) stewards weren't interested in promotion, in becoming 'dedicated Ford men'. For them to take the white coat at Halewood would be to join the other side. 'I couldn't do that. Leave the lads? Not in this firm anyway. They're a crowd of gangsters here'.[37]

Here we have the kernel of the notion, which slips through the net constructed by the sociologists of the 1960s, which is that individualism need not be at odds with a form of class awareness.

One of the advantages of talking about individualism rather than instrumentalism is that it offers an alternative framework for thinking about one of the intriguing findings of the *Affluent Worker* studies: the lack of interest which workers had in promotion. The instrumental worker should, one might imagine, be interested in earning promotion. However, in practice, workers tended to be reluctant to think about earning promotion into foremen or white collar jobs. Goldthorpe and Lockwood claimed that the reasons for this were to do with instrumental calculations, since workers felt that the extra effort involved in being a foreman was not worth the extra income which might result. What they fail to bring out, however, even though they directly quote the evidence in their own work, is how this was linked to this notion of the 'sell out' involved in being a supervisor:

> A foreman's money is no more than a skilled man's and he takes his worries to bed.
> I think I could have been a foreman – but I probably get more money anyway. I like to know when I'm coming in and out: I like to be an ordinary worker.
> All the foreman here is, is a dish rag – pushed around by people who don't know what they are talking about. And financially he's no better off.

33

In fact, as they show, the main reason given by the Luton respondents as to why they do not seek promotion is that the foreman's job involves too much responsibility, stress, pressure.[38] The important point here is that the instrumental cost/benefit analysis needs to be understood as an instrumental calculation which defined costs in terms of the loss of individuality and autonomy which supervisors possessed.

Ramifications of 'rugged individualism'

In this final section I want to open out my speculative exploration somewhat more and offer some thoughts about what my discussion suggests are the ways we should analyse male, manual work cultures in this period. There are a number of ways in which the points I have developed above allow us to rethink the dimensions of male manual work cultures.

Firstly, we can see these values not as new, modern creations, but as embedded in the 'deep history' of working-class culture. Rather than seeing individualistic work cultures as some kind of 'modern' phenomenon, as some kind of response to new forms of production methods (e.g. the assembly line) or particular living conditions (e.g. the suburb), we might emphasize how they draw on older cultural motifs and repertoires. E.P. Thompson's familiar argument that working-class culture was formed around the figure of the 'Freeborn Englishman' reminds us that in Britain struggles to advance democratic freedoms fell, by default, to male manual workers.[39] Joyce has recently shown, in an illuminating study of the nineteenth century Lancashire dialect poet, Edwin Waugh, how a strongly individualized sensibility could be associated with a plebeian, even working-class identity.[40] The instrumental workers examined by Goldthorpe and Lockwood might, in a sense, be seen as part of the broad working-class tradition. If this point is granted, then an interesting corollary follows. Joyce emphasizes how Waugh wanted workers to be admitted to equal status with the middle and upper-classes, to be individuals in their own right. Yet, as Wahrman suggests, it can be argued that there was a sense that the British middle-classes had sold themselves out, and were unable to carry the mantle of individuality.[41] Wahrman points to this with respect to the way that the idea of middle-class was assimilated to a status-based conception of hierarchy during the agitation around the Great Reform Bill. The instrumental workers of Luton may then be part of the historical mainstream of working-class values, rather than a departure from them.[42]

This suggests that the period after the Second World War was distinctive in seeing a 'reformation' of working-class 'rugged individualism' in a culture increasingly dominated by large corporate structures. The bureaucratization of employment relations which reached its height in these years allowed the relational culture of individuality to be enhanced. As manual workers compared their position with that of the salaried white collar and supervisory middle-class, they came to recognize their own distinctive potential to stand against conformity. The case of banking is undoubtedly peculiar but it is worth reiterating that the bank clerks' lives outside their work were highly regulated and controlled. Clerks had to live at an address approved by the bank; they had to ask permission from the bank manager to get married; they had to have 'appropriate hobbies'; and they were evaluated once a year for such qualities as their appearance, their demeanour, and their loyalty. Even matters such as occupational pension schemes, which were closely associated with enjoying 'staff status', were part of the culture of dependence in which white collar workers were enveloped. To be a salaried worker did indeed involve selling your self: in this respect the perception of male manual workers was entirely accurate.

This leads us further to suggest that it is so much of an historical and sociological orthodoxy that the salience of class is premised on the clear distinction of ownership of capital, that the extent to which class awareness and identity actually depended on an awareness of, and opposition to, organizational hierarchy, has been less well documented.[43] Yet taking this last point would allow us to make sense of some interesting features of worker aspirations. Take, for instance, a survey carried out in 1949 of people's work histories. In this study, the majority in all occupational groups wanted to do the kind of job they were currently doing. This is not surprising, since respondents were given the option of stating they were happy in their current job and this may have been the easiest answer. But there were two types of jobs which people generally held in high esteem, categories of work that significant members of other groups wished to move into. These two groups were 'professionals' and 'skilled, male, manual work'. Interestingly, very few people who were not clerks wished to become clerks, similarly, *very few male manual workers of any description wished to become managers, supervisors, or owners.* And indeed, some 'middle-class' men continued to aspire towards skilled, male, manual jobs. What this survey illustrates is the remarkable cultural approbation which British society accorded to the virtues and values of skilled, male, manual labour. To be a skilled worker, with the appropriate dignity coming from having a 'trade' and the likelihood of obtaining a relatively good male, manual job, was the summit of many people's aspirations. Only around 5 per cent of male manual workers wished to move into any kind of 'middle-class' occupation.[44]

It needs to be recognized that the rugged individualism I have outlined here was compatible with collective action. One of the problems involved in counterposing individualist against collectivist modes of male, manual work cultures is the assumption that collective identities somehow subsume individual ones, that the two are necessarily at odds with each other. This 'zero sum' formulation is, I would argue, mistaken. It is more useful to see how collective identities emerge through the mutual connection of multiple indi-

35

vidual identities, so that they take on an associational form. In other words, collective identities and organizations become strong when they recognize individuals rather than take them for granted or see them as subsidiary to the organisation or the 'movement' as a whole. Given this insight, we might point to the fact that one of the interesting aspects of male, manual work cultures was the way that workers were highly attuned to and recognized the individual. Male, manual workers marked out, ritually, many of the key transition points in an individual's life: marriage, coming of age, and death (through collections given to the bereaved's family).

Hitherto I have only talked implicitly about gendered notions of individualism. It is however vital to recognize the fundamental, constitutive role of gender-defining, individualistic identities in terms of autonomy and independence. This is now a fairly familiar point. What may be important in the post-war workplace is the way that notions of male, manual masculinity, asserting independence, had fewer resonances with women. This may ultimately have sown the seeds of this culture's own downfall in later years. There is also a less well developed idea, however, concerning the way in which the acquisition of adult status – and hence the ability to achieve individual autonomy – was linked to male, manual work cultures. The ritual elements of male, manual work cultures are of particular importance here. The role of apprenticeship, even in its increasingly debased and deskilled forms, was crucial in providing a 'rite of passage' for a young man to become a man. The link between apprenticeship training systems, trade union organisation, and work culture perhaps helped secure a cultural link between the very acquisition of adult masculine status and particular forms of work culture. As Willis showed in his famous study of working-class lads leaving school, the taking on of male, manual work was an integral part of achieving adult masculine autonomy.[45]

Runciman's study of *Relative Deprivation and Social Justice* emphasized that male, manual workers in Britain did not compare themselves with the middle-classes but worried more about distinctions within the working-class. Gallie's comparative study indicated that British workers, unlike their French counterparts, possessed little interest in reducing inequality. Runciman's explanation of these findings lay in the fact that the British working-class had restricted reference groups, but this would go against my suggestion that it was out of a sense of class awareness that male, manual cultures derived their strength. And in fact Runciman's analysis can be read in this way. He argues that British male, manual workers tend not to see themselves as doing worse economically than male, non-manual workers, a point which surprises him because he clearly regards them as being worse off. In particular, he notes the tendency for male, manual workers to claim that other male, manual workers, rather than non-manual workers are better off than they are. However, if my argument about the way that salaried employment was defined in ways which reduced its autonomy, and hence its attractiveness, holds good, then this does not turn out to be very surprising. Subsequent evidence from his surveys shows that a majority of male, manual respondents in his sample agreed that 'male, manual workers are doing much better' than male, non-manual workers, and only around 13 per cent felt that this was wrong.[46]

Conclusions

Let me return to make a few general points in conclusion. Whilst I am aware that the material covered here is in some ways familiar, I hope at least to have opened up some intellectual space for us to examine notions of working-class, 'rugged individualism'. My main point is that we need to avoid counterposing individual and class identities, so that it is assumed, almost by definition, that any developed individual awareness is wrapped up with the weakness of class awareness. Thus to see the class awareness of British, male, manual workers in the post-war period as somehow 'stunted', 'restricted' or somehow problematic, as was the case for many researchers from different theoretical perspectives in the 1960s, rather misses the point.

What might need further elaboration is the very strong sense of pride in the way that the individuality and autonomy of (male) workers could be exercised, a pride born from a comparative frame of reference in which salaried workers were regarded as being 'dependent'. The 1950s and 1960s may not, therefore, have seen any radical remaking of male, manual work cultures, but in fact the powerful reassertion of traditional ideals in a period whose bureaucratic features gave them extra poignancy. Undoubtedly, there were changes taking place in labour processes and labour markets. The sense of individual, male pride was nourished best in the craft tradition, and by the post-war period this tradition was losing touch with the reality of the working conditions of many workers. It became more difficult to hang on to the notion of individuality when working conditions were increasingly brutalized, automated, and deskilled, as Beynon, for example, showed to be the case in the automobile industry. But in this case, it might also be suggested that trade union militancy could be the last hope for sustaining and renewing the tradition: the last vestige of the values of 'rugged individualism'.

Returning to the themes of this book, it seems that if the argument developed here has any value, we might point to the continued relevance of class-based identities in this period, albeit not class identities which appealed to the collective so much as individual sentiment. In this respect the cultural foundations for trade unionism may well have been strong. Further research might usefully explore the changing nature of individualized identities, and their overlaps with gender, age, work and consumerism, as well as consider how trade unions themselves attempted to build on these identities and values. Notions of the collective working-class were not confined to academic circles, and the evocation of these images by leaders at all levels in the labour movement may have posed problems in appealing to workers whose attraction to trade unions and to class sentiments drew on other sources. But this is a very large question which I need to leave hanging here. What is certainly important, when drawing upon the sociological research of the time, is to be cautious of the conceptual coding of collectivism as the prime way in which class sentiments were articulated. Freeing historians and sociologists from this assumption may allow us a much more subtle account of male, manual work cultures which allows us to recognize the real historical rupture which the politics of the Thatcher period represented.

Notes

I would like to thank Fiona Devine and John McIlroy, as well as contributors to the discussion at the conference at Warwick in September 1997, for comments on an earlier draft of this paper.

1. See M. Jacques and F. Mulhern (eds), *The Forward March of Labour Halted?* (1981) and M. Savage and A. Miles, *The Remaking of the British Working-class, 1840–1940* (1994).

2. See K. Middlemas, *Politics in Industrial Society: the experience of the British system since 1918* (1980), and A. Warde, *Consensus and Beyond: the development of Labour Party strategy since the Second World War* (Manchester, 1982).

3. See A. Giddens, *Modernity and Self-Identity* (Oxford, 1991), and U. Beck, *Risk Society* (1992). To be sure, this assertion should be unpacked more carefully than I have space to do here. Another current of contemporary work has examined and critiqued the very idea of the (cohesive) 'individual'; for example, see M. Strathern, *Partial Connections* (Savage, Maryland, 1991). None the less, the point still stands since these writers are in a sense simply taking the critique of the idea of collective values one stage further in a more thoroughgoing and radical direction.

4. See E. Phelps Brown, 'The counter revolution of our time', *Industrial Relations*, 21, 1990; N. Bacon and J. Storey, 'Individualism and collectivism and the changing role of trade unions', in P. Ackers, C. Smith and P. Smith (eds), *The New Workplace and Trade Unionism* (1995); I. Kessler and J. Purcell, 'Individualism and collectivism in theory and practice', in P. Edwards (ed.), *Industrial Relations: theory and practice in Britain* (Oxford, 1995). For some criticisms of this work, see J. Waddington and C. Whitson, 'Why do people join trade unions in a period of membership decline?', *British Journal of Industrial Relations*, 35, 4, 1997.

5. There are three other essays which have similar aims to mine and which are useful guides to these issues: C. Critcher, 'Sociology, cultural studies, and the post-war working-class', in J. Clarke, C. Critcher and R. Johnson (eds), *Working-class Culture*, (1979) offers a left historical critique of sociologi-

cal writing; J.H. Goldthorpe, 'Intellectuals and the working-class in modern Britain', in D. Rose (ed.), *Social Stratification and Economic Change* (1988) offers a mirror-image account – a sociological critique of leftist accounts of working-class culture; G. Marshall, 'Some remarks on the study of working-class consciousness', in Rose (ed.), *Social Stratification*, offers an intermediary account of working-class consciousness which has informed several aspects of this current paper.

6.   See G. Marshall, H. Newby, D. Rose, and C. Vogler, *Social Class in Modern Britain* (1988).

7.   Useful surveys of the sociological debate include, R. Crompton, *Class and Stratification* (Oxford, 1998) and D. Lee and B. Turner, *Contests over Class* (1996). For a very interesting parallel critique from the perspective of debates about class in nineteenth-century Britain, see P. Joyce, *Democratic Subjects* (Cambridge, 1994).

8.   E. Yeo, *The Contest for Social Science: relations and representations of gender and class* (1996); see also R. McKibbin, *The Ideologies of Class* (Oxford, 1990).

9.   The word 'male' is used advisedly. Very few of these studies examined women's manual work in any depth (though see Lupton below). The main studies of male work were, N. Dennis, F. Henriques, and C. Slaughter, *Coal is our Life* (1956); T. Lupton, *On the Shop Floor: two studies of workshop organisation and output* (Oxford, 1963); J.H. Goldthorpe, D. Lockwood, F. Bechhofer, J. Platt, *The Affluent Worker* (Cambridge, 3 vols, 1968–9); W. Runciman, *Relative Deprivation and Social Justice* (1966); H. Beynon, *Working for Ford* (1973), are some of the important examples. But they were only the tip of the iceberg. Other important studies which might be mentioned include R.M. Blackburn and M. Mann's survey analysis of male, manual labour market structures, *The Working-class in the Labour Market* (1979); D. Wedderburn and R. Crompton's organizational case studies of technology and worker attitudes; Newby's account of 'deferential workers', *The Deferential Worker* (1979); D. Gallie's comparative work on British and French work cultures, *Social Inequality and Class Radicalism in France and Britain* (Cambridge, 1983). All these studies were rigorous, innovative, studies of diverse aspects of work cultures. There are few contemporary studies of work cultures that are so detailed or methodologically sophisticated.

10.   See D.V. Glass, *Social Mobility in Britain* (Oxford, 1954), and D. Lockwood, *The Blackcoated Worker: a study in class-consciousness* (Oxford, 1958).

11.   See M. Abrams, R. Rose and R. Hinden, *Must Labour Lose?* (Harmondsworth, 1960).

12.   R. Hoggart, *The Uses of Literacy* (1957); R. Williams, *Culture and Society* (1958); Dennis et al., *Coal is our Life*.

13.   Yeo, *The Contest for Social Science*.

14.   The proportion of miners in England and Wales fell steadily from 7.1 per cent in 1921, to 3.9 per cent in 1951 and 1.7 per cent in 1971. The textile workforce fell less dramatically from 5.9 per cent (1921) to 4.5 per cent (1951) and 2.4 per cent (1971).

15. See G. Routh, *Occupation and Pay in Great Britain, 1906–79* (Basingstoke, 1980), Table 2.27. Between 1955–6 and 1960 male manual wages rose less sharply than did average incomes. Between 1960 and 1970 male semi- and unskilled wages rose faster than the average wage but only marginally. Male manual wages rose less than the average women's income, except for unskilled women between 1960 and 1970. It was the 1970s which saw male manual wages rise markedly in relative terms.

16. See P. Anderson, 'Origins of the present crisis', *New Left Review*, 23, 1964, pp. 26–53; P. Anderson, 'Problems of a socialist strategy', in P Anderson (ed.), *Towards Socialism* (1965); T. Nairn, 'Anatomy of the Labour Party', *New Left Review*, 27, 1964, pp. 38–65; T. Nairn, 'Anatomy of the Labour Party', *New Left Review*, 28, 1964, pp. 33–62; R. Miliband, *Parliamentary Socialism*, (1961); E.P. Thompson, 'The peculiarities of the English', *Socialist Register*, 1965.

17. See Abrams et al., *Must Labour Lose?*

18. An interesting example of this point can be found if one reads the first five or so years of the journal *Sociology*, launched in 1967 as the official journal of the British Sociological Association. Here one finds abundant occupational case studies; for example, I.C. Cannon, 'Ideology and occupational community: a study of compositors', *Sociology*, 1, 2, 1967, pp. 165–85; A.J.M. Sykes, 'Navvies, their social relationships', *Sociology*, 1, 3, 1970, pp. 157–72; S. Cotgrove and C. Vamplew, 'Technology, class and politics: the case of process workers', *Sociology*, 6, 1972, pp. 169–85. There is also a deep-rooted interest in class; for example, D. Toomey, 'Home-centred working-class parents' attitudes towards their sons' education and careers', *Sociology*, 3, 3, 1969, pp. 299–320. Figures such as John Goldthorpe also exercised major influence over the journal in this period.

19. For one indication of this point, see Critcher's 'Sociology, cultural studies and the post-war working-class', n.5, which can be read in part as a 'slapping down' of the pretensions of sociological research.

20. Goldthorpe, 'Intellectuals and the working-class'.

21. G.W. Horobin, 'Community and occupation in the Hull fishing industry', *British Journal of Sociology*, 8, 4, 1957; Cannon, 'Ideology and occupational community'.

22. Hoggart, *Uses of Literacy*, pp. 68, 70.

23. Williams, *Culture and Society*, p. 327. This theme also plays a key role in Williams' novels which examine the relationship between communal ties and individual liberties, in ways which often conflate these issues with those of class. See the interesting discussion in D. Harvey, *Justice, Nature and the Geography of Difference*, (Oxford, 1996).

24. R. Harrison (ed.), *Independent Collier: the coalminer as archetypal proletarian reconsidered* (Hassocks, 1978); P.J. Waller, *The Dukeries Transformed* (Oxford, 1979); A. Campbell, N. Fishman, D. Howell (eds), *Miners, Unions and Politics, 1910–47* (Aldershot, 1996).

25. On the docks, see University of Liverpool Department of Social Science, *The Dockworker*, (Liverpool, 1956); G. Phillips and N. Whiteside, *Casual*

Labour: the unemployment question in the port transport industry (Oxford, 1985). On shipbuilding, see K. McLelland and A. Reid, 'Wood, iron and steel: technology, labour and trade union organization in the shipbuilding industry, 1840–1914', in R. Harrison and J. Zeitlin (eds), *Divisions of Labour* (Brighton, 1985).

26.   See A.J. Davies, *Leisure, Gender and Poverty* (Milton Keynes, 1993); J. Bourke, *Working-class Cultures in Britain, 1890–1960: gender, ethnicity and class* (1995); M. Tebbutt, *'Women's talk': a social history of gossip in working-class neighbourhoods* (Aldershot, 1996); S. Fielding, *Class and Ethnicity*, (Milton Keynes, 1993).

27.   See Marshall et al., *Social Class in Modern Britain*, ch. 8, for a powerful elaboration of this argument.

28.   There is of course a complex methodological debate about some of the issues raised by *The Affluent Worker* study which I do not want to focus on here. It is worth briefly mentioning the 'action frame of reference'. This idea, championed particularly by Goldthorpe, emphasized that workers have 'orientations to work' which affect their perception of their working environment. Attempts to see worker attitudes as passive responses to their work situation were therefore misguided, and neglected the agency of these workers. Goldthorpe used this emphasis on 'orientations to work' to provide a critique of deterministic thinking in industrial sociology, for instance, the technological determinism associated with Blauner. It led to a debate between Daniel and Goldthorpe concerning whether a form of 'voluntarism' was embedded in the claims about 'orientations to work'. The issue here was that since the idea of 'instrumental orientations to work' became the main critical test case for the broader perspective associated with the 'orientations to work' approach, the idea of individual agency became linked, if only indirectly, with that of instrumentalism. See F. Devine, *Affluent Workers Revisited*, (Edinburgh, 1992) for a discussion.

29.   D. Lockwood, 'Working-class images of society', *Sociological Review*, 14, 3, 1966; Goldthorpe et al., *Affluent Worker*.

30.   J. Westergaard, 'The rediscovery of the cash nexus', *Socialist Register* (1970).

31.   Goldthorpe, 'Intellectuals and the working-class', p. 47.

32.   Westegaard's account of the Vauxhall incident follows R. Blackburn, 'The Unequal Society' in R. Blackburn and A. Cockburn (eds), *The Incompatibles: trade union militancy and the consensus* (Harmondsworth, 1967), pp. 48–51. R. Pahl, 'Is the emperor naked? Some questions on the adequacy of sociological theory in urban and regional research', *International Journal of Urban and Regional Research*, 13, 4, 1989; D. Lockwood, 'The weakest link in the chain? Some remarks on the Marxist theory of action', in Rose (ed.), *Social Stratification*.

33.   See, among many other studies, H. Beynon and R.M. Blackburn, *Perceptions of Work: variations within a factory* (Cambridge, 1972); M. Mann, *Consciousness and Action amongst the Western Working-class* (Basingstoke, 1970); M. Bulmer (ed.), *Working-class Images of Society* (1975).

34.   Marshall 'Some remarks', and Marshall et al., *Social Class in Modern Brit-*

ain.

35.   S. Halford, M. Savage and A. Witz, *Gender, Careers and Organizations* (Basingstoke, 1997).
36.   This is an anonymized interview from the research project reported in note 35.
37.   Beynon, *Working for Ford*, pp. 123–4.
38.   Goldthorpe et al., *Affluent Worker*. Their Table 57 also shows that purely financial reasons for not becoming a foreman were not especially important, being mentioned in only around 10 per cent of occasions.
39.   E. P. Thompson, *The Making of the English Working-class*, (1963).
40.   Joyce, *Democratic Subjects*.
41.   D. Wahrman, *Imagining the Middle-classes*, (Cambridge, 1994).
42.   This is also one of the arguments of M. Grieco, 'The shaping of a workforce: a critique of the affluent worker study', *International Journal of Sociology and Social Policy*, 1, 1, 1981, pp. 62–88.
43.   There are of course many sociological issues which have been debated in recent years concerning organizational hierarchy and class analysis; for example, see E.O. Wright, *Class Counts* (Oxford, 1996); M. Savage, J. Barlow, P. Dickens and A.J. Fielding, *Property, Bureaucracy and Culture: middle-class formation in contemporary Britain* (1992).
44.   Reported in D.V. Glass, *Social Mobility* (1954).
45.   P. Willis, *Learning to Labour* (1977).
46.   Runciman, *Relative Deprivation*, p. 200.

CHAPTER TWO

Women in the Labour Market and in the Unions

Chris Wrigley

British trade unionism slowly, hesitantly and often very reluctantly began to come to terms with some of the requirements and growing expectations of women workers in the third quarter of the twentieth century. By the final quarter of the century the trade unions were jolted into action by changing circumstances which concentrated their minds, much in the manner of Dr Johnson's celebrated remark that 'when a man knows he is to be hanged in a fortnight, it concentrates his mind wonderfully'. In the case of trade unionists, the jolts included increasing proportions of female members amidst a rising percentage of women in the labour force and, after 1979, declining overall memberships as well as an increasingly hostile political climate.

Trade union interest in issues of special importance to their women members was not notably greater – or for that matter less – than it was for most other groups in British society. Although there was some coherence of shared concerns in many unions, nevertheless unions generally incorporated a variety of political and social attitudes. In many unions there was a conservative, even macho, male culture in which women were often at best patronized and more usually belittled. Yet, at the same time, the British trade union movement had a progressive and sometimes socialist tradition, which did not necessarily entail an awareness of gender but was often more sympathetic than some other traditions. This could be appealed to by those proposing resolutions, often with some success, at conferences of individual unions or at the annual TUC. It could also be invoked at trades councils and, perhaps less confidently, at union branches and in the workplace.

Many of the issues of concern to women trade unionists had long been aired, not least at the TUC's women's conferences. However, what mattered was not winning votes on such issues but getting union leaders and, through them, union negotiators and politicians to prioritize them. Women's issues were ventilated at national level throughout the 1945–79 period, for among trade union activists there were always some, often female, sometimes male, who pressed the needs of female members. However, advances of substance only came when educated public opinion more generally, and thus politicians of all parties, were more sensitive to women's rights and so provided a supportive context for state action. Such changed attitudes first came with regard to clerical and professional workers. Left to themselves, British trade union leaders repeatedly backed away from taking decisive action to bring about equal pay or to remedy other female inequalities. Indeed, in the 1945–79 period, there was almost a compulsive readiness to agree to unequal settlements for women workers while voicing aspirations for equal pay in the future. This essay focuses on national union developments in regard to homeworking, equal pay, and representation within unions after first commenting on the changing position of women in the labour market after 1945.

Women in the labour market

Following the Second World War, as after the First World War, there was a return to 'normalcy' for women, marked by an exit from many better-paid and male-reserved occupations. However, from 1948 the percentage of women in the insured labour force rose until the mid-1950s, when it stabilized around 35 per cent, before increasing again slowly from 1960, and then more markedly from 1966–8 (see Table 2.1). Women constituted the major part of the increase in the labour supply needed for economic expansion during the 'Golden Years' (1950–73) of the international economy.[1] The percentage of women aged 15–64 working in the UK was, according to Organization for Economic Co-operation and Development (OECD) figures, among the highest in Europe through the period 1950–80, with only Denmark in 1970–80 having a notably higher percentage. The UK was also notable for a fairly rapid increase in the percentage of women working between 1960–80, though there were even more rapid increases during these years in Denmark and Belgium and also in the USA.[2]

The growth in female employment in these years was more than echoed by an expansion in the number of female trade unionists (see Table 2.1). There was a slower rise between 1946 and 1965 than between 1966 and 1979. While the overall number of trade unionists grew by 16.5 per cent, the number of female trade unionists increased by 39.5 per cent; the proportion of trade unionists who were female rose from 18.4 to 21.7 per cent. Between 1966 and 1979 the number of trade unionists grew more rapidly – by 31.1 per cent in a shorter period. The increase of female trade unionists was 73 per cent (compared with a male 19.3 per cent), while the proportion of trade unionists who were female reached 29.4 per cent and was to rise for the rest of the century. Between 1966 and 1979 the increase in the number of women trade unionists provided a little over half (51.6 per cent) of the whole increase in trade union membership, whereas between 1946 and 1965 it had been under half (43.8 per cent).

The greatest part of the increase in female employment came in part-time work, which suited the needs of many women and also many employers. It is estimated that 922,000 of one million additional female jobs between 1971

44

and 1978 were part-time. However, statistics under-record part-time work, especially before the 1980s. Nevertheless, it is clear that there was a steady growth of part-time work in Britain and other countries in the decades after the Second World War. OECD figures suggest that in Europe Britain had the second highest level of part-time work after Denmark in the 1970s.[3] In 1979 women constituted 92.8 per cent of the part-time workforce in Britain.[4]

The numbers of female part-time workers in Britain rose five-fold between 1951 and 1981 (Table 2.2). In the 1950s and 1960s part-time work (up to 30 hours a week) was predominantly work in manufacturing industry, with the percentage of women involved rising after 1959, and more markedly so after 1963 (Table 2.3). Within manufacturing, the greatest number of these women worked in the metal and engineering trades, followed by the food, drink and tobacco sector. In the 1960s, according to the census and other surveys, between 76 and 82 per cent of all recorded women part-time workers were in manufacturing industry.[5] However, thereafter there was substantial growth of part-time working in the service sector. By the 1980s roughly 90 per cent of all part-time workers were employed in this sector, which had a high demand for part-time workers who were not carrying out work which was simply fractions of full-time work. Such demand included peak-time work at cash-tills in supermarkets and garages or meal-times in the catering trades.[6]

Women, unions and part-time work

Employing part-time workers could also be attractive as a source of cheap labour. For those working short weekly hours were often not covered by legislation relating to redundancy, unfair dismissal or maternity pay as well as not often being entitled to holiday pay. By the 1980s, this was so for those working less than 18 hours per week (if not in continuous employment for five years or more). The desire to avoid such costs encouraged a growth in employment of people for less than 18 hours a week.[7] Yet part-time working, including 'twilight' shifts, suited many women, especially those with young children.[8] This was a fact which many male trade union leaders were very slow to grasp. Indeed, there was only sporadic trade union interest in part-time workers. As Sheila Lewenhak has commented, many union activists took a 'dog-in-the-manger' attitude, seeing part-time workers as a threat.[9]

For women trade unionists, however, it was a key issue. In 1965 the TUC's Women's Advisory Committee prepared a survey of women's employment in Britain which highlighted both the increase in part-time employment as well as an increasing proportion of older married women in the workforce. The following year, the Committee warned their male colleagues: 'There must be wider acceptance of the fact that increasing numbers of married women will wish only to work part-time', and that they were being encouraged to do this by the Ministry of Labour and the National Economic Development Council in order to alleviate a labour shortage. The Women's Advisory Committee pressed their case, using an argument which was likely to assure male (and female) trade unionist support: 'While part-time women remain unorganized the committee believe they constitute a threat both to the effectiveness of the union machinery and to the security and working conditions of other workers'.[10]

Nevertheless, this was an issue which required raising repeatedly. In 1974, when the TUC's annual women's conference debated a composite motion on minimum requirements for women's employment, a central demand was for 'organization of suitable work on a part-time basis for those who are unable to work full-time because they have children or elderly parents to care for'. D. Lancaster (Society of Civil Servants), who moved the motion, argued:

> [young mothers] have very little hope of resuming mind-stretching employment although they can probably find a good-deal of mind-bending employment. This is not only frustrating for them but it is also wasteful from an economic point of view. Therefore, working conditions must be reorganized to recognize that the working life of most women will consist of periods of work interrupted, but not broken, by spells at home to bear and bring up their children ... What we need to consider is how to make the necessary changes, how to make working life possible, even to make it attractive, and to offer worthwhile work with decent career opportunities, and opportunities for development of potential ... Very often a woman needs a period of part-time work, and flexi-hours are not the answer, because however late you may arrive in the morning you have got to stay late at night to make it up. Part-time work is really needed, but it is extremely difficult. The men do not like it; they are jealous of the idea. The employers do not like it; it is difficult to organise. On the other hand, if working women are able to continue their careers organization of part-time work is absolutely essential. It is not part-time work either of a purely casual or repetitive nature. There is plenty of responsible work capable of being organized on a part-time basis if there is the will.[11]

Lancaster naturally spoke for her own clerical constituency. Nevertheless she put very clearly the needs of women-centred, not purely male-centred, organization of work.

In responding to this resolution, the TUC Women's Advisory Committee could draw on a supporting statement made by the Employment and Social Services Sub-Committee of the House of Commons Expenditure Committee which recommended that 'consideration should be given to the organization of work so that flexible working hours and the choice between full- and part-time work can be made available to the maximum number of women'. The TUC General Council referred the issues raised by the Expenditure Committee to unions with experience of flexible work-time. After consultations they found both opposition to flexible work-time and that 'a number of unions had concluded satisfactory agreements for flexible hours of work'. These responses appear to have influenced the TUC to treat part-time work similarly. The 1975 report of the TUC Women's Advisory Committee noted that 'the General Council had said they recognized that for women – and particularly those with children – there were sometimes decided advantages in being able themselves to choose the hours they work but that, nevertheless, it was important that any change in working hours should be subject to the agreement of the unions concerned'.[12] While demonstrating caution towards the motives of employers, this response indicated extremely clearly that female concerns still came a very poor second to those of male members.

By the end of the 1970s, part-time workers remained poorly unionized and some unions continued to pay little or no attention to recruiting part-time women workers. Even by the early 1980s, trade union membership was under 10 per cent among part-time sales staff and secretaries, at about 17 per cent for clerical workers but about 27 per cent for those in health and over 30 per cent for skilled operatives. Of the 15 trade unions with the largest proportions of female members, in the early 1980s two offered no special membership rate to part-time workers: the National Union of Tailors and Garment Workers and the National Union of Footwear, Leather and Allied Trades. Five related subscriptions to earnings (which helped part-timers), while seven did by this time offer reduced part-time subscriptions.[13]

Trade unions and homeworking

The trade union leaders were also reticent concerning the special needs of homeworkers. Like part-time workers, most homeworkers were women, often with young children, sometimes elderly or incapacitated. Or they were immigrants with similar family commitments and with additional language and cultural restrictions. Indeed, a survey carried out for the Department of the Employment in 1979–80 found just one male homeworker. This survey by Cragg and Dawson estimated that in 1971 some 1.5 million people (6 per cent of the labour force) worked at home. Their occupations were distributed between manufacturing, white–collar office, needlework, professional and child-minding.[14] However, the statistics on homeworking are far from reliable. Pennington and Westover, writing of the 1980s, commented: 'The collection and collation of statistics has remained unreliable and erratic, complicated by a lack of a generally accepted definition of the term, the high labour turnover and the clandestine nature of much home industry'.[15] In 1980 estimates of the number of homeworkers in the traditional manufacturing sector nationally varied between 150,000 and 400,000, although even the higher figure was probably far too low.[16]

47

Homework posed a traditional dilemma for trade unionists. Should they welcome and help homeworkers as fellow workers? Or should they be hostile to them as a source of cheap, non-union labour which could undercut the jobs of factory employees? Such protection as there was for some homeworkers came from Winston Churchill's Trades Board Act 1909 and its successors. The TUC very much supported wages councils. They applauded the extra powers given to them under the Wages Council Act, 1945 and the setting up of several new councils to cover sections of the retail trade and hairdressing under Attlee's governments.

As for homeworkers, there was a division of opinion within TUC affiliates. In both the late 1940s and early 1970s when the National Union of Hosiery Workers had called for a common trade union policy towards homeworking, the thrust of its comments had been explicitly antagonistic to the practice – as it represented cheap labour working under dangerous conditions – and implicitly protective of the position of factory workers. At the 1971 TUC Harold Gibson, General Secretary of the National Union of Hosiery and Knitwear Workers, moved a motion calling upon the General Council to press for new legislation to cover homeworking. Gibson complained that it was 'almost impossible to obtain any reliable information' as to what the piece-rates were and that there were no controls of hours, hazards and safety or the possibility of children carrying out some of the work.[17] His members had been moved away from national piece-rate agreements because of changing fashions and machinery since the mid-1950s. In the face of overseas competition productivity had risen very substantially, with night work introduced (as part of three shift working) and with a seamless knitter supervizing not 12 but 40 or even 60 machines. From 1968 the union strived to replace piece-rates with a guaranteed wage. Hence the renewed concern about competition from outside the factory. In Leicestershire, for instance, some 60–70 per cent of homeworkers were in hosiery, knitwear and other clothing work, and many of them were Asian women.[18]

In contrast to this hostility to homeworking on the part of the hosiery unions, the TUC's women's conferences and its Women's National Advisory Committee eschewed direct opposition. Instead they called for homeworking to be carried out under safe and less exploitative conditions. After the 1968 TUC women's conference passed a resolution concerning the problems of homeworking, the TUC Women's Advisory Committee contacted 60 affiliated unions to ask them about their experience. In searching for information the Women's Committee stressed that its aim was not to prohibit such work but 'to ensure that they [women homeworkers] were protected against exploitation and underpayment, bad working conditions and particularly against the risk of accidents'. As a result of the responses received, the TUC urged affiliated unions to press employers and local authorities to ensure that the 1961 Factory Act was adhered to, especially Sections 133–4 which required employers to supply the local authority with the names and addresses of all homeworkers employed in the previous six months. The Women's Advisory Committee did discover that 'one union had an agreement with an employer specifically covering homeworkers, including an agreement that they must be union members'.[19] The outcome of the Women's Advisory Committee survey was reviewed by Barbara Castle, Secretary of State for Employment and Productivity, who considered moving regulations concerning homeworkers from the Factory Acts to public health legislation. However, this was not done before the Labour Party left office in 1970.

The General Council took up the concerns expressed by Harold Gibson and the hosiery workers in the resolution passed at the 1971 TUC. When Robert Carr, the Secretary of State for Employment, responded to these representations in January 1972 by stating that a 1966 inquiry into homeworking by the Factory Inspectorate had found no evidence of substantial hazards or grounds for serious concern about the problems of homeworking, the General Council invited the hosiery and clothing unions to provide such evidence.[20] With the return of the Labour Party to office in 1974, the hosiery and clothing unions pressed for legislative changes in the Factory Acts or the Employment Protection Bill. The government declined to add provisions in the 1975 Employment Protection Bill to give allowances for overheads involved in homeworking and to set up a new register of homeworkers which would be available for trade union officials to inspect.[21]

None the less, from 1976 the TUC took the matter up with greater vigour. It set up a working party 'to formulate a more comprehensive trade union policy on behalf of homeworkers' (as the Women's Advisory Committee put it), with Audrey Hunt (ASTMS) in the chair and A. Davis (AUEW) and Ethel Chipchase (TSSA) of the Women's Advisory Committee also members. This time there was evidence. In the case of the Nottingham lace-making industry a Department of Employment enquiry discovered that 167 of 247 persons visited were being underpaid, a situation confirmed by Nottingham Trades Council. The committee gathered in further information from other trades councils as well as TUC affiliated unions. In the Women's Advisory Committee's annual report the problem was succinctly and forcefully posed:

> The enforcement of wages council orders for homeworkers is virtually impossible because of the large number of self-employed homeworkers who are specifically excluded and some method has to be found either to apply the wages council orders to the self-employed or to ensure that persons putting out the work are automatically regarded as employers.

The committee also sought to find out what Australian policy was, for it was believed that homeworking was successfully regulated there.[22]

With this working party, which first met in July 1976, and the seeking of trades councils' assistance in providing evidence of dangerous working conditions, concern became more focused on overcoming exploitation of homeworkers rather than scapegoating them as a problem for trade union-ists in factories. From the late 1970s the burgeoning feminist movement and the swing to the left in the labour movement ensured that homeworking was examined in a manner sympathetic to these workers by trades councils as well as other groups. The Long Eaton trades council carried out a substan-tial survey in the period. This revealed widespread low pay, cases of hazardous work practices (such as soldering on kitchen stoves) and use of hazardous materials (even those statutorily excluded from factories).[23] However, by the end of the 1970s the Labour Party was out of office and had been re-placed by a Conservative government immune to trade union influence and eager to promote 'flexible labour'. So the accumulated expressions of con-cern over homeworking were not translated into legislative action.

Recruiting women members

If union leaders could still be suspicious of female part-time workers and exhibit hostility to homeworkers, the rising numbers (and proportion) of women workers forced a change in attitudes to recruiting women workers from the 1940s. As in the First World War, the need of the British economy for more workers had seen women enter in large numbers occupations usu-ally held to be male preserves, though in some cases the most skilled work remained a male prerogative. The most dramatic change in membership policy regarding women came at the start of 1943 when the AEU, which had been determinedly exclusionist in its membership policies during the First World War, began recruiting women members. By the end of 1943 the number of women employed in engineering and allied trades was 1,544,000 (39 per cent of the workforce), up from 411,200 in June 1939, with 138,000 en-rolled in the union. For the women involved there still needed to be a 'cap-in-hand' approach to the men for acceptance, as is indicated by a real-istic speech made by Joan Henry, a Manchester shop steward, at an AEU women's shop steward conference. She said:

> The whole status of women in the industry will be decided by the wisdom with which we set about the job of organization now. If we are content to allow our-selves to be used as cheap labour we become a threat to the men employed along-side us. If we are able to secure a decent return, based on the men's wage we give a feeling of security to the men, while ensuring a proper standard of living for our women members. The modern methods have made it certain that the women nec-essary in industry will increase enormously over the pre-war figures. Only by trade union membership, vigilant work in the factories by the women shop stew-ards and the sympathetic help and understanding of the men, can we hope to attain the position to which our importance entitles us.[24]

After the Second World War, however, the 'boys' club' mentality of most unions was reinforced. The marginal position of women is readily apparent when reading trade union journals of the post-war years. But the growing numbers of female employees, together with changing attitudes in Britain and other western countries, began to make it untenable for trade unions to belittle women workers and to make no attempts to address their concerns. George Crane (AEU), a member of the Communist Party who exemplified the support many male militants gave to women's struggles, moved a motion at the 1955 congress calling for action by the TUC both to secure equal pay and 'to organise a nation-wide recruiting campaign among women in industry and the professions'. Crane pointed out that it had taken many years to organize 45 per cent of male workers yet only a million and a half of the seven million working women were unionized. He continued:

> The question is how we can organise women with their special problems. Some are married and have to run the home and have no time for meetings. It is much better to call small meetings. We could have more entertaining meetings, with music and entertainment provided. It is along these lines that we have had a measure of success. But, of course, above all it is a question of policy. Have we got confidence in the policy of equal pay? Do we regard it as of the utmost importance? Do we really believe it is possible to accomplish it? If it is possible to accomplish it for non-manual workers then I say it is equally possible to accomplish it for our women employed in industry and those who are producing the wealth of this country.

Crane's call for a TUC national campaign to recruit women was rebutted by Dame Florence Hancock who argued that past national membership campaigns had been expensive and ineffective and argued that the best way was for it to be done by the individual unions in cooperation 'with the local machinery of the TUC, our trades councils and our women's advisory committees'.[25]

However, most of the TUC's local women's advisory committees had a short and precarious existence, though 57 existed at various times. At the end of the Second World War there were 23, and with some difficulty the TUC pushed the number up to over 30. By the mid-1950s many had collapsed. A further drive resurrected some, and by 1958 it was claimed that recruiting members to them had been more successful. When the organizers combined a programme of distinguished trade union speakers, trade union question sessions and brains trusts with 'attractive "feminine features" such as fashion shows, beauty culture demonstrations, cookery exhibitions and so on. These methods have proved outstandingly successful'.[26] If so, the success did not last, for by 1963 only ten local women's advisory committees remained in existence. Then the Women's Committee decided to disband them. Instead selected trades councils were invited to set up *ad hoc* committees which would be disbanded after serving their purpose. In reviewing their failure the Women's Advisory Committee observed,

The two main difficulties of local women's committees have been the high turno-ver among delegates and the fact that the voluntary officers have often been women fully committed to work within their own unions. In addition, women undoubt-edly have greater claims on their time outside working hours than have men and therefore it is not always possible for women to play as full a part as they would wish in union work ... The committee did not find that any local committee had died because of lack of encouragement from the trades council.[27]

The recruitment of women into unions did not depend on the TUC's local committees but relied more on the energy and initiative of individual un-ions, locally and nationally. Recruitment depended very much on the perceptions of women workers as to the value of trade unionism to them: to expectations of protection should they hit difficult times and hopes of the collective achievement of better pay and working conditions. It also depended on prevailing social attitudes to unions, including whether women were employed at workplaces where many were already in unions, as well as po-litical views on unions and economic conditions. Recruitment was given a fillip in the late 1960s and the 1970s by the rapid growth in female employ-ment generally, and in particular, in the private services, hitherto little unionized. Workers here, as elsewhere, were encouraged to join unions by inflation. They not only feared being left behind in terms of real wages but also felt more insecure in regard to keeping their jobs.

Equal pay at a snail's pace

For much of the 1945–79 period most unions appeared far from serious in championing important issues for women workers. In a 1949 TUC debate on equal pay, F.O. Bonsor (Civil Service Clerical Association) bluntly com-mented,

> I do not propose to deal with the principle of equal pay – it has been agreed to by this Congress and by the government – but I would reiterate ... that there is very strong feeling up and down the country that nothing has been done to implement the principle. You cannot live for ever on principles that have no tangible applica-tion ... I am aware that in some outside industries the differential is worse [than in the Civil Service]. When I think of how my blood boils when I consider my own differential, I am amazed that other people who are even worse off have not died of blood pressure before now.[28]

Mel Read, who joined her union in 1965 and was on its executive 1975–90, recalls:

> In my early days as a trade union member at Plessey things were dire in some respects. For example, there were separate grades for women in that most women

were classified as female laboratory technicians or female technical operators. The lowest male grade was technician. To be a female laboratory technician you needed 5 'O' levels. To be a male technician you needed no qualifications whatsoever. The pay differential was about £2 a week ... You can imagine as a single parent with two children to bring up on my own, £2 a week made a great deal of difference. I was eventually regraded, as were a small number of other women, but this was regarded as a major advance ... It was interesting that when I approached the union about this matter their response was to suggest that women union members might perhaps pay a lower subscription and that this would deal with the problem! It was also noteworthy that these pay scales and grade descriptions were negotiated by the union, not imposed by the company.

She also remembered that one of her earliest campaigns was to go round the factory talking to all AScW (later ASTMS) women and pointing out this anomaly.[29]

Equal pay came in stages, beginning in local and central government for white collar workers. This was broadly in line with the recommendations of a Royal Commission on Equal Pay, set up in 1944 and which reported in 1946. After the Labour-controlled London County Council made a beginning in 1952 with teachers, other local authorities followed suit. In 1954 R. A. Butler, the Conservative Chancellor of the Exchequer, agreed to phase in equal pay in the Civil Service over the six years to 1961. This was later extended to administrative grade workers in local government, the health service, gas and electricity as well as to teachers and nurses. Equal pay assisted the public sector in holding clerical and other staff in a period of labour shortage. It also met the Conservatives' need to maintain the voting loyalty of many clerical and white collar workers, a loyalty which they feared was being undermined by a high-profile trade union campaign which had been launched in 1951 and which included using the logo 'Equal Pay – When?' on much of its material.[30]

While the unions campaigned publicly for equal pay, many of their negotiators still concluded wage agreements which failed to end or narrow gender differentials and, in some cases, actually widened them. Many looked to the big unions with considerable 'industrial muscle' to use their power to negotiate away such differentials. In 1954, in engineering, where over a fifth of the labour force was female and earning £11.50p less a week than their male equivalents, the AEU put forward a claim for the women to receive not less than the average male labourer's rate, a claim which would be a stage in eliminating the gender differential. In late 1956 agreement was reached that improved the relative average weekly wage rate compared to men's. Even so, in 1959, the women's average hourly pay was 77.4 per cent of that of the men and there was much to suggest union leaders saw realizing the aspirations of their female members as a low priority.[31]

Nevertheless, the AEU's record in moving towards equal pay through collective bargaining was attractive to women elsewhere in the private sector of the economy. At the 1967 TUC Marion Veitch, the Chief Women's Officer of the NUGMWU, warned Congress that while women did not 'expect equal pay to be realized overnight', they were 'not stooges ... you cannot kid them for ever'. She commented,

> Let me tell you what things women want. They want an end to the differentials. They want something like what is happening in engineering, where women's rates have risen to 92 per cent ... [of] the male labourers' rates. We want to see the next package deal in engineering closing the differential even more, and we want to see this in other industries as well, industries where the ... [differential] is 66 per cent ... against the male workers. We want to see that as a first step, and we want to be able to catch up with our European and American sisters. Then we want to see merit payments, bonuses and the rest.[32]

However, the General Council was less optimistic that equal pay could be secured through collective bargaining. After a survey of 48 affiliated unions in 1961, the General Council noted,

> Most of the unions reported failure in their attempts to secure equal pay for industrial workers though a few had succeeded in narrowing the gap between male and female rates in some industries and trades ... The absence of equal pay was a serious trade union problem in the engineering and other industries, where a considerable number of women were doing complex work for wages lower than those of less skilled male workers ... in the light of the limited success of unions in achieving equal pay and the continued opposition of most employers, the TUC should accept the need for government action in this field and should urge the government to ratify the ILO Equal Pay Convention.[33]

This report, apart from being notably frank about how limited and how dilatory progress in moving towards equal pay by collective bargaining had been, was also revealing in indicating that inequality was characterized as 'a serious trade union problem' largely because of the dangers it held for male trade unionists. Clearly lack of equal pay in other circumstances did not merit being deemed such a problem.

There was a great deal of insight in a trenchant assessment of low pay made in a Fabian Society pamphlet in 1968 by John Edmonds and Giles Radice. In arguing for a minimum wage, they observed of women and young people,

> Unions may have voted repeatedly for equal pay for women ... But both sides [management and unions] operate in a society which broadly accepts that as women and juveniles have fewer financial responsibilities than men, it is tolerable that they should be paid less, irrespective of the value of the work. In any bargain there is a tendency for both these groups to be quietly put to one side and only considered after the 'real' discussion (which, of course, concerns the pay of men) has been concluded. And since neither group is particularly active in pressing its own interests, their pay quietly stays well behind ... It is arguments like these

which reinforce the case for some sort of guaranteed national minimum, set independently of collective bargaining.[34]

A national minimum wage was still some thirty years away but equal pay legislation came in 1970. It covered not only pay but sick pay, pension benefits and holiday entitlements. The legislation was brought in by Barbara Castle, a past advocate of the need for it and generally a radical presence in Harold Wilson's Cabinet. The time was propitious for action on the issue for several reasons. During the 1960s part of a general revolt against past assumptions regarding young people and women included rejection by many of notions that women should receive inferior pay simply because they were women. With Britain appearing likely to join the EEC, there was awareness of the EEC's commitment (under Article 119 of the Treaty of Rome) to equal pay.

In Britain the issue of equal pay had emerged into public attention and debate as a consequence of a major dispute involving women sewing machinists led by Rose Boland, a shop steward, at Ford's Dagenham in June 1968. Although in this case some male trade unionists were anything but sympathetic – Alf Roberts of the National Union of Vehicle Builders being 'annoyed that the equal pay issue had been raised at all' (according to Barbara Castle) – the outcome was that Barbara Castle's intervention resulted in the women at Dagenham receiving 92 per cent of the men's rate (as at other Ford factories) instead of 85 per cent. Barbara Castle, in the course of her work as Secretary of State for Employment and Productivity from April 1968 had become convinced that the main trade union leaders were not seriously interested in prioritizing women's pay. In her memoirs she observed, 'For years the union had tolerated a pay-structure hierarchy which descended in the following order: skilled workers, semi-skilled, labourers and women'. When Hugh Scanlon of the AEU protected gains for the skilled men at the expense of his women members, Barbara Castle concluded 'that left to themselves the unions would never do anything serious about equal pay and that the government had to legislate'.[35] The fact that Barbara Castle was in the Department of Employment and Productivity, was forceful and articulate, was a long-time associate of the Prime Minister and wished to implement Labour's 1964 election pledge, ensured that the Equal Pay Act 1970 was prioritized. However, had membership of the EEC not been on the horizon, it is less likely that the measure would have reached the statute book before the 1970 general election.

While the Equal Pay Act did not come fully into effect until the end of 1975, its implementation appears to have had an early impact in speeding up the gradual erosion of gender differentials in pay. This is shown in Department of Employment and New Earnings Survey statistics. Table 2.4 shows that there was some move towards greater equality in manual workers' pay. However, in terms of closing the gender differential between male and female manual labourers it was small. In terms of weekly UK wages, women's earnings moved as a percentage of men's from 48.8 to 51.1 per cent between October 1969 and October 1971, while women's hourly earnings moved as a percentage of men's from 59.5 to 60.6 per cent in the same period. Between 1970 and 1971 there was also some closing of the gap between non-manual men's and women's wages, but this was smaller than for manual workers.[36]

In the six years after 1970, with the full implementation of the Equal Pay Act, the sex differential in earnings narrowed more markedly. According to New Earnings Survey data, women's earnings as a percentage of men's (based on hourly earnings excluding overtime) rose from 64 per cent in 1970 to 74 per cent in 1976 (see Table 2.5), but remained static thereafter until the late 1980s. Such rises in women's relative wages occurred in other Western European countries and also, although to a lesser extent, in the USA.[37] Nevertheless, compared to most Western European countries the pay of women relative to men in the UK remained notably poor throughout the whole period 1945–79.[38]

In spite of anti-discrimination legislation, women earned only about 70 per cent of men's hourly earnings from the late 1970s. One reason for this was employers' avoidance of assessing equal value in the work of women. In this they were helped by pay structures segregated by gender. Most of the women in a firm could be in a clerical pay structure while the men might be in a managerial or a skilled labour pay structure. Women were also disadvantaged by grading structures. These were usually shorter for women than for men, and where both sexes were covered, women were concentrated at or near the bottom of the scale. They were also less likely to receive merit or other additional payments. However, the equal pay legislation encouraged the spread of job evaluation. The 1980 Workplace Industrial Relations Survey found 21 per cent of establishments had job evaluation schemes. For unions with large female memberships job evaluation often proved an effective way of gaining substantial improvements in women workers' pay. They have also used the courts to pursue improved pay on the grounds of equal pay.[39]

The Sex Discrimination Act 1975 (which complemented the 1970 Equal Pay Act), was important. However, it failed to be as effective as most of its supporters hoped, not least because it placed the onus on individuals to secure legal redress if they suffered from sexual discrimination. The Equal Opportunities Commission, after six years' experience of the 1975 Act, called for the burden of proof to be moved from the person complaining of discrimination to the employer. Between 1976 and 1983 only 11 per cent of sex discrimination cases which reached tribunals were successful. Even then, the sums awarded were small (half of successful applicants in the period 1976–83 gaining less than £300) and for many the experience of going to the tribunal was exhausting and stressful. Those remaining in the same employment, not surprisingly, found that it did much harm to their subsequent work prospects. Equally, as one would expect, the numbers of people going to tribunals dropped: from 401 in 1976 to 264 in 1979. Where those going to tribunals sought union support, the unions were deemed helpful by most questioned in an Equal Opportunities Commission survey (18 of 21) and a third or more (14 of 21) in a survey by Jeanne Gregory, but with a substantial number (15 of 36) feeling the unions had been unhelpful. In one case a woman pointed out that her branch committee included men with whom she was seeking to achieve equal pay.[40]

Prioritizing women's issues

The TUC's women's conferences wanted more than equal pay. Following a resolution at the 1962 conference, the Women's Advisory Committee drew up for the 1963 conference the Industrial Charter for Women which dealt with women's employment, pay, training, promotion and working conditions. The charter consisted of six demands:

1. Equal pay based on the value of the job done and not on the sex of the worker.
2. Opportunities for promotion for women.
3. Apprenticeship schemes for girls in appropriate industries.
4. Improved opportunities for training young women.
5. Re-training facilities for older women who return to industry.
6. Special provisions for the health, welfare and care of women workers.[41]

The charter was revised in 1968, 1975 and 1977. In 1975 the revised version was published on International Women's Day (8 March) with 75,000 copies thereafter distributed via the trade unions. At the TUC Women Workers' Conference at Hastings on 13 March Len Murray, the TUC General Secretary, moved a motion welcoming the United Nation's declaration of 1975 as International Women's Year, calling on the unions to make special efforts to achieve objectives for women workers during the year and approving the revision of the TUC Charter of Aims for Women Workers. The revised charter dealt with (1) education, (2) starting work, (3) pay, (4) promotion, (5) sick pay and pensions, (6) maternity, (7) returning to work, (8) health and safety at work, (9) family responsibilities, (10) care of children, (11) marital status, and (12) women as members of the community.[42]

In 1977 it was further revised, in the wake of the Equal Pay Act 1970 which came into force in 1975, the Sex Discrimination Act 1975 (which came into effect that year) and the passage of maternity leave provisions in the Employment Protection Act, 1975. The 1977 TUC Charter of Aims for Women Workers added a section on family planning and abortion which stated 'that unions recognize that the decision whether or not to use such facilities is completely a matter for the individual but that unions oppose any move to restrict women's access to any family planning or abortion services and support the extension of such services'. (In 1979 the TUC acted vigorously when a private member's bill in the House of Commons threatened to undercut the 1967 Abortion Act, a TUC campaign ending with a major demonstration in London.) The other additional section dealt with part-time work, stating 'that part-time workers should receive pay and conditions at least pro rata to the full-time workers with whom they work'.[43]

The TUC charters for women workers had set out an important and challenging agenda for affiliated trade unions. But, as with equal pay which the TUC had first demanded in 1888, the big question was whether the unions would practise what they preached and prioritize these issues. As with so many other matters in British trade union history, there was also the contentious issue of whether these objectives should be pursued through collective bargaining or pressure for legislation. This is well illustrated by the example of maternity leave. In 1970 the Women's Advisory Committee prepared a memorandum on this at the time the Wilson government (and then the Heath government) was considering amending the Redundancy Payments Act. Robert Carr, the Conservative Secretary of State for Employment and Productivity, responded by stating that it would be too difficult to frame and then enforce legislation to protect further pregnant women in the UK. However, he did point to the fact that maternity leave agreements had been negotiated only for the public sector. As a result the Women's Advisory Committee and Vic Feather, the TUC General Secretary, urged that affiliated unions operating in the private sector should negotiate such agreements. The TUC obtained copies of agreements relating to maternity leave from 21 unions operating in national and local government, the health service, the post office, gas, electricity, water, broadcasting and atomic energy. Subsequently in the private sector there were some maternity agreements negotiated which (as in the public sector), secured advances on the minimum statutory provision.[44]

The unions generally appear to have begun to prioritize women's issues in the late 1960s. Mel Read's recollections are probably representative:

Things did change in the 1970s and I think many trade unions, including my own, were acutely aware that they had fairly radical policies with regard to women but relatively few active women certainly at regional and national level ... In 1974–5 the union [ASTMS] set up its first ever Women's National Committee. There was a considerable battle about this but eventually it was established and I was its first chair. I held this office probably for eight or nine years and this saw a time when women's structures were established, sometimes at branch, more usually at divisional or regional level. The Women's TUC also became more militant and campaigning at this time and there were various struggles around attempts to reform the 1967 Abortion Act and centring on linking various demands of women, i.e. childcare and the right to a job were linked as was the campaign for a living wage ... All of this coincided with the growth of the women's movement generally and a much more vigorous agenda for and by women.[45]

Other unions established national women's committees earlier. SOGAT, one-third of whose membership were women, set up a women's advisory committee in 1968 to advise its executive committee on all issues affecting women workers. As in so much else, a very great deal depended on the union leadership's intent. In this case the proposal had come as a branch motion to the union's delegate conference and had not been well-received by the union's executive committee (22 of its 24 members being men). The women's advisory committee only met five times before being disbanded in 1972. Its members were dissatisfied with the role permitted to it by the union leadership, deeming the committee to be merely tokenistic. It was not until 1983 that, in response to TUC moves, SOGAT established a 'positive action committee'.[46]

Indeed, for much of this period, those seeking equality for women in British society could readily see that the trade unions themselves were bastions of inequality. When in October 1946 the Attlee government abolished the marriage bar (i.e. women leaving employment on marriage), the Union of Post Office Workers (UPW) made it clear it regretted the move and its annual conference in 1953 passed the motion:

> In view of the rising unemployment figures and the consequential effect on the careers of single women, conference instructs to EC to seek agreement to the reimplementation of the marriage bar in the Post Office.

This was revoked at the 1954 annual conference. Yet the union did not repeal the policy of a marriage bar for its own employees until 1964.[47] This was an extreme case. However, beyond the TUC's affiliates, there were other notable oddities in employee representation. In 1970 Clive Jenkins, General Secretary of ASTMS, was surprised to find two staff associations for the Prudential Assurance: the Prudential Assurance Male Staff Association and the separate Ladies' Welfare Association.[48]

What was common to most unions was the simple fact that very few women held office even in organizations with high proportions of female members. In 1970, of 148 TUC affiliated unions, 107 had women members and 25 of these had more women members than men. The distribution of women's membership at the end of 1969 is shown in Table 2.6. Women's trade unionism was concentrated in relatively few unions, with 39 unions having more than 5,000 members. By 1978 this number had risen to 43 (out of 117 TUC affiliated unions). By the end of 1969 there were three unions with over 200,000 women members, by 1978 there were six, with one having over 400,000 women members and three had 3,000–4,000 members. .

The very small proportions of women playing senior or major roles in their unions is displayed in Table 2.7, which provides figures for 1976 for eleven substantial trade unions which had a majority of female members. In these only 15.1 per cent of national executive members, 7.1 per cent of full-time trade union officials and 15.4 per cent of TUC delegates were women.[49] Hence, it is not surprising that many women workers believed that the trade unions were not working for them in any seriously committed way. In 1971 such sentiments even produced a brief-lived, breakaway union, the Women's Industrial Union, initiated by Pat Sturdy, a Lucas worker in Burnley. The rebellion against the GMWU succeeded in making the union more responsive to its female members and to women's issues.[50]

The scale of the gender balance in several unions where most members, or a near majority, were women, made representation of women by women an issue that could not be dodged by the 1970s. Table 2.8 provides details of the ten unions with the greatest increases in women's membership for 1950–70 and 1968–78. In the 1970s the National Union of Public Employees (NUPE) responded to its massive recruitment of female members, which had turned it from a predominantly male union into one with a majority of female members, by adopting quotas for its executive committee. Five additional places were added, all reserved for women (with women continuing to be eligible for the others).[51]

By the late 1970s active female trade unionists were well aware that the need was not only for TUC charters of general aims for women workers but also for a charter of action for changes within trade unions. It was also a priority for the Women's Committee of the European Trade Union Confederation which in 1979 called for women to be included at all levels of responsibility in trade union organizations. Britain was the European country with the greatest number of female trade unionists. In 1979 the TUC's Women's Advisory Committee drafted a ten-point Charter for the integration of women into the trade union movement.[52] This called for action on representation at all levels, negotiating time off without loss of pay for union meetings, the provision of child-care facilities for either parent for those attending branch meetings out of working hours as well as for all other levels of union meetings and training courses, the giving of special encouragement for women to be involved in union activities and training, and the contents of union journals and other literature to present their contents in non-sexist terms.[53]

Conclusions

Brief consideration of relations between unions and women workers in this period demonstrates that unions only gradually and half-heartedly came to terms with important economic and social changes which saw women enter the labour force and the working-class at the point of production in greater numbers than ever before. No major union leader grasped the positive possi-

60

bilities for trade unionism and embraced in practice the cause of women as central to union activity. Inside the unions there was always a mix of conservative, hostile, restrictive attitudes as well as strong support for women's rights. Through these years, at local and national level, there were women and men who pushed forward the agenda of equality. And there were always men and women who opposed it, or who accepted things as they were, or, perhaps more typically, were prepared to do little to realize progress. The conventional response of union leaders was to support change in principle but to do far too little to implement those principles. Examination of a range of issues – part-time employment, homeworking, equal pay, discrimination, union recruitment policies and the representation of women in unions – demonstrates that advances were painfully slow and remained restricted. Progress was bound up with intervention by the state and the development of feminism rather than simply stemming from the ideology and activity of working-class collectivism.

By 1979, while the British trade unions were not 'user friendly' for women, most unions were beginning to get more than an inkling that responding to the needs of their female members was very important. There was some belated recognition that male workers' norms might not meet the needs of women workers, be it hours or patterns of work or child-care requirements. Progress remained pitiful in many sectors in closing the pay gap. The TUC did not take up the issues in the women's charters with any urgency and it had taken a long time before the leaderships of many unions realized that firm and decisive action for equality needed to start in their own front rooms, let alone backyards. In the subsequent two decades, with serious membership losses and continuing rise in the proportion of women, responding to women workers' priorities became not options for several unions but crucial survival strategies.

Table 2.1 Women as insured members of labour force, trade unionists and TUC members, UK 1945–79

Year	Insured labour force (in 000's)	(%)	TU members (in 000's)	(%)	TUC members (in 000's)	(%)
1945	5,398	38.6	1,638	25.0	1,341	20.4
1946	4,925	31.6	1,617	24.5	1,242	18.6
1947	4,820	30.3	1,662	25.0	1,217	16.1
1948	6,954	33.5	1,685	24.2	1,220	15.7
1949	6,954	33.5	1,674	24.1	1,237	15.6
1950	7,118	33.8	1,684	23.7	1,217	15.4
1951	7,271	34.3	1,790	24.6	1,220	15.6
1952	7,286	34.3	1,792	24.6	1,318	16.4
1953	7,351	34.4	1,778	24.2	1,315	16.3
1954	7,535	34.8	1,810	24.0	1,301	16.1
1955	7,689	35.1	1,867	24.3	1,332	16.4
1956	7,791	35.1	1,907	24.5	1,384	16.7
1957	7,848	35.1	1,894	24.1	1,402	16.9
1958	7,778	34.9	1,850	23.8	1,387	16.6
1959	7,864	35.1	1,868	25.1	1,336	16.3
1960	8,098	35.5	1,951	25.4	1,339	16.5
1961	8,242	35.7	2,005	25.6	1,403	16.9
1962	8,368	35.7	2,054	25.8	1,452	17.5
1963	8,414	35.7	2,104	26.2	1,481	17.8
1964	8,543	36.0	2,174	26.7	1,516	18.2
1965	8,677	36.3	2,241	27.0	1,691	19.3
1966	8,845	36.8	2,256	26.6	1,747	19.7
1967	8,751	36.8	2,286	27.2	1,753	19.9
1968	8,766	37.0	2,364	28.0	1,767	20.2
1969	8,839	37.4	2,507	29.4	1,842	20.8
1970	8,842	37.7	2,743	32.1	2,168	23.1
1971[1]	8,781	37.8	2,753	32.3	2,395	23.9
1972	8,512	38.5	2,907	33.6	2,418	24.4
1973	8,891	39.2	3,006	33.5	2,556	25.6
1974	9,131	40.1	3,178	34.5	2,613	26.0
1975	9,174	40.4	3,427	36.7	2,773	26.8
1976	9,151	40.6	3,561	37.6	3,034	27.5
1977	9,255	40.9	3,775	38.9	3,235	28.1
1978	9,372	41.2	3,874	37.5[2]	3,411	28.7
1979	9,641	41.8	3,902	39.4[2]		

Notes: 1. The basis of the statistics changed in 1971. Under the new basis the figures for insured labour force members and percentage were 8,408 and 38 per cent.
2. Female union density for Great Britain is estimated by Jeremy Waddington at 37.5 or 39.1 (using two alternative approaches) for 1978, and 39.4 and 40.4 per cent for 1979.
Sources: B.R. Mitchell, *British Historical Statistics* (Cambridge, 1988); *Employment Gazette,* 1983; J. Waddington, 'Trade union membership in Britain 1980-1987: unemployment and restructuring', *British Journal of Industrial Relations,* 30, 2, 1992, pp. 287–324.

Table 2.2 Female part-time workers in Britain, 1951-81

1951	779,000
1961	1,851,000
1971	2,757,000
1981	3,781,000

Source: P. Thane, 'Towards equal opportunities? Women in Britain since 1945', in T. Gourvish and A. O'Day, (eds), *Britain Since 1945* (1991), p.193.

Table 2.3 Percentage of female part-time workers in manufacturing industry in Britain 1950-68

	Per cent (¹)		Per cent (²)
1950	11.8	1959	11.7
1951	12.2	1960	13.2
1952	10.5	1961	13.7
1953	9.7	1962	13.8
1954	10.3	1963	13.8
1955	11.4	1964	15.0
1956	11.8	1965	15.9
1957	12.0	1966	17.7
1958	11.9	1967	17.0
1959	11.9	1968	17.7

Notes:
1. Column 1 (1950–9) is based on the 1948 Standard Industrial Classification.
2. Column 2 (1959–68) is based on the 1958 Standard Industrial Classification.
Source: Department of Employment, *British Labour Statistics: historical abstract 1886–1968* (1971), p. 275.

Table 2.4 Male and female manual workers' rates of pay and hours of work: UK indices 1950-71

Year	Basic weekly wage		Normal weekly hours of work		Basic hourly rates of wages	
	men	women	men	women	men	women
1950	100.0	100.0	100.0	100.0	100.0	100.0
1955	138.3	137.4	99.9	99.8	138.5	137.7
1960	169.3	170.5	97.0	97.6	174.6	174.6
1965	207.3	213.0	92.1	92.1	225.2	231.3
1970	280.4	284.8	90.3	90.0	310.7	316.4
1971	312.5	329.7	90.1	89.8	347.1	367.0

Source: Office of Manpower Economics, *Equal Pay: First Report* (1972), p. 12 (based on Department of Employment statistics). The figures are for October.

Table 2.5 Women's average earnings as a percentage of men's in the UK, 1970 and 1976

	Basic weekly wage rates		Basic hourly wages rates	
	1970	1976	1970	1976
Manufacturing:				
manual	48.1	60.0	57.1	69.4
non-manual	42.7	53.3	45.1	56.6
all	47.0	58.1	54.1	66.2
All industries:				
manual	49.6	60.5	61.3	71.1
non-manual	50.0	59.8	53.2	62.6
all	53.7	64.3	63.7	73.5

Source: Adapted from Appendix A, TUC, *TUC Women's Conference* (1977), p. 23.

Table 2.6 Women's membership of TUC affiliated unions, 31 December 1969

Number of women members	Number of unions	Total women's membership
0 – 100	14	400
101– 500	12	3,900
501– 1,000	12	8,900
1,001– 5,000	30	74,100
5,001– 10,000	13	88,700
10,001– 20,000	7	103,800
20,001– 50,000	8	307,000
50,001– 100,000	3	214,400
100,001– 150,000	3	390,300
150,001– 200,000	2	331,000
over 200,000	3	645,800
TOTALS	107	2,168,300

Source: TUC, *TUC Women Workers' Conference* (1971), p. 2.

Table 2.7 Representation of women in unions with a majority of women members, 1976

Union	% of women members	Executive committee		Full-time officials		TUC delegates	
		male	female	male	female	male	female
NUTGW	88	10	5	36	6	11	5
NUT	75	41	7	24	2	30	1
NUHKW	73	23	2	29	2	11	1
COHSE	70	27	1	35	5	8	0
CPSA	68	18	8	24	4	22	8
NUPE	65	20	6	120	2	29	4
TWU	65	18	1	6	3	4	1
USDAW	59	16	1	129	4	21	5
IRSF	58	25	3	6	1	9	0
APEX	55	11	4	5	1	10	3
CATU	53	16	2	6	0	7	2

Source: Adapted from a table in J. Hunt, 'A woman's place is in her union', in J. West, (ed.), *Work, Women and the Labour Market* (1982), p. 166.

Table 2.8 Trade unions with the largest increases in women's membership, 1950–78

(a) 1950–70 (in 000s)

Union	1950	1970	increase	% increase
NUPE	40	173	133	332.5
AUEW	35	125	90	257.1
TGWU	129	213	84	65.1
GMWU	152	220	68	44.7
CPSA	73	117	44	60.3
CAWU	16	52	36	225.0
EETPU	6	41	36	720.0
NUBE	7	41	34	485.7
USDAW	136	158	22	16.2
UPW	34	50	16	47.1

(b) 1968–78 (in 000s)

Union	1968	1978	increase	% increase
NUPE	136.0	457.4	321.4	236.3
NALGO	132.1	318.8	186.7	141.3
TGWU	194.7	317.9	123.2	63.3
COHSE	38.9	159.4	120.5	309.8
GMWU	199.9	318.2	118.3	59.2
USDAW	155.6	270.5	114.9	73.8
ASTMS	9.4	77.2	67.8	721.8
CPSA	100.0	158.8	58.8	58.8
AUEW(E)	97.4	148.3	50.9	52.3
APEX	38.7	83.7	45.0	116.3

Sources: TUC, *TUC Women Workers' Conference* (1971), p. 3 and TUC, *TUC Women Workers' Conference* (1979), p. 43.

Notes

1. C.P. Kindleberger, *Europe's Postwar Growth: the role of labor supply* (Cambridge, Mass., 1967), pp. 82–3 and 153–4. See, more generally, B. Eichengreen, 'Institutions and economic growth: Europe after World War II', in N. Crafts and G. Toniolo (eds), *Economic Growth in Europe Since 1945*, (Cambridge, 1997), pp. 58–60.

2. See A. Maddison, 'Macroeconomic accounts for European countries', in B. Van Ark and N. Crafts (eds), *Quantitative Aspects of Post-War European Economic Growth* (Cambridge, 1996), pp. 46–8; OECD, *Manpower Statistics 1950–62* (Paris, 1963); OECD, *Labour Force Statistics 1959–70* (Paris, 1972); OECD, *Labour Force Statistics 1969–80* (Paris, 1980).

3. For comparative figures on part-time workers in Britain and other European countries, see A. Gregory and J. O'Reilley, 'Checking out and cashing up', in R. Crompton, D. Gallie and K. Purcell (eds), *Changing Forms of Employment* (1996), p. 212.

4. Industrial Relations Services, 'Part-time work: a survey', *Industrial Relations Review and Report*, 320, 1984, pp. 2–9.

5. Department of Employment, *British Labour Statistics: Historical Abstract 1886–1968* (1971), Tables 142 and 143, p. 275.

6. An Industrial Relations Services survey published in 1984 provides support for stressing the importance of flexibility to employers of part-time workers (Industrial Relations Services, 'Part-time work', p. 4).

7. O. Robinson and J. Wallace, 'Growth and utilisation of part-time labour in Great Britain', *Employment Gazette*, September 1984, pp. 391–7; O. Robinson, 'The changing labour market: the phenomenon of part-time employment in Britain', *National Westminster Quarterly Review*, November 1985, pp. 19–29; C. Wrigley, 'Trade unions, the government and the economy'. in T. Gourvish and A. O'Day, *Britain Since 1945* (1991), p. 81.

8. P. Dawkins and D. Bosworth, 'Shiftworking and unsocial hours', *Industrial Relations Journal*, 11, 1980, pp. 32–40.

9. S. Lewenhak, *Women and Trade Unions* (1977), p. 267. However, the growth in women's membership of trade unions suggests this was not uniformly the case and points to the need for further research on the topic.

10. TUC, *Report*, 1965, pp. 141–2; TUC, *Report*, 1966, pp. 143–4.

11. TUC, *Report of the 44th annual conference of representatives of trade unions catering for Women Workers* (hereafter *Report of TUC Women Workers' Conference*), 1974, pp. 82–8.

12. TUC, *Report*, 1973, p. 257; *Report of TUC Women Workers' Conference*, 1975, pp. 11–12.

13. Industrial Relations Services, 'Part-time work', p. 7.

14. A. Cragg and T. Dawson, *Qualitative Research Among Homeworkers*, Research Paper 21, Department of Employment (1981).

15. S. Pennington and B. Westover, *A Hidden Workforce* (1989), p. 157.

16. Leicester Outwork Campaign, *Annual Report 1985–6* (Leicester, 1986) p. 2.

17. TUC, *Report*, 1971, p. 417.

18.	R. Gurnham, *A History of the Trade Union Movement in the Hosiery and Knitwear Industry 1776–1976* (Leicester, 1976), pp. 167–78; Leicester Outwork Campaign, *Annual Report 1985–6*, pp. 2–3.
19.	TUC, *Report*, 1969, pp. 198–9.
20.	TUC, *Report*, 1972, pp. 132–3.
21.	TUC, *Report*, 1974, pp. 387–8; TUC, *Report*, 1975, p. 331.
22.	*Report of TUC Women Workers' Conference*, 1977, pp. 17–18.
23.	Information from Mel Read and personal knowledge.
24.	Quoted in H.A. Clegg, *A History of British Trade Unions Since 1889, Vol. 3, 1934–51* (Oxford, 1994), p. 215.
25.	TUC, *Report*, 1955, p. 330.
26.	TUC, *Report*, 1958, p. 122.
27.	TUC, *Report*, 1963, p. 136.
28.	TUC, *Report*, 1949, p. 482.
29.	Mel Read to Chris Wrigley, 21 July 1998.
30.	Lewenhak, *Women and Trade Unions*,, pp. 252–4; N.C. Soldon, *Women in British Trade Unions* (Dublin, 1978), pp. 172–4; S. Boston, *Women Workers and the Trade Unions* (1980), pp. 252–4.
31.	Soldon, *Women in British Trade Unions*, pp. 172–3.
32.	TUC, *Report*, 1967, p. 532.
33.	TUC, *Report*, 1961, p. 281. The ILO Convention of 1951 was on Equal Pay for Work of Equal Value.
34.	J. Edmonds and G. Radice, *Low Pay* (1968), pp. 16–17.
35.	B. Castle, *The Castle Diaries 1964–70* (1984), diary entry, 22 June 1968, pp. 467–8; B. Castle, *Fighting All The Way* (1993) pp. 409–12. On the Fords sewing machinists dispute, see H. Friedman and S. Meredeen, *The Dynamics of Industrial Conflict*, (Oxford, 1980).
36.	Office of Manpower Economics, *Equal Pay; First Report* (1972), pp. 16–17.
37.	C. Hakim, *Key Issues in Women's Work* (1996), pp. 174–7.
38.	For a variety of figures, but all pointing in the same direction, see Soldon, *Women in British Trade Unions*, p. 179; OECD, *The Integration of Women into the Economy* (Paris, 1985), pp. 69–91; OECD, *Compendium of Statistics and Indicators on the Situation of Women* (Paris, 1986), pp. 264–5; Labour Research Department, 'Gender pay gap worse in UK', *Labour Research*, 87, 4, 1998, p. 7.
39.	This paragraph draws much from Industrial Relations Services, *Pay and Gender in Britain*, 1 (1991) and 2 (1992). These were reports prepared for the Equal Opportunities Commission.
40.	A.M. Leonard, *Pyrrhic Victory: winning sex discrimination and equal pay cases in the industrial tribunals 1980–84* (1987), especially pp. 1–2, 9–11, 20–32 and 53; J. Gregory, 'Equal pay and sex discrimination: why women are giving up the fight', *Feminist Review*, 10, 1982, pp. 75–89.
41.	TUC, 'Industrial Charter for Women', *Report of TUC Women's Conference*, 1963, and TUC, *Report*, 1963, p. 134.
42.	TUC, *Report of TUC Women's Conference*, 1975, pp. 4 and 48–51; TUC, *Report*, 1975, pp. 83–5. The TUC also marked International Women's Year

by holding a procession from Hyde Park to Trafalgar Square on 25 May, which was joined by some 6,000 trade unionists.

43.   TUC, *Report of TUC Women's Conference*, 1977, pp. 7–8, 17 and 19.
44.   TUC, *Report of TUC Women's Conference*, 1971, pp. 12–13; TUC, *Report*, 1971, pp. 90–1. In a short essay it is not possible to review other areas such as child-care. For a brief survey of some other women's issues, see V.R. Lorwin and S. Boston, 'Great Britain' in A.H. Cook, V.R. Lorwin and A.K. Daniels (eds), *Women and Trade Unions in Eleven Industrialized Countries* (Philadelphia, 1984).
45.   Mel Read to Chris Wrigley, 21 July 1998.
46.   J. Gennard and P. Bain, *A History of the Society of Graphical and Allied Trades* (1995), pp. 487–8. I am grateful to Peter Bain for letting me see his fuller typescript of the history of SOGAT.
47.   A. Clinton, *Post Office Workers: a trade union and social history* (1984), pp. 432–3.
48.   C. Jenkins, *All Against the Collar* (1990), p. 115.
49.   Even though discrimination against women was a high profile issue during the last three decades of the twentieth century a major study of trade union officials in 1991 found that in that year 62 unions employing 2,564 full-time officers still only had 302 (11.8 per cent) who were female (J. Kelly and E. Heery, *Working for the Union*, Cambridge, 1994, pp. 57 and 82–3).
50.   Boston, *Women Workers and the Trade Unions*, pp. 294–5.
51.   TUC, *Report of TUC Women's Conference*, 1979, pp. 37–8.
52   These proposals were strengthened by the 1980 TUC Women's Conference.
53.   TUC, *Report of TUC Women's Conference*, 1979, pp. 38–9; TUC, *Report of TUC Women's Conference*, 1981, pp. 73–81.

CHAPTER THREE

Complex Encounters: Trade Unions, Immigration and Racism

Ken Lunn

Given the wealth of literature which has been generated by the so-called 'race relations industry' over the last thirty or so years, it is striking how little of it has focused on the trade union movement. Hardly any specific studies have been devoted to the ways in which immigration and racial and ethnic issues have impacted upon the labour movement or how the movement, in its different component elements, has contributed to the development of policies and discourses around issues of race and ethnicity in post-war Britain. The main body of published work has tended to rely upon what have become standard accounts and interpretations, repeating both detail and assertion from a few sources and thus creating limited, if any, space for new interpretation or analysis. It is also the case that major work on trade union history has neglected these dimensions and thus created the impression of their marginal significance. In a collection of essays such as this one, which is seeking to open up new avenues of discussion, it is vital that issues of race and immigration are part of any overall re-evaluation.

As has been suggested, existing work has tended to fall into two categories: either consideration of the unions' role combined with a blanket condemnation of trade union racism or the omission of any significant analysis. In the former, the overarching hostility displayed by the predominantly white British majority of trade unionists towards other ethnic groups of workers is the consistent emphasis: '... history shows the record of the trade union movement to be characterized at worst by appalling racism and often by an indefensible neglect of the issues of race and equal opportunity'.[1] Such a model builds upon a very conventional and much-reproduced version of that history. It tends to highlight earlier manifestations of hostility, such as that displayed towards Jewish immigrants in the 1880s and 1890s and campaigns mounted by the seamen's union against the employment of 'ethnic' seafarers in the first half of the twentieth century. It assumes, or implies, a unilinear set of negative images and attitudes on the part of the trade union movement.[2] Whilst not wishing to argue that the labour movement has not displayed these kinds of characteristics at any number of points in its development, it is important to stress that 'history' ought not to be represented in such a static and one-dimensional fashion.

The second approach, one which excludes any detailed consideration either by neglect or intent, is often encountered in survey texts. For example, for all its value as a key source of reference and its admirable coverage of many other issues, Wrigley's recent reader on British trade unions since 1945 devotes only five pages to 'race', three of them based around the Mansfield Hosiery Mills strike of 1972, and has nothing on the complex history of the labour movement's policies and debates around immigration and race relations attitudes.[3] Other texts on race relations since the end of the Second World War, such as that of Layton-Henry, have only passing and very cursory references to trade unions.[4] Thus, there is a real danger that the general reader, from whatever perspective, is left with the impression that 'race' themes played only a scant part in trade union history during these years and that unions were mere bystanders in these wider debates.

What this chapter seeks to do, therefore, is to offer some alternative to both approaches. This is not to deny explicit examples of racist attitudes in the words and actions of trade unionists, and an overall tendency to play down issues of racism and immigration in favour of white British (and male) concerns. I shall attempt, however, to move away from an overly-reductive approach, from whatever political or ideological perspective, and to indicate the much more complex processes and sets of ideas at work within the trade union movement during these years. I shall also seek to demonstrate that the movement and its members have contributed significantly to debates on immigration and racism since 1945. In this respect, a more careful reading of research and writing from the 1960s and 1970s will be part of that reappraisal. One of the most effective contributions of that work was to draw attention to the dynamic process of the articulation of attitudes within the labour movement, to indicate the shifting terrain of political and economic positions and the constant reformulation of viewpoints. Thus, for example, Paul Foot in 1965 could refer to the 'knife edge' of race relations and to contradictory reactions towards an immigrant presence.[5] Equally, Peter Wright, from field research conducted in the early 1960s, could point to the complexities of white workers' responses to other ethnic groups:

> You can't take what they say at face value. They talk like that [on job acceptance] when they are on their own and believe it, but it is a very different story when they get together, say at a union meeting. A few people, about 10 per cent, will take a much harder viewpoint and the rest will fall into line with the others for fear of being out of step.[6]

In trying to offer a perspective which identifies and articulates this complex set of experiences, and attempting to explain some of the differences, I hope that an agenda for more detailed and imaginative analysis of the period under consideration will emerge.

The importance of the Second World War

Post-war attitudes were necessarily shaped to some extent by pre-war and war-time experiences.[7] The years of the Second World War brought issues of ethnicity, race and identity to the fore in a number of ways. Indeed, one historian has recently claimed that the war represented 'a watershed in the formation of the specific ethnic and cultural character of the multiracial Britain that developed in the last half of the twentieth century'.[8] There were substantial contributions to the British and Allied war effort from the Commonwealth countries, despite restrictions on aspects of recruitment into the armed services.[9] Substantial numbers were also recruited into the civilian services in Britain. West Indian employment in the war industries, particularly those in and around Liverpool, has been identified in the literature and racial tensions within the various workplaces identified.[10] The role of unions in these incidents has still to be definitively researched but some preliminary work suggests that there were important interventions during these years. The Whitley Council at the Royal Ordnance Factory, Kirby, agreed after, some lobbying, to include two black representatives in its ranks, although they were only authorized to deal with issues of 'colour discrimination'. A Colonial Office official, Ivor Cummings, felt this was a significant breakthrough: 'As far as I can find out this is the first time any branch of the Whitley Council had admitted to its ranks any persons other than men or women of the United Kingdom'.[11]

Another group whose presence constituted a vital contribution to the war effort was that often delineated as 'ethnic seafarers'. There had been a long history of antagonism, frequently racialized, towards the employment of Chinese, Lascar and Arab seamen in the British merchant marine. The main union, the National Union of Seamen, had taken a key role in campaigns throughout the pre-Second World War period, shifting the focus from one group to the next as the employment situation altered.[12] The period of the war saw many merchant seamen drawn into the Royal Navy and thus a continuing demand for replacements, which helped to direct growing numbers of ethnic seafarers into the civilian service. Wartime conditions and the question of pay and bonuses highlighted the ways in which shipping employers, the state and the NUS collaborated in preserving differentials between white Europeans, British citizens of Empire origin or descent, and 'foreign' sailors. A war ostensibly fought in defence of democracy produced strong challenges from a number of ethnic groups to these forms of discrimination and a strengthening of organizations such as the All-India Seamen's Federation and the Chinese Seamen's Union. Seafarers based in Britain also developed their own structures for defence against continued exploitation, most notably in Liverpool.[13]

Conspicuously absent from any of these activities was the NUS. Given the well-established patterns of hostility by the union leadership towards 'for-

72

eign' workers, this absence might seem surprising. Their support for discrimination might have been expected. However, as Tony Lane has argued, the union was almost inert during the war years and lost much support from rank and file seafarers.[14] For many of the ethnic workers, faced with discrimination and differentials in pay and conditions, membership of the NUS was denied. Only those employed at full National Maritime Board rates of pay were eligible for NUS membership and so many of the wartime disputes were technically of no concern to the union. Thus, the strengthening of ethnic unions and the continued divisions within an international workforce escalated.

The other major group drawn into civilian work came from Ireland.[15] Here, again, the long history of discrimination and racism directed against the Irish might have been thought to have contributed to trade union hostility. However, the particular circumstances of war-time recruitment, with, from 1941 onwards, far greater state intervention and controls, saw a positive promotion of Irish workers, male and female, and their contribution to the British war effort. The government's efforts were not always met with like-minded responses. Employers, civil servants and many of those in the communities in which the Irish settled could exhibit forms of negative stereotyping and overt hostility. There was evidence of cultural clashes and of conflict at work in the Midlands munitions industry and in shipbuilding in the West of Scotland.[16] However, indications of formal union involvement in the racialization of either work or community situations were rare and it does seem that, in this sense, the labour movement was working alongside the government to mediate forms of popular hostility towards Irish workers, given the specific conditions of their employment in these years.

The experience of white immigration

When we move into the post-war period, the temptation is to direct attention exclusively upon immigration from the 'New Commonwealth' and to note the racialization of attitudes towards that immigration. Indeed, much of the literature has adopted this emphasis. However, as part of the wider argument, with its focus on the construction of racial attitudes, due recognition of 'white' settlement and its impact on labour attitudes needs to be made. The bulk of recent research has devoted itself to examining the recruitment and assimilation of workers from continental Europe. The essential points of that history are relatively uncontested: the labour shortages and the requirements for the kind of planned reconstruction of the economy identified by the new Labour government meant that the state was attempting to recruit workers from almost every conceivable source. Initially, the 'foreign' recruits came from the Polish Resettlement Corps, those who did not wish to return to a post-war Poland under communist domination. There was also

73

a broader constituency of displaced persons, largely from Eastern Europe, identified as European Volunteer Workers (EVWs). The recruitment of these temporary workers was controlled by the state, after extensive negotiation with the trade union movement in Britain.

A number of writers, from Tannahill in the 1950s to Kay and Miles in the 1990s, have tended to emphasize the overt hostility of the unions towards this recruitment as the dominant feature of labour responses.[17] This view was the consequence of working from very general and institutionally-based sources. Clearly, these present a conception of what was happening based on national negotiations and policy-making, important elements in the overall picture, but they do not necessarily represent adequately the responses of trade union members to the employment of these European workers. The significance of the negotiations, as outlined by Kay and Miles, is that the TUC leadership was concerned to support the Labour government, in return for the fulfilment of union ambitions such as nationalization, full employment and welfare reform.[18] The leadership of the TUC and the various unions concerned then engaged in internal struggles, trying to convince the rank and file that adequate safeguards to protect 'British' jobs were in place. These debates took place within the main sectors of employment; agriculture, textiles and coal-mining. Some voiced suspicions about threats to jobs and conditions of employment and the potential threat to the politics and culture they saw as associated with the labour movement. The controls over the terms of engagement, therefore, set out the temporary nature of such employment, requirements that full union rates of pay and union membership be agreed, and that foreign workers were only to be employed in the absence of suitable British labour. Often, the consent of the local union branch was required before European workers were accepted.

It is this 'inferior and secondary position' of the EVWs, often involving the racialization of attitudes towards them, which led Kay and Miles to their wider conclusions.[19] However, local studies, particularly of the Scottish coalfields, have suggested a much more complex interaction between union members, the union apparatus, local communities and employers. Tensions over questions such as the availability of jobs and housing could sometimes lead to racialized responses but these could be challenged by local union officials and members. Evidence of positive support for Poles involved in industrial disputes by NUM branches is clear and the Scottish district made considerable efforts to inform its members of Polish culture and the problems of assimilation to try and ease the process of transition.[20] The strength of the local labour movement helped facilitate the relatively harmonious settlement of those Europeans who agreed to accept and abide by the terms of that culture.

Similar conclusions would seem to apply to other 'white' immigrant groups who were part of this immediate post-war recruitment strategy. Once again, the government made concerted efforts to organize schemes, particularly in the Irish Republic, for a number of industries, most notably coal-mining. As with the Poles and EVWs, a vital part of the scheme was trade union acceptance, yet there were fears that this might not be forthcoming. The Ministry of Labour suggested that any men from Eire, either recruited there or in mainland Britain, should be registered as 'normal' rather than 'foreign' labour and thus implied that there was no obligation to consult with the NUM. Discussions did, however, take place, particularly in the coalfields where Irish workers were allocated. In Scotland, concerns expressed at an Area Conference in 1947 were defused by William Pearson, the Scottish NUM secretary, who pointed to the urgent need for miners and the illogicality of accepting Poles and displaced persons yet refusing Irish workers.[21] Thus, with a degree of scepticism about the reliability of these new recruits, the union accepted Irish miners and there is little evidence of any racialized responses towards their employment as such. By the early 1950s, the NCB had ended its formal recruitment campaigns because of the dwindling number of volunteers and the low retention rates of the scheme. The NUM was clearly more comfortable with its demise but had not sought to oppose this experiment on ethnic or racial grounds.

Also significant was the recruitment of Italians in the early 1950s for work in a number of British industries, most notably the brickworks of Bedfordshire.[22] As with other European recruits, these schemes were tightly controlled and monitored by government agencies. Little work has yet been published on trade union reactions but it is possible to cite examples of instances where organized labour was able to intervene and to challenge certain racialized assumptions and stereotypes.[23] For example, some Italians were employed in Cornish metal mines. Early in 1954, there was considerable publicity over the case of two Italian miners alleged to have had sexual relations with a local thirteen-year-old girl. No formal action was taken against the two miners, since little corroborative evidence was produced. The issue was, however, pursued by the local Labour MP in the House of Commons and a 'moral panic' was generated locally, focusing on the loss of British/Cornish jobs and the corruption of young girls by 'foreigners'. The issue came before the Camborne-Redruth Trades Council, in the form of a resolution broadly supporting the populist sentiments. Other delegates opposed its tone and content, anxious to counter its more xenophobic content. Whilst the initial resolution was eventually carried by a narrow majority, the debate indicated the kind of divisions within the ranks of the labour movement and the degrees of opposition towards more conventional forms of racial antipathy.[24]

In short, the importance of the 'white' recruitment schemes in the immediate post-war period is that they focus trade union attention upon notions of identity, belonging and ethnicity. Through complex negotiations between state officials, trade union hierarchies, local branches and communities, there were outlined and reinforced sets of ideas about 'foreign' workers and the terms of acceptance for their introduction into the British economy. Through this process, concepts of 'Britishness' were re-stated and thus was made available images and ideas which could be re-invoked as other ethnic groups became more visible from the 1950s onwards. As an illustration of this argument, Mark Duffield's work on Indian foundry workers in the Midlands after the Second World War is particularly revealing. He notes that, as black workers were taken on in various enterprises in the area, trade unionists looked on them as having the same status as foreign nationals: 'This assumption was common until the end of the 1950s and is illustrated in the numerous domestic agreements between employers and trade unions which sought to extend the restrictions previously placed on foreign workers to blacks'.[25] The case of the NUM, who opposed the placing of more than three black miners per colliery in 1948, at the height of the employment of Poles and EVWs, is a further indication of this blurring of the distinctions between the various groups.[26]

Unions and Black and Asian immigration

There was undoubtedly a very specific set of populist notions directed at black and Asian immigrants, drawing upon cultural and political images associated with imperialism, amongst other forces. Nevertheless, the processes of identifying 'others' and of constructing ways in which 'they' were to be contained and admitted into British society were very much a part of these years. The labour movement, and the unions in particular, had a central role in these debates and the evidence suggests that they responded, and sometimes led, in complex ways. Challenges to populist racism could be reinforced by union positions and declarations but also undermined by the individual and group actions of trade union members. It is this mixture and range of attitudes that was also to characterize the way that the labour movement dealt with black and Asian immigration from the 1950s to 1979.

A more detailed consideration of trade union responses to these later years requires some basic narrative of post-1945 immigration. As has been demonstrated, there is a much longer history of black and Asian migration into Britain but the phase of population movement symbolized by the arrival of the SS *Empire Windrush* in 1948 has a dramatic historical significance.[27] Whilst it is important to emphasize that the majority of immigrants continued to come from the Irish Republic, from 'white' Commonwealth countries and from other European locations, it was the focus on black and Asian immigrants which became the issue of debate.[28] This applied as much to the labour movement as it did to the rest of British society.

The literature chronicles in more than adequate detail the development of the exodus from the West Indies from the late 1940s and from the Asian subcontinent by the 1950s.[29] Government officials, particularly in the Colonial Office, were keenly aware of the population movements and sought to ease the process of settlement as much as possible. At various stages between 1945 and 1962, Labour and Conservative governments discussed the 'problems' of this immigration and ways in which reductions or, indeed, a complete halt might be introduced. A number of administrative measures were brought in, such as much stricter interventions over stowaways and discussions with colonial authorities about stemming the exit of emigrants from their territories. However, no significant legislation was ever implemented to match the defining of the growing problem. Most commentators have emphasized the way in which this particular phase of immigration became identified as problematic. The racialization of this dimension of immigration – the identification of the cultural clashes between the established and essentially white communities and the newly-arrived black and Asian workers and their dependants – is the key element of historical significance.

From a trade union perspective, this latest phase of immigration seemed initially unproblematic. In some cases, as with London Transport and the National Health Service, since there were official recruitment schemes in the Caribbean to help fill specific labour shortages and, given the relatively full employment conditions of the 1950s, it has been assumed that there was no general outcry about the threat to British jobs. Indeed, the first tensions are generally described as being cultural ones; in the case of transport workers, triggered by clashes over the wearing of turbans and notions of special treatment. The usual argument has been that it took the disturbances at Nottingham and Notting Hill to highlight the racial disharmony and emergence of ethnic conflict within British society.

This notion is one which deserves to be challenged. It is also one which indicates the importance of being able to distinguish between two rather different foci in the literature. On the one hand, a number of texts have concentrated on the central institutional debates around race and immigration from the 1950s onwards.[30] The other approach is represented by a myriad of local studies and by documentation of individual responses. The latter are in some ways inconclusive and it is difficult to formulate any general conclusions from them. It is, however, the case that this latter category constitutes a very significant and sometimes overlooked element in any discussion of trade union attitudes towards race and immigration. This study will try to draw on both approaches to suggest a general model.

For example, whilst it can be argued that the TUC paid little attention to issues of race and immigration in the 1950s until the Notting Hill disturbances, which actually took place while the 1958 Congress was in session, there is evidence that at a local level, even in sectors where there were apparent labour shortages, black and Asian recruitment produced hostile responses.[31] In the mid-1950s, hospital branches of the Confederation of Health Service Employees passed resolutions objecting to the employment of coloured nurses.[32] In public transport, the employment of immigrant workers also involved trade union intervention in the 1950s. For example,

Beetham's study, published in 1970 notes 'strong resistance' from the local union in the West Midlands in 1955, with a series of strikes and stoppages over the employment of immigrants in public transport. In West Bromwich and Walsall, the objections were to proposals to employ immigrants.[33] In Wolverhampton, where immigrants had been employed since 1948, the union was seeking to have a 5 per cent quota imposed and banned all overtime working when management refused to discuss the proposal. The TGWU delegates to the Midlands Federation of Trades Councils proposed a resolution in September 1955, calling for the control of immigration.[34] This localized response, however, raised some problems for the union centrally and its national delegate conference in 1955 passed a resolution stressing its opposition to 'any form of colour bar'. But, as Duffield has pointed out, the resolution also noted the 'grave situation which is revealed by uncontrolled immigration from any source' and thus demonstrates the ambiguity of the union's stance even in these early years.[35]

At a national level, the TUC had effectively ignored these social and political developments. In what still remains a significant study of TUC responses to issues of race and immigration, Miles and Phizacklea suggest that, prior to 1955, there was no formal reference in any of the Congress proceedings to race relations, racial discrimination or immigration into Britain.[36] However, this was not to say that the TUC was unaware of the developing significance of such issues. The incidents noted above in the early 1950s began to push various unions, such as the TGWU, towards national discussion. Thus, as Miles and Phizacklea themselves observe, at the 1954 Congress, a motion from the Ministry of Labour Staff Association (MLSA), representing a group of workers most closely associated with the placing of immigrants into employment, was withdrawn on the understanding that Congress would pursue issues about immigrant employment. The MLSA subsequently set out its concerns in a memo to the General Council, alerting them to the difficulties of placing immigrant workers (as perceived by their members). Consequently, TUC representatives met with officials from the Ministry of Labour and produced a statement which effectively called for immigration controls and defined New Commonwealth immigration as a 'problem'.[37]

The essentials of the Miles and Phizacklea study, which covers the period up to the early 1970s, are fairly straightforward and uncontroversial. They argue that the TUC consistently failed to recognize and accept white trade unionists' hostility towards black and Asian workers and claimed in contrast that tensions were due to the immigrants' refusal or inability to integrate into a British way of life. Secondly, they suggest that the main manual unions, those where immigrant workers were most likely to be potential or actual members, failed to support any significant moves within the TUC towards wider anti-racist strategies, at least for the period under consideration. Thirdly, they argue that between 1968 and 1973, the TUC's constituency

78

broadly fell in with the policy of control of immigration on a racial basis. They do recognize that there were dissenting voices within the ranks of the Congress delegates over the years and identify a broad pattern of anti-racist sentiments and political platforms, such as a growing hostility towards South Africa and a steady, albeit minority, voicing of criticism directed at the labour movement itself for its downplaying of British racism. However, these alternative views are seen as relatively unimportant and certainly ineffective for the bulk of the period under consideration.

The weakness of this kind of analysis is, in part, acknowledged by Miles and Phizacklea. They accept that their work is based almost totally upon the institutional proceedings of the TUC's annual conferences and that it takes little account of the positions and policies of individual unions in these years. Indeed, their view that union histories have little illuminating to offer on this subject is still broadly the case. What is also lacking, however, in the Miles and Phizacklea approach is any real recognition of the dynamics of the process, the relationship between events and attitudes at a local level and the formal pronouncements of the TUC General Council. Lone or minority voices at the annual Congress, as well as the majority perspective, are indicative of a series of interlinking forces. Local union officials or groups of individuals were able to shape regional and local policy and practice, either following patterns of previous responses to 'new' workers or by pursuing policy strategies in the relative vacuum which existed for many unions in the 1950s and 1960s. It is this complex set of relationships that will be the concern of the remainder of this essay.

It has already been demonstrated that, from the early 1950s, trade unionists at a local level were involved in debates about the employment of black and Asian workers and that these incidents were impinging upon unions at a national level. For example, the TGWU, having had its membership in the Midlands involved in action against the employment of immigrant workers, was forced to state publicly its opposition to any colour bar, whilst emphasizing elsewhere the need for some kind of immigration control. It is this fundamental dichotomy which began to display itself more and more within the ranks of organized labour throughout the 1950s. At national TUC level, the Civil Service Clerical Association moved a general motion condemning 'all manifestations of racial discrimination or colour prejudice' at the 1955 Congress.[38] The motion was formally seconded and carried without any debate – an indication of the relative lack of importance given to combating discrimination at this stage.

It was the Notting Hill disturbances in the late summer of 1958 which led to a more explicit concern with both racism and immigration. As had been the case for a number of years, any reference to immigration was dealt with under the heading of the 'International Report' of the General Council and it was in the review of this report that a more balanced analysis from outside the Council was produced. Again, it was led by a representative from a white collar union, perhaps less directly involved in day-to-day engagement with the employment of immigrant workers. P. Maurice, from the Clerical and Administrative Workers' Union (CAWU), argued a powerful case.

> We have got to face the fact that racial prejudice does still exist among some of our people. We have got to face the fact that the activities of a minority of the coloured people may cause antagonism against coloured people in general. We have got to face the fact that unemployment, bad and inadequate housing, are going to make these prejudices and antagonisms come to the surface.[39]

In response, Vincent Tewson, on behalf of the General Council, paid more attention to the alleged fascist involvement in the Notting Hill case and rather complacently claimed that the trade union movement was positively strong on race issues and that integration of new workers was taking place quite effectively. He then pronounced his support for immigration control, in words that have often been cited as evidence of the TUC's evolving support for these measures: '... there should be gates in their land of origin and here through which people must pass. Consideration will have to be given to the real problems which arise in ensuring the well-being not only of people here but of those who come here'.[40]

The following year, the ambiguities of these differing perspectives were seen again. J. Mellors, for the CAWU, pointed to the irrelevance of motions carried at conferences if they were not observed on the shopfloor. She asked all delegates if they felt they had honestly challenged every instance of racial prejudice they had encountered in the last twelve months: 'It might even mean that for a time we have to be temporarily unpopular with certain sections of our members ... '.[41] Yet, in the same debate, T. Patterson, of the Transport Salaried Staff Association, talked of the efforts that the Birmingham Trades Council was involved in to promote racial harmony, including the organization of a social evening for 'all colours'. Rather grandly, he felt that this work had been very positive: 'I say we hold second place to none in terms of our understanding and toleration, which we have gained from our vast experience'.[42]

By the end of the 1950s, the TUC was caught up in the wider debate about immigration controls. As Spencer has noted, the pressure on the Conservative governments for restrictive measures was increasing dramatically, both within Cabinet and from a group of back-bench MPs (and some Labour backbenchers). Public opinion surveys also seemed to suggest a powerful lobby for controls.[43] At this stage, however, both the Labour Party and the TUC were prepared to challenge the proposed legislation. In December 1961, the General Council sent a statement to the Home Secretary, affirming its opposition to the planned controls. Whilst its language in this statement appears to have been concerned essentially with discrimination against 'coloured Commonwealth citizens' and the social issues of poor housing conditions and the fear of unemployment, there was also a sub-text to the message. Although the TUC stated its belief that immigration controls would not do anything to deal with the existing shortage of housing, it clearly felt that some intervention must be made to stem the flow of immigration and called on the government to enter into discussion with the other Commonwealth states to this end. Thus, its opposition to what became the Commonwealth Immigrants Act of 1962 was a qualified one and one in keeping with its general position on race and immigration issues.

From this date, Miles and Phizacklea have traced quite clearly the pattern of TUC policy during the 1960s and demonstrated its growing support for the Labour government's gradual acceptance of immigration controls. Highlighting the key years of 1965 and 1966 as revealing of the shift from the 'ambiguity of its 1962 position to open support for legislative control of immigration,' they stress the TUC's concern with growing numbers of Commonwealth immigrants who, in their estimation, lacked both a knowledge of the English language and of British culture.[44] This situation made integration, the desired outcome for the labour movement, a much more complex and difficult task and, Miles and Phizacklea argue, was a key reason for the TUC's alignment with state policy on immigration control, whilst still allowing some space for a general anti-racist sentiment during conference proceedings.

What this approach does not provide is any evidence of the impact of immigrant workers on their indigenous counterparts at workplace level by the 1960s and the ways in which this increasing contact began to produce a range of reflections on race and identity, ideas which began to impinge upon union hierarchies as well. Thus, there is evidence of conflicts in a number of locations throughout Britain which drew the labour movement at all levels into wider discussions on race issues. For example, in Manchester there were clashes in the public transport service over the employment, or more precisely, over the uniform regulations, for Sikh workers, along very similar lines as those in the Midlands in the 1950s. Beetham's study suggests that strong-willed individuals on both the union side and within the Sikh community were able to widen the debate and to racialize its implications, forcing the union concerned, the TGWU, to engage in formal resolutions and to begin a process of implementing more race-aware strategies both locally and at regional level.[45]. It was certainly the case that racial animosity was generated by the various incidents in Manchester but it also helped to develop and clarify union responses.

Similarly, writers such as Peter Fryer have identified a number of industrial incidents in the 1960s organized by immigrant workers. Many of them were sparked off by and directed against 'trade unions, and trade unionists, who failed to support their strikes or actively opposed them'.[46] The cataloguing of these incidents can make depressing reading and no doubt has prompted the kind of sentiment which Wrench and others have used to describe blanket hostility within the labour movement. Yet, it is possible to find evidence of positive comment and challenge to the forms of cultural and institutional racism within the labour movement during these years. The voices of critique and of positive urging of the need to take seriously the combating of racism at the level of TUC Congress discussion were mirrored or perhaps generated by localized contacts and responses. For example, a major study of London Transport, carried out in the mid-1960s, revealed not merely examples of individual and institutional prejudice but also ways in which the major unions at a local level acted as barriers to the spread of, and impact of, racial animosity. One West Indian motorman felt very positive about the union's role: 'It's turned out very well: you have the trade unions, and no one can say "you have to go back"'.[47] An oral history programme carried out in the 1990s for London Transport could also provide evidence to support such a view: 'In the early 1960s union members voted for anti-discrimination measures and for equality for members of all races'.[48]

Racism and its alternatives: the contradictions of the 1970s

Such evidence is cited not as a fundamental challenge to the notion of the widespread existence of racism within the many dimensions of the British labour movement in the 1960s. In that sense, it does not undermine the kind of general thesis put forward by Wrench, Miles and Phizacklea and many others. What it does suggest is the need for an expanded and less than deterministic approach, one which can recognize the structuring of racist sentiments but also the complexities of that structuring and the asymmetrical nature of its development. This can be further demonstrated by moving the analysis into the 1970s.

Here, although the early work of Miles and Phizacklea dealt only with the period up to 1973, they were bold enough to suggest that significant shifts had taken place. Citing a motion at the 1973 TUC Congress which called on the next Labour government to repeal the 1971 Immigration Act, the authors suggest that this was the first time that the General Council's policy on race relations or immigration had been altered by delegate action and see this event as a 'turning point in the TUC's policy toward black workers in Britain'.[49] In their later work, they argue that pressure from rank and file campaigners and the threat of the National Front produced a sea-change within official TUC strategy and in public responses to issues around race and immigration.[50] Again, whilst not discounting these dimensions in any evaluation of the 1970s experience, it is important to recognize the uneven processes of the preceding years, which makes the concept of a turning-point a rather over-stated assessment of what was taking place and devalues the long-term complexities of the historical construction of trade union responses.

Indeed, it is possible to write two very different histories of the attitudes and responses of trade unionists during the 1970s. One narrative would support the Miles and Phizacklea conception of a turning-point and catalogue the positive developments taken at all levels within the broad labour movement to promote race equality and anti-discriminatory procedures. The other version catalogues the continued existence of racist sentiments and the refusal to accept the need for positive action and direct challenge to the institutionalized forms of discrimination both in society in general and particularly within the labour movement. Both versions are valid and demonstrate the very different voices still present within what might be defined as a trade union discourse.

Using the Miles and Phizacklea approach, it is possible to trace through TUC Congress proceedings a degree of commitment to more positive race relations. In October 1975, the TUC established an Equal Rights Committee and in December of the same year, it was agreed to initiate a Race Relations Advisory Committee under the broader control of the Equal Rights Committee.[51] In July 1976, the General Council announced a programme 'to promote equality of opportunity and good race relations in industry and in the community generally', and was to cooperate with the Labour Party in a campaign against racialism.[52] It was also developing educational courses on 'Equal Opportunities in a Multi-Racial Workforce'.[53] The Conference proceedings in September of that year involved a long debate on the threat of racialism and fascism which produced unanimous support for the TUC campaign. In October, the TUC sponsored a large demonstration in Manchester which some 20,000 attended and it was reported that 200,000 copies of a leaflet 'Trade Unions and Race Relations' had been circulated within the movement. The Labour Party was approached early in 1977 for a joint anti-fascist leaflet and a model article for circulation to all union journals and local and national newspapers was distributed.[54] A further motion to escalate the anti-racist campaign was passed at the 1977 Congress.[55] The following year, a joint leaflet with the Labour Party directed at the National Front was produced, which had to be reprinted due to demand, and the TUC lobbied the Home Secretary, the Education Minister and the BBC about giving freedom of expression to NF speakers.[56] In the 1979 report to annual conference, there were details of meetings with the Home Office about racial violence in the East End of London and further calls for action against racialists within the labour movement, as well as a demand for greater state intervention on issues of public order and incitement to racial hatred. Bill Keys of SOGAT, on behalf of the Equal Rights Committee, made what could be defined as a very significant speech, one which clearly indicated a change of emphasis within the labour movement:

> My colleagues and I are sick to death of those people who continue to talk about the immigration problem when the real issue that is facing this nation and society at large – it has been ignored for the last decade or so – is the deteriorating pattern of race relations within this country.[57]

This could be said to indicate the extent to which trade unions had come to terms with the issues of racism and moved away from defensive support for immigration controls.

The other version of that 1970s history, based on the same TUC sources, reveals a reluctance to become involved in race issues except on very narrow labourist concerns and a set of values about issues of race which demonstrate little change from the 1950s or indeed from earlier years. In the 1974 Congress report, 'race' was still being dealt with under the aegis of the International Committee. It was also reported that, in evidence to the Select Committee on Race Relations and Immigration, the TUC wanted issues of discrimination settled through 'ordinary industrial grievance procedures' and was not in favour of racial quotas or special studies on racism within the workplace.[58] In the Congress proceedings of that year, Stan Jefferson of ASTMS noted that the Select Committee Report had been condemnatory towards the TUC for its lack of action in the field and called for more positive intervention: 'There have been too many instances recently when black workers have had to struggle alone. They must be given the support of the whole trade union movement'.[59] Early relations with the Race Relations Board were difficult. In 1975, the General Council was not prepared to allow the Board to circulate material on the need to avoid race discrimination in any cases of redundancy.[60] The following year it opposed what it defined as careless selection of 'racial minorities' for industrial tribunals, stressing the need above all for members to have industrial experience.[61] This appeared to reinforce the stand of the TUC against outside interference in what was deemed to be its own areas of industrial concern and perhaps a refusal to give recognition to what was already being defined as the 'race relations industry'.

The TUC was also slow or reluctant to confront issues of overt discrimination in particular spheres of employment. In the case of seafarers, despite an NUS lobby about 'overseas seamen' and the competition from their adverse conditions of employment and lower wages, the General Council accepted the government's claim that conditions could not be changed without 'causing serious economic damage'. After a further exchange with the Home Secretary in July 1976, the TUC acceded to the response to exempt the shipping industry from the discriminatory legislation and to accept the long-term promise 'to eliminate this practice with the minimum of disruption'.[62] In the case of the hotel and catering industry, the TUC was more directly involved in the restriction of immigrant labour, and ultimately discrimination, to protect what it saw as the interests of white British workers. The Hotel and Catering Industry Committee reported in 1977 that it had pressurized the government into reducing the number of work permits for immigrants under the special quota scheme from 6,000 down to 2,000. It gained further reductions, from 2,000 to 1,500 in December 1977, with no permits within the quota for unskilled workers, and was seeking to eliminate the special arrangements altogether.[63]

As further corroboration of implicit racism within the movement, evidence can be cited from Congress proceedings in 1978 and 1979. In the former, Bill Taylor from the AUEW, whilst claiming that the actions of Grunwick workers had done more for race relations than any statements or resolutions, added a note of criticism. The previous day, there had been an announcement in the hall that an Irish delegation would be late, having suffered a delay. A number of delegates were then heard to make Irish jokes and Taylor highlighted the dangers of racial humour. Irish jokes were, he pointed out, racist and stereotypes of Paddy or Mick could easily be substituted by black or Jew.[64] The following year, following Bill Keys' speech cited above, Danny Brown, a black worker from the Bakers, Food and Allied Workers Union, applauded the sentiments but pointed out the absence of ethnic minorities from the union delegations present. He stressed the need to ensure that unions were encouraging ethnic membership and involving them fully in trade union issues: 'Until you start doing that, then you are lacking in your endeavours'.[65]

These conflicting voices reflected the complex nature of events in the 1970s and drew out the differing perspectives within the labour movement. There can be no doubt, as Miles and Phizacklea and many others have suggested, that the rise of fascist groups, in particular the National Front, produced strong responses within trade unionism. In many cases, the growth of an anti-racist sentiment was a genuine reflection of worries about the impact of the Front's racism. There must, however, be some concern that what certain union officials were anxious about was the loss of influence which a populist racism might threaten in key areas. These are difficult areas to quantify but these fears can be detected in some of the TUC proceedings during these years. Anti-fascist activity also added to political divisions within the labour movement. Time and again, Congress delegates and union officials railed against the 'extremism' of the Socialist Workers Party and the Anti-Nazi League and suggested that the overt politics of the far-left groups was a barrier to 'ordinary' trade unionists and discouraged them from involvement in anti-racist activities. Whilst this kind of contention is difficult to analyse in any significant fashion, there was real concern about the propensity of left groups to use violence and to deploy anti-racism as a stalking horse for their own agendas.

Similarly, trade union activism by black and Asian workers in these years could both strengthen and detract from union solidarity. The incidents examined by writers such as Ramdin, Fryer and Sivanandan are now so well-known as to preclude further detailed analysis.[66] What can be offered

85

again is a perspective on the very different outcomes from these kind of events. Two examples have been chosen here, because they illustrate the range of responses. The first is the Imperial Typewriters dispute in Leicester in May 1974.[67] This unofficial dispute, largely involving workers of Asian origin, was ostensibly about bonus rates and payments but rapidly escalated into an exposure of the TGWU's lack of local support for Asian workers and its poor record in allowing Asians to become union officials. Whatever the merits of the various protagonists in the dispute and the demonstration of militancy and commitment by the strikers, there can be little doubt that it pushed the TGWU into a defensive and unhelpful position. A Midlands Regional Inquiry by the union accepted that its communications had been poor and that its barring clauses requiring length of service qualifications for shop stewards had prevented adequate representation of its Asian membership and perhaps inhibited union membership generally. However, the inquiry claimed that it had received no complaints about 'colour discrimination'.

Given that the Race Relations Board was also carrying out an investigation, the TGWU opted out of the wider issues and withdrew into its conception of 'separate spheres': '... we considered it appropriate to concentrate our attention on aspects of the problem which were of an industrial character'.[68] The inquiry also chose to comment on 'outside forces' influencing members to strike, presumably a reference to left factions and once more focused on the general charge of extremists' associations with debates and activity around issues of racism.

The other example is the Grunwick dispute, which took place in 1976. Again, there are very different versions of its significance. Ron Ramdin, for instance, has been keen to emphasize the widespread support from many sections of the labour movement throughout Britain. Local involvement was also very positive: 'Encouraged by the strong commitment of the strikers for trade union recognition, both APEX and the local Brent Trades Council became involved'.[69] There is no doubt that Grunwick served as a focal point for many strands of the anti-racist movement and for trade unionists who saw their basic rights as under real challenge. Roy Grantham, General Secretary of APEX, speaking at the 1977 TUC conference, lavishly praised his members involved in the dispute: 'They suffer all the disadvantages of immigrants ... Through it all they stood undaunted, united as trade unionists'.[70] But, once more, Grunwick highlighted the association of race issues with conflict and, however much the broader issues were drawn out, there is evidence of dissension and tension caused through this association. Charges of extremism were once more levelled at sections of the strikers' supporters and this could detract from generating wider sympathy for anti-racism.

Reflections on complex encounters

What could be seen, therefore, by the end of the 1970s was a continuation of the historical tensions within the labour movement over questions of immigration, race and ethnicity. In the light of this discussion, it is important to reflect upon the significance of this longer-term history and the influence which it had in shaping attitudes from the 1950s onwards. Any attempt to assess 'progress' by 1979 needs to take into account the extent to which trade union attitudes were part of a much wider political and cultural debate about the changing ethnic composition of British society and the responses to these changes. In some senses, the labour movement led by example in challenging the politics of racism; in others, it continued to replicate the institutional racism which had been constructed over some hundred years.

Indeed, the issue of the representation of ethnic groups and the strength of racist and racialized sentiments within the labour movement is still very much alive. Arguments in the 1980s and early 1990s about separate black sections, as a response to the perceived continuation of racial discrimination, have continued to be articulated up to the present day. At the 1997 TUC Congress, there was a strongly-contested debate over the question of whether delegates to the Black Workers' Conference should be black workers only. Judy McNight, from the National Association of Probation Workers, moving the motion, called for parity with the Women's Conference, which from 1993 had seen all women delegations. The General Council opposed the motion and Bob Purkiss of the TGWU, speaking on behalf of the Council, arguing that ostensibly the proposal would limit participation from unions unable to find black delegates and thus restrict their participation in the fight against racism.[71] The motion was defeated, and its points of contention, raising again issues of 'special' representation, reflect very much the kind of discussion seen some forty years earlier at TUC Congresses and internal union debates. Similarly, there was a fierce reminder from the Scottish Trade Union Congress Black Workers' Committee in 1998 against the often-misconceived notion that Scottish society lacked a racist culture – that 'it disnae happen here', as it was phrased – and warned of the continuing struggle faced by ethnic minority workers both in the workplace and for recognition within the movement.[72] Both the positive and negative dimensions of this long and complex history are still very much live issues.

Notes

I would like to thank all those who offered responses to my original paper at the University of Warwick conference in September 1997 and to Peter Alexander and Satnam Virdee, who re-awakened my interest in race and labour issues since 1945.

1.	J. Wrench, *Unequal Comrades: trade unions, equal opportunity and racism* (Policy Papers in Ethnic Relations, no. 5, Centre for Research in Ethnic Relations, University of Warwick, 1986), p. 3.

2.	For an example of this uncritical perspective, see P. Panayi, *Immigration, Ethnicity and Racism in Britain, 1815–1945* (Manchester, 1994).

3.	C. Wrigley, *British Trade Unions 1945–1995* (Manchester, 1997), pp. 157–9, 187–8.

4.	Z. Layton-Henry, *The Politics of Immigration: 'race' and 'race' relations in post-war Britain* (Oxford, 1992), makes very little reference to the trade union movement.

5.	P. Foot, *Immigration and Race in British Politics* (Harmondsworth, 1965), p. 235.

6.	Foreman, 'Pentland Alloys Ltd', quoted in P. Wright, *The Coloured Worker in British Industry* (1968), p. 172.

7.	This argument will be developed more fully in K. Lunn, *Race and Labour in Britain, 1830–1980*, Forthcoming.

8.	I. Spencer, 'World War Two and the making of multiracial Britain', in P. Kirkham and D. Thoms (eds), *War Culture: social change and changing experience in World War Two* (1995), p. 209.

9.	For details, see C. Holmes, *John Bull's Island: immigration and British society, 1871–1971* (1991), pp. 167–8.

10.	For details of these events, see A.H. Richmond, *Colour Prejudice in Britain* (1954); R. Ramdin, *The Making of the Black Working-class in Britain* (Aldershot, 1987); Holmes, *John Bull's Island*.

11.	Public Records Office (hereafter PRO), LAB 26/53, Report by I. Cummings, 18 February 1942.

12.	For an outline survey, see A. Marsh and V. Ryan, *The Seamen: a history of the National Union of Seamen* (Oxford, 1989). More specific studies include D. Frost (ed.), *Ethnic Labour and British Imperial Trade: a history of ethnic seafarers in the UK* (1994) and L.Tabili, *'We Ask for British Justice': workers and racial difference in late imperial Britain* (New York, 1994).

13.	The most useful work here is T. Lane, *The Merchant Seaman's War* (Manchester, 1990); other details can be found in Frost, *Ethnic Labour*.

14.	Lane, *Merchant Seaman's War*, p. 146.

15.	See Lunn, *Race and Labour*, for more details.

16.	For details, see K. Lunn, '"Good for a Few Hundreds At Least": Irish labour recruitment into Britain during the Second World War', in P. Buckland and J. Belchem (eds), *The Irish in British Labour History* (Liverpool, 1992), pp. 106–10.

17.	J.A. Tannahill, *European Volunteer Workers in Britain* (Manchester, 1956); D. Kay and R. Miles, *Refugees or Migrant Workers? European volunteer workers in Britain, 1946–1951* (1992).

18.	Kay and Miles, *Refugees or Migrant Workers?*, pp. 23–5.

19.	Ibid., p. 94

20. K. Lunn, 'Immigration and reaction in Britain, 1880–1950: rethinking the "Legacy of Empire"', in J. Lucassen and L. Lucassen (eds), *Migration, Migration History, History: old paradigms and new perspectives* (Berne, 1997), pp. 335–50.

21. National Library of Scotland (hereafter NLS), Dep 258/37, Scottish Area NUM Conference, 1946.

22. Holmes, *John Bull's Island*, pp. 215, 229, 232, 242.

23. See Lunn, *Race and Labour*, for more details.

24. *Cornishman*, 7, 14 January 1954.

25. M. Duffield, 'Rationalization and the politics of segregation: Indian workers in Britain's foundry industry, 1945–62', in K. Lunn (ed.), *Race and Labour in Twentieth-Century Britain* (1985), p. 159.

26. E. Pilkington, *Beyond the Mother Country: West Indians and the Notting Hill white riots* (1988), p. 31.

27. The fiftieth anniversary of the arrival of the *Empire Windrush* saw much celebration in many dimensions of the British media; two examples of the literature are V. Francis, *With Hope in Their Eyes: the compelling stories of the Windrush generation* (1998), and M. Phillips and T. Phillips, *Windrush: the irresistible rise of multi-racial Britain* (1998).

28. J. Solomos, *Race and Racism in Contemporary Britain* (1989), p. 45.

29. The literature in this field is now so extensive that citation of sources is virtually impossible in any significant form. Holmes, *John Bull's Island* remains a useful summary of the key features of immigration history for these years.

30. Two recent works – K. Paul, *Whitewashing Britain: race and citizenship in the post-war era* (New York, 1997) and I. R. G. Spencer, *British Immigration Policy since 1939: the making of multi-racial Britain* (1997) – deserve attention.

31. For details of discussion during the proceedings, see TUC, *Report*, 1958.

32. S. Bentley, 'Industrial conflict, strikes and black workers: problems of research methodology', in P. Braham, E. Rhodes and M. Pearn (eds), *Discrimination and Disadvantage in Employment: the experience of black workers* (1981), p. 240.

33. D. Beetham, *Transport and Turbans: a comparative study in local politics* (1970).

34. Ibid., p. 14

35. Duffield, 'Rationalization and the politics of segregation', p. 171.

36. R. Miles and A. Phizacklea, *The New TUC, Black Workers and Commonwealth Immigration 1954–1973* (Warwick, 1977).

37. Ibid., pp. 5–6.

38. Quoted in ibid., p. 6.

39. TUC, *Report*, 1958, pp. 378–9.

40. Ibid., p. 460.

41. TUC, *Report*, 1959, p. 426.

42. Ibid., p. 428.

43. Spencer, *British Immigration Policy*, pp. 120–8.

44. Miles and Phizacklea, *TUC*, p. 17; for a study of how these developments were reflected in the political trajectory of one trade unionist, later a Labour MP, see J. McIlroy, 'Adrift in the rapids of racism: Syd Bidwell (1917–97)', *Revolutionary History*, 7, 1, 1998.

45. For details, see Beetham, *Transport and Turbans*.

46. P. Fryer, *Staying Power: the history of black people in Britain* (1984), p. 385.

47. D. Brooks, *Race and Labour in London Transport* (1975), p. 300.

48. London Transport Museum, *'Sun a-shine, Rain a-fall': London Transport's West Indian workforce* (1994), p. 12.

49. Miles and Phizacklea, *TUC*, p. 32.

50. See, for example, A. Phizacklea and R. Miles, *Labour and Racism* (1980); R. Miles and A. Phizacklea, *White Man's Country* (1984).

51. See TUC, *Report*, 1976, p. 106.

52. Ibid., p. 107.

53. Ibid., pp. 182–3.

54. TUC, *Report*, 1977, p. 60.

55. Ibid., pp. 403–6.

56. TUC, *Report*, 1978, pp. 76–8.

57. TUC, *Report*, 1979, p. 455.

58. TUC, *Report*, 1974, pp. 211–13.

59. Ibid., p. 536.

60. TUC, *Report*, 1975, p. 74.

61. TUC, *Report*, 1976, pp. 84–5.

62. Ibid., pp. 109–110; see also Marsh and Ryan, *The Seamen, passim*; P. Gordon and D. Reilly, 'Guestworkers of the sea: racism in British shipping', *Race and Class*, 28, 2, 1986, pp. 73–81.

63. TUC, *Report*, 1978, p. 340.

64. Ibid., p. 492.

65. TUC, *Report*, 1979, p. 563.

66. Ramdin, *The Making of the Black Working-class*; Fryer, *Staying Power*; A. Sivanandan, *A Different Hunger: writings on black resistance* (1983).

67. For a detailed account of the Imperial Typewriters incident, see Ramdin, *The Making of the Black Working-class, passim*.

68. University of North London, TUC Archives, HD6661, TGWU Midland District Inquiry Report.

69. Ramdin, *The Making of the Black Working-class*, p. 289.

70. TUC, *Report*, 1977, p. 399.

71. Ibid., pp. 148–151.

72. *Glasgow Herald*, 21 August 1998.

PART TWO

Survey

CHAPTER FOUR

The High Tide of Trade Unionism: Mapping Industrial Politics, 1964–79

John McIlroy and Alan Campbell

These years witnessed the zenith of what Eric Hobsbawm termed 'the golden age' of capitalism. The new order underpinned by the Bretton Woods Agreement and the International Monetary Fund, growth of international trade, state management of the economy based upon Keynesianism, an extended welfare state, integrated trade unions and exploitation of new technology flourished into the 1960s. Full employment, an expanded public sector, increasing real wages, enhanced access to new consumer products, education, health care, social security and pensions recharged and remoralized capitalism and retooled social democratic ideology and politics. Western capitalism seemed to have solved its contradictions, reconciling its legitimation to the working-class with the demands of capital accumulation. By the late 1960s, signs emerged that it was all coming apart. Profit rates were falling in Europe and the USA. The 1970s began with 'stagflation', the oil crisis of 1973, the economic recession of 1974 and a dramatic decline in global profitability. The decade ended with increased unemployment and pressure for welfare cuts in the advanced economies and a turn, in some of them, from state economic management towards neo-liberalism and free market economics in an attempt to squeeze out inflation and restrict aggregate increases in real wages.[1]

It was in the years 1968–79, as the state attempted with limited success to use trade unions as an instrument of increasingly deflationary economic management, that the fortunes of the unions' reached their meridian – numerically and, more arguably, in terms of power. This book discusses aspects of industrial politics in these years. This survey situates the chapters against the wider background.

Capital, class and the state

The benefits of the golden age were restricted in Britain by the traditional complex of problems, deeply rooted in its history as the first industrial nation, which impaired economic performance. In consequence, growth rates, productivity and investment remained low in comparison with competing nations. The annual rate of growth of total output in Britain was 2.8 per cent in the 1960s compared with 4.8 per cent in Germany and 6 per cent in France. Between 1973 and 1979 the British figure fell to less than 2 per cent. The net profit rate in manufacturing fell from 14 per cent in 1964 to 9.9 per cent in 1973, crashing to 3.9 per cent in 1975 and recovering to only 4.8 per cent in 1979. Trade unions were increasingly implicated in economic decline.[2] Capitalism's post-war compromise with labour demanded responsibility in collective bargaining from union leaders in exchange for consultation over the management of the economy and the maintenance of the new, caring capitalism. By 1964 the autonomy that the traditional voluntary system of industrial relations granted collective bargainers to determine the level of wages, the unions' cherished freedom from legal regulation and the historical emphasis of both parties on the workplace, were increasingly challenged. In conditions of full employment, the distinctive role the British system accorded shop stewards and workplace bargaining was viewed as disruptive in its generation of inflationary wage increases, restrictive practices and unofficial strikes, and generally deleterious to economic performance.[3]

The appointment of the Royal Commission on Trade Unions and Employers' Associations in 1966 was a watershed. Thereafter the state intervened incessantly to reform trade unionism and the institutions of industrial relations, to manage the small but significant increment to bargaining power that the arrangements of 'the golden age' permitted the organized working-class. The state attempted to reach into the workplace to control unofficial strikes, wage drift and restrictive practices and reconstitute the shop steward through bodies such as the Prices and Incomes Board, the Commission on Industrial Relations and the National Enterprise Board, through continuing legislation intended to stimulate responsibility, efficiency, and new forms of productivity bargaining. The 'corporate bias' of the British state, its tendency to progress policy by involving capital and labour in informal consultation, bargaining and compromise in 'the corridors of power', blossomed.[4]

This period saw the apogee of the social democratic state. Labour was in power for some eleven of these sixteen years. It also saw strains imposed on consensus and on the Conservatives' role as a social democratic opposition during Edward Heath's albeit brief apotheosis as 'Selsdon Man' and more permanently in the drift of Conservative policy under Margaret Thatcher after 1976. But the initiatives of both major parties to remould trade unionism oscillated between the restrictive, legislative pole, represented not only by the Conservatives' Industrial Relations Act 1971 but to a lesser degree by Labour's *In Place of Strife* (1969), and the corporatist pole, represented not only by the Social Contract but by Heath's attempts to involve the unions in dialogue in the autumn of 1972. Both parties continued to accept the unions as an established, if precariously established, estate of the realm: their moderate, corporatist initiatives legitimized the union leaders as political actors to an extent hitherto unknown. Fragile corporatist alignments intensified the ambiguities of trade unions as both helpmates and antagonists of capitalism, and

94

identified unions with failures of policy. When things went wrong, union leaders were cast as aggressive protagonists in a power struggle with the state and as scapegoats for the breakdown of corporatist initiatives. They were only legitimate actors when their behaviour coincided with state objectives. 'Get your tanks off my lawn, Hughie', Harold Wilson snapped at AUEW leader Hugh Scanlon when he opposed *In Place of Strife*. Yet Scanlon's support for the Social Contract produced encomia to his 'strength and subtlety' and his successors were deemed to be lacking his 'political sophistication' because they bowed to the wishes of their members in the 'Winter of Discontent'.[5]

These issues and the response of the unions are examined in Chapters Five and Six of this volume. Labour's progress 1964–79 is sometimes conceived in terms of an organic development of a corporatism fated to fail, from the establishment of the Department of Economic Affairs, the Prices and Incomes Board and the National Plan of the 1960s, through the 1974–79 Social Contract and the unions' receipt of the keys to 10 Downing Street, to its furthest if futile reaches in the Industry Act, Planning Agreements, the Bullock report of 1977 which recommended worker directors, and the 'Winter of Discontent'. Andrew Thorpe's essay emphasizes the continuities and consensus as well as the disjunctures and conflicts that existed in the democratic coalition centred on the unions that then constituted the Labour Party. He stresses the political weaknesses of the Wilson governments 1964–70, the agency of union leaders in repairing the ravages wrought by the *In Place of Strife* episode, and of trade unionists generally in doggedly supporting the 1974–79 Labour governments to the bitter end. Labour's problems of the 1970s have to be contextualized in the very difficult economic situation faced by what became a minority government. The denouement in the 'Winter of Discontent' has to be related to the miscalculation of the politicians rather than a simplistic focus on selfish union militancy. The politicians' wider responsibility lay in the way the inflation after 1975 was handled, as in the 1960s, by short-term initiatives rather than strategic address of alternatives and the development of institutions and education to nurture policy.

In his complementary consideration of Conservative policy, Andrew Taylor highlights continuity. Legal restriction remained the party's favoured option throughout: prior to 1979 it lacked the conditions for successful implementation. Thatcherism has to be depicted in the detail of its evolution within this framework rather than decontextualized and presented as a sudden rupture with the past. Heath's failure is located in the contradictions of attempting substantial reform of the unions at a stroke, through the Industrial Relations Act, whilst remaining committed to the economic settlement that nourished the unions' power to resist it. Heath's lack of statecraft, his determination to convert union leaders exceeded only by his inability to understand them, stood in clear contrast to Thatcher's cautious, qualified turn to the market before 1979. For Taylor, the sea-change in Conservatism came later.

These accounts, together with other evidence, suggest the burgeoning of 'corporate bias' but also its limits. The reality of the state's links with capital and labour in Britain in the 1970s failed to meet the conceptions of neo-corporatism as a complex, formal system of interest representation expounded by Phillip Schmitter, or the emphasis on the integration of capital and labour through representation at leadership level and mobilization and social control 'at the mass level' favoured by left theorists.[6] In comparison, British corporatism was *ad hoc* and vestigial. True, the state attempted to assemble interests: the CBI was the product of state stimulus, there was a refusal to admit competitors to the TUC to the NEDC, 100 per cent trade unionism was given legal underpinning. And it attempted to integrate them. The Ministry of Labour in its various guises through the period was a firm supporter of tripartism and modified voluntarism. The involvement of employer and union representatives in state bodies was unprecedented.[7] From the Industrial Training Act 1964 and Redundancy Payments Act 1965 to the Employment Protection Act 1975, corporatist legislation flourished, intended to stimulate more effective management through peripheral power-sharing with trade unions. Whilst union gains were restricted, the view that 'the traditions and values of voluntarism were largely untouched' is questionable.[8]

But what it all amounted to was a pragmatic tripartism in which the singular emphasis was on relations between two of the actors, the state and the unions. There was no well publicized National Economic Forum, no full-blooded National Economic Assessment. And whilst the failings of Britain's hesitant, halting quasi-corporatism are often laid at the door of the unions, the position of the state and capital are central to the argument. The British state never evolved the strategic, long-term policies, forward planning and integrative mechanisms necessary for fully fledged political exchange as distinct from short-term crisis management. The NEDC, a shallow substitute, conducted, in TGWU leader Jack Jones' phrase, 'polite conversations': its deliberations were 'an excuse for an industrial strategy', it did not hammer out agreements binding on the parties, including the state. The tacit understanding, the gentlemen's agreement, binding in honour only and frequently disregarded, was not only confined to the collective bargaining arena. Incomes policies, focused firmly on wage restraint and pushed for insistently by the Treasury, were presented as temporary expedients and they worked as such. Their articulation with profits, prices, the social wage and the distribution of income and wealth was slight and rhetorical.

Failure fed on failure. The most developed instrument of concertation, the Social Contract, makes the point: in intensive negotiations over its content between 1972 and 1974, capital was largely excluded. The unions' insistence that there should be no discussion of incomes policy prevailed. Labour entered government with no strategic plans and in a rerun of the 1960s proceeded to bounce the unions into successive, crisis management bouts of wage restraint. It was only in 1978, when three years of pressure on pay had killed the possibility, that the Prime Minister, James Callaghan, who had condemned incomes policy up to 1975, campaigned for a long-term approach.[9]

Nor was capital equipped to play a viable part in concertation. The majority of significant employers continued to work with unions, to accept, even foster, membership, and support collective bargaining. Strinati has analysed the difficulties the CBI faced in uniting the competing interests of sectors of capital. Powerful US multinationals inclined towards corporatism because they could afford concessions; key sections of domestic capital in vehicles and engineering, prompted by hardening international markets, advocated state restriction of trade unionism.[10] By 1979 employers had actively responded to the Royal Commission's scathing summation: 'many companies have no effective personnel policy to control methods of negotiation and pay structures and perhaps no conception of one'. They did so, albeit unevenly, by concentrating on the enterprise, reforming and formalizing industrial relations at company level and diminishing the regulative reach of employers' organizations and national agreements.[11] At the very time government and corporatism demanded greater uniformity and centralization, capital was moving in the direction of greater autonomy and decentralization.

By 1979 capital's need for freedom to adjust more efficiently to a newly emerging world economic order and the necessity for a leaner, harder, more unambiguously capitalist state were gaining ground.[12] After 1975, for all its quasi-corporatist trappings, Labour's policy moved in this direction. But emphasis through this period was on consent rather than coercion. Dave Lyddon's chapter examining the events of 1972 affirms the cautious response engendered by the emergence of mass picketing and occupations. In comparison with the 1920s or the 1980s, this was a 'soft state'. But the period opened and closed with the courts questioning legislative indulgence of the right to strike and championing the freedom of the individual over collective association. States of Emergency were still declared and troops were used four times between 1975 and 1978 to break strikes. Trade unionists continued to suffer surveillance from the 'secret state'. And a harder attitude to policing industrial disputes was discernible after the 1972 miners' strike and demonstrated by 1977 in the Grunwick dispute.[13]

Class structure and traditional patterns of inequality demonstrated resilience and continuity. The statistical evidence is complex, but Atkinson's findings that by 1972 the top 5 per cent of the population owned 57 per cent of total wealth, the top 10 per cent owned 72 per cent, and the top 20 per cent, 85 per cent, were persuasive. The distribution of income also remained relatively stable.[14] By 1977 the bottom fifth of the population received 0.8 per cent and the top fifth 44 per cent of total income. Life chances, access to education, social mobility, health and longevity remained patterned by class location, overlaid by gender and ethnicity. While the percentage living below poverty levels only begins to increase at the end of this period, exacerbated by the reappearance of significant unemployment, low pay remained a problem throughout.[15]

Concentration of capital continued and, by 1975, 100 companies owned 80 per cent of the net assets of quoted commercial and industrial firms. The capitalist class, entrepreneurs, financiers and senior executives with substantial share-holdings, continued to constitute less than 1 per cent of the population, their strategic control of resources exercised through the larger group of managers, officials and professionals, often referred to as 'the new middle-class'. Approaches to the management of labour remained extremely variable: what was modern was soft, sophisticated and integrative, attempting to utilize the unions to manage their members. But an alternative if ancient strand of management strategy was foreshadowed by George Ward of Grunwick.[16]

The working-class experienced continued decline in the number of manual jobs while employment increased in the white collar sector and in professional and managerial occupations. There was a decrease in employment in manufacturing and an appreciable increase in the service industries. The movement away from areas of union strength – by 1979 only a third of workers were employed in manufacturing – to areas of union weakness accelerated in the 1970s. Also important was the growing feminization of the workforce and the entry into work of significant numbers of immigrants and their children. As in the past, the majority of workers possessed minimal control over the labour process and worked in poor conditions with few fringe benefits.[17]

Three of our chapters relate to these developments. In Chapter One, Mike Savage explores the work cultures of male, manual workers and their depiction in influential sociological studies in the 1960s and 1970s. He argues against the construction of class-based identities centred upon simplistic conceptions of collectivism which neglect the relevance and validity of individualism. Measuring work cultures against these identities and finding them wanting in terms of a class consciousness formulated by left-wing researchers or political activists can be an unsatisfactory exercise. 'Rugged individuals' and 'individual male pride' may, he suggests, have proved resilient through the post-war decades. Perhaps, he hazards, certain forms of individualism are integral, rather than antagonistic, to solidarity. Union leaders and sociologists may have missed the significance of varieties of individualism which can strengthen collectivism and mobilization.

The feminization of the workforce represented a stern challenge to labourism's fissure between home and work, domestic carers and breadwinners, and to trade unionism as a male preserve. Chris Wrigley surveys this development and the response of trade unionists to it, concentrating on homeworking, equal pay, union strategies for female recruitment and the adaptation of union structures to women members. Progress, he concludes, was slow and hesitant: it was the 1970s before such matters were taken seriously. Unions did not adequately avail themselves of the opportunity to establish themselves as the champions of what was to become more than half the labour force. Ken Lunn engages with what has in some ways become orthodoxy: the response of indigenous trade unionists to immigrants

98

was on the whole grudging, hostile and racist. Reviewing work focused on the policies of the TUC and national unions, he suggests that a simultaneous analysis of the workplace and local union organization situates official policy pronouncements and provides us with a more nuanced appreciation of what were complex engagements. There was hostility and racism but there was also solidarity and goodwill, and successful attempts to bring black and Asian workers into union struggles. Short-sighted eschewal of 'special treatment' rubbed shoulders with sincere but sometimes counterproductive anti-racism. The problems and contradictions remain with us today.

The politics of trade unionism

The increase in union membership during these years represented an important achievement, unprecedented in British labour history. Total membership increased from 10 million in 1964 to more than 13 million in 1979, and membership of TUC affiliates from 8.8 million to 12.1 million over the same period. Trade unionists comprised 55 per cent of the labour force in 1979 compared with 44 per cent in 1964. For the first time, unions represented a majority of the working-class. (See Table 4.1.) This was achieved against the grain of adverse change in the industrial structure: 44 per cent of white collar workers were union members in 1979 compared with 32 per cent a decade earlier, while 40 per cent of women workers were in unions in 1979 compared with 27 per cent at the start of our period.[18] By 1979, more than 70 per cent of workers were covered by collective agreements and 5 million by closed shop arrangements.[19] The unions were as never before at the heart of popular culture and discourse. On 24 February 1973, at the acme of 'glamrock', the Strawbs 'Part of the Union' deposed the Sweet's 'Blockbuster' as number one in the NME pop chart, its ambivalence towards militancy bespeaking the confused sentiments of many, including many new members, to the nature of trade unionism in the Britain of the 1970s.

The specific balance of explanatory factors driving advance from 1968 remains contentious. Key ingredients were undoubtedly the favourable posture of the state – economically, politically and legislatively; employer acceptance of collective bargaining and in some cases 100 per cent trade unionism; the insecurities of the business cycle – with wages chasing prices, the threats of an inflationary environment were combined with the countervailing empowerment of full employment; the publicity incomes policies accorded prices and wages and perceived changes in differentials which impelled workers towards trade unionism as a solution; and the success of militancy and assertive union leadership at national, local and workplace level in exploiting economic discontents and projecting membership as an answer, typified by the surge of ASTMS in comparison with its competitors in the white-collar field, and the TGWU with its rivals amongst manual workers.[20]

Union organization expanded and emphasis on workplace and company negotiation increased. The numbers of shop stewards grew dramatically from an estimated 90,000 at the beginning of the 1960s to 175,000 at the end of that decade, and more than 300,000 by 1980. In private manufacturing, stewards were present in 74 per cent of establishments with more than 50 workers. Workplace organization also spread from its heartland in engineering to reach similar levels in the public sector and through most areas of industry. There was a growth in the number of full-time stewards – estimated in 1979 to number around 10,000, a five-fold increase on 1968 – as well as facilities and rights to time off, which were granted legal status by the Employment Protection Act. Shop stewards had their fifteen minutes of fame: Dick Etheridge, the convenor of BL's Longbridge plant became a minor media figure; G.W. Targett wrote a novel entitled *The Shop Stewards*. If earlier active hostility from employers became more subdued, management harassment and victimization remained a reality – as the cases of Alan Thornett at Cowley in 1974 and Derek Robinson at BL in 1979, only the best remembered of many examples, attest. Joint Shop Stewards' Committees in the workplace ameliorated the problems of the fragmented union structure but Combine Committees, linking stewards in multi-plant firms with strong union organization, remained an unstable, minority phenomenon. Workplace organization proceeded to develop in tandem with the formalization of plant and company bargaining. It was increasingly articulated, if often inadequately, with the wider union, and by 1979 was a more professional, and for some observers, a more bureaucratic affair.[21]

Union membership became more concentrated. The total number of unions fell from 641 in 1964 to 454 in 1979. More than half of Britain's trade unionists belonged to the ten largest organizations and 64 per cent were members of TUC affiliates. This process was marked by the adhesion to the TUC of the major white-collar unions: NALGO in 1964 and the NUT in 1970. (See Table 4.2.) The number of TUC affiliates marginally increased from 175 at the start of 1964 to 183 in 1979.[22] Voluntary mergers did little to tidy up the patchwork structure of British trade unionism. Despite their increased size, unions remained organizationally fragile. Internationally low membership fees and increased growth straitened rather than stabilized finances. The entire full-time officer corps was never more than 3,000, with the 2 million members of the TGWU serviced at the end of this period by fewer than 500 officials.[23] Unions remained heavily dependent on lay workplace representatives and commentators questioned whether they possessed the strategic, research and educational resources for engagement with industrial democracy and partnership with the state.[24]

Despite the TUC's own inadequate resources – affiliation fees that failed to keep up with inflation and a total staff of less than a hundred, with only twelve in the Economic Department which sought to trade arguments with Whitehall – this was the path chosen by its leadership. Under the 1970s

Wilson and Callaghan governments the process marked by the establishment of the NEDC quickened. More than 2,000 TUC nominees sat on an increasing variety of tripartite bodies and quangoes, General Council members were firmly installed in 'the corridors of power', polls showed many believed the leader of the TGWU to be as important as the Prime Minister and the assessment that the unions were running the country was endorsed by academic commentators.[25] Yet the TUC was not, contrary to Middlemas, Britain's most powerful player in politics, its control over the state dwarfing that of capital.[26] Its access to government and the machinery of state, and its participation in a range of policies beyond the industrial grew: the TUC was consulted over the Budget and its Annual Economic Review was influential. It sought to shadow the state but its role was largely consultative in relation to it. The unions' very real influence should not be dismissed. Nor should it be confused with the power to determine contested decisions. The TUC's success over substantive issues when it disagreed with government remained limited. Its influence was greatest, if still restricted, in 1974 and 1975. Thereafter the policies the TUC had supported while Labour was in opposition were gradually discarded, as the cuts in public expenditure and the growth in unemployment demonstrated.

From the mid-1970s, the TUC and trade unionists at all levels supported variants of what came to be termed the Alternative Economic Strategy (AES). This centred on expansion of the economy, selective nationalizations, planning agreements and controls over investment, prices and imports. The programme carried by Labour's 1976 Conference was an example, with more radical variants supported by the Labour left and the Communist Party (CP). But the TUC never succeeded in getting these measures on to government agendas. In practice it accepted the government's orthodox framework. The loyalty it exhibited until 1979 attests to just how mistaken were the views of contemporary academic observers who claimed '[the] TUC response to government is crudely intransigent even though usually damaging to union purpose'.[27] As the failure of the Social Contract affirmed, the problems lay outside the General Council and Congress House. The TUC remained dependent for delivery on the leaders, stewards and members of its heterogeneous affiliates, operating in a culture of voluntarism and free collective bargaining, and increasingly facing contradictory state and inflationary pressures on wages and job losses. There was no consensus on purpose and declining support for incomes policy was expressed democratically. Far from being the nation's preponderant interest group, the unions' power, which lay in the comprehensiveness of their organization, their cohesion of ideology and purpose, and their ability to mobilize for agreed objectives, remained restricted, subordinate and dispersed. For the unions' organization was centrifugal, their membership was fragmented and there were significant cleavages over policy and purpose, all of which rendered industrial and political mobilization, either for corporatist or socialist objectives, intensely problematic.

101

In his chapter on George Woodcock and union reform, Robert Taylor demonstrates the intense difficulties which TUC general secretaries faced in attempting to develop a vision and plan of action for changing the movement and creating a united front over incomes policy. The leaders of affiliates, whatever their politics, had one thing in common: they treasured their autonomy and ensured that their own organization's interests came first, those of the TUC second. Woodcock was a thinker and would-be strategist. His very real inadequacies in the latter sphere draw attention to the structural limitations of the General Secretary's office and its position in the unions' pecking order. Emerging from the Congress House bureaucracy, its occupants lacked prestige and clout: leaders of major unions never considered taking on the job. None the less, under Woodcock's successors in the 1970s, Vic Feather and Len Murray, the TUC enhanced its position as a union centre. Its successful role in coordinating opposition to the Industrial Relations Act followed the responsibility to intervene in industrial disputes adopted as part of the bargain which secured the abandonment of *In Place of Strife*. Its involvement in negotiating the Social Contract, administering wage restraint and developing employment legislation gave it a higher profile. The growth of the services provided to unions, notably shop steward training, and the development of regional machinery signalled its enhanced ballast. Greater centralization was apparent in the role played in policy by the 'Big Six' General Council members and increased orchestration of General Council and Congress proceedings.[28] Nevertheless, Congress House remained constrained by the decentralized structures and sectional, voluntarist cultures of British unions, the state imperative of downward pressure on wages and other union-hostile policies. In 1978–9 the TUC sought yet again to construct a policy of wage restraint from the ruins of Congress decisions opposing it, and arrived at the February 1979 Concordat with the government over collective bargaining and promulgated its ill-fated Code of Practice on the conduct of industrial disputes. Support once more melted away.

A glance at the General Council in 1964 and 1979 shows some change in the politics of its personnel. In 1964 the roll call of right and centre was relieved only by Frank Cousins of the TGWU, Ted Hill of the Boilermakers and Bob Willis of the NGA. A quarter of a century later, there were two Communists from small unions, the Maoist engineer Reg Birch, a handful of lefts such as Bill Keys of SOGAT, and, reflecting the new times, Walt Greendale, a Hull docker and rank and file militant from the TGWU. The centre of gravity remained a considerable distance from the left. Firebrands were constrained by the experiences of the long march through union institutions, the Council's hierarchical ethos and their minority status. Even at the height of assumed radicalism in the mid-1970s, the policy-initiating bodies of the TUC remained numerically dominated by the right. The most visible and brief split occurred in 1979 when the General Council narrowly rejected a recommendation from the Economic Committee to shore up wage restraint and a group of moderates around Lord Allen (USDAW), Frank Chapple (EETPU) and Terry Duffy (AUEW) produced their own pro-incomes policy statement, *The Better Way*.[29] Over the period, the TUC grew closer to the Labour Party and, despite its lack of direct institutional links, it was represented together with the Parliamentary party and Labour's National Executive on the Liaison Committee which developed the Social Contract. Compared with the earlier period, by the 1970s it was, if often ineffectively, politically partisan.[30]

The politics of the vast majority of union leaders and officers were firmly bounded by labourism, even if by 1979 there was some turn to the left and support for the AES and the policies which came to be identified with Tony Benn. By 1979, less than half of TUC unions affiliated to the Labour Party, but those which did included all the major unions except NALGO, the NUT and the CPSA – the growing white collar unions accounted for less than 5 per cent of the party's affiliated membership. The unions' formal domination of the party was starkly underlined by the 6,351,000 votes out of a total of 7,070,000 they wielded at the 1979 Party Conference. The TGWU and AUEW each had more votes than the constituency parties combined and throughout this period Labour depended financially on the unions. The numbers of trade unionists paying the political levy remained high, though evidence suggests they did so with little enthusiasm, or in some cases knowledge: those actively choosing to contract out varied from 2 per cent in the TGWU to 25 per cent in the AEU and more than 60 per cent in some white collar unions. Additional channels of influence remained: the unions' voting hold over Labour's National Executive, where they decided the majority of seats, and sponsorship of Labour MPs, which increased from 38 per cent of the Parliamentary party in 1964 to 48 per cent in 1979.[31] Conventionally, this power had been exercised in support of the Parliamentary leadership. The emergence after 1968 of a new left and new leaders, such as Hugh Scanlon in the AUEW, Jack Jones in the TGWU and Lawrence Daly in the NUM, meshed with growing opposition to the Wilson government. The stable world of 'interlocking directorates' of parliamentary potentates, executive loyalists and Cold War union leaders was disrupted, and rapprochement in 1970–4 around the Liaison Committee saw trade unionists given a more significant role.[32]

In the TGWU, this period saw Jack Jones preside over a major expansion in membership accompanied by a carefully managed revision of the culture stamped on the organization by Ernest Bevin. There was a real move away from the *commandiste* ethos, with power shifting from full-time officers to stewards, although its extent should not be exaggerated. It is difficult to assess the politics of trade unionists in the same manner as political activists, constrained as they are by the requirements of trade union organization. Jones' specific concerns shifted in these years but remained centred on greater equality and the extension of industrial democracy. A prudent custodian of the TGWU's resources, he was acutely aware of the problems of militancy. He also adopted a cautious attitude to Labour's Alternative Economic Strategy and aspects of its industrial policy.[33] Like Jones, Scanlon enjoyed immense respect amongst his members, but in the context of engineering democracy he lacked the authority and autonomy accorded a TGWU general secretary. Whereas Jones was uncompromised by factional alignment, Scanlon was long involved in the Broad Left alliance and further constrained by the AEU's increasingly resilient right-wing faction. An ex-Communist, Scanlon initially appeared more of an ideologist and champion of rank and file militancy. He took a harder line than Jones over the Industrial Relations Act but followed the TGWU leader over the Social Contract, becoming increasingly less enthusiastic about state intervention in industry and industrial militancy.[34]

By 1977, far from constituting a new 'praetorian guard' – although both were intensely loyal to the Labour government, they retained links with the left – Jones was reaping the whirlwind, being overturned on wage restraint by the TGWU conference, whilst Scanlon, far from being a prisoner of the AUEW's right's resurgence, had embraced many of its ideas and seemed to the coming left 'a defeated man'.[35] Although politically in the same mould, Jones' successor, Moss Evans, adopted a more responsive line of leadership, incurring the wrath of those who welcomed the results of Jones' firmly guided democracy.[36] In the AEU, reaction against militancy, the weakening of the left group and the introduction of postal ballots saw the right-wing faction led by John Boyd, Terry Duffy and Gavin Laird firmly in the saddle.[37]

Under the leadership of Lord Cooper, the GMWU appeared a relic from an earlier, more moderate and deferential time. The changed climate, crystallized by the loss of members to the TGWU and the rank and file revolt which briefly stimulated a breakaway union at Pilkingtons, St Helens, produced a turn to modernization and the political mainstream under the guidance of establishment figure, David Basnett, who succeeded Cooper as General Secretary in 1972.[38] This left the EETPU as the standardbearer of Cold War politics and British business unionism. After Les Cannon's death in 1970, Frank Chapple combined the Presidential and General Secretary positions. He accelerated the agenda of anti-Communism and modernization through his decimation of the structures of craft union democracy, weakening local bodies, replacing election of officials with appointment by the full-time Executive and disciplining opponents of the leadership.[39]

Developments in the NUM suggest the unevenness and complexity of change across the unions in these years. The period of acquiescence in incomes policy and pit closures ended with the election of Daly, a spate of unofficial stoppages and the national strike of 1972. Whilst the left became better organized and established on the Executive, the tenacity of the right saw Joe Gormley elected as President in 1971. As Daly moved away from the left, Gormley's astute, pugnacious and at times militant moderation, facilitated by the privileged position which the distribution of Executive seats bestowed on the right, saw both the national strike of 1974 and thereafter the patiently orchestrated final acceptance of a divisive local incentive scheme, despite its rejection by conference and national ballots. In the face of the upheavals of the early 1970s, Gormley had steered the miners back into the centre of Labour loyalism.[40]

A long established union, NUPE emerged in a new guise and with new clout in the 1970s. It was firmly on the left, both industrially and politically. Alan Fisher, its somewhat volatile General Secretary from 1967, who had spent his life working for unions, and a range of full-time officers recruited from the membership of other unions were influential in a 'revolution from above' which saw the organization grow explosively. An important role was played by former members of far left groups, Assistant General Secretaries Bernard Dix and Ron Keating, younger radicals such as Tom Sawyer and university graduates, notably Rodney Bickerstaffe. By 1975, NUPE was viewed as representing the healthy future of assertive trade unionism, having introduced a shop steward system, reserved seats for women on its Executive and moved towards recruitment of NUPE members as officers. Drawing on academic advice, NUPE imaginatively pursued radical policies on the social wage, low pay and cuts in social services, drawing opposition in the TUC and the Labour Party. By 1979 it had harnessed 'the tremendous muscle of public employees who had hitherto been regarded as a rather pathetic group of workers who could be safely sat on'.[41] NUPE's white-collar counterpart, NALGO, followed, more hesitantly, a similar path. Growth was again significant and in 1970 the union witnessed its first official strike. General Secretary Walter Anderson took early retirement after he had lost the support of the Executive over cooperation with the Industrial Relations Act and Heath's ensuing incomes policy. It signified at least the denting of the old conservatism, although Anderson's successor, Geoffrey Drain, remained some distance from the left. Despite the 1977 decision to move towards a shop steward system, a high rate of internal participation and the emergence of the NALGO Action Group, the union's refusal to affiliate to the Labour Party remained a fair indicator of membership consciousness and the limits of change.[42]

Militancy over wages produced strikes amongst teachers, a more visible left on the NUT Executive and ginger groups around *Rank and File Teacher* and *Socialist Teacher*. But by 1979, over-centralized structures had been adapted to change and a new equilibrium saw a leadership still moderate but far more in the union mainstream and able to live with conference radicalism. There were similar tendencies in the civil service unions, most pronounced in the CPSA where by the end of this period the left controlled the Executive and activists threatened to outdo the AUEW in enthusiasm for factionalism.[43] In the private sector, ASTMS and its vigorous and extremely able, left-wing General Secretary, Clive Jenkins, came to symbolize the new white-collar unionism with its emphasis on membership growth and assertive wage policies. While ASTMS took up a position on the left of the TUC and the Labour Party, 70 per cent of its members opted out of the political levy. The contradictions of left leadership and conservative membership became apparent in 1976 when a flare-up on the Executive saw the union's Labour Party delegation abstain over nationalization of the banks and insurance companies.[44]

Analysis of union politics has to take account of the unions' interface with political parties and the state, their political affiliation and formal union activities. It also has to fasten on the organization, programme and activities of the internal factions touched on here. Academic studies have neglected this important facet of trade unionism. In his chapter on the Communist Party in this volume, John McIlroy surveys left factions across a range of unions which owed their initiation and much of their energy to the CP. It is worth noting that the no less important caucuses of the right still require attention from researchers. McIlroy suggests factionalism was widespread and significant, playing an increasing role, together with industrial and geographical interests, in union politics. Allowing for variation across unions, there was a tendency for these Broad Left Alliances to focus on the formal machinery of the unions and its upper reaches, on elections and resolutions at the expense of organizing the grassroots. By the time the CP looked to redress this, it was too late. As with industrial politics, so with academic analysis. A focus on union leaders tells us only part of the story of union politics in this period. Yet, although shop stewards came in for extensive attention, references to their politics are few. By the late 1970s, it is true, some shop stewards' committees were taking up the AES and looking to workers' alternative plans for companies to stave off redundancies and enhance industrial democracy. But earlier research for the Donovan Commission found that only 17 per cent of stewards belonged to a political party and in one union, the GMWU, almost half refused to pay the political levy. Studies of manual activists reported they were politically knowledgeable in comparison with their members but far from radical, while a total of 56 per cent of a survey of white-collar representatives identified themselves with the centre right, right and extreme right.[45]

Despite this, many academics and activists found little difficulty in identifying stewards as the key actors in a radical maturing of trade unionism and even as the vanguard of social change. These ideas frequently depended on fetishizing the workplace as the almost exclusive generator of class consciousness at the expense of other sites of struggle; underestimating the relevance and resilience of the existing institutions of the labour movement; imposing too great a degree of idealized uniformity on 'stewards'; exaggerating the fissures and antagonisms between workplace organization and the wider union; and identifying the latter with an essentialist bureaucratic conservatism, with which engagement should be eschewed, and the former with a reach towards socialist ideas.[46] Of course there was some truth in this picture: a steward's life was about conflict, although how it was approached was another matter. Some stewards' committees fitted the picture of autonomy and antagonism. But many stewards, particularly senior stewards, were always involved in their unions at branch and higher levels. They saw themselves as union representatives: 'the divorce between larger union and domestic organization has often been grossly exaggerated ... stewards often place great emphasis on the larger union as the embodiment of union principles and as a basis for their self identity'.[47] The full-time officer/shop steward relationship was often better conceived as a division of labour with tensions and antagonism as well as cooperation. Stewards, like officers, were subject to the pressures of trade union bargaining and directly and sharply to the influence of members whose consciousness was often less than radical. Fundamentally there is a need to depict stewards not as a cohesive layer but differentiated in values, beliefs, influence and politics, and standing in different relations to different union and managerial structures and cultures, and different industrial traditions.

To acknowledge the brittleness of stewards' influence, parochialism, workplace consciousness and 'the largely apolitical nature of many shop floor activists whose horizons are bounded by struggles over job control and wage bargaining', should not lead us to overlook the significant minority of politically committed activists who, at crucial points during these years, developed and transformed the consciousness of those they represented and mobilized during major stoppages and political strikes.[48] In both his study of the CP and his complementary chapter on the Trotskyists, John McIlroy examines how politically motivated elements organized in the unions and workplaces to develop and also to transcend the militancy of the period, suggesting that the latter in the end proved to be a labour of Sisyphus. In their contribution, John Foster and Charles Woolfson discuss the process of mobilizing and sustaining industrial action and constructing solidarity from a novel viewpoint. Success in struggle depends less on the political allegiance of its leadership and rather on a process of active, transformative interaction between leaders and their members. The success of the UCS work-in, they argue, was based on its ability to challenge state policy and project an alternative. A key to the capacity of the workers to sustain a struggle with these politics was the success of this interactive process which we can begin to understand through scrutiny of the language used in important episodes of the campaign. Distinguishing their approach from post-modernists who divorce discourse from structure and deny the salience of class, they rehabilitate the work of Vygotsky and Volosinov to illustrate the utility of a materialist understanding of language to analysis of industrial struggles.

Despite the efforts of political activists, militancy remained uneven across industry and subject to ebb and flow in its strongholds. It rarely generated sustained, radical politics. The left lost its crucial ideological battle with the right. Identification of trade unionists with the Labour Party declined but only marginally: in one study from 60 per cent in 1964 to 56 per cent in 1974. Class dealignment in voting was restrained by trade union membership, but decreasingly. In the general elections of 1964 and 1966, 73 and 71 per cent of trade unionists voted Labour, and this declined to 66 per cent in

107

1970, 55 per cent in the two elections in 1974, and a bare majority – 51 per cent – in 1979. Worryingly in view of trends in social structure and trade unionism, the alignment of white collar trade unionists was weaker than those of their manual counterparts. Dealignment was related to the alienation of trade unionists from the policies of the Labour government. The movement was to the right. The beneficiaries were the Conservatives, Liberals and Nationalists. In October 1974, CP candidates received 600 votes each, and in 1979 all the candidates lost their deposits, their share of the vote declining from 1.7 to 1.1 per cent (compared with 3.4 per cent in 1964). The Trotskyists did no better: the Workers' Revolutionary Party polled 12,600 votes in 60 constituencies and the ten Socialist Unity candidates totalled 2,800 votes. Over the period the rise in the membership of the left groups amounted to little more in aggregate than the decline in CP membership.[49]

The new militancy

The period stands out in labour history as a time of militancy. The official strike data are presented in Table 4.3. These figures exclude small strikes and industrial action short of a strike. A study in the late 1970s suggested that the former could constitute up to 75 per cent of strikes in manufacturing and that sanctions short of a strike were prevalent. In contrast, the official statistics were found to record 96 per cent of days lost, and this is a more reliable measure of the volume of strike activity, although open to distortion by major stoppages.[50] Mining stands out as a special case because of its high incidence of short, small disputes in the earlier part of the period, and aggregate figures including and excluding the industry are provided.

The statistics demonstrate first, that the total number of strikes increased significantly during the 1960s and the number outside mining trebled by 1970. Thereafter the number of strikes declined somewhat but remained higher than the average for the previous decade. Second, the number of working days lost increased generally if unevenly throughout the entire period. This measure indicates two peaks in the strike waves of 1968–74 and 1977–79, unique in the post-war period and unprecedented since 1921. In 1979 more than 29 million working days were lost, the highest figure since 1926 and the fifth largest of the century.[51] Third, in 1964 recorded strikes were typically short and small: 75 per cent lasted less than three days. They were also usually unofficial. By the 1970s disputes were longer, involved greater numbers and were more likely to be officially sanctioned. There were ten 'large stoppages' involving more than 200,000 days lost in the period 1964–9, but 54 such strikes occurred in the 1970s.[52] Fourth, striking spread from traditional battlegrounds in the mines, docks, car factories and shipbuilding to embrace the public sector, women and black workers: by 1979, 'almost every sort of labourer had become more strike prone'.[53] White collar workers, too, were increasingly involved: between 1968 and 1972, 'employees in professional and scientific services, public administration and defence achieved striker rates over ten times those of 1963-8'.[54] Fifth, the increase in strikes proceeded in tandem with the rapid increase in union membership described earlier. A final point to note is that the strike explosion was an international phenomenon and that the contemporary popular image of Britain as uniquely strike prone is not supported by statistics. Although international comparisons are fraught with difficulties, the most detailed studies confirmed that 'the "British disease" [was] neither peculiar to this country nor apparently present here in its most virulent form'. Depending on the data used, Britain ranked sixth or seventh among 15 comparator countries – 'average, rather than 'particularly bad', although the relative disadvantage with West Germany and Japan was notable.[55]

There were also important changes in the nature and conduct of industrial action. First, the majority of strikes in the 1960s were over non-pay issues, perhaps reflecting attempts by workers to regulate conditions of work, an ethos reflected in the establishment and influence of the Institute for Workers' Control and related to the extension of workplace organization. After 1968 there was a shift to strikes over wages.[56] Second, the percentage of sympathy strikes reached a post-war peak in the strike explosion of 1968–74, but thereafter fell below the figures for previous years. Such actions may plausibly be viewed as an indicator of confidence and solidarity.[57] Third, there was a revival of the political strike, shunned since the cathartic events of 1926. The most detailed study indicates that there were 19 political strikes between February 1969 and May 1974 directed against state intervention in industrial relations, primarily against the introduction and operation of the Industrial Relations Act 1971 but also against incomes policies and in support of the UCS work-in. These strikes involved a remarkable and unprecedented total of over 7 million workers.[58] This bears comparison with the 9.5 million workers involved in industrial disputes during the years 1969–74 (Table 4.3). There was no automatic relationship between industrial and political protest. Political strikes were largely confined to the West of Scotland, Yorkshire, the West Midlands, North West and South East England. Even in these areas activists were not always successful in persuading the majority of members to participate.[59] And chronologically such strikes were concentrated in the years 1968–74. Fourth, there was a willingness by strikers to engage in assertive tactics, some seen earlier in labour history but deployed infrequently in the previous post-war period. Thus flying pickets reappeared in the Yorkshire miners' strikes of the late 1960s, evolving into the mobile mass pickets in the 1972 national dispute; the GEC occupation of 1969 presaged the wave of sit-ins in 1972, concentrated during the engineering strike but extending beyond it.

In his chapter here, Dave Lyddon examines in detail the high point of the militancy, focusing on the strikes of miners, dockers, building workers and engineers. He brings out the very real active and participatory nature of these conflicts, suggesting that the use of secondary pickets and solidarity action is presently attacked and vilified precisely because it was effective. Fundamentally, members' strikes are more effective than those directed from above with minimal participation. The strikes over the Pentonville dockers represented a moment of rank and file solidarity which much contemporary analysis seeks to evade but cannot explain. Similarly, in his contributions, John McIlroy evokes the flow of militancy from below. Rank and file action taken independently of union leaders was an important if conjunctural phenomenon. He stresses it was neither general nor sustained and underlines not only the importance of bodies such as the Liaison Committee for the Defence of Trade Unions but also the primacy of the changing consciousness of ordinary workers and its relationship to wider politics. From a variety of perspectives, the radical and revolutionary left had seen militancy politicized by state intervention qualitatively strengthening the Labour and union left and/or laying the ground for a revolutionary party. Like supporters of corporatism, they were to be disappointed. By 1974 the militancy was faltering in the face of economic crisis. Those to the left of Labour were unable to transform it into socialist forms. Once again Labour succeeded in introducing temporary stability through the Social Contract.[60]

The militancy of the period remains an important and intriguing historical phenomenon. It involved 'a wave of political strike activity of a level never previously witnessed in the United Kingdom' and it represented a 'sharp discontinuity in British industrial relations'.[61] The factors driving it were rooted in the post-war settlement and the pressures being placed on it by the late 1960s. Economic rationality provides a plausible explanatory starting point. Workers might be expected to exploit labour scarcity in a situation where the state's guarantee of full employment bred consciousness of economic security. In key industries strong workplace organization, decentralized bargaining arrangements and management's willingness to pass on the costs of wage increases created a favourable environment for such exploitation. Political explanations are also relevant. Attempts by the state to solve these problems and bids by employers to resist union demands were often in conflict with the wider economic and political contexts which provided many workers with the confidence and bargaining power to repel change and others with an example to emulate in order to protect themselves against price increases. The precise nature of state intervention and its perception by workers is important. The strikes of 1968–74 coincided with estrangement from the policies of the Wilson government, followed by antipathy to the policies of the Conservatives on the part of trade unionists, while 1978–9 saw renewed suspicion of a Labour government. Political alienation may have some impact on extra-parliamentary militancy; conversely, as in 1974–8, a state perceived to be acting in ways supportive of workers' goals may function to restrain militancy. If each incomes policy had a life cycle from control to breakdown, the more favourable its perceived terms, the stronger its initial impact – as the Social Contract suggests. None the less every government which ran a 'strong' policy in the years 1964–79 failed to be re-elected.[62]

Edwards suggests that the increase in shop floor bargaining power in the 1960s, underpinned by low unemployment, was only temporarily restrained by incomes policies from 1966–8: the breakdown of these policies in 1969–70 'gave the upward trend in the number of strikes a powerful push'.[63] Similarly, for Cronin, the spread of plant bargaining combined with the surge in inflation following devaluation in 1967 led to the strike wave after 1968. This strike wave was fuelled not only by attempts to keep wages in line with price inflation but also by a wage–tax spiral. While the average manual worker had paid little income tax until the late 1950s, by 1974 nearly half his or her income was liable for the standard rate of tax: the tax and national insurance taken from the average gross wage increased from 4 per cent in the mid-1950s to 20 per cent in 1970. The sharp increase in money incomes in the 1970s increased this taxation further through 'fiscal drag', as a greater proportion of workers' wages became liable for tax. As a consequence, some union negotiators sought a money wage which provided a real increase after both price inflation and tax deductions were taken into account.[64] The Social Contract had a strong initial impact in restraining militancy. But the resurgence from 1977, culminating in the 'Winter of Discontent' in 1978–9, confirms Davies' conclusion in his analysis of the relationship between incomes policies and strikes: the 'significant impact in reducing strikes over pay issues ... is apparently achieved only at the expense of a sharp upsurge in such strikes as soon as the policy is removed'.[65] But it also suggests that attention should be paid to the overall political framework in which wage restraint operated.

Incomes policy has also been characterized as intensifying militancy through its distortion of differentials, particularly after the flat rate increases of 1975. Studies of the car industry suggest that such distortion was also exacerbated by the shift away from payment-by-results systems and certain skilled groups, notably toolroom workers, resorted to unofficial action to restore differentials. But in engineering, although there was some compression of differentials during the 1970s, there was less disturbance to pay structures than is often supposed. However, the differential between white-collar and manual workers generally narrowed sharply: 'in 1979 the mean weekly earnings of non-manual men had fallen to 122 per cent of that of manual men, compared with 125 in 1976 and 134 per cent in 1970'. There was also some tendency towards greater equality of pay for women in relation to men – average women's earnings had long been approximately half those of men, but increased to 58 per cent during the 1970s.[66]

Sociological explanations saw rising expectations and issues of status amongst workers as a specific determinant of wage increases and inflation, beyond the economists' interactions of supply and demand. State intervention and the publicity accorded not only settlements but larger wage claims were seen as further generalizing and intensifying wage expectations in an inflationary situation. Runciman's well known study of reference groups in the early 1960s recorded the restricted horizons within which workers made economic comparisons. However, work in the 1970s suggested that attempts at state regulation which failed to reshape the inflationary climate could disrupt traditional notions of fairness and economic justice. Others argued that if the depiction of 'the affluent worker' by Goldthorpe and his colleagues was faithful, then consequent emphasis on instrumentality and the cash nexus could produce a militancy which might question capitalism.[67] Phelps Brown analysed readiness to strike in historical and generational terms. By 1968 rank and file militancy represented the attitudes of union members who had entered work during the long boom and known only prosperity and security. Unlike their older counterparts, they viewed the inadequacies of the post-war compromise and attempts to restrain wages as a stimulus to militancy.[68] Others related the strike waves to the new youth culture with its momentum towards self-expression, activism and participation.[69]

Industrial relations scholars' portrayal of militancy in Durkheimian terms of anomie and disorder was taken up in a different way, with different solutions proffered, by New Right analysis. This pictured an overloaded state pump priming a swollen, union-ridden public sector, while economically corrosive welfare provision fuelled dependency by guarantees of cradle to grave security. Expectations could only be answered at the expense of ruinous tax burdens on capital, curtailment of entrepreneurial initiative and the collapse of the economy. Economic regeneration necessitated the state's renunciation of responsibilities for full employment and extended welfarism, the taming of inflation and a restoration of law and order, with legislative action against rights to strike and picket and the closed shop.[70] Again, some of the New Right's emphases were echoed in left-wing argument which singled out 'the fiscal crisis of the state' and its inability to overcome its potentially contradictory functions of guaranteeing capitalist accumulation whilst legitimizing it to the working-class.[71]

Overall, the economic success of the militancy is difficult to judge, although its relationship to increasing union membership is itself a major achievement often ignored by commentators.[72] In a study of inter-industry differentials, Saunders categorized 'winners' or 'losers', using the criterion of a gain or loss of more than 5 per cent in the relative average weekly earnings of manual adult men during the period 1970–9. Coalmining was the outstanding winner with a change of +34 per cent as a result of the miners' successful strikes in 1972 and 1974, followed by electrical supply (+9), while motor vehicles (–8) and post office engineering (–10) suffered the greatest losses. The relationship between success and militancy was therefore not straightforward.

These were extremes and the overall picture was one of relative stability, with some movement towards increased equality. A comparison of the average weekly earnings of 31 male manual negotiating groups in 1977–9 with their position in 1970–2 indicated that well over a third were classed as 'winners', more than that were 'neutral', while the proportion of 'losers' constituted only around a fifth. More generally, trade unionists were winners over non-unionists. The 'sword of justice' effect in relation to equality was complemented by the wage differential between unionists and non-unionists increasing to the advantage of the former from 28 per cent in 1964 to 36 per cent by 1975.[73]

At the national aggregate level, real wage rates showed a general upward movement of some 30 per cent in the years 1964–78. This trend was uneven, registering particularly rapid advance in 1970–3 (when real take home pay rose by 3.5 per cent a year, some four times the rate gained under Labour in 1964–70) and suffering a sharp reduction in 1976–7 as result of Phase 2 of the Social Contract.[74] More detailed figures on the growth of real earnings are available from the New Earnings Survey established in 1970 and these are given in Table 4.4. Again the general trend is upward although the deflating effect of the Social Contract in 1977 is once more readily apparent before being redressed by the strike wave of 1978–9. Despite such short-term variations, workers – particularly manual workers – were thus generally able to maintain and even improve their living standards in the face of a rate of inflation not experienced since the years before 1920.[75] Such a conclusion only applies to those in work, however. Full employment may be seen as a class achievement, potentially at least, increasing power, confidence and unity while significant levels of unemployment are conversely a class cost and handicap. The official unemployment figures recorded an increase from 600,000 in 1974 to just under 1.5 million by 1978; estimates which included those not registered as unemployed placed the real figure at 2.5 million, or some 10 per cent of the workforce. The impact of growing job losses on the move to the right should not be underestimated.[76]

Equally significant was the redistribution of income (taken as a percentage of gross domestic product) towards labour and away from property during these years, marking a rupture in the post-war equilibrium. In the period 1964–8, the percentage of GDP estimated to have been distributed to labour was 74.4, almost identical to that of 1946–9. By 1974 the estimate stood at 79.4 per cent and reached 81 per cent the following year.[77] The reasons for this shift were complex, but trade union action certainly played a part, supporting Phelps Brown's theory that strong union organization in a 'hard' market – reflected here in the squeeze on profits after 1970 – would have a redistributive effect.[78]

Assessing the period

Most estimates of trade unionism in these years have been negative. Indeed the period has typically been viewed as a necessary preface to 'the demise of the British labour movement after May 1979'. The roots of the difficulties in our period and future 'demise' can be traced to the fact that: 'Bluntly, trade unions in Britain were not organized, nor did they have the resources to become, social partners of any government'. In this problematic, the path which unions followed – hesitatingly, eventually unsuccesfully – is installed, largely inexplicitly, as the only possible path which they could have followed. In this type of analysis, alternative strategies are largely excluded from consideration. The fundamental problem for this argument, which has its roots in the ideas of industrial relations reformers and revisionist labourism of the 1950s and 1960s, is that 'the unions had too *little* power, not too much, and so were unsuited to enforcing government policy'.[79] In reality, of course, unions can never function in any sustained, meaningful way simply as enforcers of government policy. It was union purpose in the context of what many trade unionists perceived as the inadequacies of government policy that was problematic. Statements that unions were not strong enough often fail to interrogate the question, what kind of strength, strong enough *for what?* They elide the issue and the real, complex problems of the conditions necessary for effective political exchange in pervasive sub-texts impregnated with longing for leadership control of members in the interests of the economic imperatives of capital and nostalgia for the popular bossdoms of Bevin and Deakin.

In contrast, the distinguished historian Eric Hobsbawm locates trade unionism explicitly in the project of socialist advance. In his lecture, 'The forward march of labour halted?', perhaps the most influential contemporary assessment which also possessed the dual advantages of appearing in 1978 and setting its analysis in historical context, Hobsbawm asserted that the 1960s and 1970s saw continued decline in the cohesion and sense of mission of the movement, a decline which had commenced between 1948 and 1953. The 'common style of proletarian life', which he argued had underpinned the unity and progress from the end of the nineteenth century had been undermined by changes in social structure – the decline in manual work, the growth of white-collar and state employment, in the numbers of women and black workers – and affluence. Structural problems had been amplified by weaknesses in labour movement leadership and policy. The symptoms of dissipating class consciousness were stagnation in union density, militancy over wages which had dubious connections with the development of socialist consciousness, and the decline in the Labour vote.[80] Other labour historians waited for the first successes of Thatcherism before deciding that the inability of the Labour Party and the unions to work together in the late 1970s disclosed 'signs of terminal crisis' in the labour movement.[81] An enduring *motif* here is the 'Winter of Discontent'. A further strand of writing about the 1970s conceives the strikes of 1978–9 as a decisive historical moment when the state of the world changed and irresponsible trade unionism opened the door to Thatcherism.

The power of Hobsbawm's analysis lies in its wide canvas, its breadth of comparison and its insights; its problems lie in the absolutism of its periodization, its depiction of labour's fortunes ascending in the first half of the twentieth century and declining thereafter. In the period of advance, union density collapsed from 45 per cent in 1920 to 23 per cent in 1933; in the years of retreat, it increased from 44 per cent to 55 per cent in the face of adverse changes in the class structure. It is difficult to see the inter-war years, with their mass unemployment, the decline of the shop steward, dwindling membership and the vanishing strike as a period of progress compared with the 1960s and 1970s. The miners were signally defeated in 1926 and significantly victorious in 1972 and 1974. The decline in Labour's vote in these latter decades also requires contextualizing. Labour entered government in 1929 with its then highest ever share – 37 per cent – of the vote and polled 31 per cent in 1931, 38 per cent in 1935. Its share in 1966, at the height of the perceived affluence, was only marginally short of the record 48.8 per cent in 1951, and it polled 43 per cent in 1970 and 39 per cent in October 1974, the last election before Hobsbawm wrote.

Hobsbawm's critics would not allow that sectionalism, 'one of the oldest traditions of the British labour movement', had intensified in recent decades.[82] Moreover, they pointed out, quite fairly, that his parenthetical exemption of the strikes of 1970–4 from his stricture of 'economism' severely diminished his case. In terms of generating unity and class consciousness, this strike wave compared favourably with its predecessors of 1910–13 and 1915–22. One careful assessment concluded that Hobsbawm's almost Leninist conception of economism was too rigid and general: 'wages struggle is a general recipe neither for success in raising class consciousness (as economistic Marxists maintain) nor for failure (as Hobsbawm and Gramscian Marxists tend to maintain)'.[83]

Fundamentally, we cannot draw across the century to 1979 dividing lines between unity, solidarity and advance on the one hand, and proletarian division, difference and impasse or retreat on the other.[84] Throughout the century division and difference was endemic, the class structure was fluid and fractured, unity was painstakingly constructed out of diversity, only for sectionalism to resurface, as the history of both the 1920s and 1970s demonstrates. Progress was possible and achieved in both periods. The resilience of capitalism and the nature of parliamentary democracy, collective bargaining and reformism ensured it was always uneven and precarious.

If Hobsbawm's assessment was flawed by its imposition of over-generalized, unilinear conceptions of advance and retreat on to the complex, contingent flow of fortunes on industrial and political fronts, interrelated but discrete, it was immensely valuable for its suggestive analysis. The assumed identification between union membership and at least loose adherence to Labour, so dear to labour historians, was becoming increasingly strained. The quality of commitment to collectivism of many who joined unions, particularly where compulsory union membership agreements applied, was questionable. The trade unionism of NUPE dinner ladies, ASTMS managers and NALGO social workers was different in important respects from that of the miners, railwaymen and factory labourers, in the 1970s and in the past; but it was now closer to becoming the core of contemporary trade unionism.

The construction of the cultures of solidarity for this new unionism was as necessary but more difficult a challenge as it had been for the new unionism of the 1880s. Strikes of public utility workers did have a more powerful social impact immensely amenable to the manufacture of meaning by a mass media which penetrated the working-class in ways unknown in the 1920s, combated – far too strong a word – by the stunted cultural apparatus of a labour movement lacking even a daily newspaper.[85] If attention to gender and ethnicity was greater than in the past, it remained of limited significance.[86] The neglect by the labour movement and labour historians of the worker as thinker, consumer and citizen, the neglect of the home and community, and their inter-penetration with the workplace in generating working-class politics, seemed by this time to be creating a dangerous, one-sided emphasis on the worker as employee and producer. Working-class politics were significantly defined by workers' identities beyond work.

Hobsbawm was perceptive in his grasp of impasse and the multi-faceted problems that afflicted the labour movement. None the less, from inside the unions in 1978, many of these could be seen in relative terms as problems of success. More rigorous contemporary observation would have recalled the historical fragility of advance, delineated the militancy as an important but uneven minority phenomenon and depicted the movement facing a conjunctural set of difficulties – deep but not irreversible – centred on its political mission and that mission's tensions with voluntarism. But the labour movement had not suffered a decisive defeat: that would await further conflicts in the ensuing decade. Nor was it in terminal crisis.

Others have seen that kind of crisis crystallizing in the 'Winter of Discontent'. The literature provides sparse detail on the strikes of 1978–9, the motivations of workers and the development and conduct of the disputes.[87] Hard facts are sometimes replaced by caricature. The episode is presented in terms of the pathology and propensity to violence of some unions' members and 'the cowardice and irresponsibility of some union leaders' which 'guaranteed' the election of Thatcher.[88] Bernard Donoughue, Callaghan's adviser and a former Professor of Political Science at the LSE, portrayed the strikers as succumbing to 'irrational behaviour' and the labour movement as a whole to 'suicidal lunacy'.[89] His conclusion that a 'curious, feverish madness' was 'infecting industrial relations' is quoted approvingly by distinguished historian Kenneth Morgan who pictured trade unionists committing 'hara-kiri'.[90] For Robert Taylor, 'the attack on the community by public service workers was new ... and its ferocity irrational'.[91] References to 'violence' and brutality in which NUPE members uniformly 'behaved viciously throughout the dispute' freight a tale of 'anarchy' in which 'Britain in the last phase of Labour corporatism seemed close to being ungovernable'.[92] Amongst union leaders, Moss Evans and Alan Fisher are singled out. Evans was 'a sad disappointment ... a man out of his depth ... Even at this passage of time the irresponsibility of Evans' response seems astonishing'.[93] As a result, we are told, unions became 'targets of something close to hatred ... the consequence was to be eleven years of Thatcherism'.[94] The 1979 election result reflected this 'seachange' as the Conservatives 'penetrated the political thinking of the other side's staunchest supporters'.[95] Even for some supportive of trade unionists, the 'Winter of Discontent' was 'the key moment ... perhaps the only truly hegemonic moment of Thatcherism ... a strategic moment in the transformation of the British state'.[96]

More compelling explanations of what happened are to be found embedded in some of these accounts. The key points are these: the Social Contract had dwindled to an exercise in wage control, and pressure on pay, particularly in the public sector, meant that many groups of workers were not prepared to tolerate a further phase of incomes policy. In these circumstances, Callaghan's imposition of a 5 per cent limit and his refusal to seek a mandate by going to the country in October 1978 was unrealistic and perhaps inflammatory. Even Donoughue concedes that 'most of the Labour government's difficulties were of its own making'.[97] Situated in this political context, the strikers' actions were rational and so were the responses of union leaders. Union conferences, the TUC and, overwhelmingly, the Labour Party Conference rejected the wage controls and supported a return to 'free collective bargaining'. The government ignored them. Far from acting from weakness and cowardice, leaders like Evans and Fisher behaved responsibly and democratically in reaction to a political situation over which they possessed little control. Far from its influence being 'almost entirely negative', the TUC strove to cobble together a compromise culminating in the Concordat with the government in February 1979.[98] To excoriate union leaders because they failed to behave like a romanticized Ernest Bevin is to demonstrate incomprehension of, or opposition to, unions as ultimately democratic organizations responding to their members' wishes.

As for the conduct of the disputes, the literature cited provides no substantiation of the allegations of violence and brutality it makes free with, although it does in passing correct contemporary myths of food shortages and social disruption.[99] It would be naive to contend that there were no incidents of violence. However well documented, convincing critiques of media coverage of the strikes largely eschewed by most historians, demonstrate errors and distortions and cumulative, systematic bias in their presentation of events.[100]

The episode undoubtedly played a role in the Conservative victory at the polls. That does not mean that either the 'Winter of Discontent' or the 1979 General Election constituted a decisive watershed in labour history. The literature assumes rather than evidences this. The influence of the strikes on voters was real, but restricted and diminishing. Labour's autumnal 9 per cent lead over the Conservatives as the party with the best policies on strikes and industrial relations had turned by February 1979 into a 13 per cent lead for Thatcher. But by April, Labour was once more ahead and, in the election itself, 'it continued to be judged the party best capable of handling the unions'.[101] Those agreeing that unions constituted a 'good thing' rather than a 'bad thing' divided 57:31 in August 1978; 44:44 in January 1979, and 58:29 in August 1979.[102] That the virulent anti-unionism of that winter was cathartic would appear to be contradicted by the fact that workers were still joining unions in healthy numbers. What was at stake in the election was Labour's whole record, not just the strikes, whilst on the Conservative side the promise of free collective bargaining and reduced personal taxation appeared more influential amongst skilled workers than anti-unionism in general and the prospect of what most still saw as 'a few restrictions' on union activities.[103] The significance of voting trends in this latter group should not be exaggerated: whilst 33 per cent of trade unionists voted Conservative, this was only three points higher than in February 1974.[104]

That we need to look back further beyond the moment is suggested by the fact that Labour's share of the vote in 1979 was almost the same – 36.9 per cent compared with 37.1 per cent – as that in February 1974, when, as Stedman Jones points out, the disruptive impact of industrial action – and its amplification – was probably greater than it was in 1978–9.[105] That we need to look forward, further beyond the moment, is suggested by the fact that Thatcher entered Downing Street with the smallest share of the vote of any post-war prime minister except Wilson in 1974. This scarcely signified a new hegemony. The authoritative Nuffield study of the election contended against simplistic 'Winter of Discontent' explanations and doubted whether this was in any sense of the term a watershed election.[106]

The events of 1979 were not predestined nor did they determine the future decline of trade unionism, however justifiably convenient it is to date future change from Thatcher's assumption of power. They constituted one act in a much longer drama which cast the unions as *the* problem of British politics. They require integration into the political developments of the whole period and particularly the shifts from 1973–4. What was involved was the failure of the Social Contract, and that had longer and deeper roots in the enduring nature of the factors discussed in this essay which militated against making trade unions effective agents of either concertation or more radical socialist change. But all roads did not travel remorselessly towards the Thatcher terminus. A counterfactual, which contemporaries certainly conceived of, stems from Callaghan calling an election for October 1978. This was a plausible possibility which seemed to many at the time the best choice. That October Labour was ahead in the polls with a lead of up to 7 per cent and, perhaps crucially, it was ahead on the key issues of inflation and employment.[107] The social forces were available to make an alternative history.

Labour's rightward drift with a stronger Concordat with the unions continued in the new government after 1978. Callaghan and Healy pioneered the path social democracy was to take in Spain, Australia and New Zealand. There was a muted 'Winter of Discontent' with continuing mild corporatism and state management curbing the effects of global economic changes in the early 1980s. The unions, weakened at the grassroots and losing members, although not dramatically, made more effective collaborators with the state. This road has two forks. Along the first, Dennis Healy succeeds Callaghan in 1981, besting General Galtieri before going down to defeat at the hands of Arthur Scargill in the 1984 miners' strike, fatally undermined by Labour's left. Along the second fork, dissatisfaction with Labour's leaders, despite their success at the polls and in the Falklands, leads to the electoral college and Tony Benn's fractional victory over Healy which presaged AES policies after Benn's victory in the October 1982 general election. They encountered as little success as the Mitterand experiment in France. None the less, the 1980s were the great age of Labour.[108]

Things could have turned out differently. Unrealized alternatives direct us back to the fact that in 1979 unions remained powerful social actors whose record from 1964 seemed far from the tale of failure which figures in many current teleologies. In a very full sense, trade unions had achieved recognition in workplace, economy and society. If the agenda of collective bargaining remained restricted and union influence on management decisions was marginal, it was greater than in many comparable countries, greater than it had been in the past and greater than it would be in the future. In comparison with the past and the future, trade unionism was stronger in terms of its coverage, its social presence and its influence on the state. If its structures and cultures acted as an impediment to effective concertation and radical social transformation, or, as the 1980s would disclose, effective resistance to neo-liberalism, in the 1960s and 1970s this involved benefits as well as difficulties. Despite its failure to transcend particularism in any sustained fashion, the growth of the shop steward system was an increment to democratic activism in union, workplace and society. In key aspects, trade unionism was more democratic, more participative, more assertive towards management and more effective. The construction of solidarity proved possible both at national level, through TUC campaigns against legislative intervention and wage restraint and at rank and file level through the grassroots militancy that achieved its peak in the freeing of the Pentonville Five. The maintenance of full employment for most of the period was an important achievement. There was success in raising real wages and redistributing income, superior indices of success than the unions' elusive contribution to the economic health of employers.

There were of course real and significant failures: the inability to revitalize the tired union culture and fading sense of belonging to a movement, to transcend Fabianism and Stalinism and construct a superior compromise between trade unionism as the antagonist and trade unionism as the supporter of capitalism. At the end of the 1970s, the inability to combine militancy, collective bargaining and political action in an effective *ensemble* which could influence significant change represented a critical reverse. But it was a reverse in a period which had seen progress in many areas. It was, whatever we may think of the consequences and some of its manifestations, the high tide of trade unionism.

119

Table 4.1 Aggregate union membership and density in the United Kingdom, 1964–79

	Union membership (000s)	Potential membership (000s)	Density level (%)	Density annual % change
1964	10,218	23,166	44.1	+0.9
1965	10,325	23,385	44.2	+0.2
1966	10,259	23,545	43.6	−1.4
1967	10,194	23,347	43.7	+0.2
1968	10,200	23,203	44.0	+0.7
1969	10,479	23,153	45.3	+3.0
1970	11,187	23,050	48.5	+7.1
1971	11,135	22,884	48.7	+0.4
1972	11,359	22,961	49.5	+1.6
1973	11,456	23,244	49.3	−0.4
1974	11,764	23,299	50.4	+2.2
1975	12,026	23,587	51.0	+1.2
1976	12,386	23,871	51.9	+1.8
1977	12,846	24,069	53.4	+2.9
1978	13,112	24,203	54.2	+1.5
1979	13,447	24,264	55.4	+2.2

Source: G. S. Bain and R. Price, 'Union growth: dimensions, determinants, and destiny', in G.S. Bain (ed.), *Industrial Relations in Britain* (Oxford, 1983), Table 1.1, p. 5.

Table 4.2 The ten largest unions, 1964 and 1979

	1964			1979	
Rank	Union	Membership	Rank	Union	Membership
1	TGWU	1,426,424	1	TGWU	2,086,281
2	AEU	1,010,904	2	AUEW-ES	1,217,760
3	NUGMW	784,545	3	GMWU	967,153
4	NUM	479,107	4	NALGO	753,226
5	USDAW	351,934	5	NUPE	691,770
6	NALGO	338,322	6	ASTMS	491,000
7	ETU	281,773	7	USDAW	470,017
8	NUR	263,626	8	EETPU	420,000
9	NUT*	263,000	9	UCATT	347,777
10	NUPE	240,000	10	NUM	253,142

Sources: TUC *Report,* 1965, 1980.
* Non-TUC affiliate. The NUT figure is for 1965, taken from R. Undy et al.,
Change in Trade Unions (1981), p. 32.

Table 4.3 Trends in recorded strikes, 1964-79

Year	No. of strikes		No. of workers involved (000s)		No. of working days lost (000s)	
	Excl. mining	Incl. mining	Excl. mining	Incl. mining	Excl. mining	Incl. mining
1964	1,466	2,524	711	883	1,975	2,277
1965	1,614	2,354	756	874	2,513	2,925
1966	1,384	1,937	494	544	2,280	2,398
1967	1,722	2,116	693	734	2,682	2,787
1968	2,157	2,378	2,228	2,258	4,636	4,690
1969	2,930	3,116	1,520	1,665	5,807	6,846
1970	3,746	3,906	1,683	1,801	9,890	10,980
1971	2,093	2,228	1,155	1,178	13,488	13,551
1972	2,273	2,497	1,392	1,734	13,111	23,909
1973	2,572	2,873	1,481	1,528	7,107	7,197
1974	2,736	2,922	1,319	1,626	9,125	14,750
1975	2,070	2,282	781	809	5,690	6,012
1976	1,740	2,016	630	668	3,214	3,284
1977	2,441	2,703	1,113	1,166	10,054	10,142
1978	2,133	2,471	938	1,042	9,210	9,405
1979	1,782	2,080	4,555	4,608	29,361	29,474

Source: P. K. Edwards, 'The pattern of collective industrial action', in G. S. Bain (ed.) *Industrial Relations in Britain* (1983), p. 211.

122

Table 4.4 Indices of real earnings for males and females, 1970–79

Year	Males			Females		
	All	Non-manual	Manual	All	Non-manual	Manual
1970	53.5	65.3	47.6	29.3	32.8	24.0
1971	53.6	65.4	47.6	29.9	33.1	24.5
1972	55.8	68.1	49.5	31.3	34.6	25.8
1973	58.4	68.9	52.7	32.3	35.2	27.2
1974	57.1	67.2	52.6	32.6	35.2	28.3
1975	58.6	67.9	54.0	36.3	39.3	30.9
1976	59.4	69.5	54.3	38.5	41.6	32.7
1977	56.2	65.5	51.5	36.7	39.6	31.3
1978	58.7	68.3	53.6	37.5	40.0	32.8
1979	58.7	67.6	54.4	36.8	39.4	32.2

Note: Figures refer to gross weekly earnings for full-time employees (males 21 and over, females 18 and over) deflated by the index of retail prices (1975 = 100).
Source: M.B. Gregory, 'The economic context', in M.B. Gregory and A. J. W. Thompson (eds), *A Portrait of Pay, 1970–1982: an analysis of the New Earnings Survey* (Oxford, 1990), Table 2.6, p. 45.

Notes

1. E. Hobsbawm, *The Age of Extremes: the short twentieth century* (1994), pp. 257–86; P. Armstrong, A. Glynn and J. Harrison, *Capitalism since World War II: the making and breaking of the great boom* (1984), pp. 309–50.

2. Armstrong *et al.*, *Capitalism*, p. 464; A. Glynn and B. Sutcliffe, *British Capitalism, Workers and the Profits Squeeze* (Harmondsworth, 1972). The essential historic problems are pithily outlined in R. Hyman, 'The historical evolution of British industrial relations', in P. Edwards (ed.), *Industrial Relations: theory and practice in Britain* (Oxford, 1995).

3. See H. A. Clegg, *The Changing System of Industrial Relations in Britain* (Oxford, 1979), chs 2 and 8.

4. K. Middlemas, *Politics in Industrial Society: the experience of the British system since 1911* (1979).

5. P. Jenkins, *The Battle of Downing Street* (1970), p. 140; R. Taylor, 'The winter of discontent: Symposium', *Contemporary Record*, 1, 3, 1987, p. 36; R. Taylor, *The Trade Union Question in British Politics: government and unions since 1945* (1993), pp. 252–3.

6. P. Schmitter, 'Still the century of corporatism', *Review of Politics*, 36, 1, 1974 ; L. Panitch, 'Trade unions and the capitalist state', in L. Panitch, *Working Class Politics in Crisis: essays on labour and the state* (1986).

7. D. Barnes and E. Reid, *Government and Trade Unions: the British experience, 1964–79* (1982); R. Martin, *TUC: the growth of a pressure group, 1868–1976* (Oxford, 1980), pp. 338–40.

8. P. Maguire, 'Labour and the law: the politics of British industrial relations', in C. Wrigley (ed.), *A History of British Industrial Relations, 1939–79* (Cheltenham, 1996), p. 59.

9. J. Jones, quoted in TUC, *The Trade Union Role in Industrial Policy: report of the conference of affiliated unions* (1977), p. 33; D. Marquand, *The Unprincipled Society* (1988), pp. 40–62; J. Goldthorpe, 'Industrial relations in Great Britain: a critique of reformism', in T. Clarke and L. Clements (eds), *Trade Unions under Capitalism* (1977); B. Castle, *Diaries, 1974–76* (1980), p. 10; B. Donoughue, *Prime Minister: the conduct of policy under Harold Wilson and James Callaghan* (1987), p.p. 169–73.

10. H. Gospel, *Markets, Firms and the Management of Labour in Modern Britain* (Cambridge, 1992); D. Strinati, *Capitalism, the State and Industrial Relations* (1982).

11. Royal Commission on Trade Unions and Employers' Associations, *Report* (Cmnd 3623, 1968), p. 262; W. Brown (ed.), *The Changing Contours of British Industrial Relations: a survey of manufacturing industry* (Oxford, 1981), pp. 5–31.

12. A. Booth, 'Corporatism, capitalism and depression in twentieth century Britain', *British Journal of Sociology* , 33, 2, 1982; D. Coates, *The Crisis of Labour: industrial relations and the state in contemporary Britain* (1980), pp. 79–83.

13. J. A. G. Griffith, *The Politics of the Judiciary* (4th edition, 1991), pp. 93–9;

R. Geary, *Policing Industrial Disputes, 1893–1985* (Cambridge, 1985), pp. 67–115; M. Hollingsworth and R. Norton-Taylor, *Blacklist: the inside story of political vetting* (1988), pp. 122–6.

14. A.B. Atkinson and A.J. Harrison, *Distribution of Personal Wealth in Britain* (Cambridge, 1978), p. 218.

15. T. Bilton *et al.*, *Introductory Sociology* (1981), pp. 83ff; J. Mack and S. Lansley, *Poor Britain* (1985); C. Pond, 'Low pay and unemployment', *Low Pay Review*, 2, 1980.

16. S. Aaronovitch *et al.*, *The Political Economy of British Capitalism: a Marxist analysis* (1981); J. Scott, *The Upper Classes: property and privilege in Britain* (1982); J. Westergaard and H. Resler, *Class in a Capitalist Society* (Harmondsworth, 1976), pp. 90–6; J. Purcell, 'A strategy for management control in industrial relations', in J. Purcell and R. Smith (eds), *The Control of Work* (1979).

17. G. Routh, *Occupation and Pay in Great Britain* (1980); Clegg, *Changing System* , p. 179, Tables 7 and 8; K. Coates, 'Wage slaves', in R. Blackburn and A. Cockburn (eds), *The Incompatibles: trade union militancy and the new consensus* (Harmondsworth, 1967).

18. G.S. Bain and R. Price, 'Union growth: dimensions, determinants and destiny', in G.S. Bain (ed.), *Industrial Relations in Britain* (Oxford, 1983), pp. 4–10.

19. W. Brown, 'The contraction of collective bargaining in Britain', *British Journal of Industrial Relations*, 31, 2, 1993; S. Dunn and J. Gennard, *The Closed Shop in British Industry* (1984).

20. Bain and Price, 'Union growth', pp. 12–31; R. Richardson, 'Trade union growth: a review article', *British Journal of Industrial Relations*, 15, 2, 1977; R. Undy, V. Ellis, W.E.J. McCarthy and A.H. Halmos, *Change in Trade Unions: the development of the unions since 1960* (1981), pp. 163–6.

21. M. Terry, 'Shop steward development and managerial strategies', in Bain, *Industrial Relations*; J. McIlroy, *Trade Unions in Britain Today* (2nd edition, Manchester, 1995), pp. 100–2; M. Terry, 'Combine committees: developments in the 1970s', *British Journal of Industrial Relations*, 23, 3, 1985, pp. 67–8.

22. Undy et al., *Change in Trade Unions*; TUC, *Report*, 1964 and 1980.

23. P. Willman, T. Morris and B. Aston, *Union Business: trade union organization and financial reform in the Thatcher years* (Cambridge, 1993), pp. 7–20; J. Kelly and E. Heery, *Working for the Union* (Cambridge, 1994).

24. T. Lane, 'Economic democracy: are the unions equipped?', *Industrial Relations Journal*, 17, 1986.

25. McIlroy, *Trade Unions*, pp. 188–94.

26. Middlemas, *Politics in Industrial Society*, pp. 396–400; D. Coates, 'The question of trade union power', in D. Coates and G. Johnston (eds), *Socialist Arguments* (1983); G. Murray, 'Trade Unions and Incomes Policies: British unions and the Social Contract in the 1970s', unpublished PhD thesis, University of Warwick, 1985.

27. Martin, *TUC*, pp. 338–40; G.A. Dorfman, *British Trade Unionism Against*

the Trades Union Congress (1983), p. 4.

28. R. Hyman, 'Trade unions: structure, policies and politics', in Bain, *Industrial Relations*, pp. 54–7.

29. TUC, *Report*, 1964, p. 3; TUC, *Report*, 1979, p. iii; L. Minkin, *The Contentious Alliance: trade unions and the Labour Party* (Edinburgh, 1991), pp. 162, 186.

30. J. Hatfield, *The House the Left Built* (1978).

31. Minkin, *Contentious Alliance*, pp. 116, 124, 132; R. Taylor, *The Fifth Estate: Britain's unions in the modern world* (1980), pp. 110–11.

32. L. Minkin, *The Labour Party Conference: a study in the politics of intra-party democracy* (Manchester, 1980), pp. 90ff; R. McKenzie, *British Political Parties* (1955), p. 495.

33. J. Jones, 'Unions today and tomorrow', in Blackburn and Cockburn, *Incompatibles*; J. Jones, *Union Man: an autobiography* (1986); Minkin, *Contentious Alliance*, ch. 6; information from Regan Scott, TGWU.

34. 'The role of militancy: interview with Hugh Scanlon', *New Left Review*, 46, 1967; P. Ferris, *The New Militants: crisis in the trade unions* (Harmondsworth, 1972), pp. 55–8; J. McIlroy and A. Campbell, 'The Communist Party and industrial politics, 1964–75', unpublished paper, conference on 'British Trade Unionism, Workers' Struggles and Economic Performance, 1940–79', University of Warwick, September 1997.

35. T. Benn, *Conflicts of Interest: Diaries 1977–80* (1990), p. 147.

36. R. Undy, 'The devolution of bargaining responsibilities in the Transport and General Workers' Union, 1965–75', *Industrial Relations Journal*, 9, 3, 1978; J. England, 'Shop stewards in Transport House', *Industrial Relations Journal*, 12, 5, 1981.

37. M. Bray, '"Democracy is what you make it": union democracy and postal ballots in the AUEW', unpublished MA thesis, University of Warwick, 1979.

38. T. Lane and K. Roberts, *Strike at Pilkingtons* (1971); M. Fore, *GMWU: Scab Union* (n.d. [1970]).

39. J. Lloyd, *Light and Liberty: a history of the EETPU* (1990), pp. 506–97; P. Wintour, 'How Frank Chapple stays on top', *New Statesman*, 25 July 1980.

40. V. Allen, *The Militancy of British Miners* (Shipley, 1981); A. Campbell and M. Warner, 'Changes in the balance of power in the British mineworkers' union: an analysis of national top-office elections, 1974–84', *British Journal of Industrial Relations*, 23, 1, 1985; Benn, *Conflicts of Interest*, pp. 166, 240.

41. NUPE, *Organization and Change in the National Union of Public Employees* (1974); B. Fryer and S. Williams, *A Century of Service: an illustrated history of the national Union of Public Employees, 1889–1993* (1993), pp. 71–108; Benn, *Conflicts of Interest*, p. 526.

42. G. Newman, *Path to Maturity: NALGO, 1965–1980* (1982); R.H. Fryer, 'Public service trade unionism in the twentieth century', in R. Mailly, S. Dimmock and A.S. Sethi (eds), *Industrial Relations in the Public Services* (1989); Undy *et al.*, *Unions and Change*, pp. 80–1.

43. R.D. Coates, *Teachers' Unions and Interest Group Politics* (Cambridge,

1972); R. Seifert, 'Some aspects of factional opposition: *Rank and File* and the NUT, 1967–82', *British Journal of Industrial Relations*, 22, 3, 1984; Undy et al., *Unions and Change*, pp. 251–61.

44. C. Jenkins and B. Sherman, *White Collar Unionism: the rebellious salariat* (1979); C. Jenkins, *All Against the Collar* (1990), pp. 98–129; Undy et al., *Unions and Change*, pp. 67–74.

45. H. Wainwright and D. Elliott, *The Lucas Plan: a new trade unionism in the making?* (1982); W.E.J. McCarthy and S.R. Parker, Royal Commission on Trade Unions and Employers' Associations, Research Paper 10, *Shop Stewards and Workplace Relations*, (1968) p. 14; Taylor, *Fifth Estate*, p. 203; P. Fosh, *The Active Trade Unionist* (Cambridge, 1981); W. Nicholson, G. Ursell and P. Blyton, *The Dynamics of White Collar Unionism* (1981), p. 80.

46. See, for example, T. Cliff and C. Barker, *Incomes Policy, Legislation and Shop Stewards* (1966), p. 106; T. Cliff, *Productivity Deals and How to Fight Them* (1970); Clarke and Clements, *Trade Unions*.

47. E. Batstone, I. Boraston and S. Frenkel, *Shop Stewards in Action* (Oxford, 1977), pp. 179, 185; N. Millward and M. Stevens, *British Workplace Relations, 1980–84* (1986), p. 85.

48. J. England and B. Weekes, 'Trade unions and the state: a new view of the crisis', *Industrial Relations Journal*, 12, 1, 1981, p. 25.

49. McIlroy, *Trade Unions*, pp. 286–8; D. Butler and D. Kavanagh, *The British General Election of 1979* (1980), p. 420; D. Butler and D. Stokes, *Political Change in Britain: the evolution of electoral choice* (1969); J. B. Freyman, 'When Labour votes: an analysis of the partisan alignment of British trade unionists, 1964–1974', unpublished PhD thesis, George Washington University, 1980.

50. Brown, *Changing Contours*, pp. 100–1.

51. J. Cronin, *Labour and Society in Britain 1918–1979* (1984), pp. 241–3, Table A2.

52. P.K. Edwards, 'The pattern of collective industrial action', in Bain, *Industrial Relations*, p. 211; 'Large industrial stoppages, 1960–1979', *Employment Gazette*, September 1980, p. 994.

53. K. Coates and T. Topham, *Trade Unions in Britain* (2nd edition, Nottingham, 1982), pp. 225–6.

54. J. Cronin, *Industrial Conflict in Modern Britain* (1979), p. 185.

55. C.T.B. Smith et al., *Strikes in Britain: a research study of industrial stoppages in the United Kingdom* (1978), pp. 18–20, 88.

56. D. Gilbert, 'Strikes in postwar Britain', in Wrigley, *History of British Industrial Relations*, pp. 134–6, Table 6.2; Edwards, 'Collective action', p. 218.

57. J. Kelly, *Trade Unions and Socialist Politics* (1988), p. 142.

58. Calculated from A. Troup, 'The Mobilization of and Responses to "Political" Protest Strikes 1969–84', unpublished PhD thesis, CNAA, 1987, Series A, pp. 49–50.

59. Troup, pp. 95, 112, 141.

60. For good discussions of the role of militancy from a revolutionary perspective, see P. Anderson, 'The limits and possibilities of trade union action', in

Blackburn and Cockburn, *Incompatibles*; R. Hyman, *Marxism and the Sociology of Trade Unionism* (1971).

61. J.W. Durcan, W.E.J. McCarthy and G.P. Redman, *Strikes in Post-War Britain: study of stoppages of work due to industrial disputes, 1946–73* (1983), p. 168; Cronin, *Industrial Conflict*, p. 141.

62. M. Kidron. *Western Capitalism since the War* (Harmondsworth, 1970); Freyman, 'When Labour votes', pp. 315–16.

63. Edwards, 'Collective Action', p. 218.

64. Cronin, *Industrial Conflict*, p. 141; K. Hawkins, *Trade Unions* (1981), pp. 188–90; C. Saunders et al., *Winners and losers: pay patterns in the 1970s* (1977), pp. 30–1; 81.

65. R.J. Davies, 'Economic activity, incomes policy and strikes: a quantitative analysis', *British Journal of Industrial Relations*, 17, 2, 1979, p. 220.

66. Saunders, *Winners and Losers*, pp. 28–9; H. Scullion, 'The skilled revolt against general unionism: the case of the BL Toolroom Committee', *Industrial Relations Journal*, 12, 3, 1981; J. Waddington and C. Whitson, 'Trade unions: growth, structure and policy', in Edwards, *Industrial Relations*, p. 170; W. Brown, 'Engineering wages and the Social Contract, 1975–77', *Oxford Bulletin of Economics and Statistics*, 41, 1, 1979; C.T. Saunders, 'Changes in relative pay in the 1970s', in F.T. Blackaby (ed.) *The Future of Pay Bargaining* (1980), pp. 197–201.

67. J.H. Goldthorpe, 'The current inflation: towards a sociological account', in F. Hirsch and J.H. Goldthorpe (eds), *The Political Economy of Inflation* (1978); W.G. Runciman, *Relative Deprivation and Social Justice* (1966); R. Hyman and I. Bough, *Social Values and Industrial Relations: a study in fairness and equality* (Oxford, 1975), especially pp. 233–53; J. Westergaard, 'The rediscovery of the cash nexus: some recent interpretations of trends in British class structure', in R. Miliband and J. Saville (eds), *The Socialist Register, 1970* (1970), p. 120.

68. H. Phelps Brown, *The Origins of Trade Union Power* (Oxford, 1983), pp. 164–5.

69. S. Barkin, 'Summary and conclusion', in S. Barkin (ed.), *Worker Militancy and its Consequences* (2nd edition, New York, 1983), p. 381.

70. A. Flanders and A. Fox, 'Collective bargaining: from Donovan to Durkheim', in A. Flanders, *Management and Unions: the theory and reform of industrial relations* (1970); A. King, *Why is Britain becoming Harder to Govern?* (1976).

71. J. O'Connor, *The Fiscal Crisis of the State* (New York, 1972); I. Gough, *The Political Economy of the Welfare State* (1979).

72. The case is well stated in Kelly, *Socialist Politics*, especially pp. 115–16.

73. Saunders, 'Changes in relative pay', pp. 195, 205; R. Layard, D. Metcalf and S. Nickell, 'The effects of collective bargaining on relative and absolute wages', *British Journal of Industrial Relations*, 16, 3, 1978.

74. Calculated from Routh, *Occupation and Pay*, Table 3.1, pp. 134–5; A. Glynn and J. Harrison, *The British Economic Disaster* (1980), p. 90.

75. Routh, *Occupation and Pay*, pp. 169, 180.

76. Glynn and Harrison, *Economic Disaster*, p. 127.
77. B. Burkitt and D. Bowers, *Trade Unions and the Economy* (1979), p. 62.
78. Ibid., pp. 65–72.
79. Taylor, *Trade Union Question*, pp. 2, 338; N. Tiratsoo, *From Blitz to Blair* (1997), p. 179, following Taylor, *Trade Union Question*, pp. 1–4 and *passim*.
80. E. Hobsbawm, 'The Forward march of labour halted?' [1978], in M. Jacques and F. Mulhern (eds), *The Forward March of Labour Halted?* (1981); E. Hobsbawm, 'Response' [1979], in ibid.; E. Hobsbawm, 'The 1970s: syndicalism without syndicalists' [1979] in E. Hobsbawm, *Worlds of Labour: further studies in the history of labour* (1984).
81. J. Hinton, *Labour and Socialism: a history of the British labour movement, 1867–1974* (1983), pp. viii–ix, 198.
82. R. Harrison, untitled contribution in Jacques and Mulhern, *Forward March*, pp. 55–7.
83. Kelly, *Socialist Politics*, p. 118; see also Cronin, *Labour and Society*, pp. 19–34.
84. For a criticism of Hobsbawm's historical method, see D. Howell, 'When was the forward march of labour?', *Llafur*, 5, 3, 1990.
85. Cf J. Saville, *The Labour Movement in Britain* (1988), pp. 140–2; R. Hyman, *Strikes* (3rd edition, 1984), pp. 226–9.
86. Hinton, *Labour and Socialism*, pp. 198–9.
87. For brief accounts of particular disputes, see J. Suddaby, 'The public sector strike in Camden': winter 1979', *New Left Review*, 116, July–August 1979; P. Smith, 'The road haulage dispute 1979', unpublished paper, conference on 'British Trade Unionism, Workers' Struggles and Economic Performance', University of Warwick, September 1997.
88. D. Healey, *The Time of My Life* (1989), p. 462.
89. Donoughue, *Prime Minister*, pp. 157, 165.
90. Ibid., p. 171; K.O. Morgan, *Callaghan: a life* (Oxford, 1997), pp. 657, 650.
91. Taylor, *Trade Union Question*, p. 258.
92. B. Rodgers, 'Government under stress: Britain's winter of discontent', *Political Quarterly*, 55, 2, 1984, p. 71; Donoughue, *Prime Minister*, pp. 178, 176, 188; Morgan, *Callaghan*, p. 673.
93. Taylor, *Trade Union Question*, pp. 252–3; Morgan, *Callaghan*, p. 663.
94. Morgan, *Callaghan*, pp. 673, 635.
95. Callaghan, quoted in Taylor, *Trade Union Question*, p. 260; Anthony Seldon, quoted ibid.
96. C. Hay, 'Narrating the crisis: the discursive construction of the "winter of discontent"', *Sociology*, 30, 2, 1996, pp. 253–5.
97. Donoughue, *Prime Minister*, p. 188; for background, see Dorfman, *British Trade Unionism*, pp. 18–19.
98. Dorfman, *British Trade Unionism*, pp. 62–91.
99. Taylor, 'Winter of discontent', p. 42; Morgan, *Callaghan*, p. 668.
100. TUC Media Working Group, *A Cause for Concern: media coverage of industrial disputes, January–February 1979* (1979); Glasgow Media Group,

More Bad News (1980).

101. Butler and Kavanagh, *British General Election*, pp. 131, 345.
102. Taylor, *Trade Union Question*, p. 371, Table A3.3.
103. Butler and Kavanagh, *British General Election*, p. 338.
104. McIlroy, *Trade Unions*, p. 287.
105. G. Stedman Jones, 'Why the Labour party is in a mess', in G. Stedman Jones, *Languages of Class: studies in English working class history* (Cambridge, 1983), p. 243.
106. Butler and Kavanagh, *British General Election*, pp. 340, 336–47.
107. See, for example, Donoughue, *Prime Minister*, pp. 163–5; Morgan, *Callaghan*, p. 638.
108. See, for example, Tony Benn's comment as early as September 1978: 'I yearn for the day when Arthur is President of the NUM' (*Conflicts of Interest*, p. 342).

PART THREE

Case Studies, 1964–79

CHAPTER FIVE

The Labour Party and the Trade Unions

Andrew Thorpe

The general election of October 1964 brought the Labour Party back to power with an overall majority of five after thirteen years of opposition. The previous month the party leader, Harold Wilson, had made a powerful speech at the Trades Union Congress (TUC) in which he stated that a Labour government and the unions would be 'partners in a great adventure'. Enthused by Wilson's vision of a new, modern, purposeful Britain, delegates rose at the end of his speech and sang 'For He's A Jolly Good Fellow'.[1] The atmosphere at Congress fifteen years later, after the fall of Wilson's successor, James Callaghan, and the election of a Conservative government under Margaret Thatcher, could hardly have been more different. Now, the leaders of two major unions, the train drivers' union (ASLEF) and the National Union of Public Employees, put forward a motion demanding that the party ensure that the next Labour government would follow policy as laid down by the party conference.[2] Although the motion was ruled out of order on the grounds that it was not the business of the TUC to tell the Labour Party what to do, there was no singing, least of all in praise of the Labour leadership.

Indeed, for Britain as a whole, the years 1964 and 1979 seem poles apart. In the space of only fifteen years, it went from the fading afterglow of 'You've Never Had It So Good' to a real sense of malaise. The Labour Party, which at the start of the period had seemed to be the party of a glowing technological future, had, by its end, an image of being worn out and discredited, with few, if any, concrete answers for the problems of the modern world. Worse still, the link with the trade unions, which had served Labour well at various points in the past and which had still been seen as worth boasting of at the 1964 election, now appeared to be a millstone around the party's neck.

It is, of course, possible to overplay the extent to which change took place in the relationship between party and unions in this period. There were, for example, no significant changes to the party's constitution. Institutional relations in 1979 remained, formally, much as they had been in 1964. At every level from constituency party to conference, there remained the potential for the unions to dominate Labour. The party continued to be heavily reliant on the unions' coffers for its funding. The union section of the party's 27-strong National Executive Committee (NEC) remained at a complement of 12 throughout the period. Trade unionists continued to sit in Labour cabinets, although the extent of their live links with the union movement varied. The proportion of Labour MPs sponsored by trade unions varied between 36.3 per cent (in 1966) and 49.6 per cent (in 1979). But this reflected, to a large extent, the fact that these tended to be the safer seats: the actual number of such MPs varied between 114 and 133 (again in 1966 and 1979 respectively).[3] Fraternal delegates continued to be exchanged during the conference season. Overall, there was little real challenge to the view that the unions and the party were symbiotically linked. As Roy Jenkins, later a founder of the Social Democratic Party (SDP) but at the time a leading Labourite, wrote in 1972, 'both wings of the alliance are as necessary to each other now as they were when the Labour Representation Committee [LRC] was founded 72 years ago'.[4]

The formation of the LRC (which became the Labour Party in 1906) had come about, primarily, as a result of trade unions' anxieties about their legal status. From the start, the unions had always played a major role in the party's affairs. The warmth of the relationship had varied over time; its maintenance had rarely been seriously questioned, certainly after 1918. Even so, there had been periods of real difficulty, most notably during the two interwar Labour governments (1924, 1929–31).[5] Even in the supposedly halcyon days of party–union cooperation during under the Attlee governments of 1945–51, there had been times of stress in the relationship.[6]

The 1950s formed a curious period for party-union relations. On the one hand, most trade unionists continued to vote Labour, and their leaders to support the party. Many played a significant role in the party and in various of the disputes and arguments that periodically enlivened it. Yet the conciliatory policy of the Churchill government (1951–5), particularly its Minister of Labour, Walter Monckton, suggested to many trade unionists that life could be at least bearable under a Tory government.[7] There was no attempt to introduce anti-union legislation. Full employment was maintained. Real wages rose.

The conciliatory, consultative strand remained a part of government–union relations down to 1964: the establishment of the National Economic Development Council (NEDC) formalized consultative procedures, and seemed to confirm that the unions were now part of the national decision-making process. But another strain also began to assert itself. The Eden government (1955–7) was a good deal less conciliatory at times than Churchill's administration had been, and although Macmillan (1957–64) tried to avoid confrontation, there was no return to the days of Monckton. Attacks on trade unions remained part of the sub-text (and sometimes more) of Conservative rhetoric.[8] Union discontent rose as Macmillan's government ran into economic trouble. And the legal position of the unions came into question once more. The House of Lords's judgement in February 1964 in the *Rookes v. Barnard* case, which impeded the right to strike, was the most notorious of a series of judicial decisions that seemed to threaten the legal position of the unions as established under the 1906 Trades Disputes Act.

Harold Wilson and the modernization of industry

The return of a Labour government in 1964, then, was heartily welcomed by the trade union movement. The Labour manifesto promised full employment and faster economic growth, engineered by planning in partnership with the unions; although it stated that 'all of us, individuals, enterprises and trade unions' must be 'ready to re-examine our methods of work, to innovate and to modernise', this could be seen as a rhetorical flourish or something which carried little if any threat to the unions.[9] When the new Prime Minister, Harold Wilson, came to appoint his Cabinet, trade unionists could feel encouraged. Wilson himself had no union background. But both the deputy premier, George Brown, and the Chancellor of the Exchequer, James Callaghan, came from the union wing of the party; and the appointment to the cabinet of Frank Cousins, leader of the Transport and General Workers' Union (TGWU), as Minister of Technology, sent out the right signals. It seemed that the government would be looking to work closely with the trade union movement.

The basis for all the government's policies was faster economic growth. Only in this way, it was believed, could the economy become more healthy and desirable social reforms be achieved. But, as is well known, the economy stubbornly refused to grow much beyond its normal levels of expansion. The National Plan, published in 1965, was a bold attempt to address the problem.[10] Its force, however, was vitiated by one of its own key objectives. In order to sustain the Plan, it was agreed – at the initial stage, at least – that the value of sterling had to be maintained. But this in turn meant that the government had to satisfy the markets, and the only way in which this could be done was to show that it was tough on inflation, which had been creeping upwards.

It was felt that the way to resolve this conundrum was to impose limits on the extent to which incomes could rise. The Plan itself had stressed that 'planning for economic growth requires policies for price stability and the orderly growth of money incomes' and hence the need for 'a positive policy for prices and incomes'.[11] This, however, was controversial within the labour movement. Broadly, three strands of opinion could be discerned. For some, particularly within the trade unions, any incomes policy was anathema. It was the role of unions to secure the best possible deal for their members, without any interference from the state. At a union conference in 1965, for example, Ted Hill of the Boilermakers, while straining himself to the utmost to sound loyal, could not resist referring to incomes policy as 'this doubtful venture'.[12] At the other extreme there were those within the party leadership who believed that incomes policy was a political impera-

135

tive in its own right, and might need to be applied regardless of deals with the unions. At first, though, both these views were very much in the minority. There was a fairly broad section of the movement which saw the value of incomes policy as part of 'socialist planning'. Thus, when the National Plan was launched, there appeared to be a fairly broad coalition, in favour of its policies on prices and incomes. The 1965 TUC Congress, doubtless encouraged by the government's Trades Disputes Act which nullified *Rookes v. Barnard*, voted by a three-to-one majority against a resolution criticizing incomes policy out of hand and calling for a return to free collective bargaining.[13] Meanwhile, the same year's party conference carried a resolution calling for a 'Socialist incomes policy', which, at this stage, could be seen as a vote in support of the government.[14]

Initially, there were high hopes that this socialist planning approach could be sustained. Many trade unionists needed little convincing that incomes policy was a price worth paying for the social and economic benefits that would follow from price control and a 'forward' social policy.[15] It was possible to get agreement to a voluntary pay norm of 3.5 per cent in April 1965. However, pressure on sterling meant that the government came increasingly under pressure to focus most closely on incomes. The result was that in September 1965, with the pound under pressure, Callaghan called in Cabinet for a full statutory policy.[16] Although this was avoided, the government had some difficulty in persuading the TUC to accept compulsory notification of price and pay increases.[17] In the event, pay increases continued to exceed what the government deemed prudent.

To some extent the government had been able to point to its weak parliamentary position, the obvious imminence of a further election, and the 1965 Act as reasons for the unions not to rock the boat. Most unions were prepared to go along with this, albeit with a degree of resentment. Cousins, who opposed incomes policy instinctively and had soon started hankering for a return to the TGWU, stayed on in the Cabinet until the 1966 general election so as not to open any wounds.[18] However, the results of the March 1966 general election changed matters. Labour now had an overall majority of 97, and a full term ahead of it. Ironically, given that the Labour governments of the 1970s would suffer for their small or non-existent parliamentary majorities, that of 1966–70 almost certainly suffered because its majority was so large.

But it also suffered because of changes within trade unionism and industrial relations more generally. Previously, Labour leaders had felt able to deal with trade union and industrial relations policy by reference to union leaders. The impression that this kind of dealing worked had probably reached its peak during the 1950s. Then, a bloc of right-wing union leaders – Arthur Deakin (TGWU), Tom Williamson (National Union of General and Municipal Workers) and Will Lawther (National Union of Mineworkers) – had been seen as the essential power-brokers of Labour politics, each handling hundreds of thousands of votes at party conference with impunity, and always casting them in favour of the leadership. This had been a little misleading even then; by the 1960s there could be little doubt that serious changes were taking place. Even before 1964, there had been a growing *de facto* decentralization of power, with significant increases in the number and density of shop stewards in, for example, engineering, and a significant growth in workplace bargaining.[19] Part cause and part effect of this, some unions were electing more left-wing leaders who were more responsive to workplace power than hitherto. This was typified by the election of Hugh Scanlon as President of the AEU and Jack Jones as General Secretary of the TGWU in 1967 and 1969 respectively. The TGWU and some other unions sought to begin to decentralize, in order to enfranchise shop stewards and recognize workplace realities.[20] When it is remembered that this was a period of significant union expansion – membership rose from 10.2 million in 1964 to 11.2 million in 1970 and peaked at 13.5 million in 1979 – and that the increasing power of unions, combined with turbulent economic times, led to greater militancy, it is clear that it was likely to be a time of great difficulty for Labour in government.[21]

The years between 1966 and 1970 were a period of exceedingly hard going for the government on the economic front. Up to November 1967, the emphasis was on trying to save the pound; the effort failed. But then the stress had to be on running a tight ship in order to sustain sterling at its new level. All of this, naturally enough, increased pressure for strict incomes policies. The seamen's strike in the spring of 1966 was the occasion for sharp rhetoric on Wilson's part and the announcement of a six-month wage freeze, to be followed by six months of 'severe restraint'.[22] Although the policy became less stringent in July 1967, statutory controls remained in place until early 1970. At a time when the government was trying to take a strong line of limiting public expenditure, it was not surprising that dissension within the party, and between party and unions, developed. Indeed, Minkin has argued that the 1967 party conference represented a watershed in the politics of the labour movement. Until then, the party leadership had generally been able to mobilize enough support to secure the decisions it wanted from the wider party. But now, two big unions, the Engineers and the Transport Workers, were on the left, and increasingly critical of Labour's leaders. Thus there was 'a powerful base at the Conference for the government's critics to go over to the offensive', and, in a situation of general union disillusionment on numerous aspects of government policy, 'the rest of the unions could not be relied upon to mobilize in its favour'.[23] This meant, too, that from then onwards the NEC was to have fewer ministerial loyalists as members, so that it became increasingly prone to acting against the wishes of the party leadership from the later 1960s onwards.[24]

Thus pay restraint was not the only issue in government–union relations. But a deteriorating situation was made even worse when the legal position of the unions, which had been periodically threatening to erupt onto the political agenda, particularly from the 1950s, was promoted to centre stage. This was not entirely the doing of the government. The challenges presented by judge-made law in the early 1960s had necessitated piecemeal legislation to regularize matters. The 1965 Act, for example, restored the legal immunities which it had been believed the 1906 Act had guaranteed. But there was a general feeling that further investigation was needed, although the grounds for this varied from those who hoped such an enquiry would merely underpin the *status quo* to those who hoped for a quantum leap towards greater rights and responsibilities for unions. The result was the establishment of the Royal Commission on Trade Unions and Employers' Associations, under Lord Donovan. The Donovan Commission sat for three years before reporting in June 1968.[25] Its conservative conclusions were such as to hearten those who had looked for an authoritative restatement of the existing situation. Overall, Donovan broadly accepted the *status quo*, recommending voluntary reform of collective bargaining as against a new legal framework.

It is important to note, however, that Donovan did call on government 'to codify in one Act of Parliament the principles relating to collective bargaining, to industrial relations in general ... and to trade unions and employers' associations'.[26] At the very least, there was a need for 'a comprehensive measure for the consolidation of the statute law'.[27] Thus even a document seen by the minister responsible, Barbara Castle, as having '[TUC General Secretary] George Woodcock's fingerprints all over it' and as no real help in facing the actual situation did, all the same, open the door to some form of legislation.[28] It was now up to ministers whether they simply consolidated the law, or whether they sought to give it a more substantial tweak.

Castle and her officials were particularly alarmed by the growth in unofficial, or 'wild-cat', strikes. These disputes offended Castle's conceptions of socialist responsibility and the need for constitutional majority decisions: they could also be seen as threatening the very basis of ordered trade unionism. They also appeared to damage the nation's economic prospects, undermining productivity and hence the chances of the fruits of prosperity being used for desirable social reforms.[29] Successive retreats – on health service charges, on the raising of the school-leaving age in 1967–8 – had seared deep into the collective psyche of ministers. Castle's firm, innovative attempt to bring order to industrial relations was one response to this.

More broadly, a number of ministers were beginning to see that electoral nemesis might be looming. Election results were abysmal: in the period 1951 to 1964 the Conservatives had lost only ten seats at by-elections, yet between July 1966 and November 1968 Labour lost eleven of the seventeen seats it was defending.[30] Furthermore, the May 1968 local elections proved disastrous: for example, Labour lost control of Sheffield for only the second time since 1926. One way to avoid disaster might be for the government to take on, and beat, the unions, something on which the Conservative opposition under Edward Heath was now making the running. This would show that the party was its own master, and reassert the government's political virility at a time when devaluation had made it look impotent. Thus it was for a combination of reasons that the White Paper *In Place of Strife* was published in January 1969.[31] This document proposed new rights for unions, such as compulsory recognition, but also new responsibilities. In particular, any unofficial action was to be subjected to a compulsory 'conciliation pause' of twenty-eight days; the Secretary of State would have the power to order a ballot before any strike could take place; and the decisions of the new Commission on Industrial Relations (CIR) would be legally binding.

The story of this document's fate is too well known to require extensive recapitulation here.[32] Initial misgivings soon blossomed into a full-scale revolt as first the TUC, then the NEC, and then the PLP came out against it, with Callaghan, in particular, playing a leading role in the resistance. But to focus solely on the high politics of *In Place of Strife* would be to tell only part of the tale. Castle saw unofficial strikes as a breach of labour movement discipline, and she shared with her officials the view that they were often undertaken for narrow and mean motives. But this was to downplay the significant changes that had been taking place in trade unionism and industrial relations, noted earlier. A quasi-corporatist vision of deals being struck between unions, employers and government at the highest levels, and then being simply applied to the workforce, went against the grain of those developments. When the increasing hostility of trade unionists towards incomes policy, broader disillusionment with the government's performance, and the general leftward swing of the unions are added into the equation, it becomes fairly clear that such a 'top-down' solution as *In Place of Strife* had very little chance of being effective.

One result was a degree of union militancy directed squarely at the White Paper. This came at all levels. By the end of April 1969, fourteen union executives had supported a call for a special Trades Union Congress to be held to condemn the plans.[33] There were demonstrations, and even occasional strikes, on the issue, although the question of how far it led to a longer-term increase in strike activity remains controversial.[34] It was not, then, just 'The Battle of Downing Street', as one commentator defined it.[35] Rather, as Panitch has written, 'it was the more militant sections of the rank and file rather than the union leadership that initiated the main challenge to *In Place of Strife*'.[36] But the repercussions were felt at the very highest levels, with political humiliation for Castle, and severe embarrassment for Wilson, who had supported her. On 17 June the Cabinet, at a 'very, very tense meeting' decided, against the Prime Minister's opposition, to abandon the plans.[37] Next day a face-saving agreement was reached, with union leaders promising to do all they could to contain unofficial strikes.

Relations between the party and the unions had been greatly strained, but they did improve somewhat over the next year. So far as the unions were concerned, the crisis showed that they were still strong enough, in matters directly concerning them at least, to prevent the government doing things they did not want done. For their part, the unions appear to have made greater, and partially successful, attempts to reduce the number of demarcation disputes.[38] On the other hand, events thereafter suggest that there was a degree of distrust entering into party-union relations. The whole affair had been a fiasco. Even if *In Place of Strife* had been enacted it is doubtful whether it would have been effective, given the changes that were taking place in industrial relations and union attitudes. It is questionable whether it would have even drawn the Conservatives' teeth on the issue of the reform of union law. The then Defence Secretary, Denis Healey, went so far as to suggest that 'permanent damage' was done to the relationship, and that the episode 'did for Wilson what the hopeless attempt to delete Clause Four from the party constitution had done for Hugh Gaitskell'.[39] Like Callaghan, he came to believe very quickly that legislation on union affairs was best avoided.

But, just as Gaitskell had recovered from his battle with Labour theology, the next few months saw a surprising revival of Wilson's, and the party's, fortunes. The ending of statutory wage controls in January 1970 was a clear play for the union vote at the next election, and when that election came, in June 1970, most observers expected Labour to win. However, it failed to do so, and Heath came back with an overall majority of 30.

Rebuilding bridges and the Social Contract

In the aftermath of defeat, leaders and members began to differ more and more on the question of trade union policy. Any attempt to identify different strands of thought is hazardous. None the less, a section of the party's right wing was by now heartily sick of the compromises that were needed to keep the unions on board, worried about the inflation and low productivity they believed were being caused by excessive wage settlements, and determined to impose strict wage policies whenever Labour came back into office. Many, though by no means all, of these people would find themselves in the SDP little more than a decade later. Left-wingers, on the other hand, suggested the need for socialist planning of wages as part of broader economic planning and transformation. At the same time, though, the impressive manifestations of wage militancy (most notably among power workers and miners) during the period of the Heath government persuaded some that a return to free collective bargaining was the most desirable route forward.

140

The problem for the party leadership was that, once in office, it would have actually to carry out policy. It had to steer between the extremes in party thinking. To simply try and impose wage restraint would hardly make life easy; nor, in the long term, could it be effective. Then again, to associate the party with all kinds of wage militancy hardly looked like responsible statecraft, and would be sure to fuel the inflation that was becoming endemic under Heath. The years of opposition between 1970 and 1974 provided a stern test for the Labour leadership.

But the test of the leadership, and of the party–union relationship, was not as stern as it might have been. Even at this distance in time it is hard to imagine any Conservative government doing so much in so short a space of time as Heath's to restore a close relationship between the Labour Party and the trade unions. The Conservatives' 1971 Industrial Relations Act was a supremely effective tool in achieving this goal, even though it was a disaster in almost every other sense.[40] This vast and unwieldy statute, introduced on the back of the Conservatives' explicitly critical approach towards the unions at the 1970 election, included various rights for unions and their members, but it also impinged significantly on established union freedoms, and therefore it was hardly surprising that trade unionists were virtually united against it. Predictably enough, too, their view of the Labour Party became more favourable once again. For sure, the party's leader had favoured *In Place of Strife*, but he had at least had the good sense to retreat. In any case, people like Callaghan, seen by many as having been heroic in their resistance, were still prominent in the leadership of the party. At the 1971 party conference a resolution calling for the Act to be 'completely repealed in the first session of a new Labour government' was passed 'without dissent'.[41] The following year's conference strengthened Labour's position still further by reiterating the pledge to repeal within the first year and also to make the policy a 'major item' of the next general election manifesto.[42] And the parliamentary report to the 1973 conference earned some easy points with trade union delegates by stressing that PLP speakers had continued 'at every opportunity' to demand repeal.[43]

Labour policy also changed in ways that suited trade unionists. In part, this reflected a swing to the left that was a natural reaction partly to the performance of the Wilson governments and partly to the active support of some trade unions, like the TGWU, for a more radical stance. In January 1972, the establishment of a TUC-Labour Party Liaison Committee, with representatives from the Parliamentary Labour Party, the NEC and the TUC, symbolized a new degree of consultation and cooperation.[44] Meanwhile, the NEC (which, as noted above, had moved leftwards since 1967) launched a major redefinition of party policy, culminating in *Labour's Programme 1973*. This contained a great deal to appeal to trade unionists. The Industrial Relations Act would be repealed. Price controls, the extension of industrial democracy and more state control of industry were all promised. Perhaps more significantly, there was an explicit commitment that pay restraint would not be a one-way street. Instead, the idea of a Social Contract was put forward, whereby unions would take responsibility for moderating wage claims in return for, first, various social goods, such as food subsidies, redistributive taxation, increased social expenditure, second, the extension of public ownership, and, third, legal reforms, of which more later.[45]

Labour made an unexpected return to office in March 1974, following the previous month's general election at which no party had emerged with an overall majority. Heath's decision, in the face of a miners' strike, to call a general election on a 'who rules Britain' ticket has usually been seen as a grievous error, and it is a conclusion that is hard to resist. It has to be said that it was an election in which neither of the major parties looked particularly compelling, but Labour fared well enough to return to office. The government started brightly, so far as the unions were concerned, by settling the coal dispute on terms favourable to the miners and repealing the Industrial Relations Act. Castle was appointed Secretary of State for Health and Social Security and distanced from industrial relations matters. Michael Foot was appointed as Employment Secretary after consultations with Jack Jones of the TGWU: the latter had been very keen on Foot, whom he saw as sympathetic and much preferable to the possible alternative, the right-winger Reg Prentice.[46] Foot was to prove amenable towards the unions, and his performance at Employment between 1974 and 1976 was to be a significant factor in his leap up the Labour hierarchy in the remainder of the decade, culminating in his election as party leader in 1980.[47] Healey became Chancellor.

From Social Contract to 'Winter of Discontent'

The Labour governments of 1974–9 were not to attempt any further 'once-and-for-all' pieces of legislation on industrial relations. None the less, the government did have a view of the way in which industrial relations should develop, and was not slow to move in a quasi-corporatist direction in order to realise it. The key here was the Social Contract. So far as the Labour leadership was concerned, this implied a new raft of laws. Thus the Advisory, Conciliation and Arbitration Service (ACAS) was set up, as a body to which industrial disputes could be referred by the parties concerned if they so wished. There was a new Trade Union Act, and acts on health and safety at work, employment protection, equal pay, and so on. The establishment of the Bullock Commission on Industrial Democracy in 1974 was another radical new departure. All this looked impressive, as did the growing trend for the government to deal with the TUC General Council on a regular basis.[48] At the same time, though, it brought the issue of trade union power still more to the centre of the political agenda: increasingly, critics (some of them within the Labour Party, but many more outside) argued that the unions, not the government, were running the country. In a January 1977 poll, 53 per cent of respondents stared that Jack Jones was the most powerful person in the country, with just 25 per cent naming Callaghan, the Prime Minister.[49] This view was undoubtedly false: certainly so far as the latter part of the government's tenure is concerned there is much truth in David Coates's contention that there was a 'striking ... gap between the public *image* of trade union power and the private *reality* of waning trade union influence over public policy'.[50] But it was an image which was very difficult to shake off.

If corporatist legislation on unions and industrial relations was one side of the Social Contract, pay restraint was another. In particular, largely external forces, admittedly fuelled by loose monetary policies, meant that inflation was rampant by 1975, culminating that August in an annual rate of 26.9 per cent. In the face of this, most union leaders were agreed that something had to be done. High inflation meant high stakes in the wages round: one year's poor settlement could mean members being severely disadvantaged vis-à-vis other workers, the erosion of differentials, and so on. It was thus that the Social Contract became a reality. Under Phase I of the government's pay policy (July 1975–July 1976), increases were limited to a maximum of £6 per week, and there were to be no increases at all for those earning more than £8,500 a year. In return the government implemented various policies, such as subsidies on food, rent controls, tax concessions, and higher pensions, to increase the value of the 'social wage'.[51] Healey has claimed that the policy was 'a resounding success' in its first year. While he can hardly be cited as an impartial observer, it is true to say that the rate of earnings growth and inflation did fall under Phase I.[52] The TUC agreed to Phase II, which ran from July 1976 to July 1977: under this agreement, wage increases were limited to a maximum of 5 per cent, subject to weekly minima and maxima of £2.50 and £4 respectively.

The results of all this were not unimpressive, although there is debate as to how far it was incomes policies, as opposed to world economic trends and increasing fear of rising unemployment, which led to the moderation of wage demands.[53] Still, the government could claim some credit for the reduction in the increase in earnings from 30 per cent in 1975 to 13 per cent in 1976 (and, later, 10 per cent in 1977).[54] The relationship between the unions and the government continued to function, although not without difficulty; and the succession of Wilson by Callaghan in April 1976, and the promotion of Foot to be effectively deputy premier, augured well for a continuing close relationship. Even so, union pressure on incomes policy was growing. One problem was that national agreements on wage restraint could not be particularly effective in a situation where so much wage bargaining had become decentralized.[55] Indeed, the Social Contract itself had the effect of further stimulating the growth and 'officialization' of shop stewards.[56] The Trades Union Congress of September 1976 did reject a motion which criticized incomes policies for lowering living standards and doing nothing to prevent increasing unemployment, and which called for an immediate return to free collective bargaining. But it also carried a resolution demanding 'a planned return to free collective bargaining' during 1977.[57]

Within months of Callaghan's succession to the premiership, the government was faced with what seemed to be a very serious crisis. A run on the pound began in the summer, and Treasury projections (later proved to be grossly over-pessimistic) suggested that the government was heading towards a major budget deficit.[58] Here is not the place to rehearse the details of the crisis of autumn 1976 which led the government to seek a loan from the International Monetary Fund, but two points need to be made. The first is that, although Callaghan handled the crisis superbly, bringing an initially hostile Cabinet round to a package of spending cuts and suffering not one resignation as a result, the crisis marked an end·to the expansive stage of Labour's social expenditure and created a strong undertow of tension and resentment within the Labour movement. The second is that the cuts effectively marked the end of the government's side of the Social Contract, but necessitated a stern fiscal stance in which the restraint of income growth would prove more of a priority than ever. In this sense, incomes policy once again became a one-way street, at just the time that the TUC was moving its position back towards full support for free collective bargaining.

The results of this were not immediate. The downturn in the economy and increasing fear of unemployment meant that unions had to curb their wage demands. Thus, although Phase III of the incomes policy (August 1977–July 1978, allowing a maximum increase of 10 per cent) was not formally accepted by the TUC, earnings growth was generally held down. But the signs were ominous. The 1975 party conference had 'overwhelmingly' carried a resolution in favour of the Social Contract and flat-rate (rather than percentage-based) pay settlements as being 'in accordance with our socialist beliefs'; a motion calling for a return to free collective bargaining had been easily defeated.[59] The following year's conference passed a resolution, again without the need for a card vote, supporting the efforts of the government and the TUC to 'beat inflation' and avoid 'a wages free-for-all which would be injurious to weaker members of the community and which would destroy or jeopardize our long-term objectives'.[60] At the 1977 conference, incomes policy was not discussed as such, but even there, a left-wing resolution condemning, *inter alia*, falling real wages was defeated.[61] Perhaps too much should not be made of this: had there been a debate, the government might well have faced at least a sizeable hostile minority, because, by now, it was only with great difficulty that many groups of trade unionists were persuaded to moderate their demands. Skilled workers began to complain that their differentials had been eroded. Unskilled workers, particularly in the public sector, were feeling increasingly that they were falling even further behind in the wages race. The Social Contract might (although it might not) have helped to assuage some of these fears, or at least have offered a figleaf behind which the more moderate union leaders could have hidden. As it was, however, it was to assert a fairly naked truth to argue that, for many workers, years of pay restraint had brought few real benefits and not a few costs. Significantly, that year's Trades Union Congress passed by 7.1 million to 4.3 million votes a resolution calling for an immediate return to free collective bargaining. As Hugh Scanlon put it in proposing the motion, grassroots union members had made clear 'their revolt against any question of a Phase III'.[62]

The expiry of Phase III in the summer of 1978 ushered in a commitment by the government to limit pay increases to 5 per cent in Phase IV (1978–9). This time there was no question of union agreement. To most informed observers, the new limit seemed utterly unrealistic: if anything, now was the time to move away from incomes policies altogether or at least to relax the position somewhat. Instead, it was decided to go for a still tighter limit. Most people saw the new limit, though, as pre-election window-dressing.[63] Callaghan had lost his parliamentary majority in April 1976, and the position had worsened since then; given that another election would have to come before the end of 1979, it seemed that the autumn of 1978 would be as propitious a moment as any to go to the country. The government would demonstrate its toughness by stating the aim of 5 per cent, win the election, and then, once back in office, take a somewhat more sensible stance. This, certainly, appears to have been the view of delegates at the September 1978 TUC, who voted through with some enthusiasm a resolution pledging support for a Labour victory at the next election.[64] It seemed inconceivable, to most people, that there could be any other explanation: after all, surely Callaghan, of all people, was not trying to face the unions down as Wilson had tried to do over *In Place of Strife*?

There were, of course, other reasons for Callaghan's decision not to call an election. The legislation on devolution still had to be completed, and, given the massive time and effort that had been invested in it, it was understandable that the cabinet was reluctant to simply throw it all up in the air again. Callaghan was pessimistic about the prospects of Labour gaining an overall majority, even though it seemed that the party should return as the largest in parliament: and the thought of more years of the febrile atmosphere of minority government hardly appealed to a man in his late sixties. All the same, the government's decision to face the winter with a pay limit of 5 per cent signalled fairly clearly that it was to be on his ability to 'control' or 'tame' the unions that Callaghan was asking to be judged. The most favourable interpretation is probably that ministers hoped or expected that union leaders and members would see it as being in their own self-interest to toe the line. After all, the alternative – a rampantly right-wing Conservative Party under Margaret Thatcher, who had succeeded Heath in 1975 – seemed so patently unappealing that even a Labour government with a 5 per cent pay limit would seem a better option. Labour movement solidarity within a year of a general election would surely hold the line.

But this analysis was flawed. There had been plenty of signs of restlessness among union members, even when their leaders had tried to play the government's game. The leader of the biggest union, Jack Jones, had been an architect of the Social Contract. But he had no choice but to back away from the kind of 'one-way' incomes policies which came to dominate the scene after 1976. He retired in March 1978 and his successor at the TGWU, Moss Evans, was a good deal less favourably disposed towards incomes policies of any kind.[65] In addition, while it was axiomatic to ministers that ordinary trade unionists should prefer a Labour government, increasing numbers of rank and file members were not seeing it that way. As long ago as the early 1960s, Goldthorpe et al. had found, in their study of Luton, that car workers were voting Labour less through any kind of class solidarity than because they were acting 'instrumentally': that is, they saw a Labour government as being most likely to deliver a better standard of living.[66] By the late 1970s that was no longer the case, so far as many trade unionists were concerned, and Thatcher's rhetoric of self-reliance, tax cuts and the like did appeal to many members of the working class. Even those who had no great affection for Thatcher's Conservative Party might be prepared to vote for it; others – perhaps more – could not see such a great difference between the monetarism of Healey and that of Howe, Thatcher's Shadow Chancellor. They were not prepared to forego gains at this stage: indeed, the pessimism regarding Labour's electoral prospects represented by Callaghan's decision not to call an election might even have convinced some to push hard for a decent wage increase now, rather than wait for less propitious times under a Conservative government. It must also be said that ministers underestimated the extent to which some union leaders were prepared to go in securing decent wage increases for their members. And they overestimated those leaders' ability to deliver their rank and file even if they were willing to do so. In a sense, labour movement solidarity on the one hand and corporatism on the other blinded the government.

Even the party conference, which had, up to 1976, been squared on incomes policy, now joined in to kick the government. Callaghan's broadcast, announcing that there would be no election before 1979, was made on 7 September 1978. But within a month, the party conference had passed, by a two to one margin, a resolution which 'totally reject[ed] any wage restraint by whatever method ... and specifically the Government's 5 per cent' and called for a full return to free collective bargaining.[67]

This vote presaged a period of severe difficulty for Callaghan's administration. Motor workers at Ford were awarded 10 per cent by the company, and when the government tried to impose sanctions it was defeated in parliament, some of its own left-wingers voting with the opposition. The lorry drivers went on strike, with inevitable disruption of supplies to shops. And

146

public sector manual workers also struck, feeling that they had a very strong case for a substantial rise after years of limited increases on already poor wages. The winter of 1978–9 saw a dramatic falling away in the government's public opinion poll rating, as a 48–43 per cent lead over the Conservatives in November 1978 became a 33–53 per cent deficit by February 1979. And, crucially, it was given too little time to recover, since it was defeated in the House in March on a vote of confidence, and forced to call an election for 3 May 1979. The election was duly lost; it would be many years before Labour ministers and trade unionists would have the chance to face each other again.

Conclusions

The relationship between unions and the party had shown few signs of obvious strain in 1964. Trade unionism was still well-regarded by public opinion at large, and the government started brightly, with proposals likely to benefit unions and their members. But the period between 1964 and 1979 did not prove to be an easy time to be, in Wilson's phrase, 'the natural party of government'. The economic context, certainly by 1974, was as difficult as that faced by any peacetime twentieth-century British government, with the exception of the Attlee government after 1945. Rising, and then soaring, inflation, and mounting unemployment, were largely due to world trends over which the Labour Party's leaders could have little real influence. But they provided a dismal backdrop against which to work. Furthermore, changes within the party and the unions, and in industrial relations, all meant that quasi-corporatist 'solutions' favoured by the Labour leadership when in government had little real chance of success.

Indeed, the very fact of being in office for two significant periods, so close together and so long, induced immense tensions in the labour movement. By the early 1970s there was potential for conflict, which would almost certainly have been much worse had it not been for the shotgun remarriage which took place thanks to Heath's Industrial Relations Act. In the short term this worked to the party's benefit; it stimulated greater unity and policy coherence. But in the longer term it simply meant that the underlying problems festered, to erupt from autumn 1978 onwards. By 1979 there were those in both wings – party and unions – who had little regard for the difficulties of the other side, and who perhaps welcomed a showdown, particularly once Labour had been roundly defeated at the polls.

The results of all this for the labour movement were sombre. In the first place, divisions at every level provided the context in which Thatcher's rhetoric, until recently still seeming arch and uncertain, could flourish, and helped the Conservatives to win the 1979 election despite the real achievements of the Callaghan government. Secondly, the movement's problems meant that, once in opposition, irritations and hatreds could come to the surface in a severe bout of internal infighting from which neither the left nor the right of the party emerged with much credit. Ultimately, Labour's attempts to find a new *modus vivendi* with trade unionism in this period failed. Ironically but predictably, it was the party's attempts at 'corporatism' that aroused particular ire, not just from the renascent political right under Thatcher, but also from left-wing critics of the record of the Wilson and Callaghan governments of the 1960s and 1970s.[68] It would be a rather different Labour Party, and a much-changed trade union movement, that would come together again to try to reformulate government–union relations in the aftermath of the economic and legal changes of the Thatcher and Major years.

Notes

1.   TUC, *Report*, 1964, pp. 384, 386.
2.   TUC, *Report*, 1979, pp. 614–17.
3.   Calculated from figures given in Labour Party, *Annual Reports*.
4.   R. Jenkins, *What Matters Now* (1972), p. 117.
5.   A. Thorpe, *The British General Election of 1931* (Oxford, 1991), pp. 14–17, 88; N.B. Riddell, 'The second Labour government 1929–1931 and the wider Labour movement', unpublished PhD thesis, University of Exeter, 1994, pp. 13–89.
6.   V.L. Allen, *Trade Unions and the Government* (1960), pp. 290–1; J. Davis Smith, *The Attlee and Churchill Administrations and Industrial Unrest, 1945–1955* (Oxford, 1990), pp. 38–40; K.O. Morgan, *Labour in Power, 1945–1951* (Oxford, 1984), p. 80.
7.   R.M. Martin, *TUC: the growth of a pressure group, 1868–1976* (Oxford, 1980), p. 300.
8.   P. Dorey, *The Conservative Party and the Trade Unions* (1995), pp. 59–60; J.A. Lincoln, 'Unions and the law', in A. Seldon (ed.), *Rebirth of Britain* (1964), pp. 115–23.
9.   F.W.S. Craig (ed.), *British General Election Manifestos, 1900–1974* (Chichester, 1975), p. 272.
10.   *The National Plan* (Cmnd. 2764, 1965).
11.   Ibid., p. 65.
12.   Confederation of Shipbuilding and Engineering Unions, *Report of the Thirtieth Annual Meeting* (1965), pp. 17–18.
13.   TUC, *Report*, 1965, pp. 473, 496.
14.   Labour Party, *Annual Report*, 1965, pp. 229, 231, 247.
15.   Ibid., pp. 238–9.
16.   R. Crossman, *The Diaries of a Cabinet Minister* (3 vols, 1975), I, p. 316, 1 Sept. 1965.
17.   A motion condemning the move at the party conference was only defeated by 3,635,000 votes to 2,540,000: Labour Party, *Annual Report*, 1965, p. 247.

18. Crossman, *Diaries*, I, p. 321, 12 Sept. 1965.
19. R. Price, *Labour in British Society* (1986), pp. 215–16.
20. K. Middlemas, *Power, Competition and the State* (3 vols., 1986–91), II, p. 223.
21. R. Taylor, *The Trade Union Question in British Politics: government and unions since 1945* (1993), pp. 381–2.
22. P. Ziegler, *Wilson: the authorised life* (1993), pp. 251–2.
23. L. Minkin, *The Labour Party Conference: a study in the politics of intra-party democracy* (1978), p. 322.
24. Ibid., p. 297.
25. Royal Commission on Trade Unions and Employers' Associations, 1965–1968, *Report* (Cmnd. 3623, 1968).
26. Ibid., p. 204.
27. Ibid.
28. B. Castle, *Fighting All The Way* (1993), p. 413.
29. Ibid., p. 416.
30. D. McKie, 'By-elections of the Wilson government', in C. Cook and J. Ramsden (eds), *By-Elections in British Politics* (2nd edn, 1997), pp. 180, 191.
31. *In Place of Strife: a policy for industrial relations* (Cmnd. 3888, 1969).
32. A contemporary account is P. Jenkins, *The Battle of Downing Street* (1970); see also L. Panitch, *Social Democracy and Labour Militancy: the Labour Party, the trade unions and incomes policy, 1945–1974* (Cambridge, 1976), pp. 171–203; C. Ponting, *Breach of Promise: Labour in power, 1964–1970* (1989), pp. 350–71; B. Pimlott, *Harold Wilson* (1992), pp. 528–44. For a trenchant critique, see D. Coates, *The Labour Party and the Struggle for Socialism* (Cambridge, 1975), pp. 126–7.
33. Panitch, *Social Democracy and Labour Militancy*, p. 179.
34. Ibid.; J.W. Durcan et. al., *Strikes in Post-War Britain: a study of stoppages of work due to industrial disputes, 1946–73* (1983), p. 377.
35. Jenkins, *The Battle of Downing Street, passim*.
36. Panitch, *Social Democracy and Labour Militancy*, p. 179. For grassroots opposition to the proposed legislation, see J. McIlroy, 'Notes on the Communist Party and industrial politics' in this volume, and J. McIlroy and A. Campbell, 'Organizing the militants: the Liaison Committee for the Defence of Trade Unions, 1966–79', *British Journal of Industrial Relations*, 37, 1, 1999.
37. T. Benn, *Office Without Power: diaries 1968–1972* (1988), p. 187, 17 June 1969.
38. Durcan et. al., *Strikes in Post-War Britain*, p. 160.
39. D. Healey, *The Time of My Life* (1989), p. 341.
40. P. Whitehead, *The Writing on the Wall: Britain in the seventies* (1985), pp. 72–9.
41. Labour Party, *Annual Report*, 1971, pp. 168, 187.
42. Labour Party, *Annual Report*, 1972, pp. 122, 133.
43. Labour Party, *Annual Report*, 1973, p. 85.
44. TUC, *Report*, 1972, p. 105; L. Minkin, *The Contentious Alliance: trade un-*

ions and the Labour Party (Edinburgh, 1992), pp. 118–19; Minkin, *The Labour Party Conference*, pp. 337–8; Middlemas, *Power, Competition and the State*, II, pp. 372–3.

45. M. Hatfield, *The House the Left Built: inside Labour policy-making 1970–75* (1978), pp. 112–31; Whitehead, *Writing*, p. 118.
46. M. Jones, *Michael Foot* (1994), pp. 350–1.
47. Ibid., p. 451.
48. Taylor, *Trade Union Question in British Politics*, p. 228.
49. Ibid., p. 231.
50. D Coates, *Labour in Power? A study of the Labour government, 1974–1979* (1980), p. 82.
51. M.W. Kirby, 'Supply-side management', in N. F. R. Crafts and N. Woodward (eds), *The British Economy since 1945* (Oxford, 1991), p. 256.
52. Healey, *Time of My Life*, p. 396.
53. N. Woodward, 'Inflation', in Crafts and Woodward, *The British Economy since 1945*, pp. 203–5; P. Ormerod, 'Incomes policy', in M. Artis and D. Cobham (eds), *Labour's Economic Policies 1974–1979* (Manchester, 1991), pp. 56–72.
54. D. Porter, 'Government and the economy', in R. Coopey and N. Woodward, *Britain in the 1970s: the troubled economy* (1996), p. 46.
55. Price, *Labour in British Society*, p. 223.
56. Ibid., p. 238.
57. TUC, *Report*, 1976, pp. 521, 523, 541.
58. Healey, *Time of My Life*, pp. 427, 423.
59. Labour Party, *Annual Report*, 1975, pp. 166, 148, 150, 167.
60. Labour Party, *Annual Report*, 1976, pp. 137, 155.
61. Labour Party, *Annual Report*, 1977, pp. 164–5, 182.
62. TUC, *Report*, 1977, pp. 467, 486.
63. E. Dell, *A Hard Pounding: politics and economic crisis, 1974–6* (Oxford, 1991), p. 285.
64. TUC, *Report*, 1978, pp. 523, 526.
65. J. Callaghan, *Time and Chance* (1987), p. 520.
66. J.H. Goldthorpe et al., *The Affluent Worker: political attitudes and behaviour* (Cambridge, 1968), esp. pp. 79–80.
67. Labour Party, *Annual Report*, 1978, pp. 230, 214.
68. T. Benn, *Arguments for Socialism* (1979), esp. pp. 144–6.

CHAPTER SIX

The Conservative Party and the Trade Unions

Andrew Taylor

Between 1964 and 1979 there was no dramatic shift in the Conservative Party's attitude to the unions. When the Conservatives left office in 1964 they were convinced of the need to 'do something' about the unions and that this something required the legislative reformation of the voluntarist tradition of non-intervention in industrial relations. Between October 1964 and April 1965 the Conservative Party adopted a legislative solution to the union problem and this remained the basis of subsequent policy. The failure of Heath's Industrial Relations Act did not lead to a fundamental reappraisal of the legal approach but rather to reconsideration of how change was to be achieved. After the disasters of 1970–4 the party élites also recognized that law would have to be backed by increased state capacity to resist trade union disruption, coupled with a willingness to use this power. The Conservative analysis of the unions under both Heath and Thatcher was based therefore on a substantial degree of common ground. Their different responses reflected the reactions of party élites to changes in the political environment after 1964.[1]

The Conservatives and the union problem

Robert Taylor's view that the Conservatives 'began to abandon their previous reluctance' to contemplate union reform after their 1964 election defeat is a common one.[2] In fact the Conservatives were re-thinking policy well before their defeat, *A Giant's Strength* (1958) was the first Conservative attempt since the General Strike at formulating a radical programme of reform. It called for pre-strike tribunals of enquiry, the withdrawal of immunities from anyone who struck while the tribunal was sitting, a Restrictive Practices Court, and the vigorous regulation of the closed shop but proposed no action on compulsory secret ballots or the political levy.[3] This programme was largely based on a reaction against Sir Walter Monckton's policies at the Ministry of Labour between October 1951 and November 1955. Monckton had been instructed by Churchill not to antagonise the unions. In more than following these instructions, Monckton became identified as the arch-appeaser of the unions.[4]

By 1962 there was considerable interest in reform in the Conservative Research Department (CRD), the Ministry of Labour and the party (in and out of Parliament). However this was tempered by political caution.[5] The CRD argued for an initiative similar to *The Industrial Charter* (1947), which sought to convince the unions and their members of the Conservative Party's sympathy for them and encourage cooperation in industry. The resulting statement, *A Tory Look at Industrial Relations*, which was intended to foster a greater sense of security amongst workers, led to the Contracts of Employment Act (1963) and the Redundancy Payments Act (1965). CRD's Industrial Relations Committee was revived in November 1962. In May 1963 it issued a report advocating that unofficial strikers should lose social security benefits and that pre-strike ballots should be introduced. But it argued that the TUC should be encouraged to impose order on the union movement. The closed shop would remain legal but the report suggested that the Ministry of Labour become a Ministry of Employment promoting good industrial relations and an active labour market policy, in return for union acceptance of compulsory conciliation and pre-strike cooling-off periods. If the TUC did not respond, then pressure from public opinion might be used to justify more extensive legislation.[6] Reflecting this shifting mood, and worried by a loss of public esteem and the ETU scandal, George Woodcock, the TUC General Secretary, famously asked the 1962 TUC, 'What are we here for?'[7]

The 1961 Conservative Conference had rejected union legislation but party opinion had now shifted decisively in favour of action on the unions.[8] John Hare, the Minister of Labour, warned that unless the unions put their house in order, they risked legislation.[9] Harold Macmillan's observation on incomes policy: 'colleagues are all confused – so is the Party in the House. We must try to work out something rather more imaginative than we had done so far', might have applied equally to union policy.[10] The Cabinet recognized that *Rookes v Barnard* undermined the union immunities under the 1906 Act and the Ministry of Labour was attracted to the proposal for a wide-ranging inquiry into the industrial relations system, which would also appeal to the party. The TUC were demanding action on *Rookes v Barnard* and the Cabinet believed the TUC's support could be won if any inquiry embraced the employers' associations.[11]

The TUC would not cooperate before a general election and the government believed it was unwise to appoint a Royal Commission in the face of TUC hostility. There had been no enquiry into the unions since the early 1900s. Public opinion would support an inquiry but union consent was politically essential.[12] The government's hope that 'the law in relation to trade unions should be reviewed in an atmosphere free from political controversy' was unrealistic. Nevertheless, a Royal Commission would appeal to the party, public opinion and moderate union opinion, so the Cabinet felt able 'to accept the risk that their proposal might be misrepresented as an attempt to undermine the industrial power of the unions'.[13]

Ian Macleod confessed he 'felt frankly schizophrenic' about legislation on unofficial strikes: wanting action but fearing the political consequences. Rab Butler expressed similar doubts about the proposals in *A Tory Look at Industrial Relations*. Macleod agreed with Butler that any suggestion of compulsion 'would lose us the backing in the trade unions upon which our victory at a General Election ultimately depended'. Hare concluded,

> legislation would cut across the present policy of trying to bring about a general improvement in industrial relations on a voluntary basis ... it would end the prospect of further progress [and] cause a head-on collision with the trade union movement. It might lead them to withhold their cooperation over the who'': field of relations with the government and withdraw from the [National Economic Development Council].[14]

Macleod and Robert Carr accepted the need for the reform of industrial relations law but there were no plans or even an agreed approach.[15] Even Macmillan was forced to concede that the unions were structurally and politically incapable of engaging in a stable, long-term political exchange with government.[16] By the end of his premiership, Macmillan was lamenting the government's powerlessness in the face of union militancy.[17] Despite the Advisory Committee on Policy's (ACP) recommendation that the 1964 manifesto, *Prosperity with a Purpose*, include a 'statement on trade union law', party leaders refused to go beyond calling for 'an early inquiry'.

By the early 1960s there was a widespread perception that industrial relations and union behaviour needed attention. There was a developing, but not a general, consensus that the system of law based on the 1906 Act was in urgent need of reform. Whilst the TUC was willing to consider legal changes, it remained totally opposed to legal regulation of the unions' activities. Similarly, the twin economic policy goals of full employment and economic growth were increasingly perceived to be threatened by a collective bargaining system which promoted wage inflation. There was a consensus that the only response was incomes policy, but again the unions were deeply and instinctively hostile to statutory wage regulation. By the time the Conservatives left office in 1964 the unions were perceived by many to be a developing threat to political and economic stability.

1964–70: the Conservative adoption of legislative reform

Only eleven days after the general election, Sir Alec Douglas Home appointed Heath to chair the ACP, with a wide-ranging brief to reappraise party policy. Between 1964 and 1970 three groups worked on industrial relations and trade union reform. This effort enjoyed Heath's personal support. He had a vision of unions drawn 'out of their outdated posture of obstructiveness and persuade them to become partners in industry on the German or American model. He tried constantly to assure the unions that his intentions – and hence the intentions of the Tory party – towards them were friendly'.[18]

The Trade Union Law and Practice Group appointed by Heath made very rapid progress, issuing its interim report in April 1965, five months after its inception, and its final report in September. This report represented a decisive break with the voluntarist approach of post-war Conservatism, the only dissent coming from those who felt they might be attempting too much too quickly. There was, however, a serious weakness at the heart of the statement which attracted little attention at the time: what was the political objective of reform? From one angle, the recommendations sought to strengthen the authority of trade union executives over their members in order to impose discipline within industrial relations so that unions could engage in corporate bargains with government. Another strand in the report suggested that the purpose of reform was to transform the unions' environment to such a degree that their ability to disrupt the economy would be undermined.

When Heath was elected leader, he replaced Joseph Godber with Sir Keith Joseph as front bench spokesman for employment and Joseph became chairman of the study group. An important shift in this period was a new emphasis on withdrawal from incomes policy and the promotion of labour market efficiency, but it was suggested that the powers of the Registrar of Friendly Societies (who exercised light supervision of union rules) should be increased to cover internal union procedures and the legal enforcement of collective agreements. If workers refused to abide by these agreements their unions would have to discipline them, if necessary by expulsion, and failure to do so would risk fines. Special Industrial Courts would be created to deal with procedural disputes and appeals from the Registrar of Friendly Societies (who exercised a light supervision of union rules and finances). Many of these proposals derived from the established traditions of industrial relations and government–union relations, but their tone was different, as was the emphasis on legal remedies, which was coupled with a moral critique of union power over both individuals and the economy. The proposals were enshrined in the policy document, *Putting Britain Right Ahead* (September 1965), which set out Heath's new style of Conservatism.

The 1966 manifesto, *Action Not Words*, contained a commitment to legal reform proposing legally enforceable collective agreements, a Registrar for union rules, an Industrial Court, action on restrictive labour practices, and action to prevent intimidation. When Carr replaced Joseph as front bench employment spokesman in 1967, the party's basic policy and intention to legislate were clear and one month before the publication of the Donovan Report the Conservatives published *Fair Deal At Work*.[19] This document advocated a legal framework to ensure unions operated in the public interest and provided a clear definition of rights and duties in industrial relations. It proposed a sixty-day cooling-off period for certain strikes, the registration of unions, and a more precise definition of a trades dispute. Union-recruitment procedures, relations with members, collective bargaining, and industrial action would be regulated by new legal institutions. A Registrar would approve union procedures and rules, and the legislation would be policed by a new National Industrial Relations Court (NIRC), with the powers of the High Court. The purpose of these proposals was to strengthen union leaders against shop-floor militancy. Robert Carr preferred a piecemeal approach as politically safer. But he was ultimately committed to radical reform and by the time he became responsible for the policy it was too late to undertake major revisions.[20] Disquiet remained within the party élite as to the reaction of the unions, but this was counterbalanced by the perception that union reform was electorally popular, especially after the fiasco of Labour's own reform proposals, *In Place of Strife*, in 1969.[21]

Instead of trying to make the system work better, others, such as Timothy Raison, argued for an assault on the 'One-Nation-Spirit-of-Dunkirk' and its obsession with stability. Moncktonism might have been appropriate for the early 1950s but was no longer so. A 'firmer, but not unfair' approach to the unions, involving the law, was, he argued, now needed. Strikes, the closed shop and collective agreements would all benefit from codification and greater flexibility. Ideally the changes would be negotiated with the unions, 'but if agreement is impossible they must be achieved without it. Again this may arouse accusations of class warfare, but that cannot be helped – the sores in our economy must not be left to fester indefinitely, even if it hurts to cure them'. This also entailed abandoning incomes policy as the exemplar of the illusory search for harmony and equality.[22]

The reaction against Macmillan's controversial drift towards corporatism was clearly reflected in the 1964 and 1966 manifestos as well as the 1965 policy statement *Putting Britain Right Ahead*. Inflation had to be controlled but Conservative and Labour experience with incomes policy, together with the growing neo-liberal rhetoric, pointed to the fallibility of direct state intervention. The Shadow Cabinet split over incomes policy with Reginald Maudling in favour and Macleod (no crude economic liberal) opposed largely for reasons of party management.[23] Initially Heath was agnostic (personally and politically he was closer to Maudling) but became anti-incomes policy as Labour's difficulties increased, though without articulating clearly how a Conservative government would handle inflation. For most of the period in opposition Heath strove to avoid opting for either Maudling's or Macleod's position. The consequence was, despite the ringing delaration in the 1970 manifesto that 'We utterly reject the philosophy of wage control', the Conservatives simply 'failed to prepare for what turned out to be the central issue, economic management'. The hope was that *Fair Deal At Work* would provide the answer by reducing the unions' monopoly power through restrictive legislation rather than formal wage restraint.[24] There was a contradiction between the proposals for a radical shift in trade union law and the reluctance to sanction the abandonment of incomes policy and neo-corporatism on the one hand, and using the threat of unemployment to control inflation on the other. The latter raised sensitive political questions of acceptability and enforceability: public opinion would not accept unemployment as an economic regulator whereas it approved of legal reform (see Table 6.1). It is worth stressing at this point that the much discussed conference held at the Selsdon Park Hotel in January 1970 which was seen as ushering in a new, harder line, did not represent the articulation of a clearly worked out neo-liberal political project. In fact, it left many issues – most importantly incomes policy – unresolved.[25]

The 1964 manifesto had contained a vague intention to inquire into the union problem and that of 1966 a commitment to legal reform. This was reiterated by the 1970 manifesto, *A Better Tomorrow*. It stated that a Conservative government 'will introduce a comprehensive [Bill] in the first Session of the new Parliament. It will provide a proper framework of law within which improved relationships between management, men and unions can develop'. TUC cooperation was welcomed, but as a complement to, not a substitute for, legal reform. The Bill's purpose was 'to strengthen the unions and their official leadership' and control 'irresponsible action by unofficial minorities'. By 1970, therefore, Conservative policy remained essentially that of 1966, modified only by the deterioration of union–government relations under Labour.

1970–74, crisis and conflict: the Heath government

The Conservatives came into office proclaiming a radical new departure in policies for dealing with the unions. Legal reform would modernize the unions and the rejection of incomes policy, coupled with a non-interventionary industrial policy, would induce the unions to behave responsibly in preserving full employment and improving living standards.

The Industrial Relations Act

The Industrial Relations Bill was one of the cornerstones of Heath's 'quiet revolution'.[26] The decision to go for one bill was justified on the grounds that reform was urgent and there was great pressure from the party. The TUC was opposed in principle to the proposals and bitterly resented the absence of consultation which it regarded as a serious breach of constitutional proprieties.

Vic Feather had been told by Heath there would be genuine consultation 'and that its proposals will be susceptible to change in response to reasoned argument ... I hope though that the document will not look anything like ... *Fair Deal At Work*'. The TUC would have to once more, as it had with Wilson

156

and Castle, undertake 'the tedious process of educating the politicians about industry'. Although the TUC was not seeking confrontation, Feather believed that if 'the Movement is forced into such a situation ... They will find a TUC which in a hundred years has seen thirty Governments come and go and which will see yet another thirty vanish from the scene'.[27] At a meeting between Robert Carr and the TUC's Finance and General Purposes Committee on 13 October, the TUC were told that that the Bill's 'eight pillars' were non-negotiable. This confirmed their worst fears.[28] Some of the Bill's proposals were welcomed by the TUC as a basis for voluntary agreement but they opposed legislation. Their case was that the Bill would undermine union authority, restrict individual freedom and introduce political dogma into the workplace. The government's refusal to negotiate was condemned as a breach of thirty years of constitutional practice which suggested that Heath's real intention was politically to marginalise the unions.[29] Feather described the Bill as 'a major challenge to the trade union movement'. Overall the voluntary system was working well and the 'Government's proposals [were] oppressive, irrelevant and positively dangerous'. Feather offered TUC and union cooperation in improving industrial relations 'provided that it is a part of an overall plan for faster economic growth and that it covers profits, prices, dividends and the distribution of wealth'.[30]

The Consultative Document was published on 5 October 1970. The Bill itself, (193 clauses, 8 schedules and 97 amendments) was published on 3 December and had its second reading on 14–15 December. The committee stage lasted from 18 to 24 February 1971, and there were 63 divisions at the report stage. Only 39 of 288 clauses were debated before a guillotine was imposed. It received the Royal Assent on 5 August. This speed has been identified by one its authors, Geoffrey Howe, as a major weakness, given the complexity and sensitivity of the Bill. However, justifying this timetable the Cabinet claimed an unequivocal electoral mandate and public support (see Table 6.1). They pointed out that the proposals had been known and intensively discussed since the publication of *Fair Deal At Work*. Their first decisive action stemmed from within the party and evidenced government intentions to act resolutely in addressing the country's problems.[31] The TUC's response was determined by a Special Congress (18 March 1971) at the Fairfield Hall, Croydon. Unions were advised not to register under the Act, not to enter legally binding agreements, not to use any of the right enshrined in the Act, and to refuse to recognize the National Industrial Relations Court. This advice was approved by 5 million to 4.2 million votes, and it subsequently became mandatory at the 1971 TUC where Congress rejected the platform's advice that its proposals remain persuasive. TUC leaders were, in effect, pushed into a more militant posture by their activists. The 1972 Congress suspended 32 unions with a membership of some 500,000 and a year later expelled 20 covering about 4 per cent of the TUC's affiliated membership. Non-registration severely circumscribed the Act's effectiveness, and its implementation and enforcement became dangerously politicized with the creation of the NIRC which raised the possibility of trade unionists being imprisoned.

In March 1972 the NIRC ordered the TGWU to stop 'blacking' (an 'unfair industrial practice' under the 1971 Act) Heaton Transport's lorries as part of the dockers' campaign against containerization. Thus began the dramatic industrial, legal and political entanglements which led to warrants for the imprisonment of five dockers – the 'Pentonville Five' – being issued on 21 July. Consequent widespread strike action resulted in the intervention by the Official Solicitor which led, in a humiliating climb down, to the release of the dockers on 26 July, despite the fact that they had not purged their contempt.

The Engineers also fell foul of the 1971 Act. In late 1972 James Goad appealed against his expulsion, and therefore loss of employment, from his AUEW branch. Unlike the TGWU, the AUEW refused to recognize the NIRC and was fined £5,000 and then £50,000 for contempt. When the AEU continued to refuse to pay, its assets were sequestered resulting in a series of one-day protest strikes. In late 1973 the AEU was ordered to end its boycott of Con-Mech, a non-union firm. Again it refused and was fined £75,000, the fine being paid by an anonymous group of businessmen anxious to avoid a national engineering strike.

Even when the Act was invoked and its procedures followed, it produced unexpected results. In April 1972 an overtime ban and work-to-rule on the railways led Maurice Macmillan, Carr's successor as Employment Secretary, to ask for a twenty-one day cooling-off period under the Act. The NIRC granted fourteen days which the NUR observed but when this came to an end it reimposed the overtime ban and work-to-rule; Macmillan returned to the NIRC and asked for a compulsory secret ballot to test opinion. The result was that 80 per cent of those who voted backed the union, the leadership's position was significantly strengthened and the episode culminated in a 13 per cent pay increase. The cooling-off and balloting provisions were never to be used again and, by the summer of 1972, the Industrial Relations Act was effectively crippled.[42]

The Conservatives' 1970 manifesto rejected incomes policy (except in the public sector) but this was negated by events. The power workers' overtime ban in late autumn 1970 produced power cuts for which government had no response (although a State of Emergency was declared). Lord Wilberforce's report legitimized surrender. Although Wilberforce did not concede the power workers' full claim, his report crippled Heath's public sector incomes policy of 'N – 1' – in which each offer to successive bargaining groups was reduced by 1 per cent – despite the defeat of the postal workers in a six-week strike in 1971. Private sector employers paid little attention to Heath's exhortations for restraint and by the end of 1971 wage inflation was nudging 20 per cent. These controversies were typical of government–union relations of the mid-1960s to early-1970s. But the situation was transformed by the eruption of the NUM onto the scene in the Autumn of 1971.

The first miners' strike

A grassroots rebellion in 1969 in reaction to stagnating pay and job losses culminated in the mineworkers voting by a small majority in favour of industrial action in support of a pay claim in the autumn of 1970. But union rules called for a two-thirds majority for a strike and this fuelled pressure for change. This came together at the July 1971 NUM Conference which approved a 47 per cent pay claim and called for a strike ballot. The majority needed for strike action was reduced to 55 per cent. The resurgence of the NUM was unexpected and ministers did not regard the mineworkers as a threat.[33] As Carr later admitted: 'our intelligence about the strength of opinion within the miners' union generally was not as good as it should have been ... We just didn't know the miners. They hadn't been to St James's Square, the old home of the Ministry of Labour, for nearly fifty years'.[34] The NUM's President, Joe Gormley, although an orthodox but canny right-winger, realized the direction of opinion in the NUM and, unlike his predecessors, was not afraid of industrial action. At pit level, a new generation of activists were emerging who regarded industrial action as the miners' best and only weapon.

Press opinion was unanimous that a miners' strike would have little or no effect other than to close more pits and on an 86 per cent turnout the NUM secured a bare 55.8 per cent vote in favour of strike action. The NUM did have, however, a number of advantages. Firstly, despite coal's decline, the interdependence of electricity generation and coal had actually increased. As the power workers had demonstrated, a highly centralized power generation and transmission system was vulnerable to disruption. This vulnerability was amplified by the level of coal stocks which were not only low but in the wrong locations. Secondly, the unofficial strikes of 1969 and 1970 saw a new tactic: the mass, mobile picket. Stopping coal production was not a problem so the mass picket would be used to blockade the distribution of coal to power stations, many of which were located outside the coalfields. There was a widespread feeling in the coalfields (disguised by the narrow majority) that the time had come to take a stand. Finally, public opinion (in contrast to a critical attitude to the unions in general) was sympathetic towards the miners.

The NUM's strategy was designed to increase pressure on the NCB and government (an overtime ban began in November), maintain unity and keep the support of public opinion. Once the strike began, however, the NUM fought a short, sharp campaign which benefited from the support of transport workers (especially railway workers), who were instructed by the TUC to observe NUM picket lines. The strike, which began on 8 January 1972, was devastatingly effective, causing a major crisis which shook the political establishment severely. Brendon Sewill, a Treasury special adviser, draws a vivid picture of Whitehall in this period:

> The lights went out and everybody said that the country would disintegrate in a week. All the civil servants rushed around saying, 'Perhaps we ought to activate the nuclear underground shelters and the centres of regional government, because there'll be no electricity and there'll be riots in the streets. The sewage will overflow and there'll be epidemics'. The result of all that was that the government had to give way and pay up to the miners.[35]

The mass picket at the Saltley coke depot in Birmingham cruelly exposed the state's vulnerability. Neither the police nor politicians had experience of dealing with such a crisis. Furthermore, the police lacked the political support and technical means for confrontation with the NUM. Maudling, the Home Secretary, wrote in his memoirs: 'I remember when during the miners' strike pickets threatened to close [Saltley] ... the then Chief Constable of Birmingham assured me that only over his dead body would they so succeed. I felt constrained to ring him the next day after it happened to enquire after his health!' Given the Chief Constable's tactical situation – 800 police facing 15,000 pickets – it is difficult to see what other option he had, a point conceded by Maudling: 'Some of my colleagues', he wrote, 'asked me afterwards, why I had not sent in troops to support the Police, and I remember asking them one simple question, "If they had been sent in, should they have gone in with their rifles loaded or unloaded?" Either course could have been disastrous'.[36] On 8 February a State of Emergency was declared. But the damage had been done and the following day Carr summoned the NUM for negotiations. The NUM, scenting victory, stood firm on its demands. The government had no option other than surrender. On 11 February Lord Wilberforce was again called upon to work his special magic. Douglas Hurd wrote in his diary, 'The Government now wandering vainly over the battlefield looking for someone to surrender to – and being massacred all the time'.[37] Wilberforce conceded the NUM's case, recommending a 20 per cent pay rise phased over sixteen months which the NUM's Executive rejected by 10 votes to 15. Subsequently at 10 Downing Street further concessions were wrung from a humiliated Cabinet and on 28 February (the day the Industrial Relations Act's final provisions came into force) the strike ended.

The return to corporatism

The Cabinet resolved to use its defeat to re-establish relations with the TUC. This shift was underpinned by the inexorable rise of unemployment towards the symbolic one million mark. The 27 per cent awarded to the NUM did not open the floodgates to wage inflation, the public sector average was 9 per cent, the private sector 13 per cent. The period between the end of the miners' strike and the summer was dominated by the Industrial Relations Act but this was speedily followed by a dramatic switch to tripartite politics of a type undertaken by no previous government.[38] Jack Jones, the TGWU General Secretary, found Heath 'not unsympathetic', believing 'he genuinely wanted to get on with working people'.[39] Vic Feather was convinced that Heath could be won round, largely as a result of participating in a year-long series of meetings under the ambit of the NEDC with the objective of working out a common approach to the economy. Heath's desire for a new start and these talks enabled Feather to persuade the TUC to engage in the tripartite Downing Street-Chequers talks.[40]

Neither Feather nor Heath appreciated fully the political limits under which the other operated. Feather was faced by considerable suspicion from union leaders such as Jack Jones and Hugh Scanlon and downright hostility from other General Council members. He could not guarantee to deliver the unions and misinterpreted the extent to which Heath could ditch policies in pursuit of an agreement. Equally, Heath felt strongly that he could not be seen to be negotiating with the TUC on policies which had received an electoral mandate and to which the party was committed.[41] Nevertheless, Jones later wrote: 'No Prime Minister, either before or since, could compare with Ted Heath in the efforts he made to establish a spirit of camaraderie with trade union leaders and to offer an attractive package which might satisfy large numbers of work-people'.[42] However, the Industrial Relations Act and the TUC's insistence on statutory price control and voluntary pay restraint remained insuperable obstacles to an agreement. Jones blamed the breakdown on Heath's sudden reversion to a hostile and rigid attitude. Heath's biographer judged that the talks broke down because the Prime Minister recognized that an agreement would not be forthcoming and that it was his duty to impose a solution in the national interest. Feather's biographer concluded, 'the division was not between two habits of mind or two modes of life. It was a division between men answerable to different constituencies'.[43] On 2 November the talks broke down and on 6 November Heath announced a statutory price and wage freeze which led Enoch Powell to ask Heath if he had taken leave of his senses.

Heath's incomes policy was divided into three stages: Stage 1 was a 90-day statutory freeze on wages, prices, dividends and rents. The policy was administered by a Price Commission and a Pay Board. Stage 2, introduced in January 1973 was to last until November and provided for a maximum pay rise of 4 per cent plus £1.00 per week and an average upper annual limit of £250. Heath's attempt to secure union cooperation in Stage 2 failed but he continued to try and win their cooperation for Stage 3 which was regarded as the most critical phase of the policy. Despite the unions' hostility there was no offensive against Stage 1 or 2 but incomes rose faster than anticipated.[44] Stage 3 was to last from the autumn of 1973 for twelve months.

The main difficulty was expected to come from the NUM which had approved demands for pay increases ranging from 22 to 47 per cent at its July Conference. On 16 July Heath and William Armstrong (Cabinet Secretary and Heath's main adviser) secretly met Gormley to find a means whereby Stage 3 could be made acceptable to the NUM. Gormley did not negotiate but suggested a way out, telling Heath and Armstrong that the NUM would not only seek money but improvements in unsocial hours payments. 'As far as I was concerned', Gormley claimed, 'I had given them the biggest possible hint, because they turned to each other and said, "We never thought of that. We never thought of that at all"'.[45] Heath and Armstrong believed they had a deal. But Gormley saw it rather as an understanding. In any case, he could not guarantee to deliver the NUM's Executive and much depended on the course of negotiations with the Coal Board. Nevertheless, Stage 3 was written with the NUM in mind.[46]

The policy was launched with great pomp by Heath at Lancaster House on 8 October 1973 and was greeted with open hostility by the TUC General Council. Ominously the Electrical Power Engineers' Association banned overtime in response to the non-implementation of an agreement which fell foul of Stage 2 and on 1 September the NUM had presented its claim, rejecting an NCB offer of about 13 per cent and imposing an overtime ban from 12 November. On 13 November the government declared a State of Emergency giving it wide powers over electricity use.

The second miners' strike and the fall of Heath

Gormley was willing to work for a revised settlement given the political sensitivity of the dispute, whilst the outbreak of the Yom Kippur War in the Middle East on 6 October transformed the political-economic environment and the economic position of coal, giving the government a plausible excuse to declare the NUM a 'special case'. Some ministers and civil servants supported this. Others argued the government had to stand firm behind Stage 3, otherwise the inflationary floodgates would be opened and government authority would collapse, precipitating a governability crisis.

Securing the NUM's adherence was made more difficult because in public the policy gave no hint that the NUM was a special case. Gormley saw this as a critical failure but more serious were the NCB's negotiating tactics. On 10 October the NCB made its full (and final) offer amounting to about 16 per cent, the maximum allowed under Stage 3. Hurd was aghast as the negotiations,

> showed how little had been learned about the tactical handling of public sector disputes. Once again the crucial opening rounds were in the hands of the nationalized board. Once again the Board decided to give everything at once ... Once again the [NUM] accustomed to negotiate, rejected this first offer as wholly inadequate.

Similarly, Robert Carr described the NCB's tactics as 'most unfortunate' because 'they put everything into the shop window at the beginning, and they had an unusually long bargaining period to get through [they] left no room for negotiation and bargaining ...'.[47] On 13 December further emergency measures were introduced, notably a three-day week from the end of the month which was designed firstly to impress on the country and the unions the seriousness of the situation and shock them into settling under Stage 3 thereby isolating the miners from the unions and public opinion; and second, to conserve fuel stocks. Nevertheless, the government was full of foreboding:

> The Conservative Party, its Leader, its Ministers, its backbenchers and its supporters in the country had already been beaten on this very ground in 1972. We had most dreaded, beyond anything else, a further engagement with the miners. Yet here we were being manoeuvred once again towards the same fatal field, still littered with relics of the last defeat.[48]

The NUM Executive met the full Cabinet and Heath held out the hope that the Pay Board's enquiry into relativities would produce more money, coupled with a long-term investment plan in the coal industry. Armstrong remembered an NUM member asking Heath "'Why can't you pay us for the coal what you are willing to pay the Arabs for oil?" And although it was put in that way, not put as an economist would put it, that was bang on the economic nose ... And the Prime Minister really had no answer'.[49] When the NUM Executive rejected Heath's offer by 18 votes to 5 (Gormley was in favour of putting it to the members) the suspicion, never far from the surface, that the NUM was engaged in a political crusade to destroy the Heath government grew rapidly. Nevertheless, Heath continued to pursue a settlement, bringing Willie Whitelaw back from Ulster to replace Maurice Macmillan as Employment Secretary, largely because of his negotiating skills. But as Whitelaw later admitted, the expectations placed in him were impossible to realize as he was exhausted from his Ulster posting and Gormley made it clear in a confidential meeting that the NUM would not settle under Stage 3. If the NUM was made an exception he could probably swing his Executive. The Cabinet could not agree.[50]

There were other attempts to find a settlement. The most important was the TUC offer, made by Sir Sidney Greene of the NUR to Anthony Barber (Chancellor of the Exchequer) at the NEDC on 9 January, that if the NUM was made a special case, given the changed circumstances, other unions would not cite this in their own pay negotiations. Barber consulted Armstrong (who was at the meeting) and rejected the offer out of hand. There is some confusion as to whether Barber consulted Heath. But Campbell concludes Heath understandably doubted the TUC's ability to deliver the unions, especially the power workers. Even if correct (which it probably was), Heath could have used the TUC's offer to strengthen his position by challenging the TUC to deliver.[51] On 23 January 1974 the NUM Executive voted by 16 to 10 to ballot its members on strike action. There was an 81 per cent 'Yes' vote and the strike was called for 9 February. The NUM Executive subsequently rejected a personal appeal from Heath and a final meeting between Heath and the TUC produced nothing.

From mid-November 1973 the possibility of a general election had been discussed sporadically within the government. In early December Hurd warned:

> It would be a highly charged and violent election, and it would of course be impossible to confine it to any one issue. The Government's election campaign would only be credible if it included proposals which would bring to an end to the industrial action. It is not easy to see what these would be.

Until early-February 1974 Heath did not want a general election as he feared the polarization of politics. But on 7 February he called the election for 28 February, not to defeat the NUM but to secure a new mandate to meet the economic crisis.[52] Whatever Heath's intention, the February 1974 election has gone down in history as the 'Who Governs?' election.

At the heart of the Conservative manifesto, *Putting Britain First*, was an attack on the trade unions as 'the danger from within'. But it also contained a plea for government and unions to establish a new collaborative relationship to meet the crisis facing the country. Government must govern, but would do so by cooperating with the unions and would amend the Industrial Relations Act. The manifesto distinguished between the mass of ordinary members and the politically motivated minority of militants and stressed that the government wanted a fair and just settlement with the NUM, based on the Relativities Report. This emphasis on involving the rank and file rather than strengthening the official leadership represented a major change from previous policy. It was difficult for observers to see how the Conservatives could lose the election but lose it they did. Events intervened: Campbell Adamson, CBI Director General, called for the repeal of the Industrial Relations Act, whilst the Pay Board's report on the NUM's claim revealed that the NCB's statistics were wrong and the miners could have been offered more at the outset. Enoch Powell declared the election was fraudulent and urged his supporters to vote Labour. Meanwhile the NUM's conduct of the strike was far more low key than in 1972. Gormley was anxious to damage Labour's electoral prospects as little as possible and also to undermine the government's claim that the strike was a politically motivated assault on the democratic process. As Hurd had predicted and Heath feared, the election was not fought on 'Who Governs?' but essentially on the government's record. The Conservatives polled more votes than Labour, losing seats because there was an upsurge in votes for the Liberals and for the Nationalists in Scotland

and Wales, but Labour formed a minority government.[53]

Why did the Heath government fail so disastrously in its relations with the unions? First, the growing pressure within the unions from the grassroots made it impossible for ministers to impose 'order' in industrial relations and, later, for ministers and union leaders to cooperate. Second, there was a powerful legacy of mistrust between Heath and the unions. Although this was eroded to some extent by personal contact, both sides had constituencies which they could not ignore. Third, there was a lack of effective policy instruments. Neither voluntary nor statutory incomes policy worked. Nor did statute law in the form of the Industrial Relations Act and there was no ideological or political consensus to govern government–union relations. The Heath government lacked the means and the political will to restructure radically industrial relations and there were no collectivist impulses or sympathies sufficiently powerful to bind the putative social partners into corporate politics.

Heath's experiences as Chief Whip, Minister of Labour, President of the Board of Trade and Macmillan's chief negotiator in Brussels had wedded him to a rationalist style based on negotiations with corporate élites. Heath's public persona and political style were not suited to managing an upsurge of grassroots unrest fuelled by inflation and his government seriously underestimated the reaction of the TUC.[54] Ministers really believed their vehement protestations that the 1971 Act was not intended to weaken the unions and that a legal framework would benefit the unions would be taken at face value, and that the unions would acknowledge the authority of the government's electoral mandate.[55] This paralleled the TUC's belief that ministers would bow to its expertise and, confronted with reality, would modify their proposals. Neither expectation was realized and both the Cabinet and the TUC found themselves in a confrontation neither desired. Given these weaknesses and the reluctance of public opinion to countenance confrontation with the unions during these years, it is difficult to see what Heath could have done differently. Even if, for example, the Conservatives had won the February election would this of itself have persuaded the NUM to end its strike or resolved the wider political-economic crisis?

Facing the enemy within: Thatcher and the unions, 1975–79

The trauma of the events of 1974 for the Conservative Party and the State cannot be overestimated: 'if you ask them ... what they thought of 1973–4 they thought it was the bloody trade unions out of control full stop. They didn't think, wouldn't it be nice if we were French or German and we had social partners. They thought it was all breaking loose because of bloody flying pickets'.[56] What, then, was to be done about the 'bloody flying pickets'?

After decades of relative industrial peace, the state had lost the capacity and will to respond to large-scale industrial disruption. Hurd admitted this at the time of the power workers' dispute in December 1970: 'It is clear that all the weeks of planning in the civil service have totally failed to cope ... and all the pressures are to surrender'.[57] After 1972 the state concentrated on mitigating the effects of Saltley-type events and, although this underpinned the State of Emergency called in 1974, no real thought was given to the fundamental questions involved in neutralizing trade union power. Indeed, this was thought to be politically and practically impossible to achieve. Not surprisingly, 'conventional wisdom in Whitehall has it that the central government's handling of the 1972 miners' strike was a shambles ...'.[58] Heath commissioned a review of the civil-emergency planning machinery, which resulted in the 'Winter Emergencies Committee' which became the Civil Contingencies Unit (CCU) located in the Cabinet Office. The CCU's first task was to prepare a list of vulnerable industries and possible counter-measures.[59]

This machinery was predicated on the assumption that it was the state's task to mitigate the effects of large-scale industrial action but that trade union power *per se* was a political given. Yet a very different strategy from conciliation plus emergency powers was emerging in the Conservative Party. Throughout the post-war period there was always a powerful undercurrent in the Conservative Party which rejected the consensual approach to the unions. The Institute for Economic Affairs (IEA) played a crucial role in systematizing the traditional suspicion of unions into a powerful political-economic critique which seemed confirmed by events. By the mid-1960s the unions were clearly identified as major threats to monetary (and therefore political) stability.[60] The IEA's attack on union power – vital for labour market flexibility, monetary inflation and individual freedom – was extremely radical in the 1960s and culminated in Hayek's *A Tiger By The Tail* (1972). The subsequent events of 1972–4 moved the IEA's critique from the fringes of Conservative politics into the mainstream.

In contrast, Heath completed his journey to tripartism between February and October 1974. The October 1974 manifesto, *Putting Britain First*, was a curious mixture. It promised the Industrial Relations Act would not be re-introduced and a Conservative government would seek 'Partnership In Industry'. Large and medium-sized companies would be required to consult employee representatives, employees would have the right to hold union meetings on company premises, union leaders would be elected in secret ballots (funded by government), government would assist in the training of shop stewards and union officers, the NUM's picketing code would become the basis for picketing, and social security payments to strikers would be restricted. This corporatist flowering was neutralized by defeat: the general election reverse – the second in nine months – forced the removal of Heath as party leader and his replacement by Margaret Thatcher. In the resulting debate over the post-1974 response to the unions, Thatcher's personal hostility to collectivism was of pivotal importance.

Elected to Parliament in 1959, Thatcher quickly revealed her hostility in a private member's Bill, The Public Bodies (Admission to Meetings) Act in 1960. This measure was apparently motivated by a desire to promote press freedom but 'a more potent influence was the desire to turn back trade union power. During the newspaper strike of 1958, certain Labour councils had voted to support the strikes by excluding from council meetings reporters who worked for papers being produced with strike breaking labour'. Thatcher wanted to make this unlawful. Between 1964–70 she said little in public about union power but her 1968 Conservative Political Centre (CPC) Lecture *What's Wrong with Politics?* expressed hostility to incomes policy and consensus politics.[61] In her memoirs Thatcher claims she and many other younger Conservatives were deeply concerned about the unions, knew of and had discussed *A Giant's Strength* and had wished to use her 1960 private members' Bill to 'break or at least weaken the power of the closed shop'. The 1958 newspaper dispute was an example of 'civil liberties under threat from collectivism' and 'socialist connivance with trade union power', but the Whips made it clear such a Bill would not be helpful.[62]

The pay pause and major disputes in the engineering and shipbuilding industries made 1962 the worst year for strikes since 1926. Thirty years later Thatcher blamed the government. She claimed: 'Rather than deal with the roots of the problem, which lay in trade union power, the Government moved towards corporatist deals with organized labour ... accepting a fundamentally collectivist analysis of what was wrong with Britain'.[63] The fundamental error of 1964–70 was the Conservatives' failure (apart from Powell) to formulate a clear position on incomes policy, a failure replicated in the Industrial Relations Bill, of which Thatcher was a keen supporter. She has accepted that 'the philosophy of the Bill was muddled' but the Act's most serious weakness was political,

> We did not recognize that we were involved in a struggle with unscrupulous people whose principal objectives lay not in industrial relations but in politics. Had we understood this we might have embarked upon a step-by-step approach, fighting on our own territory at our own timing, *as we were to do after 1979.*[64]

This political failure was reflected in the government's handling of the industrial disputes of 1970–4, a failure Thatcher was determined to avoid. In opposition Conservative thinking focused on four issues: endurance, policy, strategy and consent.

Endurance

There was a general agreement the state had been badly prepared for the scale of industrial conflict. Prior, for example, noted that despite sufficient coal, power cuts were caused by NUM pickets preventing supplies necessary for burning this coal entering the power stations. He recalled: 'We vowed that never again would we "do a Wilberforce"'. Thatcher later argued that, despite government being aware of the power of strategic groups in the electricity industry, no counter-preparations were made. She concluded: 'what subsequently happened [does not] suggest that any monitoring was accompanied by forward thinking'.[65] This omission, she felt, was yet another illustration of the corrosive effect of consensus politics on government authority. Faced by the threat of politically motivated industrial action, the 'moral force' of declaring a State of Emergency (or even a general election) would have little effect. It could make matters worse as an ineffective State of Emergency undermined government authority and, as Heath discovered, general election campaigns were unpredictable. Neither incomes policy nor tripartism offered a solution. So, as Nicholas Ridley told Cecil King, government could 'neither confront the unions nor ... be submissive':

> Powerful unions that demanded more money would get it ... Strikes should only be seriously fought when they are political – and he doubted if trade union members would have their hearts in a political strike. This is essentially Powell's point of view. It would mean widespread bankruptcies and unemployment instead of – or perhaps even associated with – inflation.[66]

All sections of party opinion conceded the party's difficulties with trade union reform. A CPC contact programme, *Tories and the Trade Union* (1975) found general hostility to the unions, but back-benchers and the ACP were undecided on the wisdom of attacking the unions or seeking to work with them. In the aftermath of February 1974 Lord Carrington was asked by Heath to analyse the unrest and the nature of the union threat. Carrington concluded that industrial society had a number of strategic points which if disrupted would affect society as a whole. The threat to these points could be eased, however, by careful planning and preparation, reinforced by support for resistance from political leaders.[67] Twenty years after these events Thatcher reflected:

> Looking back, and comparing 1972 with the threatened miners' strike of 1981 and the year-long strike of 1984–5, it is extraordinary how little attention we gave to 'endurance' – the period of time we could keep the power stations and the economy running with limited or no coal supplies – and how easily Cabinet was fobbed off by assurances that coal stocks were high, without considering whether those stocks were in the right locations to be usable, i.e. actually at the power stations. The possibility of effective mass picketing, which would prevent oil and coal getting to power stations, was simply not on the agenda.[68]

Under Thatcher these issues were definitely on the agenda. The Ridley

Report was primarily concerned with the financial viability of the nationalized industries but its annexe considered the measures that would be needed to meet the industrial disruption which would flow from a tighter financial regime.[69] Ridley argued such a challenge could be met by (i) paying above average wages in strategic industries to buy peace or at least time; (ii) any confrontation should be on ground of the government's choosing; (iii) every precaution should be taken to avoid the disruption of electricity by amassing coal at power stations, importing coal, encouraging the use of non-union lorry-drivers to move coal by convoy and expand the CEGB's dual coal/oil-fired capacity; (iv) cut supplementary benefits to strikers and their families; and (v) counter mass, mobile pickets with mass, mobile police units. Many of these measures had already been identified by the CCU and had become part of the state's analysis. Although the Ridley Report was never formally adopted as policy, it none the less expresses with great clarity the direction of Conservative thinking.

Policy

The agenda of the Conservative opposition remained dominated by familiar but tantalizing questions. Should a future government introduce an Industrial Relations Act Mark II? What role should incomes policy play? Prior, Thatcher's Employment spokesman, remained convinced of the need for incomes policy whilst others, notably Keith Joseph, were hostile. It took three years to find a workable solution. The Economic Reconstruction Group, chaired by Geoffrey Howe, was the main forum for working out economic strategy, and, in the turf war over anti-inflation and industrial relations policy, the initiative remained with Prior. Thatcher opposed incomes policy but for political and electoral reasons she accepted Prior's line. Howe argues this was unsustainable in the long run, given the shift in party policy and the centre of political gravity, as the Labour government's Social Contract disintegrated. Statements such as *The Right Approach* (1976) pointed to the policy changes under way in the Conservative Party. Whilst *The Right Approach to the Economy* (1977) stressed the need for tripartite consultation, the monetarist stamp was dominant. Furthermore, it warned of the dangers posed by politically motivated trade unions and it condemned Labour's legislation (notably the Trade Unions and Labour Relations Act, TULRA) as a threat to personal liberty and employment. At Prior's insistence (endorsed by Thatcher) no legislative commitments on, for example, the closed shop, were made. However, neither of these documents represented 'official' policy, in fact they acted as a screen for a deeper policy debate within the Conservative élite.[70]

Central to the debate over union policy was the conversion of Sir Keith Joseph to monetarism in the aftermath of 1974.[71] Joseph was instrumental in shifting policy towards monetarism as a cure for inflation but it was soon apparent that the pure quantity theory of money offered no immediate response to disruption on the scale of 1970–4. Francis Pym notes that there was a general agreement in the Shadow Cabinet on the objects monetarism sought to deliver but there were grave doubts about relying on an untested theory.[72] Thatcher retained Prior as Employment spokesman 'as a signal that I had no immediate plans for a fundamental reform of trade union law'. The 1971 Act had been neutralized, Heath destroyed by industrial militancy and public opinion was wary of the Conservatives. Prior's conviction was that:

> our aim should be to establish both that we accepted the existing trade union law, with perhaps a few alterations, and that we saw the union leaders as people with whom we could deal. Such an approach made more sense at the beginning of the period in Opposition than at the end of it.

Prior saw himself 'fight[ing] on two fronts – I was striving to impose some form of legislation on the union while repelling right-wing demands for extreme measures'.[73] He argued that courting the union leaders might contribute to an agreed reform programme and in January 1977 the General Council met members of the Conservative front-bench after eighteen months' cultivation by Prior. Prior warned there would be reform but this would be incremental and limited to the closed shop and secondary picketing. He could cite, in support of his stance, Thatcher's speech to the 1976 Conservative Trade Unionists' conference in which she called for a strong, responsible trade union movement. He confidently pledged that a future Conservative government would not seek revenge for 1970–4 and TULRA would not be repealed. Nevertheless the meeting was a failure.[74]

Joseph conceded that monetary policy could not of itself resolve the union problem, especially as it would lead to an increase in unemployment and pressure on pay which the unions would resist. As a monetarist, Joseph accepted that, whilst the unions did not of themselves cause inflation, their behaviour 'makes the cure of inflation more difficult'. In seeking higher wages, the unions were reacting to their economic environment. If government policy transformed this, a further barrier remained: union power was buttressed by the legal framework,

> Our unions have been uniquely privileged for several decades, but Labour's more recent legislation – all at the request of the TUC – seems designed to ensure that a strong union can almost always win any dispute, regardless of its economic case. The predictable result has been the growing use of strike and the strike threat. In a trade dispute most things seem permitted for the union side; breaking contracts; inducing others to break contracts; picketing of non-involved companies; secondary boycotts.

The result was, Joseph asserted, a 'militants' charter'. Control was slipping away from union leaders to left-wing militants. The first step in solving this problem was the creation of a new fiscal, monetary and legal framework. The 'replacement of the militants' charter by a moderates' charter' was an immense task and would require further action on *inter alia* secret ballots, picketing, the closed shop, and limits on the right to strike in essential services. This project carried great political risks particularly if 'union leaders or activists succeed in persuading the majority of their members that we are wrong to propose changes in the law and that they are right to resist them, then it will be difficult to legislate successfully'. Public opinion had to be convinced of the need for legislation and the depth of this commitment could only be tested in a general election.[75] This analysis was the surface reflection of a major strategic debate which crystallized around the Grunwick dispute. This was a union recognition battle marked by confrontation between police and pickets on the streets of north London which seemingly confirmed the perception of those who saw the unions as tyrannies above the law.[76] Whilst organizations such as the IEA and another right-wing think tank, the Centre for Policy Studies, promoted an intellectual critique of trade unions, it was the National Association for Freedom's (NAFF) organization of resistance at Grunwick which was of crucial importance for Conservative policy. The Grunwick dispute,

> was the first time that the power of the union had been challenged at a practical level since the victory of the miners in 1972 and 1974, and the NAFF won a conclusive victory – it was also a portent of the industrial strife that was to characterize the Thatcher government's attempt to repeat the success of Grunwick on a national scale against the miners in 1984–85.[77]

This, however, required a strategy.

Strategy

In November 1977, Joseph invited John Hoskyns and Norman Strauss to prepare a report on the trade union problem and how it might be turned to the Conservative advantage.[78] The result was the *Stepping Stones* report which has been described as the blueprint for the 1979–83 Conservative government but more accurately was the basis of the government's anti-union strategy. *Stepping Stones* provoked a major internal debate in 1978: 'a ritual unfolded in which those who took the Hoskyns view, like Geoffrey Howe, pushed forward the frontiers of the thinkable, while those who took the Prior view sought to dampen expectations and fears alike ... the leader steadily maintained the same posture; publicly on Prior's side, privately with Hoskyns'.[79] Hoskyns and Strauss argued reversing national decline required not just an election victory but a pre-election strategy to ease the implementation of future policy. Public opinion was shifting decisively against the unions and this could be exploited by laying to rest the public's fear that a

Conservative government would result in catastrophic conflict.

Thatcher claims not to have been initially impressed by the proposed strategy but she changed her mind. Thatcher met Hoskyns at the House of Commons in November 1977 and set up a Steering Group (which met in January) to explore how the strategy might be implemented. Union reform was at the centre of what the Conservatives wanted to achieve but they had to win the argument with public opinion which meant openly confronting the union question. In these discussions considerable disquiet was expressed about launching an aggressive critique combined with a prescription for cure. According to Thatcher's account, this disagreement took a month to sort out but even then Prior remained strategically placed to delay the adoption of *Stepping Stones*. In effect, a decision was taken to circumvent him. Howe, for example, made two speeches in August and September 1978 which explicitly questioned the representativeness and political role of trade union leaders.[80] *Stepping Stones* contended the reversal of national economic decline required more than 'good housekeeping'.[81] These policies could only be effective 'in an economy which is above some threshold of structural health' but Britain was below that threshold and locked into 'the self-fuelling momentum of decline' which was pushing it into further decline despite growing North Sea Oil revenues.[82] This required 'turn-around' policies to create social and economic stability by defeating inflation and the unions were the main obstacle. The unions were not 'the sole cause of our problems ... but because they are the only group whose leaders' political convictions and lack of economic understanding could pit then against any government which dares to do what has to be done'. In other words, through a combination of self-interest and ignorance the unions would resist policies designed to reverse national decline.

Stepping Stones then identified the Conservative Party's main political problem:

> Anti-union hysteria gets us nowhere, but the unions do pose a real dilemma ... the Tories can either challenge the trades union status quo – and risk losing the election in the subsequent rumpus; or they can promise to govern on the unions' terms, and probably win the election on safer issues, knowing that they are then almost certain to fail the country in office. *Any move to break out of this trap has, so far, been successfully altered by the unions shouting 'Confrontation'!*[83]

The party needed to show 'that we understand the real complexity of Britain's decline, that it won't be arrested by Callaghan's good housekeeping or left-wing panaceas; to demonstrate intellectual honesty, fairmindedness (the unions not [sic] the sole culprits, management and all governments share the blame)'.[84] *Stepping Stones* would resolve this electoral dilemma by challenging the unions but in a way that enhanced the Conservative's electoral prospects. Election victory had to be based on a positive rejection of socialism and union power rather than a vote against the Labour Party. This would provide a Conservative government the legitimacy it needed to institute its radical 'turn-around' policies.

By 1978 a wealth of opinion data gave some support to this move to frontal attack. It showed the electorate (and a majority of trade union members) to be hostile to union militancy although this was counterbalanced by a fear of the consequences of confronting the unions. 'The Stepping Stones Programme', therefore, 'concentrate[d] on linking socialism and Labour with the union leadership' (what Hoskyns and Strauss described as 'The Sick Society') in comparison to 'something better – unity, effort, quality of work, fairness, trust, straight dealing' ('The Healthy Society').[85] This was to be achieved by,

> ... call[ing] the 'confrontation' bluff; to show fairmindedness and objectivity on the union issue; to inform the public, factually, of all privileges, immunities, and the inevitable abuses; to explain the unique link with the Labour party and show how Labour and union left work together, regardless of which party is in power, for a socialist Britain.

> ... to show how collective bargaining, as currently practised in the public and private sector, is now the biggest single obstacle to achieving the very objectives the trade unions hold most dear – economic growth, full employment, stable prices ...

> ... to create a feeling of exasperation and disillusionment among union members with the unions' failure to increase real take-home pay; to show that this failure was inevitable because the commitment to socialist policy meant that government spent most of the new wealth with little to show for it; ... to increase the frustration further by acknowledging that there have been real 'winners' e.g. printing unions and miners, where monopoly power has been ruthlessly exercised by a minority and paid for by the rest of us.

Central to this approach was the contention that unions were controlled by politically motivated, unrepresentative oligarchs. Their autonomy was limited for they were themselves in thrall to tiny coteries of left-wing extremists who dominated the passive rank and file. A stark choice was to be given to the electorate:

> ... the two existing options – putting the clock back to 'Class Struggle', or cosy corporatism – are useless; the public have had enough of the former, the rank and file of the latter, the economy isn't strong enough to stand either. ... All, especially rank and file members, must be involved in the great debate, for the unions belong to the country; the country doesn't belong to the union leaders. Those pursuing socialism will do anything to silence the debate, for they want to use the power of the union movement to destroy the free enterprise system, not to rebuild it.

The party had to 'tackle, head on, the fear in peoples' minds that the unions are already effectively in power. Get this issue out into the open, first to make it less alarming, and second, to show how close the Left have got in their check-mate strategy'. This meant the Conservatives had to go on the offensive over trade union power 'to put left-wing union leaders in an impossible position and to do so visibly in front of the electoral audience ...'.[86] The unions would either have to fight or surrender. If they chose the former, then *Stepping Stones*, the Ridley Report, and public opinion would be crucial resources. If they opted for the latter, the unions would be revealed to be boneless wonders. Either way, the Conservatives would win.

How influential was *Stepping Stones*? Nigel Lawson believes it stimulated debate but 'cannot recall the "Stepping Stones" papers having much practical influence in Government, except in so far as they helped maintain the momentum for a radical reform of trade union law'. Howe believes 'The "Stepping Stones" analysis remained available to offer guidance through the years ahead [and] the Winter of Discontent [was] the most strategically placed Stepping Stone we could have wished for'.[87]

Consent

Commenting on Heath's experience, Hurd wrote:

> If the Government found public opinion hostile, then it was unlikely to persevere for very long ... If a union found public opinion hostile, this might or might not affect its stand, depending on the actual power of that union to disrupt the economy ... The Government had to have public opinion on its side if it was to hold.

The key was avoiding disruption to everyday life; once the lights flickered public opinion would clamour for government to settle. So the lights had to stay on.[88] However, an aggressive stand by the Conservatives on union power might have serious electoral consequences, an argument which Thatcher appreciated. The 1976 IMF crisis seemed to offer the Conservatives a political opportunity but 'because the trade unions were seen by people as all-powerful ... we were constantly put at a disadvantage by the question: How would *you* deal with the unions? Or more ominously: How would the unions deal with *you*?'[89]

In 1964, 70 per cent of those polled by Gallup believed the unions were a good thing; by 1979 this had declined to 53 per cent; those regarding them as a bad thing rose from 12 to 33 per cent. In 1964, the difference between those who thought them a good thing over those who regarded them as bad was 58 per cent, but by 1979 this lead had more than halved to 20 per cent (see Table 6.2). This decline in public esteem was a vital underpinning of the growing belief that a challenge to the unions might not have the serious adverse political and electoral consequences usually predicted for the Conservative Party. Norman Tebbit, for example, wrote: 'On the doorsteps in the 1979 campaign Tory canvassers were asked, "What if the trades union leaders won't talk to Mrs Thatcher if she was the Prime Minister?" The right answer to that question was and is "So what – who cares?" But it was an answer which seemed credible only to a few radicals in 1975'.[90]

Between 1972 and 1974 the percentage thinking the unions were too powerful rose from 63 to 77 per cent and the net balance of those who thought them too powerful/not powerful enough rose from 55 to 72 per cent. Of great political importance was the fact that this change in attitude was common to all classes. The British Election Survey found a convergence of opinion amongst all voters on the question of union power between 1974 and 1979. This perception increased by 14.7 per cent amongst Conservative voters, 20 per cent amongst Labour voters, and a dramatic 29.7 per cent amongst trade union members. This convergence obviously operated in the Conservatives' favour. The perception that unions were too powerful increased by 15.2 per cent amongst professional and managerial groups, 9.7 per cent amongst intermediate and routine non-manual groups and by a huge (and politically crucial) 21.9 per cent amongst the manual working-class.[91] The proportion of trade union members who identified themselves very or fairly strongly as Conservatives averaged 20 per cent between 1964 and 1979 with the largest percentage in 1970 (24.3) and the lowest (17) in the two 1974 elections. An average of 26 per cent of trade unionists voted Conservative: in 1964, 26 per cent; 1970, 28.7 per cent; 1974 (February), 23 per cent; 1974 (October), 20 per cent; and 1979, 31.6 per cent. Labour's lead over the Conservatives in the trade union electorate collapsed between 1974 and 1979. In 1964 Labour led the Conservatives in trade union votes by 39 per cent, in 1970 by 35.4 per cent, 1974 (February) by 33.9 per cent, 1974 (October) by 41.8 per cent and in 1979 by only 18.3 per cent. Labour's lead was to fall even lower – 5.7 per cent – in 1983.[92]

In 1964 public opinion discerned no real difference in handling the union issue between the Conservative government and Labour opposition: although Labour enjoyed a slight lead, both enjoyed substantial approval. In the fifteen years covered by this chapter, a social, electoral and political consensus, aided by the media and the unions' behaviour, developed that the unions were too powerful and that, by extension, this was damaging the country. The difficulty in demonstrating the shift in opinion is the lack of a consistent time-series. But what can be determined from the available data is that Labour progressively lost its image of being able to manage the unions, whilst the Conservatives were increasingly perceived as hostile to the unions. The Conservatives derived little long-term benefit because of the countervailing view that the Conservatives enjoyed poor relations with the unions and that (in the late 1970s) relations would worsen. Dislike of union power was therefore tempered, in part, by the perception that Labour was able to handle the unions whereas a Conservative government would provoke confrontation.

175

The 'Winter of Discontent' was vital in eroding this perception. In the dying months of 1978–9, Labour's handling of the unions was, not surprisingly, strongly disapproved of. Public hostility peaked in February 1979 with a massive net disapproval rate of 68.7 per cent. After the General Election, disapproval of the government's handling of industrial relations continued, although at a much reduced level.[93]

The Winter of Discontent

The Callaghan government's 5 per cent pay rise target of July 1978 lit the fuse to the 'Winter of Discontent'.[94] This came after four years of restraint; it was not discussed with the TUC; and even the Cabinet was divided on the policy's merits and wisdom. Few took the target seriously, as it was universally believed that Callaghan would call an autumn election, so when he did not do so conflict became inevitable. On 17 November Ford ended a nine-week strike of its workers by conceding pay increases of 16.5 per cent, and the Conservatives blocked an attempt to impose financial penalties on the company. Oil and petrol tanker drivers threatened to strike in pursuit of a 25 per cent pay claim and were bought off with a 20 per cent increase. On 3 January lorry drivers struck, using secondary picketing to block the movement of food. This dispute was settled with a 21 per cent pay rise. So the 5 per cent pay policy was effectively dead before the end of the year. But the most damaging dispute began on 22 January when public sector workers struck in favour of a £60.00 per week minimum wage.

The economic impact of the public sector workers' action was nothing compared to its political impact and it proved a propaganda gift to the Conservatives:

> Do they really think we have forgotten last winter? We have seen the gravediggers refusing to bury the dead. We have seen the refuse accumulating in the streets. We have seen the schools shut in the face of children because the caretaker has walked off with the key. And now we see the teachers making them do without their lunches. We have seen cancer patients having to postpone their operations because hospital laundry is not done, floors not swept, or meals not cooked ...[95]

These disputes confirmed the *Stepping Stones* analysis and, thanks to the images generated, simplified matters enormously for the Conservatives.[96] Thatcher believes the Conservatives would have won an autumn election but that it would have been close; moreover her government would have been saddled with the political fall-out of Labour's pay policy without public opinion being forced to recognize the problem of union power. This would have been disastrous, 'confirm[ing] in the public mind the impression left by the three-day week in 1974 that Conservative Governments meant pro-

176

voking and losing confrontations with the trade unions'. Without the 'Winter of Discontent', 'it would have been far more difficult to achieve what was done in the 1980s'.[97] The 'Winter of Discontent' eroded one of Labour's most powerful weapons: that only they could deal effectively with the unions. So, although the unions had been unpopular with the public since the 1960s, the shift in opinion (especially amongst working-class voters and trade union members) in this period was of great political significance. During 1978–9 and through the election campaign itself, Labour was still regarded as the party best able to handle industrial relations and strikes. However, its lead over the Conservatives narrowed dramatically and a majority of voters (including union members) approved of the Conservatives' reform proposals. Labour's links with the unions and the unions' behaviour were a major factor in Labour's defeat.

After Christmas, Thatcher 'came back to London determined on one thing: the time had come to toughen our policy on union reform'.[98] This required the outflanking of Prior, who was fighting a rearguard action against *Stepping Stones,* and other measures such as providing government money for union secret ballots and restrictions on social security payments to strikers' dependants. The result was 'considerable friction' with Thatcher who 'wanted to take much tougher measures than [he] was prepared to support...'. Prior's approach remained 'that we should take things steadily, and not believe that we could solve all the problems by draconian legislation'.[99] Under the influence of events, however, party policy and strategy moved decisively in Thatcher's favour. Comparing the 1978 draft and the final version of the manifesto, Butler and Kavanagh comment, 'The only significant addition ... was the section dealing with trade union power. The events of the winter made a tougher line acceptable. The proposals on picketing and taxation of strikers' benefits were new and placed at the forefront of the manifesto'. Politically and electorally it became clear to Thatcher 'that we could and should obtain a mandate to clip the wings of the trade union militants' and the result was a manifesto with which she was 'very happy'. The 1979 manifesto was unequivocal: 'We cannot go on, year after year, tearing ourselves apart in increasingly bitter and calamitous industrial disputes'.[100]

The Conservatives returned to government with a clear analysis of, and strategy to deal with, the union problem. But they did not have a timetable. Internal politics whilst in opposition revealed considerable, residual hostility to confrontation as a legacy of 1970–4. Thatcher herself, conscious of her still vulnerable position as party leader and that precipitate action might endanger her government's long-term plan to regenerate Britain, was cautious. She did, however, believe confrontation to be both inevitable and desirable if government authority was to be reasserted and this was reflected in the Ridley Report and *Stepping Stones*. The battle-lines were drawn.

Conclusions

Between 1964 and 1979 the Conservative Party moved from a resigned acceptance that little could be done about the unions to a determination to radically reform both them and industrial relations more generally by the creation of an innovative legal framework. The first key period was that between the October 1964 General Election and the publication of the initial report in April 1965. This saw the party adopt a legislative solution and thereafter the debate concerned the extent and philosophy of reform. Originally the intention was to strengthen official leaderships against the grassroots, to impose 'discipline' from the centre, a strategy and philosophy which failed with the Industrial Relations Act and the industrial unrest which took place under the Heath government. As a corporatist politician, Heath's intention was not to marginalize the unions but to ensure their responsible participation in the political status quo as recognized social partners.

What endured through this period was evolution and continuity. There was no abrupt disjuncture after 1975. Ideology was a talisman rather than the forge upon which policy was radically recast. It is difficult to discern, for example, either authoritarian populism or a new accumulation strategy dictating policy creation.[101] Rather Thatcher's strategy, in reaction to these failures, moved cautiously towards a more radical policy designed to neutralize the unions' power by encasing them in a highly restrictive legal framework and removing the unions from the political process. This approach was outlined in opposition but was hidden by the continued prominence of Prior's accommodationist strategy which Thatcher accepted for pragmatic reasons. It did not reflect the strategy expressed by the Carrington, Ridley and *Stepping Stones* reports, nor Thatcher's preferences, but this alternative strategy was only 'firmed up' in late 1977 and early 1978, particularly with the 'Winter of Discontent'. The 'Winter of Discontent' and changes in public opinion, especially amongst trade union members, provided a degree of consent for change which had not been available to Heath. Nevertheless, mindful of Heath's fate, the Thatcher governments moved cautiously but irresistibly against the unions after 1979.

Table 6.1 Public attitudes to the Industrial Relations Bill, December 1970

Do you approve or disapprove of the following proposals outlined in the Government's Industrial Relations Bill?	Approve	Disapprove	Don't know
A 'cooling-off period' where a strike might harm the national interest?	73	9	17
Fines for unions who break the new rules and commit unfair industrial practices?	65	16	19
A secret ballot of members to be made before a strike?	69	17	14
A worker to be able to decide whether to join a trade union or not?	76	12	12

Source: Attitudes Towards Trade Unions in Great Britain, 1946–1987 (Gallup, September 1987).

Table 6.2 The public esteem of trade unions, 1964-79

Poll date	Good thing	Bad thing	Don't know	Net good
1963 Sept.	65	15	20	50
1964 Aug.	70	12	18	58
1965 Aug.	57	25	18	32
1966 Mar.	60	21	19	39
1967 Aug.	60	23	17	37
1968 June	65	23	12	42
1969 May	63	18	19	45
1970 Aug.	60	24	17	36
1971 Aug.	62	21	17	41
1972 Aug.	56	32	12	24
1973 Aug.	61	25	14	36
1974 Aug.	54	27	19	27
1975 Aug.	51	34	16	17
1976 Aug.	60	25	14	35
1977 Aug.	53	33	14	20
1978 Aug.	53	33	14	20
1979 Aug.	53	33	14	20

Source: Attitudes Towards Trade Unions in Great Britain, 1946–1987 (Gallup, September 1987).

Notes

1.   For an overview see A.J. Taylor, 'The party and the trade unions', in A. Seldon and S. Ball (eds), *Conservative Century: the Conservative Party since 1900* (Oxford, 1994), pp. 499–543; P. Dorey, *The Conservative Party and the Trade Unions* (1994).
2.   R. Taylor, *The Trade Union Question in British Politics: government and unions since 1945* (Oxford, 1993), p. 117.
3.   *A Giant's Strength* (Inns of Court Conservative Association 1958). A young Geoffrey Howe played a role in preparing the report.
4.   A. Seldon, *Churchill's Indian Summer: the Conservative government, 1951–55* (1981), pp. 196–207; and A. Roberts, *Eminent Churchillians* (1994), pp. 243–85, for a more splenetic view of Monckton.
5.   Conservative Party Archives (hereafter CPA), ACP/2/2/50, Advisory Committee on Policy (ACP), Minutes, 2 May 1962.
6.   CPA, ACP/3/10/(63)/105, 'Report of the Industrial Relations Sub-Committee', 8 May 1963.
7.   *TUC Report 1962*, pp. 298–9. For the ETU scandal see, C.H. Rolph, *All Those in Favour? The ETU trial* (1962), and E. Wigham, *What's Wrong With the Unions?* (Harmondsworth, 1961).
8.   National Union, *Report of the 80th Conference 1961*, pp. 109–18.
9.   CPA, CCO/503/2/4, Press Release, Speech by John Hare to CTU Conference, 9 March 1963.
10.   H. Macmillan, *At The End of the Day 1961–1963* (1973), Diary 27 May 1962, p. 69.
11.   Public Record Office (hereafter PRO) CAB 128/38, C.M. 11 (64), 13.
12.   PRO, CAB 128/38 C.M. 17 (64), 5 March 1964 conc. 2, February 1964 conc. 9. In law *Rookes v. Barnard* was not about the closed shop (Rookes was dismissed after being expelled from his union) but about the right to strike, as the House of Lords judgement implied that a strike threat could be construed as a threat to carry out an illegal action and damage a third party. Thus, unions would be opened to crippling damages (K.W. Wedderburn, *The Worker and the Law*, 1971, pp. 361–71).
13.   PRO, CAB 128/38, C.M. 18 (64), 13 March 1964 conc. 6.
14.   CPA, ACP/2/2/50, ACP Minutes, 2 May 1962; ACP/3/10/63/103, memo by Hare, 'Industrial Relations – Unofficial Strikes', 28 January 1963.
15.   D. Butler, '1961–64: did the Conservatives lose direction?', *Contemporary Record*, 2, 5, 1989, pp. 2–8.
16.   H. Macmillan, *Pointing the Way 1959–61* (1972), p. 375.
17.   Macmillan, *End of the Day*, Diary 14 May 1962, p. 66. 18; J. Campbell, *Edward Heath: a biography* (1993), p. 219.
19.   Conservative Political Centre, *Fair Deal At Work: the Conservative approach to modern industrial relations* (1968).
20.   Interview with Lord Carr by author. The definitive study of the genesis and failure of the Industrial Relations Act is M. Moran, *The Politics of Industrial Relations* (Macmillan 1977).

21. On *In Place of Strife*, see, P. Jenkins, *The Battle of Downing Street* (1970); B. Castle, *Fighting All The Way* (1994); and G.A. Dorfman, *Government Versus Trade Unionism in British Politics since 1968* (1979).
22. T. Raison, *Conflict and Conservatism*, Conservative Political Centre (CPC) Pamphlet 313, March 1965.
23. J. Prior, *A Balance of Power* (1986), pp. 45 and 48.
24. Campbell, *Edward Heath*, pp. 230–3, and 'Symposium: Conservative Party Policy making 1965–1970 (II)', *Contemporary Record*, 3, 4, 1990, p. 34.
25. B.J. Evans and A.J. Taylor, *From Salisbury to Major: continuity and change in Conservative politics* (Manchester University Press, 1996), pp. 150–2.
26. G. Howe, *Conflict of Loyalty* (1994), p. 47. Geoffrey Howe had been involved in *A Giant's Strength*, had written extensively on the unions in *Crossbow*, and as the *Daily Telegraph's* legal correspondent had dwelt at length on *Rookes v Barnard*.
27. TUC, *Report*, 1970, pp. 566–7. Feather's comments were followed by a long debate rejecting legal intervention (pp. 581–8). For their part the government never imagined the unions would so strenuously oppose an elected government (Campbell, *Heath*, p. 234).
28. *The Times*, 14 October 1970. The eight pillars were: a statutory right to belong (or not belong) to a trade union, a right to union recognition, registration, collective agreements would be legally enforceable unless both parties contract out, limitations on the unions' immunity for damages, safeguards for the community where a dispute could cause a national emergency, selective enforceability of procedural agreements, and machinery to determine which union in a workplace would have bargaining rights.
29. *TUC Industrial News 16*, 20 October 1970, for example.
30. *TUC Press Release*, 12 November 1970. The TUC's case against was set out in the pamphlet, *Reason*.
31. Howe, *Conflict of Loyalty*, p. 65; Taylor, *Trade Union Question*, pp. 185–6.
32. See Moran, *Politics of Industrial Relations*, pp. 124–48, and Dorfman, *Government Versus Trade Unionism* pp. 58–65. For revisionist accounts of these events, see J. McIlroy, 'Notes on the Communist Party and industrial politics' and D. Lyddon, '"Glorious Summer" 1972: the high tide of rank and file militancy', both in this volume.
33. Campbell, *Heath*, p. 412.
34. P. Whitehead, *The Writing on the Wall* (1985), p. 74. MI5 and Special Branch surveillance of the NUM was reduced as the mineworkers' disruptive potential was seen to have diminished from its high point in the 1940s and 1950s. The CEGB transferred resources from the coalfields to the 'new working-class' in the Midlands car plants.
35. Whitehead, *Writing on the Wall*, p. 76. See also Campbell, *Heath*, p. 417, for the Cabinet's sense of powerlessness.
36. R. Maudling, *Memoirs* (1978), pp. 160–1. On this episode, see Prior's testimony in Whitehead, *Writing on the Wall*, p. 75. A similar episode occurred during the work-in at the upper Clyde Shipbuilders, when the Chief Constable of Glasgow warned of the likelihood of serious civil unrest if the yards

were closed.

37. Hurd, *An End To Promises*, p. 103.
38. *The Chequers and Downing St Talks* (TUC, 1972) gives a useful account of these talks. This shift in attitude was reflected in the abandonment of the 'lame duck' industrial policy (allowing bankrupt industries to collapse) with the nationalization of Rolls Royce, intervention to preserve upper Clyde Shipbuilders and the passage of the highly interventionist Industry Act (1972).
39. J. Jones, *Union Man: an autobiography* (1986), p. 255. Hugh Scanlon, the other half of 'the terrible twins' and AUEW President, formed a similarly sympathetic view of Heath (*Listener*, 27 September 1979).
40. E. Silver, *Victor Feather, TUC: a biography* (1973), pp. 207–10.
41. Campbell, *Heath*, pp. 471–5.
42. Jones, *Union Man*, p. 259.
43. Jones, *Union Man*, p. 257; Campbell, *Heath*, p. 478; Silver, *Feather*, pp. 212–13.
44. D. Barnes and E. Reid, *Government and Trade Unions: the British experience 1964–79* (1980), pp. 170–4, for Stages 1 and 2. Individual unions, such as NHS ancillary workers, did resist stage 2 but received little support.
45. Whitehead, *Writing on the Wall*, p. 100; J. Gormley, *Battered Cherub* (1982), pp. 124–5. Gormley, like Jones, 'got on perfectly all right with Heath. I found him neither stubborn nor unapproachable ... I knew he was listening, whereas Harold Wilson often gave the impression of being somehow detached, not really listening at all' (p. 124).
46. See the White Paper, *Counter-Inflation Policy: Stage Three* (Cmnd 5446), and Consultation Document, *The Price and Pay Code for Stage Three* (Cmnd 5444). The basis of the NUM's claim was that since the Wilberforce award in 1972 their position relative to comparable groups of workers had declined drastically. Relativities played a crucial role in the 1973–4 dispute.
47. Gormley, *Cherub*, p. 127; Hurd, *An End To Promises*, 116; Whitehead, *Writing on the Wall*, p. 102.
48. Hurd, *An End To Promises*, pp. 114–15.
49. Whitehead, *Writing on the Wall*, p. 104; Gormley, *Cherub*, p. 131.
50. W. Whitelaw, *The Whitelaw Memoirs* (1989), pp. 126–7; Gormley, *Cherub*, pp. 132–3.
51. *The TUC's Initiative* (1974), p. 8; Campbell, *Heath*, pp. 580–5.
52. Hurd, *An End To Promises*, p. 119; Campbell, *Heath*, pp. 594–5. The best account of these events is S. Fay and H. Young, *The Fall of Edward Heath* (1976). Specifically on the unions, see the excellent ICBH Witness Seminar, 'The Trade Unions and the Fall of the Heath Government', *Contemporary Record*, 2, 1, 1988, pp. 36–45.
53. D. Butler and D. Kavanagh, *The British General Election of February 1974* (1974) chronicles the 'Who Governs?' election; for an overall analysis, see D. Kavanagh, '1970–1974', in A. Seldon (ed.), *How Tory Governments Fall: the Tory Party in power since 1783* (1996), pp. 359–86. The Heath government is treated sympathetically and at greater length in S. Ball and A. Seldon (eds), *The Heath Government 1970–74: a reappraisal* (1996).

54. It also underestimated the unhappiness of the employers and the CBI with its policies and attitudes towards the TUC and organized labour.

55. Interview with Lord Carr by author.

56. P. Hennessy, 'Review Article: K. Middlemas, power competition and the state', *Contemporary Record*, 5, 3, 1991, p. 535.

57. Hurd, *An End to Promises*, p. 99. See also, C. Townshend, *Making the Peace: public order and public security in modern Britain* (Oxford, 1993), pp. 143–5.

58. K. Jeffery and P. Hennessy, *States of Emergency: British government and strikebreaking since 1919* (1983), p. 236.

59. Jeffery and Hennessy, *States of Emergency*, pp. 237–40. See also, P. Hennessy, *Whitehall* (1990), p. 236. In fact power station coal stocks were lower in December 1973 than in December 1971.

60. R. Cockett, *Thinking the Unthinkable: think-tanks and the economic counter-revolution 1931–1983* (1995), p. 148.

61. H. Young, *One of Us: a biography of Mrs Thatcher* (1989), pp. 45, 65. For the development of union policy under Thatcher, see R. Behrens, 'Blinkers for the carthorse: the Conservative Party and the trade unions', *Political Quarterly*, 49, 1978, pp. 457–73; M. Moran, 'The Conservative Party and the trade unions since 1974', *Political Studies*, 17, 1979, pp. 38–53.

62. M. Thatcher, *The Path to Power* (1995), pp. 110–11.

63. Thatcher, *Path to Power*, p. 128.

64. Thatcher, *Path to Power*, p. 205, my emphasis.

65. Prior, *Balance of Power*, p. 73; Thatcher, *Path to Power*, p. 215.

66. C. King, *The Cecil King Diary 1970–1974* (1975), entry for 28 June, p. 370.

67. A.J. Taylor, 'Terrible nemesis? The miners, the NUM and Thatcherism', *Teaching Politics*, 15, 2, 1986, pp. 294–5. Lord Carrington has confirmed that this was the gist of his report in a letter to the author, 20 April 1998. See also H. Beynon and P. McMylor, 'Decisive power: the new Tory state against the miners', in H. Beynon, *Digging Deeper: issues in the miners' strike* (1985), pp. 29–45.

68. Thatcher, *Path to Power*, p. 216.

69. 'Appomattox or civil war?', *Economist*, 27 May 1978; N. Ridley, *My Style of Government: the Thatcher years* (1991), pp. 13–16, 66–7; Young, *One of Us*, pp. 114–18.

70. Howe, *Conflict of Loyalty*, pp. 100–2; Prior, *Balance of Power*, p. 109; Young, *One of Us*, p. 108; Thatcher, *Path to Power*, p. 299.

71. M. Halcrow, *Keith Joseph: a single mind* (1989), pp. 56–76; J. Ranelagh, *Thatcher's People* (1991), pp. 120–41.

72. F. Pym, *The Politics of Consent* (1984), p. 6.

73. Thatcher, *Path to Power*, p. 228; Prior, *Balance of Power*, p. 154.

74. TUC, *Report, 1977*, para. 490, p. 309; *The Times*, 28 December 1976; *Guardian*, 30 December 1976; E. Jacobs, 'Margaret makes peace with the unions', *Sunday Times Business News*, 29 February 1976; Thatcher, *Path to Power*, p. 312.

75. This paragraph is derived from K. Joseph, *Solving the Union Problem is the Key to Britain's Recovery* (1979).

76. *Sunday Times*, 8 January 1978; Prior, *Balance of Power*, pp. 154–5; N. Tebbit, *Upwardly Mobile* (1989), pp. 192–6. For the union view, see J. Dromey and G. Taylor, *Grunwick: the workers' story* (1978).

77. Cockett, *Thinking the Unthinkable*, pp. 221–2.

78. After leaving the Army, Hoskyns went into computing later selling his company to IBM. Obsessed with Britain's decline he had connections in both major parties. He met Thatcher via Joseph and was very impressed with Conservative attempts to formulate a coherent strategy. Norman Strauss spent his business career with Lever Brothers and was closely involved with the Centre for Policy Studies, Joseph's and Thatcher's personal think-tank. After 1979 Hoskyns and Strauss served in the Number 10 Pol'cy Unit until 1982 (see Ranelagh, *Thatcher's People*).

79. Young, *One of Us*, p. 117.

80. Howe, *Conflict of Loyalty*, pp. 106–7; Thatcher, *Path to Power*, pp. 421–2.

81. *Stepping Stones* acknowledged the policies outlined in *The Right Approach to the Economy* (monetary and fiscal discipline, minimal economic intervention, a stable tax system, incentives for wealth creation, a refusal to subsidies dying industries, and deregulation) which had been central to the 1970 manifesto.

82. *The Stepping Stones Programme*, para 2.1.

83. Ibid., para 2.2, my emphasis.

84. Ibid., Appendix A, para A.3

85. Ibid., paras 4.1–4.

86. Ibid., Appendix A, paras E.3 4.

87. N. Lawson, *The View from No.11: Memoirs of a Tory Radical* (1992) p. 18; Howe, *Conflict of Loyalty*, pp. 108, 113.

88. Hurd, *An End to Promises*, p. 97.

89. Thatcher, *Path To Power*, p. 310, emphasis in original.

90. Lawson, *The View from No. 11*, p. 30; Tebbit, *Upwardly Mobile*, p. 193.

91. The media played a crucial role in these changes. See, for example, Glasgow Media Group, *More Bad News* (1980); J. Seaton, 'Trade unions and the media', in B. Pimlott and C. Cook (eds), *Trade Unions in British Politics: the first 250 years* (2nd edition, 1991); N. Jones, *Strikes and the Media: communication and conflict* (Oxford, 1986). Labour's sensitivity on strikes can be seen in its complaint to the IBA about the planned broadcast of *I'm All Right, Jack* on Easter Sunday; LWT cancelled the film's showing in the London area. In election news broadcasts, unions and industrial relations ranked fourth in overall coverage (D. Butler and D. Kavanagh, *The British General Election of 1979* (1980), pp. 204, 211).

92. Psephological data is taken from I. Crewe, N. Day and A. Fox, *The British Electorate 1963–1987: a compendium of data from the British Election Studies* (Cambridge, 1991).

93. This analysis is based on data provided by the ESRC Data Archive, University of Essex.

94. Insider accounts of the 'Winter of Discontent' can be found in J. Callaghan, *Time and Chance* (1987); D. Healey, *The Time of My Life* (1990); B.

Donoughue, *Prime Minister: the conduct of policy under Harold Wilson and James Callaghan* (1987); T. Benn, *Conflicts of Interest: diaries 1977–80* (1990); W. Rodgers, 'Government under stress – Britain's Winter of Discontent 1978–79', *Political Quarterly*, 55, 2, 1984.

95.   Lord Hailsham, quoted in Butler and Kavanagh, *British General Election of 1979*, pp. 189–90.

96.   Howe, *Conflict of Loyalty*, p. 107, for example. Public discomfort was increased by atrocious weather and the failure to grit many roads. The public mood was not improved when Callaghan returned from Guadeloupe and (according to the *Sun*) asked 'Crisis, What Crisis?'

97.   Thatcher, *Path to Power*, p. 414.

98.   Ibid., p. 423.

99.   Prior, *Balance of Power*, p. 111; Howe, *Conflict of Loyalty*, p. 108; Young, *One of Us*, p. 117. Prior (p. 155) suggests that he could have resisted this pressure in the run-up to the election as Thatcher could not have afforded his resignation and admits he did not appreciate the strength of his position.

100.   Butler and Kavanagh, *British General Election of 1979*, p. 155; Thatcher, *Path to Power*, pp. 435, 438. Conservative reform plans attracted stable, high levels of public support. In October 1970 Gallup found 46 per cent of those polled approved of the government's plans, 22 per cent disapproved, and 32 per cent didn't know. In August 1979 the respective percentages were remarkably similar: 54, 20, and 26.

101.   For discussion of various characterizations of Conservative politics from 1977 onwards, see A. Gamble, *The Free Economy and the Strong State: the politics of Thatcherism* (1988).

CHAPTER SEVEN

'What are we here for ?': George Woodcock and Trade Union Reform

Robert Taylor

> The character of our trade union movement has been moulded by conditions and not by theories. It has taken shape and its purposes and practices from the circumstances in which it grew. (George Woodcock, 12 December 1960)[1]

> We are a voluntary body. We have no sanctions and even if we had, we have no power to enforce them. (George Woodcock, April 1972)[2]

George Woodcock's time as General Secretary of the Trades Union Congress from September 1960 until March 1969 is often characterized as a period of unfulfilled promise, a lost opportunity for the trade unions to modernize themselves and become a necessary partner in the management of the British economy. An undisputed if insecure Estate of the Realm, the TUC in the 1960s was given the opportunity to become a crucial institution in helping to resolve the country's economic problems, so it was argued. However, the TUC failed to seize the challenge. Woodcock himself is often blamed for what happened. 'He is a cynical man – maybe if you get to the top in the trade union movement you have to be cynical but not as much as he is', Anthony Wedgwood Benn, then Minister of Technology, wrote in his diary.

> He once made a speech saying that life was full of shoddy compromises and I think, early on, he had a conception of how the trade unions should develop and be run which never came to reality, partly because history was not ready for it and partly because he did not have enough drive. It has made him very bitter. He is also a terrible old bore.[3]

George Brown, a man whom when Secretary of State for Economic Affairs Woodcock initially admired for his energy and optimism, took an equally unfavourable view of Woodcock's role at the TUC, although he was later to acknowledge Woodcock had been right. 'He is a most up and down fellow; even in his most enthusiastic comments, he sounds rather like an undertaker. One day he would be for it but the next day while he was still for it, he now saw all the snags and possibilities', complained Brown,

Woodcock was always sure I was in too much of a hurry – that if only one would do things in a fairly leisurely way over the next fifty years, then one could bring it about. He professed to be well aware that you had to make 'shoddy, shabby compromises'. It was only naive fools like me who thought you might do something rather better.[4]

Richard Crossman, senior cabinet minister in the Labour governments of the 1960s and one of Woodcock's former tutors at Oxford, was relieved to see him go. Of Vic Feather who became TUC General Secretary in March 1969 on Woodcock's departure, he wrote in his diary: 'He is far more vigorous and far less neutral than Woodcock, far more solidly pro-Labour and pro-government'.[5] Barbara Castle, impatient of trade union ways when Secretary of State for Employment and Productivity, was exasperated by Woodcock who had given her the impression he agreed with her *In Place of Strife* proposals to reform the trade unions. Woodcock had told Denis Barnes, the department's Permanent Secretary, that he believed 'Barbara has done a first-class job of work. The policy is excellent – very skilful'. As she noted in her diary, 'It will be the day when he says that to the press and I will believe it when I hear it'.[6] She was tired of union leaders saying one thing in private and another in public.

Woodcock could irritate even friendly Conservative government ministers who wanted to help him as much as they could to draw the TUC into an acceptance of wider public policy responsibilities. Reginald Maudling, expansionist Chancellor of the Exchequer under Harold MacMillan in the early 1960s, testified to the 'cordial relations' he established with the TUC General Council, not least with Woodcock. But he was taken aback by Woodcock's sardonic sense of humour. 'I remember him once saying – "Well Reggie, I have come to the conclusion that if achieving greater productivity means getting up half an hour earlier in the morning, I am against it". Could there have been a better incapsulation of the views of the English people at that time?' ruminated Maudling.[7]

Many of his contemporaries came to regard Woodock as a strange, cautious, introspective political recluse, ill-equipped to become the modernizer of the trade union movement. More Hamlet-like philosopher than ideologist, he appeared to stand aloof and somewhat apart from the pragmatic, earthy and tough world of trade union power-brokering. Woodcock was the first to recognize his own personal limitations. 'I was a little bit of an austere person at the TUC. I hope not grumpy but a little remote', he confessed in retirement.

There is a tendency in these big organizations for people to want to do the fixing with you behind the scenes and that was why I shied away a little bit from people. I prefered not to fix. If there was anything to be done it should be discussed by the appropriate committee or by the TUC General Council without any prior commitment with any member of the committee.

Woodcock admitted, 'I never made any friends in the sense of personal friends. I took the view you were there to advise the General Council as a whole and your advice should never be tinged by your belief that you had blue-eyed boys on the General Council'.[8] Despite this, union leaders respected his intelligence.

But Woodcock had his coterie of admirers, especially among national newspaper labour editors such as Eric Wigham of *The Times* and Geoffrey Goodman, then of the *Daily Herald* and later the *Sun*. John Cole at the *Guardian* was a particular friend. In his memoirs he describes Woodcock as the trade union movement's 'last, best hope to avoid its later unpopularity and decline ...'. He had a mind of great clarity, illuminated by a powerful imagination and human sympathy'.[9] Not all labour editors were so sympathetic. Peter Jenkins of the *Guardian* believed Woodcock became TUC General Secretary 'too late' in life. He had grown 'gravely introspective, radical in thought but cautious (some alleged plain lazy) when it came to action'. Jenkins portrayed him as 'deracinated, sick in his heart', a man whose abilities and sense of purpose had 'atrophied'.[10]

However, it was Woodcock – more than any other trade union leader of his generation – who sought to prepare and challenge organized labour into playing an increasingly demanding role in a post-war economy where governments committed themselves to the creation of economic growth, full employment, high public spending, and the development of a welfare state based on universalist principles of provision. He agonized over what the relationship of trade unions should be with a democratic state that extended responsibilities for managing the economy. Woodcock tried to discover how trade union autonomy could be reconciled with industrial efficiency and innovation, how unions ought to practise voluntary restraint in pay bargaining to prevent the outbreak of damaging wage-push inflation. He wrestled with trying to balance the defence of trade union custom and practice with the need for unions to accept workplace reform and help improve labour productivity. During the 1960s Woodcock attempted – but only sporadically and perhaps always unduly aware of the obstacles to change – to find answers to such crucial questions. If he failed ultimately to do so, it is arguable this was as much the fault of the times and the pecularities of the British industrial relations system as his own weaknesses and personal idiosyncracies.

The formative years

Woodcock's difficulties in office undoubtedly stemmed, at least partly, from the comparative lateness of his arrival as TUC General Secretary. He had spent 13 years in the shadows as the frustrated assistant secretary to Sir Vincent Tewson, a mediocre consolidator, a man Woodcock openly despised.

Woodcock was indeed an extraordinary man. Born in 1904 the son of a weaver in Walton-le-Dale outside Preston in Lancashire, he left school at twelve to work in the trade of his parents. A keen footballer, he almost turned professional. But then illness struck him and he was confined to bed for many months. It was during that crucial formative period that Woodcock read his way out of weaving. Through diligent hard work he won a scholarship to working-class Ruskin College, Oxford, in 1929. From there he advanced to New College where he secured a first-class honours degree in politics, philosophy and economics. Surprisingly, he did not believe he suffered from any class prejudice. 'I thought Oxford was a wonderful place as though it were built for me', he recalled. 'It was ideally the kind of place that I wanted'. He thrived on the tutorial system. 'At no point anywhere, either among the undergraduates or among the dons did I ever get the impression of a distinction based on class', he claimed. 'I was aware of a distinction in my maturity and experience but apart from that, at no stage was I ever made aware that I was a working man and they were of another kind'.[11]

After twelve months on a scholarship at Manchester University, Woodcock took a job in the Civil Service. But after two years, in 1936, he was appointed head of the TUC's research and economic department after the sudden death of the legendary Milne-Bailey, taking over as Assistant General Secretary in January 1947. In the small TUC policy-making secretariat under Sir Walter Citrine, a TUC general secretary he admired and who influenced him enormously, Woodcock thrived. During the Second World War, the TUC played an active and crucial part in decision-making through a network of joint consultative committees that covered a wide policy area including manpower problems, productivity, trade, price and wage stability. Woodcock came to know both the economist John Maynard Keynes and the social reformer William Beveridge very well. He was heavily influenced by their economic and social thought with its strong emphasis on the need for taking personal responsibility and devotion to the concept of public service. Woodcock played a key role in the efforts to develop a tripartite reconstruction programme which paved the way for the domestic policies of the 1945 Labour government.

It was during the period of total war that Woodcock began to develop his underlying views of what the TUC's role ought to be in a modern democracy with an activist state. In the late 1940s he became an often robust and influential voice at the TUC in its dealings with a Labour government in economic crisis although he was compelled to play second fiddle to Tewson. The TUC archives reveal how young Woodcock argued its case effectively and bluntly with Prime Minister Clement Attlee, Chancellor Stafford Cripps and Ernest Bevin, the Foreign Secretary. In a note written in November 1950 he assessed the increasing importance of the TUC, pointing out that before 1940 its discussions with ministers had usually been 'ad hoc and limited to one particular matter' and employers had not been present.[12] With the war came continuous, formalized and structured discussions between the TUC, government and employers. After 1945 the TUC made itself indispensable in economic management, industrial policy and the development of the welfare state. Its influence was especially vital in ensuring a period of voluntary wage restraint in support of government economic policy in 1948–49, although the TUC approach fell apart in 1950 under shop floor pressure against any form of wage control. Woodcock acknowledged the post-war state had come to recognize that it should not challenge the TUC's enhanced authority but instead try to use it more effectively in the achievement of its own economic and social objectives. As he later explained:

> From the end of the First World War to the beginning of the Second, the trade union movement had great difficulty in getting governments to accept more than a narrowly limited degree of responsibility for the level of employment, economic growth and industrial efficiency. ... That attitude has changed. Since the end of the war all political parties accept – at least in principle – that it must be a responsibility of a modern government to maintain a high level of employment and to promote a constant and steady improvement in our standards of living. The TUC was not alone in trying to bring about this change of attitude. Yet the change can fairly be reckoned by the TUC as one of its major achievements of the inter-war years.[13]

A more interventionist state required a TUC response. 'A government needs these days the advice and the assistance of the trade union movement in determining the practical means of achieving desirable objectives', Woodcock explained in 1968. But for their part, the trade unions needed the government to pursue economic growth strategies in order to help their members secure more stable employment and higher pay. 'We spent years in getting government round to the view they ought to set for themselves these objectives and at this stage we cannot just stand back and say "yes, we expect you to get to those ends and we are not going to help you in doing what we ourselves say we ought to do"'.[14]

However, Woodcock always retained a deeply sceptical view of the direct role of the state in the industrial relations system. His own background made him an eloquent supporter of the so-called 'voluntarist' tradition which believed trade union freedom meant trade unions should be allowed to pursue their basic collective bargaining purposes without fear of any outside legal or political interference. 'The attitude of the trade unions towards the government is that we should be just as lief you left us alone. If you do not think it is possible for you to help the trade unions then the least you can do is not to impede us', he declared. 'Trade unions expect of the law only that it should sustain their legal immunities'.[15] Woodcock's TUC colleagues were often irritated by his provocative suggestion that as a result trade unions were 'outlaws'.

Woodcock was always acutely sensitive to what he regarded as the ultimate purpose of trade unionism. He may have sought new responsibilities for the TUC in its relations with government but he never lost sight of the realities of collective bargaining in the workplace. As he broadcast on the BBC Caribbean service in 1959:

> The short and important point about trade unions is that their essential function is to look after the interests of the workpeople who are their members. In a democratic society it is the workpeople themselves who decide what are the interests of workpeople and it is therefore they who determine the functions of trade unions.[16]

Woodcock was no Marxist class warrior but a devout Roman Catholic, although unlike other union leaders of that faith this did not turn him into an obsessive anti-Communist. It is true he was ready to press strongly for the expulsion of the Communist-dominated ETU as his first important task as TUC General Secretary. On that issue, there could be no room for any equivocation. Woodcock believed the misbehaviour of the ETU leadership over ballot-rigging threatened to drag the entire trade union movement into public disrepute and this was simply unacceptable.

But in his philosophical approach to industrial relations he was close to being a Marxist in his bleak analysis of the political economy. Woodcock harboured no comforting illusions about eradicating the inequalities of power that existed between capital and labour. Comforting terms such as 'social partnership' and 'industrial consensus' were absent from his vocabulary. He argued from what he believed to be a self-evident truth – that there were always two sides in industry. The primary objective of industrial relations was to secure through negotiation practical and voluntary agreements between employers and unions based on a recognition of that unequal relationship. As he explained:

> The idea that there is a natural and close affinity of interest among all those engaged in any given undertaking or industry which, if not distorted by ignorance or greed, will almost automatically ensure a common approach to problems, is deceptive. The idea of a common purpose in industry is not of itself an illusion but it can be and sometimes is used to justify conclusions which are childish or even dangerous.[17]

The abiding relevance of trade unions arose from the existence of conflicting interests in the workplace and not simply from the traditional aim of protecting working people from exploitation by their employer:

> There are two sides in industry whose interests and objectives do not automatically coincide and differences between the two sides are best dealt with by negotiation and agreement. As long as there are two sides in industry there will be trade unions.[18]

It was a theme he returned to constantly. 'Unions and management exist – not as part of the same team but as two separate groups with different aims working in the same sphere', he explained. This did not necessarily mean endless disruption. 'All that happens is that the people involved have a clearer idea of their respective roles in collective bargaining. They accept their position and that of the other side and seek to reconcile the outstanding differences in frank negotiations. Dismissing the fanatasies of what might be they concentrate on what is'.[19] Woodcock did not believe such conduct represented any stubborn resistance to modernization. On the contrary, he believed workers were readier to accept the need for technological innovation and work reorganization if employers bargained with their trade unions to secure their active cooperation through negotiation and joint consultation.

Woodcock's view of trade unionism stemmed in part from his Roman Catholicism, although he never spoke out openly about its influence on his public life. As he explained although he did not grow up in a home that was 'in any sense of the word fanatically religious – it was part of your life. We were Catholics and we were aware we were Catholics. We didn't flaunt it on our sleeves. We just were so', he recalled.[20] But it also reflected much of his personal experience as a young weaver. It was those years of grinding poverty and exploitation that gave him a deeply held moral view of what it was to be a trade unionist.

> Throughout my life I have been impressed, perhaps I have even become obsessed, with this idea of a good trade unionist as a person with a high sense of his responsibilities. It seemed to me that even as a weaver we had an obligation to each other and if mill-managers were inclined to discriminate against trade unionists it was better for all of us to join the union and make that sort of discrimination impossible.

Woodcock believed most employers realized the 'best and most reliable workpeople were those who had some pride in themselves and in their work ... and that these people were also usually the keenest trade unionists'.[21]

Woodcock's constant preoccupation with the relations between the TUC and the state was therefore underpinned by a deeply ethical and conservative view of what he believed was possible under the voluntarist system of industrial relations. In his solitary eyrie in Congress House, he was as keen to devolve power to the workplace as he was to enhance the TUC's position vis-à-vis its affiliate member unions. Woodcock was more sympathetic than most national union leaders in his understanding of the rise of shop steward power and the so-called 'threat from below' during the 1950s. However, by the time he succeeded Tewson in September 1960, he was also well aware of the difficulties that lay ahead in turning his philosophical insights about trade unionism into any kind of programme of effective action. Woodcock became TUC General Secretary without any detailed blueprint for trade union reform waiting in his bottom drawer.

But he was conscious of the high public expectations encouraged by his arrival at the top of Congress House. During the 1950s the public image of the trade unions was deteriorating. They were no longer admired and respected institutions as they had grown to be during the war. Now they were being turned into the scapegoats of relative economic decline, blamed for economic stagnation, wage inflation, unofficial and inter-union strikes, low productivity, and obstruction to industrial change. Their critics demanded urgent reform from the trade unions and if they did not respond then many urged the state must intervene and regulate their affairs. Some wanted the TUC to acquire greater centralized power and authority over its affiliate members to discipline errant unions and make corporatist deals with government on economic policy, as it allegedly explained the success of economies like Sweden and West Germany. Others on the left favoured 'all power to the shop stewards' and enhanced industrial democracy, a delegation of power to the workplace and an end to the rigidities of national and industry-wide wage bargaining. There were also calls from all sides for internal modernization of the trade unions, to make them more professional and centralised bodies with greater financial resources.

Woodcock was sensitive to the widely diverse range of critics. He recognized the trade unions enjoyed a less sympathetic public opinion than they had done during the war and its immediate aftermath. He also believed the courts were growing more hostile to the trade unions with adverse judgements that might eventually threaten their legal security. Woodcock believed the main reason for such growing disenchantment stemmed from the shift in the power balance in post-war industry due to full employment. Workers were more prosperous, more secure and enjoyed an improved bargaining position in a tight labour market. Although the relative affluence of many workers could not be taken for granted, their newly-found strength encouraged forms of trade union behaviour such as enforcement of closed shops and pursuit of sectionalist wage demands that the wider public found hard to sympathize with. 'It is only when the public is generally favourable to trade unions that the unions can expect them to accept with good humour and tolerance trade union activities which, on the face of them, are bound to seem to people not directly involved to be difficult to understand perhaps foolish, selfish or even unreasonable,' he observed. And he emphasised: 'Without goodwill, the public soon loses patience.' [22]

Woodcock was prepared to defend the closed shop although he agreed it was open to abuse. He wanted trade unions to curb their excesses themselves, accept wider responsibilities and justify their behaviour by reason and common sense, not through the threat or use of industrial muscle. He believed public opinion would not stand for that and would turn against trade unions, demanding the state should restrict their activities. He had in mind

194

the demarcation disputes, 'noisy demonstrations' and unofficial stoppages that were starting to concern the government from the mid-1950s. Woodcock accepted national union leaders were keen to stop such militancy by an 'undisciplined minority' in giving the unions 'a bad name' and he urged them to do so, although he dismissed as simplistic those who believed such industrial unrest was due to any Communist conspiracy.

Trade union structure and the limits of self-reform

Woodcock's first priority after September 1960 was to launch a wide-ranging TUC inquiry into trade union purpose and structure 'with a view to making trade unions better fitted to meet modern industrial conditions'.[23] In an interview with Hugh Chevins, industrial correspondent of the *Daily Telegraph*, he explained that he believed trade unions would have to reform their structures to respond to new circumstances and this meant launching a wide-ranging public debate about trade union purpose. Woodcock confessed he was unable to do this by throwing down a direct challenge to the affiliated unions. 'Simply to say "I believe in big unions or craft unions or industrial unions" will get you nowhere. We must ask first of all – "What are we here for? What is your job?" If you can get that understood then there is the lever for changes that have naturally to follow'. But from the outset Woodcock seemed full of self-doubt. 'I have got nine years in this job', he explained,

> This may be conceit on my part but I really want to do something and I feel that nine years is not a long time. I want to get things moving. I want to see the TUC as a central organization representing not only eight million affiliated members but the whole of Britain's twenty three million working people. I want to elevate the TUC to a position where it can bring influence to bear on the country's industrial and economic development'.[24]

In an undated *aide-memoire* entitled 'What are we here for?' Woodcock sought to articulate his thoughts.[25] 'The whole point and purpose of unions', he ruminated, 'is to protect the interests of workpeople; to advance, to safeguard. Trade unions exist to interpret workpeople's experiences; to discover their real interests; to be their advocates and to administer in their behalf'. The core of the paper concerns Woodcock's familiar preoccupation with state–trade union relations. It justifies extended quotation:

> There can be no formal limits or restrictions on wage bargaining; on trade unions having the right to get as strong as they can by a system of voluntary association including the closed shop. There can be no justification at all for any external limitation of a legal or any other kind upon a union's right to organise, to formulate their policies and to pursue them as relentlessly as they can. In the past,

circumstances were the limiting factor. But today there is a limit to what unions should do – can rightly do – without making it impossible for the government to do the right things too. This is what I call the practical limits of regulation that we want to find. It is not a question of form but it is the principle of the acceptance of the idea that there are limits and it is for us to see if we can define those limits. We cannot define them precisely. I am thinking about a conception at a point to which the unions are obliged to restrain the full use of their authority in a full employment society with due regard to the wider national effects of their individual actions. I am trying to achieve the establishment of an idea that there is an obligation upon unions to conform to a national policy which covers situations wider than the ones with which the unions are dealing.

Woodcock also made it clear in the document that unions must be concerned with much more than collective bargaining:

If unions keep using their strength to push up wages to the point at which inflation is a constant feature and a constant danger to the maintenance of our exports and of the ability to maintain our position as an exporting nation, then the only thing we can do is to induce deflation – deliberately to restrain price movements even when it means inducing unemployment to be abler to do it. That is the heart of the matter. A union ought to reflect upon the imposition or the acceptance in principle of a limit to what they can do. The limit is not what they can get out of the employer without having to strike but it does involve reactions all round. If a key body in an industry or firm exploits its strength to the full, then the rest of the workers in that firm have a limit imposed upon them by the action of that key body that went ahead regardless of anyone else's interests. I am thinking of arguments that will be needed to establish what will be considered a new principle of trade unionism – that unions do not ruthlessly exploit their strength. I want to make them more powerful instruments, improve their structure, improve their knowledge of the possibilities. But if as a result of the enquiry all that we did was to improve the competence of trade unions within their preconceived field of getting the most they can for their workpeople; for streamlining their negotiations, or devolving responsibility downwards by giving full authority to people at the shop level to go ahead; if, as a result, all that we can do is to make them more dangerous in terms of rocking the national boat, then we should not have done enough. My object is not simply to improve the unions as instruments for doing what they want without reflection on the consequences of their actions.

At the initial stage of the TUC enquiry Woodcock wanted agreement from union leaders on these ideas: 'Eventually we shall have to get formal machinery, some power by which we impose conceptions but the first thing is to get the conceptions accepted as part of the belief of trade unionism ... We are not going to jump in straightaway with purely structural talk. The first thing is to establish the essential functions of trade unionism'. Woodcock also used the oppportunity of his undated *aide-memoire* to define what the TUC's relationship should to be in politics. 'The TUC is in politics – there is no question at all about that', he wrote. 'But we are not going to take our policy from anyone else. When I say we have to fit in with a conception of national interest, I do not mean a conception of national interest given to us by anyone else, neither by the Labour Party nor the Conservative government'.

In this key document Woodcock laid out what was a bold and radical challenge to the trade unions but his exposition remained confined to the privacy of Congress House. Woodcock never revealed to the wider outside world his vision of modern trade unionism in such a startling and perceptive way. It is also strange that he did not decide to launch the inquiry he wanted until two years after his arrival as TUC General Secretary. Indeed, it was not until a meeting of the TUC's Finance and General Purposes Committee on 10 December 1962 that he explained to senior union leaders what he sought in an oratorical *tour de force* on trade union purpose that seemed to bewilder his audience.

A minute of the occasion provides a cogent account of what Woodcock had to say. If his aim was to win support for giving the TUC a greater authority over its affiliate members in the wider interests of the trade union movement, he was to find it a futile effort. Woodcock contrasted the trade unions before and after the Second World War. As he explained:

> In the pre-1939 period there was a constant striving for national agreements and a common rate. The direction of union power was upwards; unions were conscious of seeking to be nationally controlled. At that time the state accepted no responsibility and we were constant in wanting no interference ... But since 1944 successive governments have accepted the necessity for full employment: in the future it is certain that governments will continue this policy. We are adamant that government should accept its obligations in such matters as trade and finance: is there no obligation on trade unions?

The TUC had an obligation to help unions by continuing to impress on the government the need for full employment, which was the 'greatest objective of the TUC. Surely this means that unions have an obligation to the TUC or are they to exercise complete freedom at whatever cost to full employment or whatever cost to other unions? We should not always resist government interference'.

Woodcock argued that 'if every union was a law unto itself with no responsibility for outside, then it was not the kind of trade unionism on which we were brought up to believe in ... There was an interdependence of the trade union movement at the present time. Men on strike can put thousands out of work'.

> There is a serious disparity in wages, for example, between the car industry and railways. Coordination has never been possible. Last year the nurses, miners, engineers and railwaymen showed that a common effort was desirable and we could have done a great deal for the nurses and railwaymen if the miners and engineers had held off.

Full employment had given to many unions the power to 'go it alone' but 'unions should not appeal to man's worst instincts. It is not simply a matter of the highest possible wage; man is concerned with continuity of employment and purchasing power. The free-for-all cannot continue unabated; it will bring regulation by unemployment or legislation'. Noting the devolution of authority to local groups on the shop floor, he insisted that:

> These groups should be within the general supervision of the unions. We should not encourage workers to exploit ruthlessly their strength in some sectors; this would lead to fragmented unions. Indeed, if we concentrate on wages no one will take any notice of us on 'government' matters. In a free for all we must be part of the all but is the free for all to continue for ever?[26]

For Woodcock, the 'heart of the matter' lay in a crucial question: 'Could the unions say we look to you to press the government to maintain economic conditions, to see that the demand for labour is maintained, and yet at the same time say but the TUC can have no concern at what we do however it may affect your function?'[27] He said that he was worried at what would happen if the unions did not seek to work to change the 'free-for-all society'. 'If people ruthlessly exploited their economic strength created by community action and by the TUC's action in some cases, the community would not tolerate the circumstances which lead to instability', Woodcock continued. Even a government committed to full employment might not accept the responsibility 'if the trade union movement ruthlessly exploited to the full its strength in separate groups'. It is important to underline the fact that Woodcock pinned the main blame on employers because they had agreed to wage increases on a 'kind of cost-plus basis'. His conclusion was grave:

> If this problem were not solved, the government would solve it by putting employers back into the position of having to be tough. Industrial discipline should not be enforced by regulation or by unemployment. If they ever came up against disastrous economic conditions, there would be nothing they could do, no matter how they organized themselves.

Woodcock found no supporters around the table for his cause. Frank Cousins, the left-wing General Secretary of the TGWU, was dismissive of what he had heard. 'It is impossible to make trade unionists into idealists', he warned Woodcock. Cousins suspected the TUC General Secretary wanted more power at the expense of affiliated union leaders and if this was so there would be little role left for men like him. Cousins' view was: 'In a system of free for all unions must be part of the free for all. Unions should not be commercial undertakings; they should use power for the people they represent'. William Carron, right-wing President of the AEU, used the occasion to attack wage disparities between skilled workers and what he deemed the irresponsibility of militant shop stewards. Nobody was ready to engage with

Woodcock's philosophy about trade union purpose. His bold initiative was almost over before it had begun.

Later Woodcock blamed himself for trying to initiate the debate about union structure ahead of that of purpose. In fact, he had not done so. But the minutes of that December 1962 TUC meeting suggest he stood alone in his attempt to debate in a serious, fundamental fashion what the unions were there for. Woodcock was right to feel that moving on to union structure was a pointless exercise if no agreement had been reached about union purpose. Nevertheless, that is what he proceeded to do. Again, he failed to make any headway with the leaders of affiliated unions. In May 1963 Woodcock virtually ended the possibility of any significant advance for the inquiry by submitting a paper to his colleagues advocating industrial unionism. It should have been no surprise to him that such an argument fell on deaf ears. In 1927 and again in 1944 internal TUC inquiries had discussed the idea of industrial unionism but without reaching any agreement. Yet now Woodcock argued in his paper:

> Industrial unionism is the only basis on which it would be possible to make continuous and substantial progress towards structural integration. Organization on any other basis, short of a single union for all workpeople, is bound to result in diversity of structure.[28]

Woodcock did not accept industrial unionism was a Utopian proposal if the unions were 'prepared to take time, patience and flexibility' in trying to bring it about. 'It has been done in other countries and the widely held belief if we in Britain were starting from scratch we would build trade unions on an industrial basis surely implies these technical questions are not insoluble'. He accepted it might take forty to fifty years to achieve industrial unionism but believed it was well worth laying it down as a TUC objective. However, Woodcock conceded that such a change would inevitably involve the demise of two of the largest, multi-industry based unions in the country, the TGWU and the GMWU whose mainly manual worker members were spread right across the labour market. 'This difficulty could only be overcome, if at all, by a scheme framed in such a way as to allow unions to make the required changes gradually over a long period of time', he admitted. He thought the example of the British Iron and Steel and Kindred Trades Association might be considered: 'In that recruitment into a number of separate unions was stopped and though the unions carried on with their existing membership they were eventually superseded in the natural course of events by the new association'. His paper failed to find the slightest support among other union leaders. Cousins again lost no time in rejecting his arguments. He pointed out his own organization was a splendid example of industrial unionism with 54 former unions united in one body. Not to be outdone by this, Fred Hayday of the General and Municipal Workers said his union consisted of 300 different unions.[29]

Congress House continued to discuss the nature of structural reform by looking at possible areas where the TUC could encourage trade union mergers and amalgamations. But the inquiry was virtually at an end by the time of the TUC's Finance and General Purposes Committee on 10 February 1964. For that meeting, at Woodcock's direct insistence, the secretariat added a section to a memorandum, calling for the abolition of the TGWU and NUGMW with a transfer of most of their members to new industry-based organizations. They would then merge to represent 'miscellaneous industries and groups of workpeople not easily classified for attachment to the main industrial unions' such as chemicals, paint, rubber and plastics.[30] This was not a prospect likely to find any favour with the large unions concerned. By the time of the 1964 Congress Woodcock admitted defeat on trade union reform. 'I was perhaps wrong to speak of industrial unionism and ought to have spoken more about coordination or amalgamation leading to one bargaining unit for each area of industrial negotiations either for a whole industry or more in line with présent day thinking', he admitted.[31]

The inquiry into trade union structure and purpose was not entirely barren of achievement. In 1964–6 the TUC held 24 conferences on union structure to encourage union mergers and amalgamations. While in 1962 there had been 182 TUC affiliates, that number had fallen to 170 four years later. In addition union density rose by 2 per cent, and there was a net gain of 450,000 members for TUC affiliates. Yet it was a sad outcome for what Woodcock had begun in 1962 with such high hopes. He does not seem to have found the time, the energy or the organizational means for turning his insightful analysis of the trade union problem into practical and successful policymaking. A TUC office note dated 4 August 1967 on 'Woodcock's main achievements' ought to provide a final word on his famous inquiry. As it explained:

> In 1962 the General Secretary persuaded the annual TUC to agree to a thoroughgoing examination of trade union structure. The intention of the General Secretary was to secure by amalgamation a considerable reduction in the number of trade unions and more particularly to get unions formed on the basis of industries as against the craft basis of many of the older unions or the heterogenous spread of the general labour unions. This proved to be too ambitious or precipitous for most of the unions. Nevertheless, structural reform by amalgamation and closer association has recently proceeded on an *ad hoc* basis more speedily than for many years.[32]

The state steps in: Donovan and *In Place of Strife*

'I desperately wanted all the time I was at the TUC and still want to try to get a clearer and more widely acceptable understanding of what trade unions are for', Woodcock told Harold Webb, the BBC's industrial correspondent in 1970, when reminiscing as Chairman of the newly formed independent Commission on Industrial Relations.[33] Thwarted by his failure to win over his TUC General Council colleagues, he saw the Wilson government's appointment of a Royal Commission on Trade Unions and Employers' Associations as an alternative way forward. Perhaps a broader forum could begin to answer the 'what are we here for?' question: 'I looked on that commission as an instrument from which I could get this discussion and this clear statement of trade union purpose'. This is why he insisted he should become a member of the proposed commission chaired by Lord Donovan, the well known and respected judge. Without his presence on the body he feared the other Commission members might not deal with the crucial problem that continued to trouble him. As he explained to Webb:

> I did not think that what I wanted the Donovan Commission to do could be done simply by writing a memorandum of evidence and appearing on one or two days to be questioned by a committee over which I had not got some continuous influence. I will put it as conceitedly as that: I wanted to be there in the detailed discussions.

But Woodcock confessed to Webb that after all the Commission failed to address the question of what trade unions were here for:

> The Donovan Commission became mainly (though not exclusively) a commission on the structure of industrial relations, on collective bargaining. And all the things that oppressed me at the TUC – our relations with government, our responsibility shared with government for the development of our social services, education, hospitals, National Health Service and so on – those things were not touched on in the Donovan Commission. I failed to get the discussion I wanted.

But the question is – did Woodcock ever really try? He had served on the Royal Commission on Taxation and on the Radcliffe Committee on the working of the monetary system so he was not inexperienced on what being on such a commission involved. From the start, however, Woodcock turned out to be a surprisingly infrequent attender at the Donovan Commission's meetings. And the minutes of the Commission give no sign that when he did bother to turn up he ever raised that 'what are we here for?' question. He certainly never submitted a memorandum of his own. It was Andrew Shonfield, the incisive Economics Editor of the *Observer*, who produced a trenchant analysis that ended up almost as a one-man minority report. The intellectual firepower behind the mainstream work of the commission came from the so-called Oxford University industrial relations school of Professor Hugh Clegg, Allan Flanders and Otto Kahn-Freund. It was Clegg's draft that formed the core of the final report with little sign of any involvement from Woodcock.

Indeed, Woodcock and his TUC colleague, Lord Collison of the Agricultural Workers' union, appear to have adopted a wholly negative attitude to the Commission's suggestion that it should widen its investigations to cover unofficial strikes and restrictive labour practices. This was partly due to the growing concern inside the TUC that initial evidence before the Commission seemed to be hostile to trade unions. Woodcock claimed that the TUC had been 'put on the defensive by criticisms arising in evidence heard so far; this might be an accidental result of the way evidence has so far come in since the first union had only been heard that morning and the Commission had previously been reluctant to hear individual unions in advance of the TUC'.[34] But this was entirely Woodcock's own responsibility. The long delay before the TUC itself produced its own written evidence to the Commission remains baffling. Woodcock himself could hardly have endeared himself to his Commission colleagues when he told them:

> The setting up of the Commission could perhaps be attributed to the efforts of the TUC more than anyone else and they had had high hopes of what an inquiry which would essentially be into industrial relations might achieve; but now that the Commission was receiving many (often ill thought-out) proposals, for example on the legal enforceability of collective agreements, whose object was to put pressure on the unions they were naturally wary. This inclined them to wait and see what criticisms were made before putting in their own evidence. In any case the TUC staff was under severe strain at present and this was holding up work on its evidence.

Woodcock explained he found it 'quite impossible to attend meetings of the Commission more than once a week'.[35]

Even more surprisingly, he seemed keen to limit the areas of inquiry of the Commission away from his own 'what are we here for?' question. He explained to his colleagues that:

> It was questionable whether it was really for the commission to deal for example with some of the vast questions raised under the heading of incomes policy. Fundamentally the Commission's job was to examine industrial relations. It should not act in the belief that it could direct the two sides of industry in any particular direction.[36]

When the Donovan Commission eventually held a discussion on 10 May 1966 over the role of unions and employers in 'accelerating the social and economic advance of the nation', Woodcock was conspicuous by his absence. By early autumn of that year Lord Donovan was starting to lose patience with the TUC because of its continuing failure to produce any of its long-awaited evidence. He told his colleagues that the Commission was 'now reaching the end of its hearings of oral evidence and was about to embark on discussions on the problems before it and these discussions would concern matters of great moment to the trade union movement. It would be unfortunate if the Commission had to do this without having had both the written and oral evidence of the TUC'.[37]

When the TUC evidence did eventually reach the Commission in November 1966, eighteen months after the Commission had started its work, it devoted little space to a discussion of Woodcock's 'what are we here for?' question. He wrote the first chapter of the TUC's written submission himself but its reflections on the relationship between the trade unions and the state were rather perfunctory. Indeed, Woodcock seemed to visualize government intervention in industrial relations only as a complement or a second-best alternative to the strengthening of employer–trade union agreements. The government's attitude, he argued, was 'one of abstention, of formal indifference'. In any future development of the relationship the 'respective responsibilities of trade unions and government' should be made 'quite distinct' to avoid 'dangers of.misunderstanding'.[38] Woodcock at no time sought to demand a direct TUC role in the administering of public policy. The TUC evidence was highly circumscribed on what it visualized the TUC's relationship ought to be with the state. There were few signs of the more radical analysis contained in Woodcock's earlier memorandum in 1962 on 'what are we here for?'.

In 1971 Woodcock reflected on the outcome of the Royal Commission. 'If the Commission failed to deal with an important question it was this question of incomes policy or more correctly the relationship of trade unions and the state', he said.

> I would have been willing for the commission to discuss all aspects of incomes policy within a discussion of the wider question. I tried, though perhaps not hard enough, to get the commission to examine the essential role and responsibilities of modern governments. But by the time we had done with 'relations between management and employees' and might have gone on to the closer examination of the role of trade unions and employer associations in accelerating the social and economic advance of the nation, the commission had had enough.[39]

And yet Woodcock had plenty of opportunity during his time on the Donovan Commission to pursue the issue that agonized him. His apparent indolence and lack of interest contrasts sharply with Shonfield's hyperactive contribution.

The final outcome of the Commission's deliberations, the Donovan Report, was concerned overwhelmingly with the problem of how to reconcile what it called the 'formal' with the 'informal' system of industrial relations, through acceptance of a more structured approach to workplace bargaining by the encouragement of company-wide collective agreements. The document had surprisingly little to say about the role of the state in industrial relations or the impact of trade unions on the wider political economy. The TUC's own rather churlish response to the Donovan Report hardly suggests Woodcock was part of the final outcome. But by the summer of 1968 Woodcock seems to have grown tired of TUC General Council attitudes, no doubt due in part to his increasing difficulties in maintaining its support for relations with the Labour government over incomes policy. The General Council statement on Donovan suggested it would give 'further consideration' to establishing basic principles to cover union admission, discipline and elections, with the TUC providing a 'last resort for individuals who have a complaint under existing procedures'. The TUC document went on: 'The General Council would be seriously concerned by any government commitment in this particular area in advance of their own examination of the issues involved'.[40] Woodcock wrote angrily in the margin of his copy; 'Government will not, however, wait for ever or be satisfied with the pussyfooting pace of the General Council'.

Indeed, he seemed to be moving towards a sympathetic view of the need for government action to reform the trade unions. Barbara Castle, the Secretary of State for Employment and Productivity, recalls that Woodcock appeared ready to swallow whole her new radical plans. As she noted in her diary on 19 December 1968 : 'On an impulse I have decided to take him completely into my confidence about what I am proposing over Donovan. He listened to my full resume in silence and then to my surprise said he didn't think there was anything there that need alarm the trade union movement. I could hardly believe my ears!'[41] 'I don't remember the exact words I used', Woodcock later recalled, 'But what I think I said was "well I am not surprised that we are faced with this"'.[42] It was Woodcock who persuaded her to reveal her plans to the TUC Finance and General Purposes Committee before she presented them to the full Cabinet. 'He knew I would be taking a risk in talking fully to the TUC before going to the Cabinet but he was sure it would reap dividends', said Mrs Castle. 'The TUC would then never be able to say they had not been consulted fully before the government had made up its mind'.[43] Again, she recalls in her diary on 2 January 1969 that Woodcock called her White Paper, *In Place of Strife,* 'excellent': 'He went on almost passionately to say I had given the trade unions the opportunity he had always wanted them to be given and that our approach had been better than Donovan's'. Woodcock informed her: 'I wanted the Commission to be more forthcoming but I had to compromise'. However, Mrs Castle was dubious as to Woodcock's practical utility as an ally:

> He clearly inferred my penal powers would act as an incentive to the unions to do the job themselves and for this reason he welcomed them and I hinted hard that he could save an unnecessary cleavage with the unions if he would only say as much. He obviously intends to help but no doubt he will do so in his own obscure way.

Nevertheless, she believed him when he assured her there was 'no violation of trade union principles in my package'.[44]

Woodcock had always wanted the TUC to take a direct role in influencing government decisions, especially in the making of macro-economic policy. But he recognized the difficulties of persuading the TUC General Council to become involved in such a development if this meant any abrogation of the power of affiliate unions over their collective bargaining. Trade union suspicions of the state were based on tradition and practical experience. As Woodcock accepted: 'Our movement is clannish, inbred. It prefers to stick to itself and avoid outside influences. It is a bit afraid of entanglements'.[45] The TUC's strategic shift from mass demonstrations and marches to behind-the-scenes lobbying in Whitehall departments did not take place without years of agonized debate and indecision. Woodcock's attitude was similar to that of his mentor Sir Walter Citrine, who during his period as TUC General Secretary between 1926 and 1946, had sought to broaden the TUC's influence over public policy so that it would have 'power to act on policy issues in a cohesive manner'.[46] During the 1930s – from the 1932 Ottawa conference which introduced Imperial preference to the 1939 government preparations for war – the TUC established a limited access to consultation.

But it was the Second World War that accelerated this process. The new mood of self-confidence and realism during those years can be detected in the pages of the TUC's increasingly voluminous annual reports. By 1945 in Citrine's words the TUC had established the right to be heard on 'those questions of general policy which were of common interest'.[47] In reality, the practice never matched the ideal. This was partly due, in Woodcock's opinion, to the calibre of the trade union leaders who joined the multiplicity of public service posts offered to them after the war. 'Seniority, union muscle, competence. You needed one of those assets to get a job and in that order', he explained. Woodcock disliked what he regarded as the improper way in which public appointments were treated as perks of office by union leaders. He recalled receiving a complaint from John Hare, Minister of Agriculture in the 1950s, that the union nominees on the marketing boards were not making an effort. 'It was true. There was no reporting back. We never knew what they were doing. In fact they did damn all'.[48]

As TUC General Secretary, Woodcock was determined to try and change such attitudes. He was also keen to encourage a more active role for the TUC in its relations with government, even a Conservative one. His aims were assisted enormously by Prime Minister Harold MacMillan's decision to form the National Economic Development Council in 1962, a tripartite forum designed to develop a wider understanding of the economy in a systematic way. Woodcock later believed one of his greatest achievements had been to persuade the unions to agree that the TUC should participate in the NEDC at a time when state–union relations were strained by a government clamp-down on public sector pay and growing pressure for the creation of a national incomes strategy. In many ways the NEDC was the institutional expression of Woodcock's philosophy for it gave the unions the opportunity and responsibility to play a significant role in public policy. 'It was the reflection of my attitude', he explained. 'It was the outward sign of the inward grace'.[49] Woodcock told the 1962 Congress:

> We must not as a trade union movement give the impression that we are claiming absolute, unfettered, unqualified freedom, to do what we like and to hell with the rest. That is not trade unionism, never has been. The whole point and purpose of trade unionism is for people to get together and collectively come to a common policy. That is what the NEDC is for in intention.[50]

The new body was seen as the instrument that would gradually break down the defensive attitudes of the trade unions and make them ready to take what Woodcock called 'a completely impartial, coldly analytical view of all our problems'. He visualized the NEDC playing an educative role in the modernization of trade unions by making them much more aware of the wider concerns of the political economy beyond collective bargaining. The structure of the NEDC owed much to the strength of his own arguments in convincing Selwyn Lloyd, the Conservative Chancellor of the Exchequer, that the proposed body should be much more than a device for simply 'extending and regularising the consultative system' and providing the Treasury with advice.[51]

From the outset, Woodcock insisted that the six union members of the NEDC must be chosen by the TUC General Council and not the government. This was made a condition for TUC involvement in the new tripartite organization. Moreover, the TUC nominees were to sit on the NEDC as a collective group not as individuals, and they were to report back and be accountable to the TUC Economic Committee and the General Council. Woodcock described them once as the 'ambassadors of the movement' who were 'engaged' but not 'committed', because that would have suggested that union leaders were under some 'absolute obligation' which was never possible. It was unclear where the NEDC was leading under the Conservatives. Woodcock admitted to a meeting of union research officers in November 1963, fifteen months after its creation, that it remained an 'open question' how the NEDC would develop. 'When they had come to really difficult problems they had tacitly side-tracked them but they were at least still together', he admitted:

> The TUC had never wanted a 'talking shop', doing nothing but produce reports on the economic situation and a yearly economic survey. Economic surveys, as such, were an important and indisputable part of planning but the most important part of planning was agreeing to make things happen.[52]

The 1967 TUC assessment of his 'achievements' highlighted the importance of his role in the creation of the NEDC. The TUC's involvement was seen as a reflection of 'a greater willingness on the part of the trade union movement to cooperate with governments and employers in the formulation and administration of economic policy and in economic planning in particular'.[53] The monthly NEDC meetings were useful, often informative, gatherings that dealt with the familiar long-term ills which impeded economic growth such as poor productivity, lack of workers' skill training and education, too little industrial investment and lack of financial incentives for companies. More detailed, practical work was done by what were known as the 'little NEDDYS', the sector or industry-based economic development committees serviced by the NEDC secretariat. Union officials sat on those bodies but their performance was inevitably uneven in quality. Woodcock acknowledged the difficulties this presented to the TUC itself as it attempted to support their activities with its own limited resources.

Critics of the NEDC complained that the body was toothless because it lacked executive powers and was more of a talking shop than a body capable of effective action. Its early agenda was concerned with looking at ways of improving economic growth and examining the obstacles to better performance. It is true the Conservative government had no wish to strengthen the NEDC in economic policy-making in such a way that it could usurp or challenge the powers of the state and parliament. But Woodcock was much more upset by the attitude of the Labour government after October 1964, when it downgraded the NEDC's strategic role through a reassertion of executive authority. George Brown's newly formed Department of Economic Affairs and the resulting ambitious 1965 National Plan were to be the dynamos for the new growth strategy, not the NEDC. Woodcock's ambivalent attitude to the Labour Party was confirmed by his experiences of working with Harold Wilson and his ministers on economic policy. In retrospect, he believed he found it easier and more congenial to work with Reginald Maudling as Chancellor of the Exchequer than his Labour successors. 'When Labour came in they wanted to hog everything, do everything their way', he remembered. 'They met an enormous amount of goodwill and got a lot of support in the early stages'.[54]

In fact, Woodcock held a low opinion of most politicians, Labour as much as Conservative. He disliked the TUC being overly committed to Labour. He wanted to establish an enhanced role for Congress House as the representative national federation for organized workers, whatever their political loyalties might be, and he never visualized the TUC as a servile wing of the Labour party. He regarded the affiliation to the TUC of NALGO, the white collar local government trade union which was not affiliated to the Labour Party and did not even have a political fund at that time, as one of his greatest achievements while General Secretary. In the TUC's evidence to the Donovan Commission the arms-length nature of its relationship to Labour was emphasized as 'a significant divergence of function'. The TUC memorandum reflected: 'The existence of common roots yet distinct functions is the most important feature of the relationship. The relationship becomes strained if either attempts to capitalise on the loyalties which exist and the strength of the relationship lies paradoxically in the looseness of the ties'.[55]

Woodcock made it clear that he would not have considered joining the Labour government in October 1964 even if he had been asked. Frank Cousins was to suffer an unhappy period as Minister of Technology until he resigned in protest at the government's economic crisis measures in July 1966. In his philosophy Woodcock may have been keen to develop close state–union relations. But during Labour's years in office there was a serious lack of cohesion between the TUC and government. The absence of a figure like Bevin who could straddle the two sides was to prove a real weakness.

The rise and fall of incomes policy

The focus of friction between the two wings of the labour movement centred around the tangled and ever-present issue of incomes policy. This was due to the almost persistent pressure from the Labour government after October 1964 on the TUC to seek to moderate the wage claims of its affiliated unions as a way of convincing the international financial community that the UK economy was basically sound. Woodcock had always been, in his own words, 'very much an incomes policy man ever since September 1939'. He regarded reaching common agreement over wage determination between the TUC and government as 'an essential part of a full employment policy'. But he also admitted union leaders were always less convinced than he was about the need for any form of incomes policy. 'All through, there was reluctance, distrust, dislike, opposition, certainly always uneasiness about any talk or any attempt to control wages'.[56]

Woodcock understood trade union reluctance to engage in wage restraint even if he did not really share such doubts or resistance himself. He failed to see how it was possible for the TUC to gain any credibility in pressing its own economic agenda with governments if it failed to address the wages question in a serious manner. To militant union leaders like Frank Cousins the whole purpose of trade unionism was to gain more money for the members. But Woodcock recoiled from what he considered such an uncomplicated view, although he bewildered rather than convinced his colleagues over what actual role he envisaged for the TUC in the development of a permanent incomes policy. His own personal experience in the 1930s, as well as his backroom work at the TUC during the war and with the Attlee government, had strengthened his belief that wage stability was necessary in a democratic society to ensure there could be no return to the ravages of mass unemployment. He regarded a voluntary incomes policy as an essential pre-requisite to prevent such a catastrophe. But Woodcock was never favourable to the idea of a statutory incomes policy legislated by government and backed with penal sanctions to be used against unwilling employers or workers. After 1964 he spent much of his time arguing as best he could against a Labour government which increasingly believed the UK economy faced ruin unless curbs were placed on pay bargaining to prevent wage push inflation.

But Woodcock also recognized that governments were not over-impressed by the TUC's capacity to deliver its side of any economic bargain. Ministers under stress sought TUC consent, or at least acquiescence, in incomes re-straint as a matter of urgency in the national interest. Woodcock did not believe such pressure was conducive to economic success. Union leaders might respond favourably to Labour government exhortations, but through a sense of political loyalty to the Labour party rather than from any convic-tion that wage restraint made much industrial or economic sense.

Woodcock regarded incomes policy as a long-term objective not a short-term fix. It would take time to convince union leaders that a national understanding over pay was in the best interests of their members, he be-lieved. He was opposed instinctively to wage restraint imposed by government through fiat or threat. During his years as General Secretary, Congress never defeated resolutions favourable to the principle of incomes policy. 'Through-out my time we adhered to the view that an incomes policy was desirable and was compatible with proper trade union objectives', he said. 'We had perhaps disagreements sometimes among ourselves about methods'.[57] In the early 1960s Woodcock endeavoured to stimulate 'a mood, a sense of respon-sibility' on pay among union leaders. But his efforts were continually challenged by Frank Cousins. At the 1963 Congress Woodcock gave articu-late expression to the need for a voluntary incomes policy and its connection to his wider concerns about union–state relations. In doing so he laid bare the tangled difficulties of resolving the problem of reconciliation between the demands of the state and the aspirations of union members which was never to be resolved. As Woodcock told the delegates it was,

> entirely foreign to trade union tradition and practice for there to be any interfer-ence whatsoever at any time with unions in their right to pursue on behalf of their members claims for improvements in wages and working conditions. It is a tradi-tion of the trade union movement. This is why we were formed. This is what we have done all our lives.

Woodcock agreed that it was 'wrong and certainly dangerous even to at-tempt to interfere with unions in this bargaining process'. But then he went on to point out as a result of the TUC's own success since 1945 in increasing its power and influence over governments in the making of economic policy, it was impossible for the unions to exclude the wages question from the

209

public policy agenda. He asked: 'Are we when these big issues come up, to sit supine and dumb and mute, to have nothing at all to say?'. In his view the days of TUC protest were over. He asserted: 'We left Trafalgar Square a long time ago'. Now the TUC should use its influence in the commitee rooms sitting opposite the men with power in government and this meant having to discuss pay as well as prices, profits, rents and the rest.[58]

Although he was reluctant to admit it publicly, Woodcock believed the trade unions would never move over pay and perhaps over anything else unless they were subjected to external pressures. Governments needed to confront the TUC with problems to which it would have to respond. Unity at the TUC came from the dangers posed to it by outside threats or blandishments. On the other hand, Woodcock found it hard to balance that belief with his intellectual fastidiousness over any crude use of political power. In the autumn of 1965 he had to tolerate the bullying style of George Brown who had demanded the TUC General Council must accept the introduction of a compulsory early warning system for price rises and pay settlements. Woodcock believed that no incomes policy stood much chance of success if it was divorced from any genuine commitment to economic growth and became an instrument that sought to impose deflation on working people. But out of the 1965 crisis came the TUC initiative to create its own committee to vet wage claims and settlements presented to it by affiliated unions, a move that in the words of the then Chancellor Jim Callaghan 'attracted favourable coverage in many countries and improved sentiment markedly'.[59] The TUC's creation of a 'distinctive, self-administered incomes policy' involving the notification by unions of their wage claims through a vetting procedure was a clear intrusion into union autonomy.

However, Woodcock remained sceptical of the government's broad economic strategy. In the July 1966 crisis he was inclined to call inside the TUC for a rejection of the government's proposed wage freeze. Woodcock believed it would serve the unions little purpose if they swallowed the government's package and then found it was rejected by work groups through aggressive shop floor bargaining over which neither the TUC nor its affiliate unions could exercise effective control. But the wage vetting process continued to provide the TUC with a semblance of influence over pay, even if the government was unimpressed by the outcome in restraining union bargainers. The 1967 assessment of Woodcock's 'achievements' argued that the TUC had strengthened its position as the 'authoritative voice of the British trade union movement' in its dealings with governments by its role in the development of incomes policy.[60] It emphasized that this did involve a clear TUC intervention in the domestic affairs of the unions by bringing wages and the working conditions of their members into scrutiny.

On the other hand, Woodcock saw no point in mobilizing the TUC to confront the government's incomes policy as the growing left in the unions demanded. In his last speech as General Secretary to the 1968 Congress, he returned to old themes. He argued that although the TUC had to oppose government policies, there was no future in getting into fights with governments 'in the kind of world in which we live today'. In the long run, the TUC had to work with governments. He told delegates that what Britain needed was 'a better ordered and more methodical, sensible and more just system of collective bargaining and wage settlement'. He developed his now familiar text: while unions existed as 'custodians of the principle of collective bargaining', this did not mean collective bargaining was about 'simply strengthening little groups to do what they like and to hell with the rest of us'.[61] But by 1968 such sentiments found limited support among union leaders. Cousins, backed by the newly elected left-wing President of the AEU, Hugh Scanlon, successfully moved a resolution that rejected any legislation designed to restrict pay on the grounds it curtailed basic union rights. A motion that merely reaffirmed Congress support for the TUC's voluntary system was carried only narrowly by a 34,000 majority.

None the less Woodcock was successful in winning over the TUC General Council to a more systematic approach to economic policy-making which would strengthen Congress House in its relations with government. This came with agreement on the publication of an annual TUC economic review. 'The success of the TUC in making a deal with government depended upon the TUC's internal competence and their ability to have something to give as well as to take in a bargain', Woodcock told a TUC conference of union executives on 17 January 1968. The TUC needed to have the right to commit unions on economic policy and to 'speak with a union about attitudes and practices which impeded the realization of the objectives of the trade union movement as a whole'. The TUC annual economic review was regarded by Woodcock as the culmination of a process that went back to the Second World War. He saw its introduction as an important stage in turning the TUC from being a 'self-centred pressure group' into an organization that could offer government 'a coherent, competent, sensible, intelligent view', reflecting the TUC's position as a 'responsible and permanent part of a civilised community'.[62] The annual review did bring a greater intellectual coherence to TUC economic thought. Long after the tedious battles over incomes policies were forgotten, that publication remained an important part of the TUC public policy process, ensuring union leaders were better equipped to argue their case in the trade union interest against the restrictive views of the Treasury.

Assessment

Woodcock regretted he did not serve long enough as TUC General Secretary. But it is doubtful whether he would have achieved much more than he did if his term at Congress House had lasted fifteen rather than less than nine years. The job of TUC General Secretary is almost an impossible one to carry out with success at the best of times. There are no big battalions that the General Secretary can mobilize. Moreover, the General Secretary is very much the servant of Congress, the collective voice of the movement. This imposes severe limits on his or her capacity to lead the unions too far in any particular or distinctive policy direction. Ideally, the TUC General Secretary requires powerful allies on the General Council to be effective. Citrine was able to find such a partner in the massive TGWU union leader, Ernest Bevin, after 1926. For almost twenty years the two men – despite their personal differences of style and character – worked together in a formidable alliance that helped to transform the TUC into an increasingly respected and influential national institution. Woodcock's trouble was that he was to enjoy no similar relationship with any senior union leaders on the General Council. It is true Frank Cousins of the TGWU was a man he respected, but he also had very different ideas about what trade unions were for than Woodcock. 'He was an influence against me. But I admired the man', admitted Woodcock.

> He read his papers. He knew the subject and his arguments were not to be thrown away. They were not trivial. They were related to a basic belief and principles just as I believe mine were. Mine was a principle of elevating the TUC to be the voice of the trade union movement in the field of economic policy. His belief was that individual unions existed to protect the working interests of their members. Now those two things were not immediately reconcilable.[63]

The truth is that Woodcock lacked the personal and political qualities needed to cajole and gladhand, to flatter and manouevre. He was conceited about his own cleverness and scornful of those who were less intelligent than he was himself. But this made it very difficult to exercise any positive influence over the thinking of the TUC General Council, although he was respected and often feared by its members and emphatically by the able Congress House secretariat. As Woodcock admitted: 'I would float a proposal. It would be chewed over in committee, then it would go to the General Council and finally to Congress by which time it was unrecognizable from what I first envisaged'.[64] He was as much aware of his own personal failings as his critics. But it is debatable whether anybody else could have made much difference to the evolution of the TUC during the crisis years of the 1960s.

What Woodcock did, however, was to ask the crucial questions about the future of trade unionism. He may not have been able to translate his own answers into effective action but he was more aware than others about the importance of establishing a stable and credible relationship between the trade unions and the state in a full employment economy. This involved a difficult balancing of interests. As he explained in 1968, the TUC performed two distinct and conflicting functions. It was there to represent the 'common interests of working people'. But it was also established that it would not interfere in the 'domestic affairs of the unions'. 'We have to find a way of reconciling these two apparent opposite and contradictory obligations'.[65] Woodcock warned the TUC it would have to persuade its affiliate unions to adapt their own divergent policies to conform with the commonly agreed objectives of the movement as a whole. If this was not done, then severe troubles lay ahead. Unless the TUC was modernized by the unions themselves to take on more collective responsibility, then a future government was likely to introduce industrial relations laws to restrict their activities and disengage the state from economic management with a resulting abandonment of any commitment to full employment. Events under Margaret Thatcher's premiership in the 1980s confirmed Woodcock's realistic analysis.

The August 1967 TUC briefing note on his achievements summarized the Woodcock era:

> Generally Mr Woodcock has tried to make the individual unions less self-centred and more willing to make their individual policies and practices fit in with the broader objectives of national policy. The ultimate practical outcome of all this in terms of structure and practice is still uncertain but what is certain is that the trade unions have become more receptive to change during Mr Woodcock's period as General Secretary.[66]

The outcome may have fallen far below Woodcock's idealistic ambitions. The TUC, as a loose confederation of disparate interests, was at its best when faced by external adversity. During the Second World War and in its efforts at developing credible incomes policies culminating in the Social Contract of the 1970s, the TUC was able to mobilize an impressive if temporary unity to combat with some effect the impact of national crises. But the UK's social and economic structure was not conducive to the emergence of a fully-fledged corporatist system with a TUC equipped with the centralized powers enjoyed by other western European national union bodies such as the West German DGB and the Swedish LO. Woodcock realized this full well, despite his admiration for Swedish trade unionism. He tried, in his own particular way, to persuade the TUC into shouldering wider responsibilities while always acknowledging the strength of the voluntarist tradition of industrial relations. If he was unable during the 1960s to reconcile the genuine tensions between voluntarism and regulation that lay at the heart of British trade unionism, this turned out in the end to be as much a tragedy for the wider political economy as for either the TUC or himself.

Notes

The author would like to thank Vilja Woodcock, the daughter of George Woodcock, for access to her father's papers. Most are to be eventually deposited at the Modern Records Centre at Warwick University. Some are in the temporary possession of the author and remain uncatalogued. They will form part of a wider project on a modern history of the Trades Union Congress at present underway by the author.

1. Woodcock Papers (hereafter WP), G. Woodcock draft article, 12 December 1960.
2. WP, G. Woodcock, interview with Tony Lane, April 1972.
3. A. Benn, *Out of the Wilderness 1963–1967* (1987), p. 486.
4. G. Brown, *In My Way* (1970), p. 155.
5. R.H.S. Crossman, *Diaries of a Cabinet Minister, Volume 3*, (1977), p. 915.
6. B. Castle, *Fighting All The Way* (1994), p. 420.
7. R. Maudling, *Memoirs* (1978), p. 187.
8. WP, Interview with H Webb, April 1970.
9. J. Cole, *As It Seemed To Me* (1995), pp. 54–7.
10. P. Jenkins, *Battle of Downing Street* (1970), p. 76.
11. WP, Interview with B. Mycock, 8 October 1968.
12. WP, G. Woodcock, The Function of the TUC, 3 November 1950.
13. WP, G. Woodcock, 'Trade unions in the 1970s', transcript of BBC Broadcast, 22 May 1968, pp. 4–5.
14. WP, G. Woodcock, 'Trade unions and government', Leicester, 1968, p. 6.
15. Ibid., p. 10.
16. WP, G. Woodcock, Broadcast, BBC Caribbean Service, 6 February 1959.
17. WP, G. Woodcock, Broadcast, BBC Caribbean Service, 13 February 1959.
18. Ibid.
19. WP, G. Woodcock, Memorandum, 7 November 1964.
20. WP, Interview with B. Mycocks, 8 October 1968.
21. WP, G. Woodcock, Broadcast, BBC Caribbean Service, 13 February 1959.
22. G. Woodcock, 'Trade unions and public opinion', *Listener*, 23 July 1959, p. 119.
23. TUC, *Report*, 1962, p. 244.
24. H. Chevins, 'British unions on the move', *Free Labour World*, February 1963.
25. WP, 'What are we here for?', Undated Memorandum, c. 1963.
26. WP, 'Trade union structure and purposes', Notes for TUC Finance and General Purposes Committee, 10 December 1962.
27. WP, 'Trade union structure and purposes', Condensed Points made at TUC Finance and General Purposes Committee, 10 December 1962.
28. WP, 'Trade union structure', Memorandum by G. Woodcock, 10 May 1963.
29. WP, Minutes of TUC Finance and General Purposes Committee, 10 May 1963.
30. Published in R. Taylor, *Fifth Estate* (1978), p. 42.

31. TUC, *Report*, 1964, p. 261.
32. WP, 'Main achievements', 4 August 1967.
33. From BBC Interview, published as 'The time of my life', *Listener*, 10 September 1970, pp. 338–40.
34. Modern Records Centre, University of Warwick, Minutes of the Donovan Commission, 18 January 1966, para. 7.
35. Ibid., para. 11.
36. Ibid., 6 September 1966, para. 5.
37. Ibid., 5 October 1966, para. 2.
38. 'Trade unionism', TUC evidence to the Donovan Commission, November 1966, p. 31.
39. WP, G. Woodcock in conversation with R. Shackelton, 11 December 1971.
40. WP, Draft Consultative Document by TUC on Donovan, 7 October 1968.
41. Castle, *Diaries*, p. 574.
42. WP, Conversation with H. Webb, April 1970.
43. Castle, *Diaries*, p. 574.
44. Ibid., p. 582.
45. Quoted in Taylor, *Fifth Estate*, p. 87.
46. W. Citrine, *Men and Work*, (1964), p. 228.
47. Ibid., p. 230.
48. Quoted in Taylor, *Fifth Estate*, p. 90.
49. WP, Conversation with the Open University, June 1972.
50. TUC, *Report*, 1962, p. 291.
51. WP, Economic Planning, Woodcock meeting with union research officers, 8 November 1963.
52. Ibid.
53. WP, 'Main achievements', 4 August 1967, pp. 3–4.
54. WP, Conversation with the Open University, June 1972.
55. TUC evidence to Donovan Commission, p. 56.
56. WP, G. Woodcock, interview with Tony Lane, April 1972.
57. WP, G. Woodcock, conversation with R. Shackleton, 11 December 1971.
58. TUC, *Report*, 1963, p. 392.
59. J. Callaghan, *Time and Chance* (1987), p. 5.
60. WP, 'Main achievements', 4 August 1967.
61. TUC, *Report*, 1968, p. 550.
62. TUC Congress of Executives, 17 January 1968, pp. 96–105.
63. *Listener*, 10 September 1970, p. 338.
64. Quoted in Taylor, *Fifth Estate*, p. 104.
65. WP, G. Woodcock, lecture to Institute of Personnel Management, 1968.
66. WP, TUC Memorandum, August 1967.

CHAPTER EIGHT

Notes on the Communist Party and Industrial Politics

John McIlroy

The role of Communist Party (CP) activists in industry has been long disregarded by industrial relations academics and political scientists. Neglect is rooted in the constitution of industrial relations and politics as academic subjects centred respectively on the institutions of collective bargaining and Parliamentary politics. Where recognition occurs it is slight. In his respected study of the Industrial Relations Act 1971, for example, Michael Moran has two references to the party, two more than appear in the other well known study of the legislation by Brian Weekes and his colleagues. Moran mentions that the Communists were the best organized left group in industry, influenced the Liaison Committee for the Defence of Trade Unions (LCDTU) and were active in the docks, a key site of struggles against the Act. He tells us nothing more about these matters, although they are, without question, highly germane to the episodes he is analysing.[1]

Such texts are often dehumanized, at least in partial fashion, their top-down vision locating senior politicians and sometimes union leaders as individual actors seeking to elicit consent and support from 'workers', 'shop stewards', 'Communists', depicted *en masse*. Once we vacate 'the corridors of power', personalities and their influence on events tend to vanish from the literature of political science and industrial relations. It is futile to ignore high politics: but explanation requires forays beyond its boundaries, particularly where rank and file leaders played an appreciable role in struggles. The influence of political activists in industry should not be exaggerated. Nor should their activities be studied in isolation from the policies and organization of the party to which they adhered. The political allegiances of trade unionists and their impact – in conjunction with other pressures – on their values, motivations and actions must be acknowledged and explored if we are properly to understand trade unionism and its development. While such sentiments would be increasingly endorsed by students of trade unionism, we still lack studies which take this approach.

The demise of the CP has, in contrast, stimulated a flourishing literature on its long march and final implosion. Writing general histories, Willie Thompson and Francis Beckett, perforce, devote only limited attention to the party's presence in industry.[2] Almost all of the work addressing the

CP's terminal crisis neglects its industrial involvements and concentrates on the internal factional struggles of the 1980s, often abstracted from the party's practice. There is a need to situate these problems both in a longer perspective and in the party's external activity.[3] For most of its history, the CP saw the unions as the primary arena for political intervention. It is my contention that the ultimate failure of the party's industrial initiatives and the weakness of its base in workplace and unions in the decades before the fall was a significant factor in its ultimate dissolution. In this context, I survey the CP's industrial politics in the 1960s and 1970s; sketch the work of its members in key unions and industries; outline their role in important struggles; and conclude with a brief assessment of the position on the cusp of the decade of disintegration.

The party and its politics

CP politics were codified in *The British Road to Socialism* (1951), revised in 1968 and 1977. *The British Road* envisaged a peaceful transition to socialism. The motor of development was conflict between 'the people' and monopoly capitalism which facilitated creation of a 'Broad Popular Alliance' centred on the traditional working class but mobilizing small capitalists and the middle class. In partnership with a mass movement outside Parliament, a left government, representing a radicalized labour movement hinging on Labour Party–CP unity, would begin the structural reforms that would produce a people's democracy. The 1977 redraft replaced the 'Anti-Monopoly Alliance' with the conception of a 'Broad Democratic Alliance'. This reflected greater recognition of the importance of civil society, democracy and oppression, enhanced emphasis on the role of the 'new social movements' – women's liberation, anti-racism, gay and environmental currents, and an expanded definition of the working class to include white collar groups.[4]

The extent to which the anti-monopoly alliance infused industrial strategy is questionable. But *The British Road* provided a broad frame for industrial policy and privileged it. The unions were seen as crucial to radicalizing the Labour Party, and the way to change the unions was through left unity and industrial militancy. This position was developed and fleshed out from the early 1960s:

> The trade unions are decisive for any real change. To achieve this it is necessary to win left progressive majorities (socialist, Communist and non-party) in all the main trade unions. Because of the decisive influence of the trade unions in the Labour Party and the grip of the right-wing, the position can only be changed by winning the main unions for progress.[5]

217

The CP campaigned for its members to have the right to attend Labour Party meetings as union delegates, for closer cooperation between CP branches and CLPs and, more realistically for trade unionists, 'to exercise their democratic rights in the Labour Party ... to ensure the development of socialist aims'.[6] The assertion that the Labour Party could be transformed by external pressure was an essential component of CP politics.

From 1964 left unity was pushed into the foreground. Party leaders reiterated, 'we cannot go it alone. We can only advance as a component, a leading component, of the great and growing body of trade union militants'.[7] This approach was reinforced by the waning of Cold War antipathies, the development of state intervention in industrial relations providing a focus for unified opposition, and the growing disillusion with the Wilson governments. The ballot-rigging in the ETU stimulated the quest for more broadly based, more open forms of work. The failure to ensure the removal of the ban on CP members holding office in the TGWU; the extension of proscriptions to the ETU in 1964; the continued inability to shake the right-wing regime in the AEU and the disciplinary action taken against CP cadres; these all demanded 'some broader relationship of a permanent character with the left forces'. The new approach to left unity and building Broad Left alliances in the unions was affirmed by the Political Committee in May 1964.[8]

The thrust of CP industrial politics centred upon defence of collective bargaining and the shop steward system, seeking to insert into this defence an advocacy of broader industrial and economic policies. State intervention was defined as a corporatist attempt to domesticate the unions in response to capitalist crisis. In consequence: 'we face the gravest concerted attack on the trade union movement in this century'.[9] Incomes policy was a mechanism for wage cutting which eroded union independence. Reform of industrial relations and its charter, the Donovan report, was dismissed as a means for undermining stewards, facilitating wage restraint and opening the door to restrictive legislation.[10] Productivity deals were strongly opposed. Opposition to *In Place of Strife* in 1969, the Industrial Relations Act (1971), and Heath's incomes policy culminated in rejection of the industrial policies of the 1974 Wilson government.[11]

The leftist caste of CP politics, cutting in practice with the grain of militancy despite the popular frontism of *The British Road*, is readily evoked by the position on industrial democracy. The strategies of structural reform adumbrated by the Institute for Workers' Control were rejected with disdain. Whilst worker directors were seen as useful in nationalized industries, the TUC proposal for representation of workers on the boards of private enterprises and the later recommendations in the 1977 Bullock Report were dismissed:

It is class collaborationist in character, dampens the class struggle, leads to

218

corruption of workers' representatives, and is a deceptive sham of industrial democracy; its primary objective is to enmesh workers in running industry to provide maximum profit for the shareholders.[12]

Congress resolutions chimed discordantly with past support for collaboration with management in the interests of increasing productivity: 'We should oppose all inroads into the rights of workshop organisation by the so-called production committees ... we will never allow ourselves to become sponsors of capitalist rationalisation'; 'This Congress rejects the conception that advance of wages and working conditions will be brought about through productivity, work study and rationalisation policies in industry'; 'The right to strike is the be all and end all of industrial trade union struggle'.[13] Despite the cross-class formulations of the anti-monopoly alliance, the CP's industrial politics largely rejected the popular front orientations which re-emerged in the 1980s.[14]

Alternative policies included a freeze on redundancies, a 35-hour week and equal pay. Support for free collective bargaining always lay at the core of immediate demands. The broader framework included extension of public ownership, cuts in military spending, increased social expenditure, and new taxes on the rich. Controls over prices, imports and investment became more prominent. By the early 1970s this package of measures was referred to as the Alternative Economic Strategy (AES). In relation to the unions, there were demands for amalgamations, democratization and election of full-time officials.[15]

For the CP, internal conflict in the unions hinged on politics, relatively autonomous from structure and material interests. There was sustained insistence on the importance of leadership and official positions. Electing lefts 'should not be divorced from the mass struggle', and in turn it was essential that militancy be reflected in the higher levels of union leadership.[16] There was a strong belief in rank and file mobilization – even in its initiation outside official structures – but controlled mobilization, targeted at specific objectives under favourable conditions. Militancy was a component in overall strategy: its purpose was to stimulate official action, not to supersede it. Rank and file action was the forward moment in the mobilization of the official machinery, not an alternative to it, a stimulus to the leadership, not its antagonist. Providing the base and context for winning positions and reminding leaders of their responsibilities, militancy required organization and guidance. The party's conception was described in 1970 by its Industrial Organizer:

Militant struggle from below, far from creating difficulties for the official leaderships of unions, is of positive assistance to those trade union leaders who are actively fighting to advance the interests of their members. Such militancy and action by the membership strengthens the bargaining position of the official negotiators.[17]

219

Bert Ramelson, Industrial Organizer from 1966 to 1977, had no background as a union activist but he enthusiastically grasped the opportunities of militancy. The industrial struggle was fundamental: 'In the course of pursuing it, the workers, learning the lessons of the struggle, would deepen their political awareness of the nature of capitalism and the need to replace it by a new society ...'.[18] As militancy declined from 1974, Ramelson emphasized the need for a political programme and the role of the CP:

> ... there are limitations to militancy; it is a vital first step but they then need to go a stage further and recognize the need to transform society and change capitalism into a socialist system of society and to deepen their understanding that it can only be achieved through struggle led by a revolutionary political party.[19]

The sense that the CP was not benefiting sufficiently was reflected in discussions led by Ramelson on the theme 'Militancy is not enough'.[20] A more fundamental critique was developed from 1974 by CP economists Dave Purdy, Mike Prior and Pat Devine. Opposing the view of Ramelson and the party leadership that the Social Contract was cosmeticized wage-cutting, they argued, first tentatively then forcefully, that it provided an opening to assess the allocation of social resources and project structural reforms. The role of wages in generating inflation and the problems inflation caused had to be acknowledged. A 'socialist incomes policy' could bargain wage restraint and a reduction in inflation for aspects of the AES, planning agreements and industrial democracy.[21] Hitherto, criticism had been limited to the small group around Sid French who argued for more attention to building the party in the factories. Opposition was checked at the 1975 Congress.[22] But matters were not concluded. As the 1970s progressed, there was growing interest in sections of the party in the ideas of Eurocommunism, Gramsci and the new social movements, and growing criticism of the 'economism' of the party's industrial work.[23]

The politics of industrial organization

After discussion in 1964–5 of more open forms of work, it was decided that the CP's industrial advisory committees would continue alongside the Broad Lefts. Ramelson revamped the committees embracing union activists and party full-timers so that they covered all major unions and industries. Their staple appears to have been union elections, although other issues were addressed. Ramelson's stance was that the advisories should take decisions but that members might change their positions as discussion developed in the wider forums.[24] He believed that the CP should be 'strong at the top as well as the bottom' of the unions. His circular, 'Needs of the Hour' listed model motions for union and Labour Party conferences, and he developed close personal links with union leaders as well as lay activists both inside and outside the party.[25] Eschewing rank and filism but seeing the need to channel rank and file resistance against state intervention, the CP created a mechanism to coordinate militant struggles from below in order to pressurize the official movement. The LCDTU was launched in 1966 and whilst Ramelson was careful to stay in the background, it operated as an arm of his department. Its conferences acted as a conveyor for CP policies, a means of extending party networks and a pressure point on union leaders.[26]

As militancy and success diminished from 1974, concern developed that the Industrial Department had become dedicated to winning influence with union leaders rather than making Communists and winning recruits. There was a minority of union activists on the Executive, where perforce discussion on industrial issues was broad, and some expressed concern at the limited role trade unionists played in party activity.[27] As early as 1964 it had been asserted that:

> ... our methods have had the effect of creating 'TU Comrades' and 'TU work' that is often cut off from the Party as a whole and the Party branches in particular ... We have 'specialists' in TUs working on a very narrow basis, some of them winning leadership and position with nothing much as a basis by work as individuals ... election to some TU posts has led to the corruption of some of our comrades ... our comrades tend at times to get immersed completely in the day-to-day problems of the routine work of the TU jobs.[28]

This dual problem – members' tendency to absorption in trade unionism, reinforced by the organization of industrial work – was submerged in the heady successes between 1968 and 1974. The Social Contract and the blue water Hugh Scanlon (AUEW), Jack Jones (TGWU) and Lawrence Daly (NUM) now put between themselves and the CP, unveiled the shaky foundations of party strategy. It was all too often fragile and contingent on forces outside the party. By the mid-1970s more than 100 CP members spread across 30 unions were delegates to the TUC Congress. But on the General Council there were only Ken Gill of TASS (from 1974) and George Guy of the Sheet Metal Workers (from 1977). They were dependent for minority influence on sympathetic representatives from small unions – Alan Sapper (ACTT), Ray Buckton (ASLEF) and Ken Cameron (FBU).[29] As the tenuous nature of the gains of the upturn since 1968 became apparent, so did criticism that the industrial leadership had leant too much, and too unsuccessfully on establishing its *bona fides* with union leaders – and allowing CP trade unionists too long a leash – at the expense of sustained work amongst the rank and file.[30]

For it was also apparent that the upturn had not significantly augmented the party's union cadre. The third arc of party activity, intersecting with the advisories and Broad Left in each union and the LCDTU operating across the unions, the indispensable means of ensuring that the party grew and reaped the benefit of its intensive efforts, was the workplace branch. The Committee on Party Organization which reported in 1965 reiterated the importance of such branches in developing political activity in the workplace. But a National Factory Conference in 1966 attracted only 86 delegates from 62 factory branches, despite insistence that the workplace was the key site for struggle.[31]

The importance of workplace organization was stressed in 1967 and 1968. But it then slipped down the agenda, attracting little more than passing reference at Congresses until 1975. The CP Congress that year demanded greater efforts 'to improve the work and extend the membership and activity of existing workplace branches and establish many more new ones'.[32] The lack of progress over the previous decade was highlighted by a 1975 conference on workplace organization. The first such initiative for nine years, it was attended by only 91 representatives of workplace branches. Sustained initiatives such as factory branch cadre schools and the drafting of full-timers to work with established branches yielded little fruit. A national conference in April 1978 saw only 26 branches represented and 17 of the 52 delegates held no union position. Activists expressed doubts whether the leadership and membership at local level really supported the extension of industrial work.[33]

The number of workplace branches declined between 1964 and 1979 from 265 to 126, despite intensive efforts after 1975. Of course this was part of the general deterioration in membership, but it underlines clearly the party's failure to benefit in terms of membership growth from the role it played in the militancy of these years. Indeed the percentage of members organized at the workplace declined from ten per cent in 1963 to 8.3 per cent in 1976. Furthermore the evidence demonstrates the impermanence of CP workplace organization: of the 115 such branches existing in London at some point in this period, only 24 were in existence in both 1966 and 1979.[34] Personal observation suggest there was some inflation of membership figures if we are talking of even minimal activism. This is supported by some of the party's own surveys. A 1968 listing of 47 branches in London recorded only 21 met regularly and a 1975 report characterized only 16 out of 43 workplace branches as carrying out 'regular work of all types'.[35]

The picture suggested was not a national community of political branches but rather a shallower, personalized network of trade union militants – individuals or handfuls – largely concerned with industrial issues, sometimes with limited attachment to the CP and 'deep-seated caution in showing the face of the party'. The extent and depth of workplace organization and the degree to which it developed beyond a small industrial pressure group in the workplace, selling CP literature, making the occasional recruit, the degree to which workplace branches acted as a political alternative to left labourism rather than its industrial organizer, is questionable. The verdict of the Scottish Organizer from 1968 could do service across different areas through this period: 'the majority carry out little or no political activity ... although most handle some *Morning Stars*. Some carry out limited, sporadic activity. Only a few do consistent all-round activity'.[36]

These problems were underpinned by a structural fissure. The responsibility for prosecuting party policy in the unions lay with the Industrial Department. But the Organization Department had responsibility for workplace branches, formally the bedrock of industrial work. A further fundamental tension which should not be overlooked in any assessment of industrial work was the sustained haemorrhage of the energies of trade unionists, and the party as a whole, into local and national elections – with barren effect.[37] By 1977, with membership declining from 34,000 in 1964 to 25,000, conflicts intensified. Purdy returned to the attack with articles in *Comment* and *Marxism Today* in late 1976.[38] Ramelson responded by denying wage increases any significant role in inflation. Free collective bargaining was the essential means of pressuring the state, pumping demand into the economy and reducing unemployment. Militancy must be complemented by ideological struggle over the AES. But industrial struggle created fertile conditions for political progress.[39]

So long as Ramelson continued as Industrial Organizer, critics registered few gains. He combined powerful argument, charm and bullying. He had close rapport with the party's trade unionists, the confidence of the leadership, the respect of antagonists, and an easy dominance of the party's Economic Committee. On the brink of his retirement, debates about industrial strategy were fanned by the discussion around the 1977 Congress. And when Mick Costello moved from the *Morning Star* to the Industrial Department in late 1977, he was inheriting a difficult situation inside and outside the party.[40]

The discussion spilled over into the *Morning Star* with a confrontation between trade unionists and academics. Ken Gill repeated: '... the wages struggle can mobilize millions of workers and the true nature of the crisis can be grasped. A mass militant wages movement is therefore the key to winning the labour movement for the left alternative strategy'.[41] The sociologist Alan Hunt countered: 'we should get away from the naive position of supporting every act of trade union militancy and make political judgements ... Communists must shed the illusion that has dominated the British left that wage militancy has some necessary or automatic connection with the struggle for socialism'.[42] The CP's leading intellectual, Eric Hobsbawm, proffered the popular front as a far from exhausted, if in Britain far from successful, exemplar. He followed this with a re-assessment of the British labour movement through the century. The publication of 'The forward march of labour halted' in September 1978 prompted wide-ranging discussion about industrial militancy and the current predicament of the labour movement which was to have perhaps greater resonance in the 1980s.[43]

Mick Costello was in the same political mould as Ramelson, but lacked his prestige. He was faced with the burgeoning judgement that the industrial work was both 'economistic', neglecting wider political issues, and conducted as 'a party within a party'.[44] The National Organizer, Dave Cook, enthused by the new 'Broad Democratic Alliance' (BDA), argued that CP members should raise their political profile in the unions. Alternative plans for companies and industries should be elaborated. Local communities should be involved in union struggles, alliances built with the new movements:

> workers can be politicized by all the concerns of the broad democratic alliance as well as their reaction to class exploitation. Therefore the second great question of unity with which our strategy is concerned is that between the class organizations, the trade unions, etc, and the various movements against oppression, women, youth, black people, etc.

Cook stressed new forms of action, 'the Anti-Nazi League, cultural sponsorship and involvement (Rock Against Racism, actors, sports festivals, etc)'. The old axis of the unions, Labour Party and CP was seen as inadequate. In the CP itself,

> the various specialist advisory committees within the party need to become more concerned with policy development ... the compartmentalized nature of much of our work comes out most strongly in the separation of many comrades in industry from the rest. This impoverishes both groups. The structure of industrial advisories exists alongside the branch, area, district organization but does not often interact with it. Many comrades active in industry work through the advisories but only rarely attend branch meetings.[45]

Yet if the big industrial struggles of the 1970s had failed to qualitatively advance socialist consciousness, it was difficult to see what 'Rock Against Racism', laudable in its own terms as it was, added to the equation. If the power of the TUC could not extract significant concessions from the state in return for wage restraint, it was very difficult to see how adding the CP to its supporters would produce a 'socialist incomes policy.' What fundamentally concerned the 'traditionalists' was the autonomy from class and capitalism which they saw some interpretations of the BDA granting the new social movements and the inflated significance accorded them as partners in alliances with the labour movement. They worried that the intimate relation of ethnic or gender oppression to class exploitation was being deflated, that its patterning beyond class and capitalist domination was being accentuated. Costello laid the fundamental weakness of the workplace branches at the door of the Organization Department. In a critical response to Cook, he asserted the pre-eminence of class politics, the leading role of

224

the traditional working class and the centrality of the unions. He was prepared to concede the virtues of a broader political approach which addressed the organization of production, alternative plans and controls over new technology. But issues of ethnicity and gender were best prosecuted inside the unions, the fundamental class organizations. And unions should not be confused with political parties: inside them Communists could raise political issues and reshape, but never replace, the economic struggle.[46]

By January 1979, as the 'Winter of Discontent' raged, sufficient unity was achieved for a new turn to industry. Costello's report which launched the new initiative accepted that progress over the previous decade had been limited and uneven. The right-wing was still dominant. De-industrialization was striking at the strongest sections of the working class. He, too, advocated more open campaigning for party policies, popularizing the AES and pursuing 'an ever widening conception of free collective bargaining'. There was a need for more grassroots work to counter the new anti-union 'commonsense'. He noted, 'The broad left is not something that starts or ends among the higher reaches of trade union organizations. We see it as based in the rank and file ... providing forums for debate on policy and criticism, as above all a fighting and campaigning living body'. The LCDTU was urged to greater efforts amongst white collar and public sector workers. Workplace branches were too small and too few:

> We are paying a high price for long neglect of our workplace organizations and for the widespread failure to integrate the factory branches into the campaigning by the party as a whole ... An interesting illustration of the complexities is the fact of our strength within the trade union movement continuing alongside growing problems in securing workplace branch organization. I am not arguing for less attention to the former but to paying more attention to Party building and branch building at the places of work. We are paying the price for this one-sidedness in an ageing of our leadership in the field of industry, in the fact that a growing proportion has never been in a workplace branch of the Party. The effects of this for developing a new generation of young, all round Communist cadres in industry must be obvious.[47]

This analysis contained very strong elements of self-critique. Even as moves to implement it began, the campaign which would see Thatcher installed in government was beginning.

Inside the unions

Within the broad-left approach there existed diversity both in style of organization and its relationship to the party. In the TGWU the party strengthened its position. The ban on CP members holding office was only lifted in 1968 and it cast a long shadow in terms of the low key, inclusive style of work and enduring gratitude to the new General Secretary, Jack Jones. The CP had allocated a full-time worker to the campaign against the ban, and contacts made bore fruit with the election of six members to the Executive in 1970. The Broad Left remained CP-dominated and clandestine, a loose network lacking democratic structure or formal programme. The TGWU leadership was seen as progressive and the left focused on elections, appointments and resolutions, seeking to represent all viewpoints outside the hard right. Despite conflicts over incomes policy after 1974, the general stance was to sustain the General Secretary. Praise for Jones was lavish and concern was expressed at even mild rebukes. Even over the Social Contract, criticism was measured, although the resolution which broke with incomes policy at the 1977 TGWU conference against Jones' opposition was motivated by the Broad Left.[48]

The CP was far from a strategic, creative force influencing policy in the TGWU: its representation on the Executive never exceeded five or six members, although sympathizers doubled the figure. Only a handful of full-time officers – notably Sid Staden in London and Hugh Wyper in Scotland – were members, and the party exercised real influence only in London, the Midlands, Scotland and Ireland. In contrast, in the other general union, the GMWU, it remained unable to transcend its historically negligible purchase. The search for 'progressives' settled upon unlikely figures: the *Morning Star* was reduced to recommending support for David Basnett in the 1972 contest for General Secretary. Its most obvious successes were in smaller unions such as the Constructional Engineering section of the AUEW, where Eddie Marsden was General Secretary from 1968–75; the Sheet Metal Workers, where George Guy was General Secretary; the Furniture Trade Workers where CP member Ben Rubner filled the top post; and the Lightermen, whose President was Harry Watson. Insiders felt the position in the NUR, where the CP had a strong minority position on the Executive in the 1960s, weakened after Dave Bowman, later the union's President, left in 1970. The party also maintained a presence amongst leading officials in ASLEF.[49]

At the opposite pole, the *Building Workers' Charter* was a powerful, militant and rank and file organization. The CP had always had support in this conflict-prone industry and it developed a power base in disputes such as those at Myton's Barbican site and Sunley's Horseferry Road in London in the mid-1960s. The growth of the unofficial Joint Sites Committee in London intensified conflict with union leaders, particularly in the Amalgamated Society of Woodworkers (ASW). Disciplinary action against CP stewards, Jim Hiles, Jack Henry and Lou Lewis, stimulated further agitation. The active merger policy pursued by the ASW, which culminated in the creation of UCATT in 1971, was accompanied by centralization. Amalgamation weakened the ASW right and the abolition of district organization stimulated the rank and file. By 1970 the CP was far stronger at site level than it had been a decade earlier. The *Charter* group, chaired by Lou Lewis, which was established that year grew out of the conflict between enhanced grass-roots strength and the increasing remoteness of the leadership.

Charter was a cross-union organization, based on stewards. It operated on a long leash from the party, although contact through the advisories and with the Industrial Department was regular. The group popularized a pro-gramme of demands on wages, hours, pensions, union democracy and the abolition of labour-only subcontracting – 'the lump'. The *Charter* was led by CP members but involved a wide range of militants. It published a news-paper with a circulation of 10,000, organized conferences attended by up to 900 delegates, and its supporters became a force on the UCATT Execu-tive and a majority, or near majority on its Regional Councils in London, Manchester, Scotland and Birmingham. According to Lou Lewis, the *Char-ter* peaked in 1972 when it played a key role in the first national building strike for fifty years, and built its momentum from the ground up. By 1974 it had secured a base on the UCATT Executive, a third of Conference del-egates were *Charter* supporters and the left was able to reverse leadership policies on wages, union structure and the Shrewsbury pickets, convicted for their role in the national dispute. Despite successes in 1975 over elec-tion of officials and lay involvement at district and regional level, the *Charter* was losing impetus. Encouraged by the party, key activists such as Hiles and Lewis became full-time officials. By 1979, the party was en-trenched in the union structures with three members on the Executive. But its rank and file organization had faded.[50]

Work in the growing white collar unions provides further contrast. In those historically moderate, centralized organizations, the party was often living off human capital accumulated twenty years earlier. In the NUT, the CP had failed to renew its base. The Broad Left was small and secretive, an amorphous coalition which included Liberals as well as the Labour left. It was heavily oriented towards winning Executive positions, although tak-ing an interest in broad educational issues through the CP journal, *Education Today and Tomorrow*. The most prominent cadre, Max Morris, elected NUT President in 1972, was a pillar of respectability who took little account of party policy and was out of touch with the restive mood amongst younger teachers. The emergence of the paper, *Rank and File*, supported by the International Socialists and dissident CPers sharpened conflict. The group was condemned by the CP, whilst former party mem-bers who joined believed that the CP:

> increasingly saw its role in the teachers' movement as winning positions in the union and had gradually begun to behave as a left extension of the progressives on the NUT Executive. The fundamental fight was increasingly seen as taking place on the latter rather than any mobilization of the rank and file teachers.[51]

There were few CP members in ASTMS: around 25 attended national meetings in the early 1970s. Whilst five or six full-time officers and two to three executive members were in the party's ranks, it was never a significant influence on union policy. In NALGO, the CP's reliance on informal links between key activists and a moderate, cautious approach oriented towards Executive elections saw the emergence of the NALGO Action Group. Here the party's stance was more adept. Whilst they advocated disciplinary action against *Rank and File*, they joined the Action Group. Although the party regrouped towards the end of the 1970s, their neglect of the significant unrest in these growing unions meant they had lost ground to the Trotskyist organizations. Similarly in NUPE, which was also in the throes of qualitative transformation, the opportunity to influence the new culture passed the party by.[52]

In this context of pragmatism and diversity, we turn to briefly examine four different cases which demonstrate the party's differing fortunes:

(i) The NUM – constructing left unity

The 1960 elections which saw CP members competing against each other, and the return of the right-wing Sid Ford as President, were later seen as a watershed in developing left unity.[53] Its creation was a complex process. The party's inability to impose unity on its own members was highlighted again in 1963 with the emergence of an autonomous left group led by CP members Will Paynter, NUM General Secretary, and Bill Whitehead, President of the South Wales Area, involving ex-CP members such as Bert Wynn and left-wing academics. The group held meetings in Derbyshire and Yorkshire, eventually producing in 1964 *A Plan for the Miners*. It was viewed with hostility by CP members in the Yorkshire and Scottish areas who regarded it as 'motivated by anti-communism that held back the development of a genuine left'. The Scottish Area President, Alex Moffat, who had reservations about unity with the Labour left, refused to attend and there were allegations that party members were excluded.[54]

A new formation crystallized the following year around the election of a successor to Paynter as General Secretary. Lawrence Daly's name was mooted. He had left the CP in 1956 and a CP candidate had opposed him in bitter struggles in 1965 for the General Secretaryship of the Scottish Area and for a National Executive seat. Owing to painstaking work by Mick McGahey, now the Acting President in Scotland, the new line won out. The leading CP miners in Scotland and Yorkshire threw their weight behind a united national left with Daly as its candidate.[55]

The inaugural meeting in August 1967 demonstrated the CP's strength in the coalfields. It was attended by McGahey, Daly and Bill McLean from Scotland, Dai Francis, the CP General Secretary of the Welsh Area, Emlyn Williams, a Labour left who became Welsh Area President, Jack Dunn, the

CP Secretary of the Kent miners, and two CP full-time officers from Yorkshire, Jock Kane and Sammy Taylor. There were officials from Derbyshire and Lancashire, as well as rank and file miners. The successful campaign which saw Daly defeat Joe Gormley solidified support. The bargain was sealed when McLean, a CP member, replaced Daly as Secretary of the Scottish Area.[56]

There was no formal democratic structure. Meetings were summoned by a self-appointed but generally accepted leadership when they felt it appropriate. Attention was focused on elections, but sought to relate positions to policy. Daly launched his campaign with a pamphlet, *The Miners and the Nation*, calling for public ownership of all energy industries and guerilla strikes against closures. When McGahey unsuccessfully fought Gormley for the Presidency in 1971, he too published a manifesto, *Miners and the Energy Crisis*.[57]

There was by 1970:

> a cohesive alliance between members of the Communist Party and the Labour Party which political allegiance only rarely obstructed. There were open, sometimes disturbingly frank discussions between them. They never voted but always argued until a consensus emerged. There were of course personal rivalries but members were quick to jump on those who were seen to subordinate policy matters to their own interests. It was not until later when left-wing influence had been consolidated that personality differences emerged in the juggling for official position.[58]

The Broad Left was only occasionally complemented by regional organization, notably the Barnsley Miners' Forum which from 1967 forged links to form a Yorkshire left caucus. By the eve of the 1972 strike there was a left grouping of eight – including six CP members – on the 26-person National Executive. Further progress in Yorkshire saw Arthur Scargill and Owen Briscoe replacing right-wingers as President and Secretary. This was the high point of CP influence and the left group on the Executive increased to eleven. With the General Secretary increasingly detached from the left, progress was stemmed and the second half of the 1970s saw important defeats for the left. Rallied by the adroit Joe Gormley, the right won the battle over Area incentive schemes – a mechanism which increased fragmentation.[59]

In-fighting continued over vacant positions. It has been claimed that such conflicts in Yorkshire weakened the campaign for McGahey in 1971 and that the CP was determined to dominate the alliance there.[60] A current around Scargill, distinct from the CP and sometimes in conflict with it, emerged. In 1964 it was observed of the CP's emphasis on key positions:

> We have also seen how fatal it is to depend on that leadership without developing the movement from below. There needs to be a drastic improvement in the

organization and work of our pit branches and pit groups. Only if the Communists in the pits work in an organized way can the political understanding of the miners be deepened and expressed in powerful mass pressure.[61]

But progress from 1968 was not accompanied by growth in CP membership in the pits. By 1979, the only CP members at the top were McGahey (National Vice-President), Joe Whelan (Nottinghamshire), Jack Collins (Kent), and George Rees (South Wales). Squabbling reasserted itself: Davey Bolton saw off the challenge for the Scottish Vice Presidency of fellow CP member George Bolton. But in 1977 he was defeated for the Area Secretaryship by Labour Party member Eric Clarke, supported by McGahey; in consequence he quit the party. Unity had to be defined and redefined within as well as without the CP. Throughout this period party members defended local interests and individual viewpoints. Critics asserted that politics were inadequately articulated in an electoral machine, neglecting grass roots issues.[62]

(ii) The ETU – a caucus for union democracy

Confidence eroded by exposure of the ballot-rigging and its members barred from office, the CP was faced by a leadership as ruthless as that it had displaced. Yet the 90 branches which followed its line at the 1965 Rules Revision Conference demonstrated there was still support. The approach was low key and defensive: reacting to policy, supporting mildly left candidates in elections, and the issue of internal democracy. In 1965 the party supported Eric Hammond for the Executive, only to see him succumb to the new leadership; in 1966 they mounted a campaign for George Tillbury, defeated by Frank Chapple in the election for General Secretary, but he also soon joined the establishment. Agitation against the three-year deals in. contracting and supply provoked demonstrations and disciplinary action. This provided some basis for a campaign for Fred Morphew, who ran against Les Cannon for President in 1968. But that same year the *Power Worker*, the CP-backed rank and file paper in electricity supply, faded away after disciplinary action against contributors.[63]

In 1969, the ETU leadership overplayed its hand at the Rules Revision Conference, producing an opposition of around one-third of the delegates and rejection of key changes. The decision to press the rule changes in a national ballot saw the party move into its highest gear since 1962, organizing a 'no' vote around a new journal, *Flashlight*. There were *Flashlight* groups in major cities, dominated by the CP but including independent lefts and Trotskyists.[64] The model of organization was analogous to that of the reform caucus in American trade unions. *Flashlight* put forward no detailed political programme and declared itself concerned essentially with democratic reform. The paper was published:

not because we believe in a rank and file movement or a rank and file journal written by and for members of our union. When union democracy flourishes there is little need for a paper such as this ... This paper is not dedicated to any faction or aspirant to union office. It is dedicated to the best interests of all the members of our union irrespective of differing viewpoints ... Our policy therefore is simply – transform our union into a fighting instrument democratically run by the membership so that all of us have a greater say in our union affairs.[65]

Flashlight activists achieved success in the 1970–1 executive elections. Bill Gannon won the plumbers' seat, Charlie Montgomery defeated a leadership supporter only to have his election invalidated. Disciplinary action commenced against *Flashlight* supporters, underlining the difficulties of opposition, especially an opposition saddled with the baggage of the CP's malpractice. However, opportunity beckoned with a split in the ETU leadership over who should succeed Cannon, who died in 1970, as President. Fred Gore, who stood against Chapple for General Secretary in 1971, was widely supported on the left. CP electricians again floated Eric Hammond. Despite the adoption of Gore at a *Flashlight* meeting, the paper was less than forceful in endorsing him against the right-wing Hammond.[66] The CP's search for a reform candidate who could attract wide support continued with an infatuation with Mark Young, an early supporter of Cannon. The episode ended when he left the union in 1974.[67]

On difficult terrain, the CP subordinated left politics to the building of a ginger group dedicated to democratization and the search for allies across a broad spectrum. *Flashlight* was essentially an electoral enterprise. Success proved elusive. In 1973 three lefts were elected to the executive: they were isolated and pilloried by the leadership. In 1976, when Harold Best stood unsuccessfully for General Secretary against Chapple, he was found to be in breach of rule as he had received CP support. By 1979, some were looking beyond the CP, as witnessed by the election of independent left Wyn Bevan to the Executive in 1979 and the closure of the Cardiff branch because of SWP activity.[68]

(iii) DATA/TASS – the Party in control

In the draughtsmen's union the Broad Left Group developed through the 1950s as a well organized opposition to the right-wing leadership of the AESD (which became DATA in 1961). Embracing CP and Labour Party members, as well as independent socialists, it was largely a lay member organization with groups in the union's sixteen divisions. The Broad Left did not organize around a paper but focused on Executive elections, annual conference and the lay presidency. With growing representation at conference, the left made increasing inroads on the Executive and influenced the appointment of organizers. By the 1960s, Labour left George Doughty was long established as General Secretary, three CP members had served as President, and there was an established cadre of CP members among the full-time officers.[69]

From 1966, the Broad Left was dominant: its connections with the CP remained relatively low key. Despite success in winning full-time positions, it reflected the ethos of a decentralized union where, in the 1960s, one in seven members held lay positions. Officers did not attend meetings and the left cultivated lay member democracy. The initial phase of left leadership was accompanied by new strategies developed by the CP: aggressive and successful wage bargaining, targeting key employers, preparing for strikes with work to rules and go slows, and supporting strikes with full wages. Conference decisions reflected socialist policies and found their way on to the agendas of the TUC and Labour Party.[70]

Critics argued that after 1968 full-time officials began to try to control the Broad Left: 'CP members believed that the important political role was to seize as many positions as possible ... Those who had been leading members of the left began to try and play the same role when they became full-time officials ...'.[71] A more moderate industrial policy and progressive reductions in strike benefit were seen as financially necessary to stimulate and sustain membership growth – from 73,000 to 105,000 between 1967 and 1970 – in a harder climate with closures in the engineering combines which constituted DATA's heartland. Militancy was viewed as presenting an unappealing image to potential members while there was also concern that DATA should cut an attractive figure as potential partner in amalgamations. The right-wing threat was no longer a bonding force. Left unity increasingly *excluded* those to the left of the CP who had previously played an important role: the Maoist group around Dick Jones, expelled from the party in 1965, Mike Cooley who left in 1970, and members of Trotskyist organisations. An academic observer noted:

> The Rolls Royce dispute was a watershed. from then on divisions inside the Broad Left intensified and between 1970 and 1973 the left opposition was systematically removed from the EC and most Divisional Councils. 1970–73 marks a transition period in the union ... A three line Communist Party whip began to operate on the EC, at Conference and on Divisional Councils. Ken Gill had become the first CP national official in 1968. After 1970 he was the key figure in changing the political climate in the union ... The Broad Left broadened out, assimilating a lot of the old right in the process to form a new alliance against what was becoming labelled as the 'adventurism' of the 'ultra-left'. The CP became a conservative centre in the union.[72]

Amalgamation with the AUEW in 1970 intensified this process. The number of full-time officers was doubled before an agreement in principle was reached that election would apply to new appointments, as in the Engineering Section. Members complained of the lack of consultation over the

232

merger and viewed it as an attempt to consolidate CP power and present Gill as Scanlon's successor. By 1975, the EC was dominated by CP members and supporters, and critics estimated that at least 17 out of the 28 organizers were party members.[73]

The main pockets of opposition were now outside the Broad Left which tended towards a support network for the leadership. The CP had been the organizing force within the Broad Left and its members now dominated the union. CP politics were expressed in conference resolutions. The limits of this approach was demonstrated by TASS acquiescence in the AUEW delegation's failure to oppose the Social Contract at the 1974 TUC. This underlined the boundaries of party control over its leading members. There were close personal relations with Ramelson (who even sat in on negotiations over the AUEW merger). But he was perceived as having a voice which would be listened to rather than the purveyor of a line which demanded allegiance. And some CP members felt the TASS leadership enjoyed privileged autonomy from party policy.[74]

(iv) The AEU – the ruling party?

The central formative event was the 1967 Presidential election in which Hugh Scanlon defeated John Boyd. In the early 1960s, CP organization was in some disarray. The long established Engineering and Allied Trades Shop Stewards' National Council, along with its paper *The Metalworker*, went out of existence by 1962. There were divisions over its viability in relation to disciplinary action taken against its supporters and fears of proscription. There was a feeling that there was a need to 'get inside' and use the official machinery.[75] In the 1964 presidential election, the CP stuck with the hardy perennial, Reg Birch, as its candidate. He did remarkably well, and, despite his breach with the CP, subsequently won the executive seat left vacant by CP veteran Claude Berridge in 1966. This success augmented the left presence of Scanlon on the executive, sometimes joined by the moderate Len Edmondson, and the two CP National Organizers, Les Ambrose and John Foster.[76]

National unity found a focus in the collaboration of the CP with the Labour left in Manchester, which had seen Scanlon to his executive seat in 1963. The Broad Left in Manchester developed from 1947 around an alliance which saw Scanlon, then a CP member, and Alf Jones, a Labour left, elected as Divisional Organizer and Assistant Divisional Organizer. It was 'very much set up on the basis of an electoral machine', an informal network based on the full-time officers which threw up a committee with contacts in branches and factories around elections. By 1966 this machine had placed Labour lefts such as Jones and Bob Wright, and CPers such as Eddie Frow and John Tocher, in full-time positions, whilst the legal battle over Scanlon's election to the executive had enabled them to achieve wider prominence.[77]

This coalition contrasted with CP activity in engineering in London and Sheffield where the thrust was towards independent operations. Nevertheless, by 1966 Scanlon presented himself as a potential national leader. There was hostility to Birch in sections of the party and the Manchester members were pushing for Scanlon. Ramelson, a proponent of *realpolitik*, was impressed by the size of his potential vote, while Scanlon's Labour Party credentials would minimize anti-Communist clamour.[78] An additional factor favouring unity and Scanlon was the newspaper, *Voice of the Unions*, which from 1965 published *Engineering Voice*. Partly aiming to fill the vacuum left by the *Metalworker*, the paper's sponsors included left-wing MPs and prominent trade unionists. The CP welcomed a non-party paper which would support left candidates and mobilize Labour supporters in the AEU, disgruntled by the policies of the Carron leadership. None the less, divisions remained. The vote for Scanlon at the CP national advisory was a relatively close 24–16, primarily on the criterion that he stood the best chance of winning.[79]

Ramelson insisted on the need for discipline amongst CP members:

if there is going to be left organization it means that when differences of opinion have been expressed and argued out and decisions taken by a majority vote then they must be carried out by everybody including the minority otherwise there is no point in meeting at all ... in that direction lies chaos and anarchy and handing a gift to the right-wing.[80]

However, there was a need to be sensitive in Broad Left meetings:

it was pointed out that the final decision would have to be taken at the broader meeting including Party and non-Party lefts which was to be held in Birmingham and that while all comrades would go to that meeting to put the point of view for the one decided upon, they should also go there ready to listen to arguments and if necessary be flexible so that it was seen that the choice made in Birmingham was united choice of the left as a whole.[81]

At the Birmingham 'assemblage' in June 1966 the CP successfully nominated Scanlon. His subsequent victory was seen as affirmation of the benefits of left unity. The CP had brought to the alliance a revived national network of militants but the Manchester group and the *Voice* both possessed constituencies. It was a genuine coalition but one in which the politics of left Labourism remained dominant. The left now went from strength to strength. Ken Brett, another CP member, won the second Assistant General Secretary post, Bob Wright took Scanlon's seat on the Executive and Tom Walmsley became an additional National Organizer. In 1970, CP member Les Dixon was elected to the Executive. Progress was significant but circumscribed. Left supporters held the Presidency but only two out of seven EC seats, dependent on the votes of Birch and Edmondson for a majority, two out of three Assistant General Secretaryships, and three out of seven National Organizers' posts. The National Committee remained delicately poised, but with changes in divisional and district positions, there was, by 1972, a clear political shift in which the Broad Left played a vital role.[82]

The Broad Left was informal and top-down, with the full-time officials at AUEW headquarters assuming leadership. Its national organizer, Ken Brett, liaised with Ramelson, whilst John Hampton, AUEW National Organizer from 1970 liaised with *Engineering Voice*. Local organization was rudimentary and episodic. A survey in the early 1970s found regular meetings in only four out of 25 key districts with 11 meeting at election times. *Engineering Voice* appeared infrequently. Policy making focused on the National Committee in the context of Scanlon's electoral pledge to uphold its decisions: 'The Broad Left didn't have a policy distinct from the union. We never had to formulate it – discussions took place on the National Committee, etc'.[83]

Until 1974, this situation had its strengths. The AUEW's structure was democratic. Its leading committees reflected the politics of its activists, and its leadership reflected the policies of these committees. The AUEW received strong leadership over the Industrial Relations Act. There was more cause for criticism over the 1968–71 package deal, the limited success over the 1972 national claim, and the leadership's insistence on plant-by-plant bargaining to achieve it. Feeling over these issues, particularly in Manchester and Sheffield, where the leadership prohibited district-wide action, may have contributed to the disillusionment with the left discernible from 1973. Some pointed to rank and file disgruntlement at the resolute stance against the state compared with bread and butter issues. The introduction of postal ballots in 1972 has been seen as decisive in this rightward shift, but it should be viewed as occurring within a specific context.[84]

Retreat was gradual. In 1973, CPer Bernard Panter lost the Manchester District Secretaryship and Tocher was stretched in the Divisional Organizer contest. This was put down to discontent over the left's inability to deliver improvements in wages. In 1975 Boyd defeated Wright for General Secretary and the hardly known Terry Duffy overwhelmed Wright to win his Executive seat. Gavin Laird defeated Jimmy Reid for Boyd's vacant Executive seat and Broad Left supporter Len Brindle lost to Laurie Smith for the National Organizer's post vacated by Ambrose.[85] Under the editorship of Walter Kendall, *Engineering Voice* became more critical of the CP, to the consternation of Ramelson and Brett, who, after discussions with Ernie Roberts and Scanlon in 1975, gained agreement on producing a new newsheet, the *Engineering Gazette*. This was specifically geared to elections, funded by collections among left officials, and 'more under the control of the CP'.[86]

But decline continued. In 1976 a layer of AUEW cadres – Pat Farelley,

Cyril Morton, Reid, Panter and Tocher – left the party. By 1977 political estrangement with Scanlon was complete as he cast the delegation's vote at that year's TUC Congress for continued wage restraint in defiance of established policy. The following year Duffy defeated Wright to become Scanlon's successor. The period ended as it began with the right-wing in the saddle. Not a single left sat on the Executive; they were in the minority on the National Committee, and, with Boyd as General Secretary and Duffy as President, their influence at the top was reflected only through Assistant General Secretaries, Brett and Wright.[87] The AUEW left was often seen as a model for other unions: its success was tenuous, dependent on allies outside its control. In the end the CP may have paid a heavy price for this dependence and the fact that it cultivated no strong independent political presence.

This brief survey demonstrates that the relationship between creation of policy and its articulation inside the unions was far from automatic. Translation into practice required complicated transactions, both with party members, for democratic centralism was now dilute, and potential allies. In some unions left unity was long established, in others its initiation was belated. Its development took different forms in the variegated structures, traditions and politics of British unions. Tensions between policy and practice were, from the CP's vantage point, far from uniformly benign. Pragmatism entailed divisive squabbles over elections and the violation of policy over the Social Contract.

Within heterogeneity and complexity, we can isolate a common core to Broad Leftism: a drive to 'get inside' and operate the official machinery of the unions, viewed uncritically as neutral engines of class advance with the correct hands on the wheel. Despite the CP's avowed leading role, there was some tendency to defer to Labour lefts. Creation of a politically developed membership was often subordinated to electoral manoeuvres with little attention to the conservatizing aspect of machine politics. The energies of the CP's limited forces were concentrated on building the Broad Lefts as electoral organizations with less emphasis on recruiting trade unionists into the party. The stress on official machinery had its strengths against leftists who argued it was useless to engage 'the bureaucracy'. It also had its problems. In conditions where CP control of its own militants was brittle, the Broad Left was unable to bind lefts to the CP line and there was no powerful base to hold them to account. The white collar unions were neglected and younger members often found little identification with the sedentary Broad Lefts. Influence was real but circumscribed: even in the AEU and NUM it proved fragile after 1974.

236

Party strongholds

Most observers would agree that by 1970,

> the Communist Party was still the major activist force in the engineering industry in Sheffield and Manchester, in shipbuilding on the Clyde and in the Scottish and Welsh coalfields, and was influential in the British Leyland Longbridge plant in Birmingham, the Ford plant in Dagenham, the engineering union throughout London, the building industry in London and Birmingham.[88]

This assessment evokes the uneven, variable nature of the CP network, its concentration in old industries and manual worker unions, and its relative antiquity. It is noteworthy that the party never built the base in Ford Halewood, Standard Speke, the Vauxhall factory at Ellesmere Port, or even the new Scottish car plants which it constructed in Dagenham or Longbridge around the Second World War. The picture requires some supplementing. The CP was also influential in the vehicle plants in Coventry and Birmingham and in engineering in Scotland. In contrast with its diminished presence in Wales the party's greatest strength was in the West of Scotland industrial belt and it exercised significant pressure through the STUC. Its single largest workplace branch was in Rolls Royce Hillington, and whilst such figures must be viewed critically, party veterans recall 70 members at its zenith, of whom 15 were shop stewards. Scotland was the only area where there was, by the 1970s, a network of pit branches. From the 1950s the party had also made incursions into the Yorkshire coalfield, with little success in building pit branches, and strengthened its position in the London docks. As its weakness in other ports testifies – by 1980 only nine members were listed in Liverpool docks – party strongholds were scattered. Even its heartlands boasted few 'Putilov works'.

In Manchester the CP dominated engineering trade unionism until the mid-1970s through a focus on the apparatus and the role of key activists in the union and important factories rather than through a network of strong workplace branches. There were a few such branches – at Shell Carrington, Massey Ferguson, Hawker Siddley, Ward and Goldstone, and Ferranti – but only one, GEC Openshaw, seems to have functioned significantly throughout this period. The Roberts Arundel strike in Stockport in 1966 was the herald of the new militancy. Prosecuted with imagination and mass and mobile picketing by the local CP industrial leadership, it produced membership gains and the development of a branch at the Mirlees factory, but nothing of long-term significance. By 1976 its key leaders had left the CP.[89]

In Sheffield workplace organization was stronger. Again it was concentrated on a number of key engineering and steel factories: Firth Brown, Firth Brown Tools, Davey United, BSC and, especially, Shardlows, a CP 'fortress' with a sizeable membership – at its height, over 70, including important stewards. Here power on the ground – around half of the CP's 600 members worked in engineering in the 1960s – was reflected in continued strength at district and divisional level in the AEU, closer links with the Labour left and the ability to mobilize industrial action. By 1976 the number of functioning workplace branches had declined to eight. Thereafter, restructuring and redundancies, and changes in the market position of Shardlows, a strategic factory which made crankshafts for the motor industry, saw a decline in membership.[90]

In the mines, the CP resurgence in Yorkshire from the 1950s had a powerful impact on the fortunes of the left. Here again, we encounter the paradox for a party whose imperative was to root itself in the workplace: it remained numerically weak in the pits but influential in the union. The organizational lessons learnt in the unofficial strike of 1969 bore fruit with the flying pickets and mass picketing which characterized the 1972 strike – tactics used in Yorkshire since the 1950s. Despite internal differences, the CP members on the NUM Executive played a role in legitimizing rank and file initiatives, as did strategically placed regional personnel such as CP member Jock Kane, the Yorkshire Financial Secretary.[91] As with other key incidents of these years, the closure of the coke depot at Saltley, Birmingham, on 10 February 1972, of tremendous significance in both the strike and the wider militancy, was not produced by a spontaneous eruption. It had to be organized. It represented a united effort by the miners and the Midlands labour movement. Nevertheless the role of CP engineering advisories, their important contacts at district and shop steward level, and the links local CPers such as Frank Watters and Peter Carter enjoyed with influential figures such as Brian Mathers, the TGWU Regional Secretary, and Arthur Scargill, were instrumental in organizing latent support. In 1974, in contrast, the three CP members on the National Strike Committee appear to have provided no opposition to centralization of control of the stoppage.[92]

Accident was sometimes allied to opportunity. In 1969 Jimmy Reid resigned as Secretary of the Scottish CP and went to work as a fitter in Upper Clyde Shipbuilders, playing, together with other party members Jimmy Airlie and Sammy Barr, a vital part in the 1972 work-in which stimulated an unprecedented wave of occupations throughout Britain. Nevertheless the CP again failed to benefit in terms of membership growth and in 1976, amongst recriminations, Reid left the party. Similarly the presence of a CP contingent on Brent Trades Council enabled party veterans such as Tom Durkin and sympathizers such as Jack Dromey to become involved in the Grunwick strike in 1976–7.[93]

Party members also played a significant role in the docks struggles. Party reports list membership only in London, claiming 34 members in 1966 and 75 in 1968. The party was strong in the TGWU on the London docks but more influential in the tiny NASD and the Lightermen (both later absorbed by the TGWU). They dominated the unofficial Port of London Liaison Committee and with the introduction of shop stewards to the docks in 1968, party members Micky Fenn, Vic Turner, Buck Baker, Jack Dash, Ted Kirby, Danny Lyons and Bernie Steer were elected. The removal of the ban on party members avoided conflict with the TGWU and CPers went on to play a substantial part in the National Port Shop Stewards' Committee.[94]

On the whole, the docks activists kept their distance from the party. Many of them had a limited relationship with the CP, although Lyons served a term on the Executive. The containerization campaign, the issuing of injunctions prohibiting blacking of container depots and road haulage firms, and the imprisonment of five dockers on 21 July 1972 for flouting these orders, brought the dockers into the centre of industrial politics. Chris Harman alleges that in order not to offend union leaders, '... the Liaison Committee for the Defence of Trade Unions failed to take any initiatives at all during the struggle of the dockers against the law – even though one of the imprisoned dockers, Bernie Steer, was a Communist Party member'.[95] In fact the CP supported the dockers throughout their campaign. The party pressurized lorry drivers' leader and CP member Eric Rechnitz to drop opposition to the dockers' containerization campaign and resisted pressure from the TGWU by arguments of principle and expediency – while the majority of the dockers were in the TGWU, Steer, secretary of what was a joint shop stewards' committee, and two others of the 'Pentonville Five', Con Clancy and Derek Watkins, were members of the NASD.

At a conference on 10 June, the LCDTU urged solidarity action if the dockers were imprisoned. As soon as the five dockers were gaoled, the LCDTU's leaders called for this decision to be implemented. CP members were instrumental in spreading stoppages to the national newspapers, engineering and building. At an emergency industrial aggregate on 23 July, Ramelson called for members to spread the strikes to force the TUC to call a general strike until the dockers were released. There can be little doubt that the CP played an appreciable part in the July events which represented the zenith of 1970s militancy: the purchase of the CP's industrial network was demonstrated in the groups of workers on strike from 22 July onwards.[96] But nor can there be doubt as to dockers' dissatisfaction with the CP. The distance between the party and its docks activists caused terminal problems. In the aftermath of 1972, the CP docks branch collapsed – only 13 members are listed – and by 1975 it was very weak. Veterans such as Kirby and Dash had already retired and younger members such as Fenn and Eddie Prevost joined IS.[97]

Figures for the late 1960s demonstrate that the party's greatest numerical strength lay in the car factories. Some believed that the party's influence at Fords Dagenham was never as great after the victimization of stewards in 1962. None the less the CP maintained a branch of 40 members on the

Dagenham estate and members such as Sid Harroway and Danny Connor played a leading role as stewards through the 1970s and it was one of the few branches to periodically produce a factory bulletin.[98] The party also had a strong base in Longbridge and Leyland's Tractors and Transmissions plant in Birmingham, both of which, in the late 1960s and early 1970s, had workplace branches of up to 60 members, although these figures represented different levels of activism, allegiance and turnover amongst members. Both stewards' organizations bore the imprint of strong leaders, AEU members Dick Etheridge at Longbridge, a canny, folksy pragmatist with a suspicion of mass democracy, and Arthur Harper at Drews Lane, an able, charismatic eccentric. Throughout these years, the CP remained the dominant force in the BL Combine. They took a cautious line. Despite opposition from some stewards, Measured Day Work was accepted by the Longbridge leadership, and alliances were developed with right-wing convenors, notably Eddie McGarry from Standard Triumph, Coventry.[99]

When Derek Robinson replaced Etheridge as convenor in 1975, the CP still dominated the Joint Shop Stewards' Committee and the Works Committee. With the advent of the Ryder Report, the party became enthusiastic supporters of increased productivity and workers' participation, and key CP convenors – Robinson, Peter Nicholas (Rover Tyldsley) and Tom Steward (Coventry Engines) – sat on the BL Cars Council. Tensions developed between the lay leadership's emphasis on company survival and opposition to strikes, in which they identified themselves with Jones and Scanlon, and growing shop floor opposition to the Social Contract. Other CP convenors, such as Len Brindle from the Truck and Bus Division, denounced participation as weakening the stewards' role. Robinson's condemnation of the BL toolmakers' strike in early 1977 produced further dissension and led the Combine to call a national conference, 'a rank and file TUC', in Birmingham in April. The CP was in a difficult position: calling for a united front against any Phase III of incomes policy, it opposed struggles taking place under Phase II – the strikes of the BL toolmakers and the Port Talbot electricians. Seeking to impose unity and avoid sectionalism, it impaired the potential for mobilization. This was underlined by the absence of a strike on the 20 April Day of Action supported by the Birmingham conference.[100]

Events moved swiftly from the installation of the hard-line management of Michael Edwardes through the CP's move to withdrawal from participation to the dismissal of Derek Robinson on 19 November 1979 for signing a Combine Committee pamphlet opposing the restructuring plans. The lack of support for strike action from AUEW leaders and the impact their manoevrings and delays had upon workers facilitated the victimization. The divisions and disillusion which CP opposition to strikes and support for breaking picket lines in the toolroom dispute had reinforced, also played its part. The victimization underscored the weakness of the CP in its strongholds by the end of the 1970s. Despite strength in the factories, the left had always been in a minority on the two Birmingham AUEW District Committees, although with their appeal crossing political boundaries, Etheridge and Harper could be elected to office there. The CP was constrained by vigorous right-wing opponents, notably Bill Jordan, later AUEW President, which limited their participation in the strikes against anti-union legislation. Harper's desertion to IS suggested the fragility of the party's base. In 1979 it still had a branch of around 30 members in Longbridge. But despite repeated exhortations by Mick Costello, it never met throughout the Robinson dispute. Robinson's supporters were also critical of the inability of the local party to mobilize.[101] The contrast with 1972 was stark. By 1979 growing unemployment, the disputes over the Social Contract and the inability to find political answers beyond wage militancy had taken their toll on grassroots mobilization.

The party against the state

When Harold Wilson attacked the CP's role in the seamen's strike in June 1966, he was frustrated and looking for scapegoats. Apart from occasional phrase-mongering, his statements were measured. As a 'tightly knit group of politically motivated men', party leaders certainly supported strikes against the government's wages policy and the Prime Minister took pains to stress he was not condemning 'militant trade unionism' or suggesting the party was behind the stoppage – and again this was fair comment – they were 'exploiting' it. CP documents confirm his assessment of links between the Industrial Department and NUS activists over a number of years, and the strike suggested the strengths, weaknesses and *modus operandi* of the CP at the start of this period. They had a tiny membership amongst seafarers and nobody on the NUS Executive. But CP members Jack Coward and Roger Woods chaired the two key strike committees in London and Liverpool, Gordon Norris was a leading member of the negotiating committee and the party was able to mobilize the contacts of the National Seamen's Reform Committee, a body they had allowed to collapse in 1964 in order to 'get inside the union machine'. Respected activists gave the party a voice out of proportion to its numbers and they had close links with Executive members Joe Kenny and Jim Slater who were willing to discuss strategy with Ramelson. Kenny and Slater, in their turn, were powerful voices in the union leadership. In this way the party was able to exercise influence on the progress of the dispute whilst attempting to involve the dockers and other groups in its support.[102]

Enthused by this publicity, by the growth of militancy and the right-wing trajectory of the Wilson administration, the party launched the LCDTU in September 1966 to coordinate opposition to state intervention in industrial relations. It was sponsored by CP-dominated lay bodies such as the Joint Sites Committee and the London Docks Liaison Committee and its first conference in December 1966 was attended by an encouraging 671 delegates representing 130 trade union branches, 201 shop stewards' committees, 15 district committees and 16 trades councils. There were also representatives of 9 local union defence committees which the CP and the Trotskyists were both seeking to establish. Further conferences in 1967 and 1968, again sponsored by shop stewards' committees under CP influence, showed no growth in numbers or representation and demonstrated the limits of the party's base. The conferences were organized by London-based militants. Jim Hiles was the Secretary with Lou Lewis, later replaced by Kevin Halpin, as chair, working closely with the Industrial Department. The conferences carried declarations opposing wage controls and legal intervention in the unions, and urging the need for an alternative economic policy. They were forums for propaganda, enthusing the troops and extending the CP's industrial network.[103]

But the publication of the White Paper, *In Place of Strife* in 1969, with its plans for legal controls over union activity, fulfilled party prophecies and announced new opportunities. Hitherto, the special conference of union executives called by the TUC on 27 February would have seen only the call for a lobby. But in the context of an educational campaign against the proposals in its press, the party now campaigned for industrial action on the day of the conference. This took the form initially of publicizing calls for action from union bodies amenable to party influence, with the importance of industrial action subsequently emphasized by CP General Secretary John Gollan. As calls for actions developed, the LCDTU declared support not simply for a lobby but for stoppages. Success was limited: estimates of the number on strike ranged from 65,000 to 150,000. Troup, who makes the most careful estimate, suggests around 70,000 were involved and that strikes were largely limited to Scotland and Merseyside. In the face of opposition from the major unions, there was no industrial action in party fortresses such as the Welsh mines, Manchester, Sheffield or the Midlands.[104]

Rather than writing it off as an unsuccessful adventure, the party decided to go forward. An LCDTU conference in April 1969 was attended by an impressive 1700 delegates and gave carefully phrased support for strikes on 1 May which might mobilize the historic connotations of May Day. Once again there was a finessed build up in the party press, with publicity for calls from union bodies for stoppages on 1 May. Again there was opposition from major unions including the AEF, only SOGAT, the NASD and the Lightermen gave official support. Around 200,000 took industrial action. This time big car plants at Longbridge and Cowley were out and in Sheffield thirteen factories closed. Dockers and printers were prominent whilst action was again extensive in engineering and the mines in Scotland. But there was little response in CP bastions such as the Manchester engineering industry.[105]

Willie Thompson asserts that after 1963 the CP made a final break with early traditions in that it sought 'to mobilize its members at large to support action by workers rather than to instigate workers to industrial action in pursuit of its own policies and aims'.[106] As a characterization of its position during these years, this is plainly mistaken. The party sought consistently to mobilize workers to take industrial action against state policies. It did so, however, on the basis of calculated, limited objectives, with caution and finesse, and through a series of interlocking dialogues between its militants on the ground and the Industrial Department which enabled it to select engagements with some prudence. Calls to action followed careful soundings and were developed when there appeared to be reasonable chances of success. The emphasis was always on moving the official machine, on attempting to pressurize unions and the TUC to act. But the CP demonstrated it was willing to develop independent action to this end.[107] Whilst its success was circumscribed and pointed up the weaknesses in its own ranks as well as sources of militancy independent of the party, it made a real contribution to the defeat of *In Place of Strife*. The strikes themselves involved a small minority. But they were the first strikes against state policy since 1926. The arguments at workplace level which calls for action – successful or not – ignited; the publicity accorded the strikes; the educational impact of campaigns; the pressure the action put upon union leaders and Labour MPs; all suggest that any account of this episode bound by Labour Party in-fighting and parliamentary manoeuvrings falls several chapters short of the full story.

The LCDTU was tested further by the announcement of the Heath government's Industrial Relations Bill. The party could now avail itself of the experience of the previous period and anti-Toryism. The LCDTU conference in November 1970 was well prepared, attracting a record 1,800 delegates. Whilst the LCDTU agreed education and agitation were important, it criticized the TUC for failing to understand they were best developed through mass action. Encouraged by a wide range of calls for industrial action, it was more forthright than 18 months earlier in calling a one-day strike on 8 December, the day the Bill was to be published.[108]

Chris Harman's claim that 'once the struggle against the Industrial Relations Bill involved spreading industrial action in defiance of the officials it [the LCDTU] abstained', is fundamentally misplaced.[109] The 8 December initiative was condemned as illegitimate use of industrial action for political ends by the TUC General Secretary. Opposed by the TGWU, the GMWU and the ETU, it again received no support from the AEF which left the decision to District Committees. The strikes were now reaching significant proportions: the official estimate was that 350,000 workers were involved; the most balanced suggests almost 440,000 were on strike. The usual qualifications have to be made: the stoppages were again generally limited to

243

engineering, print, the docks and mines, and largely within these occupational categories to Scotland, Merseyside, Manchester, Sheffield and London. The message that the legislation was injurious to the health of unions, specifically shop stewards, and that it could be successfully opposed was reaching more and more workers in areas of traditional militancy rather than hitting schools and hospitals and bringing out members of NUPE and NALGO or even the ETU. The unevenness of the CP's base, the difficulty of convincing workers to strike, and the importance of imaginative leadership as well as conditions on the ground were once more underlined by the fact that Manchester engineering factories were heavily affected whilst key Midlands car factories stayed at work.[110]

Whatever the qualifications, 8 December was a triumph. Independently, in the teeth of official opposition, although it remained careful to emphasize it was seeking to move the official movement not transcend it, the CP through the LCDTU had motivated significant stoppages. In familiarizing workers with political industrial action, the strikes had incalculable impact in stiffening and extending opposition to the proposed legislation. In February 1971 the party's work in the AUEW Broad Left bore fruit when the changing balance of forces and the conversion of wide sections of the traditional right to active opposition to legislation saw the National Committee call two one-day strikes in March. With the Bill now set to become law and a major union set on defiance, the LCDTU conference in April, attended by only 700 delegates, understandably directed its attention to stiffening TUC policy. However, there was now an unfortunate loss of momentum. In June the LCDTU called for lobbies of the TUC and Labour Party conferences. It took no further initiatives for the remainder of 1971, suggesting an, at least reactive, response to the fact the Bill had now become law.[111]

Despite the upsurge in struggle announced by the miners' strike, the LCDTU's next national conference in February 1972 was attended by representatives of a mere 80 shop stewards committees. Its endeavours to realize the party slogan 'For a General Strike on May Day' were conspicuously unsuccessful. The humiliating mothballing of the call due to lack of enthusiasm in the workplaces denotes again the volatility of the militancy, its relative resistance to sustained campaigns and the brittleness of the CP's base when too many demands were placed upon it.[112] The initiatives of the NUR and TGWU in diluting TUC policy to facilitate involvement with the legislation and the National Industrial Relations Court (NIRC), and the progress of the containerization dispute sparked the crisis that disabled the Industrial Relations Act.[113]

The circumscribed part the LCDTU played in the events of July 1972 underlines its nature as an extension of the party. It was never an independent, even quasi-independent, rank and file movement. It took no initiatives without the *imprimatur* of the Industrial Department. The Committee was shadowy, consisting of party-influenced stewards' committees carefully selected by the officers. The conferences blended with the lack of democratic structure: declarations prepared by the officers and the Industrial Department were placed before the meetings with no amendments or alternative resolutions allowed. The LCDTU was a CP franchise: the party was not prepared to risk losing control of a customized, precision instrument in the gamble that an autonomous organization with real democracy might attract greater support. We have to recognize both the successes of the LCDTU in opposing state policies and the limits of that success, and we have to locate its activities as organic to the party's industrial work.[114]

The boundaries of that work became clearer as the decade developed. The LCDTU played little role in the continuing resistance to the Industrial Relations Act, the brunt of which was borne by the strikes called by the AUEW against judgements of the NIRC. The success it achieved over anti-union legislation eluded its attempts over the next five years to construct a unified opposition to incomes policy. Decline preceded the Social Contract. Despite an impressive platform, the LCDTU's October 1973 conference was attended by only 515 delegates with representation from only 35 stewards' committees. The June 1974 conference was attended by less than 100 delegates and the LCDTU was forced to reassume its pre-1969 role as a vehicle for propaganda and lobbying.[115]

Its last throw in this period came in early 1977 as militancy revived in opposition to Phase II of Labour's incomes policy. The LCDTU conference in February 1977 followed the pattern of earlier initiatives with the *Morning Star* recording an impressive build-up of support. The conference attracted 1,300 delegates from 272 branches and 132 stewards' committees and 61 trades councils. The conference called for a day of action for a return to free collective bargaining, but with calculated caution and the desire to build a secure platform, waited on the BL Combine's 'rank and file TUC' on 3 April before naming the day. The party campaigned for support for action on 20 April demanded by the BL conference. The response in terms of strikes was derisory. Although there were small stoppages in Scotland and Sheffield, the BL Combine stayed at work.[116]

A party already in trouble?

This period emphasized the CP's appreciable if minority role in industry and the limits of that role. Whilst its influence in the unions was greater than at any time since the 1940s – perhaps, as some suggest, than at any time in its history – the fragility of that influence and the boundaries of it were discernible in 1979. In the decade 1964–74 the party cut with the grain of ascending militant radicalism and left its mark on the struggles, particularly the fight against legislation. The CP's purchase historically

245

had been greater in building trade unionism rather than moulding its politics. In these episodes it played a remarkable political role. The party lacked the Bolshevik machine attributed to it by Harold Wilson in 1966. But it remained unique in possessing an industrial network which could mobilize defiance. The party punched well above its weight: it influenced the response of workers and the fate of legal reform, and registered real impact on industrial politics. The tide turning in favour of the Social Contract and, perhaps more pertinently, away from the left in general, saw the CP increasingly marginalized. It disclosed the limited foundations of CP organization and the failure to significantly refurbish and extend it on the ground, in the workplace, in apparently propitious circumstances.

By 1979 membership had declined to 20,500. Whilst we have no specific statistics on the numbers of trade unionists in membership, figures on workplace branches for eight party districts (including London) show that by 1979 all but two had fewer members than in 1963 (and these two had only one such branch in 1979).[117] Many industrial members had tenuous links with the party. CP documents confirm the impression of the industrial organizer that union activists were ageing and that their numbers had not been replenished. The cadre had not been qualitatively developed and renewed in the good years: 'people used to say to me sometimes, "Christ, you've got seven people on the General Council", or five or whatever it was, and I said, "That's work of ten years ago, fifteen years ago" '.[118]

There was success in winning positions in the unions – although the lion's share seems to have gone to non-party lefts – but after 1974 the going again got harder. The absence of a strong participative CP presence in the Broad Lefts representing rank and file workers meant there was an insufficiently powerful countervailing force to arrest left leaders who felt the pull of the state. The CP's weakness here was essentially political given the absence of a viable alternative to the Social Contract. The 1974 TUC illustrated the magnetic force ran through Hugh Scanlon to Ken Gill not *vice versa*. The power of trade unionism to absorb politics is evoked by Gill's explanation of the withdrawal of the TASS motion: consideration of the AUEW merger was uppermost in his mind. If the CP could not motivate its own leading members, how could it influence those independent of it?

As it concentrated on the corridors of union power, the party's weight at the grass roots, the essential *avoirdupois* it could bring to bear on high union politics, was withering. The party paid a high price for its influence on the higher echelons of the unions. The CP's historic aim, bar oscillations immediately after 1945, had been a political organization rooted in the workplace. On the face of it, the years after 1964 provided the most favourable opportunities since the 1920s for realizing this project. Yet by 1975 Ramelson admitted at a conference on workplace branches to the 'glaring gaps regionally and industrially in our organization and was self-critical on behalf of the leadership on the priority that had been given to this work'.[119] By 1979 the party still possessed only a network of industrial militants, fraying, patchy, under pressure. This suggests once again that the oxygen of industrial militancy is less conducive to the radical restructuring of political consciousness than many believed, and may stimulate, amongst some sections of workers, a move to the right. And of course by the mid-1970s structural factors – the decline of manufacturing industry, shifts in the workforce and trade unionism, from areas where the CP was strong on the ground such as engineering to areas where it was weak such as public utilities – were militating against party growth.

The nature of the CP as the ideological agent for socialist transformation of militants also requires more address. In the workplaces its members rarely played the revolutionary agitator. The CP's complex history had produced gradualism and a restrained, realistic style. They more typically pushed militant trade unionism than *The British Road*. They built shop stewards' committees not 'Little Moscows'. Then there was the party itself. To read, for example, the pre-congress discussions in *Comment* through the 1970s is to gather the impression of a divided and troubled organization, not in the best condition for recruiting and educating members. If attention cannot simply be concentrated on the industrial work, it is difficult not to endorse the view that that work remained focused on bread and butter issues and on the union hierarchies at the expense of ideological struggle to make Marxists. But the blame for difficulties cannot simply be attached to the Industrial Department. We come back to the party.

The party as a whole, specifically its Organization Department, was ultimately responsible for recruitment and workplace organization, while education of members was neglected. The resources devoted to work in local and general elections, draining and unfruitful, cannot have helped. Criticism of the Industrial Department has to be related to the relaxation of discipline and the weakening of democratic centralism in relation to the party's trade unionists and others. This is often viewed benignly, even celebrated. Yet it surely played a role in the tendencies to assimilate to trade unionism which critics of the industrial work deplore. As the former Industrial Organizer recalled:

And you would have a position where there was a constant battle of the Industrial Department with particularly our leading trade unionists, general secretaries and such people, a constant battle never made public for obvious reasons, to winning them, which is what their branches should have been doing, for political approaches on a number of questions, rather than what trade unionism teaches you and that is to compromise at every stage: 'We can't win it, don't fight it'. Now that's a logical thing sometimes at the workplace but if it comes to a resolution at the TUC on incomes policy it is not a logical decision. And you had that constant battle.[120]

247

If the relationship between militancy and socialist politics proved less intimate than Leninist theory conceived, the alternatives proffered by critics were scarcely more compelling. The militancy did broaden beyond 'economism' to briefly embrace struggles against the state and challenges to the logic of capitalism. The encouragement of radically new forms of struggle linking conflict at the point of production to social oppression and hegemonic politics has always been part of Marxist approaches and has always encountered stubborn resistance, not only from the pressures of union practice under capitalism but from groups outside the unions who stubbornly refuse to be mobilized. Even if such groups united with trade unionists, it is not cynical to inquire precisely what muscle they would add to struggles against the employers or the state. In the 1970s, this project required stronger sinews than parsons, pop concerts, protest marches and the often arid circumlocutions of *The British Road*. Unlike industrial militancy, the 'socialist incomes policy' lacked the social forces to realise it: qualitative concessions from the state in return for wage restraint were not on offer while, on all the evidence, sustained wage restraint without significant concessions was a vote loser amongst workers. The new social movements, with their insubstantiality and their inherently sectional demands, lacked the universality and power that the labour movement could at least aspire to.

What was distinctive about the party and what for many remained its *raison d'être* was its work in industry. By 1979 this was in decline, it no longer anchored the party, it was decreasingly at the centre of members' preoccupations and, again in contrast with the past, its fundamental premises, its relationship to socialist transformation, came under fierce criticism. By 1979, the makings of party crisis were already in place. The CP did not face the new decade in a strong position, though it did not necessarily appear so at the time. The future was not determined: it had overcome problems often enough in the past and a Tory government might stimulate renewed militancy. But in the forcing house of Thatcherism the CP's difficulties would worsen and play their part in the party's final chapter. They have to be related to fundamental long-term aspects of its position as a small reformist party competing with Labour (and now to a limited extent with the far left) saddled with the Soviet connection and a consequent history of unprincipled politics. The party was usually significant, but it was never strong outside the conditions of wartime. And it was soon to prove one amongst many casualties as the consensus forged in wartime unravelled.

Notes

I would like particularly to thank Alan Campbell, my co-researcher on a wider study of the Communist Party, who has provided many of the materials for this chapter and discussed the issues with me. Thanks also to Nina Fishman for her incisive comments on an earlier draft, and to Andrew Flinn and Stephen Bird, custodians of the CP Archive at the National Museum of Labour History.

1. M. Moran, *The Politics of Industrial Relations* (1977), pp. 114, 141. Cf J. Kelly, 'Social democracy and anti-communism: Allan Flande.. and British industrial relations in the early postwar period', in A. Campbell, N. Fishman and J. McIlroy (eds), *British Trade Unionism and Industrial Politics, 1945–79, vol. 1: 1945–64* (Aldershot, 1999).

2. W. Thompson, *The Good Old Cause: British Communism 1920–1991* (1992); F. Beckett, *Enemy Within: the rise and fall of the British Communist Party* (1995).

3. See, for example, J. Callaghan, 'The long drift of the Communist Party of Great Britain', *Journal of Communist Studies*, 1, 1985, pp. 3–4; M. Kenny, 'Recent changes in the Communist Party of Great Britain', *Journal of Communist Studies*, 7, 3, 1991; K. Hudson, 'Communist and former Communist organizations in Britain', *Journal of Communist Studies*, 10, 4, 1994. N. Fishman provides some historical background in 'The British Road is resurfaced for new times: from the British Communist Party to the Democratic Left', in M. Bull and P. Heywood (eds), *Western European Communist Parties after the Revolutions of 1989* (1994). There is brief allusion to the need to set the turmoil of the 1980s in an understanding of the party's industrial work since the 1940s in L. Pitcairn, 'Crisis in Britain [*sic*] communism: an insider's view', *New Left Review*, 153, 1985, p. 113. See also R. Hyman, 'Trade unions, the left and the Communist Party in Britain', in *Journal of Communist Studies*, 6, 4, 1990.

4. *The British Road to Socialism* (1968); *The British Road to Socialism* (1977).

5. National Museum of Labour History, CP Archive, CP/CENT/CONG/15/06, Report of 29th Congress, 1965, 'Political Resolution', p. 40.

6. CP/CENT/CONG/14/01, Report of 28th Congress, 1963, Resolution: 'The future of trade unionism', p. 77.

7. CP/CENT/CONG/14/01, Report of 28th Congress, 1963, J.R. Campbell, 'Reply to discussion' on 'The future of trade unionism', p. 43.

8. CP/CENT/CONG/13/01, Report of 27th Congress, 1961, 'Political Resolution', p. 53; CP/CENT/PC/07/17, Political Committee, 7 May 1964, 'Trade union problems in 1964'.

9. Report of 29th Congress, 1965, John Gollan, 'Turn left for progress', p. 4.

10. Ibid., p. 5; Report of 30th Congress, 1967, 'Incomes policy: speech by David Bowman introducing the resolution to Congress', pp. 771–4; B. Ramelson, *Incomes Policy: the great freeze trick* (1966); Report of 31st

Congress, 1969, 'Defence of the trade unions: speech by Mick McGahey moving the resolution', pp. 755–6; J. R. Campbell, 'The movement and the commission: delusions about Donovan', *Marxism Today* (hereafter *MT*), September 1968.

11.	Ibid., pp. 755 and Resolution: 'Defence of the trade unions', p. 758; B. Ramelson, *Productivity Agreements: an exposure of the latest and greatest swindle on the wages front* (1970); B. Ramelson, *Bury the Social Contract: the case for an alternative policy* (1977), p. 2.

12.	B. Ramelson, 'Workers' control? Possibilities and limitations', *MT*, October 1968, republished with other contributions in *The Debate on Workers' Control: a symposium from Marxism Today* (Nottingham, 1970); B. Ramelson, 'Public ownership and industrial democracy: the report of the Communist Party's Executive Committee, March 8th/9th', *Comment*, 22 March 1975, p. 82.; CP, *Evidence to the Committee of Inquiry on Industrial Democracy* (1976); *Morning Star* (hereafter *MS*), 27 January 1977.

13.	Report of 29th Congress, 1965, J. Gollan, 'Turn left for progress', p. 5; Report of 31st Congress, 1969, Resolution: 'Defence of the trade unions', p. 758; Ramelson, 'Workers' control', p. 25.

14.	The substance of the party's industrial politics in the period 1964–75 – as distinct from the formulations in *The British Road* – again raises questions about the organic, sustained, privileged relationship of popular frontism to CP politics suggested by so many students of the party. However this strand does re-emerge in the late 1970s, particularly in relation to events at BL, described below. See J. McIlroy, 'The Communist Party: From World War to Cold War', *Labour History Review*, 63, 3, 1998.

15.	See, for example, Report of 31st Congress, 1969, Resolution: 'Defence of the trade unions', p. 758; Report of 32nd Congress, 1971, Resolution: 'Unity, the Communist Party and the struggle for socialism', p. 456; Ramelson, *Incomes Policy*, pp. 19–21; Ramelson, *Bury the Social Contract*, pp. 21–35; CP/CENT/PC/07/17, Political Committee, 7 May 1964, 'Trade Union Problems in 1964'; CP/IND/MATH/05/06, 'Trade Union Problems in Britain Today': Memorandum submitted by the Communist Party to the Royal Commission on Trade Unions and Employers' Associations, September 1965.

16.	*British Road to Socialism* (1968 edition), p. 19; J. Bloomfield, 'The myth of rank and filism', *Comment*, 30 November 1974; G. Roberts, 'The strategy of rank and filism', *MT*, December 1976; Report of 31st Congress, 1969, pp. i–ii.

17.	Ramelson, 'Workers' control', p. 23.

18.	B. Ramelson, 'Politics and the trade unions', *Comment*, 9 February, 1974; Ramelson, *Productivity Agreements*, p. 24; B. Ramelson, 'TUC assessed: Bert Ramelson's report to the Communist party Executive Committee, September 10th', *Comment*, 29 September 1977, p. 340; Ken Gill, Interview with J. McIlroy and A. Campbell, 2 June 1998. Baruch 'Bert' Ramelson (1910–94) was born in the Ukraine and raised in Canada where he became a barrister. After service in the Spanish Civil War and the British Army during World War Two, he remained in Britain. From 1952 to 1966 he was a CP organizer in Yorkshire.

19. Ramelson, 'Politics and the trade unions', p. 35.
20. Ibid.
21. See, for example, P. Devine, 'Inflation and Marxist theory', *MT*, March 1974; D. Purdy, 'Some thoughts on the party's policy towards prices, wages and incomes', *MT*, August 1974; M. Prior, 'Discussion on inflation and Marxist theory', *MT*, April 1975. For a good discussion, empathic with these views, see G. Andrews, 'Intellectuals and the CP leadership in the 1970s', in G. Andrews, N. Fishman and K. Morgan (eds), *Opening the Books: essays on the social and cultural history of the British Communist Party* (1995).
22. CP/CENT/EC/11/07, Executive Committee, 12–13 November 1966; Report of 32nd Congress, 1971, Amendment 55, Conference Papers, p. 7; New Communist Party, *The Case for the New Communist Party* (1978), p. 13; 'The crisis, left unity and the Communist Party: Tony Chater's reply to the discussion', *Comment*, 15 December 1975. The French group, based on the Surrey District, split away prior to the 1977 Congress to form the New Communist Party.
23. For discussion of these debates, see Thompson, *Good Old Cause*, pp. 164–77, and Andrews, 'Intellectuals', pp. 237–45.
24. CP Archive, Uncatalogued industrial file, Documents on discussion of industrial work and the role of advisory committees, 1964–5; CP/CENT/PC/07/17, Political Committee, 7 May 1964, 'Trade union problems in 1964'; Gill interview; interview with Mick Costello by J. McIlroy and A. Campbell, 27 April 1998. Throughout this period, there were two, sometimes three, full-time workers in the Industrial Department, as well as other cadres who worked full-time on particular projects. Ramelson also strongly influenced the network of organizers in the regions (interview with Mike Power by J. McIlroy and A. Campbell, 11 November 1997). In the 1960s, Ramelson was assisted in the Department by Dennis Goodwin and Julie Jacobs, later by Jim Saunders; Costello was assisted by Gerry Pocock.
25. Modern Records Centre, University of Warwick (hereafter MRC), MSS 202/CP/61, Etheridge Papers, B. Ramelson to D. Etheridge, 'Notes for meeting to be held 24th September 1966; interview with George Anthony by J. McIlroy and A. Campbell, 13 July 1998; Gill interview; Costello interview. Beckett, *Enemy Within*, pp. 174–9, provides a somewhat exaggerated account but it captures the flavour of Ramelson's attempts to win friends and influence amongst union officials; see also S. Milne, 'Bert Ramelson: shop floor strategist', *Guardian*, 16 April 1994.
26. J. McIlroy and A. Campbell, 'Organizing the militants: the Liaison Committee for the Defence of Trade Unions, 1966–79', *British Journal of Industrial Relations*, 39, 1, 1999.
27. This is the recollected view of current supporters of both the Communist Party of Britain and the Democratic Left: interview with Mike Hicks by J. McIlroy and A. Campbell, 14 July 1998; Power interview; 'My view at the time was that the industrial workers didn't bother with the party machine,

they went to the advisories, they sorted out who was going to run for office, they discussed the resolutions to annual conference, they discussed inner trade union activities, but when it came to the party struggle they weren't really all that interested' (Anthony interview).

28.   CP Archive, Uncatalogued industrial file, H. Green, 'Industrial Work. From North-East District', and F. Miller, 'Industrial Work'.

29.   Ramelson, 'TUC assessed', p. 341; M. Costello, 'The TUC/Lab Pact', *Comment*, 30 September 1978; Gill interview; Power interview. Power estimates the number of CP delegates at the TUC as nearer 200 by 1979.

30.   Hicks interview; Power interview.

31.   CP/CENT/COMM/09/01, Report of the Committee on Party Organization to the Executive Committee, April 1965, pp. 14–15; CP/CENT/IND/1/2, 'Report of factory branch conference 1966'; CP/CENT/IND/1/3, 'Communists and the factories: The speech of Frank Stanley, chairman of the Communist Party, to the Communist Party's factory branch conference held in London, June 11th–12th, 1966'.

32.   CP/CENT/CONG/19/07, 34th Congress report, 1975; pp. 396–7.

33.   CP/CENT/PC/13/22, Political Committee, 2 and 16 October 1975; CP/CENT/ORG/3/1, 'Workplace branch conference, Birmingham, 8th/9th April 1978'; 'Regional Conference', 1 September 1979'.

34.   1963 and 1976 figures calculated from information in CP/CENT/IND/1/2, 'Report of Factory Branch Conference, June 1966' and CP/CENT/ORG/3/1, 'Conference on Workplace Branches, October 1976'; London figures calculated from information in CP/LON/BRA/1/8, 'London factories, February and June 1966'; CP/CENT/ORG/3/1, 'London District Committee. Workplace branches as at October 1979'.

35.   CP/LON/BRA/1/8, 'Factory branches in London 1968'; CP/LON/BRA/1/19, 'Position of Workplace Branches, London, 27 October 1975'.

36.   CP/CENT/ORG/3/1, 'Regional Conference, Birmingham, 1 September 1979'; CP/CENT/IND/1/2, Political Committee, 29 February 1968, 'Draft Report to EC, 9/10 March: Factory Organization'.

37.   Costello interview; Thompson, *Good Old Cause*, pp. 139–44.

38.   D. Purdy,'Viewpoint', *Comment*, 26 June 1976; D. Purdy, 'British capitalism since the war, parts 1 and 2', *MT*, September and October, 1976.

39.   B. Ramelson, 'Letters', *Comment*, 10 July 1976.

40.   Gill interview; Power interview; Costello interview; Andrews, 'Intellectuals', p. 237.

41.   K. Gill, 'Letters', *MS*, 30 November 1977. Similar points were made by other trade unionists; see, for example, *MS*, 6, 7 and 19 December 1977 for the views of George Bolton, NUM, George Jerrom, NGA, and Frank Watters.

42.   A. Hunt, 'Letters', *MS*, 7 December 1977; see also *MS*, 30 November (D. Purdy) and 21 December (P. Devine), 1977. The debate was not simply a matter of workers versus intellectuals. Some university lecturers, notably Ron Bellamy, John Foster and Lawrence Harris, were vigorous supporters of 'class politics' whilst UCATT activists Peter Carter and Lou Lewis and BL shop stewards Roger Murray and Jack Adams, were advocates of 're-

visionism'. But it seems clear that in the late 1970s the bulk of the trade unionists remained wedded to the Industrial Department's approach.

43. E. Hobsbawm, 'The forward march of labour halted', *MT*, September 1978. See also the comments by Ken Gill, *MT*, December 1978, and Peter Carter and Kevin Halpin in the January and February 1979 issues. Together with later contributions, they are collected in M. Jacques and F. Mulhern (eds), *The Forward March of Labour Halted?* (1981), In 'Forty years of popular front governments', *MT*, July 1976, Hobsbawm noted: 'The issues raised are not merely historical but belong to practical politics' (p. 221). This emphasis was to inform much of the discussion in *Marxism Today* in the 1980s.

44. Power interview; G. Andrews, 'Re-assessing the CPGB's strategy in the seventies: some preliminary thoughts', unpublished paper (n.d.), p. 7. Mick Costello, born 1942, was the son of a New Zealand diplomat, later Professor of Russian at Manchester University. He was partly educated in the Soviet Union and after leaving university in 1964, worked for the party in Kent. He became the *Morning Star's* Industrial Correspondent in 1969, switching to the Industrial Department in early 1977 and succeeding Ramelson in 1978.

45. D. Cook, 'The British Road to Socialism and the Communist Party', *MT*, December 1978, pp. 374, 372, 378.

46. Costello interview; M. Costello, 'The working class and the Broad Democratic Alliance', *MT*, June 1979. Costello was in turn criticized by S. Aaronovitch, 'The working class and the Broad democratic Alliance', *MT*, September 1979, and G. Charing, *MT*, October 1979, whilst class politics was defended by L. Harris, *MT*, December 1979.

47. CP/CENT/PC/14/32, M. Costello, 'Development of work in industry. Notes for Political Committee, 15.2.79'; CP/CENT/EC/17/01, 'Report to EC, 11 March 1978. Communist Work in Industry: Mick Costello', pp. 5–6; M. Costello, 'Politics of the workplace', *Comment*, 31 March 1979.

48. G. Stephenson (ed.), *The Life and Times of Sid Easton, 1911–1991* (n.d.), p. 44; Cf. R. Undy, V. Ellis, W.E.J. McCarthy and A.M. Halmos, *Change in Trade Unions: the development of UK unions since the 1960s* (1981), p. 94; telephone interview with Sean Morrissey by A. Campbell, 18 August 1998; Cf. IRIS, *In Perspective: concerning the role of the Communist Party and its effectiveness*, February 1972, pp. 8–10; G. Sinfield, 'Jack Jones: instincts will always be with rank and file', *MS*, 12 December 1968; CP/CENT/EC/13/20, Notes of Executive Committee, 9/10 September 1972, Address by Eddie Marsden; CP/CENT/EC/13/20, North West District Committee to John Gollan, 6 September 1972; B. Ramelson, 'Don't bow to CBI', *MS*, 14 October 1977.

49. The highest estimates are 11 – more than a quarter of the Executive – and 10 in 1975: Morrissey interview; P. Shipley, *Revolutionaries in Modern Britain* (1976), p. 53; an examination of TGWU Executive Committee minutes and discussion of them with TGWU official Regan Scott (13 November 1998) suggest that the number of CP members on the committee was never more than six at any one time in the 1970s. *MS*, 15 September 1972. Basnett was

reported as voting against the General Council's call for a one day general strike in July 1972: *Labour Research,* September 1972; Costello interview; a report to the government detailing links between the CP and its members in the 1966 railway dispute is in Public Record Office, PREM 13/786, 'The Communist Party and the threatened railway strike, 22 February 1966'.

50. Interview with Lou Lewis by J. McIlroy and A. Campbell, 14 July 1998; *Building Workers' Charter,* various issues; A. Goulding, 'The building industry: background to a rank and file movement', *International Socialism,* no. 75, February 1975; T. Austrin, 'The lump in the UK construction industry', in T. Nichols (ed.), *Capital and Labour: a Marxist primer* (1980); T. Austrin, 'Industrial Relations in the Construction Industry', unpublished PhD thesis, University of Bristol, 1978; J. England, 'How UCATT revised its rules: an anatomy of organizational change', *British Journal of Industrial Relations,* 17, 1, 1979.

51. Interview with Ruth Frow by A. Campbell, 16 January 1998; A. Boys, 'The changing union: a study of the NUT 1960–74', unpublished MA Thesis, University of Warwick, 1974; R. Seifert, *Teacher Militancy: a history of teacher strikes, 1896–1957* (1987), pp. 124–5. The CP Executive heard complaints that Morris contradicted party policy in press interviews (CP/CENT/EC/14/12, Executive Committee, 13–14 July 1972); R. Seifert, 'Some aspects of factional opposition: Rank and File and the National Union of Teachers, 1967–1982', *British Journal of Industrial Relations,* 22, 3, 1984, pp. 375, 383; *MS,* 14 July 1972; *Rank and File,* January 1969, p. 2.

52. Anon., 'A call to AEF members', *mimeo,* June 1970, pp. 1–2, 6; 'Homewood', 'NALGO at the crossroads', *Comment,* 12 July 1975. See also J. McIlroy, 'Trotskyism and the trade unions' in this volume.

53. J. Edelstein and M. Warner, *Comparative Union Democracy: organisation and opposition in British and American unions* (1975), pp. 224–5; P. Kahn, 'Essay in oral history: interview with Frank Watters', *Bulletin of the Society for the Study of Labour History* (hereafter BSSLH), 43, 1981, pp. 59–60.

54. V. Allen, *The Militancy of British Miners* (Shipley, 1981), pp. 6–8, 126; Kahn, 'Watters', p. 60; F. Watters, *Being Frank: the memoirs of Frank Watters* (Barnsley, 1992), pp. 17–18. 'Criticism of negative aspects of the CP's role' is reported in P. Kahn, 'Essay in oral history: Tommy Mullany', *BSSLH,* no. 44, Spring 1982, p. 54.

55. Edelstein and Warner, *Union Democracy,* p. 248; Allen, *Militancy,* p. 130; Kahn, 'Frank Watters', p. 60.

56. Allen, *Militancy,* pp. 125–35; *IRIS News,* October 1968, p. 5; *MS,* 25 March 1969.

57. P. Routledge, *Scargill: the unauthorised biography* (1993), p. 86; Edelstein and Warner, *Union Democracy,* pp. 250–1; Watters, *Being Frank,* pp. 19–20.

58. Allen, *Militancy,* pp. 145–6; Routledge, *Scargill,* p. 86.

59. Kahn, 'Mullany', p. 54. Mullany suggests the forums were viewed with suspicion by the national left. Allen, *Militancy,* p. 187; J. and R. Winterton, *Coal, Crisis and Conflict: the 1984–85 miners' strike in Yorkshire* (Manchester, 1989), pp. 9–11; M. Crick, *Scargill and the Miners*

(Harmondsworth, 1985), pp. 69–77.

60. Watters, *Being Frank*, pp. 20–22; Kahn, 'Mullany', p. 54.

61. CP/CENT/PC/09/03, Political Committee, 10 December 1964. 62.Costello interview; C. Woods, *The Crisis in Our Communist Party: cause, effect and cure* (1983); A. Mitchell, *Behind the Crisis in British Stalinism* (1984); *MS*, 27 December 1977; Kahn, 'Mullany', p. 54.

63. CP/CENT/EC/04, Executive Committee, 14–15 November 1964; CP Archive, uncatalogued industrial file, 'Industrial Work' from L.W. Dawson, 12 November 1964; J. Lloyd, *Light and Liberty: the history of the EETPU* (1990), pp. 485–6, 509, 532, 534–6.

64. Lloyd, *Light*, p. 537; interview with Ian Brown by J. McI'roy, 17 June 1989.

65. *Flashlight*, 1 December 1969.

66. Lloyd, *Light*, p. 578; Brown interview.

67. *The Ugly Face of Chapple's Union*, (Rank and File Pamphlet, 1975).

68. Brown interview; *Rank and File Contact*, no. 1, Summer 1975; P. Wintour, 'How Frank Chapple stays on top', *New Statesman*, 25 July 1980.

69. G. Wootton, 'Parties in union government: the AESD', *Political Studies*, 9, 2, 1961; B. Parkin, 'The Broad Left in TASS', *International Socialism*, no. 74, January 1975; Gill interview.

70. T. Foley, *A Most Formidable Union: the history of DATA and TASS* (1992), pp. 14–16; Parkin, 'Broad Left', pp. 16–17; C. Smith, *Technical Workers: class, labour and trade unionism* (1987), pp. 272–3; C. Smith, untitled, unpublished paper on the Broad Left in TASS, March 1982; G. Jenkins, 'The carving-up of Mike Cooley', *Socialist Review*, September–October 1981, p. 27.

71. H. Wainwright, 'Mike Cooley's colleagues asks [sic] if union is willing to fight', *New Statesman*, 31 July 1981, p. 1.

72. Parkin, 'Broad Left', p. 18; Smith, *Technical Workers*, p. 289; Smith, untitled paper, p. 5.

73. Smith, untitled paper, p. 7; Smith, *Technical Workers*, pp. 285–6; Parkin, 'Broad Left', pp. 19–20; Ken Gill denied that a majority of the full-time officers were ever members of the CP (Gill interview).

74. Smith, untitled paper, p. 8; Smith, *Technical Workers*, p. 275; Foley, *Formidable Union*, pp. 45–7; Gill interview; Hicks interview; Costello interview.

75. Interview with John Tocher by J. McIlroy, 2 June 1989; cf E. and R. Frow, *Engineering Struggles: episodes in the story of the shop stewards' movement* (Manchester, 1982), pp. 258–9. The last issue of the *Metalworker* appeared in March 1963.

76. Birch lost by 44,599 votes to 31,213 in the second ballot; see M. Bray, '"Democracy is what you make it": union democracy and postal ballots in the AUEW', unpublished MA thesis, University of Warwick, 1979, p. 75.

77. Alf Jones, quoted in M. Armstrong, 'The history and organisation of the Broad Left in the AUEW (Engineering Section) until 1972, with special reference to Manchester', unpublished MA thesis, University of Warwick,

1978, pp. 17–20, 23.
78. Interview with Bill Moore by J. McIlroy and A. Campbell, 14 July 1997; Tocher interview; MRC MSS 202/CP/61, Etheridge Papers, B. Ramelson, 'Notes for meeting to be held 24th September 1966'; Tocher interview.
79. Edelstein and Warner, *Union Democracy*, pp. 284–5; Armstrong, 'Broad Left in the AEU', pp. 6–9.; 'Agitation in the engineering industry', *AEU Journal*, July 1966, p. 273. MRC MSS 202/CP/61, Etheridge Papers, B. Ramelson, 'Notes for meeting to be held 24th September 1966'; Tocher interview.
80. Ramelson, 'Notes', p. 2.
81. Ibid., p. 3.
82. 'Agitation in the engineering industry', pp. 273–4; Bray, 'Democracy is what you make it', pp. 28–30; R. Undy, 'The electoral influence of the opposition in AUEW (ES) 1960–75', *British Journal of Industrial Relations*, 17, 1979, p. 25.
83. Armstrong, 'Broad Left in the AUEW', p. 9; information from Tony Carew, September 1997; J. Deason, 'The Broad Left in the AUEW', *International Socialism*, 79, June 1975, p. 9; Eddie Frow, quoted in Armstrong, p. 26.
84. For discussion of these developments, see Deason, 'Broad Left', pp. 10–15; G. Chadwick, 'Manchester engineering sit-ins, 1972', *Trade Union Register* (Nottingham, 1973); Undy, 'The electoral influence of the opposition in AUEW (ES)', p. 31.
85. Deason, 'Broad Left', p. 9; 'The AUEW defeat and after', *International Socialism*, 84, December 1975, p. 4.
86. 'Interview with Bob Wright', *MT*, September 1978, p. 271; Ernie Roberts, quoted in Armstrong, 'Broad Left', pp. 9–10.
87. P. Wintour, 'The battle for the AUEW', *New Statesman*, 17 March 1978; *New Statesman*, 7 December 1979, 29 february, 25 April 198C.
88. C. Harman, *The Fire Last Time: 1968 and after* (1988), p. 237.
89. CP/CENT/IND/1/2, 'Party factory organization in engineering and transport', n.d., 1968; George McCormack, interviewed by A. Campbell, 1 May 1998; Armstrong, 'Broad Left'; Frow interview; J. Arnison, *The Million Pound Strike* (1971).
90. CP/CENT/IND/1/2, 'Party factory organization'; CP/CENT/ORG/3/1, Information on Workplace Organization, April 1976; interview with Vi Gill by J. McIlroy and A. Campbell, 21 April 1998; interview with Walt Moore, Les Warsop and Cliff Wright by J. McIlroy and A. Campbell, 21 April 1998; Bill Moore interview.
91. CP/CENT/ORG/1/3, 'Yorkshire: Information for PC, June 1976'; Allen, *Militancy*, pp. 186–92; Watters, *Being Frank*, p. 63.
92. Costello interview; F. Watters, 'Victory at Saltley', *Comment*, 25 March 1972; Watters, *Being Frank*, pp. 63–4, 66–72; Allen, pp. 247–8.
93. J. Reid, *Reflections of a Clyde-built Man* (1976), pp. 42–5, 154–66; J. Foster and C. Woolfson, *The Politics of the UCS Work-In* (1986); Costello interview; J. Rogaly, *Grunwick* (Harmondsworth, 1986), pp. 60–9, 197–8.
94. CP/LON/BRA/1/8, 'London factories February and June 1966' and 'Fac-

tory branches in London 1968'; CP/LON/MEMB/1/18, Membership registration 1972; CP/LON/BRA/1/19, 'Position workplace branches, London, 27 October 1975'; J. Dash, *Good Morning Brothers* (1969), pp. 38ff, 171–3; Stephenson, *Sid Easton*, pp. 42–3; interview with Kevin Halpin by J. McIlroy and A. Campbell, 15 April 1998.

95. Halpin interview; Harman, *Fire Last Time*, p. 261; Vic Turner of the Pentonville Five was also a CP member. For further information see D. Lyddon, '"Glorious Summer" 1972: the high tide of rank and file militancy', in this volume, and the sources cited there.

96. Costello interview; Hicks interview; Lewis interview; LCDTU, 'Report of emergency national conference, 10 June 1972; CP/LON/IND/2/10, 'Notes of emergency industrial aggregate, 23 July 1972'.

97. CP/LON/MEMB/1/18, Membership registration 1972; CP/LON/BRA/1/19, 'Position workplace branches, London, 27 October 1975'; *Socialist Worker*, 14 April 1973; Harman, *Fire Last Time*, p. 265; Halpin interview.

98. Halpin interview; CP/CENT/IND/1/2, 'Party factory organization'; H. Friedman and S. Meredeen, *The Dynamics of Industrial Conflict: lessons from Ford* (1980).

99. CP/CENT/IND/1/2, 'Party factory organization'; interview with Derek Robinson by J. McIlroy and A. Campbell, 8 January 1998; S. Jefferys, 'The changing face of conflict: shopfloor organization at Longbridge, 1939–80', in M. Terry and P. K. Edwards (eds), *Shop Floor Politics and Job Controls: the post-war engineering industry* (Oxford, 1988); interview with Jim Denham by J. McIlroy, 8 January 1998.

100. J. Bloomfield, *British Leyland: save it* (1976), with a foreword by D. Robinson; J. Denham to J. McIlroy, 29 October 1997; Robinson interview; A. Thornett, *Inside Cowley. Trade Union Struggle in the 1970s: who really opened the door to the Tory onslaught?* (1998), pp. 112–14, 151–4; *MS*, 28 March 1977; R. Falber, 'Report to Executive Committee, 14/15 May 1977', *Comment*, 28 May 1977.

101. M. Edwardes, *Back from the Brink* (1983), pp. 107–30; Robinson interview; Watters, *Being Frank*, pp. 102–11; H. Scullion, 'The skilled revolt against general unionism: the case of the BL Toolroom Committee', *Industrial Relations Journal*, 12, 3, 1981; P. Willman and G. Winch, *Innovation and Management Control: labour relations at BL Cars* (Cambridge, 1985), pp. 81–3. Robinson was himself a toolmaker.

102. *Parliamentary Debates*, 1966–7, vol. 729, col. 1242–7, vol. 730, col. 1610–27; PRO PREM 13/1228, 'Note of a meeting between the Prime Minister and Mr Heath ... Tuesday 21 June 1966'; CP/IND/GOLL/04/07, Gollan Papers, Handwritten notes; J. Hemingway, *Conflict and Democracy: studies in trade union government* (Oxford, 1978), p. 70. Joe Kenny was not a CP member in 1966 although he later joined the party.

103. McIlroy and Campbell, 'Organizing the militants'.

104. *MS*, 9–27 January 1969; Halpin interview; *Financial Times*, 28 February 1969; A. Troup, 'The Mobilization of, and Response to, "Political" Protest Strikes, 1969–1984', unpublished PhD thesis, CNAA, 1987, pp. 49–52, 86–89.

105. K. Halpin, 'Trade unions' hour of decision', *Labour Monthly* (hereafter LM), June 1969; LCDTU, 'Declaration of National Conference, 12 April 1969'; *MS*, 14 March 1969; B. Panter, 'Action decided', *LM*, July 1971; Troup, 'Political Protest Strikes', pp. 49–52.

106. Thompson, *Good Old Cause*, p. 136.

107. Halpin interview; Power interview.

108. *MS*, 16 November, 4 December 1970; LCDTU, 'Declaration of National Conference, 14 November 1970'.

109. Harman, *Fire Last Time*, p. 238.

110. J. Jacobs, 'Trade unions: the fight back', *LM*, December 1970; K. Halpin, 'Act now to save the unions', *LM*, January 1971; *The Times*, 18 November, 1, 2, December 1970; Troup, 'Political Protest Strikes', pp. 106–11; Moran, *Politics*, pp. 114–16.

111. LCDTU,'Declaration adopted at Conference on 24 April 1971'; B. Wright, 'The Tory onslaught', *LM*, March 1971, pp. 16–17; Tocher interview; *MS*, 26 April 1971; LCDTU 'Statement', n.d., July 1971; Moran, *Politics*, p. 115.

112. B. Ramelson, 'Report to Executive Committee, January 8th/9th 1972', *Comment*, 12 February 1972; LCDTU, 'Declaration presented to the Conference on 12 February 1972'; LCDTU, 'Report of Conference on 12 February 1972'; LCDTU, 'All out on May 1st', n.d., 1972; Halpin interview.

113. Moran, *Politics*, pp. 138-40; J. Jones, *Union Man: an autobiography* (1986), pp. 248-9; Troup, 'Political Protest Strikes', p. 130.

114. McIlroy and Campbell, 'Organizing the militants'; Halpin interview; Power interview.

115. LCDTU, 'Report of National Delegate Conference, 20 October 1973; LCDTU, 'Statement on Meeting of 19 January 1974'; LCDTU, Circular on Conference, 6 April 1974; LCDTU, 'Report on LCDTU Conference, Salford, 29 June 1974'.

116. *MS*, 10 January 1977; D. Cook, 'Report to Executive Committee, 8th/9th January 1977', *Comment*, 22 January 1977; K. Halpin, 'Who broke the contract?', *MS*, 4 February 1977; LCDTU, Circular re. conference on 26 February 1977; LCDTU, 'Report of Conference, 26 February 1977'; *MS*, 28 March, 3, 7 April 1977; R. Falber, 'Report to Executive Committee, 14th/15th May 1977', *Comment*, 28 May 1977; *Financial Times*, 21 April 1977; *MS*, 21 April 1977.

117. CP/CENT/ORG/3/1, Communications from districts re. workplace branches, 1979.

118. Costello interview. This view is confirmed by the age of trade unionists on the executive and lists of 'younger' leading comrades produced in the 1970s, many of whom were well into their forties and had been in the party since the 1950s: see, for example, papers in CP/CENT/ORG/1/07.

119. Quoted in D. Cook, 'Every factory must be our fortress', *Comment*, 15 November 1975, p. 380.

120. Costello interview.

CHAPTER NINE

'Always Outnumbered, Always Outgunned': the Trotskyists and the Trade Unions

John McIlroy

These years witnessed a surprising phenomenon: the flowering of Trotskyism in Britain during the high tide of affluence. At the very moment academics were affirming the quiescence and political instrumentality of the working-class, the development of industrial militancy and disillusion with the Wilson governments of 1964–70 saw thousands of young workers turn away from the Labour Party in search of radical alternatives.[1] The war in Vietnam, 1968 in France, events in Ireland, Chile, Portugal, the worldwide student revolt – all fed a mood of optimism, rebelliousness and desire for fundamental social change. This was particularly so amongst the generation born in the 1940s. For many, the Communist Party (CP) was compromised by Stalinism, and the reformist complexities of *The British Road to Socialism* unattractive. Whilst the CP exercised greater influence than at any time since 1945 amongst union officials, its emphasis on winning official positions, the extension of the 'union machine' into the workplace and the incorporation into the structures and conventions of 'responsible' collective bargaining of many of its key lay activists strengthened the resolve of some to look further left.

In an era of escalating social conflict, questioning of established authority, structures and creeds, invocation of the efficacy of direct action and faith in activist democracy, Trotskyism flourished. Its growth was facilitated by the most sustained militancy since the early 1920s, economic decline, state intervention in the unions, the leftwards trend and the legitimation of lay activism in key unions such as the AUEW and the TGWU. The idealistic, dedicated young people who joined the Trotskyist organizations remained a small minority. The stubborn allegiance of the bulk of trade unionists to labourism proved enduring. However, if the Trotskyists remained a marginal force in industrial politics, their influence stretched beyond committed adherents. In many workplaces and unions they stimulated solidarity, created or recreated a tradition of active, aggressive collectivism and provided a radical cutting edge to the sudden, exciting extension of trade unionism after 1968.

For many beyond their ranks, the Trotskyists portrayed the problems of the period and propounded solutions in compelling fashion. At the heart of their vision lay pervasive, unrelenting conflict between capital and labour, but also a trade unionism fissured by an endemic clash of interests between a privileged bureaucracy, vacillating between employers and the working-class, and a rank and file whose essential, inscribed interests lay in the destruction of capitalism. The path to socialist consciousness and replacement of the bureaucracy, which held back struggle and in decisive conflicts sided with capital, lay through intensification of militancy. Strikes were the best method of securing concessions. Further, they facilitated awareness of the role of union leaders and the need to transcend capitalism and drew workers closer to the revolutionary party. Strong, independent, democratic, outward-looking, steward organization, rooted in the workplace, the cockpit of class struggle, was the first building block in socialist strategy in the unions.

Powerful organization, whether in the workplace or wider combine committees, was essential but inadequate. It was necessary to deploy the second and third building blocks: independent rank and file factions within unions and grouping together revolutionary militants and militant reformists across unions and industries in sectoral and national rank and file movements. Such movements must preserve their independence from the union bureaucracy, formulating a programme of economic and political demands to fill the vacuum left by the incorporation of the bureaucracy, and create a new leadership. The national rank and file movement would constitute a two-way bridge between industrial struggles and the final crucial building block, the revolutionary party. It would carry the party's politics into industrial struggles and militants into membership of the party.

Militancy and strikes held these building blocks together and moved them forward. The rank and file worker was depicted as a natural, noble militant if freed from the artificial constraints of union leaders. There was little consideration of the limits of union action and steward power in capitalist enterprises. The tendency was towards optimistic estimation of the balance of forces and the room available to extend workers' power in industry. As against precise, hard-headed, conjunctural analysis of capitalist upturns and downturns, of the ebb and flow of influence in particular workplaces and industries, of the fragility of workers' power in capitalism, the problems of the system were exaggerated, its resilience played down. There was a widely held view that state intervention would *itself* politicize workers. Faith in the efficacy of permanent militancy flourished. The relationship between strikes and the evolution of socialist consciousness was magnified. There was a tendency to minimize workers' consciousness of the difficulties, the losses as well as benefits which strikes entailed, the onset of war weariness if industrial action was sustained, and the ability of capital to manoeuvre through closures and relocation.[2] The tactical compromise, the honourable retreat, nevertheless remained in the Trotskyist armoury.[3] And if they were often over-generous in estimating the parameters of the possible, at times their opponents, may have taken too limited a view.[4]

These ideas, particularly the centrality of the rank and file movement, were attributed, in different degrees, to the National Shop Stewards and Workers' Committee Movement of the First World War and the early Minority Movement in the 1920s. They were legitimized by politically partial historical excavations which commenced with the publication of Brian Pearce's *Some Past Rank and File Movements* by the Socialist Labour League (SLL) in 1959.[5] The CP was characterized as having long deserted its revolutionary heritage; making its peace with the bureaucracy; renouncing the materialist understanding that structural location and function inside the unions ultimately prevailed over political differences in motivating behaviour. The party stood indicted of neglecting the essential task of building an independent rank and file movement, in favour of cultivating left officials and subordinating strategy and organizations such as the Liaison Committee for the Defence of Trade Unions (LCDTU) to their requirements.[6]

In practice numerous problems remained. The actions of union leaders were explained as stemming, alternatively or simultaneously, from material interests, social function or corruption. There were differing assessments of the possibilities of transforming the unions or replacing them. There was unresolved disputation on a range of issues from the nature of the programme of a rank and file movement – reformist or revolutionary, limited to industrial demands or going beyond them – to the nature of the exercise, as an independent united front or the industrial wing of the revolutionary party. This sketch glosses over significant differences between – and within – the Trotskyist groups which we cannot fully explore here. The SLL, later the Workers' Revolutionary Party (WRP), insisted on adherence to Trotsky's 1938 'Transitional Programme'. The International Socialists (IS), who later became the Socialist Workers' Party (SWP) were explicitly revisionist.

The SLL/WRP brandished the writings of Lenin and Trotsky on the labour aristocracy and emphasized the pre-ordained nature of bureaucratic betrayal. IS sought to update the sacred texts and stressed far more the vacillations of union leaders and their potential responsiveness to militancy. The SLL/WRP placed more rhetorical emphasis on the established labour movement, on demands and denunciations which it saw as bringing workers into conflict with union and Labour Party leaders, thus 'exposing' them. IS/SWP politics were rooted in building an alternative at the base: they downplayed the domination of Labour and engagement with it. By 1970 and 1980 respectively, the WRP and SWP had largely abandoned their conceptions of rank and filism in favour of direct party work in the unions. Other groups had their own totems and shibboleths. The politics of groups changed over time. They have to be related to their small size and limited implantation in the labour movement. The relative absence of members in key situations and influential positions posed problems in the generation of strategic intelligence of movements and workers' consciousness and hard assessment of possibilities, pressures and constraints. The small size of these organizations moreover made it easy to confuse relative growth or success with progress in the wider movement.

In 1964 there were only a few thousand Trotskyists in Britain. The three main groups traced their origins to the Revolutionary Communist Party, the unified organization of British Trotskyists, which broke up in 1949. The largest organization, the SLL, had around 500 members with possibly 2,000 in its high-turnover adjunct, the Young Socialists. The SLL had been formed in 1959 after the earlier, entrist organization, 'the Club', recruited a number of CP cadres – in total around 200 members – in the aftermath of the events of 1956. Among them were a number of industrial activists, although the only militant of the first rank was building worker Brian Behan. Out of Behan's work in the Shell Mex strike, the League was able to organize rank and file conferences with up to 500 delegates in 1958 and 1959. The chronic factionalism which dogged Trotskyism saw the opportunity squandered. By 1960 most of the cadres recruited in the aftermath of 1956 – Peter Fryer, Brian Pearce, Alasdair McIntyre, Peter Cadogan, Ken Coates and Behan and his supporters – had left or been expelled.

The IS, which unlike its competitor failed to benefit from 1956, had around 200 members in 1964. The *Socialist Review* Group, as the organization was known until 1962, had barely kept going through the 1950s. Despite the temporary adhesion of various groups, notably Eric Heffer and the remnants of the Socialist Workers' Federation, several Prospective Parliamentary Candidates and, for a few days until he was expelled from the organization in 1966, an MP in the shape of Syd Bidwell, IS remained in the shadow of the SLL. Although it benefited in the early 1960s from the recruitment of a number of young workers in Glasgow and London, it possessed little industrial base. The Revolutionary Socialist League (RSL) was led by veteran RCP leader, Ted Grant, and organized inside the Labour Party around the paper *Militant*, founded in 1964. The Grant group, too, struggled to keep going through the 1950s and had no more than 40 members in 1964. The International Marxist Group (IMG) formed in 1965, enrolled ex-members of the CP, SLL and RSL. It had briefly and unsuccessfully fused with the Grant group in the early 1960s and only reached a membership of 40 in 1968.[7] Taken together, the influence of the Trotskyists was negligible. Only the SLL had achieved fleeting prominence in its earlier incarnation through its involvement in the breakaway of dockers from the TGWU to the National Amalgamated Stevedores and Dockers (NASD) in 1954–55.[8]

After 1968 each group increased in size and influence. The IS and IMG followed the SLL out of 'entry work' in the Labour Party and became fixtures on the industrial scene. The SLL, transformed in 1973 into the WRP, peaked at around 2,000 members. The IS, which in 1977 became the SWP, had over 4,000 members by 1979. The *Militant* Group grew to 770 members in 1975 and 2,000 in 1980, while the IMG increased to 400 in 1972 and 800 in 1978.[9] By that time all these groups produced a weekly paper except the SLL/WRP which launched the daily *Workers' Press* in 1969. They were joined in the 1970s by neophytes based on splits from the WRP and IS, such as Workers' Fight, later Socialist Organizer, the Workers' Socialist League (WSL) and Workers' Power.

The IMG's base in industry remained limited: its membership was largely composed of students and white collar workers. A split in 1967 ensured it lost out on the development of the Institute for Workers' Control which its members, notably Ken Coates, had pioneered. In the early 1970s using the tactic of 'colonization' – sending members into key industries – they developed a base in Rover Solihull where one of their supporters became a senior steward, and a presence in British Leyland's Cowley assembly plant.[10] The IMG admitted their inability to construct fractions in the engineering and car industries. Working within IS/SWP-dominated groups, *Redder Tape* in the CPSA and *Red Collar* in ASTMS, they sought to broaden their politics and make them more inclusive. They were active in groups such as the Campaign for Action in NUPE and the COHSE Socialist Alliance. Their most successful intervention was in the NUT where they took a leading role in the Socialist Teachers' Alliance (STA). Established in 1976 as an alternative to the IS-initiated *Rank and File* group, the STA quickly overtook its rival.[11] *Militant's* work in the unions was also handicapped by its small size and by concentration on Labour Party activity. In the late 1960s it had a smattering of members in print and engineering and a presence on the trades council in its Liverpool heartland. Reports of meetings of its industrial caucuses in 1975 show 16 in attendance from the AUEW, 11 from the EETPU, 14 from the railway unions, 12 from ASTMS and 21 from NALGO. Two influential senior stewards at Rover Solihull were *Militant* supporters and its presence in the unions was growing, particularly in the CPSA. It was only in the 1980s it reaped greater success, presaged by winning the leadership of the CPSA's biggest branch, full-time officer posts, and four seats on the union's executive in 1978, and the election of Joe Marino as General Secretary of the Bakers' Union in 1979.[12]

The SLL/WRP was the only group to establish a significant base and sustained leadership role in an important industrial workplace. The IS/SWP were singular in attracting workers across a range of industries and constructing the beginnings of a shop steward network. This chapter, therefore, provides case studies of the industrial politics of what, for most of the period, were the best known Trotskyist organizations. It provides a general introductory survey rather than a comprehensive account of the complex politics of the Trotskyists and the experiences and impact of their activists in particular unions and industries.

Crisis ... what crisis? the industrial politics of the SLL/WRP

The politics of the SLL/WRP hinged on catastrophism: capitalism had entered permanent crisis, a pre-revolutionary situation lay around the corner. The major barrier to resolving the crisis of leadership lay not in the consciousness of the workers but in the venal manoeuvres of Labour Party and union leaders, Stalinist counter-revolutionaries, and other Trotskyist groups. The group's politics echoed third period Stalinism.[13] As early as 1969 the SLL was posing 'either the dictatorship of Wilson followed by fascism, or socialist revolution'.[14] By the early 1970s the approach of military dictatorship was an insistent theme.[15] These perspectives justified continual exhortation to 'build the party', hyperactivity, driven by the need to sell a daily paper, and a harsh internal regime based on the developing dictatorship of Gerry Healy.[16] By the early 1970s, membership requirements were diluted and activity focused on campaign politics, rather than sustained work in the labour movement. Up to 8,000 could be mobilized for rallies, less than a quarter of that number were active in the WRP.

Industrial politics centred on placing demands on leaders to expose them. These demands focused on the fight for a socialist programme and a general strike which would bring down the government and develop the irreconcilable antagonism between the reformist labour bureaucracy and the objective interest of the working-class in the destruction of capitalism.[17] By the late 1960s the SLL was moving away from its earlier conception of an independent rank and file movement, emphasizing the dangers of 'syndicalism', and stressing the need for the direct leadership of the League in industrial struggles.[18] The SLL initially viewed the CP's vehicle for gingering up the union leadership, the LCDTU, as a forum in which to intervene to build in this direction and was a force in establishing local committees in Leeds and Sheffield.[19] The Oxford Liaison Committee was dominated by the SLL and its conferences attracted national support.[20] But the impetus was sectarian: Vauxhall stewards walked out over the imposition of the League's positions and Healy moved to transform the committee into a national competitor to the LCDTU.[21] The All Trade Union Alliance (ATUA) was launched in February 1968, attracting around 2,000 to its conferences. Almost from its inception, it discarded any semblance of independence:

> The All Trade Union Alliance was formed in order to organize together all those trade unionists moving towards the political struggle of the Socialist Labour League. It is not, therefore, simply an alliance of all these who agree on one or more immediate policy questions in industry. This is what is meant by saying that the Alliance is the political arm of the League in the trade unions. In this sense the Alliance, like the Young Socialists for the politically developing youth, is a training ground and preparation for League membership.[22]

The officers of the ATUA were SLL members and it was firmly under the control of the League's leadership.[23] Its role as an annexe of the party was reflected in its declarations: 'A new world economic crisis is beginning to take root in all the major capitalist countries. As in 1931 the capitalists have only one solution to offer ... creating a world recession. This will bring millions of unemployed with the dangers of a third world war'.[24] The ATUA excluded other tendencies and the SLL polemicized against rank and file movements asserting the primacy of penetrating formal union organization rather than creating alternatives at the base, whilst setting about the creation in practice of its own private labour movement.[25] A contemporary critic observed:

> [The ATUA] seems to have few branches, its main activity seems to be the frequent conferences. These however very rarely get down to any discussion of building a movement. The last all industry conference consisted of a long speech by Gerry Healy ('Be Prepared to Give Leadership') followed by a series of soliloquies by various militants and also by the other two Triumvirs, Central Committee members Mike Banda and Cliff Slaughter.[26]

Success remained elusive after 1964 when the SLL contained only a handful of industrial militants.[27] The view that 'Healy built up serious forces throughout the Midlands (Britain's industrial heartland), with a party membership there of around 200 and these were mostly industrial workers' is exaggerated for the Midlands and even more so nationally.[28] The pattern in cities such as Birmingham or Coventry was of isolated militants in membership. There was a small base in the railway workshops in Swindon where Frank Willis and Ray Howells were shop stewards. The situation was similar in Lancashire, with a few temporary members in Vauxhall's Ellesmere Port plant and groups of building workers in Liverpool and Wigan. The remnants of the old Trotskyist base in the Birkenhead NASD, built in the 1950s, lingered on: SLL militant Peter Kerrigan (not to be confused with the CP's Industrial Organizer of the same name) was briefly a full-time officer in Liverpool in the late 1960s. But after Larry Cavanagh dropped out in the early 1970s, there was nothing left amongst the Merseyside dockers. In Yorkshire, miners joined and left but no serious base was built. In Scotland there was again a sprinkling of members in engineering and the car factories. The SLL/WRP availed itself of union elections. Jimmy Dormer was a regular candidate in the EETPU, as were Alan Wilkins and Jim Bevan (successfully) in the AUEW, where Healy pulled off a coup in the early 1970s by recruiting the experienced ex-CPer Laurie Smith, later elected as a national organizer of the union. That was largely it: recruitment of individuals and dependence for sustained work and influence in particular areas on a handful of experienced militants, such as Bill Hunter on Merseyside, who were respected, often in spite of their politics. The group was not in a position to lead struggles, it recruited in ones and twos – Gerry Caughey from the 1970 Pilkington dispute, Des Warren from the Shrewsbury Pickets – through sustained support for strikes. It rarely held new members for long.[29]

The industrial work was not organic to party activity. It was often conducted under the personal auspices of Healy who claimed credit for breakthroughs in ACTT and Equity. In 1968 a group around David Mercer, Tony Garnett, Ken Loach, for a time Stuart Hood, were recruited, largely through the influence of the playwright Jim Allen and were active in the ACTT. Another group, most famously Corin and Vanessa Redgrave, was active in Equity. Even here Healy's manipulative approach spelled disaster. The WRP controlled the ACTT Freelance branch and held three Executive positions. When the right-wing and CP put a motion to an emergency meeting to remove the branch committee, the WRP faction was instructed to rule it out of order, rather than fight it out. As a result of this personal decision by Healy, the WRP lost all its positions in the ACTT. In Equity the Gorst affair, in which a WRP sympathizer spoke to the press about her experiences, had negative repercussions.[30] By the mid-1970s there was minimal horizontal contact between WRP trade unionists and the party's union work was in disrepair:

> ... the National Committee of the ATUA has also ceased to function ... major policy decisions on TU work are taken without discussion on any of the TU committees of the party ... The non-functioning of party TU committees has meant that wrong policies have been pursued with no opportunity for the TU comrades to fight to challenge them ... there has been no organization for TU elections.[31]

The main exception was the work in the car industry in Oxford.

Trotskyism in a British car factory

Employment in the Oxford car factories of British Leyland fluctuated between 22,000 and 29,000 in the decade to 1975, with 95 per cent working in the Body and Assembly Plants in Cowley. Separated by a road, the two plants possessed very different union traditions. The Body Plant (the former Pressed Steel, taken over by BMC in 1965) was a strategic factory, producing bodies for all the car firms. The unions possessed the leverage they lacked in the labour-intensive Assembly Plant where wages were a more important factor in costs, and rises could not be easily passed on to customers. Unionization came early to Pressed Steel, after a militant strike in 1934, although a management offensive in 1938, centring on the victimization of the senior steward, Tom Harris, subsequently undermined the left. The Assembly Plant, in contrast, needed the Second World War to obtain shallow recognition, and 100 per cent membership was only gradually achieved in the decade after 1956.

266

McCarthy suggested militancy over the closed shop which developed after the 1956 strike against redundancies, may have generalized the 'protest strike' to other issues in the 1960s. Certainly by 1966, strikes in the plant were averaging 300 annually, although the majority were of brief duration. Wages in this period were often lower than in the body plant, although there were often strikes over conditions.

Although the CP lacked any strong presence, the Assembly Plant leadership adopted a militant approach from the early 1950s. This was typified, on the one hand, by Labour activist Frank Horsman, TGWU Convenor from 1953, and, on the other, his deputy, Bob Fryer, who came from a Hungarian Communist background. The unsuccessful strike over Horsman's victimization in 1959 consolidated the tradition of leadership militancy. It was based on the preponderance of the TGWU, a strong Joint Shop Stewards' Committee, independence from full-time officers, and support from the Combine Committee of which Assembly Plant steward and CP sympathizer Les Gurl was for long the secretary. The Body Plant, in contrast, sought to reap the rewards of conciliation and exploit that real if elusive factor: management's willingness to reward moderation. From the 1950s, the plant leadership was actively hostile to the left and close to the full-time officers. They refused to participate in the Combine Committee and resisted successive attempts at cooperation initiated by the Assembly Plant stewards.[32]

Two immediate events pushed a group of stewards who had left the CP further left: the 'Noose Trial', in which strike breakers were required by a mass meeting to contribute a day's pay to charity, prompting a virulent press campaign during the 1966 General Election, and the sacking of 1,300 workers that autumn. A further factor was the presence in Oxford of SLL students and the considerable attention Healy devoted to the group.[33] A factory branch of the League was formed in 1967:

> Those of us who were attracted to the Socialist Labour League in Cowley were attracted by what we saw as the relevance of its politics to the problems we faced in the unions. After a group of us joined, a branch was established covering the various car plants which grew to about 40 members. The majority were shop stewards and included convenors and deputy convenors from the TGWU, the AUEW and the ETU. We saw [the SLL] as a serious organization dedicated to the struggle for socialism and keenly interested in trade union issues ... that trade union officials represented class compromise and the interests of union establishments more than their own members was confirmed by our own experience.[34]

The key leaders initially were John Power, AUEW Convenor of the Service Division and the 'Mr X' of the Noose Trial; Reg Parsons, the TGWU Deputy Convenor in the Assembly Plant; and Alan Thornett, another ex-CPer who developed as the key SLL cadre and organizing force inside the factory. Fryer, the TGWU Convenor, never joined but remained an intimate collaborator of the League, as did the TGWU 5/55 Branch Secretary Tony

267

Bradley. By 1970 Power and Parsons were the main speakers at ATUA conferences and nine out of thirteen of the branch delegates to Oxford Trades Council were SLL members. From their base in the massive 5/55 branch, they sought unsuccessfully to secure closer relations with the right-wing leadership in the body plant; organized canteen and component workers; fought for strike action over *In Place of Strife* in 1969 and the Industrial Relations Bill in 1970; broke the colour bar in the plant; and took up issues of international solidarity.[35]

A management offensive began in 1968, centred on the replacement of piece-work with measured day work (MDW), a vehicle for weakening the stewards and reimposing managerial control over wages and productivity. The SLL's position was to defend piece-work in principle. A six-week strike in autumn 1970 was defeated after the intervention of the full-time officials and the new system was forced in. Events proved what many had argued: outright opposition to MDW was not a viable option. The stewards were forced to revise their position and sign a new agreement.[36] Defeat was not without its price: both Parsons and Power broke with the SLL over the uncompromising struggle over MDW and opposition based on the costs of militancy began to develop in sections of the plant.[37] Stereotypes of the Trotskyists as self-interested 'wreckers' mingled with material concerns over wages lost by lay-offs through the plant induced by sectional action. Moreover the Body Plant, which didn't lose a day over MDW, ended up with an earlier and similar agreement to the Assembly Plant. By 1973 Parsons had moved dramatically to the right: correspondence with Jack Jones led to links with local and regional full-time officials determined to combat the Trotskyists.[38]

Management's attempts to break the mutuality agreement, which required union consent before any changes in jobs or track speed were introduced, and the powerful resistance of Thornett, led BL to withdraw his recognition as Deputy Convenor and Chair of the Joint Shop Stewards' Committee in the spring of 1974. A strike by the transport section, where Thornett was steward, closed the plant and provoked a backlash and media witchhunt of the strikers. This was spearheaded by the Cowley Wives' Group – mostly wives of workers laid off. In the face of TGWU refusal to make the strike official and lack of support from the BL combine committee, the drivers reluctantly returned to work and accepted a compromise recommended by Thornett by which he kept his steward's card but the company refused to recognize him as a full-time convenor.[39] At regional level the TGWU moved against the factory leadership. An officer recalled two decades later how they organized to 'break the power of the Trots – we did everything we could to try and break the backs of these people'.[40] A regional inquiry split their power base, the 5/55 branch; Fryer was found to have brought the union into disrepute; and new convenor elections were called on the basis of secret ballot of all the members, rather than a vote by stewards. In the face of intense adverse publicity the left were defeated and Parsons elected as convenor.[41]

The WRP characteristically assessed these events as a victory. They were criticized by others on the left for inflexibility over MDW, reliance on sectional, minority action to stop production, and over-dependence on the union branch, which determined formal policy, to impose decisions on the workforce, rather than fighting for them amongst the inactive membership.[42] It is easy to criticize from the sidelines events in the sprawling jungle of this massive plant. The plant leadership achieved significant success in welding a diffuse membership together. But some of these criticisms were justified. For example, in August 1972, the branch took a decision to strike in solidarity with the occupation at the BL Thorneycroft plant at Basingstoke threatened with closure. The night shift was refused a separate vote and when they held a meeting and voted against a strike, the convenors simply ruled it out of order.[43] Obsession with 'leadership' and 'crisis' could easily produce overestimation of the consciousness of the membership and the belief that action – even if members had to be pushed into it – would radicalize them. By 1974 the Cowley leadership itself felt that 'Healy's political line was seriously damaging to us in Cowley and was undermining our credibility'.[44] Reaction to the WRP's ultra-left crisis-mongering in the face of support for the new Labour government, and the party's authoritarian regime led to the Cowley carworker members, bar one steward, Tom White, breaking from the WRP to establish the Workers' Socialist League which sought a return to the allegedly healthy SLL of the 1960s.[45]

The events of 1974 underlined the tremendous problems in establishing Trotskyist leadership in the workplace on a sustained footing. In a large car plant there would always be groups who would read the equation between the costs of militancy and militancy's benefits negatively. The determination of management to uproot Trotskyism was finally complemented by full-time officers whose own role was, in contrast with the body plant, circumscribed by steward leadership and they, too, moved to harness internal dissatisfaction. Despite representation on the District and Regional Committees, the plant leadership lacked the resources and numbers to make a sustained impact on the higher echelons of the TGWU. Without this, and given the enmity of the right-wing and the CP at regional level, they would always remain open to attack. Yet against all odds the left fought back. By December 1977, with a number of young WSL shop stewards grouped around Fryer and Thornett, they had won control of the new 5/293 branch and Fryer was re-installed as Convenor after defeating Parsons. The left had won two out of the seven deputy convenor positions.[46]

They had also survived almost three years of disciplinary inquiries by both District and Regional Committees and the victimization of Trotskyist stewards. They were charged by the TGWU with a variety of vexatious offences of which the most serious was 'disruption', for challenging minutes and 'breach of rule', for distributing branch bulletins on the factory gates when management refused to allow distribution inside the plant, and harassed through exclusion from stewards' meetings and denial of facilities. There was continuing Regional Committee supervision of the plant and close alliances between Reg Parsons' moderate faction within it and full-time officers. And on the key policy issues the Trotskyists were pushed back as determination of the BL agenda moved from plant to national level. The Cowley left were defeated over union involvement in participation bodies and the move to corporate bargaining. They maintained a minority position in the BL Combine Committee, embracing unpopular causes, such as the BL toolmakers in 1977, and opposing the welcome the Combine leaders initially gave to Michael Edwardes.[47]. The 5/293 branch continued to make an important contribution to the local labour movement: it was involved in organizing workers in the university and hospitals and gave significant support to recognition struggles in Blackwell's Bookshop and the Oxford hotels.[48] The breakdown of the Social Contract and the withdrawal of the BL unions from the company's employee participation process in 1979 proved a false dawn. By that time the WSL was in decline and the WRP had degenerated into a bizarre cult financed by Colonel Gaddafi and devoid of any working-class base.[49]

A study of the Cowley assembly plant demonstrates that despite eccentric politics, the SLL/WRP was able to achieve some success through sustained advocacy by able supporters of militant policies, perceived by sections of the workforce as some answer to harsh working conditions and aggressive management. It affirms the limited tolerance by union leaders of effective militants and the fragility of management acceptance of strong workplace organization – as well as the boundaries to Jack Jones's empowerment of stewards in the TGWU. The most recent war on stewards did not begin in the 1980s: as early as 1974 those at Cowley were under attack, and by 1978 it was reported that new investment in BL was dependent on the hope that '… militant moderate union officials can destroy the Trotskyite power base in the vital Cowley plant'.[50]

The International Socialists and revolutionary realism

IS in the 1960s provided a contrast with the orthodox Trotskyists in its rejection of dogmatism and its willingness to analyse changes in capitalism and class. Whatever its inadequacies, Tony Cliff's analysis of Russia as state capitalist identified socialism with workers' control. There was an insistence that revolutionaries should not substitute themselves for the working-class, a preference for Luxembourg over Lenin, and adoption of flexible, federal organization, with a libertarian ethos. Members contrasted themselves with the 'toytown Bolsheviks' of the SLL: there was a stress on the need to develop theory beyond the inheritance of Lenin and Trotsky and on modest initiatives, underpinned by the belief capitalism had temporarily stabilized through the growth of the 'permanent arms economy'. During the post-war boom, it was claimed, the labour movement had undergone decomposition. Workers no longer looked to the Labour Party for advance: 'the locus of reformism' had shifted to the point of production where fragmented steward organization employed 'do it yourself reformism'. The group's politics always emphasized the workplace, stewards and 'linking up the fragments'.[51]

As militancy developed from the mid-1960s there were small successes. In 1965 the group formed a workplace branch in the ENV engineering factory in Willesden, which had a long history of both Stalinist and Trotskyist activity, based on leading stewards recruited from the CP. The following year IS was involved in the Myton strike of building workers at the Barbican where a member, Frank Campbell, was a steward, and the bitter Roberts Arundel engineering dispute in Stockport.[52] Although the CP led both these strikes, the new situation prompted IS to launch the London Industrial Shop Stewards' Defence Committee (LISSDC), in January 1966, aimed at developing opposition to incomes policy. A brief marriage of convenience, involving Reg Birch, who was then championing China in the CP and Jim Hiles, later secretary of the LCDTU, the LISSDC briefly produced a paper, *Resistance*, and similar committees were launched in Newcastle and Liverpool. In the building industry IS members sold *Rank and File*, 'journal of the militant building worker', an initiative from shop stewards in Lancashire.[53] Sustaining these developments proved beyond the capacity of a small group, although they may have galvanized the CP which withdrew from the LISSDC and mustered its resources to establish the LCDTU as a national alternative in 1966.[54] In 1966 the ENV factory was threatened with closure. IS members were unable to convince the majority on the stewards' committee to take action and their leading stewards, Geoff Carlsson and Geoff Mitchell, were sacked. This led to some heart searching: the view that minority action was legitimate and essential to ignite wider militancy was suggested. It was argued that substitutionism was not the only danger, '... an unwillingness to lead even from a minority position is a definite weakness ... the ENV stewards were open to criticism: they should have done something'. The factory branch had not proved a solution and 'the group did not act in a very organized way on the stewards' committee'.[55]

The LISSDC gave IS the opportunity to expound its politics in a pamphlet on incomes policy which assessed the weaknesses of workplace union organization but saw state intervention welding the fragments into a broader movement. Stewards were 'the potential builders of the mightiest movement yet in the history of Britain', leading 'the most potentially revolutionary working-class in the history of Britain'. The political limitations of stewards were acknowledged but it was concluded that, 'wherever do-it-yourself reforms are won, the seeds of socialism are being sown'.[56] Commending the

271

text, Birch rebuked the authors for syndicalism: 'I do not accept that the extension of shop stewards' organizations, their increase in number will automatically lead to the development of a socialist movement'.[57] Already in 1967 internal opponents of the view that militancy solved all problems pushed their objections to the point of resignation. The group was condemned for,

> submerging itself in the fragments and failing to take the next step and attempt to politicize the fragmentary rank and file organizations that exist. The group has taken the opposite view: that the necessity is simply to foster rank and file militancy ... Reformism from below is only marginally better than reformism from above.[58]

Resistance was condemned as, 'not of a sufficiently deep theoretical level to appeal to industrial and political militants'. The LISSDC, deserted by the CP, was soon a 'front shell', while papers for dockers, busworkers and engineers, 'completely independent of the group', were shortlived.[59]

These problems were to recur: the development of the group was now overtaken by student radicalization and the French events of 1968. IS recruited heavily from the student milieu and the Vietnam Solidarity Campaign. The group grew to over 1,000 members but industrial workers remained a small minority. Work inside the Labour Party faded away, *Labour Worker* became *Socialist Worker* in 1968, and Cliff deduced from the failure of revolution in France the necessity for a democratic centralist party. The turn to Leninism was accompanied by a 'turn to the class': the leadership attempted to orientate new recruits towards the factories.[60] By 1970 membership was rising again. (See Table 9.1.) Ironically the first success came with the establishment of *Rank and File* in the NUT from 1967, a group consisting of IS members, ex-CPers and independent left teachers.[61] A small number of ex-students went into industry and an important initiative was the development of factory bulletins produced on a sustained basis which built up an increasing readership and a path into many workplaces. There was over-estimation of the situation: the decline of Labour and the CP was seen as creating 'a vacuum on the left'. The new emphasis on the party was located in IS tradition: it was seen more as an organizational coordinator of struggles rather than as an ideological action mechanism for their transformation.[62] However, Cliff's 1970 book on productivity deals was very important in placing IS in the vanguard of organizations seeking to deepen the militancy and creating connections with stewards.[63] One recalled:

> we were flogging it around the union branches and the factories and people snapped it up ... this was a book that outlined a real strategy, how to negotiate, how to withdraw the teeth of prod deals ... it provided practical advice, so that's how I initially became involved with IS.[64]

IS was doing what no one else, significantly the CP, was doing: providing analysis and information for stewards in the front line. But once again the accent was almost exclusively on the existing industrial struggle. Little more than a page at the end of the text announced abstractly: 'We need politics, we need socialist politics, we need a revolutionary socialist movement'.[65]

Towards a rank and file movement

As the new decade began, IS met the heady mood of the times and aspirations for a new political beginning. It was increasingly seen as a novel, exciting organization. Its newly minted politics, untainted by Stalinism or the excesses of orthodox Trotskyism, were for many commendably summed up by its refusal of allegiance to either Washington or Moscow or Wilson's Labour Party, its belief in socialism from below, and its stress on the creative potential of workers' own activity. Its ability to rework theory to meet the needs of the hour was witnessed by Richard Hyman's exploration of the writings of Lenin, Trotsky and Gramsci to suggest the possible pliability of union leaders in the face of militancy, and the potential of 'ordinary' trade union struggles to stimulate simultaneously socialist consciousness and capitalist crisis. Rather than rattle the bones of Trotsky, IS intellectuals critically examined the past, imaginatively analysed the contemporary world, and collaborated with worker members to provide ammunition to change it.[66]

In the turbulent atmosphere of 1971, sections of the leadership urged an ambitious expansion of industrial work and talked extravagantly of creating a revolutionary party as a 'current aim'. IS had fewer than 2,000 members.[67] The success of the 'turn to industry' was reflected in the establishment of industrial fractions covering the major unions and eight rank and file papers: 'these together with factory branches or groups and a national all trade union organization are the principal fighting units of a working-class party'.[68] Yet despite the accent on the factories, under 30 per cent of the membership were manual workers and 30 per cent students or lecturers. Amongst the 500 manual workers in the group there were only 13 convenors and 81 shop stewards. The situations where members could be numbered in more than ones or twos, such as Chrysler Coventry with 10 members and 4 stewards, were rare. A sense of proportion would have suggested caution. But at both the 1971 and 1972 conferences there were resolutions, albeit defeated, for the creation of factory branches. And in 1972 the group adopted the perspective of creating a rank and file movement.[69]

IS politics remained bound up with the industrial struggle. As against the SLL's overestimation of the need for leadership, IS tended to follow events, to argue for 'more militancy for more pay', for more support for existing strikes, for immediate demands, with slogans such as 'Defend the Unions', 'Victory to the Miners'. A maximum position – the need to abolish capitalism – was put forward with few links between the present and the future.

273

The group eschewed demands on the Labour Party on the grounds that the struggle was taking advanced workers past the Labour leaders, and rejected calls for a general strike as posing prematurely the question of power: it was only raised fleetingly, after the Pentonville Five were imprisoned. Rejection of the orthodox Trotskyist emphasis on timeless transitional demands rooted IS in the problems of the here and now. The weakness lay in the absence of any political bridge between militant trade unionism today and socialism tomorrow. Revolutionary realism became economism. More militancy of the same kind became the answer to everything, to economic problems, to sexism, to racism, to national divisions. As workers became concerned about the inability of militancy to solve the problems of inflation, IS still rejected transitional politics: '... the best advice we have to give now, apart from "put in a big claim and fight for it" is "establish the right to put in another claim whenever the workers decide". This is the only method of defending workers' wage packets against the effects of inflation'. The political and practical benefits of militancy were overestimated, the real problems that it caused for many workers underplayed. Revolutionaries were urged to adapt to the existing consciousness of militants: 'care has to be taken to involve broad support even if it means keeping relatively quiet about our distinctive ideas'.[70]

The development of a rank and file movement was seen as initially dependent on intervention in the LCDTU. Here IS called for more precise, ambitious demands for strike action and permanent democratic organization. Little impact was made in LCDTU conferences in 1970–1, 'because we lacked delegates representing organizations of substance'.[71] By the June 1972 LCDTU conference IS had 150 delegates (out of more than 1,000) but were able to muster the support of a further 150. This was impressive, particularly in view of CP hostility. It demonstrated IS had the energy and capacity to mobilize an increasingly significant membership and periphery. It was backed by shrewd assessment of the balance of forces:

> We do not yet possess the strength to act independently of the Liaison Committee ... we should continue to work within it whilst demanding it adopts a real programme of struggle, democratizes itself, builds local committees and acts as a genuine rank and file movement by organizing Liaison fractions in every union.[72]

This represented healthy realism. In the big disputes of 1972 only a handful of IS members were involved. There was one member in the docks. In the engineering struggle in Manchester, IS had one AUEW steward and an ETU convenor; the AUEW steward broke ranks and supported the CP in a crucial meeting. In disputes such as Fine Tubes and Fisher Bendix where IS had one or two members, it was difficult to go beyond servicing the struggle.[73] But there was progress: by the end of the 1972 building strike there were forty IS members in the industry.[74] Progress fuelled impatience: in August 1972 it was decided to establish factory groups with members being reassured this was not an attempt to introduce factory branches by the back door.[75]

But this was the next step, with a debate conducted under the shadow of workerism orchestrated by Cliff and his supporters.[76] It was argued there was a need to concentrate membership at the point of production for efficient intervention and enhanced recruitment. Workplace branches were essential to a combat organization; they facilitated more effective links between the leadership and key members; and workers preferred them to the discussion circles of middle-class branches.[77] Opponents counter-claimed that the small numbers of workers in IS, their lack of concentration and their level of development rendered these arguments abstract and premature. Workplace branches would segregate union activists, intensify social divisions and strengthen economism. The cadre, as Lenin affirmed, was not simply a union leader but a 'tribune of the people', fighting exploitation in the workplace and oppression in the community.[78] A serious debate leavened by Cliff's demagogy – 'Most of the opponents of factory branches didn't have a clue about industry and have a patronizing attitude to workers' – produced a majority for factory branches at the 1973 conference.[79] This 'indispensable first step towards building a revolutionary party' was taken in 1973 with a national membership of 2,667. However, an encouraging factor was the continued growth of a network of rank and file papers spanning a range of industries and unions, although they were highly dependent on the efforts of IS members.[80] (See Table 9.2.)

There was continuing growth to March 1974, but the industrial membership remained stubbornly at around a third of the organization. However, 56 factory or industrial branches had been formed, organizing ten per cent of the membership, with 16 in the car industry, including six in BL, three in Chrysler and three in Ford. They sold IS literature and produced factory bulletins with the aim of becoming 'the true leaders of the left in the factory and then the true leaders of the factory'. The evidence suggested the new branches were not firmly rooted: within the year 18 out of 56 had gone out of existence. A study of the strongest branch judged its activities to be at the level of militant trade unionism with only a third of its members active. The Industrial Organizer's view that the branches had 'stood the test of time' was, on the reported facts, over-optimistic.[81]

Branch A reports: The Branch was formed with about eleven members. This rose to fourteen members. Three or four dropped out after one and a half months ... The branch now has seven members. The majority left because they thought IS was something else. There was no real discussion or education. The branch was set up (in the opinion of the members left) too quickly. 'We know very little about Marxism and even less about revolutionary politics ... it would have been better if we had joined the local branch first' ... The secretary of Branch B set up in February this year describes the development of the Branch starkly, 'three then, six now, lost three. Two were not political'. In Factory Branch D there were bigger problems: 'At best we have ten members lost five members. Two of them senior stewards' ... Factory Branch J writes: 'We have five members now and had eight at one time. The main reason for losing three was that they were not interested in trade union work ... Factory Branch M writes: 'We had nine members. However some dropped out of IS ... too much commitment needed ... Present membership stands at four with little chance of recruiting more'.[82]

IS lacked the experienced cadre to present a rounded view of the complex changes occurring across industry, let alone carry through a project of this ambition. A smaller number of workplace branches or factory cells linked to broader branches, preserving the advantages of interpenetration and cross fertilization with other groups of workers, intellectuals, women, might have produced more firmly founded progress. Yet despite the retrospective view of Jim Higgins, then National Secretary but shortly to become an opponent of the leadership, that 'the job was rushed and half the time botched', the lessons were not learned.[83] Instead of retrenchment, the aim of doubling the branches over the next year was adopted.[84]

It was not simply that IS did not have enough worker members: those they did have were dispersed and were far from cadres. On the brighter side the group had established a presence in key trade unions. (See Table 9.3.) There were, by early 1974, 16 fractions compared with 10 a year earlier, and they covered all the major unions and industries, embracing almost 2,000 members. There were 275 engineering workers, 180 carworkers, 70 miners and 7 dockers. IS was recruiting in what it regarded as the key, powerful sections of the proletariat. Driven by a tremendous level of membership activism, it was beginning to recruit out of important struggles: two stewards in Con-Mech, where fines on the AUEW under the Industrial Relations Act led to a strike by the union, joined.[85] It was breaking out of the ghetto on a front no Trotskyist group had reached hitherto. But what was true of the AUEW was even more true of the other unions such as the TGWU, the EETPU, the NUM, UCATT and TASS: '... we have a number of comrades with considerable experience at the local level especially in terms of shop floor work. We have a sprinkling on District Committees. We have no one with any national experience. No National Organizers, no NC or EC members'.[86]

In the white collar unions – where the CP was weaker and in some cases, such as the NUT, increasingly conservative, and the existing left more fragile – growth was even more impressive. There were 330 teachers in IS and two members on the executive of each of the NUT, EIS and NUJ.[87] A little later it was observed that as white collar militancy developed:

our influence was unquestionably stronger at that time in the white collar unions than it ever was in manual unions where we had some strength. We played a role in these unions not unlike the role of the 'broad lefts' in manual unions where the right-wing dominated. We became the natural focus for wide layers who were in opposition and wanted the unions to act more effectively.[88]

276

By 1974 *Rank and File* in the NUT, the NALGO Action Group, and *Redder Tape* in the CPSA were the main left opposition to the union leaderships. Rank and filism was making significant inroads in conservative, public sector, white collar unions with centralized structures and centralized collective bargaining amenable to incomes policy controls.[89]

Whilst IS saw its growing impact confirmed by the expulsion of its members from the national executives of ASTMS and the Dyers and Bleachers' Union, all of this represented a small beginning not a consolidated achievement. It was driven politically by a changing appreciation of the period: as the 1970s developed, rejection of catastrophism, impending general capitalist crisis and mass worker radicalization, was replaced, as IS veteran John Palmer recollected, by 'an almost millennial expectation of breakthrough from Cliff and the IS majority'.[90] The group now saw a 'deepening of the crisis facing British capitalism ... we are facing years of relative instability. The crisis the system has entered is serious and most probably irreversible ... We are at the beginning of a period of revolutionary possibilities'.[91] Its former caution and modesty dissipated, IS saw itself as the core of the revolutionary party. Conformity was strengthened by the expulsion of oppositions in 1971 and 1973 and delusions of grandeur were stimulated by small but relatively significant growth.

IS's analysis of reformism was at times superficial. It focused upon the decline of Labour Party membership, activism and electoral results, and an over optimistic estimation of trade unionists' propensity to turn left. This was at the expense of an appreciation of workers' resilient attachment to reformism, with its intrinsic antipathy to revolutionary policies, even when reforms were limited. Within these shallow organizational conceptions of reformism, the election of a Labour government in February 1974 promised further progress: 'The residual illusions which many workers still have in Labour and in the possibilities of reform will be put to the test'.[92]

The decision to proceed with building a national rank and file movement in late 1973 produced differences in the leadership. The hitherto unanimous view had been that progress on recruitment, creating fractions and developing the rank and file papers, was such as to make this the logical next step. Moreover, although IS had become the recognized opposition at LCDTU conferences, it was unable to overcome the CP's manipulative control of the organization and its political domination of the gatherings themselves. Now, however, Cliff and his supporters began to perceive a conflict between devoting resources to direct recruitment and putting effort into what would be a longer-term project with more indirect impact on growth.[93] None the less the 'most important venture we have ever undertaken' went ahead with a conference in March 1974 sponsored by several of the rank and file papers.[94] There were 500 delegates from 270 union bodies, 51 from the AUEW, 37 from the TGWU, 7 from UCATT and 6 from the NUM – the remainder came from white collar unions. Two thirds of the delegates were manual workers and 36 stewards' committees applied for credentials. The conference adopted a programme of opposition to incomes policy and anti-union legislation. It pledged itself to organize rank and file groups in each union and build a movement to 'organize against the union leaders' failure to defend workers' rights and living standards'.[95] It elected an organizing committee which convened a second conference in November 1974, attracting 468 delegates from 313 union bodies, with the number of stewards' committees represented increasing to 49.[96]

The creation of a National Rank and File Movement (NRFM) had always been an IS aspiration. The argument proceeded from principle and history. For example, there was little consideration as to whether the decentralized structures of British trade unionism in this period circumscribed both the need for a rank and file movement and the possibilities for building it. Assertions of its necessity were, however, hedged round by warnings against substitutionism and the danger of declaring 'meaningless paper organizations', by acknowledgment that revolutionaries, themselves, lacked the base to create such a movement. IS, moreover, theoretically conceived the NRFM as a bridge between party and class, not an appendage of the party. It should constitute an alliance of revolutionaries and militant reformists in which revolutionaries would seek to win over reformists.[97] The factors now seen as justifying its launch were, according to the Industrial Organizer Andreas Nagliatti, the growth of IS, the continuing militancy, and the limitations of the LCDTU.[98] But the initiative in 1973–4 was put forward cautiously: 'only modest steps are possible which can begin to lead in the right direction'. The new enterprise was 'a statement' by IS of the need for such organization and 'the conductor of the main industrial initiatives of IS'.[99] None the less the NRFM was now in existence and questions were soon being asked of its viability, orientation and independence.

The CP criticized its basis in a crude conception of union bureaucracy and IS control of the new organization.[100] Other Trotskyist groups criticized its failure to seek alliances with left officials.[101] The organizing committee consisted entirely of IS members, despite reiteration of the maxim that the NRFM should include not only revolutionaries but 'all those sections of the class who are prepared to fight'.[102] Inside IS, some saw the fact that only seven out of thirteen on the committee were manual workers as a sign of weakness. Opponents of the Cliff leadership argued:

> The requirement for independence was not understood or was ignored. The organizing committee was staffed by IS members whose qualifications were more their IS cards than their ability to lead in the workplace. The clear need to bring in non-IS militants was seen as subversive of IS control.[103]

IS dominance took on an element of workerist substitutionism when group members voted down attempts to commit the NFRM to nationalization of industry under workers' control, on the grounds that it was too political. Internal critics opined: 'IS in its efforts to look like a collection of trade unionists wanting unity in struggle took up a position to the right of many trade union rule books'.[104] Instead of struggling to bring militants to revolutionary politics, IS was fighting to keep the movement's programme at the level of economistic reformism. The real problem, however, was the absence of a strong independent group of workers willing to combine with it in struggle. This reflected the weaknesses of the militancy in general and the limited weight of IS in the working-class. The contemporary view of Hinton and Hyman that conditions were more favourable for the NRFM than they had been for the young Minority Movement was arguable. The judgement that 'the vast amount of delegates represented little or nothing in terms of leadership of the working-class' may have been a trifle harsh on an infant organization: in broad sweep it was correct.[105] The times were inauspicious. The NRFM was established in the year militancy began to decline. IS now had to work against the grain as union leaders won the ideological debate over the Social Contract.

Yet its leadership was seeking short cuts when the necessary mentality was that of the long haul, the marathon not the sprint. Vic Collard, one of the engineering stewards won to IS in 1970 later reflected:

> Around 1973 things began to go off the rails. I got the distinct impression that the leadership became impatient. I remember thinking: what Cliff and co don't seem to understand is that the reason we're doing so well is because of the very long, hard, patient work we're doing. All of a sudden things had to move fast.[106]

Destructuring Lenin's work into a series of quotes to justify every new turn, Cliff reacted to the more difficult situation under a Labour government by proposing new approaches. He argued that more workers should be drafted into the leadership, that *Socialist Worker* should become a more basic paper written by workers, and that the group should orientate itself away from experienced militants, as stewards became incorporated, towards young workers unsullied by reformism. Attempts to replace experienced leaders with his supporters produced the IS Opposition, the strongest faction yet, consisting of a layer of IS's most experienced cadres who defended the earlier traditions. None the less populism and the internal restructuring of the organization in a more authoritarian mould proceeded. By the end of 1975 debilitating tendencies were affirmed by the expulsion of the opposition and other opponents of the leadership.[107]

The decline of the SWP

In retrospect 1974–5 marked a watershed. As the industrial struggle subsided with the economic downturn and the initial success of the Social Contract, the weaknesses of workerism and economism became more apparent and continued to alienate many women, black workers and those with a broader conception of politics.[108] In the manual unions progress was reversed. Their insubstantial foundations exposed, and hastened by victimizations such as those of John Worth in Chrysler and Jock Wight in BL, the factory branches collapsed. In the white collar unions, IS began to lose influence to broader formations involving the CP, IMG and *Militant*. The IS leadership remained optimistic and sought to keep the NRFM alive whilst acknowledging its weakness.[109] Retrospectively it was admitted:

> Almost as soon as the second Rank and File conference wound up its business towards the end of 1974, the Rank and File Organizing Committee it elected was isolated and left on the shelf, inevitably so as the level of industrial struggle dropped from year to year (thirteen million strike days in 1974, eight million in 1975, three million in 1976).[110]

The industrial struggle has always waxed and waned. If the NFRM had real roots, a decline in militancy would still have suggested its maintenance for retrenchment and reflection. There had been no decisive defeat. Its shelving underlined the brittleness of IS's working-class base.

The consequences of the Social Contract and the decline in militancy were serious for IS. The average weekly paid sale of *Socialist Worker* peaked at 20,500 in 1974 and dropped to around 13,000 in 1976. With the collapse of the factory branches and the fragility of its base in the workplace exposed, 'leading IS members in the AUEW, building workers, CPSA, EETPU and NALGO left the organization'.[111] The new line, 'steering left', as advanced workers were seen as moving to the right, was based on recruiting inexperienced youth, on replacing work in broader organizations such as the Broad Left in the AUEW and EETPU with work in IS-dominated groups, the creation of IS fronts such as the Right to Work Campaign and the Anti-Nazi League, and 'building the party'. The declaration of the transformation of IS into the SWP from January 1977, produced another 'turn to industry'. But by the following year the emphasis was on the degeneration of shop steward organization and the leadership was beginning to claim a period of defeat had begun in 1974.[112]

The situation in the AUEW typified problems. The group's strength in 1975 had been overestimated with a tendency 'to confuse the 250 AUEW members in IS on paper with the 25 to 30 in any way active in the fraction'.[113] Those who were active, particularly the group of experienced shop stewards recruited in the early 1970s in the Birmingham area, remained opposed to breaking with the CP-dominated Broad Left (BL). In 1974–5, they committed the fraction to working within it, only to be overturned by the leadership who argued the BL had lost its ability to mobilize. In Birmingham, where IS had its strongest base, the members were already committed to supporting a BL candidate, Phil Higgs of the CP, for the post of AUEW National Organizer; they refused to accept the new line and were expelled. This exemplified the way in which the progress of the early 1970s was shattered not simply because of the new situation but because of the IS leadership's impatient, sectarian response to it.[114] A new rank and file organization, Engineers' Charter, was launched around the candidature of Chrysler Linwood steward Willie Lee for AUEW National Organizer in 1975 which yielded 10,000 votes. Events proved the SWP was unable to mobilize in superior fashion to the BL. Subsequently, leading SWP engineers reflected in 1978:

> convinced that we could do even better a further six elections were fought over the next eighteen months, hardly stopping for breath – although the vote did increase in some cases, it was not accompanied by a parallel growth of our base in the localities. In fact we had started to go along the same road as the Broad Left while hardly noticing it ourselves ... The Charter itself, although it attempted to raise the shop floor issues, was unable to because of the lack of base and therefore suffered from some of the worst faults of a rank and file paper. Non-IS people were not drawn into writing for it and only a handful of our own people contributed. Almost without exception Charter was not built in the districts.[115]

By 1978 the verdict on the AUEW experience was: 'our decision was right but we failed miserably to put it into practice ... we have wasted two years'.[116] The alleged wisdom of the decision was based on the decline of the Broad Left but of course this might have been limited or have held advantages, had the IS/SWP worked within it.

In 1977 there were only 30 SWP members in the TGWU scattered through seven regions and six trade groups, and despite a sizeable vote for Tommy Riley in the election for General Secretary – he received 27,500 votes compared with 349,000 for Moss Evans and 75,000 for third-placed candidate Alex Kitson – no advances were made.[117] In the EETPU there was a breach with the Broad Left around *Flashlight* in favour of a new group around *Rank and File Contact* which supported SWP candidates.[118] In the Building Workers' fraction, sectarian impatience again took its toll. Until 1974 leading members felt:

> We were building slowly and surely but confidently. Then a political clanger was dropped. At the 1976 IS conference, without any prior consultation with the Building Workers Fraction, the group was accused and held up as a supreme example of comrades who were accommodating to the CP by refusing to break away from the CP – dominated London Joint Sites Committee. In the argument that followed some leading comrades felt so strongly about the unjustified criticism that they left IS. Their loss was a serious political and especially organizational blow to our attempts to build an SWP faction.[119]

In other manual unions it was observed: 'we have only handfuls (in some cases individuals) in these unions scattered all over the country'.[120] The situation was also grim in the white collar sector. A review by Industrial Organizer Steve Jefferys in 1977 concluded:

> ... our impact at union conferences has declined in 1975/6 ... The rank and file groups have either stagnated in terms of membership or actually declined ... The circulation of rank and file papers has fallen; we have produced them less regularly ... opposition groupings to the right of us have been organized in almost every union ... we have lost quite a large number of members who were very active when we were playing pressure group politics within the union but who couldn't stomach the increasing isolation as we have attempted to continue to steer left.[121]

In NALGO, 'fraction organization has collapsed', whilst in the CPSA, *Redder Tape*'s meteoric rise was threatened by the CP-*Militant* Broad Left. In the schools the STA was outflanking *Rank and File* and work in the hospitals was also in decline. In white collar unions the rank and file challenge was to some extent absorbed as their leaders renovated centralized structures and developed systems of workplace representation.[122]

Confused debates as to the independence of the rank and file groups from the IS/SWP were resolved by their reduction to vassalage: 'steering left would place more emphasis on party building. Rank and file groups were to become periphery organizations of the IS/SWP'.[123] Despite these setbacks, the upturn in militancy in 1977 saw the SWP attempt to relaunch the NRFM, shelved since 1975 in favour of the Right to Work Campaign, as a party front.[124] The shrewder observed that 'to relaunch the NRFOC before we have recreated effective rank and file movements is to put the horse before the cart'.[125] Accompanied by unsuccessful overtures to the CP, the November 1977 National Rank and File Conference drew 522 delegates from 251 union bodies and issued a call for a day of action over the national fire-fighters' strike. The resulting fiasco, with no workers striking, was retrospectively characterized by SWP leaders as 'a humiliation' and 'ultra-left substitutionism'.[126]

The government held the line on incomes policy, the predicted New Year offensive of 1978 failed to appear and the NRFM once again dropped out of the picture. Through the temporary, single issue, Right to Work Campaign and the Anti-Nazi League, which played a significant role in anti-racist work, the SWP was able to maintain a national presence of sorts and recruit among youth. This was no substitute for sustained work to secure a base in the unions. The SWP reached the end of the decade bigger than ever; but in terms of trade union work, it was weaker than it had been since the 1960s. An autopsy of the NRFM by the SWP Central Committee in early 1978 lamented:

... despite the increase in membership we have not gained a proportionate increase in striking power. We are very weak in the workplaces. The November Rank and File Conference was not a significant advance on its predecessors held when we were smaller. We are not stronger and may well be weaker at shop steward and lower echelon trade union machine level. Our gains have come through what has been called (not altogether correctly) street politics i.e. RTW [Right to Work Campaign], anti-fascism [Anti-Nazi League] and so on ... Our lack of industrial muscle was starkly illustrated by the dilemma of the R & F conference: what concretely can we call for to support the firemen? What can we actually deliver? The answer turned out to be in terms of industrial action, as opposed to lower level solidarity work, effectively zero.[127]

As the 1970s ended only half of the SWP's members sold *Socialist Worker* and around a quarter didn't even read it. The number of rank and file papers had dwindled, print orders were declining, membership was stagnating. Only four central committee members had any significant union experience.[128] The SWP was resolved on a party rather than a class approach to union work, and moving towards the conclusion that the working-class had suffered defeat coincidental with the downturn in the fortunes of IS. The retrospective verdict of one who played a key role through the 1970s was damning: 'Just at the very moment that the British working-class was heading towards a major confrontation with the Tories ... Cliff announced that the battle had already been lost in 1974 because the shop stewards had become incorporated into the trade union bureaucracy'.[129] From promising beginnings in the 1960s the SWP was on the way to becoming just another sect.

The prophet betrayed?

In many workplaces and unions, the presence of Trotskyists, their exemplary action as trade unionists, the regular bulletins they produced, ensured socialist arguments were heard, democratic tendencies in trade unionism were strengthened, militancy was sustained. In several unions such as the Post Office Engineering Union and in car factories in Oxford, the Midlands and Scotland, activists acted to constrain accommodation. In the docks and engineering a small layer of militants began to look past the CP towards left alternatives. In unions such as the CPSA, NALGO and the NUT, the presence of Trotskyists influenced the changing patterns of union culture. Their presence made a difference. Some would argue that the activities of the IS/SWP, in particular, stiffened resistance to the Social Contract and spurred on support for militancy in the CP.[130]

Former CP activists disagree: they claim the Trotskyists exercised real if minority influence only in the white collar unions. Others concede that by the mid-1970s, IS was making inroads in engineering and printing.[131] Certainly in terms of gaining key positions, leading significant disputes or achieving appreciable impact on policy, the Trotskyists never achieved substantial advance in the key unions of the period – the TGWU, AUEW, NUM, or, in a different way, the EETPU or TASS. Progress in the white collar unions was curbed by their leaderships' ability to respond structurally and politically. The workplaces in which the Trotskyists led were few. They never overtook the CP in terms of political influence or membership. And that – making and recruiting revolutionary socialists – was in the end what it was all about. By 1976, despite hyper-activism and high ratios of full-time organizers to members, Trotskyist influence was ebbing, and much of what they had begun to establish was swept away in the 1980s.

Already by 1975 the favourable conditions which facilitated advance were beginning to dissolve. A Labour government; the developing sense of a harder world economic climate; growing unemployment and consequent insecurity on the shop floor; loyalty to left leaders; the absence of a compelling political alternative to the Social Contract; and changes in employer strategies underlining the brittleness of union power in the workplace; these factors combined to produce a new situation. Militant stewards accepted the changing politics of Jones and Scanlon. The far-left groups were pushed further into the fringes of union power politics. What was in play was not simply objective circumstances but also political reactions to them. If our account affirms the limits of the revolutionary potential of the twentieth-century working-class in Britain and the rooted nature of its acceptance of capitalism, it nevertheless suggests something more substantial and enduring could have been constructed in these years. If, and it is a very big if, a more patient, propagandistic, inclusive approach to constructing socialist networks had been deployed, organizations more organic to the tempo and ethos of British trade unionism might have been constructed. Many thousands became members of the groups to the left of the CP and many more were influenced by their politics. Yet it was a case of promise unfulfilled. Too often the Trotskyists magnified the potential of militancy and the consciousness of trade unionists, minimizing the constraints of trade unionism, the supple power of reformism, the tempo of change. By the 1980s the WRP represented the 'lunatic left'. The SWP was immured in the dogmatic tradition it had threatened to transcend: it possessed little weight in the unions and was isolated from the developing Labour left. Unlike the CP, the Trotskyists had demonstrated a lack of staying power, the ability to sustain militants and maintain influence over the long haul, the ups and the downs.

The years the forerunners of IS and the WRP spent quarantined from the labour movement stored up problems for the future. Personalities were important in small group contexts. The deficiencies of orthodox Trotskyism refracted through Healy's personality produced a religious cult once the ice broke. In the years after 1968 the fragility of IS's politics – the underestimation of labourism, the complexities of class consciousness and structural changes within the working-class; the customized economism which privileged the exploitation of manual workers at the expense of the oppression of other social groups and the workplace at the expense of the labour movement –were exposed by events. Filtered through Cliff's impatience and his conception of Leninism as a recipe book, they produced sectarianism. To read Cliff on industrial politics is to register inspirational impressionism: he never understood the labour movement.[132] The resulting *ersatz* Leninism was not malignant like Healy's, but just as politically disabling. Dogmatism won out over creative politics and real influence in the trade unions.

Table 9.1 IS/SWP membership, 1964–80

Year	Membership
1964	200
1966	200
1967	447
1968	1,000
1969	N/Λ
1970	880
1971	1,830
1972	2,351
1973	2,667
1974	3,310
1976	2,500
1977	4,000
1978	4,200
1980	4,100

Sources: I. Birchall, *Building the Smallest Mass Party in the World: Socialist Workers' Party, 1951–79* (1981); IS, *Internal Bulletin*, June, December 1971; April 1973; Pre-conference Issue 1974; No. 3, May 1978, No. 6, 1978; No. 3, August 1979.

Table 9.2 Rank and file papers at March 1973

Paper	Issues	Latest print order
Car Worker	9	6,000
Collier	6	5,000
Hospital Worker	7	6,000
Platform	3	3,000
Textile Worker	1	1,500
Case Con	4	5,000
Journalists' Charter	4	2,000
NALGO Action News	8	6,000
Rank and File Teacher	13	10,000
Redder Tape	4	3,000
Scots Rank and File	3	2,000
Tech Teacher	4	2,500
Dock Worker	12	5,000
GEC Rank and File	5	8,000
Building Worker	6	2,000
Electricians' Special	3	2,000

Source: IS, *Internal Bulletin*, 'Pre-conference Issue', n.d., [1974]

Table 9.3 IS trade union fractions and membership, 1973–4

	Membership March 1973	Membership Dec. 1973	Membership June 1974
Manual fractions:			
AUEW (Engineering)	200	235	275
Buses	25	35	37
Building		70	70
Docks	3	6	7
EETPU	40	60	90
Motors	150	180	
NUM	50	67	70
Steel		20	
UPW		30	
Manual and white collar fractions:			
Health	30	100	130
White collar fractions:			
APEX			30
ASTMS		150	150
ATTI		150	150
AUEW (TASS)	30	50	70
Civil Servants	40	46	56
NUT		260	230
NUJ		37	48
NALGO	120		160

Total members in fractions, June 1974: 1,908

Source: IS, *Internal Bulletin*, 'Pre-conference Issue', n.d. [1974].
Note: There is some overlap between the AUEW and Motors fractions.

Notes

Thanks to my co-editors, to Dave Lyddon and Steve Jefferys for comments on this chapter and to all mentioned in the notes who provided information. The papers of the SLL/WRP are stored in Newcastle but not open to inspection. There are a few conference documents and reports from the early 1960s in the Purdie Papers, MSS 149, Modern Records Centre (MRC), University of Warwick. Collections there relevant to the IS/SWP in this period include the papers of C. Barker (MSS 152) R.Hyman (MSS 84), S. Jefferys (MSS 244) and R. Kuper (MSS 250). For the IMG, see the Purdie Papers, and also MSS 95 and MSS 128. Unless specifically noted internal material cited here is in the author's possession. Printed materials relevant to this subject are cited in the following notes.

1. There is only cursory reference to this subject in the literature. There is brief reference in R. Hyman, 'Trade unions, the left and the Communist Party in Britain', *Journal of Communist Studies*, 6, 4, 1990, pp. 148–9, 155; and R. Taylor, *The Trade Union Question in British Politics: government and unions since 1945* (Oxford, 1993), p. 173. The first two volumes of J. Goldthorpe *et al.*, *The Affluent Worker* were published in 1968. For a critical comment on this analysis based on an earlier article by Goldthorpe, see R. Blackburn, 'The unequal society', in R. Blackburn and A. Cockburn (eds), *The Incompatibles: trade union militancy and the consensus* (1967). For the history of Trotskyism in Britain, see S. Bornstein and A. Richardson, *Against the Stream: a history of the Trotskyist movement in Britain, 1924–38* (1986); S. Bornstein and A. Richardson, *War and the International: a history of the Trotskyist movement in Britain, 1937–49* (1986). For the general background to the developments discussed here see J. Callaghan, *British Trotskyism: theory and practice* (Oxford, 1984). J. Callaghan, *The Far Left in British Politics* (Oxford, 1987), largely rehashes the same material. Both texts draw on limited sources and are far from reliable on detail.

2. For an example of a detailed statement of this kind of approach, see T. Cliff, *The Crisis: social contract or socialism* (1974). 'Fraction' usually denoted the group's members in a particular union, as distinct from 'faction', a grouping of revolutionaries and reformists. The term 'faction' could also be used to describe a specific political alliance of members within the group itself.

3. See, for example, F. Dobbs, *Teamster Rebellion* (New York, 1972), often used as a handbook by revolutionary trade unionists in the 1970s. On tactical retreats, see also J. Kelly, *Trade Unions and Socialist Politics* (1988), pp. 181–2; A. Thornett, *Inside Cowley. Trade union struggle in the 1970s: who really opened the door to the Tory onslaught?* (1998), pp. 48–9.

4. For critiques of the constraints on collective bargaining conventionally accepted by union officers, see V. Allen, *Militant Trade Unionism* (1966); J. Kelly, 'Union militancy and social partnership', in P. Ackers *et al.* (eds), *The*

New Workplace and Trade Unionism (1996).

5. B. Pearce, 'Some past rank and file movements', *Labour Review*, April–May 1959, reprinted in M. Woodhouse and B. Pearce, *Essays on the History of Communism in Britain* (1975); J. Higgins, 'The Minority Movement', *International Socialism*, November–December 1970; M. Banda, *Marxism or Rank and File-ism* (1972); A. Nagliatti, 'Towards a rank and file movement', *International Socialism*, February 1974; S. Jefferys, 'The challenge of the rank and file', *International Socialism*, March 1975.

6. Trotskyist critiques of the CP in this period include 'Editorial: the Communist Party', *International Socialism*, Winter 1967–8; R. Black, *Stalinism in Britain* (1970); D. Hallas, 'The CP, the SWP and the Rank and File Movement', *International Socialism*, February 1977.

7. Anonymous, 'The disunity of theory and practice: the Trotskyist movement in Great Britain since 1945', n.d., [1964], reprinted in *Revolutionary History*, 6, 2/3, 1996, p.227; I. Birchall, *Building the Smallest Mass Party in the World: Socialist Workers' Party 1951–1979* (1981), pp. 1–4; J. McIlroy, 'Adrift in the rapids of racism: Syd Bidwell, 1917–97', *Revolutionary History*, 7, 1, 1998; P. Taafe, *The Rise of Militant* (1995), p. 18; P. Peterson, 'Aspects of the history of the International Marxist Group', Pre-Conference Discussion, *Internal Bulletin*, 3, 1972, p. 12.

8. B. Hunter, 'The dockers and trade union democracy', *Labour Review*, 3, 1, January – February 1958; B. Pennington, 'Docks: breakaway and unofficial movements', *International Socialism*, 2, Autumn 1960; J. Phillips, 'Interunion conflict in the docks 1954–55', *Historical Studies in Industrial Relations*, 1, March, 1996.

9. A. Thornett to author 6 October 1997; National Museum of Labour History, CP Archive, CP/Cent/PC/13/05, Draft Report to EC, 1974, 'Ultra-leftism in Britain', p. 3; A. Callinicos, 'The rank and file movement today', *International Socialism*, 17, Autumn 1982, p. 21; P. Taafe, *The Rise of Militant*, p. 111, 166; IMG, *Pre-conference Bulletin*, 1, 1978, p. 1; *Socialist Challenge*, 2 February 1978.

10. *National Conference Draft Document on Organization*, IMG 1968; Peterson, 'Aspects of the history of the IMG', pp. 11–12; T. Ali, *The Coming British Revolution* (1972), pp. 137–40; A. Thornett to author 6 October 1997; K. Sinclair interview with author, 2 October 1997.

11. IMG, *Pre-Conference Bulletin*, 8, 1978, pp. 3–4, 10; R. Seifert, 'Some aspects of factional opposition: Rank and File and the National Union of Teachers 1967–1982', *British Journal of Industrial Relations*, 22, 3, 1984, pp. 380–1.

12. *Bulletin*, December 1975 (RSL Internal Document) pp. 3–7; *Bulletin*, July 1975, pp.3–4; Taafe, *The Rise of Militant*, p. 141; MRC, MSS 356, Interviews with B. Ashworth, B. Mullins;

13. MRC, MSS 149, Box 1, File 1, SLL 1964 Conference, 'On work in the trade unions'; 'The role of the Labour Government'. And see generally, E. Germain, *Marxism vs Ultra-leftism: the record of Healy's break with Trotskyism* (1967); T. Polan, *The SLL: an autopsy* (1969); T. Whelan, *The Credibility Gap – The*

Politics of the SLL (1970); D. Hallas, 'Building the leadership', *International Socialism*, October/November 1969.

14.   *Newsletter*, 19 April 1969.

15.   Thornett, *Inside Cowley*, p. 13.

16.   Gerry Healy (1913–89). Born in County Galway, Ireland, Healy joined the Trotskyist movement in 1937. He led the opposition to the leadership of the Revolutionary Communist Party, supported by the Fourth International. On the breakup of the RCP in 1949 he was installed as leader of 'the Club', doing entry work inside the Labour Party. With the recruitment of ex-CP members after 1956, Healy launched the Socialist Labour League in 1959. Healy was a gifted organizer but an authoritarian devoid of theoretical ability. He was expelled from the WRP in 1985 for sexual abuse and violence against members.

17.   See note 12; C. Slaughter, *Who Are the International Socialists?* (1971); Banda, *Marxism or Rank and File-ism?*.

18.   MRC MSS 149, 'Draft resolution on trade union work', Eighth Annual conference of the SLL, 1966, p. 3. As the different initiatives of the CP, SLL/WRP and IS/SWP demonstrate, there were a variety of conceptions of how a rank and file movement should be organized and what it should do. This was sometimes justified by different readings of the pre-1920 shop stewards' movement and the Minority Movement, and different estimations of the extent to which unions had changed since the heyday of these movements. There were of course differing assessments of the role of these movements at the time: see J. Hinton and R. Hyman, *Trade Unions and Revolution: the industrial politics of the early British Communist Party* (1975), pp. 54–5.

19.   'British Perspectives 1967', SLL. For the LCDTU, see the preceding chapter.

20.   P. Shipley, *Revolutionaries in Modern Britain* (1976), p. 85; MRC MSS 149, Documents re. Oxford Committee.

21.   *Newsletter*, 9 September, 1967; K. Weller, 'The Oxford fiasco', *Solidarity*, 4, 8, 1967.

22.   *Newsletter*, 21 June 1969.

23.   Interview with A. Jennings, Sheffield, 20 October 1997, by J. Halstead and J. McIlroy. Jennings was Healy's secretary for much of this period.

24.   *Newsletter*, 4 January 1969.

25.   See note 17.

26.   Whelan, *Credibility Gap*, p. 45.

27.   Anonymous, 'The disunity of theory and practice', p. 222.

28.   T. Wohlforth, *The Prophet's Children: travels on the American left* (New Jersey, 1994), p. 203.

29.   The foregoing section is based on Jennings interview; A. Thornett to author, 6 October 1997, 18 October 1997; Workers' Socialist League, *The Battle for Trotskyism: documents of the opposition expelled from the Workers Revolutionary Party in 1974* (1976), pp. 36, 83; M. Shaw, *Fighter for Trotskyism: Robert Shaw 1917–1980* (1980), p. 164; J. Lloyd, *Light and Liberty: the history of the EETPU* (1990), pp. 509, 536. For Kerrigan, see B. Hunter,

They Knew Why They Fought: unofficial struggles and leadership on the docks, 1945–89 (1994), *passim*, and for Hunter, see B. Hunter, *Lifelong Apprenticeship: the life and times of a revolutionary* (1997).

30. Jennings interview; WSL, *Battle for Trotskyism*, pp. 146–7. The SLL's theatrical adventures were memorialized in Trevor Griffiths's play, *The Party*, first performed in December 1973 with Laurence Olivier playing John Tagg, a character modelled on aspects of Gerry Healy.

31. WSL, *Battle for Trotskyism*, pp. 4–5.

32. H. A. Turner *et al.*, *Labour Relations in the Motor Industry* (1967), pp. 29, 240–1; W. E. J. McCarthy, *The Closed Shop in Britain* (Oxford, 1964), pp. 119–22; N. Fishman, *The British Communist Party and the Trade Unions, 1933–45* (Aldershot, 1994), pp. 68, 216; S. Ward *et al.*, 'Cowley in the Oxford economy', in T. Hayter and D. Harvey (eds), *The Factory and the City: the story of the Cowley automobile workers in Oxford* (1993), p. 79; A. Thornett, 'History of the trade unions in Cowley' in *ibid.*, pp. 95–6; R. Whiting, *The View from Cowley: the impact of industrialisation upon Oxford, 1918–39* (Oxford, 1983).

33. Royal Commission on Trade Unions and Employers' Associations 1965–68, *Report* (1968), p. 106; WSL, *Battle for Trotskyism*, pp. 77–8; information from D. Lyddon, May 1998.

34. Thornett to author, 18 October 1997.

35. A. Thornett, *From Militancy to Marxism: a personal and political account of organizing car workers* (1987), pp. 81, 106, 117–18; Jennings interview; CP Archive, CP/CENT/ORG/13/3, J. Tarver to H. Bourne, 19 February 1970; A. Sweeney, 'Women making cars, making trouble, making history', in Hayter and Harvey, *Factory and City*, pp. 132ff.

36. S. Johns, *Victimization at Cowley* (1974); IMG, *Leyland in Crisis: Cowley under fire* (1974).

37. WSL, *Battle for Trotskyism*, pp. 81–2.

38. Thornett, *Inside Cowley*, pp. 16–17.

39. Johns, *Victimization*, pp. 61–2, 72.

40. D. Buckle, speaking on Radio Oxford, 1992, quoted in Thornett, 'History', p. 106.

41. Johns, *Victimization*, pp. 68–79; IMG, *Leyland in Crisis*, pp. 44–9.

42. Johns, *Victimization*, p.11; *Workers Press*, 10 August 1974; *Red Weekly*, 19 April 1974; IMG, *Leyland in Crisis*, pp. 49–50.

43. IMG, *Leyland in Crisis*, pp. 19–20.

44. Thornett, *Inside Cowley*, p. 13.

45. WSL, *Battle for Trotskyism*, pp. 75 ff.

46. *Trotskyism Today*, March 1978.

47. These events are detailed in Thornett, *Inside Cowley*.

48. Hotel and Catering Workers' National Committee, *The Hotel Strikes: lessons for unionization* (1978); Sweeney, 'Women making cars'.

49. T. Crawford, 'Political and religious sectarianism: a comparison and contrast', *New Interventions*, Summer 1997; C. Smith, 'Some reflections on the Healy group', ibid.

50. P. Wintour, 'A star chamber for the red mole of Cowley', *New Statesman*, 7 April 1978.

51. Tony Cliff was born Yigael Gluckstein in Palestine in 1917. He joined the Trotskyist movement *c.*1935 and came to Britain in 1946. On the breakup of the RCP he founded the *Socialist Review* Group with 33 members in 1951. The group rejected the degenerated/deformed workers' states analysis that the Fourth International applied to the USSR and its Eastern European satellites, the International's assimilation to Stalinism, and the undemocratic nature of the Healy regime, in favour of a state capitalist analysis. In the 1950s, Gluckstein published books on China and Eastern Europe, toyed with Luxembourgism and maintained links with Max Shachtman's groups in the USA. IS's key texts were: T. Cliff, *Russia: a Marxist analysis* (1955, 2nd edition, 1964); M. Kidron, *Western Capitalism Since the War* (Harmondsworth, 1968); and for the Leninist turn, T. Cliff et al., *Party and Class* (n.d., [1970]). For the group's earlier history see R. Kuper (ed.), *The Fourth International, Stalinism and the Origins of the International Socialists: some documents* (1971); Birchall, *Building the Smallest Mass Party in the World*; J. Higgins, *More Years for the Locust: the origins of the SWP* (1997).

52. J. Rosser and C. Barker, 'A working class defeat: the ENV story', *International Socialism*, Winter, 1967–8; Higgins, *More Years for the Locust*, pp. 66–71; P. Foot, *The Anti-Cameron Report* (n.d., [1967]); International Socialism Group, *Bulletin*, March 1967, pp. 8–9. The group was known as 'International Socialism' from 1962 until the late 1960s when it became 'the International Socialists'.

53. ISG, *Bulletin*, February 1967, pp. 9–10; *Bulletin*, March 1967, p.10; Higgins, *More Years for the Locust*, pp. 66–71; Foot, *Anti-Cameron Report*, p. 2.

54. See J. McIlroy, 'Notes on the Communist Party and industrial politics' in this volume.

55. J. Higgins to author, 15 July 1997; Rosser and Barker, 'A working class defeat', p. 32.

56. T. Cliff and C. Barker, *Incomes Policy, Legislation and Shop Stewards* (n.d., 1966), pp. 106, 135.

57. Ibid., p. 3.

58. I. Birchall, 'Resignation letter', ISG, *Bulletin*, 1 February 1967, p. 1.

59. Report on 'Resistance', *Bulletin*, 1, p. 10. MRC MSS 149, Box 1, File 1, C. Lever, untitled document, 1968; MSS 84, Box 1, T. Hillier and R. Cox, 'Proposals for the engineers', *Bulletin*, May, 1969.

60. T. Cliff and I. Birchall, *France: the struggle goes on* (1968); Cliff *et al.*, *Party and Class*; T. Cliff, 'The class struggle in Britain', in N. Harris and J. Palmer (eds), *World Crisis: essays in revolutionary socialism* (1971).

61. D. Hallas, 'White collar workers', *International Socialism*, October 1974, pp. 18–21.

62. Cliff, 'The class struggle', p. 266.

63. T. Cliff, *The Employers' Offensive: productivity deals and how to fight them* (1970).

64. V. Collard, 'When IS turned to the workers', *Workers' Liberty*, April 1995, p. 26.
65. Cliff, *The Employers' Offensive*, p. 232.
66. R. Hyman, *Marxism and the Sociology of Trade Unionism* (1971); J. Hinton, *The First Shop Stewards' Movement* (1973); P. Foot, *Race and Immigration in British Politics* (1965); P. Foot, *The Politics of Harold Wilson* (1968); Harris and Palmer (eds), *World Crisis*; N. Harris, *Competition in the Corporate Society: British Conservatives, the state and industry, 1945–64* (1972); M. Kidron, *Capitalism and Theory* (1974). Cliff's book on productivity deals was in fact the outcome of extensive collaboration amongst IS members. The extent to which IS drew on the ideas of others – for example, the followers of Shachtman for 'Neither Washington nor Moscow' and the Permanent Arms Economy, a variety of earlier theorists for state capitalism, the French group *Lutte Ouvriére* for workplace bulletins – requires further consideration.
67. *IS Internal Bulletin* (hereafter IB), May 1971, p.13.
68. 'Industrial subcommittee: notes on fractions', *IB*, August 1971, p. 12.
69. 'The Organizer', *IB*, June 1971; *IB*, May 1971, p.13; 'Conference report', *IB*, May 1972, p. 3; National Committee Minutes, June 1971, reprinted in *IB*, June 1971.
70. *Socialist Worker*, 21 August 1974; Nagliatti, 'Towards a rank and file movement', p.13.
71. See, for example, *Socialist Worker*, 21 November, 12 December, 1970, 9 January, 16 January, 24 April 1971, 17 June 1972; J. Townshend, 'SW on liaison committees', *IB*, May 1971; 'EC Minutes 26.4.71', reprinted in *IB*, May 1971, p. 6; 'EC 3.5.71', *IB*, May 1971, p. 9.
72. 'Industrial subcommittee', *IB*, June 1972, pp. 5–6.
73. G. Carver, 'IS intervention in the Manchester engineers' struggle', *IB*, June 1972; M. Auton *et al.*, 'Fisher Bendix and IS', *IB*, May 1972; 'NC [National Committee] perspectives for industrial work', *IB*, September 1972, p. 11.
74. 'Report of IS building workers' meeting', *IB*, October 1972, p .7.
75. 'National Secretary's Report, Policy statement adopted by August NC', *IB*, September 1972, pp. 9–13; C. Williamson, 'Factory discussion groups: a critique', *IB*, October 1972; J. Higgins, 'A reply to Williamson', ibid.
76. T. Parker, 'Recruitment and ideological struggle', *IB*, June 1971; K. Crowe, 'Workers vs students', *IB*, September 1972; M. Shaw, 'The making of a party? the International Socialists 1965–1976', in R. Miliband and J. Saville (eds), *The Socialist Register* (1978), pp. 114–18.
77. See, for example, J. Prus and K. Hulme, 'Factory branches now? sometime? never?', *IB*, May 1972; J. Macey, 'Why we need factory branches', *IB*, August 1972; 'Industrial Report', *IB*, April 1973, p.10.
78. R. Hyman, 'On factory branches', *IB*, May 1972; J. Lake, 'On factory branches', *IB*, September 1972.
79. 'Conference Report 1973', *IB*, April 1973, p. 13.
80. 'Conference Document: Industrial Report', *IB*, March 1973, p. 2; 'National Secretary's Report, Conference Report', *IB*, April 1973.

81. *IB Pre-Conference Issue*, 1974, pp. 14, 16, 18, 19; A. Cleminson, 'The Coventry car industry and the intervention of the Communist Party of Great Britain and the International Socialists', unpublished MA thesis, University of Warwick, 1987, pp. 89, 95–8.

82. *IB Pre-conference Issue*, 1974, pp. 16–17.

83. Higgins, *More Years for the Locust*, p. 97; *IB Pre-conference*, 1974, p. 22.

84. *IB Pre-conference*, 1974, p. 28.

85. Ibid., p. 27. There was overlap between engineering and carworker members.

86. A. Nagliatti, 'The rank and file conference', *IB*, April 1974, p. 9. IS did enjoy influence with one national leader, Vincent Flynn of SOGAT – cf. Interview with Mike Hicks by J. McIlroy and A. Campbell, London, 14 July 1998.

87. *IB Pre-conference*, 1974, pp. 30, 36.

88. S. Jefferys, 'Our work in the white collar unions', Pre-conference discussion, *SWP Bulletin*, May 1977, p. 3.

89. Ibid., p. 4; Hyman, 'Trade unions, the left and the Communist Party', p. 155.

90. S. Jefferys, 'The challenge of the rank and file', p. 15; J. Palmer, 'A relapse into the worst of Trotskyism', *Workers' Liberty*, September 1995, p. 34.

91. Nagliatti, 'Towards a rank and file movement', p. 7.

92. 'Notes of the Month', *International Socialism*, March 1974, p. 3; *International Socialism*, February 1974, p. 6; 'Perspectives for 1974–5', *IB*, June 1974.

93. *IB*, March 1973, p. 25; *IB*, April 1973, p. 11; Higgins, *More Years for the Locust*, p. 100; S. Jefferys, 'How the SWP narrowed into a sect', *Workers' Liberty*, June 1995, p. 30.

94. Nagliatti, 'The rank and file conference', p. 9.

95. *IB Pre-conference*, 1974, pp. 22–3; Jefferys, 'The challenge of the rank and file', p. 14.

96. EC Pre-conference Discussion Documents, April 1975, p. 13; Jefferys, 'The challenge of the rank and file', p. 14.

97. See R. Hyman, Review of N. Fishman, *The British Communist Party and the Trade Unions 1933–45*, *Science and Society*, 61, 1, pp. 145–6; Higgins, 'The Minority Movement'.

98. Nagliatti, 'Towards a rank and file movement', pp. 11–13. See also Jefferys, 'The challenge of the rank and file'; K. Appleby, 'The rank and file movement yesterday and today', *International Socialism*, November 1975; D. Hallas, 'The CP, the SWP and the rank and file movement'.

99. Nagliatti, 'Towards a rank and file movement', pp. 11, 12; *IB Pre-conference*, 1974, p. 24.

100. J. Bloomfield, 'The myth of rank and filism', *Comment*, 30 November 1974; G. Roberts, 'The strategy of rank and filism, *Marxism Today*, December 1976.

101. Callinicos, 'The rank and file movement', p. 23.

102. *IB Pre-conference*, 1974, p. 23.

103. 'The platform of the IS Opposition', *Pre-conference Discussion Documents*,

1975, p. 33.

104. D. Cattell, *IS and the Rank and File Movement* (n.d., [1974]), p. 9; J. McIlroy, 'Rank and File - not far enough!', *Socialist Worker*, 20 April 1974.

105. Hinton and Hyman, *Trade Unions and Revolution*, p. 74; Cattell, *ibid.*, p. 7.

106. Collard, 'When IS turned to the workers', p. 26.

107. National Secretary's Report, *IB*, April 1974; 'NC Report', *IB Pre-conference*, 1974; 'The platform of the IS Opposition'; Birchall, *Building the Smallest Mass Party*, pp. 23–4; Higgins, *More Years for the Locust*, pp. 104–23; Shaw, 'The making of a party?', pp. 128–30.

108. The arguments are put well in Shaw, *ibid., passim*.

109. *Pre-conference Discussion Documents*, 1975, pp. 13–18.

110. Central Committee (hereafter CC), 'Rebuilding the national rank and file movement', *SWP Bulletin Pre-conference issue*, 4, May 1977, p. 1.

111. 'Building the periphery: a discussion document', *IB*, May 1978, 3, p. 7; Glasgow District Committee, 'Our industrial strategy', *IB*, October 1979, p. 24.

112. CC, 'Now is the time to recruit: towards the Socialist Workers' Party', *IB*, September 1976; CC, 'Time to change gear', *SWP Bulletin*, February 1977; Industrial Discussion Document, *SWP Bulletin*, 6, 1978, p. 6; 'Steve Jefferys April 22 1979', *IB*, 2, May 1979; CC, 'Where we have been and where we are going', *IB*, 3, August 1979.

113. CC, 'Charter', Pre-conference discussion, *IB* , May 1978, 3, pp. 3–4.

114. M.Rice, *Birmingham AUEW Expulsions* (1975); Collard, 'When IS turned to the workers' p. 27; J. Higgins, 'The end of the "rank and file"', *Workers Liberty*, March 1995, p. 26. For an unconvincing defence of the break with the RL, see I. Birchall, 'The premature burial: a response to Martin Shaw', in R. Miliband and J. Saville (eds), *The Socialist Register, 1979* (1979), p. 29. For the Broad Left in the AUEW see the preceding chapter.

115. CC, 'Charter', p. 3.

116. Ibid.

117. S. Jefferys, 'Building in the TGWU', *Pre-conference Bulletin*, 3, May 1977; D. Lyddon, 'Our work in the TGWU', *Pre-conference Bulletin*, 4, May 1977.

118. *The Ugly Face of Chapple's Union and How to Change It* (n.d., [1975]); *Rank and File Contact*, 1, Summer 1976.

119. B. Higgins, 'The building industry', *IB*, 2, May 1979, p. 7.

120. CC, 'Charter', p. 4.

121. Jefferys, 'Our work in the white collar unions', p. 4.

122. A. Potrykus, 'NALGO fraction', *IB*, May 1977, 3; I. Ferguson, 'NALGO and 9 March – the case for the NALGO action group', *IB*, May 1977, 3, pp. 6, 8; M. McGrath, 'The broad left in the CPSA – a discussion document', *IB*, May 1977, 3; J. Hurford, 'The teachers' fraction: a discussion document', *IB*, Pre-conference discussion, May 1977, 4; Seifert, 'Some aspects of factional opposition', pp. 380–1; 'Industrial discussion', *IB*, May 1978, 3, p. 6. Hyman, 'Trade unions, the left and the Communist Party', p. 155, emphasizes the process of reform in white collar unions as undermining the left. But this has to be related to the other factors discussed here.

123.   S. Freeman, 'Steering left', *IB*, November 1979, 5, p. 47; Jefferys, 'How the SWP narrowed', p. 30; S. Jefferys, 'A note on the NUT article', *IB*, May 1977, 4.

124.   CC, 'Rebuilding the national rank and file movement', *IB Pre-conference issue*, 4, May 1977, p. 3.

125.   M. Shaw, 'Time to change course', ibid., p.30.

126.   *National Conference Report*, 1977, p. 3; *Socialist Worker*, 9 July 1977; *Comment*, 20 August 1977; 'Rank and file work in the downturn', *IB*, June 1982, p. 7; Callinicos, 'The rank and file movement', p. 29.

127.   CC 11.1.77 [sic], 'The next six to nine months', *IB*, 1, 1978, p. 1.

128.   CC, 'State of the organization', *IB*, 7, 1978; CC, 'Rank and file work in the downturn', p. 7; *IB*, 2, May 1979, p.20.

129.   Jefferys, 'How the SWP narrowed', p. 32.

130.   S. Jefferys to author, 17 March 1998.

131.   Interview with M. Costello, London, 27 April 1998, by J. McIlroy and A. Campbell; interview with M. Power, London, 12 November 1997, by J. McIlroy and A. Campbell.

132.   S. Newens, 'Cliff never really understood the British labour movement', *Workers' Liberty*, February 1995.

CHAPTER TEN

How Workers on the Clyde Gained the Capacity for Class Struggle: the Upper Clyde Shipbuilders' Work-In, 1971–2

John Foster and Charles Woolfson

The UCS work-in was the largest and most successful of the 190 work-place occupations between 1971 and 1975, and took place during a key period in the politicization of industrial action in early 1970s. It began in Summer 1971, three months after the last of the one-day strikes against the Tory Government's Industrial Relations Bill and during a period in which resistance to it appeared to be on the decline. The work-in provided the focus for two major one-day strikes against unemployment in Summer 1971. By the time of the first miners' strike in January 1972, the workers of UCS had already forced major concessions out of the government. The workers were still in occupation when the Pentonville dockers were jailed in July 1972, and the work-in only terminated when the future of the fourth yard was finally guaranteed by the government in October 1972. (See Table 10.1 for a chronology of the main events.) Our concern here is with *how* these shipyard workers were able to sustain this struggle for so long and on terms that provided a radical critique of the existing economic order – in other words, how they gained a capacity for *class*, as against purely economic, struggle.

In terms of method we seek to show the potential of language and its analysis for revealing key turning points, identifying areas of causality and assessing subjective perceptions. This approach draws on the work of Vygotsky and Volosinov and more recently Wertsch, Collins and others. It is an approach that is particularly appropriate to the study of industrial relations. It focuses on timing, interrelationships and contexts: on the way the unfolding of a dispute can turn on the particular formulations and how these are received and debated by workers and others. It is, as we will see later, an approach that is in direct contradistinction to those applied recently in cultural and social history by Patrick Joyce, James Vernon and Geoff Eley.

Posing the questions

In the July 1971 the 8,000 shipyard workers on the upper Clyde took possession of the shipyards. By October 1972 they had forced the Conservative government to abandon almost all its original objectives. Most of the 8,000 jobs remained. Four yards were in operation. Worse still for the government, it had been pushed into a much wider reversal of regional policy. Its original intention in ending credits to the publicly-owned Upper Clyde Shipbuilders (UCS) had been to demonstrate its determination to stop support for all ailing industries. Now it had to reverse its entire regional policy and pay for a massive refloatation on the Clyde.

Even at a superficial level the UCS work-in therefore poses some interesting questions. The Conservative government was never soft on its working-class opponents. It bankrupted councillors and imprisoned shop stewards. Yet nothing whatever happened to the UCS stewards. There was never any attempt at eviction, arrest or other legal sanctions. Four years later a number of leading Conservatives were asked for their explanation. All of them blamed the threat to public order posed by the workers in the yards. The minister directly responsible, Nicholas Ridley, spoke of the danger of 'civil violence' spreading from Belfast to Glasgow. Another ex-minister much closer to the prime minister, Peter Walker, claimed that there was a real fear of 'social disorder of a kind not seen in this country'. The Parliamentary Private Secretary to the Secretary of State for Scotland, Jock Bruce-Gardyne, said the critical moment came when the Chief Constable of Glasgow said he would need 15,000 extra men if instructed to clear the yards[1].

It is the argument of this paper that these explanations bear only passing resemblance to the truth. The UCS stewards were not involved in any physical confrontation with the forces of the crown. They never made any threat of violence. They did, on the other hand, represent a challenge of a far more subtle and far-reaching kind. This was to the social legitimacy of the government.[2] This challenge was so difficult to handle precisely because it was multi-dimensional and operated on at least three fronts simultaneously. First, it threatened the assumptions of social democracy: that trade unionists should never use industrial action 'unconstitutionally' to oppose the policies of the elected government. This had been central to the practice of government in Britain over the previous half-century. The work-in challenged this convention at just the moment when the government required at least the neutrality of the TUC leadership to carry through its Industrial Relations Act. Second, the work-in visibly challenged the authority of management. The rationale of the government's industrial relations policy was that shop floor power had to be curbed if managements were to secure higher productivity. Ostensibly, the work-in seemed to prove that workers ran things better. Third, and probably most seriously of all, the politics of the work-in threatened to dissolve the social base of the Conservative Party. The party's electoral support, still strong in the West of Scotland, rested on an amalgam of large and small business, the professions and sections of the working-class. It combined patronage, deference and populism. Edward Heath's policies, on the other hand, were in essence quite inimical to such regional constellations of influence. EEC membership meant concentrating resources in the hands of the largest of British firms. The arguments of the UCS stewards directly exposed this conflict of interest.

Other industrial struggles of the time challenged one or other of these systems of authority. What made UCS unique was that it challenged all three at once. Moreover, it did so at precisely the wrong time for the government: in a way that interacted in a particularly destabilizing fashion with the other major salients of struggle. It was this, in combination, that made it possible for the UCS workers to defeat the government. Our direct concern, however, is with what gave the UCS workers the capacity to do it. Clydeside shipbuilding was a by-word for sectionalism. Its industrial relations had long been dominated by conflict between different trades over demarcation and relative pay levels. Attitudes and allegiances were, on the surface at least, socially conservative, sometimes sectarian and in trade union terms tending towards support for the social democratic right-wing. Yet for these two years Clyde's shipyard workers sustained a unity articulated in explicitly class terms and provided a platform for a radical critique of the capitalist order. This is the paradox we want to address.

Materials for an answer

Before embarking on our analysis, we will outline the kind of answer we want to sustain. It has two elements. One derives from shipyard labour relations themselves. The other concerns their interaction with developments outside the yards. At the level of the shipyards three initial points can be made. First, the trade identities in the yards were sectional but also collectivist and activist. They were about group power, used collectively and directly, and exercised in the first instance against management. And although these identities were defensive, focused on rights defined against other groups of workers, they were also expressed in terms of the right of workers to take action as they saw fit without any necessary permission from formal trade union structures.[3]

Second, there had always existed within the yards, and within each trade, a dimension of explicitly socialist analysis and argumentation. It had been present since before the First World War and by the 1960s was largely (but by no means exclusively) carried forward by Communist Party (CP) members. Such politics had in themselves only limited purchase on shipyard industrial relations. Their adherents were tolerated as shop stewards and conveners – as long as their personal politics did not become too obtrusive. Their views existed alongside a cocktail of other personal religious and political identities, Catholic, Protestant, Labour, Conservative, Nationalist, none of which had a determining influence on the conventionally 'non-political' politics of the yards. But their presence was acknowledged none the less.

Thirdly, this array of sectional trade identities and generally 'non-political' trade union politics did not exist outside history. Shifts occurred, and these had been fairly significant over the previous ten years. Technological advance had altered the balance and character of different trades. Welding was now the key skill among the traditionally dominant metal crafts. The outfitting trades, engineers, electricians, wood workers, had become numerically more important. So also had the technical and scientific grades involved in design. At the same time, the general contraction in shipbuilding employment on the Clyde, from almost 30,000 in the late 1950s to 20,000 in the late 1960s, had led to intensified conflict over who controlled the technologically new or modified processes. By the mid-1960s shipbuilding was Britain's most strike-prone industry. And initiatives to 'reform' these industrial relations produced, as far as managements were concerned, somewhat unhelpful results. This was particularly so for the 'Fairfield Experiment' of 1966 when a partly government-funded consortium took over the biggest yard on the upper Clyde. The objective was to test the effectiveness of plant-based productivity bargaining techniques in an industry hitherto operating through a cumbersome national bargaining structure based on individual trades. The end result was, perhaps predictably, to consolidate the authority of the stewards at yard level, lessen that of trade union officers and produce an even bigger wage differential for the upper Clyde over the lower Clyde (focused on the Scott Lithgow yards at Greenock). When in 1969 the government consolidated the five remaining upper Clyde yards into Upper Clyde Shipbuilders, in line with the recommendations of the Geddes Report, these new practices spread. By the end of the decade all the yards on the upper Clyde had joint shop stewards committees covering all grades from technical and scientific to labouring.

So it was not totally surprising, when in 1969 the Labour government published *In Place of Strife* and sought to introduce legislation to curb unofficial industrial action, that the shipyards on the upper Clyde were among the first workplaces to endorse the call for a one-day general strike. The proposals were directly targeted at the workplace rights of groups such as the boilermakers and electricians. Nor was it altogether surprising, given the loss of jobs over the previous decade, that in April 1970, just after the Conservatives came to power, the upper Clyde yards took the lead in supporting the first regional one-day general strike on the issue of employment. These developments in turn undoubtedly made the upper Clyde yards a likely target for the incoming Conservative government. But the transformation of the yards into a base for advanced class politics resulted from something much more than a simple response to attack. Critically important were the external circumstances in which the attack took place. Three can be singled out.

One was the scale of conflict that existed, at least potentially, within the Conservative Party and its regional base in the West of Scotland. Heath's government saw the way ahead in terms of Britain's big transnational companies in chemicals, oil, pharmaceuticals, electrical, aerospace and motor manufacturing. These firms had to grow fast to become dominant players in the Common Market. Traditional industries and regional blocs of capital would need to make way. This conflict was never spelt out. Indeed, it was quite elaborately concealed by the incorporation in the government of politicians, like Nicholas Ridley, who represented traditional industries, and in the adoption in 1970 of the hard-line, proto-monetarist positions of the Selsdon group. But the conflict none the less remained.

The second was the restriction placed by the new political situation on the traditional role of social democratic functionaries in the trade union movement and the Labour Party. The Conservative government had taken over many elements of the Labour Party's industrial relations strategy. In essence this strategy sought to curb shop floor bargaining by reasserting the authority of the official movement. Opposition to the Conservative's Industrial Relations Act, and to the actions of an elected government, posed deep problems for the philosophy of the right-wing.

The third dimension was the emergence in 1971 and 1972 of other struggles which also generalized class issues. Some, like the strikes against the Industrial Relations Act, arose as a direct response to government policy. Others were more contingent. The miners' strike of winter 1972 was largely dependent for its success on the rise in oil prices and the resulting fuel crisis. But in combination, a point we will come back to, these struggles created an environment in which the wider power of a working-class could be readily identified.

This, then, very schematically, is the framework of our answer. Within the yards there existed the raw collectivism inherent in sectional identities, the gradual consolidation of the authority of the stewards at yard level and the limited presence of some form of socialist critique. Outside the yards there were the fissures that existed within the national and regional base of the Conservative Party, the limitations placed on the effective exercise of social democratic politics and the contingent existence of other major industrial struggles. It was by no means obvious, however, that these materials would ignite. And once ignited there was every possibility, in terms of the general balance of forces, that they would be extinguished long before the government had been forced into retreat. So the basic question remains: that of the capacity of the workforce. How, then, was it possible for it to sustain for so long, for months not weeks, a base for the deployment of advanced class politics? It is to help resolve this question that we want to introduce at this stage the analysis of language.[4]

Putting the meaning back into language

Probably the best starting point is with some of the currently familiar works of the post-modernist school, those of James Vernon, Patrick Joyce and Geoff Eley.[5] These authors have pioneered the 'linguistic turn' in the writing of recent British history, and their methodology is so far the direct opposite of that adopted here that it usefully highlights the particular characteristics of our approach.

Vernon, Joyce and Eley have sought to contest reductionist interpretations of political behaviour in terms of 'underlying' economic and social forces. Specifically they wish to oppose 'the primacy of class' by which a person's attitudes are 'read off' from their social position. This, they argue, is to demean the autonomy of individuals. Instead they radically counterpose social structure and language: 'it is language and not some prior social structure that creates the unstable, diverse and often contradictory identities.[6] The key to understand these identities is the 'reading of politics as an attempt ... to make identity fixed, stable and coherent (however provisionally) through the narrative forms of its language'. These political languages or 'narrative forms', 'radical, Liberal, Conservative or classical', have their own autonomous existence across history. 'Individual actors are constrained by the finite subjectivities of political languages' – although they can 'play at the margins of these languages'. This ultimately enables us to 'see politics as a discursive struggle to empower people by imagining them as legitimately acting subjects around specific fixed identities'.[7] As Gareth Stedman Jones famously argued in *Languages of Class*, Chartist leaders were only successful in so far as they were able to inhabit and use a 'political narrative', or language form, that of radicalism, which had been in existence for the previous century.[8]

The origins of this approach, as Perry Anderson demonstrated in his critique of Stedman Jones, goes back through Foucault, Lacan and Derrida to De Saussure's original distinction between *langue* and *parole* at the beginning of this century. *Parole* represented the amorphous, fluid utterances of every-day speech – which, for De Saussure, was scarcely susceptible to systematic analysis. *Langue*, on the other hand, provided the proper field for scientific linguistics. It represented the continuing structures of a language, its rules of deployment and organization in which the sign existed apart from any specified use or point of reference. Any scientific analysis of *langue*, De Saussure argued, required its abstraction from the contingencies of its day-to-day use. Systems of signs must be analysed on their own terms and on the basis of their own inherent structures. The discussion of subjects, the attempt to explain a text by reference to its readers or the creation of relativities between texts would violate the integrity of a given language.[9]

The approach used here is one that actively contests the exclusions imposed by De Saussure's distinction between *langue* and *parole*. It focuses

302

on meaning *in contexts,* on language as the medium by which human beings actively and experimentally make sense of themselves and their environment. It goes back to the 1920s and 1930s and the endeavour of Vygotsky and Volosinov to create a Marxist psychology which developed the original perspectives of Marx and Engels on the social role of language. After the war this approach was continued by Leontiev, Luria and, on a different front, by Ilyenkov. More recently, this approach has been adapted and developed by a series of Western social scientists – among others Wertsch, Bakhurst, Collins, Huspek and Brandist.[10] None offers exactly the same approach methodologically. But there is a basic commonality that is best captured by a couple of initial paradoxes – statements which will also, we hope, make clear how different this approach is to that just mentioned.

The first is that the basic unit of its analysis is not language structures or 'political narratives', but individual 'word meanings' – which must be understood, at one and the same time, as *common* and *continuing* and also constantly undergoing *change.* Language is seen to represent the common social tool which is integral to the process by which human beings develop their fundamental and distinguishing potential for labour – their ability actively, socially, to understand and control themselves and their environment. And in line with this, at the level of individual psychology, the word meanings which the child assimilates within its early social interactions are exactly the medium by which conceptual thought is developed and knowledge inherited. Yet, within this commonality, meanings also change. The very process of developing the capacity for labour requires a constant interrogation of received knowledge. And this expectation of fluidity and experimentation is itself is a key part of the way language is learnt and used in everyday speech. This first paradox interlocks with a second.

Within any society there will be a *coexistence* of different, socially-bonded *types* of speech. On this front there is indeed an element of commonality with 'language forms'. But it is qualified. Such types of speech, or speech genres, will be socially-rooted and be part of a process which seeks to distinguish, insulate and control those who use them – not just by inflections of spoken accent and idiom but by seeking to construct meanings in ways that give the world a different significance. Yet, although this is their aim and function, such socially-bonded speech genres are *not* impermeable. They cannot be 'read' in isolation. On the contrary, their ability to survive depends precisely on their tacit *inter-relationships*: their constant modification and redefinition of positions in line with what other groups say and do. Nor can they themselves and their specific content be understood outside their interaction with wider social forces. It will be the *relative* distribution of a society's material resources which will inform particular identities – and similarly with the corresponding 'reification' of word meanings that provides these identities with coherence and justification. Within such reified speech, meanings which separate and distinguish groups socially must also

303

possess a measure of commonality. Volosinov spoke of 'the inner dialectic quality' of words by which they take on a multifaceted, socially fluid significance directly contingent on the changing balance of class forces. A ruling class will, for instance, always seek to impart an eternal 'non-class' or 'supra-class' meaning to words and so stress the immutable, unchangeable nature of social reality. Any analysis which challenges this has itself to be made illegitimate. By contrast, those who do not rule, but suffer the consequences, will equally often seek to exclude this knowledge by modifying the way they construct their own understanding of the world. External holders of power either disappear from discourse or are familiarized as fallible individuals, 'Maggie' or 'Tony'. But no group, in terms of the very nature of language, will be able to use it in a way that is ultimately impenetrable. Word meanings are learnt and used experimentally and actively. They depend on contexts, and contexts change.

Finally, to complete the contrast with those, like Joyce and Vernon, who stress the equal legitimacy of any 'political narrative', types of language can and must be defined, ranked, to use Huspek's phrase, on the basis of their *emancipatory* potential – or, in Ilyenkov's terms, by their relative ability to reveal causes, to perform the basic function of language in advancing the human potential for knowledge. This contest between languages of differing emancipatory potentials is, for this approach, the central axis of analysis.

It is our contention that this methodology has particular merits for the study of industrial relations. It captures the importance of timing, conjuncture and the flux of contested meaning on which the unfolding of any dispute depends. More importantly still in terms of our current subject, it opens up the study of how analyses of society are actively changed in the course of a dispute: how workers widen their horizons to those of class struggle. We will now seek to use this methodology more practically. First we will look at how the shop stewards initially set up the clash of meanings between the government and themselves, and the way in which they sought to relate the differing 'levels' of language in the yard in a way that would also paralyse the government outside. We will then look at a converse incident in which the government sought to retrieve the situation. In doing so, we will also seek to point up the contrast between this methodology and the other.

Levels of language

The reason for this government's anti-working-class policy is to be found in the deepening crisis and sickness of the British capitalist economy. Its aim is to solve that crisis at the expense of the people, and to do so in such a way as to reinforce the big monopolies. Much of Tory policy can be seen as a preparation for entry into the Common Market. Tory policy is hostile to the vast majority of the British people – industrial workers, farmers, professional people, small business and trad-

ers alike ... The movement must openly proclaim the clear political character of the struggle. The goal must be to drive the Tories out; to advance ... alternative policies; and challenge the monopoly control of our economic resources ...
The establishment of Scottish and Welsh parliaments would give the Scottish and Welsh people greater democratic opportunities to fight for the planned development of their countries, so as to overcome to neglect and exploitation of the past and present. In the course of this struggle the great monopoly concerns and the ruling class will be exposed as the chief threat to genuine popular and national interests.

The above quotations are fairly recognizably Communist. They have all the hall-marks of the rather comfortable, inner-party style of discussion which assumes that a ruling class exists, that monopolies control the economy, that divisions within society on the basis of class interest colour other issues such as nationality and that it is feasible to call for some sort of broad popular alliance involving small business which can 'challenge' monopoly rule. As general formulations, they might have been plucked from party documents at any time between the 1950s and the 1980s. In fact they come from speeches made by Jimmy Reid in the years immediately before the work-in. The first comes from his Political Report to the party's National Executive in March 1971; the second from Reid's speech to the party's Congress in 1969. The main resolution at that Congress continued: '... the new authoritarianism of the trusts is the menace today. This is not only a working class issue. It involves all the middle strata, the professions whose future is threatened, the small capitalists and shopkeepers. These are the force which the working-class must win in a broad anti-monopoly alliance.'

Let us now consider two other snatches of language from Reid. The first comes from his speech to the mass meeting of 30 July which announced the work-in:

The world is witnessing the first of a new tactic on behalf of workers. We are not going to strike. We are not even having a sit-in strike. We are taking over the yards because we refuse to accept that faceless men, or any group of men in Whitehall or anywhere else, can take decisions that devastate our livelihoods with impunity ... The shop stewards representing the workers are in control of this yard. Nobody and nothing will come in and nothing will go out without our permission ... And we want to make this public announcement here today. There's been talk in the press about redundancies at Connells. This liquidator can do what he wants, but we are not accepting redundancies ... if necessary, we'll line up in South Street and we'll identify ourselves with them and we'll march into this yard, because, brothers, I want to make this point. Everybody talks about rights. There is a basic elementary right here – that's our right to work. We are not strikers. We are responsible people and we will conduct ourselves with dignity and discipline that we have all the time expressed over the last few weeks. And there'll be no hooliganism. There'll be no vandalism. There'll be no bevvying ... The existing

305

managerial people who are with us will continue to function in this capacity and their instructions, decisions will be adhered to as long as they are consistent with the general strategy ...'[11]

Our second quotation comes from Reid's call to the all-Britain meeting of shop stewards on 10 August 1971:

... on the part of the working people of Britain to put an end to policies and practices whereby decisions can be taken by a group of men either in government or in a board room that can decimate communities and cast thousands of workers on to the dole queue and blight the future of the younger generation, forcing social upheaval and people leaving their communities in search of a future.

Now for too long we have tolerated such policies and such practices, for too long they've been getting away with it and at last a section of the workers have rejected and repudiated such social, economic and political theories, have reasserted the dignity of working men to establish that they've got rights, and they've got commitments and privileges and principles, and they are going to utilise their ability and capacity to resist these measures, to fight and to unite around them their brothers and sisters.

So that in winning this victory, and that's what we should be speaking about today, it is not a narrow victory for the UCS workers, but a victory for the British working people that can reverse the whole trend that's been obvious in our country for the last years, and indeed, create a situation where no more can such decisions be taken.

Because I want to say this: the policies of the government in relation to the UCS indicate a mentality ... it raises the question of there being people in this government who represent financial interests, whose sole concern is maximising their profits, and if this can be done by investments abroad or by chewing gum plantations in Timbuktu, they're not interested in the devastation that their policies will wrought in terms of the economic structure of Britain – the social malaise and desert that these policies will create.

... there is no trade unionist will defend the record of the UCS of about 1968 to half-way through 1969 for reasons which Joe touched upon. The money was squandered, compensation given to previous owners, too many of them. Too many of these previous owners who had brought shipbuilding and the upper reaches of the Clyde to the sorry state they were in, as a result of their neglect, were represented on that board and I'm saying this to you quite bluntly. The record of the shipbuilding families of the Clyde, that's the owners, is such as they shouldn't be allowed to manage a bingo hall, let alone an industry fighting for its community ... (Cheers and applause.)

We are asking that you respond to our call not only for financial assistance, but at some stage in the relatively near future, to demonstrate beyond all shadow of doubt where you stand, you and your workers stand and you and your organizations stand, by giving the most visible, physical demonstration that on this issue, the workers of Britain recognize it's a trial, it's a test case, that if it's won can galvanise the whole progressive working-class movement in Britain that contains men of goodwill and can take this country on a new course, where the people matter, where the people come first, where elementary rights and decencies take a

306

higher priority than the economic dogma and greed of a tiny section of the community. (Applause and Cheers.)[12]

Reid's first speech was to the yard workers and was intended to win commitment to the terms of the work-in as agreed by the shop stewards. The second was to shop stewards assembled from across Britain in solidarity – although Reid was also speaking with an eye to the mass media and to how its reportage would be received in the yards.

One thing is immediately clear from any comparison between what Reid said in inner-party discussion and what he said during the work-in. The words addressed to Reid's 'fellow workers' contain not one mention of capitalism, monopolies, the ruling-class or alliances. In fact, the first excerpt contains no reference even to the working-class. There was good reason. Reid was speaking as a shop steward. Any suggestion that he was doing so as a Communist would immediately have divided his hearers and brought accusations that he was bringing 'politics' into the dispute. Yet it is equally clear that the content and assumptions of Reid's statements as a shop steward were constructed on a scaffolding of meaning drawn from the way he and others on the UCS leadership thought as Communists. It should be no less clear that without this underlying scaffolding the conduct of the dispute would have been quite different.

The instinctive response of right-wing trade union officers would have been, and in fact was, to negotiate the best deal in the immediate circumstances: to accept some redundancies as inevitable but to limit the number. The battle would then have become internalized and sectionalized: which yards would go and which workers would lose their jobs. Reid and his colleagues sought to generalize the dispute: to kill any suggestion of compromise or internalization at the outset and to establish a tactic of response that progressively ate into the social and political base of the government. The ploy of 'working-in', which forced the government to accept the continuance of the yards as a going concern, immediately ranged behind the workers the 700 creditor firms which stood to lose all they were owed as well as the custom they depended on for the future. It forced local authorities, even the Conservative/Progressive-controlled Glasgow Council, to confront the dilemma of supporting 'their communities' or the government. It took leadership of the dispute out of the hands of the official movement and temporarily neutralized a Scottish press which tended towards the Conservative Party (*Herald* and *Scottish Daily Express*) or right-wing Labour (*Record*). This response, of seeking to work upon and include the specific interests of local business and the professions in the regional economy, was based precisely on what Reid reported to the CP national executive: an analysis of the specific contradictions of monopoly capitalism. By contrast the social democrat position made no such an analysis. It talked in terms of a 'managed economy'. Conflicts of class interest no longer figured. Government was a tripartite partnership with business and labour, and Labour's industrial policies through the 1960s were founded on modernizing the economy in cooperation with the biggest of Britain's transnational firms. Any talk of alliances based on the class interests of anti-monopoly forces, let alone anything seeking to change the balance of class forces by direct action from below, was totally alien.

In this very important sense the two types of language, social democratic and Communist, were not just different. They did represent different levels. In terms of 'emancipatory potential', or in Ilyenkov's terms of penetrating into contradictory processes of social change, the system of meanings used by Reid and his colleagues proved (if we are to rule out a purely random serendipity) a more accurate and hence effective guide to how workers could best exploit the weaknesses of the government.[13]

This, however, brings us to a further key dimension of level and to the issue of process. Most workers in the yards did not, in their daily intercourse, speak the language of social democracy – let alone Marxism. As we have said, the sectional identities which composed the basic units of yard life were founded in particular crafts and grades and sought to defend their specific interests. They were collective as well as sectional. Their intense parochialism was mixed with a deep suspicion of management. Winning compliance with the idea of the work-in posed formidable difficulties. The very thought that it formed part of a wider picture framed in Marxist terms would have killed it dead from the start. No less difficult was the idea of obeying management. Workers' immediate instinct would have been to take strike action. To win acceptance of what was an ostensibly highly unnatural tactic, Reid and colleagues somehow had to build a bridge, in the forum of language and argument, between the existing worlds of caulkers, joiners and draughtsmen, and another dimension in which it was possible to do more than simply fight a sectional corner in a world of finite possibilities.

To understand how this was done we need to return briefly to the earlier theorizations of the way everyday language is used. It was Volosinov who first analysed this type of transformative process in terms of the dialectic of 'theme' and 'meaning'. 'Meaning', for Volosinov, represented the standard, received, socially-endorsed significances which existed within a word or phrase. Such significances will usually be multiple and always somewhat general – with a force derived from this generality and even more, on occasion, from the reified, socially endorsed convention of particular speech genres. Yet the actual meaning, the 'real' meaning taken at any particular moment, will depend on how the word is used, on its context. The act of comprehension involves the constant search to find context, of aligning the immediate usage with previous knowledge. It is 'dialogic' in the sense that the process of understanding another person requires an answering set of 'words' or meanings. It is within this process that Volosinov identifies his dialectic of theme and meaning.[14] 'Theme' represents the way in which speak-

308

ers actively seek to construct contexts to *transform* meaning – with context representing not just the changing flux of material circumstance but also the way in which speakers from different positions will seek to link and connect or to by-pass and omit.

Here Volosinov stresses, in terms that are very similar to those of Vygotsky, the special character of 'inner speech' as thought – as abbreviated, short-hand, seeking the 'sense' of a word or phrase through a conjunction of images in which affective, emotional associations will be particularly powerful.[15] The capacity of 'theme' to transform 'meaning', of a speaker to be able to fragment existing received notions and rearrange them in a new way, will depend directly on the skill with which they can identify and use those core meanings which have the greatest affective power. This skill will in turn depend on a first-hand knowledge of how, for any individual or group of individuals, existing systems of meaning have, to quote Leontiev, dug them-selves into 'his connections with people forming the real circle of his contacts'.[16] No less critically, it will require an element of appraisal: an ability to stand outside this circle as well as within it. The capacity to transform in an 'emancipatory' direction will depend precisely on a knowledge of how to harness those elements of meaning which – within the wider tensions of a class society – represent the defence of rights and material expectations.

Let us now look at the way Reid deployed his rhetoric to win the workforce for the idea of a 'work-in'. The term itself is of no small importance pre-cisely because it had no previous meaning or existence. It was a non-word which gave Reid and his colleagues, initially at least, the power to fill it with the meaning that they chose. The world was witnessing the launch of a 'new tactic on behalf of workers'. Reid moves quickly back and forth be-tween galvanizing anger not at management but at 'faceless men', in Whitehall (outside Scotland) and invoking an all-encompassing solidarity that outflanks sectionalism. If Scotstoun men are made redundant, 'we will all march together' back into the yard. He defines the work-in as not being a strike – but does so in a context that stresses the power of the workers. They have 'taken over yards'. Nothing will come in or go out without 'their' per-mission. He seizes on the core of sectional identities, 'rights' within a specified order, and generalizes it in a quite new way: 'the right to work'. In doing so Reid mixes in a series of powerful 'universal' word meanings: dig-nity, responsible, disciplined. He uses them to frame and introduce the critical relationship that will continue between workers and management.

Much of the same rhetoric is present in the second speech. Although Reid is now talking to shop stewards who have come from across Britain, and who thereby represented a somewhat higher level of class understanding, he still strenuously avoids anything reminiscent of 'party' language. On the other hand, he does use the occasion – and the opportunity the media pro-vided to talk back to the workers in the yard – to heighten his previous formulations. He still does not use the term 'class'. But he does repeatedly invoke 'the working people of Britain' and the 'trade union and labour movement' – usually linking these terms to 'Scotland' and 'community'. He also talks about power in societal terms: the unaccountable power of 'men in a board room' to 'decimate' communities – as against the power of workers to 'reassert the dignity of working men'. It is the workers who are moved by 'commitments' and 'principles' – whereas it is the owners, 'a tiny section' who are motivated by 'economic dogma' and greed. He also uses this discussion to give a greater depth of meaning to the 'faceless men' of the previous speech. He explores the collusion between the state and finance capital: the people in government who represent financial interests, whose 'investments abroad' will create deserts at home, and pillories the old shipbuilding families, central figures in old systems of local patronage and dependence, as unfit to run a bingo hall. Reid then ends by posing the alternative: taking Britain 'on a new course', where people come first and 'elementary rights and decencies take a higher priority'. In this the external support of the trade union movement is made to play a critical role: the physical presence of hundreds of stewards is made to embody the force that can make alternatives possible.

Both these speeches come from the early weeks of the struggle, 30 July and 10 August. This was before the shop stewards had had to face any really concentrated attack from the government or the media. The tactics of the shop stewards, and their success in rallying the workforce behind them, had taken the government by surprise. Yet it would be unwise to underestimate the difficulty of the task faced by the stewards in these early days. They had to win the commitment of the workforce to a highly innovative form of direct action – and then maintain it. Without this the struggle would have been quickly internalized and limited. In examining the process whereby this was achieved, the specific importance of language should have become clear. The ability of Reid and the other stewards to transform meaning depended on a precise knowledge of the existing array of conventional meanings. It required a capacity to create new contexts, to deploy theme against meaning, and the affective power to seize on core meanings and deploy them in support.

This brings us back to the point we began with: levels of language. Reid tailored his speech to the particular speech genres he was addressing and the conceptual challenges they presented. But the content of what he said came from elsewhere. He and his colleagues were able to draw on a level of analysis which enabled them to penetrate the real social processes, and hence open up tactics of resistance which the right-wing would never have envisaged. The invention of the 'work-in' conjured with conventional word meanings in a way that captured the ideological ground on which the government stood. It made the workers the responsible defenders of the productive economy and the government the irresponsible wreckers. The success of this inversion was not just dependent on a random play on words.

It was effective precisely because Reid and his colleagues successfully analysed the contradictions of material interest within the government's political base.

Yet, as should be readily apparent, another level in the emancipatory capacity of language was also at work. This was the skill with which Reid used language. An understanding of political economy would have been of little use unless Reid possessed the acquired skills which themselves derived largely from CP practice as it evolved during the 1930s and 1940s: its stress on working *within* the existing organizations of working people on their own terms. It was the resulting acquired knowledge that enabled Reid to use 'theme', the construction of contexts and the deployment of emotions, to transform received meaning so effectively.

At this point it is useful to refer back to our earlier comparison with the post-modernists. Superficially it might appear that our portrayal of Reid's political leadership exactly mirrors the approach to 'leaders' by Patrick Joyce and James Vernon. In fact this is not so, and an examination of the differences illuminates the core of Volosinov's method. James Vernon's *Politics and People* is centrally concerned with the iconography of leadership and in particular the propensity of 'the people' to defer to 'the gentleman leader': Hunt, O'Connor, Bright, Gladstone. This confirms for Vernon an innate need to 'create idols' from potential leaders who possessed a cross-class resonance and who clearly articulated a specific 'political narrative'. Vernon's evidence is drawn from five separate communities spread from Devon through London to Lanacashire across a time period from 1815 to the 1870s. But his use of it is detached from particular times and places – because, he claims, all five represent the same 'national political culture'. Vernon also makes a detailed analysis of the texture of speeches. His focus is on two aspects. On the one hand, he highlights the devices of rhetoric: the use of melodrama, repetition, opposition, by which speakers 'drew the audience into an imaginative world in which they became part of the performance'.[17] On the other hand, Vernon examines the response of the audience. Here he looks at reactions in terms of applause or shouting down – the oral contests between rival groups within an audience that express rival political narratives. Vernon illustrates these processes by assembling examples of such rhetorical devices and audience response from across space and time with no regard to the specific context of what was being said.

By contrast, the method of Volosinov hinges entirely on the detailed, contingent reconstruction of the contexts of 'word meanings'. It depends on the constant tension between 'theme' and word meanings and the transformative power of this tension to create new meanings and extend the level of understanding. It assumes a direct, active and immediate relationship between speaker and listener. This is not the case with the post-modernists. For all their talk of respect for the autonomy of cultures and narratives, 'the people' themselves are essentially passive – entering the imaginative play of rhetoric on the one hand and inhabiting grand 'political narratives' on the other (even though they are given the freedom to 'play on the margins'). The basic human urge for meaning, experimental, immediate, contextual, does not come in to it. The very texture of their writing debars it.

In this reconstruction of Reid's interventions we have sought to show that the material contexts of meaning were decisive. A passionate address might temporarily shift the way contexts were constructed. The real world none the less remained – as we will see in our next section which examines a far more active conflict of linguistic positions. We will end this section with an unsolicited tribute to the skills of the UCS stewards over those first weeks of the work-in between July and August. It comes from the Conservative-inclined leader writer of the *Glasgow Herald* on August:

> It might be thought that the official opposition might be winning such a game. It is not. Neither the industrial or political wings of the official labour movement can win. They have lost the leadership to the shop stewards. It is the shop stewards who best understand the rules of the UCS, and who have shown constant political and public relations skills of the highest order.

Multi-accentuality, materiality and social democracy

The announcement of the withdrawal of government support for UCS was made in the Commons on 14 June 1971. This was followed by the first mass demonstration and half-day regional strike on 23 June. The report of the 'Four Wise Men', which reiterated the original position of the government, was published on 29 July. The first redundancies and the announcement of the work-in came the following day, 30 July. Within the following two weeks there was the convening of the mass, British-level meeting of shop stewards in Glasgow (10 August), emergency meetings of the STUC (16 August) and of the TUC General Council in Glasgow (17 August), and the second regional strike and mass demonstration (18 August). (see Table 10.1).

The government undoubtedly expected trouble when they embarked on the closure. They probably hoped that the passage of time, the publication of an independent report and the offer of two yards and some jobs would sap the strength of resistance and enable the negotiations to commence through the official movement. The meeting with Heath in June and the visit to Glasgow at the beginning of August by John Davies, Secretary of State for Industry, were meant to demonstrate the government's concern and at the same time win an acceptance of 'economic realities'. By mid-August it was clear that this course was not working and that the situation was slipping out of control. The problem was not just the revolt among local business and the mutiny by the Progressive/Conservative group on Glasgow council. The real worry for the government was the loss of authority by the official trade union leadership. Neither the Confederation of Shipbuilding and Engineering Unions (Confed) nor Danny McGarvey, General Secretary of the Boilermakers, had been able to assert control over the negotiations and, no less dangerous, the shop stewards had been able to call into existence an all-Britain network of support based at shop steward level, which was raising more general issues of the right to work. For the government this could not have happened at a worse moment. The Industrial Relations Act had just become law, and its operation depended on compliance by the official movement. Ultimately, the Act required trade unions themselves to discipline unofficial action at shop steward level. Now, at this precise juncture, the actions of the UCS workers was giving the stewards movement a new moral authori.y and unofficial action a much broader social legitimacy.

It was against this background that the government began a concerted and well-planned offensive against the stewards at the end of August and into September. One front was financial: to threaten the work-in with bankruptcy. The liquidator was forced into announcing a series of redundancies which had reached nearly 500 by the beginning of September. The weekly wage packets of these workers represented a significant sum to be met from the levy on other workers and from public support. The other front was ideological and organizational. The government on its own initiative set up negotiations with McGarvey and the Confed over a 'rescue' package. In order to achieve its ends it was willing to give its negotiators some leeway in terms of jobs – although not, as we will see, on the crucial area of conditions of work. This initiative was accompanied by a combined onslaught from all sections of the press demanding that the stewards be reasonable and cooperate in the long-term interest of those they represented. The Labour-inclined *Record* ran its front-page story on 22 September as 'Speak Up Brother Dan'. On the same day the Conservative *Glasgow Herald's* editorial argued that 'the full-time trade union officials now have a duty to take over from the shop stewards and work with management to ensure that the maximum number of jobs is preserved'.[18]

The resulting struggle for control has been made the subject of an important analysis by Chik Collins.[19] This study makes pioneering use of Volosinov's theorization of speech, in terms of its practical application to live debate, and its conclusions enable us to abbreviate our own treatment considerably. Collins uses Volosinov to focus on what he described as the multi-accentuality of speech. 'Utterances', Volosinov's basic unit of analysis, are, as we noted before, dialogical. They presuppose more than one voice so that 'the voice of one speaker can be heard speaking through another speaker'. To quote Volosinov: 'class does not coincide with sign community ... different classes will use one and the same language. As a result differently oriented accents intersect ...' There will be a continual contest over meaning which will become intense at periods of social crisis. It is then that the 'inner dialectic quality of the sign' will be most apparent. But this contest is not free-floating:

> Every sign is the construct of socially organized persons in their interaction. There-
> fore the forms of sign are conditioned above all by the social organization of the
> participants involved and also by the immediate conditions of their interaction.
> When these forms change so does the sign ...[20]

Collins demonstrates the character of this multi-accentuality in his reconstruction of the debates which took place in the last week of September
1971. The government chose very carefully the character of the ground on
which it wished to fight. Its defeats over the previous two months were seen
to have stemmed in large measure from the stewards' ability to seize control
of the terms 'community', 'industry', 'Scotland', and to represent the interests of the Conservative Party's own natural constituencies among local
business and the professions. The government's response was to adopt the
language of social democracy. Just as its brokers were to be the right-wing
leaders of the Confed, so Davies and the other government negotiators now
sought to speak through and populate the concepts of the labour movement.
The proto-monetarist rhetoric of Ridley, Eden and the Seldson group, present
in the early stages of the dispute, was replaced by appeals to 'co-operation',
'reasonableness', 'flexibility', 'making the best of the situation'. As the
Sunday Times pointed out on 26 September, the consequences would be the
same:

> The hard fact is that for the first time since the start of the work-in concrete offers
> of jobs have been made ... National union leaders would doubtless like to settle
> for the jobs, and then talk of saving the others later. This sort of compromise will
> not commend itself to Airlie and Reid. Any compromise will break their grip, so
> releasing the dissident elements which have so far been kept in check...

Collins pinpoints the climax of this struggle as being at the mass meeting of
all yard workers on 24 September. Further redundancies had been announced.
McGarvey had succeeded in conducting negotiations with Davies that by-
passed the stewards. He had 'won' a deal whereby shipbuilding on the upper
Clyde would be saved. Two yards would continue. All that was needed now
was a commitment of cooperation from the workforce. Over the previous
week the press had saturated the workforce with appeals to their good sense
and increasingly explicit innuendoes that they were being led down the gar-
den path by politically-motivated groups: the work-in was a pretence, it could
never be sustained financially, workers had to face reality and make the best
of the offer on the table. In these circumstances it would be very easy for the
workers of the 'saved' yards, Govan and Linthouse, to revert to the same
social democratic but implicitly sectional language of their official leaders
and vote for negotiations.

The stewards had to try to stop this. They had three resources at their dis-
posal. The first was the workers' own class understanding. Its actual strength
depended on the degree to which the struggle over the previous three months,

especially the interaction with support from the workers and communities outside the yards, had changed horizons about what was possible and created new 'meanings' more akin to those of Reid and his colleagues. Such a transformation had undoubtedly occurred to some degree. But it was difficult to gauge just how far it had gone.

The second weapon was directly linguistic: a political timebomb which the stewards had been hoarding against hard times, the photostat copies of the Ridley Report. The government was aware that the stewards had got hold of limited extracts. These had been quoted by Benn in the original Commons debate in June. But there had been no proof of authenticity and the government was able to deny all knowledge. As the stewards did not respond, the government thought it was safe. Now in the second week of September the stewards published the undeniably authentic letters in which Nicholas Ridley, the minister directly responsible for the closure, had summed up his earlier discussions with other shipbuilders on the Clyde. Ridley, whose family had owned the biggest shipyard on the Tyne, spelled out his findings with the cynical arrogance that befitted a true son of the ruling class. The yards on the upper Clyde were a 'cancer' whose militancy was forcing wages up elsewhere. The profits of the remaining private yards, Yarrow and Lithgow, were suffering as a consequence. So, concluded Ridley, we should 'put in a government "butcher" to cut up UCS and sell (cheaply) to the lower Clyde ...'. This evidence of direct collusion – when the government had always claimed that UCS's financial crisis was self-inflicted – caused immediate outrage among the creditor firms. But it also gave the stewards the weapon they needed to take over and populate the government's chosen social democratic imagery with quite different meanings.

Finally, there was a more recent weapon of the government's own making – though one that also makes its appearance in the Ridley letters. This was the government's insistence in its negotiations with McGarvey that the conditions for the retention of jobs was the introduction of new shift patterns and new forms of wage calculation. This would more or less bring the yards on the upper Clyde into line with those on the lower. Such was the other significance of cooperation and flexibility.

It is clear from the way the stewards introduced their case at the mass meeting that they knew they would have to use all three of these weapons if they were to win the vote for no negotiations and a repudiation of McGarvey. Airlie as Chair of the Coordinating Committee introduced Reid, the spokesperson. In his introduction Airlie read *verbatim* extracts from the *Glasgow Herald* on the conditions being laid down in return for the retention of jobs – conditions apparently accepted by McGarvey, the ostensible champion of the 'rights' of shipyard sectionality:

This meeting has been convened by the UCS Joint Shop Stewards Committee and it is in reply to the Government's decision to set up a board based on Govan and

Linthouse and call the Govan Shipbuilding Company. We decided that decisions and recommendations will be made to this meeting, a meeting of all workers on the upper Clyde; they can take their decisions but we will not be divided, we will take our decisions as a whole. The Press are now parading the statements of the government and the new chairman of their so-called board Sir Hugh Stenhouse as a new initiative. This is a deception on the Scottish people. It is not a new initiative … it is the government's commitment from the start based on their White Paper, the report of the so-called Four Wise Men …We are being criticized, as we're inflexible, and the Press are saying that this is the best way forward. We are of the opinion that it is not any alternative. They are saying that half a loaf is better than nothing. It is not even half a loaf; it is part of a loaf and in order to get that part of a loaf you've got to grovel and crawl; that is not an alternative for any men or women. I would like to quote from this morning's *Glasgow Herald*:
Headline: 'Government demands pledge from Govan workers'.
We will give then a pledge, but it will be from the UCS workers in total. I would like to go on and quote the opening parts of the report:

> 'Before the government authorised a multi-million pound shipbuilding investment for the upper Clyde they are insisting on pledges of trade union co-operation with Govan Shipbuilders Limited, the successor company to UCS. Mr John Davies, Secretary of State for Trade and Industry, left the House of Commons in no doubt yesterday that the future of merchant shipbuilding on the upper Clyde depends on the workers agreeing to new commitments on "hours and wages". This means accepting competitive wage rates on the lower level of those and other shipyards and agreeing to two shift working – probably from 6 am to 2 pm and 2 pm to 10 pm'.

We are saying that it's like a burglar complaining that the housewife is trying to make her premises lockfast. We are not accepting that position. We are asking for a reiteration of our solidarity and for our demand to fight that no-one will butcher this industry. We have recommendations and the JSS Committee have decided that Jimmy Reid will put these recommendations on our behalf. I therefore call upon Jimmy Reid to put these recommendations …[21]

Reid followed:

And so we are saying to you workers the unreasonableness in the whole position is that of the Government, despite the exposure, despite the mass condemnation, they have pushed through their policy to butcher our industry and don't let any leader writer talk to us about reasonableness and inflexibility. The unreasonableness and the inflexibility is that of the Government. For our part we'll go and see Davies, Heath, anybody … on the basis … that we'll discuss any proposals … that deals with the four yards and gives guarantees to the labour force in these yards. [We'll] talk to anybody … but all the time they come back to the butchery of our industry. And I want to say here and now, don't let there be division in our ranks, I'll tell you this much, and I'm speaking personally here, if the Government succeeded in the butchery of our industry I'd rather be on the dole than be amongst the two and a half thousand that would be left to grovel, accept wages reductions and all sorts of other things, and I'm telling you it would be a short-term solution because their objective would take place in a year or so, and it would be the end of our industry in the Clyde, and its like a murderer who wants to murder us, we've found out, we've defended ourselves against the murder and people say 'please negotiate with the murderer, you might stop him from piercing your heart, but he can cut off your legs and arms and there's a sensible compromise'. And when you're lying bleeding they will tell you in a year or two, wi' you minus the legs, why aren't you standing on your own two feet? And brothers our proposals therefore spring from a sense of responsibility to ourselves and to our families and our community and in the last resort to the British working-class. It's impossible for us to accept this ... we are not capitulating to the butchery ... There will be no co-operation, and this is what we're putting to you with this board, no co-operation, that we close the ranks as a united labour force and tell them that they are not on ... So, we are appealing to you, its a simple proposal, there will be no co-operation, because that's the butchery we all reacted to on the 29th of July...[22]

The outcome was victory for the stewards. The workforce endorsed the proposal for non-cooperation and its implicit repudiation of McGarvey. There were two attempts to put the case for accepting the 'part loaf' from the floor. In both cases they failed to win a hearing. In analysing how this result was achieved, Collins highlights two things: the thematic building up of an evaluative context or theme to transform meaning and at the same time the use of one language to speak through another. Reid repeatedly links the words 'co-operation' and 'butcher'. As he does, the bland mask of John Davies is peeled away to reveal the saturnine visage of Nicholas Ridley. The language of neo-monetarist class hatred is made to speak through and annihilate the language of social democracy. At the same time McGarvey is implicitly exposed as an accomplice in a 'sensible compromise' that directly attacks the rights of his own members, the hard-fought differential in terms of wages and conditions over the lower Clyde. This then frames an appeal to identities that moves upwards from 'ourselves', 'our families', 'our community' to responsibility '... in the last resort to the British working-class'.

Collins then cites Volosinov on why linguistic analysis of this kind must be central to our understanding of history and social process. Language helps us pinpoint key moments of change:

Countless ideological threads running through all areas of social intercourse register effects in the word ... the word is the most sensitive index of social changes, and, what is more, of changes still in the process of growth, still without definitive shape and not as yet accommodated into already regularised and fully defined ideological systems. The word has the capacity to register all the transitory, delicate, momentary phases of social change.[23]

In this instance we can see this precisely. Reid and Airlie are willing to presume a certain development in wider class solidarity and understanding.

317

Responsibility to the British working-class figures in a way it did not two months before. But this presumption has to be carefully framed. The sectional understanding of rights, 'ourselves', is invoked to sustain the need for a fighting response before any use of the word 'class'. The condemnation of McGarvey is entirely implicit. The stewards could not be seen as attacking the official leadership or the Confed. Much of the finance for the work-in came from this source, and, far more important, the legitimacy of the work-in in the wider movement stemmed from the inability of the official leadership to find a pretext for any direct public attack. War could not be declared on this front. But the language of social democracy, in the mouth of John Davies, had to be destroyed.

Equally the other side of this implicit dialogue between the stewards and the government is highly revealing. Davies and his colleagues also operated within material, political constraints. On hindsight they may seem extremely stupid to have insisted on changes in wages and working conditions. If they had not, it is quite likely that Reid and Airlie would have been unable to hold the line. But Davies was also a prisoner of circumstance. The Heath government was trying to hold together quite opposed sections of British capital and of the Conservative Party. The monetarist right-wing was still present within the government. The whole point of the UCS closure had been to placate regional capital and show that the government would take action against inflationary wage pressures. This intent was spelled out in blood in the text of the Ridley letters. To attempt a resolution of the UCS dispute which failed even to remove wages differential would be to admit that the whole initiative had been a disaster – with great collateral damage to other aspects of the government's programme. Davies and the government gambled on the authority of McGarvey, the influence of the media and the fragility of any nascent development of a wider class commitment in the yards. The linguistic battle of positions on 24 September 1971 proved they were wrong.

The result left the stewards in charge. Within days Davies and his local representative Stenhouse were forced to recognize this and attempt direct approaches. The stewards used this to extract the first real concession: a tentative acceptance by Stenhouse that the new company should include three yards and that the government should take responsibility in addition for the future of the fourth yard, John Brown in Clydebank. Collins, in a further analysis, shows how the word 'cooperation' was reappropriated by the stewards as 'cooperation by and with Stenhouse and the government to save all the jobs' in an attempt to construct a new linguistic universe from which the government could not escape without further accusations of treachery. The following two months saw a waiting game. The government continued to look for concessions on wages and sought to use McGarvey as intermediary. The stewards refused to recognize the new company and continued to look for an unequivocal acceptance of a 'cumulative' retention of the four yards

318

with no concessions on wages.

By new year the stewards had won this particular round. The government could wait no longer. The miners' strike had begun. A wages offensive was expected from the engineers. A 'Scottish Assembly' was being convened by the STUC – threatening to bring together precisely the combination of trade union radicalism, national sentiment and community mobilization which would be most dangerous for the government's political base. Already in October senior cabinet figures had initiated a fundamental reappraisal of policy at a Chequers meeting organized by Lord Rothschild. This meeting had explored a return to the types of economic policy implemented by Labour: a concordat with the unions on wages in return for guarantees on regional policy and employment. By early 1972 other options had been exhausted and the urgency of a policy change had become inescapable. Ridley and Eden were thrown overboard. The government embarked on a full-scale attempt to recreate a social democratic image. This 'U-turn', involving a long-term schism within the Tory Party, was a fateful one. It meant a breach with the type of regional industrial baronage represented on the Clyde by Lithgow and Yarrow and with other Conservatives who hankered for a return to pre-Keynesian days. But at the time Heath and his colleagues saw this danger as being of less magnitude than a further slide to the left in the unions and more generally. The remainder of the year was spent attempting to buttress the position of social democracy within the trade union movement itself, and, more locally, helping Danny McGarvey emerge as the saviour of the John Brown yard.

Conclusions

We started with a hypothesis and a question. The hypothesis was that the UCS work-in was successful not because it posed some kind of threat to civil order but because its politics endangered the government's wider social legitimacy. The question followed directly from the hypothesis. If the real leverage of the work-in was based on its ability to project a sophisticated critique of government policy, one that exposed its class contradictions and posed an alternative, what was it that gave the UCS workers the capacity to sustain such politics?

Our analysis of language has sought to shed light on the process by which this was achieved. We chose two episodes. One was the projection of the work-in, internally and externally, during its very first days. The other came two months later – after a period in which the work-in had been the focus of national and international attention, but when it was meeting a far more dangerous and sustained attack from the government. In the first episode we see how carefully Reid has to approach the issue of class allegiances and any wider enunciation of a class analysis of government policy. The existence of different levels of language is palpable. But so also is the process of change. Reid's success depended on creating new contexts for conventional, received 'meanings', and doing so with all the affective force of emotion-charged linkages of 'core' meanings. Two months later this process of conceptual transformation could be referred to as a fact, something achieved: 'our responsibility to the British working-class'. Its weight was uncertain. Reid and Airlie were definitely not going into battle simply armed with appeals to class solidarity. Yet this 'class' sentiment was now seen to be part of the armoury on which they could call. It had become, at least temporarily, rooted in what Leontiev and Luria have called the 'soil' of received meaning – and to this extent, as Davies no doubt reflected, what were simply 'ideas' in June 1971 had become a material force by September.[24]

At the same time, analytically, the main point of the second episode demonstrates this process cannot occur voluntaristically, at will, as a result of the rhetorical ability of particular leaders. Language is tied 'by countless threads' to the wider unfolding of events, to the constraints of political economy and to the overall balance of class forces and prosecution of class strategies at governmental level. The use of the Ridley letters in September 1971 was so devastating because Davies remained tied to the agenda set out by Ridley in January 1970. It was not a matter of the compromising Mr Davies and the wicked Mr Ridley. In policy terms Davies *was* Ridley. He was still trying to force down wages and conditions to those on the lower Clyde.

The analysis of language in this way is therefore important not just because of what it reveals about process. It also helps pinpoint interactions and causality. Government formulations about negotiation and compromise fell precisely because they were linked materially to certain conditions that were still politically crucial in September 1971 but had been abandoned by February 1972. In the same way the analysis of language also helps frame and identify transformative processes within the working-class. Our examination here has only allowed us to explore one aspect of this: the interactions within the yard between the different levels of language and the differing conceptual constructions associated with different speech genres. This itself has had its own limitations. The analysis of language has been confined to two episodes. It rests on what was said by leaders – not the rank and file. The evidence for any conceptual change hinges on just one or two phrases. On the other hand, the language of September was perceptibly different from that of July, and would indicate that a process of transformation had begun. Further analysis of later mass meetings, specifically 21 September and 2 October 1972, shows that direct appeals to class solidarity were successful in overcoming breaches in the work-in during its final phase.[25]

So what was it, in terms of our original question, that gave the UCS workers the capacity for class struggle? It might appear that we are arguing, on the basis of different levels of language, that it was, quite simply, because they were led by Communists. Indeed, this is an explanation that has often been put forward. But this is not the intention. Our objective has been to show that the relationship was *not* a passive one. Each mass meeting was critical. A wrong step at any point, a failure to keep the initiative in debate, would have led to collapse and defeat – as did happen in so many other disputes. Success depended on an active and transformative relationship. Language is the witness to it. We will conclude with a final quotation from Reid in March 1971:

> The Tories ... in pushing ahead with their policies ... calculate on the right-wing of the labour movement playing its traditional role of holding back and dissipating the fighting potential of the working-class ... [But] masses of people have adopted slogans and attitudes which a few years ago were exclusive to the left. There is a new, profound class note running through almost every discussion among shop stewards and trade unionists. It is little wonder that right-wing Labour leaders show signs of alarm at these developments. The mass pressure from below, the new left forces that are emerging, are capable of breaking the paralysing grip of the right-wing on the movement. In other words, the present struggle has to be consciously seen as having the potential for laying the basis for a new radical left alignment within the British labour movement ...[26]

Table 10.1 UCS Work-In: summary of main events

Government announces end of subsidy	14 June 1971
First mass demonstration and regional general strike	23 June 1971
Report of the 'Four Wise Men'	29 July 1971
First redundancies: Work-In starts	30 July 1971
First all-British shop stewards' meeting	10 Aug. 1971
Emergency session of STUC	16 Aug. 1971
TUC General Council meets in Glasgow	17 Aug. 1971
Second mass demonstration and regional strike	18 Aug. 1971
STUC Inquiry begins: Ridley letters published	1 Sept. 1971
Government announces Govan Ship Builders' Board	21 Sept. 1971
Government concedes third yard, Scotstoun	29 Sept. 1971
STUC convenes first assembly	14 Feb. 1972
Government announces £35m package to finance three yards	28 Feb. 1972
White Paper on industrial and regional development	28 March 1972
Deal agreed to support fourth (Clydebank) yard; Work-In ends	9 Oct. 1972

Notes

We would like to thank Chik Collins for his comments and for permission to cite unpublished materials. Much of the substantive argument and supporting evidence for this paper can be found in J. Foster and C. Woolfson, *The Politics of the UCS Work-In: class alliances and the right to work* (1986).

1.   B. Hogwood, *Government and Shipbuilding: the politics of industrial change*, (Farnborough, 1979), p. 162

2.   B. Strath, *The Politics of De-Industrialisation: the contraction of the West European shipbuilding industry* (1987), p. 127, stresses the wider political pressure exerted by the work-in.

3.   Shipyard identities are examined at some length in Chapter 3 of Foster and Woolfson, *Politics of the UCS Work-In.*

4.   The UCS work-in provides an unusually rich resource of language. All shop stewards' meetings and mass meetings from 10 August 1971 onwards were tape recorded. This material has been transcribed together with some television coverage from June and July. The lack of comprehensive materials for the first six weeks of the dispute represents a significant loss. But what is preserved is of great analytical use. References will be either to Foster and Woolfson, *Politics of the UCS Work-In* (where materials have been previously cited) or to the Glasgow University Archive copies of the transcripts. For other important struggles in 1971–2, see McIlroy, 'Notes on the Communist Party and Industrial Politics' and Lyddon, '"Glorious Summer", 1972' in this volume.

5.   J. Vernon, *Politics and People: a study in English political culture, c. 1815–1867* (Cambridge, 1993); P. Joyce, *Visions of the People: industrial England and the question of Class, c. 1848–1914* (Cambridge, 1991); G. Eley, 'Is all the world a text? From social history to the history of society two decades later', in T. MacDonald, (ed.), *The Historical Turn in Human Sciences*, (Ann Arbor, 1992).

6.   Vernon, *Politics and People*, p. 5.

7.   Ibid., p. 6.

8.   G. Stedman Jones, *Languages of Class: studies in English working-class history, 1832–1982* (Cambridge, 1983).

9.   P. Anderson, *In the Tracks of Historical Materialism* (1983), provides an illuminating critique.

10.   L. Vygotsky, *Thought and Language* (Massachusetts, 1962, translated from 1934 Russian edition, the first major text available in the West); V. Volosinov, *Marxism and the Philosophy of Language* (1973, translation from the 1930 Leningrad edition). A.R. Luria's *Cognitive Development: its cultural and social foundations* (1976), reports research conducted as a member of the Vygotsky group in the 1930s. AN. Leontiev, *Activity, Consciousness and Personality* (New Jersey, 1978) is a post-war restatement broadly representative of the continuing thinking and research of this group in the 1950s and

1960s. A more journalistic appreciation is given in K. Levitin, *One is Not Born a Personality* (Moscow, 1982). E. Ilyenkov, *The Dialectic of the Abstract and the Concrete in Marx's Capital* (Moscow, 1980) defends important elements of the Marxist tradition within which Vygotsky worked and provides a philosophy of language and meaning that is directly parallel to Vygotsky's psychology. Ilyenkov was himself a major post-war proponent of the ideas of Vygotsky and Leontiev. C. Woolfson's 'Culture, language and human personality', *Marxism Today*, August 1977, represents an early statement in English of the importance of Vygotsky and Volosinov for social science. J.V. Wertsch, *Vygotsky and the Social Formation of the Mind* (1985) was the first major full-length study. Wertsch's *Voices of the Mind* (1991) provides a further personal development of these ideas. D. Bakhurst, *Consciousness and Revolution in Soviet Philosophy* (Cambridge, 1991) criticizes aspects of Werstch's interpretation – as does C. Collins, 'Language, ideology and the development of social consciousness: an attempted application of the theories of L.S. Vygotsky and V.N. Volosinov to contemporary sociopolitical conflict in the West of Scotland', unpublished PhD thesis, University of Paisley, 1997. C. Collins, 'Pragmatics of emancipation: a critical review of the work of Michael Huspek', *Journal of Pragmatics*, 25, pp. 791–817, provides a methodological comparison of Volosinov and Huspek. M. Huspek, 'Language and power', *Language in Society*, 20, 1, 1991, and 'Oppositional codes and social class relations', *British Journal of Sociology*, 45, 1, 1994, are the most accessible introductions to his work. See also C. Brandist, 'Gramsci, Bakhtin and the semiotics of hegemony', *New Left Review*, 216, March 1996.

11. Foster and Woolfson, *Politics of the UCS Work-In*, p. 197.
12. Ibid., pp. 227–9.
13. The liquidator, Courtney Smith, made few statements during the work-in itself and had to tread a very careful line between his legal commitments to the creditors, who wanted the UCS to maximize income from existing contracts and as far as possible for the yards to remain in operation, and the government who still remained in control of credits attached to export orders. After the work-in concluded, he gave a talk to the Publicity Club of Glasgow which was partly reported in the *Scotsman*, 18 November 1972. There he pours scorn on those in London who talked of civil conflict and 'tanks in the yards', but stresses the immense political pressures placed by the work-in on the West of Scotland community. The government were bemused 'as the wind they sowed in the liquidation of UCS reaped a political whirlwind of opposition, intrigue and of moral conflict' – reaching not just the Conservative Party and the trade union movement but the wider communities affected by the closure. He describes the clergy in Clydebank as 'perplexed and worried over losing their livelihoods or falling in with Communists'.
14. Volosinov, *Marxism and the Philosophy of Language*, p. 102.
15. R. van der Veer and J. Valsiner, *Understanding Vygotsky: a quest for synthesis* (Oxford, 1993), pp. 361–72, examine the common sources used by

324

Volosinov and Vygotsky.

16.   A.N. Leontiev, *Activity, Consciousness and Personality* (New Jersey, 1978), p. 94.

17.   Vernon, *Politics and People*, p. 119.

18.   Cited by C. Collins, 'To concede or to contest: language and class struggle', in C. Barker and P. Kennedy (eds), *To Make Another World: studies in protest and collective action* (Aldershot, 1996), p. 77.

19.   Ibid.

20.   Volosinov, *Marxism and the Philosophy of Language*, p. 21.

21.   UCS Transcripts, folder 3, tape 3, side A.

22.   As cited by Collins, 'To concede or to contest', pp. 78–9.

23.   Collins, ibid., pp. 74–5, citing Volosinov, *Marxism and the Philosophy and Language* (1986 edition), p. 19. Collins explores these issues further in 'Foregrounding language in housing and urban research', paper presented to seminar on Discourse and Urban Change, Centre for Housing Research and Urban Studies, University of Glasgow, 2–3 June, 1997.

24.   A.N. Leontiev and A.R. Luria, 'The psychological ideas of L.S. Vygotsky', in B. Wolman (ed.), *The Historical Roots of Contemporary Psychology* (1968).

25.   This analysis is made in Foster and Woolfson, *Politics of the UCS Work-In*, pp. 360–76.

26.   Ibid., pp. 221–22.

325

CHAPTER ELEVEN

'Glorious Summer', 1972: the High Tide of Rank and File Militancy

Dave Lyddon

The most enduring symbol of the industrial politics of the 1970s has been the so-called 'Winter of Discontent' of 1978–9, popularly identified with losing the Labour Party the 1979 general election. But, in another phrase from the opening speech of William Shakespeare's *Richard III*, there was also a 'glorious summer' in the 1970s – the events of 1972 referred to by Seamus Milne just before the 1997 TUC conference:

> We are ... a very long way from the high water mark of trade unionism reached by the unions in the seventies. Twenty five years ago, five ... dockers jailed for defying anti-union legislation were carried shoulder high from Pentonville prison after the Tory government was forced to release them in the face of a TUC-threatened general strike. And ... Arthur Scargill was catapulted to national fame in the first of two devastating miners' strikes that drove the Heath administration from power.[1]

The period 1968–74 witnessed the biggest strike wave in Britain for half a century.[2] But 1972 stands out as its zenith, a year distinguished by working-class victories achieved through the use of militant tactics. John Goodman summarized the main features: 'The miners made their ... strike effective by large-scale picketing of power stations, sending mobile groups of pickets to areas remote from the coal fields. The dockers and building workers copied this tactic ... Sit-ins and factory occupations occurred in the engineering disputes'. He described the events surrounding the dockers' imprisonment as 'momentous'.[3]

Many early commentators were in no doubt as to the significance of the events of that year. Before 1972 had finished, Charles Drake was claiming that it 'must go down as the year in which Britain saw some of the liveliest picketing since the General Strike'.[4] Writing after the 'Winter of Discontent', but before the 1984–5 miners' strike, James Cronin suggested that the strike wave of 1968–72 'was the most important domestic event, or series of events, in post-war British history'.[5] James Hinton was less emphatic but did argue that the 1972 miners' victory, 'after a massive and highly visible strike, marked by the use of flying pickets ... helped to generate a mood of euphoric combativity in the ranks of organized labour', and that, despite the unofficial nature of the dockers' boycott, 'escalating spontaneous strikes ... forced the General Council to threaten a general strike'.[6]

Early accounts often approved of, and sometimes even celebrated, the working-class victories of 1972. More recent commentary has been dominated by very different interpretations. The most prominent has been the demonization of the entire decade, epitomized by Labour Prime Minister Tony Blair's comments at the 1997 TUC: 'Labour would not allow a return "to the days of industrial warfare, strikes without ballots, mass and flying pickets, secondary action and all the rest"'.[7] Similar sentiments have, unsurprisingly, been staple fare in Conservative politicians' memoirs. Another response has been to sanitize the events of 1972, stressing the role of the official movement, including the TUC, and playing down the importance of rank and file activity; this has been the position of trade union leaders, particularly current TUC General Secretary John Monks, and their supporters in the press. A third reaction, typified by much recent academic work, has been either to ignore the events or, by basic errors of fact, to alter their significance. All three responses, with their different political agendas, are united in expunging the memory of the high tide of rank and file militancy in post-war Britain.

There were many important industrial struggles at the time: for example, the UCS work-in, which continued well into 1972 and which is analysed elsewhere in this book, and the successful railway workers' dispute that spring which was conducted according to the requirements of the Industrial Relations Act 1971.[8] But this chapter will confine itself to discussion of the three biggest victories of 1972 – in the docks and the mining and building industries – before contrasting them briefly with the ineffective engineering factory sit-ins in Manchester. The strikes over wages in mining and building were both extremely successful, the former obliterating the Heath government's attempts at voluntary incomes policy and the latter coming soon before a statutory pay freeze was announced. The dockers' unofficial picketing and 'blacking' activities in their campaign against the effects of containerization on their employment opportunities dealt the death blow to the Industrial Relations Act. A single chapter can only necessarily give limited detail on these four industrial movements and thus concentrates on a number of key themes.

All four were run mainly from below by rank and file activists: the coal strike was official, but was characterized by mass involvement, with some activities going well beyond official guidelines; the building strike was official, but the early strategy of limited selective strikes was superseded when rank and file members escalated it in practice into an attempted all-out strike; and the dockers' activities were totally unofficial, except for the national strike from late July to mid-August which came after the release of the dockers from Pentonville. Given that many union lay activists also hold official

327

positions or sit on union committees, there has often been some confusion
as to what is official and what is unofficial policy or action. The mass participation in the miners' strike and eventually in the building workers' strike
blurred the distinction. Sometimes full-time officials were pulled along by
rank and file initiatives though they might take credit for any successes.[9]
The action inspired by unofficial leaders in the docks was disowned by the
official TGWU leadership but, as the dockers (in both the TGWU and NASD)
supported it, this opposition had little effect; and the unofficial campaign
was a prelude to the official national strike and strengthened the officials'
negotiating position. The shorter working week national claim in engineering was pursued most vigorously in Manchester by an official district-wide
campaign of industrial action which rapidly led to a spate of factory occupations. These were necessarily led by the individual workforces, but the
explosion of militancy demonstrated in each act of taking over employers'
property was strait-jacketed by the local officials' and leading stewards' rigid
adherence to the national officials' strategy of bargaining plant by plant.

What is now called 'secondary picketing' in statute law – picketing
workplaces other than one's own – was common to three of the movements
(workers' action in the engineering sit-in strikes was confined to their own
individual workplaces). But there were important differences. The miners
were employed in large numbers at a few hundred collieries and other ancillary sites; their main picketing activities were away from the coalfields,
particularly aimed at stopping the general movement of coal and coke as
well as of other essential materials used in power stations. This required a
large number of separate picket lines trying to stop transport workers from
moving goods. These were sometimes needed at short notice (flying pickets), and occasionally in large numbers (mass pickets). By contrast, building
workers, while they did eventually picket to stop the movement of cement,
were mainly concerned to close down a huge number of often relatively
small construction sites and to win more workers to the strike. This required
mobile, sometimes mass, pickets. Picketing by London dockers was a necessary adjunct to the national unofficial policy of blacking particular
companies. Their picket lines were away from the docks, at container bases,
and again only sometimes took on a mass character (though Humberside
dockers were later involved in several large-scale confrontations).

The internal politics of the four disputes cannot be fully analysed here but
some brief observations can be made. Rank and file action lay at the heart of
all of them and was central to their success or failure, but its nature and role
differed in each. In the miners' dispute the ballot decision for a national
strike and the stance of the left on the NUM Executive ensured that rank and
file activists were able to build upon an official platform which endorsed the
need for solidarity action and picketing to achieve it. In contrast with this
relative internal unity, the dockers were in direct conflict with TGWU leaders who opposed their militant tactics. In the building strike there was an

'in-between' situation: the national leadership called for selective strikes and the activists were able to develop this into a broader stoppage facilitated by the earlier work of the *Building Workers' Charter*, a Communist Party (CP)-inspired rank and file organization with strength on the sites. In further contrast, the national leadership of the engineering dispute, having determined upon plant-by-plant bargaining, took firm steps to ensure that a more coordinated, centralized approach was not adopted. Far from providing an alternative to official strategy, as the *Charter* activists did, the engineering Broad Left loyally enforced it. The engineering dispute provides a contrast with the other three where the grass-roots left, particularly CP supporters, organized and orchestrated the militancy which sometimes developed beyond their expectations.[10]

The miners' strike

The miners' strike was the first national official strike in the industry since 1926. It lasted from 9 January to 25 February, involved 308,500 workers directly and 'lost' 10,725,000 working days.[11] The post-war period had witnessed a significant contraction in the number of collieries and miners, while the piece-work system had constrained national unity among the workforce. With the introduction of the National Power Loading Agreement in 1966, miners on all new coalfaces went on to a flat rate system of pay and by the end of 1971 almost all faceworkers were on the same hourly rate. The potential unity that this unleashed was fed by a significant material factor. The changeover involved many miners having their wages cut: first of all, cuts in money wages for those whose piece-work earnings had been higher than the new flat rates; second, cuts in real wages for miners in the higher-rated areas who received small pay rises while miners in lower-rated areas caught them up. A further 70,000 underground workers were then brought under the Third National Daywage Structure in June 1971 with a significant percentage also standing to face pay reductions when moved to a different job. Not only had miners overall slipped down the 'league table' of earnings, large numbers had experienced actual wage cuts. As the official historian of post-war mining noted: 'It was the complicating changes in the wage structure that united the interests of mineworkers in aggressive national action'.[12]

As well as having a particularly strong reason for striking against the government-dictated pay offer, the miners had also developed their own tactics which would be put to their ultimate test in 1972. In unofficial strikes in 1969 and 1970 Yorkshire miners (led mainly by the Doncaster panel) had picketed out miners in many other collieries. The 1970 strike followed a 55 per cent vote for a national wage strike at a time when the NUM still operated a two-thirds majority rule for such action; the union's 1971 annual conference changed this minimum to 55 per cent and later that year nearly

59% voted for action over their next pay claim. Vic Allen has noted that the overtime ban which preceded the strike concentrated miners' minds on 'how low their basic wages were' and hardened support for the strike.[13]

The national strike threat was not taken particularly seriously and press comment suggested that the strike itself would have limited impact. Matters turned out differently. The incumbent Prime Minister Edward Heath's recent reflections confirm the shock that the strike gave the Conservative government: 'we did not anticipate the spasm of militancy from a union which had been relatively quiet for so long, and the tactics which it was willing to adopt. The use of "flying pickets" … took us unawares'.[14] Margaret Thatcher has recalled that in Cabinet meetings before the strike, 'The possibility of effective mass picketing, which would prevent oil and coal getting to power stations, was simply not on the agenda'.[15] The Home Secretary at the time, Reginald Maudling, later wrote memorably about the police's closure of the Saltley coke depot in Birmingham on 10 February: 'Some of my colleagues asked me afterwards, why I had not sent in troops to support the Police, and I remember asking them one simple question: "If they had been sent in, should they have gone in with their rifles loaded or unloaded?"'[16]

The miners' first concern was their own collieries. During the strike, 'The [TUC] General Council were concerned that … *in spite of instructions from the NUM*, safety requirements were being met [at that point] in only 36 pits' (emphasis added).[17] By the end of the strike, only 30 of the 289 collieries had full safety cover.[18] The *Economist* claimed that Midlands miners, for example, 'had believed that the damage to underground equipment would prove to be their biggest bargaining counter' and that they were 'frankly amazed at the havoc they appear to have caused [by picketing]. None of them expected the strike to bite so deeply'.[19]

The crucial factor was secondary picketing. The union's national office issued instructions on picketing power stations but not until a few days into the strike, by which time miners in the different areas were creating their own solutions in practice.[20] Non-mining regions of Britain were allocated to different NUM areas; for example, the Barnsley panel of the Yorkshire miners was given East Anglia to picket, and Robert Taylor recounts how, when the tactic of spreading pickets thinly over too many locations there was failing, Scargill successfully pushed for mass picketing to be organized at each site in turn.[21] With similar action occurring all over the country, Allen argues that 'the scale and intensity of the miners' participation in the [1972] strike distinguished it from all other strikes in recent trade union history'. He cites an estimate of 500 establishments being picketed on a 24-hour basis by an average of 40,000 miners each day, and that some 200,000 miners were involved in strike duties. A government statement declared that 263 people (not all, but mainly, miners) had been arrested for offences connected with picketing.[22] Allen summarizes the arguments about the miners' picketing: 'The complaint' against the picketing 'was not specifically its mass scale, or its mobility or ... its legality, *but its effectiveness*' (emphasis added).[23] In fact, Lawrence Daly, the NUM General Secretary, told the Wilberforce Court of Inquiry in mid-February that: 'the Government has said that it has to act now because of the effectiveness of our pickets'.[24]

The Times noted that 'the picketing succeeded only because individual members of other unions respected the pickets'.[25] On 10 January the TUC General Council had 'requested members of its affiliated unions not to cross picket lines', but this applied only to the movement of coal.[26] In practice, union members tended to respect picket lines with other purposes. Several months after the strike *The Times* gave a graphic example:

> The driver and second man of a goods train of oil tankers ... refused to take their train out of the yards. They said there were pickets on the line. Management could see no pickets ... The driver rang ... [ASLEF] headquarters and asked for a picket. A frantic telephone call to the NUM ... led to the immediate dispatch of two 'flying pickets'. They unfurled a blanket bearing the slogan 'official NUM picket' from an overhead bridge and the train did not run.[27]

The most affected organization was the Central Electricity Generating Board which reported in early February that it was 'in a state of siege', complained of the 'unrelenting blockade' of power stations, and considered itself to be 'conducting a guerilla war'.[28] While the *Economist* pointed out towards the end of the strike that 'under existing civil law, companies whose oil has been stopped by the pickets at the power station gates could try taking them to court for inducing a breach of commercial contract', it also added that 'none has so far thought it worth a try'.[29]

Discussion of the 1972 miners' strike has increasingly revolved around the events at Saltley in east Birmingham. Engineering and car workers struck in support, with sufficient thousands of them marching to the coke depot to seal it off, forcing the police to shut it at 10.43 am on Thursday 10 February.[30] As Daly acknowledged a few days afterwards, 'the industrial workers of Birmingham marched in their thousands to join our picket line'.[31] Roger Geary's detailed account mentions Scargill's plea to the East Birmingham District Committee of the AUEW(E) on the night of Tuesday 8 February, but not the support from the NUVB and TGWU district committees or the shop stewards' meetings that occurred: 200 AUEW stewards met on the Wednesday afternoon and unanimously accepted their district committee's recommendation to join the picket line, while NUVB stewards came to similar conclusions on the Wednesday evening.[32] The importance of such outside support is underlined by the generally unacknowledged action of officers of the TGWU 5/35 branch, which organized the great majority of lorry drivers in the Birmingham conurbation. They took the decision before the end of the first day of the picket at Saltley (4 February) not to cross the line and also had a branch member permanently on the picket to turn back TGWU

drivers. This resulted in a dramatic reduction in the numbers of lorries crossing, and employers responded by using non-union firms which inevitably
led to a larger police presence.[33] One incident was recounted in *The Times*:
'pickets let down the tailboard of a loaded lorry and about three tons of coke
poured on to the road. Policemen had to shovel it on to the lorry to clear the
way'.[34]

Whatever the subsequent political symbolism of Saltley as the defining
moment in the strike, four days later, on 14 February, *The Times* reported
that 'the miners are strengthening their picket lines'. That day at the
Longannet power station in Scotland, a mass picket of some 2,000 was confronted by 400 police; thirteen pickets were arrested and charged with the
Scottish common law offence of 'mobbing and rioting'. The pickets were
detained in custody and would normally have been held until the following
week. A wave of protest saw the Lord Advocate (the senior government law
officer for Scotland) fly to Scotland on 16 February; the investigation was
speeded up and the pickets released on bail the next day.[35] By this time, as a
Court of Inquiry on the miners' claim was being held in an attempt by the
government to extricate itself from problems caused by growing power cuts,
pickets were being scaled down but not called off. Thus, for example, two of
the country's biggest oil refineries were still affected by the combination of
miners' pickets and sympathetic train drivers, who jointly stopped nearly all
oil products leaving.[36] And miners picketed the homes of three Coal Board
officials who had been doing safety work at Lewis Merthyr colliery in South
Wales (a form of picketing which would be unlawful a few days later under
the Industrial Relations Act).[37]

Stephen Milligan (Labour Correspondent of the *Economist*, later a Conservative MP) was in no doubt that picketing was the key factor which won
the strike, especially stopping oil and hydrogen from getting into the power
stations; interestingly, the Saltley incident is only singled out by him as 'the
most serious flouting of the law' during the strike.[38] Taylor's assessment of
the 1972 strike was that, 'If Heath had persisted with lorry convoys into the
power stations guarded by the police, the strike could well have gone down
to defeat'. Here, 'the massive, practical help from other trade unions and the
general public ... was crucial. The success of those flying pickets depended
on the support of the many. But the ultimate reason for victory was the spirit
of aggression and zeal displayed by rank and file miners'.[39]

Over the years there has been extensive revision by some academics not
only of the significance of the strike but also of its basic features. For example, Colin Crouch claimed that the prolonged nature of the strike led to miners
'developing new tactics to strengthen their action ... mass picketing', but
this occurred from almost the beginning of the strike.[40] One common strand
in recent comments has been the conflation of the miners' strikes of 1972
and 1974. Paul Blyton and Peter Turnbull claim that both these strikes were
'backed up by ... the use of mass and flying pickets', when that only applied

to the 1972 strike. They also claim that 'rising oil prices ... enhanced the disruptive potential of the miners' yet this feature was specific to the 1974 strike following the massive oil price rise in the autumn of 1973.[41] Derek Fatchett, a Labour MP, also wrongly made this point when arguing that in relation to the 1972 strike, 'it is ... necessary to assess coolly the contribution made by mass picketing to the outcome of the strike; other factors, particularly the dramatic shift in relative fuel prices, can be considered as of greater significance'.[42]

Most commentators on the early 1970s predictably mention the events at Saltley, though usually very briefly. Their accounts generally present a rather misleading picture of the process of picket mobilization. Thus Phil Scraton's 'From Saltley Gates to Orgreave' does not refer to the presence of non-miners on the picket that closed Saltley. Keith Middlemas mentions 'fresh waves of picket reserves' bringing the total at Saltley to 15,000 but similarly ignores the solidarity action. Kenneth Morgan writes of '15,000 massed pickets' without acknowledging outside support and of 'Arthur Scargill's massed legions at ... Saltley'.[43] Elsewhere, Morgan has referred to 'Arthur Scargill's "flying pickets"' at Saltley, which recalls Heath's biographer's (John Campbell's) phrase 'Scargill's flying pickets' and Thatcher's 'mass pickets led by Arthur Scargill ... [at] ... Saltley'.[44] This personalization and simplification of events has mainly occurred since the 1984–5 miners' strike; for example, Taylor's short 1993 account has 'an estimated 15,000 workers led by the Yorkshire miners under the Napoleonic style leadership of the young Arthur Scargill', which contrasts with his earlier detail of outside help for the miners and his earlier figure of 10,000 at Saltley.[45] John Monks of the TUC had a different agenda when arguing that the 'practical effect [of closing Saltley] was limited. But its significance was great. It seemed to say to trade unionists that the way to win disputes was by picketing in strength at key targets'. By contrast, and in a clear rebuke to the rank and file activists of 1972, he comments that:

the 1974 miners' strike did not rely on mass picketing but on TUC-supported guidelines of six pickets and agreements between the NUM and unions in transport and energy. These features did not create the same potent symbols as the 1972 strike, even though they worked faster, more effectively and more acceptably.[46]

In another vein altogether, SDP (former Labour) MP John Grant, wrote of the events at Saltley that the 'large-scale secondary picketing, intimidation and violence, was a new and brutish phenomenon in British industrial relations'.[47]

Assessing the impact of the strike, the economic historian William Ashworth has convincingly commented that 'for a number of years' one contribution to the price of coal being commercially competitive 'had been to keep the

333

lid on mining wages. In 1972 the lid was blown off and things would never be the same again'.[48] But the significance of the victory was not simply economic. Morgan argues that the miners' success in 1972 meant that 'Black Friday and the General Strike had finally been avenged'.[49] Certainly the miners' historic defeats in the 1921 and 1926 lockouts had been avenged through the first ever national strike by the NUM, whose crucial cutting edge – and we need to emphasize this point – was the inventive militant tactics of rank and file activists in the localities. Executive guidelines on safety cover were widely ignored. The Executive circulars intended to elicit solidarity from other workers at power stations, ports and oil depots, were built upon in practice. The national leadership's position provided legitimacy and officials went along with rank and file action with varying degrees of enthusiasm rather than attempting to curb it.

The dockers' entanglement with the Industrial Relations Act

By 1972 British dockers were experiencing a revolution in cargo-handling techniques. By an accident of timing, the dockers' unofficial campaign against the effects of containerization on dockers' job opportunities coincided with the implementation of the Industrial Relations Act. Although the campaign was industrial, it unleashed a train of events which became increasingly political. Fred Lindop records in some detail the main developments and demonstrates that the continuing unofficial nature of the action not only put pressure on the dockers' main union, the TGWU, to eventually call an official national strike over the issue but also inadvertently stiffened the resolve of the largest TUC unions to maintain their policy of non-registration under the Act.[50]

The unofficial national port shop stewards' committee had agreed in December 1971 that all 'stuffing and stripping' of containers should be performed by registered dockworkers. A one-day unofficial national strike and lobby of the TGWU docks trade group committee in January 1972 received widespread support. In Liverpool an unofficial joint TGWU committee of dockers and members of the union's commercial road transport trade group then drew up a document to be signed by hauliers using Merseyside docks. Most signed when their drivers were confronted at the dock gates. Heaton Transport of St Helens, however, took a case to the National Industrial Relations Court (NIRC) in March, and the TGWU was fined £5,000. Another £50,000 fine followed in April. None the less the blacking of Heaton's lorries continued despite TGWU officers' attempts to get it called off. With the threat of sequestration of assets hanging over the TGWU for its continuing contempt of court, the TUC General Council advised the union to pay the fine (and hence to recognize the court). Even with its General Secretary Jack Jones supporting the TUC decision, the TGWU General Executive

Council only agreed to this by the chair's casting vote.

The union duly paid up but took the case to the Court of Appeal in early May. By then the national stewards' committee had already extended the blacking to two firms in each port. This prompted a case against the chair of the Hull port shop stewards, Walter Cunningham (who refused to attend the NIRC), and the TGWU, which was eventually dropped by the company, Panalpina. In London, the inability to sufficiently enforce the boycott led to a decision to directly picket the depots of Dagenham Cold Storage and Midland Cold Storage and to black all firms using them. As this was not totally effective, a group of stewards from the Royal Docks picketed the Chobham Farm site in Stratford (east London) where lorries turned away from Dagenham were being diverted. When the chair and secretary of the London (and the Royal) docks stewards' committee argued against this move, their objections were overruled in practice and the site was picketed again.

On 13 June the Appeal Court (led by Lord Denning) overruled the NIRC in the Heaton case, affirming that unions were not responsible for the actions of their stewards, thus crucially leaving the way open for imprisonment of individuals. This judgment caused Heath to fume: 'This was exactly what the union militants wanted. Even though they had been using their strength to bully and blackmail the nation, they could now pose as the underdogs'.[51] The NIRC had already made an interim order against three stewards picketing Chobham Farm. This was now altered to an order threatening them with imprisonment if they did not attend the court on Friday 16 June and satisfactorily explain their conduct. Unofficial strikes broke out at most ports during Thursday and Friday. The union representing two of the men, the NASD, was not persuaded by officers from the TGWU and the TUC to agree to their members being represented in court. A large picket assembled at Chobham Farm on the Friday but no arrests took place. Lord Denning had engineered a meeting between the Official Solicitor (who acted for those unable to represent themselves in legal matters) and Peter Pain, QC (who normally acted for the TGWU). This enabled the Official Solicitor to instruct Pain to apply to the Appeal Court which set aside the committals due to a technicality.[52] Denning was aware of the dock strike and its implications. He later commented that: 'The country was at crisis point', and has claimed elsewhere that 'We'd been told there was a danger of a general strike'.[53]

The picketing continued and Midland Cold Storage applied to the NIRC, naming seven dockers. Eventually warrants went out for the arrest of five of them on Friday 21 July: four were found that day and lodged in Pentonville prison while, Vic Turner, the fifth, was arrested picketing the prison the following day! The events between the arrests of the dockers and their release on Wednesday 26 July are a subject of some debate. The TUC's eventual decision to call a one-day strike has over time been accorded the status of the key factor in the dockers' release. Yet TUC General Secretary Vic Feather was publicly arguing on the Saturday against a general strike, while Jack

Jones made it clear that the imprisoned dockers were to be given no assistance by the TGWU and its officials were not to visit them.[54] But, as with Chobham Farm, there was an unofficial national docks stoppage and this time the dockers also sought immediate support from other workers.

> The London docks stewards set up a permanent picket of Pentonville Prison. It became a focus for protest demonstrations and a centre from which delegates and flying pickets were sent out, first to every port in the country then to other sections of industry ... [A]ll the major engineering and motor plants were on holiday. Dock stewards turned their attention on the first evening to Fleet Street, knowing that if they could shut the papers they would have a massive and immediate impact. But the initial response was cool. The papers appeared the next morning, and played down the significance of the jailings, trying to kill the dockers' campaign with silence. The following day docks stewards visited virtually every father and mother of the chapel ... in Fleet Street, aided by leading print union activists ... Within two days Fleet Street was closed down.[55]

The electricians in Fleet Street were later to chant: 'We got the dockers out'.[56] While the unofficial national dock strike, combined with the shutting down of national newspapers, ensured that the dockers' imprisonment would not be sidelined, the strike movement was developing rapidly elsewhere despite the holiday season. Lindop estimates that 'at the very least, 90,000 workers, including 40,000 dockers, were on indefinite strike by the time that the five were released. As many as 250,000 had come out for one or two days by Wednesday, with longer strikes threatened if the men were not released quickly'.[57]

The dockers could not be released until they had purged their contempt, which they were determined not to do. According to Gerald Dorfman, senior ministers were confident on the Monday that the Law Lords would reverse the Appeal Court judgment on the Heaton case and 'thus open the way for the jailed workers to be released'. But they did not know when.[58] Heaton had appealed against Denning's judgment and when the Law Lords started the hearing on 11 July, it was believed that their ruling would come after the normal two-month summer break. Even by the end of an unusually short hearing, on 19 July, the judgment was expected on 31 July at the earliest. But the arrests of 21 July and the developing strike movement changed everything. Lindop suggests that 'at some time on Monday night or Tuesday morning, 24 and 25 July, the timetable was changed and the process accelerated'.[59] We now know that Lord Hailsham as Lord Chancellor told the Lord Chief Justice, Lord Widgery, early on the Tuesday morning that the Lords' judgment would be given the next day and his diary entry noted that it was 'confidently expected' that it would reverse the Appeal Court ruling.[60] Dorfman interviewed Conservative MP Nicholas Scott on the Wednesday and wrote that 'Ministers heard [on the Tuesday] that the Lords would give their judgment in the Heaton case the following day ...[and] also heard the rumour that the news would be "good"'.[61]

In an important article published several months later, John Griffith noted that the Official Solicitor had unsuccessfully attempted to get the NIRC to reconvene on the Tuesday afternoon so that he could apply for the dockers' release and 'was told to apply "not later than Wednesday afternoon"'. This was significant as the Law Lords gave their judgment 'in the late morning of Wednesday 26 July', only seven days after the hearing closed. It was a single judgment, which was 'uncommon'; and 'it was handed to counsel, shortly before it was delivered, not printed (as is usual) but duplicated and with typed and manuscript corrections'. Griffith contended powerfully that the NIRC's argument on the Wednesday afternoon that the Law Lords' decision had 'entirely changed' the situation, conveniently ignored the fact that the dockers had been jailed for contempt of the NIRC, which contempt they continued to refuse to purge, and not for 'blacking'.[62] As Michael Zander noted: 'Force of circumstances required the sacrifice of the rule of law at the risk of some lessening of respect for the courts'.[63] Reflecting on the events, the *Economist* commented that 'the government's attitude ... was remarkably relaxed and it was plain that Mr Heath had decided this was not going to be his general strike week. By Wednesday it was clear why. The House of Lords handed down its ruling'.[64] At the heart of Griffith's explanation of judicial actions concerning both Pentonville and Chobham Farm were the following observations:

> The community of rulers is a close and narrow community. Judges and politicians do not have to agree on the details of policies, they do not have to belong to the same political party. *There is no conspiracy because there is no need for a conspiracy.* All share the same fundamental premises. And one of these is the desirability of avoiding widespread industrial unrest.[65] (emphasis added)

At the present time we do not know how critical the role of the TUC was in this episode. Its most recent historian writes of 'the freeing of the "Pentonville five" following the TUC's threat of a one-day general strike' which was to take place on 31 July.[66] Heath was informed by the TUC's Finance and General Purposes Committee on the Monday that the General Council would be voting two days later on a motion (from the AUEW, the union most vociferous against the Act) for such a strike. But the TUC's hand had been forced by the developing unofficial strike movement. However, by the Wednesday the situation had changed and Peter Paterson has commented that when the TUC General Council 'decided [on Wednesday 26 July] on the strike there was no one in the room who did not realise that the Official Solicitor was about his benign and healing work, and that the dockers were likely to be released from Pentonville that very afternoon'.[67] A few years later, Michael Moran observed of Paterson's article that, 'I have received independent assurances that this is an accurate account'.[68]

337

In his attempt to play down the significance of the unofficial action around Pentonville ('to insiders these trade union victories looked a little different'), Monks confuses the actual sequence of events. He wrongly asserts that the 'Court of Appeal ... held the union to be liable for the actions of its shop stewards' and that the House of Lords reversed this, thus 'creating martyrs'. He then claims that 'Had the Court of Appeal's position been upheld ... there could have been a very different outcome'. But the TGWU had been fined by the NIRC and, ironically, without the union's appeal there would not have been the Court of Appeal decision that unions were *not* liable for the actions of their stewards, which left the way open inexorably for martyrs.[69] Dennis Kavanagh's account is bizarre: 'In August 1972 ... a major dock strike' took place over the NIRC's 'decision to fine errant trade unions, and the government backed down'.[70]

While the legal detail can certainly cause confusion, there is surprising disagreement among academics about the length of the period of imprisonment but less surprising failure to acknowledge the unofficial sympathetic strikes in protest (a point well illustrated by Lindop).[71] Keith Laybourn claims that the Pentonville five were released 'after only two days' following a national strike of 170,000 dockers (Henry Pelling had earlier also cited the same number of dockers on strike).[72] Yet this is the Department of Employment's official figure for all strikers; there were only about 40,000 dockers at the time and 35,435 took part in the subsequent official strike of registered ports. Middlemas dates the release one week after the 21 July imprisonment. Taylor recounts that 'the trade union response ... [to the dockers' imprisonment] ... was immediate. The TUC threatened to call a one day general strike ... and demonstrators gathered outside the prison as thousands of dockers around Britain stopped work'; he gives the date of release as 1 August. Peter Dorey repeats the 1 August date, as does Morgan.[73]

Morgan elsewhere refers to 'continuing industrial action by militants in London, Liverpool and Hull', but (as in his account of Saltley) makes no mention of wider support. Martin Holmes only refers to 'a national dock strike and demonstrations at the prison', while both Kavanagh and Henry Phelps Brown claim that a dock strike was only 'threatened'. Robert Currie ignores the strike movement altogether in his account, while Alan Sked and Chris Cook refer to the events at Chobham Farm in June but do not mention Pentonville at all.[74] Milligan goes to the other extreme and claims that as well as dock strikes, 'workers in ... Fleet Street and other militant industries immediately walked out', missing the point that support had to be argued for.[75] Perhaps the most factually incorrect and misleading account is one of the most recent:

> Some rank and file militants were jailed for contempt of the new act but had to be released because of protests from sympathizers. Further embarassment followed when the High Court reversed two Industrial Relations Court decisions. If this

was not enough, Heath next found himself pitched into a damaging conflict with the miners [the January–February 1972 strike!].[76]

However, all writers are happily agreed on the outcome of the Pentonville affair. As Denning's later account states: 'The political consequences were immense. The Industrial Relations Act had been shattered. The Government had set up the Industrial Court to enforce the Act. Yet it had been shown by events to be powerless'.[77] Following the dockers' release from Pentonville, Heath himself decided that the government, during the official dock strike, would not use the cooling-off and balloting powers available under the Industrial Relations Act (which measures had already backfired on the government in the earlier official railway dispute).[78] While Taylor's observation that 'a combination of fortuitous events in the spring and early summer of 1972 brought about the early demise of the Act' is uncontentious, it understates the critical importance of the dockers' refusal to call off their unofficial campaign.[79] Their dogged resistance to the blandishments and demands of TGWU and TUC leaders in this respect underlines the tenacious independence of rank and file dockers. Without this the court cases would not have occurred and the TUC policy of non-registration under the Act would have collapsed.[80]

The building workers' strike

The building workers' strike, starting on 26 June and finishing on 22 September, was estimated to involve in total 146,030 workers directly and 9,835 indirectly (i.e. laid off in the same establishments) and 'lost' 3,836,500 working days.[81] It consisted of selective stoppages for the first six weeks before it escalated into a much wider conflict, with the unions at its peak claiming 270,000 workers out at some 9,000 sites.[82]

The circumstances facing the building workers when they started their official pay strike at the end of June 1972 were very different from the those confronting the miners and the dockers. First, the majority of the workers in the industry were not unionized and huge numbers were scattered on small sites across the country: this presented a major obstacle to any national industrial action. Second, for those who were unionized, the main union in the industry, UCATT, had only just been created from the merger of three unions facing declining membership and bankruptcy, and its authority had yet to be established. Third, there had been an active rank and file organization since 1970, the *Building Workers' Charter*; but given the dominance of casual work in building, the rank and file activists' relationship with the mass of the membership in the industry was necessarily different from that prevailing among the more settled workforces in mining or even on the only recently decasualized docks.

339

The build-up to the strike saw the emergence of centres of union organization in a number of towns, notably Birmingham and Liverpool, with campaigns against 'the lump' system of paying building workers.[83] The strike's beginnings were inauspicious. The plan was to escalate slowly though selective regional strikes, with six extra sites being brought out each week in every UCATT region. The numbers on strike at any particular time were a constant bone of contention, with the employers' estimates much lower than the union's. The first few weeks of the strike were also notable for the lack of coverage in the press: 'For this relief, Mr Heath ... should be enormously grateful'. But by early August the press was reporting that there were roughly 20,000 workers on strike on about 300 sites.[84]

The period from the end of July to the middle of August was a turning point in the strike. Terry Austrin claims that at the end of July the regional action committee in Birmingham (where the *Charter* was particularly strong) moved for an all-out stoppage, first in Birmingham and then in the region, to be achieved by the use of flying pickets. This local action reflected a wider mood, and a provisional settlement of the national strike, reported on 1 August, was abandoned by UCATT a week later as a number of area meetings also voted for all-out strikes. On 9 August the president of the National Federation of Building Trade Employers was reported as claiming that 'militants were moving from site to site inciting workers into strike action' and that 'these militants have used strongarm methods. They have called strikes official when they have not been'.[85] A week later, with 'intense pressure from militants for a total stoppage', the four unions – UCATT, TGWU, NUGMW and FTAT – agreed to strike employers with between 60 and 200 workers.[86] But the momentum was with the rank and file local activists. The employers' federation sent out 15,000 letters to member firms to compile dossiers on flying pickets, claiming that 'the moderate elements ... are being forced into intemperate action by travelling groups of militants which move from site to site'. By now UCATT's selective campaign had been 'wholly overtaken by militant action' and it was 'now busily declaring more and more official strikes to keep pace with the sites being unofficially pulled out by the militants'.[87] Austrin claims that all-out stoppages were achieved in London, Bristol, Birmingham, Manchester, Liverpool, Glasgow, Edinburgh and Dundee.[88]

As with the miners, the building workers did not confine their activities to their own workplaces: pickets were arrested, for example, outside Rugby Portland Cement Company in Birmingham in late August as cement companies were targeted to cut off supplies to working sites.[89] But with only about one-third of the industry's workforce unionized, stopping work at building sites was the overwhelming priority. Sometimes the pickets had to stay outside a site, such as one at Basildon, where, after a week of being forced to cross picket lines, twenty-five workers were flown in and out of the site by helicopter.[90]

A flying picket of some 250, transported in six coaches and a number of cars, travelled to Shrewsbury early in September. In itself this was unremarkable at the time. However, there were reports in *The Times* of an 'orgy of destruction' at one site. Out of this came the conspiracy charges that were to lead to the imprisonment of three pickets.[91] The charges were not brought until several months after the events and represented a very different way of dealing with the problem of picketing. By then the strike had finished. Despite its success – the *Economist*, for example, complained that 'while the Prime Minister was talking about wage restraint to the leaders of industry and the unions ... the building employers agreed to raise their already hyper-inflationary offer' – militant mass meetings in several of the largest towns refused to go back immediately, hoping to force extra concessions, though within a week there was a full resumption.[92]

Apart from events connected with Shrewsbury, relatively little has been written about the strike. UCATT's own later official record is misleading, obscuring the role of the rank and file in escalating the dispute. Thus 'with no sign of a tangible offer forthcoming, the strike rapidly escalated from being one of a selective nature to a full-scale industrial dispute'; 'the strike proved more successful than originally anticipated because, once started, a snowball effect became apparent and this culminated in an industry wide stoppage'; 'with no positive offer forthcoming, the area of the dispute was extended to cover all forms of building'.[93] Here, the rank and file disappear as the main actors. Milligan, however, was in no doubt that the 'flying pickets had a major impact. Without their efforts, the 1972 building strike might easily have folded up'. He argued that they were 'organized, not by the union, but by the unofficial groups of militants'. His agenda, however, was to highlight the apparent violence.[94] As Hugh Clegg has argued, 'in most strikes picketing is of little importance'; a national strike in a partially organized industry was an obvious exception, and the enthusiasm for such a daunting task was unlikely to come from above.[95]

Picketing

The combination of three features in the above disputes – the centrality of rank and file involvement, the widespread use of pickets, and the successful outcomes – was responsible for the immediate shift in policing policy in industrial disputes and the Conservatives' later legislative initiatives. Before the miners' strike had even finished, but after the closure of Saltley, an editorial in the *Financial Times* opined that 'mass pickets against industries and businesses not directly involved in the dispute has set a highly dangerous precedent'. At the same time it was recognized that the Industrial Relations Act, which did not fully become law until 28 February (after the miners' strike had finished), would have been inapplicable: 'First there are

341

the large numbers of people involved in the picketing. Second, in the current situation, court orders would probably be defied'.[96] Later in the year, the *Economist* argued that 'the rewarding of the miners' violent picketing ... led directly to the picketing of the container depots this summer ... [The] spectacular rewarding of this will make it easier to arrange tougher picketing in ... [future] ... strikes'.[97] This was not long in coming, with the escalation of the builders' action. However, the *Economist* did not immediately comment on this, and continued to complain that the use of flying mass pickets, where the police were unable to mobilize enough officers, meant that 'the initiative will always lie with the militants' and repeated that 'the tactics employed by the miners ... [were] used by the dockers with almost total impunity'.[98]

With the settlement in the building industry – 'surrender ... to a strike where there has been widespread use of violence by thuggish pickets who have been travelling round the country' – there was the expected refrain: 'Ever since the miners were allowed to get away with their mass pickets ..., violence has escalated 'rapidly'. This article, entitled 'Rent-a-thug?', continued: 'The main problem is not the present law [on picketing], but the lack of enforcement of it. Thousands of miners who picketed the Saltley depot appeared to lay themselves open to prosecution but no action was taken. During the building strike, employers have again been complaining about the lack of police intervention'.[99] At the end of the building strike, a correspondent on *The Times* noted that it had been 'the third major industrial dispute this year whose course was directed largely by the concerted action of pickets'; that the 'flying pickets' had had 'considerable success'; and that while some had been prosecuted, 'the pickets had generally stopped a site and moved on before police arrived at the scene'.[100]

The unofficial strikes to secure the release of the dockers from Pentonville took place a few weeks into the building workers' strike and the two campaigns worked to their mutual benefit. Lindop has detailed how North Wales building workers and Birkenhead dockers picketed out the Shotton steelworks, while shop stewards from the World's End building site in Chelsea went round local building sites and power stations seeking support for the dockers. Building workers also left their sites to join the mass demonstratiuon from Tower Hill to Pentonville on Tuesday 25 July.[101]

Given the general success of picketing in 1972, it is not surprising that the major academic study of picketing concluded:

> If one were to search for a single event which led to the picketing provisions of the 1980 Employment Act it would be the picketing ... at Saltley Coke Depot ... [where] the police were overwhelmed by sheer numbers ... Saltley was seen by the police themselves as a defeat ... and came to epitomise a series of problems about how the state defended itself and maintained civil order.[102]

Thatcher has also claimed that: 'For me, what happened at Saltley took on no less significance than it did for the Left'.[103] In fact, following Saltley, Heath commissioned a review of the civil emergency planning machine, leading to the establishment of the Civil Contingencies Unit, which was in place by the time of the official dock strike at the end of July that year.[104] During the unofficial strike over the Pentonville jailings, Humberside dockers had picketed a number of Trentside wharves that operated outside the National Dock Labour Scheme. When eighteen pickets achieved no response on 24 July, the next day some 800 achieved a different outcome, stopping all the wharves (including one where the pickets had to force their way through the gates). With the start of the official national dock strike on 28 July (with a state of emergency declared on 3 August), there was further picketing. Following the decision of workers at Neap House Wharf near Scunthorpe to work normally from 7 August, on several occasions hundreds of pickets confronted hundreds of police, with arrests and injuries. Tony Topham saw this as the second of the 'two moments of drama' in the 1972 dockers' struggle. As Geary commented, 'this time, the police seemed determined not to be seen to lose as at Saltley'.[105]

This policy shift toward more aggressive policing was to be seen more publicly in the later stages of the Grunwick strike in 1977.[106] But the failure of the police to deal with the builders' flying pickets in 1972 was partially compensated for by the subsequent court case surrounding the alleged events at Shrewsbury during that strike.[107] The incoming Conservative government in 1979 drew attention to 'secondary action (picketing, blacking and blockading)', especially the 'greater degree of organization of picketing, which is sometimes the work of unofficial groups rather than official union leaders'.[108] This led to the Employment Act 1980. The reaction to the general success of the picketing in 1972, however, went beyond policing and legislative changes. According to Sir Otto Kahn-Freund (an academic labour lawyer who sat on the 1965–8 Royal Commission on Trade Unions and Employers' Associations), 'the word "picketing" [during the early 1970s] seems to acquire a new meaning'. Referring to the 1972 miners' strike, he wrote:

> As long as the miners did not go beyond exchange of information and 'persuasion', and as long as the information was exchanged with, and the persuasion directed to, say, men loading or unloading coal or coke on to or from lorries, they were engaged in picketing as this word has been understood for at least half a century. If however the persuasion became physical compulsion or prevention, if the picket line became a road block, this was something else than picketing ... Moreover ... if, whether by persuasion or by physical means, the pickets tried to prevent fuel oil from reaching an electrical power station, they were engaging in an activity which had no longer anything to do with industrial relations at all.[109]

Such sentiments represented more than the 'moral panic' over 'picketing as organized violence'; they typified the reaction of many 'supporters' of the labour movement to one of the few periods when trade union activity has stepped beyond its self-imposed limits and threatened the 'normal' power relations in capitalist society.[110]

Conclusions and a comparison

The industrial struggles of 1972 raise fundamental questions about the nature of workers' power and the limits of trade unionism within a capitalist economy. The three successful movements outlined in this chapter demonstrate the effectiveness of official strike action when large numbers of ordinary union members are actively engaged in the action, whether drawn in officially or unofficially; that workers' preparedness to act unofficially can help to achieve official union objectives, despite national union leaders' caution or even hostility; that 'secondary' picketing is a tactic that can dramatically shift the balance of power in a dispute in the workers' favour and accelerate its chance of success; and that solidarity action by workers not involved in the dispute – through respecting picket lines or striking themselves – can be the critical difference between success and failure.

A brief comparison can be made with the wave of engineering factory occupations in the Manchester district in the spring and summer of 1972. As an offensive movement for a shorter working week, this was a radical departure for British workers; but it also demonstrated that a daring tactic in itself is no guarantee of success.[111] The CSEU's decision in January 1972 to fight the national engineering pay and hours campaign on a plant-by-plant basis could have achieved some success if plants had been selectively targeted and levies raised in their support as they were in the later 1989–90 dispute (and as the draughtmen's union DATA, later TASS, had practised for many years by the early 1970s).[112] But even though the CSEU, and particularly its dominant constituent, the AUEW, had decided against any national coordination, there was still the possibility of successful local action given that district committees were accorded the power to sanction any plant settlements. AUEW President Hugh Scanlon even told his union's National Committee in April that it had been hoped that district committees would select firms. Yet when districts decided to take militant action they encountered an unsympathetic national leadership. Thus the Sheffield district's early decision to have a city-wide strike was denounced as unconstitutional and was abandoned. In Manchester 'carbon copy' claims were agreed at a district-wide meeting of 700 shop stewards. Once these claims were rejected by the plant managements, another meeting decided on individual factory sanctions of an overtime ban and work-to-rule and a ban on piece-work.

A number of factories did not wait until the agreed start of sanctions on 27 March and crucial features of the dispute were fixed before most factories had even started taking action. Sit-ins were used to counter management threats of lock-outs or suspensions and these were made official; at the peak

344

of the action some thirty factories in the Manchester area were occupied. As important for the character of the dispute, however, was that when the local engineering employers' association expelled a company for reducing the length of the working week the unions agreed that the terms of all future settlements in this campaign would be kept secret. The Manchester factory occupations were therefore not only isolated from other workforces within their own industry, they were isolated from each other. With the EEF funding the Manchester employers' resistance to concessions on hours and holidays, the latter determined to 'sit out' the sit-ins. A few weeks into the campaign, Scanlon told a district meeting of stewards that settlements could be made without any progress toward a 35-hour week. Despite this, a number of occupations carried on for up to three months. However, their relative failure in delivering results (Tuckman estimates a national total of 49 occupations, and these and other actions cost the AUEW £2.5 million in strike benefit) marked a turning point in the national fortunes of the Broad Left within the AUEW.[113]

The failure of this movement for a shorter working week requires more detailed address than can be attempted here. Yet some comparisons can be made with the three successful movements outlined in this chapter. The Donovan Report of 1968 had highlighted the engineering industry as representing a system of industrial relations increasingly out of the control of factory managements.[114] In its turn, the left characterized engineering as the heartland of shop steward power and prized the autonomy of stewards from the unions as a source of radical strength. The CP was at its strongest in engineering – both in the factories and in the unions. However, a number of factors militated against the types of national action demonstrated in the other industries in this chapter, particularly the sheer size of the industry, its heterogeneous character and the scale of its multi-unionism. In discarding national action in favour of a plant-by-plant strategy, union leaders and activists believed that in areas like Manchester and Sheffield, at least, they were trading in weakness for strength. These two areas were viewed as relatively homogeneous districts, with strong workplace organization and with a tenacious left, specifically CP, tradition – districts which could produce exemplary struggles, pulling other areas along behind them.

The role of the EEF in orchestrating a general response stands out and highlights the stark absence of essential coordination (either official or unofficial) beyond the plant on the unions' side. In Manchester the two leading full-time union officers were also the popular leaders of the Broad Left, typifying the fact that, unlike the *Building Workers' Charter*, the engineering Broad Left was rooted in the unions rather than in the workplaces.[115] These officers faithfully executed official strategy and opposed attempts even to organize a joint occupation committee. Leading CP stewards also continued to identify with Scanlon and the local officials and thus disarmed their supporters, unlike their counterparts in the docks and building industry. While

345

the shop steward model of workplace organization was being actively extended by both employers and unions to many other sectors of employment at this time, one of its features in engineering was that recent traditions of unofficial action had tended to be confined to individual workplaces, unlike in the mines or on the docks. Most engineering industry activists still thought parochially and believed that they could win major battles without campaigning beyond the confines of their own workplaces, even when their employers practised solidarity and their union leaders demonstrated timidity.

In 1972 these problems, which demonstrated that successful militancy was far from general, were overshadowed by the momentous victories of the miners and the dockers. Indeed, the occurrence of the sit-ins was viewed optimistically: 'the remarkable thing about the sit-ins ... is that they happened so very easily' and they 'broke new ground ... [by being] not defensive but offensive'.[116] This chapter has argued therefore that 1972 was generally a 'glorious summer' for British trade unionism and presents a very different role model to that manufactured by politicians and press in the so-called 'Winter of Discontent', which has dominated public debate ever since. The events of 1972 marked the high point of class struggle during the long postwar boom, a year when the British state's increasing politicization of industrial relations clashed with a generally undefeated and increasingly self-confident and militant working-class. It was also a vivid demonstration of the limitations of 'trade' unionism under capitalism as government and key employers took a series of beatings but were able to regroup. Yet however much commentators of different persuasions may now demonize, sanitize or ignore it, the 'sun' of 1972 still shines through the clouds of subsequent defeats.

Notes

Several people have commented on this chapter. I would like to thank all of them, particularly Tony Topham and John McIlroy. Thanks also to Ralph Darlington, my collaborator on a wider project on 1972, with whom I have since given several papers.

1. At least one industrial relations writer has cited the full quotation from Shakespeare, but without the particular use I have made of it: C. Crouch, *The Politics of Industrial Relations* (2nd edition, 1982), p. 229, n.1. S. Milne, *Guardian*, 6 September 1997.
2. J. Kelly, 'Long waves in industrial relations: mobilization and counter-mobilization in historical perspective', *Historical Studies in Industrial Relations* (HSIR), 4, 1997, pp. 9–13.
3. J. Goodman, 'Great Britain: toward the Social Contract', in S. Barkin (ed.),

Worker Militancy and Its Consequences: new directions in western industrial relations (New York: 1975), pp. 68–9.

4.   C. Drake, 'The right to picket peacefully: section 134', *Industrial Law Journal*, 1, 4, 1972, p. 212.

5.   J. Cronin, *Labour and Society in Britain, 1918–1979* (1984), pp. 191–2.

6.   J. Hinton, *Labour and Socialism: a history of the British labour movement, 1867–1974* (Brighton, 1983), p. 195.

7.   *Financial Times*, 10 September 1997.

8.   See J. Foster and C. Woolfson, 'How workers on the Clyde gained the capacity for class struggle: the Upper Clyde Shipbuilders Work-In, 1971–72', in this volume.

9.   See, for example, NUM president Joe Gormley's account of his role, in J. Gormley, *Battered Cherub: the autobiography of Joe Gormley* (1982), pp. 95–118.

10.   For the role of the Communist Party, see J. McIlroy, 'Notes on the Communist Party and industrial politics', in this volume.

11.   'Stoppages of Work due to Industrial Disputes in 1972', *Department of Employment Gazette*, June 1973, from which other figures in this chapter are also cited.

12.   W. Ashworth, with the assistance of M. Pegg, *The History of the British Coal Industry, Volume 5, 1946–1982: the nationalized industry* (Oxford, 1986), p. 305.

13.   V. Allen, *The Militancy of British Miners* (Shipley, 1981), pp. 132–9, 161–6, 176 and 178–9; A. Taylor, *The Politics of Yorkshire Miners* (1984), pp. 191–201.

14.   E. Heath, *The Course of My Life: my autobiography* (1998), p. 350; see also A. Taylor, 'The Conservative Party and the trade unions', in this volume.

15.   M. Thatcher, *The Path to Power* (1995), p. 216.

16.   Quoted in K. Jeffery and P. Hennessy, *States of Emergency: British governments and strikebreaking since 1919* (1983), p. 236.

17.   TUC, *Report*, 1972, p. 98.

18.   *The Times*, 21 February 1972.

19.   *Economist*, 19 February 1972, p. 68.

20.   R. Taylor, *The Fifth Estate: Britain's unions in the seventies* (1978), pp. 260–1, makes the point about the slowness of the national leadership in issuing such instructions; Allen, *Militancy*, pp. 201–6, reproduces various NUM circulars on picketing, dated 11–21 January 1972.

21.   Taylor, *Fifth Estate*, pp. 261–2.

22.   Allen, *Militancy*, pp. 189, 200. Taylor, *Fifth Estate*, p. 263, states that by 5 February, 11,000 miners were on picket duty every day; T. Hall, *King Coal: miners, coal and Britain's industrial future* (1981), p. 191, repeats this figure. Detail on picketing is provided in M. Pitt, *The World on Our Backs: the Kent miners and the 1972 miners' strike* (1979), pp. 122–66; Taylor, *Politics of the Yorkshire Miners*, pp. 217–29; Taylor, *Fifth Estate*, pp. 260–5; Allen, *Militancy*, pp. 181–206; interview with Arthur Scargill in *New Left Review*, 92, 1975. See also D. White, 'Picket Duty', *New Society*, 27 January 1972, p. 169.

23. Allen, *Militancy*, p. 200.
24. J. Hughes and R. Moore (eds), *A Special Case? social justice and the miners* (1972), p. 9.
25. *The Times*, 21 February 1972.
26. TUC, *Report*, 1972, pp. 97–8.
27. P. Routledge, 'Does the Triple Alliance march again?', *The Times*, 2 August 1972.
28. *The Times*, 2, 5, 15 February 1972.
29. *Economist*, 19 February 1972, p. 67.
30. *The Times*, 11 February 1972.
31. Hughes and Moore, *A Special Case*, p. 10.
32. R. Geary, *Policing Industrial Disputes: 1893 to 1985* (1986), pp. 73–8; F. Watters, *Being Frank: the memoirs of Frank Watters* (Barnsley, 1992), p. 63; *The Times*, 10 February 1972. M. Crick, *Scargill and the Miners* (1985), pp. 56–62, gives some indication of the support from the Birmingham trade-union movement. Taylor, *Fifth Estate*, p. 366, also mentions support from the electricians' union.
33. T. Corfield, *The Rule of Law: a study in trade union organization and method* (Birmingham, 1982), pp. 150–2. Hall, *King Coal*, p. 190, also mentions two groups of Birmingham workers who struck in support on the Tuesday.
34. *The Times*, 8 February 1972, cited in S. Milligan, *The New Barons: union power in the 1970s* (1976), p. 201.
35. P. Wallington, 'The case of the Longannet miners and the criminal liability of pickets', *Industrial Law Journal,* 1, 4, 1972, pp. 219–23; Geary, *Policing Industrial Disputes*, pp. 76–7.
36. *The Times*, 16, 17 February 1972.
37. *Financial Times*, 17 February 1972.
38. Milligan, *The New Barons*, pp. 108–9, 201.
39. Taylor, *Fifth Estate*, p. 265.
40. Crouch, *Politics of Industrial Relations*, pp. 74–5.
41. P. Blyton and P. Turnbull, *The Dynamics of Employee Relations* (1994), p. 285.
42. D. Fatchett, 'Ballots, picketing and strikes', in B. Towers (ed.), *A Handbook of Industrial Relations Practice: practice and the law in the employment relationship* (3rd edition, 1992).
43. P. Scraton, 'From Saltley Gates to Orgreave: a history of the policing of recent industrial disputes', in B. Fine and R. Millar (eds), *Policing the Miners' Strike* (1985), p. 150; K. Middlemas, *Power, Competition and the State, Volume 2: threats to post-war settlement Britain, 1961–74*, p. 366; K.O. Morgan, *The People's Peace: British history 1945–1989* (Oxford, 1990), pp. 326, 414.
44. K.O. Morgan, *Callaghan: a life* (Oxford, 1997), p. 383; J. Campbell, *Edward Heath: a biography* (1994), p. 415; M. Thatcher, *The Downing Street Years* (1993), p. 340.
45. Though H. Pelling, *A History of British Trade Unionism* (3rd edition, 1976), p. 281, wrote of Scargill as leading the miners' picketing generally, culmi-

nating in the closure of Saltley (which he described as a power station). R. Taylor, *The Trade Union Question in British Politics: government and unions since 1945* (Oxford, 1993), p. 198; Taylor, *Fifth Estate*, pp. 365–7.

46.   J. Monks, 'Gains and losses after twenty years of legal intervention', in W. McCarthy (ed.), *Legal Intervention in Industrial Relations: gains and losses* (Oxford, 1992), p. 211.

47.   J. Grant, *Blood Brothers: the division and decline of Britain's trade unions* (1992), p. 55.

48.   Ashworth, *History of the British Coal Industry*, p. 314.

49.   Morgan, *The People's Peace*, p. 327.

50.   The following few paragraphs draw particularly on F. Lindop, 'The dockers and the 1971 Industrial Relations Act, part 1: shop stewards and containerization', *HSIR*, 5, Spring 1998, pp. 33–72, and 'The dockers and the 1971 Industrial Relations Act, part 2: the arrest and release of the "Pentonville Five"', *HSIR*, 6, 1998, pp. 65–100. For a 'Chronology of docks dispute', see B. Weekes, M. Mellish, L. Dickens and J. Lloyd, *Industrial Relations and the Limits of Law: the industrial effects of the Industrial Relations Act* (Oxford, 1975), pp. 278–94, though note that the dates are not always accurate; for example, the date of the Official Solicitor's intervention in the Chobham Farm case is given as 17 June when it was 16 June, and that of the order for the imprisonment of the five dockers is given as 22 July when it was 21 July.

51.   Heath, *The Course of My Life*, p. 406.

52.   'Note on the Churchman case by Sir Peter Pain', in G. Lewis, *Lord Hailsham: A Life* (1997), Appendix 1, 'The Dockers' Cases of 1972', pp. 348–9; Lord Denning, *The Closing Chapter* (1983), pp. 169–73.

3.   Denning, *The Closing Chapter*, p. 171; the second quote is cited in Lindop, 'The dockers, part 2', p. 74.

4.   Lindop, 'Dockers, part 2', pp. 92, 82.

5.   C. Harman, *The Fire Last Time: 1968 and after* (1988), p. 230.

6.   Editorial, *New Society*, 3 August 1972, p. 226.

7.   Lindop, 'The dockers, part 2', pp. 84–5.

8.   G. Dorfman, *Government versus Trade Unionism in British Politics since 1968* (1979), p. 62.

9.   Lindop, 'The dockers, part 2', pp. 94–5.

0.   Lewis, *Lord Hailsham*, p. 347.

1.   Dorfman, *Government versus Trade Unionism*, pp. 62–3 and p. 162, nn. 31–2.

62.   J. Griffith, 'Reflections on the rule of law', *New Statesman*, 24 November 1972, pp. 756, 758.

63.   *Guardian*, 28 July 1972, cited in Dorfman, *Government versus Trade Unionism*, pp. 63–4.

64.   *Economist*, 29 July 1972, p. 57.

65.   Griffith, 'Reflections on the rule of law', p. 759.

66.   R.M. Martin, *TUC: the growth of a pressure group, 1868–1976* (Oxford, 1980), p. 323.

67.   P. Paterson, '1926 and all that', *New Statesman*, 4 August 1972, p. 150. The

official TUC record states that 'on [Wednesday] July 26 ... the General Council ... decided to call on all affiliated unions to organise a one-day stoppage of work and demonstrations on Monday July 31 ... [to] commence at midnight on Sunday, July 30 and terminate at midnight on Monday, July 31. All Trades Councils were asked to organise public demonstrations ... Later on July 26, the men were freed' (TUC, *Report*, 1972, p. 105).

68. M. Moran, *The Politics of Industrial Relations: the origins, life and death of the 1971 Industrial Relations Act* (1977), p. 187, n. 111.
69. Monks, 'Gains and losses', pp. 211–12.
70. D. Kavanagh , 'The Heath government, 1970–1974', in P. Hennessy and A. Seldon (eds), *Ruling Performance: British governments from Attlee to Thatcher* (Oxford, 1987), p. 225; this basically repeats his earlier assertion of a 'dock strike in August over the rights of the new Industrial Relations court to fine a recalcitrant union' (D. Butler and D. Kavanagh, *The British General Election of February 1974* (1974), p. 22).
71. Lindop, 'The dockers, part 1', pp. 36–7.
72. K. Laybourn, *A History of British Trade Unionism, c. 1770–1990* (Stroud: 1997, first published 1992), p. 196; Pelling, *History of British Trade Unionism*, p. 280.
73. Middlemas, *Power, Competition and the State*, p. 364; Taylor, *Trade Union Question*, pp. 201–2; P. Dorey, *The Conservative Party and the Trade Unions* (1995), p. 99; Morgan, *Callaghan*, p. 383.
74. Morgan, *The People's Peace*, p. 325; M. Holmes, *Political Pressure and Economic Policy: British government 1970–1974* (1982), p. 29; Kavanagh, 'The Heath government', p. 227; H. Phelps Brown, *The Origins of Trade Union Power* (Oxford, 1986), p. 196; R. Currie, *Industrial Politics* (Oxford, 1979), p. 237; A. Sked and C. Cook, *Post-war Britain: a political history* (1979), p. 297. Hugh Clegg claimed that the three dockers accused at Chobham Farm were arrested but released the next day: H.A. Clegg, *The System of Industrial Relations in Great Britain* (3rd edition, Oxford, 1976), p. 460, repeated in H.A. Clegg, *The Changing System of Industrial Relations in Great Britain* (Oxford, 1979), pp. 325–6.
75. Milligan, *The New Barons*, pp. 71–2; Campbell, *Edward Heath*, p. 461.
76. N. Tiratsoo, '"You've never had it so bad?": Britain in the 1970s', in N. Tiratsoo (ed.), *From Blitz to Blair: a new history of Britain since 1939* (1997), pp. 166–7.
77. Denning, *The Closing Chapter*, p. 177.
78. Dorfman, *Government versus Trade Unionism*, p. 64, cites an unattributable interview with a parliamentary private secretary.
79. R. Taylor, 'The trade union problem in the age of consensus, 1960–1979', in B. Pimlott and C. Cook (eds), *Trade Unions in British Politics: the first 250 years* (2nd edition, 1991), p. 181.
80. '[A] number of major unions had been flirting with the idea of registration ... But the jailed dockers put paid to all such thoughts', argued Ken Coates (K.Coates, 'Introductory review: converting the unions to socialism', in M. Barratt Brown and K. Coates (eds), *Trade Union Register* 3, (Nottingham,

1973), p. 19).

81. The building strike was reported as two separate strikes – one for England and Wales, the other for Scotland.

82. *Financial Times*, 29 August 1972; *The Times*, 31 August 1972.

83. T. Austrin, 'The "lump" in the UK construction industry', in T. Nichols (ed.), *Capital and Labour: studies in the capitalist labour process* (Glasgow, 1980), pp. 302–15.

84. T. Austrin, 'Industrial relations in the construction industry', unpublished PhD thesis, University of Bristol, 1978, pp. 288–91, 296. K. Sim, 'What building strike?', *New Statesman*, 11 August 1972, pp. 188–9.

85. Austrin, 'Industrial relations in the construction industry', p. 297; *The Times*, 1, 7, 8, 9 August 1972.

86. *The Times*, 15, 16 August 1972.

87. Ibid., 21, 22 August 1972

88. Austrin, 'Industrial relations in the construction industry', p. 309.

89. *Financial Times*, 24 August 1972.

90. *The Times*, 9 September 1972.

91. J. Arnison, *The Shrewsbury Three: strikes, pickets and 'conspiracy'* (1974).

92. *Economist*, 16 September 1972, p. 79; *The Times*, 19, 25 September 1972.

93. L. Wood, *A Union to Build: the story of UCATT* (1979), pp. 16–17, 18, 19.

94. Milligan, *The New Barons*, pp. 201–2. M. Adeney and J. Lloyd, *The Miners' Strike 1984–5: loss without limit* (1986), p. 102, also later referred to 'widespread and violent hit-and-run picketing' in the building workers' dispute.

95. Clegg, *Changing System*, p. 387.

96. *Financial Times*, 14 February 1972.

97. *Economist*, 5 August 1972, p. 13.

98. *Economist*, 19 August 1972, p. 21.

99. *Economist*, 16 September 1972, p. 79. The clear sequence of events makes it hard to comprehend Crouch's observation that: 'In 1972 building workers developed what became known as the "flying picket" ... Later the same year the coal miners used "mass picketing"' (C. Crouch, *Trade Unions: The Logic of Collective Action* (1982), p. 97).

00. *The Times*, 18 September 1972.

01. Lindop, 'The dockers, part 2', p. 87 and n. 64.

02. P. Kahn, N. Lewis, R. Livock and P. Wiles, with the assistance of J. Mesher, *Picketing: industrial disputes, tactics and the law* (1983), p. 75.

103. Thatcher, *The Path to Power*, p. 218.

104. Jeffery and Hennessy, *States of Emergency*, p. 235.

105. T. Topham, 'The attack on the dockers', in Barratt Brown and Coates, *Trade Union Register* 3, p. 227; Geary, *Policing Industrial Disputes*, pp. 78–83.

106. The policy decision to intercept flying pickets was first made in November 1973, in anticipation of the miners' strike of 1974 (T. Bunyan, *The History and Practice of the Political Police in Britain* (1977), p. 270).

107. See *R v. Jones and others* [1974] ICR 310 [CA].

108. *Industrial Relations Legal Information Bulletin*, 142, 8 August 1979, p. 5.

109. O. Kahn-Freund, *Labour and the Law* (2nd edition, 1977), p. 261.

110.   J. McIlroy, '"The Law Struck Dumb"?: labour law and the miners' strike', in Fine and Millar, *Policing the Miners' Strike*, p. 82.

111.   The following account, except where otherwise indicated, is based on several sources: G. Chadwick, 'The Manchester engineering sit-ins, 1972', in Barratt Brown and Coates, *Trade Union Register* 3; R. Rosewell, 'The AUEW: the 1972 wages struggle and the left', *International Socialism*, 57, 1973; A. Tuckman, 'Industrial action and hegemony: workplace occupation in Britain 1971 to 1981', unpublished PhD thesis, University of Hull, 1985, ch. 3.

112.   For discussion of the tactics used in these and other national engineering disputes and in draughtsmen's action, see D. Lyddon, 'Rediscovering the past: recent British strike tactics in historical perspective', *HSIR*, 5, 1998, pp. 120–3, 126–9.

113.   Tuckman, 'Industrial action and hegemony', p. 146; Taylor, *Fifth Estate*, p. 215.

114.   Royal Commission on Trade Unions and Employers' Associations, 1965–1968 (Donovan) *Report*, (Cmnd 3623, 1968).

115.   See McIlroy, 'Notes on the Communist Party and industrial politics'.

116.   Chadwick, 'The Manchester engineering sit-ins, 1972', p. 113.

Afterword: What Went Wrong?

Richard Hyman

Writing at the outset of the period covered by this book, Vic Allen began his study of union militancy with the declaration that 'it is quite clear that under conditions where labour is freely bought and sold trade unionism is endemic, universal and permanent'.[1] In the fifteen years surveyed in the previous chapters there was little in British experience which appeared to contradict this confident assertion, which now reads like an echo of a distant age. Union membership in the UK increased in all but three of these years, from 10.2 million in 1964 to 13.4 million in 1979. Aggregate employment changed little over this period, so that density increased similarly: from 44.1 per cent in 1964 to 55.4 per cent in 1979.[2] These figures were indeed open to alternative interpretations: for Eric Hobsbawn they could be viewed as relative stagnation and were one indicator of the end of labour's 'forward march'.[3] Yet this was a somewhat perverse reading: the increase of ten percentage points in union density achieved in a decade from the late 1960s to the late 1970s had been matched only twice before in this century, in the very special circumstances surrounding the wars of 1914–18 and 1939–45. This progress was the more significant given the changes in workforce composition which Hobsbawm himself noted: growing feminization, the shift from manual to white collar occupations, the decline of employment in many of the old trade union strongholds (notably mining) and the growth of the service sector.

All these shifts meant that, even to stand still, unions had to recruit in areas of employment and among types of worker, where they had traditionally been relatively weakly represented; actually to move forward, and for the first time ever to include the majority of Britain's working population within union ranks, was in many respects a remarkable achievement. One may add that this was not simply a tribute to unions' own organizing capacity: it owed more than a little to the assistance of employers. For many, in particular the largest, support for unionization – often formally expressed in closed shop agreements – was part and parcel of the reform of industrial relations, contributing to order and discipline in the workplace. The formalization of the closed shop was one paradoxical consequence of the principle of unfair dismissal which was introduced in the Industrial Relations Act: the law had to specify circumstances in which dismissal for non-membership of a union could be deemed fair, and this involved formal procedures for instituting compulsory membership. The 1971 Act defined the requirements for a legal closed shop very narrowly; but most employers still maintained existing arrangements.[4] The relaxation of the rules under the 1974 Trade Union and Labour Relations Act encouraged a substantial increase in closed shop agreements, and by 1979 nearly 5.2 million employees – almost 40 per cent of all union members – were covered.[5] As was later to become evident, relying on the employer as a recruiting agent could be a mixed blessing.

One may also note the gradual deterioration in the labour market throughout these years: a worrying trend for trade unionism. In the 'stop–go' cycle of the British economy, unemployment tended to rise sharply in the recession without fully recovering in the subsequent upturn. This was apparent at the outset of our period and was to become increasingly obvious.[6] The 1960s notion of 'redeployment' lost any of its original credibility in the 1970s when three trends coincided. First, the contraction of traditional staple industries accelerated. Second, job loss (or at best 'jobless growth') was the typical pattern in many successful industries, particularly as the corporate merger wave of the 1960s was followed by rationalization and asset-stripping, and 'new technology' was applied to displace labour. Third, the expansion of public services which had to some extent compensated during the 1960s for a reduction of jobs in the manufacturing and extractive industries decelerated under the impact of the crisis in public finances. In the process, the limits of politically acceptable unemployment were repeatedly raised: half a million in the early 1960s was an outrage; the 'intolerable' ceiling of a million was breached in 1972 (on the same day that share prices reached record heights); in 1978, the number of jobless approached two million. This provoked surprisingly little protest, beyond ritual declarations of shock, from trade unionists or others: perhaps signalling to future governments that there was no longer any politically unacceptable level of unemployment. Of the 'affluent workers' surveyed by Goldthorpe and his colleagues in the early 1960s, 88 per cent had never been unemployed and 90 per cent considered that their existing jobs were secure; far fewer of their counterparts in 1979 could have responded in similar terms.[7] The implications for the future of trade unions were at that date unpredictable.

In many respects, however, the context of trade union action still seemed comfortably familiar: 'business as usual' remained a plausible maxim. Writing in 1979, Hugh Clegg – the most experienced of British industrial relations academics, and as chair of the Comparability Commission a practical link between the old era and the new industrial relations regime under Thatcher – emphasized the probability of continuity despite a change of government. Interestingly enough, the issue which led him to essay a prediction of the future – a rare exercise for such a cautious analyst – was incomes policy:

> Everyone acknowledges the need to 'modernize' British industry so that Britain will be competitive when the oil runs out. Governments will therefore be under pressure ... to limit resources used on other items, including pay. This pressure is likely to turn their mind to incomes policy, since monetary restraint would check

the process of modernization as well as the rate of increase in pay and prices – if indeed the degree of monetary restraint which is politically acceptable would have a sufficient impact on pay settlements to hold back prices.[8]

For Clegg too, the bounds of political acceptability seemed clearly defined by a third of a century of post-war experience. There was no realistically predictable alternative to the maintenance of socio-economic stability through negotiated compromises (which given the institutional deficiencies of British industrial relations would be *ad hoc* and unstable) between organized labour and the state:

> It would ... be a bold prophet who would predict a social contract between the unions and a Conservative government. Nevertheless ... governments and unions are becoming more expert at negotiating and administering incomes policies. There is therefore a prospect that policies may be more lasting and successful in the future than in the past.[9]

Thus Clegg's tentative prognosis in 1979 was a strengthening of collective negotiation over terms and conditions of employment: reinforcing his premise 'that collective bargaining is the central process in industrial relations'.[10] If most British trade union activists in 1979 were complacent concerning the future, they were in good company.

A crisis of governability?

'Since the end of the Second World War the British working class – without itself exhibiting the will to power – has established that it cannot be governed in the old way. It is not a footsore spectator at a crisis: it is that crisis'.[11] Royden Harrison's remark at the end of the decade accorded with a widespread diagnosis in the 1970s of a 'crisis of governability' in Britain, with trade union militancy seen as its clearest expression. In blunter terms (whether or not ironically) the song *Part of the Union* summed up an attitude encouraged by the seemingly triumphant resistance to Heath's industrial relations offensive: 'although I'm a working man, I can ruin the government's plan, I'm not too hard, but the sight of my card, makes me some kind of superman'.[12] This matched the 'ideology of Labourism' defined by John Saville, also writing during the Heath government, as defensive militancy which could be obstinate but unrelated to any transformatory project.[13]

For many observers, the 'British disease' of frequent unofficial strikes was the manifest expression of an industrial bloody-mindedness which by the period under discussion had become economically destructive and socially divisive. The number of officially recorded stoppages of work had followed a complex course from the 1940s onwards.[14] The war brought an upsurge – almost without exception small, short and localized. The figure of a thousand was exceeded in 1941 (only the sixth time since records began in 1893) and never dropped below this level until 1985. From 1944 to 1946 the two thousand threshold was exceeded followed by a brief decline and then a new rise in the 1950s. At this time the statistics were dominated by coal-mining, which in the mid-1950s accounted for three-quarters of all disputes.[15] For a time the figures stabilized: but this reflected two contrary trends, a sustained decline in mining (partly because of falling employment, partly because of a change in payment systems) and an increase in other industries. By the late 1960s the total was rising rapidly, reaching almost 4,000 in 1970 before subsiding to just over 2,000 a year in most of the 1970s.

For critics, the volume of disputes – far above that in most other industrialized countries – was proof of a basic unreasonableness on the part of British trade unionists, a disposition to strike first and ask questions afterwards. Yet there were also structural explanations. In the case of engineering – from the 1960s the leading sector in terms of strike activity – the official 'provisions for avoidance of disputes' had been imposed by the victorious employers after the lock-out of 1897–98 and reaffirmed in similar circumstances in 1922; by the 1960s they held virtually no legitimacy for engineering workers and their unions.[16] Much more generally, the analysis of the Donovan Report is relevant: the official institutions of British industrial relations (the formal system') were oriented to the national, industrial level; but at least ı the core sectors of manufacturing, the real locus of employment regulaon (the 'informal system') was on the shop floor. In most key industries, ıanual production workers were paid by results under systems which of-:red ample scope for sophisticated shop stewards, perhaps representing only handful of workers, to bargain at the point of production under threat of a .toppage which might disrupt a whole factory and perhaps also those to which it was a supplier. Different groups of production workers would keep a jealous eye on their position in the earnings hierarchy (within the single workplace, the company, the locality, and the industry nationally) while off-production workers, both manual and non-manual, were also willing to act militantly to avoid falling behind in the free-for-all. The institutions of British industrial relations, in a context of relative job security, encouraged something akin to a Hobbesian war of all against all.[17] The strike pattern of the 1960s was part and parcel of this process: competitive efforts by different groups to maintain and improve their relative position in the hierarchy of pay and benefits in the absence of overarching regulatory institutions would result, according to Fox and Flanders, in an escalating process of 'normative disorder'.[18]

Yet if this reading was correct, it would be possible to pose a different question: why were there so *few* strikes? Department of Employment research revealed that in the period 1971–3, on average only 2 per cent of manufacturing establishments in each year experienced a stoppage; the authors concluded that 'Britain does not have a widespread strike problem ...

British industry in general is certainly not widely or continually affected by industrial action; it is not "riddled" with strikes'.[19] To some extent, their analysis indicated a phase in which the 'reform' of British industrial relations was already reversing the proliferation of small-scale stoppages evident in the late 1960s. The Donovan Report, as has been seen, perceived a conflict between the 'pretence' of national industry-level collective bargaining and the real decision-making power of a workplace-based system which was 'largely informal, largely fragmented and largely autonomous'.[20] The consolidation of company-level negotiation which Donovan advocated was already under way in the 1960s: formalizing the collapse of national bargaining in much of British industry, but at the same time curbing the bargaining autonomy of first-line shop stewards – particularly when linked to the abolition or at least the stricter regulation of payment by results.[21]

Yet 'reform' was itself double-edged: while inhibiting small-scale 'spontaneous' stoppages it could provoke and facilitate larger-scale, more strategically planned disputes (hence reversing in part the 'sectionalism' of traditional piecework disputes). At the same time, the earnings of different groups of relatively high-paid manual workers became more publicly visible, perhaps contributing to the aspirations of those in less favoured sectors, such as miners and a range of public-sector employees. This process, combined with the deteriorating context of the British economy in the 1970s, helps explain why the number of 'days lost' in strikes in this decade was three times the level of the 1960s.

It would be a mistake to focus simply on issues of pay, however – even though it was resistance to Callaghan's misconceived intensification of pay restraint which fuelled the 'Winter of Discontent'. Declining competitiveness within a global economy beset by a succession of crises inspired what can be defined as a systematic effort to redefine social relations in production. To a large degree (as was the argument of many of the academics associated with the Donovan Commission), shop-floor trade union power had rested on a vacuum of management: employers lacked either the will or the organizational capacity to direct the labour process to the extent normal in other countries. The years 1964–79 can in retrospect be seen as a phase in which management itself was restructured, the better to shift the frontier of control on the shop floor. Under strong government encouragement, employers (those which did not simply go to the wall) developed increased strategic sophistication, struggled to subordinate the management of industrial relations to the broader priorities of production, marketing and financial control, and confronted those principles and practices (such as the maxim of 'mutuality' in the engineering industry) which restrained the control of labour. This was a fundamental challenge to established conceptions of trade union rights, and provoked inevitable resistance.

Here we see a key transformation in the course of the 1970s. The unions defeated the Industrial Relations Act not solely – perhaps not primarily –

357

because of the force of their own opposition; most large employers did not at that stage perceive the need for a legislative assault on trade unionism. By the end of the decade the situation had changed radically. This allows us to recognise the irony of Harrison's remarks in his response to Hobsbawm: 'the unsettled character of the new social settlement was finally exposed when, by the failing light of the new technology, the British workman could still be discerned answering the foreman back'. But if British capitalism was to survive, things had to change. Here, there is a poignancy to Harrison's comment that the impasse in shop-floor relations 'poses the question: which is it to be – socialism, or the ruin of the two contending classes?' Immediately Harrison added: 'there is a third possibility. But that requires us to think of Keith Joseph in the role of the "Chicago Boys" and Mrs Thatcher in the part of General Pinochet. At the time of writing we have not come to that nor is it a denouement which I find easily imaginable ...'.[22] No longer a joke, alas. 'Solving the union problem is the key to Britain's economic recovery' was the title of one of Joseph's pre-election broadsides; and the Thatcher project was to reassert government the better to enable a reassertion of management.

Could this have been prevented? Against those who diagnose a relentless drift to destructive competitive sectionalism, it is necessary to emphasise the complex and contradictory nature of developments in this period. The guru of the International Socialists, Tony Cliff, often alluded to the 'revolution of rising expectations': a sustained experience of improving living standards would shape ideas of normal entitlement; when the objective scope for continued improvement was narrowed, the system itself would be questioned. Indeed, the central strategic issue for socialists in the 1970s was the impact on consciousness of an economic downturn, or more radically an economic crisis. In 1975, when class struggle seemed to be advancing, I wrote in a popular text: 'as bargaining *within* capitalism comes to yield shrinking gains (and indeed to require a *deterioration* in conditions) trade unionists can be expected to become more and more susceptible to the idea of its elimination'. Yet I added that 'there is nothing *inevitable* about the growth of socialist consciousness, organisation and action; as Lukacs insisted, "history is at its least automatic when it is the consciousness of the proletariat that is at issue"'.[23]

For many contributors to the 'Forward March' debate, economic crisis would lead naturally, given the British tradition of fragmented unionism and defensive sectional militancy, to increasingly divisive responses with each group possessing any strategic power fighting its own corner at the expense of others, encouraging an authoritarian political outcome.

Yet this was not inevitable (except to the extent that any historical development, being attributable to causally sufficient preconditions, must have been a necessary outcome). An important issue in the 1970s was the evidence of qualitative as well as quantitative advances in struggle. The UCS action (discussed above by John Foster and Charles Woolfson in Chapter 10) was just one manifestation of a much broader set of innovative responses to capitalist crisis. These years saw a resurgence of interest in the idea of workers' control (with the Bullock Committee enquiry into board-level employee representation a pale official response) and the development of guidelines for an 'alternative economic strategy' (AES) which combined traditional Keynesianism with the notion of shop steward and trade union involvement in company planning and local authority initiatives in shaping a local economy to democratic control. These imaginative notions (which most far-left groups perhaps dismissed in too simple a reflex) might conceivably have formed the basis for an alternative industrial politics. Two specific developments which deserve to be recalled are, first, the 'Benn co-operatives', attempts with some state sponsorship (however limited) to build islands of worker-managed enterprise to some degree shielded from the cut-throat capitalism which had brought the original companies to insolvency; second, the not merely defensive insistence on the right to work. This became imaginatively expressed in the call for the right to *useful* work when demand no longer existed for former useless production – as specifically in the case of military products. The plan developed by shop stewards in Lucas was the most famous instance of such efforts to transcend the limits of conventional trade union action.[24]

This can be seen as the 'left', 'progressive', 'solidaristic' face of trade unionism in the 1970s. Perhaps the attainment of its goals was always utopian. What was also important, however, was the eclipse in mid-decade of the efforts to unite trade union and Labour Party lefts in a common strategy. The occasion for this defeat was the referendum on membership of the European Community, when the TUC and the Labour Party left were united in an oppositional posture which proved decisively unsuccessful. The result was to strengthen right-wing tendencies in the party and government, marginalize Benn (and the AES) and facilitate subsequent capitulation to the dictates of the IMF. In retrospect – given the experience of Mitterrand in the early 1980s and the Swedish social democrats later in the decade – it is clear that Keynesianism (let alone socialism) in one country was no longer on the agenda. Pursuing the anti-EEC line, in one sense justified by the dominant capitalist bias of European integration, nevertheless involved a poisoned alliance with right-wing nationalism, the defeat of which gave Wilson and Callaghan a virtually free hand for the remainder of Labour's term of office. *If* the British left had sought an alliance with the left elsewhere in Europe in favour of a pan-European AES, the outcome might – conceivably – have been different.

1964–79: Britain in comparative perspective

How does the experience explored in the present volume compare with developments in trade unions and politics elsewhere in Europe? There are obvious parallels: most countries saw a growth in union membership, increased strike activity, and a more general, though less easily measurable, enhancement of the collective confidence and political influence of organized labour (see Table A.1). In the title of one detailed comparative investigation at the time, there was a 'resurgence of class conflict' in much of Europe, perhaps reflecting a crisis of the Fordist regime of production and challenging many features of the class compromises established in the early post-war years.[25]

Table A.1. Trade union density and strike incidence in selected countries, 1960–80

	D	DK	F	I	NL	S	UK
Union density (%)							
1960	34.7	63.1	19.3	25.0	39.4	69.4	44.2
1970	32.8	64.4	21.3	32.2	36.5	66.4	48.5
1980	36.0	79.8	17.3	43.7	31.0	78.2	52.9
Strike incidence [a]							
1961–5	18.3	107.6	146.3	648.4	8.0	3.8	127.0
1966–70	6.0	42.7	134.0 [b]	933.6	14.0	33.0	222.6
1971–5	47.7	354.5	186.7	1063.9	36.1	65.5	538.6
1976–80	44.1	75.9	154.2	940.0	27.8	220.3	521.7

Notes:
a working days lost per 1000 employees (annual average)
b excludes 1968 (year of mass general strike)

Source: J. Visser, 'Trade unionism in Western Europe', *Labour and Society*, 1988; ILO, *Yearbook of Labour Statistics*.

Trends in union organization and collective militancy were evidently uneven, variable cross-nationally, and of differing significance according to the situation in each country before the 'resurgence'. What seems to have been a common pattern, however, was a revolt against wage restraint on the one hand, rationalization and intensification of production on the other, by a generation of workers that had come to take 'affluence' and relative security of employment for granted. The assertiveness which in many countries peaked in the late 1960s and early 1970s in its turn helped accentuate national economic crisis – most spectacularly, perhaps, in Italy.

The outcome of these crises depended to a significant degree on the strategic choices made by different trade union movements. These choices were conditioned, but not predetermined, by each national institutional context. Much depended on how the labour movement had hitherto been implicated in the formulation and implementation of national social and economic policy. A familiar means of characterizing this relationship involves a distinction between labour exclusion, corporatist integration and pluralistic detachment.[26] Apart from the authoritarian dictatorships, two obvious cases of labour exclusion in post-war western Europe were France and Italy, where – at least after the onset of the Cold War – unions were weak and divided, and governments supported the dominant employers in a modernization strategy based on intensive production and low wages. Corporatist integration was characteristic of Sweden and other Nordic countries, but also of Austria and the Netherlands: typically involving wage restraint combined with significant union influence over labour market and social welfare policies; Germany in the 1960s was moving from the first pattern towards the second, after the entry of the social democrats to government. Britain stood out as a system based on pluralistic detachment between the spheres of government socio-economic policy and industrial relations.

In a number of cases, economic crisis led to a renegotiation of this relationship. The most dramatic instance was in Italy, where the 1970 Workers' Statute formalized rights of union representation and the main, Communist-led union confederation subsequently embraced the concept of 'historic compromise' and became co-sponsor of a complex set of deals with successive governments. In Sweden, the unions won substantial legislative underpinning for their rights at workplace level as the price for continued cooperation in wage policy; a process to some extent matched in Germany.

In Britain, there was far less scope for a negotiated outcome to socio-economic crisis. Industrial relations had developed on the basis of the principle of 'voluntarism': the notion that employment regulation was largely a private matter for unions and employers. As the TUC argued in its evidence to Donovan:

> no state, however benevolent, can perform the functions of trade unions in enabling workpeople themselves to decide how their interests can best be safeguarded. It is where trade unions are not competent, and recognise that they are not competent, to perform a function, that they welcome the state playing a role in at least enforcing minimum standards, but in Britain this role is recognised as the second best alternative to the development by workpeople themselves of the organisation, the competence, the representative capacity, to bargain and to achieve for themselves satisfactory terms and conditions of employment.[27]

The traditional separation between 'politics' and 'industrial relations' was mirrored in the division of labour between the unions and the Labour Party: each wing of the movement traditionally respected the other's autonomy within its respective sphere of competence. The party did not intervene uninvited on issues of industrial relations; the unions did not attempt to use their weight to dictate policy on general political questions against the wishes of the party leadership.[28] Neither demarcation made much sense in an era when governments accepted a role as macroeconomic manager and when the state was a major employer in its own right. Industrial relations was increasingly a political matter, importantly but not only because incomes policies became normal elements in governments' portfolios of options. But how politics and industrial relations should be integrated was never clarified. Despite the tentative efforts of the initial 'Social Contract' phase, the idea of a trade-off between wage restraint and government concessions on other elements of the 'social wage' – the everyday material of 'political exchange' in most European countries – never acquired real legitimacy in Britain.[29] Such an exchange remained equally suspect to governments and to the unions: partly, but only partly, because the fragmented and decentralized structure of British trade unionism made it almost impossible for the latter to deliver on any macro-political deal. The record of the 1970s was thus a 'combination of narrow trade unionism and failed state intervention'.[30]

One important feature of the response to crisis by different national labour movements was the way in which economic instability entered workers' consciousness, and the specific rhetorics available which allowed unions to address their members' fears and aspirations. In countries where unions had an established status as 'social partners', it was relatively predictable that they should become directly implicated in the management of crisis. In other contexts, deep-rooted ideals of solidarity could be deployed to legitimize the principles both of sacrifice and of workers' right to compensating concessions from government as part of an overarching union response.[31]

In this respect, a crucial dimension was trade unions' articulation with civil society. 'Social partnership' defined for unions a specific societal role. In some countries, as in France and Italy, unions were key institutions within a bifurcated civil society (but also with roots in a particular type of nationalist tradition). In England, by the 1970s unions seem to have lost their former status as influential components of civil society (though the situation in Scotland was different, as the UCS struggle showed, and Wales perhaps likewise).

By the end of the 1970s, 'pluralistic detachment' as the basis of British industrial relations had run into the sands. Rather than appearing potential contributors to the solution of economic crisis and economic decline, the unions could be readily presented as the scapegoats. The way was open for Thatcher to emulate, in some respects at least, the practices of her admired friend Pinochet.

Notes

1. V. L. Allen, *Militant Trade Unionism* (1966), p. 11.
2. G. S. Bain and R. Price, 'Union growth: dimensions, determinants and destiny' in G. S. Bain (ed.), *Industrial Relations in Britain* (Oxford, 1983), p. 5.
3. E. J. Hobsbawm, 'The forward march of labour halted?', *Marxism Today*, September 1978; reprinted in M. Jacques and F. Mulhern (eds), *The Forward March of Labour Halted?* (1981).
4. B. Weekes, M. Mellish, L. Dickens and J. Lloyd, *Industrial Relations and the Limits of Law* (Oxford, 1975), p. 42.
5. J. Gennard, S. Dunn and M. Wright, 'The content of British closed shop agreements', *Department of Employment Gazette*, November 1979; and 'The extent of closed shop arrangements in British Industry', *Employment Gazette*, January 1980.
6. See, for example, Paul Foot, *Unemployment: The Socialist Answer* (Glasgow, 1963).
7. J.H. Goldthorpe, D. Lockwood, F. Bechhofer and J. Platt, *The Affluent Worker: industrial attitudes and behaviour* (Cambridge, 1968), pp. 117–18.
8. H.A. Clegg, *The Changing System of Industrial Relations in Great Britain* (Oxford, 1979), p. 378.
9. Ibid., pp. 381–2.
10. Ibid., pp. 378 9.
11. R. Harrison, untitled comment in Jacques and Mulhern, *The Forward March of Labour Halted?*, p. 51 (originally published in *Marxism Today*, June 1979).
12. J. Ford and R. Hudson, *Part of the Union* (1973), recorded by the Strawbs on A&M AMS\7035.
13. J. Saville, 'The ideology of labourism', in R. Benewick, R.N. Berki and B. Parekh (eds), *Knowledge and Belief in Politics* (1973).
14. Official statistics exclude all strikes involving fewer than ten workers or lasting less than a day, unless 'working days lost' amount to at least 100; disputes not primarily concerned with 'industrial' issues (i.e., those judged 'political') are also excluded. Since neither party is obliged to report a dispute, many which meet the criteria fail to be recorded; survey evidence in the 1970s suggested that the majority (mainly small, short conflicts) fell through the official net.
15. Partly perhaps because the nationalized industry was more systematic than other employers in reporting stoppages, but also because of the somewhat chaotic operation of the piece work system in mining.
16. In 1971, following ineffectual attempts to renegotiate the disputes procedure, the unions withdrew from the complex provisions specified.
17. Notwithstanding the earlier reference to increasing unemployment, at least until well into the 1970s the employment of those already in jobs in the profitable sectors of British industry seemed relatively secure.
18. A. Fox and A. Flanders, 'The reform of collective bargaining: From Donovan to Durkheim', *British Journal of Industrial Relations*, 1969, reprinted in A. Flanders, *Management and Unions* (1970).

19.   C.T.B. Smith, R. Clifton, P. Makeham, S.W. Creigh and R.V. Burn, *Strikes in Britain*, Department of Employment Manpower Paper 15, (1978), pp. 63, 88.
20.   A. Flanders, 'Collective bargaining: prescription for change' (1967), in Flanders, *Management and Unions*, p. 169.
21.   See, for example, B. Ross, *Know Your Enemy: A Report on the Reports* (Coventry, 1968).
22.   Harrison, comment, pp. 52–3.
23.   R. Hyman, *Industrial Relations: a Marxist introduction* (1975), p. 202.
24.   See for example K. Coates (ed.), *The Right to Useful Work*, (Nottingham, 1978); K. Coates (ed.), *Work-ins, Sit-ins and Industrial Democracy* (Nottingham, 1981); H. Wainwright and D. Elliott, *The Lucas Plan: a new trade unionism in the making?* (1982).
25.   C. Crouch and A. Pizzorno (eds), *The Resurgence of Class Conflict in Western Europe*, 2 volumes (1978).
26.   M. Regini, 'Political bargaining in Western Europe during the economic crisis of the 1980s', in O. Jacobi, B. Jessop, H. Kastendiek and M. Regini (eds), *Economic Crisis, Trade Unions and the State* (1986), pp. 61–2.
27.   TUC, *Trade Unionism* (1966), pp. 68–9.
28.   Though it was, of course, taken for granted that the union block vote would be used to support the leadership against left-wing opposition from the constituencies. The breach of convention was only when unions applied their weight in the opposite direction, as over nuclear disarmament in 1960.
29.   A. Pizzorno, 'Political exchange and collective identity in industrial conflict', in Crouch and Pizzorno, *The Resurgence of Class Conflict in Western Europe*, vol. 2.
30.   H. Wainwright, untitled comment, in Jacques and Mulhern, *The Forward March of Labour Halted?*, p. 132.
31.   A key basis for the Italian unions' success in persuading (at least partially) the militants of the early 1970s to accept restraint at the end of the decade; see M. Golden, *Labor Divided: austerity and working-class politics in contemporary Italy* (Ithaca, 1988).

Index

366

371

374

survey 47
and trade unions 48–50
Hood, Stuart 266
Horobin, G.W. 27, 40
Horsman, Frank 267
Hosiery Mills, Mansfield, strike (1972) 71
Hoskyns, John 172
career 185
Stepping Stones 171–4
hotel and catering industry, opposition to
immigrants 84–5
Hotel and Catering Industry Committee 84–5
Hotel and Catering Workers' National
Committee, *The Hotel Strikes: lessons
for unionization* 291
Howe, Sir Geoffrey 146, 157, 169, 171, 172,
174, 181
Conflict of Loyalty 182, 184, 185, 186
Howell, David 6, 15, 16, 17, 40, 129
Howells, Ray 265
Hudson, K.J. 249
Hudson, R. 363
Hughes, J., *A Special Case? social justice and
the miners* 348
Hull, fishermen 27
Hulme, K. 293
Human Resource Management (HRM) 3
Hungary, uprising (1956) 5
Hunt, Alan 223, 252
Hunt, Audrey 49
Hunt, J. 65
Hunter, Bill 265, 289
*Lifelong Apprenticeship: the life and times
of a revolutionary 1920–1959* 291
*They Knew Why They Fought: unofficial
struggles and leadership on the docks
1945–1989* 291
Hurd, Douglas 160, 164, 174
An End to Promises 183, 184, 185
Hurford, J. 295
Huspek, M. 303, 304, 324
Hyman, Richard 4, 15, 18, 124, 126, 249, 273,
288, 290, 293, 294, 295
Industrial Relations: a Marxist introduction
14, 18, 364
*Marxism and the Sociology of Trade
Unionism* 14, 128, 293
*Social Values and Industrial Relations: a
study in fairness and equality* 128
Strikes 129

identity, and class consciousness 24
IEA (Institute for Economic Affairs) 166, 171
ILO (International Labour Organisation), Equal
Pay Convention (1951) 54, 68
Ilyenkov, E. 303, 304, 308
*The Dialectic of the Abstract and the
Concrete in Marx's Capital* 324
I'm All Right Jack (film) 185

IMF (International Monetary Fund) 93, 144,
174, 359
IMG (International Marxist Group)
archives 288
industrial fractions 263
industry base 263
Leyland in Crisis: Cowley under fire 291
membership 262–3
and the NUT 263
trade union base 263
immigration
and the CAWU 80
and the CSCA 79
Irish 73
Jewish 70
legislation 81, 82
and London Transport 77
and National Health Service 77
and public opinion 80
and the TGWU 78, 79
and trade unionism 70
and the TSSA 80
and the TUC 74, 78–9, 80–81
West Indian 76–7
white 73–6
and the TUC 74
and the workplace 81
Immigration Act (1971) 82
Imperial Typewriters dispute (1974) 86, 90
In Place of Strife (1969) (White Paper) 94, 95,
102, 139, 141, 145, 149, 155, 182
CP opposition 218, 242–3
SLL opposition 268
strikes against 242
trade union opposition 139–40
and UCS 300
income, distribution 97, 113
incomes policies 97, 110, 354–5
breakdown 111
and the Callaghan government 145
and the Conservative Party 156, 158
and Frank Cousins 209
and differentials 111, 144
and the Heath government 161–2, 327
and Sir Keith Joseph 169
and Jim Prior 169
and the Wilson government 135–6, 143
and George Woodcock 136, 208–11
Indian workers, and trade unions 76
individualism
and class consciousness 32–3
and collectivism 23–4, 29, 31–8, 97, 98, 115
industrial action, and politics 9–10
Industrial Charter for Women 57–8
industrial democracy
Bullock Report 142
and the CP 218–19
industrial relations
and linguistic analysis 297, 304

375

377

381

Polish Resettlement Corps 73
Polish workers, and trade unions 74
politics
    and industrial action 9–10
    and labour history 10–11
Pollert, A., *Girls, Wives, Factory Lives* 14
Pond, C. 125
Ponting, C., *Breach of Promise: Labour in power 1964–1970* 149
Port of London Liaison Committee 239
Porter, D. 150
post-modernism, and labour history 6–7, 16–17
postal workers, strike (1971) 158
Potrykus, A. 295
Powell, Enoch 161, 164, 167
power industry, disputes 158, 166
Power, John 267, 268
Power, Mike 251, 252, 253, 258
'Praetorian Guard' (trades union alliance) 104
Prevost, Eddie 239
The Price and Pay Code for Stage Three (consultation document) 183
Price Commission 161
Price, Richard 9, 15, 17, 18, 120, 125, 363
    Labour in British Society 149, 150
Prices and Incomes Board 94, 95
Prior, Jim 168, 170, 171, 172, 177, 178, 182
    A Balance of Power 182, 184, 185, 186
    and incomes policies 169
Prior, Mike 220, 251
Prudential Assurance Male Staff Association 59
Prus, J. 293
Public Bodies (Admission to Meetings) Act (1960) 167
public opinion
    and immigration 80
    and Industrial Relations Bill (1971) 179
    and miners 159
    and trade unions 174–6, 180
Purcell, J. 38
    The Control of Work 125
Purcell, K. 67
Purdy, Dave 220, 223, 251, 252
Purkiss, Bob 87
Pym, Francis 170
    The Politics of Consent 184

R v. Jones case, and strikes 351
race awareness
    and London Transport 82
    and the TGWU 81
race relations
    and the Labour Party 83
    and the TUC 83–4
    and trade unions 83–7
Race Relations Board 84, 86
Race Relations, Select Committee on 84
Radice, Giles 54, 68
railway industry, disputes 158, 327

Raison, Timothy 155
    Conflict and Conservatism 182
Ramdin, R. 85, 86
    The Making of the Black Working-class in Britain 16, 88, 90
Ramelson, Bert 220, 223, 224, 233, 234, 235, 239, 241, 246, 251, 252, 253, 256, 258
    Bury the Social Contract: the case for an alternative policy 250
    Incomes Policy: the great freeze trick 249
    life 250–51
    Productivity Agreements: an exposure of the latest and greatest swindle on the wages front 250
Ramsden, J. 149
Ranelagh, J., *Thatcher's People* 184, 185
Rank and File group 272, 277
rank and file movement
    and events of 1972 327, 328, 334, 339, 340, 341
    and the IS 274–9
    publications 275, 277
        list 286
    ways to organise 290
Ratner, H., *Reluctant Revolutionary: memoirs of a Trotskyist 1936–60* 18
RCP (Revolutionary Communist Party) 262, 290
Read, Mel 52–3, 58, 68, 69
Rechnitz, Eric 239
Redgrave, Corin 266
Redgrave, Vanessa 266
Redman, G.P. 128
Redundancy Payments Act (1965) 58, 96, 152
Rees, George 230
Regini, M. 364
Registrar of Friendly Societies 154
Reid, A. 41
Reid, E. 124, 183
Reid, Jimmy 235, 236, 238, 305–7, 308, 309–11, 312, 315, 316, 317, 318, 320
    Reflections of a Clyde-built Man 256
Reilly, D. 90
relativities, and pay 163, 164, 183
Resler, H. 125
Rhodes, E. 89
Rice, M., *Birmingham AUEW Expulsions* 295
Richardson, A. 288
Richardson, R. 125
Richmond, A.H., *Colour Prejudice in Britain* 88
Riddell, N.B. 148
Ridley, Nicholas 168–9, 178, 298, 301, 314, 315, 317, 318, 319, 320
    My Style of Government: the Thatcher years 184
Right to Work Campaign 280, 282
Riley, Tommy 281
Roberts, Andrew, *Eminent Churchillians* 181
Roberts, Alf 55

Printed in the United Kingdom
by Lightning Source UK Ltd.
126083UK00001B/130-132/A